Given $\mathbf{Ax} = \mathbf{d}$, where $\mathbf{A} = [a_{ij}]$, $\mathbf{x} = [x_i]$, and $\mathbf{d} = [d_i]$,

$(i = 1 \ldots n; j = 1 \ldots n)$, then $\bar{x}_j = \dfrac{|\mathbf{A}_j|}{|\mathbf{A}|}$ (solution to a system of linear equations)

Given $y = f(x)$, $f'(x) = 0$ (first order condition for critical point);
    $f''(x) > 0$ (for a relative minimum) and $f''(x) < 0$ (for a relative maximum)

$MR = MC$ (profit-maximizing output rule)

$P < AVC$ (output shut-down rule)

$MRP_L = MFC_L$ (profit-maximizing employment rule)

$ARP_L < w$ (employment shut-down rule)

$\epsilon_p^d = \dfrac{(dQ^d/Q^d)}{(dP/P)} = \dfrac{(dQ^d/dP)}{Q^d/P}$ (price elasticity of demand)

$Q = AK^a L^b$ $(0 < a, b < 1)$ (Cobb-Douglas production function)

$Q = A[uK^{-p} + (1 - u)L^{-p}]^{-r/p}$ $(0 < u < 1; p > -1$ and $p \neq 0$; and $r > 0)$
    (CES production function)

$Q = \text{minimum } [K/a, L/b]$ (fixed-coefficients production function)

$\sigma = \dfrac{d(\overline{K/L})/(\overline{K/L})}{d(w/r)/(w/r)}$ (elasticity of substitution)

$L(\lambda, K, L) = r_0 K + w_0 L + \lambda \cdot [Q_0 - Q(K, L)]$ (constrained cost minimization)

$L(\lambda, x, y) = U(x, y) + \lambda \cdot [I - P_x x - P_y y]$ (constrained utility maximization)

$A(Y, r) \overset{e}{=} Y$ (*IS* curve: Product Market Equilibrium)

$L(Y, r) \overset{e}{=} M_0^S/P_0$ (*LM* curve: Money Market Equilibrium)

$\dfrac{dK(t)/dt}{K(t)} = \dfrac{dY(t)/dt}{Y(t)} = \dfrac{dN(t)/dt}{N(t)} = s/v = n$ (steady-state equilibrium in Harrod-Domar Model)

$dk(t)/dt = sy(t) - nk(t)$ (fundamental equation of the Solow Model)

USING MATHEMATICS IN ECONOMIC ANALYSIS

PRENTICE HALL SERIES IN ECONOMICS

USING MATHEMATICS IN ECONOMIC ANALYSIS

PETER HESS

DEPARTMENT OF ECONOMICS
DAVIDSON COLLEGE

Prentice
Hall

UPPER SADDLE RIVER, NJ 07458

Library of Congress Cataloging-in-Publication Data

Hess, Peter N.
  Using mathematics in economic analysis / Peter Hess.
    p. cm.
  Includes index.
  ISBN 0-13-020026-3
    1. Economics—Mathematical models. 2. Economics, Mathematical.
  3. Econometrics. 4. Econometric models.   I. Title.

  HB135 .H48 2002
  330′.01′51—dc21

                                            2001034018

AVP/Executive Editor: Rod Banister
VP/Editor-in-Chief: P.J. Boardman
Managing Editor (Editorial): Gladys Soto
Assistant Editor: Marie McHale
Editorial Assistant: Lisa Amato
Media Project Manager: Victoria Anderson
Marketing Manager: Joshua P. McClary
Marketing Assistant: Christopher Bath
Managing Editor (Production): John Roberts
Production Editor: Maureen Wilson
Permissions Coordinator: Suzanne Grappi
Associate Director, Manufacturing: Vincent Scelta
Production Manager: Arnold Vila
Manufacturing Buyer: Diane Peirano
Cover Design: Kiwi Design
Cover Illustration/Photo: PhotoDisc
Full-Service Project Management and Composition: Compset, Inc.
Printer/Binder: Hamilton Printing Co.

Credits and acknowledgments borrowed from other sources and reproduced, with
permission, in this textbook appear on appropriate page within text.

10 9 8 7 6 5 4 3 2 1
ISBN 0-13-020026-3

With love to my wife, Boo, and sons, Jamie and Joey,
I dedicate this work

BRIEF CONTENTS

CONTENTS

Mathematics in undergraduate economics tends to be underutilized to the detriment of student comprehension of economic principles. Usually introductory texts shy away from even basic algebra, and intermediate theory texts, if using calculus at all, often relegate the mathematical treatment to appendices and footnotes. The traditional mathematical economics texts, in contrast, focus on presenting the mathematical techniques with economic applications interspersed throughout, but with no coherent progression of the economic theories.

With this text I seek to convey the utility of mathematics—the conciseness of expression, preciseness of assumptions, and the advantages in manipulation—for economic analysis. The mathematics employed (including derivative and integral calculus, exponential and logarithmic functions, first order difference and differential equations, matrix algebra, linear and nonlinear programming) are motivated by the economics. Accordingly, the coverage of economic theory is organized into three parts: "Analysis of Markets," "Optimization," and "Macroeconomic Analysis." We progress from models of perfectly competitive markets for single commodities, to the optimizing behaviors of the firms and households operating in markets characterized by perfect and imperfect competition, to the aggregate markets of macroeconomic models. Mathematical concepts and techniques are introduced at appropriate points in the presentation of the economic theories and then reinforced throughout the text. The primary objective of *Using Mathematics in Economic Analysis* is for students to develop mathematical skills that can open up a new dimension of economic analysis, thereby enhancing their understanding of economic theories.

FEATURES

The emphasis throughout the text is not on mathematical theorems and formal proofs, but on how mathematics can enhance our understanding of the economic behavior under study. The careful development of economic topics strives for a coherence not often found in mathematical economic texts. A premium is placed on clear explanation, with a blending of mathematical, verbal, and graphical exposition. Numerical illustrations of the economic models are used extensively to aid understanding. Frequent practice problems are provided throughout each chapter, with answers at the end of the chapter to give immediate feedback to students, bolstering confidence and building a secure foundation as they progress through the material. The end-of-chapter exercises are comprehensive and challenging. Moreover, key terms in economics (in bold) and mathematics (in italics) are listed at the end of the chapter (with page references), and a glossary of concise definitions is provided at the end of the text.

ORGANIZATION

In the first chapter, the construct of an economic model and the concept of equilibrium are discussed and illustrated with the example of a competitive market for a commodity. Then Chapter 2 provides a review of some basic mathematics; including sets, derivatives, limits, and integrals.

In Chapter 3, which begins Part I of the text, "Analysis of Markets," we use derivatives to establish conditions for the static stability of market equilibria and for comparative static analysis, inverse functions to illustrate different market adjustment mechanisms, and integral calculus to find consumers' surplus and producers' surplus. We shift to dynamic analysis in Chapter 4, beginning with first order difference equations. As a bridge between the discrete time of period analysis and continuous time we review exponential and logarithmic functions. The discussion of compound interest leads us to natural exponential and natural logarithmic functions, which are part of the solution of the first order differential equations also used in the dynamic modeling of a competitive market. In Chapter 5 we expand beyond a single competitive market to general competitive equilibrium. To build up to the matrix algebra needed for solving systems of linear equations, we first review vectors. A technique known as Cramer's rule is introduced, which will prove especially useful in the comparative static analysis for systems of equations.

In Part II, "Optimization," we look behind the market to the underlying optimizing behavior of firms and consumers. Chapter 6 develops the short run decision rules for a firm in selecting the profit-maximizing levels of output and labor employment. The powerful Implicit Function Theorem is introduced to enhance our ability to do comparative static analysis. Perfectly competitive and monopolistically competitive firms are addressed in Chapter 7, along with the concept of price elasticity of demand. Monopolies and monopsonies—at the other end of the theoretical spectrum—are the topics of Chapter 8. We will see how a monopolist may practice price discrimination to bolster profits and how a union can diminish, if not negate, the power of a monopsonist in a labor market. Chapter 9 completes our modeling of market structures by examining duopolies and oligopolies, where the firms in the market, few in number, are actively engaged in competition. The introduction to game theory follows naturally from the discussion of the firms' interdependent decision-making.

The progression from free optimization with one independent variable (e.g., perfectly competitive firms in Chapter 7) to two and more independent variables (e.g., a monopolist with two plants in Chapter 8) allows us to illustrate partial differentiation and the Implicit Function Theorem for the analysis of systems of equations. We then turn to constrained optimization. In Chapter 10 the long run decision of a firm in selecting the cost-minimizing input combination for producing a given output is modeled using the Lagrange multiplier method. With linear programming and nonlinear programming in Chapter 11, we extend the analysis to incorporate optimization under more than one constraint and to illustrate the concept of duality. Chapter 12 concludes Part II of the text with the application of constrained optimization to the theory of consumer behavior. In particular, the labor-leisure tradeoff of a household is modeled.

Part III, "Macroeconomic Analysis," parallels the first part of the text in that the treatment advances from static analysis to comparative statics to dynamic analysis. Chapter 13 begins with a discussion of input-output models. Then a Simple Keynesian Model is developed and applied to two countries to illustrate a phenomenon known as the foreign repercussions effect. In Chapter 14 we build up from the Simple Keynesian model (product market only), to the IS-LM model (addition of the money market), to the Aggregate Demand-Aggregate Supply Model (incorporation of the labor market and aggregate supply constraints). Again partial differentiation and matrix algebra are extensively used in the derivation of the multipliers associated with the various versions of the macromodels. The policy implications of the derived multipliers are discussed. The coverage of growth rates and growth models in the concluding Chapter 15 reinforces the use of natural exponential and natural logarithmic functions and first order differential equations, as well as derivative and integral calculus.

ALTERNATIVE ORGANIZATION

Covering all fifteen chapters in one semester may be challenging. Twelve chapters may be a more reasonable objective. Two basic options for using the text are: (I) Chapters 1–12—which emphasizes the microeconomics (leaving out Part III, "Macroeconomic Analysis"); and (II) Chapters 1–9 and 13–15—which allows for coverage of both microeconomics and macroeconomics (leaving out Chapters 10–12 on constrained optimization). Skipping the dynamic analyses in Chapters 4 and 15 would further reduce options I and II to eleven and ten chapters respectively.

INSTRUCTOR'S MANUAL

Available with the text is an *Instructor's Manual*, which provides answers to all of the end-of-chapter problems. The practice problems in the text are designed for students to work through themselves as they progress through each chapter. The end-of-chapter problems, of varying degrees of difficulty and often with several parts, can be assigned as homework exercises.

AUDIENCE

Using Mathematics in Economic Analysis can be adopted effectively for different audiences. I believe the text is most appropriate for an undergraduate course in mathematical economics where students have completed a first course in calculus and intermediate microeconomic theory and, perhaps, intermediate macroeconomic theory. The text, or individual chapters, may also serve as a supplement to the standard intermediate microeconomic and macroeconomic theory courses. And, the text might function well in the summer review courses given by graduate programs in economics and in Master's programs in business and public policy.

ACKNOWLEDGMENTS

To begin, I'd like to acknowledge all of my students in mathematical economics over my twenty years at Davidson College. You provided my motivation for writing this text. In particular, I'd like to thank one student, Jasmina Radeva, who early in the development of the text, proofed some of the chapters and developed additional exercises. I am fortunate to be teaching at Davidson College with fine colleagues in the Economics Department: Dennis Appleyard, Ben Baker, Kelly Chaston, Mark Foley, Vikram Kumar, Dave Martin, Clark Ross, and Fred Smith. I am especially grateful to Kelly Chaston for her insightful comments on drafts of some early chapters. I am indebted to Barbara Carmack, the Economics Department Assistant, who is a joy to work with and who kept the department on an even keel during the past three years.

I appreciate the support and good work of the team at Prentice Hall. Scott Sambucci, the former publishing representative and then editor in electronics technology, carried my initial project to Rod Banister, Executive Editor. Rod's insight and encouragement has made my text better. I've enjoyed working with Marie McHale, Assistant Editor, and Maureen Wilson, Production Editor, and I thank Elena Picinic and Joshua McClary for their efforts in marketing. And, it was a real pleasure working with Janet Domingo of Compset, Inc.

I am also grateful to the following people for their helpful reviews of the material:

Vic Brajer, California State University–Fullerton
Craig Gallett, University of Central Florida
Brett Katzman, University of Miami

Man-Lui Lan, University of San Francisco
Jeanette Mitchell, Rochester Institute
David Molina, University of North Texas
Kajal Mukopadhyay, University of Notre Dame
Richard Peck, University of Illinois–Chicago
Kambiz Raffiee, University of Nevada
Reza Ramazani, Saint Michael's College
Catherine Schneider, Boston College
Peter VanderHart, Bowling Green University

I hope that students benefit from *Using Mathematics in Economic Analysis*, gaining a richer understanding of economic theory.

Peter Hess

CHAPTER 1

INTRODUCTION TO ECONOMIC MODELS

Economics deals with the allocation of resources for the production, distribution, and consumption of goods and services. To explain the behavior of the households, firms, and government authorities involved, economists develop theories. The economic theories can be conveyed verbally, graphically, and mathematically. These three approaches are appropriately considered to be complements, rather than substitutes. In introductory economics, for example, we mainly rely on verbal description of the concepts, enhanced by graphical illustration, and reinforced with numerical examples. Underlying the verbal descriptions and graphical depictions, however, are mathematical formulations.

Indeed, equations are to mathematical formulation as sentences are to verbal description and as curves are to graphical depiction. The advantages of mathematical over verbal representation of theory lie in the conciseness, potential precision, and efficiency of operation. Complex relationships may be expressed concisely with equations that embody specific assumptions about the theoretical relationships under study. Often these equations may be manipulated or transformed to derive new relationships. When confined to two or three dimensions, the mathematical equations can be represented graphically. Beyond three dimensions, graphical analysis breaks down; while mathematical analysis is not limited by dimensional constraints.

This text deals with mathematical economics—the use of mathematics to convey economic theories. Econometrics, a related field, is concerned with the statistical analysis used to test economic theories. The empirical models tested, however, are derived from the mathematical models formulated.

In this introductory chapter we discuss the concept of an economic model, illustrating with a generic example of a perfectly competitive market. The types of variables and equations that embody a model are defined and the properties of an equilibrium are examined.

ECONOMIC MODELS

The basic construct of economic theory is the **economic model**, a formal framework for the representation and analysis of hypothesized relationships among selected economic variables. Examples of economic models include a firm's selection of the cost-minimizing combination of capital and labor; a perfectly competitive market for a commodity; and aggregate demand-aggregate supply in macroeconomics. The structure of the model is provided through the equations that link together the variables representing economic magnitudes. Common variables in economics are prices and quantities, outputs and incomes, and revenues and expenditures.

VARIABLES AND EQUATIONS

There are two basic types of variables. *Endogenous variables* are analogous to dependent variables, since the values of the endogenous variables are to be determined within the model. *Exogenous variables* are analogous to independent variables in that the values of exogenous variables are considered to be given or determined outside the model. Exogenous variables are used to explain the behavior of endogenous variables. In other words, we seek to account for changes in the values of the endogenous variables through changes in the values of the selected exogenous variables.

Whether a variable is exogenous or endogenous depends on the particular behavior under analysis and the complexity of the model set forth. For instance, in a perfectly competitive market for a commodity, the market price is endogenous—determined jointly by the demand and supply of the commodity in question. For an individual firm in the perfectly competitive market, however, the market price is exogenous. So too, the individual consumers would regard the market price as given. In a sense, you could argue that all economic variables are ultimately endogenous. Yet, in any economic model some variables will be selected as exogenous—implicitly, if not always explicitly. Economic theory furnishes the insight to make informed choices about the endogeneity or exogeneity of the variables included in the model.

As noted in the preceding, equations convey the theory. There are three types of equations. *Identities,* sometimes indicated by the symbol $\equiv$, represent relationships that are accepted as true by definition. For example, total revenues (TR) equal the product of the unit price received (P) and the quantity, or number of units, sold, (Q). $TR \equiv P \cdot Q$. *Behavioral equations* describe the hypothesized relationships between the variables. For example, in the simple Keynesian consumption function, personal consumption expenditures (C) are directly related to disposable personal income (Y_d). We can write this relationship as $C = C(\overset{+}{Y}_d)$, where the plus sign over the income variable indicates its hypothesized positive influence on consumption. Note that here personal consumption is clearly an endogenous variable; however, depending on the scope of the model, disposable personal income may be either endogenous or exogenous.

The third type of equation is an *equilibrium condition*, sometimes highlighted by the symbol $\overset{e}{=}$. The concept of equilibrium is very important in economics, since it indicates a particular condition that may be attained within the model. An *equilibrium* refers to a state where the interactive forces in the system are in balance. For instance, picture a tank that is half-full of water, with one pipe uniformly injecting 2 gallons of water per minute into the tank, exactly offsetting a drain at the bottom of the tank, that is uniformly discharging 2 gallons of water per minute. The level of water in the tank would be constant and could be considered in equilibrium. Economics examples would be a perfectly competitive market where equilibrium is achieved at a price which equates the quantity demanded with the quantity supplied of the commodity, or a household that, for a given budgeted income and market prices, has achieved its utility-maximizing consumption of goods and services.

CHARACTERISTICS OF EQUILIBRIUM

Three characteristics of equilibrium of interest in an economic model are *existence, uniqueness,* and *stability*. First, does an equilibrium exist? Mathematically, an equilibrium may or may not exist . . . or it may exist only under certain conditions. Moreover, even if an equilibrium exists mathematically, does it make sense economically? Many of the variables in economics (e.g., prices and quantities) tend to take on only positive values. Second, if an equilibrium exists, is it unique? Or do multiple equilibria exist in the model? Third, is an equilibrium stable? Are there forces in the system that automatically work to reach the equilibrium?

The question of stability can be addressed statically and dynamically. In *static analysis* all the endogenous variables in the model are defined for the same time period. There are no conditions imposed that relate variables at different points in time. In *dynamic analysis* the endogenous variables are dated for different periods or points in time. As such, time explicitly enters the solution of the model. In dynamic analysis we are interested in the time paths of the endogenous variables. Static analysis of a perfectly competitive market, introduced below, will be developed further in Chapter 3. Dynamic analysis of a perfectly competitive market is the topic of Chapter 4.

STATIC MODEL OF A COMPETITIVE MARKET

Below we illustrate the types of equations and variables and the concept of equilibrium with a simple static model of a perfectly competitive market for a particular commodity. A **perfectly competitive market** is characterized by the interaction of many buyers and sellers of a homogeneous or standardized good or service. None of the buyers or sellers has any significant influence over the market price; there is freedom of entry and exit into the market; and in the long run equilibrium, economic profits are zero. Examples include the markets for basic agricultural commodities like corn, tomatoes, or eggs.

To begin, we define our variables. Let

Q^d = quantity demanded of the commodity,

Q^s = quantity supplied of the commodity,

and P = unit price of the commodity.

The quantities demanded and supplied are *flow* variables, that is, they are defined for a given duration of time, and indicate, respectively, the total amounts of the commodity that the demanders are willing to purchase and that the suppliers are willing to sell over a given period, for example, a day, week, or month.[1] For example, if the commodity in question were fresh shrimp, the quantities demanded and supplied might be expressed in thousands of pounds of fresh shrimp per day in a local market, a coastal community. These quantities depend on the unit price of the commodity. In this case, the unit price may be measured in dollars per pound of fresh shrimp. Mathematically, we can write the two behavioral equations in general form as:

$$(1)\quad Q^d = Q^d(\bar{P})$$

$$(2)\quad Q^s = Q^s(\overset{+}{P})$$

where we assume the usual case of a negative relationship between the quantity demanded of a commodity and its unit price (the **law of demand**) and a positive relationship between the quantity supplied of a commodity and its unit price (the **law of supply**). These assumptions are indicated by the minus and plus signs over the price variable in the two equations. Verbally, equation (1) indicates that the quantity demanded of the commodity is a negative function of its unit price. Similarly, equation (2) indicates that the quantity supplied of the commodity is a positive function of its unit price. In Chapter 3 we will discuss some unusual cases where the quantity demanded is directly related to the price and the quantity supplied is inversely related to price.

From economic theory we know that there are additional determinants or influences on the demand for a commodity, such as the number of prospective buyers in the market; the average income of the buyers; tastes and preferences; and the prices of substitutes and complements (e.g., in the case of shrimp, other shellfish, and shrimp sauce, respectively). Similarly, there are other determinants of the supply of a commodity, including: the number of sellers in the market; the cost of the inputs used to produce the commodity (e.g., the gasoline to run the shrimp boats and the wage rates paid to the hired shrimpers); the technology of production (e.g., the sonar used to locate shrimp); and government regulations (e.g., restrictions on the size of shrimp nets) and taxes assessed on the suppliers. Here we focus on the primary relationships between the unit price and the quantities demanded and supplied of the commodity, understanding that we do so holding constant all the other relevant influences.

We can graphically depict the demand and supply equations (or schedules) as demand and supply curves. Following the convention in economics we place the unit

---

[1]The other way to measure a variable is as a *stock*. A *stock variable* is defined for a point in time. For example, the amount of money in a savings account at the beginning of a month is a stock variable. The interest earned on that savings account over the month is a flow variable.

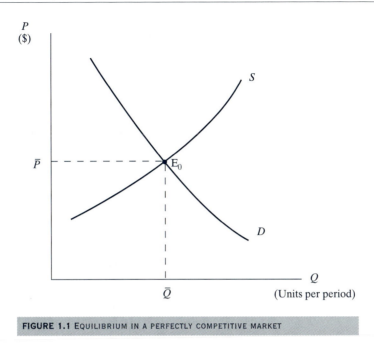

FIGURE 1.1 EQUILIBRIUM IN A PERFECTLY COMPETITIVE MARKET

price of the commodity (measured in monetary units) on the vertical axis.[2] See Figure 1.1 where D and S represent the demand and supply curves, respectively.

We complete the model with equation (3), the equilibrium condition, which states that, in equilibrium, the market price will equate the quantity demanded with the quantity supplied. In other words, in equilibrium, the market clears: there are no unsatisfied demanders or suppliers, in the sense that anyone who wants to buy or sell at the market price is able to do so.

$$(3) \quad Q^d(P) \stackrel{e}{=} Q^s(P)$$

If we define the **excess quantity demanded** of the commodity, E^d, as the difference between the quantity demanded and the quantity supplied of the commodity for a given price,

$$E^d = E^d(P) \equiv Q^d(P) - Q^s(P)$$

then we can rewrite the equilibrium condition as equation (3')

$$(3') \; E^d(P) \stackrel{e}{=} 0$$

That is, at the market equilibrium price the excess quantity demanded is equal to zero.

---

[2]In mathematics the convention is to place the dependent variable on the vertical axis and the independent variable on the horizontal axis. We will explain in Chapter 3 why economists have tended to reverse the axes. We should note now that price and the quantities demanded and supplied are endogenous variables. The exogenous variables are not explicitly defined in the model, but would be the relevant factors underlying the demand and supply curves.

Graphically the equilibrium occurs at the intersection of the demand and supply curves. See point E_0 in Figure 1.1. Dropping perpendiculars to the axes we identify the equilibrium price ($\overline{P}$) and quantity transacted ($\overline{Q}$), where we use the convention of a line over the endogenous variable to indicate an equilibrium value. Note that the quantity transacted is identical to both the quantity demanded and the quantity supplied. $Q^d(\overline{P}) = Q^s(\overline{P}) = \overline{Q}$ or $E^d(\overline{P}) = 0$. This need not always be the case. For example, as we will see later in this chapter, with market restrictions like price ceilings and price floors, the quantity demanded need not equal the quantity supplied in equilibrium.

LINEAR MODEL

Mathematically we cannot solve the model explicitly since we have not imposed specific functional forms. Often, for analytical convenience, we use the linear specification.[3] We convert the general model above into linear form as follows:

$$Q^d = d_0 + d_1\,P \qquad d_0 > 0, d_1 < 0$$

$$Q^s = s_0 + s_1\,P \qquad s_0 < 0, s_1 > 0$$

$$Q^d(P) \overset{e}{=} Q^s(P)$$

where $d_0, d_1, s_0,$ and s_1 are *parameters* or given values that define the particular demand and supply schedules. Parameters are considered as exogenous variables since their values are determined outside the model. Again we assume the usual case. Thus d_1, which represents the change in the quantity demanded per one unit change in price, is negative and s_1, indicating the change in the quantity supplied per one unit change in price, is positive. The d_0 and s_0 terms are the quantity intercepts. We expect that $d_0 > 0$; if the price for the commodity were zero, then a positive quantity would be demanded. Conversely, we expect $s_0 < 0$, if a positive unit price is required before any quantity of the commodity will be supplied. (Mathematically, if the price of the commodity were zero, then the quantity supplied would be negative.) The parameters d_0 and d_1 capture the exogenous influences on the quantity demanded of the commodity—holding constant the endogenous price of the commodity. In particular, changes in d_0 would shift the demand curve. Changes in d_1 alter the slope of the demand curve. The parameters s_0 and s_1 represent the exogenous influences on the quantity supplied of the commodity—holding constant the unit price. Changes in s_0 would shift the supply curve. Changes in s_1 would alter the slope of the supply curve. Figure 1.2 illustrates the linear demand and supply curves.

With the unit price of the commodity on the vertical axis, the slopes of the demand and supply curves are respectively $1/d_1$ and $1/s_1$. We can more easily read off the slopes of the demand and supply curves if we "solve" the demand and supply equations for

---

[3]With a linear specification, the impact of a unit change in any given variable on a dependent variable is constant, regardless of the magnitude of the given variable.

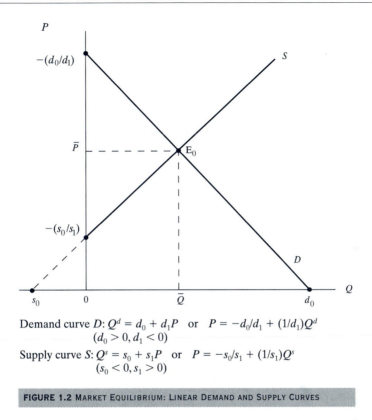

Demand curve D: $Q^d = d_0 + d_1 P$ or $P = -d_0/d_1 + (1/d_1)Q^d$
$(d_0 > 0, d_1 < 0)$

Supply curve S: $Q^s = s_0 + s_1 P$ or $P = -s_0/s_1 + (1/s_1)Q^s$
$(s_0 < 0, s_1 > 0)$

FIGURE 1.2 MARKET EQUILIBRIUM: LINEAR DEMAND AND SUPPLY CURVES

the unit price. The demand equation, $Q^d = d_0 + d_1 P$, can be written as: $P = -d_0/d_1 + (1/d_1)Q^d$. The supply equation, $Q^s = s_0 + s_1 P$, can be rewritten as: $P = -s_0/s_1 + (1/s_1)Q^s$. The coefficients of the quantities demanded and supplied, $(1/d_1)$ and $(1/s_1)$, respectively, give the slopes of the linear demand and supply curves when the unit price, P, is on the vertical axis—as is the convention in economics. The price intercepts for the demand and supply curves are $-d_0/d_1$ and $-s_0/s_1$, respectively.

The graphical solution is again found at the intersection of the demand and supply. See point E_0 and the equilibrium price, $\bar{P}$, and quantity transacted, $\bar{Q}$, in Figure 1.2.

We can also illustrate the excess demand curve. See Figure 1.3a, where the demand and supply curves are graphed, and Figure 1.3b, where the excess demand curve is derived. The excess quantity demanded at any price is the horizontal distance between the demand and supply curves. For unit prices above $\bar{P}$, (e.g., P_1), excess quantity demanded is negative, ($Q_1^d - Q_1^s < 0$), indicating an excess quantity supplied, or a **surplus**. For unit prices below $\bar{P}$, (e.g., P_2), a positive excess quantity demanded, or a **shortage**, exists. See P_2, where $Q_2^d - Q_2^s > 0$.

Mathematically, given the linear functional forms, we can solve explicitly for the equilibrium price and quantity transacted. Substituting the demand and supply equations into the equilibrium condition gives:

$$Q^d = d_0 + d_1 P \overset{e}{=} s_0 + s_1 P = Q^s$$

We have reduced the system of three equations in three unknowns (Q^d, Q^s, and P) into one equation in one unknown (P). Solving for the equilibrium price we obtain:

$$d_0 + d_1 P = s_0 + s_1 P$$

$$d_1 P - s_1 P = s_0 - d_0$$

$$(d_1 - s_1)P = s_0 - d_0$$

$$\overline{P} = \frac{s_0 - d_0}{d_1 - s_1} \quad \text{(the equilibrium price)}$$

FIGURE 1.3 EXCESS DEMAND CURVE

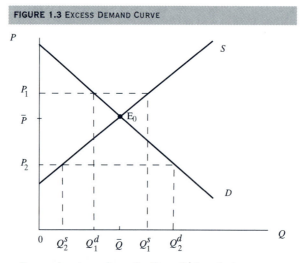

a. Demand and supply: at P_1: $Q_1^s > Q_1^d$ (surplus);
at P_2: $Q_2^d > Q_2^s$ (shortage)

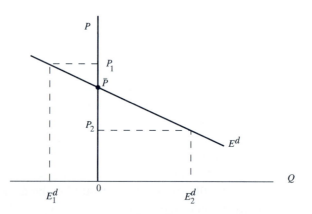

b. Excess demand: at P_1: $E_1^d = Q_1^d - Q_1^s < 0$ (surplus);
at P_2: $E_2^d = Q_2^d - Q_2^s > 0$ (shortage)

Mathematically, we cannot divide by zero, so we must restrict $d_1 \neq s_1$. In the normal case of an upward-sloping supply curve ($s_1 > 0$) and a downward-sloping demand curve ($d_1 < 0$), this condition is automatically met, since $d_1 - s_1 < 0$. Note that if $d_1 = s_1$ (meaning $1/d_1 = 1/s_1$), the demand and supply curves would have the same slopes. Either we would have an infinite number of solutions or no solution. If, $d_1 = s_1$ and $d_0 = s_0$, then the supply and demand equations would be identical and the two curves would coincide. We would have a system of one equation and two unknowns (P and Q), yielding an infinite number of solutions. If, on the other hand, $d_1 = s_1$, but $d_0 \neq s_0$, then the supply and demand equations would be *inconsistent*; the supply and demand curves would be parallel lines with no points in common; and there would be no solution.[4]

Economically, we will restrict the analysis to positive prices, that is, $P > 0$. With our assumptions here ($d_0 > 0$, $s_0 < 0$, $d_1 < 0$, and $s_1 > 0$), a positive equilibrium price is guaranteed.

To find the equilibrium quantity we can substitute the equilibrium price into either the supply or demand equation and solve for Q. (Why does it not matter which equation we use here?)

$$\overline{Q}^d = d_0 + d_1\overline{P} = d_0 + d_1(s_0 - d_0)/(d_1 - s_1) = \frac{d_1 s_0 - d_0 s_1}{d_1 - s_1} = \overline{Q}$$

$$\overline{Q}^s = s_0 + s_1\overline{P} = s_0 + s_1(s_0 - d_0)/(d_1 - s_1) = \frac{d_1 s_0 - d_0 s_1}{d_1 - s_1} = \overline{Q}$$

The same mathematical restrictions apply here, that is, $d_1 \neq s_1$. Economically we expect $\overline{Q} > 0$. Given $d_1 < 0$ and $s_1 > 0$, a negative numerator, $d_1 s_0 - d_0 s_1 < 0$, ensures a positive equilibrium quantity transacted. Note that the equilbrium values for the endogenous variables ($\overline{P}$, $\overline{Q}^d$, and $\overline{Q}^s$) are all expressed entirely in terms of the exogenous variables of the model (here d_0, s_0, d_1, and s_1).

The *structural equations* of the model (i.e., the behavioral equations for the quantity demanded and quantity supplied and the equilibrium condition), which convey the theoretical relationships, have been used to derive the *reduced-form equations* for the endogenous variables, which give the solutions for the endogenous variables. In fact, we can state that *the solution for any endogenous variable will be a function of the exogenous variables of the model.* Moreover, once an equilibrium is attained, there will be no tendency for it to change as long as the underlying exogenous variables remain constant. Or, to put it another way, only changes in the exogenous variables will cause the system to depart from the equilibrium once attained.

PRACTICE PROBLEM 1.1

Given the linear demand and supply equations for a commodity:

---

[4]A simple example of a system of one equation in two variables (x and y), yielding an infinite number of solutions, would be: $x + y = 7$. There are an infinite number of ordered pairs of real numbers, (x, y) that satisfy this equation, including $(1, 6), (2, 5)$, and $(3.1, 3.9)$. A simple example of a system of equations that is inconsistent, resulting in no solution, would be: $x + y = 7$ and $x + y = 8$. There is no ordered pair, (x, y), that simultaneously solves both of these equations.

$$Q^d = 40 - 6P \text{ and } Q^s = -4 + 5P$$

a) Determine the slopes of the demand and supply curves.
b) Solve algebraically for the market equilibrium price ($\bar{P}$) and quantity transacted ($\bar{Q}$).
c) Derive the excess demand equation, E^d, and show that the excess quantity demanded of the commodity equals zero at the market equilibrium price.

(The answers are at the end of the chapter.)

NONECONOMIC EQUILIBRIA

In this example of a typical market we have shown that an equilibrium does exist and that it is unique. Consider now two examples where mathematically an equilibrium exists and is unique, but economically it does not make sense or it is not observed in practice. We might refer to such cases as noneconomic equilibria.

First consider negative equilibrium quantities. See Figure 1.4, where the quantity transacted would be negative—suggesting a "prohibitively expensive" commodity. Given a negatively sloped, linear demand curve ($d_1 < 0$) and a positively sloped, linear supply curve ($s_1 > 0$), then a negative equilibrium quantity means that $d_1 s_0 > d_0 s_1 > 0$. Graphically, the price intercept of the supply curve is greater than the price intercept of the demand curve: $-s_0/s_1 > -d_0/d_1 > 0$. An example might be new nuclear power plants in the United States where safety and environmental concerns have escalated costs and depressed demand. Or, currently, the market for commercial space travel to the Moon does not exist—even though there may be a demand for such an experience,

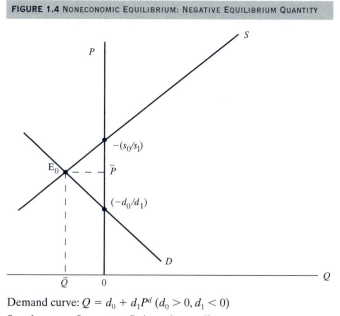

FIGURE 1.4 NONECONOMIC EQUILIBRIUM: NEGATIVE EQUILIBRIUM QUANTITY

Demand curve: $Q = d_0 + d_1 P^d$ ($d_0 > 0, d_1 < 0$)
Supply curve: $Q = s_0 + s_1 P^s$ ($s_0 < 0, s_1 > 0$)

$\bar{Q} < 0$ since $d_1 s_0 > d_0 s_1 > 0$ or $-(s_0/s_1) > -(d_0/d_1) > 0$

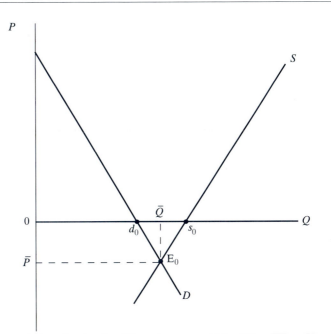

Demand curve: $Q^d = d_0 + d_1 P \ (d_0 > 0, d_1 < 0)$
Supply curve: $Q^s = s_0 + s_1 P \ (s_0 > 0, s_1 > 0)$
$\overline{P} < 0$ since $s_0 > d_0 > 0$

FIGURE 1.5 NONECONOMIC EQUILIBRIUM: NEGATIVE EQUILIBRIUM PRICE

the costs are exorbitant. Although we now observe no transactions in either market; nuclear power plants were built in the United States in the past, and commercial space travel may well take place in the future.

Consider now negative equilibrium prices. In Figure 1.5, the market-clearing price would be negative. Here the supply quantity intercept is not only positive, but greater than the demand quantity intercept: $s_0 > d_0 > 0$. This is the case of a "free good." An example might be leaves in the autumn that are more than plentiful enough to satisfy homeowners' demand for compost. Indeed, homeowners may pay someone to rake up and haul off their excess leaves.

In sum, for operative markets, with positive prices and quantities transacted, the values of the parameters underlying the market demand and market supply schedules ($d_0, d_1, s_0,$ and s_1 in our simple linear model) must satisfy certain conditions. Namely, given that $d_1 < 0$ and $s_1 > 0$, then $d_0 > s_0$ and $d_0 s_1 > d_1 s_0$. In Chapter 3 we will explore the possibility of multiple equilibria. We turn now in our introduction to equilibrium in economic models to a third characteristic, static stability.

STATIC STABILITY OF EQUILIBRIUM

An equilibrium is *stable* if any departure from the equilibrium results in adjustments to restore the equilibrium. If, on the other hand, any departure from equilibrium results in movements further away, then the equilibrium is *unstable*. Recall, with static stability we are concerned only with whether the adjustment in the system is toward or away from an equilibrium. As we will illustrate in Chapter 3, to some extent the stability of an equilibrium depends on the type of adjustment specified. Let us continue with the linear version of the static model for a perfectly competitive market.

$$Q^d = d_0 + d_1P \quad (d_0 > 0, d_1 < 0)$$

$$Q^s = s_0 + s_1P \quad (s_0 < 0, s_1 > 0)$$

$$Q^d(P) \stackrel{e}{=} Q^s(P) \quad \text{or} \quad E^d(P) \stackrel{e}{=} 0$$

In this model, an example of a **Walrasian system**, price is the adjustment mechanism.[5] In a competitive market we would expect an excess quantity demanded, indicating a shortage of the commodity, to result in a higher price—as frustrated buyers, who are unable to purchase the desired quantities, bid up the price of the commodity. In contrast, an excess quantity supplied, or a surplus on the market, would lead to a lower price—as frustrated sellers would try to reduce their accumulating inventories by lowering the price.

The requirement for **Walrasian stability** is that a price increase reduces an excess quantity demanded and that a price decrease reduces an excess quantity supplied (i.e., a decrease in price increases a negative excess quantity demanded). We illustrate this in Figure 1.6.

Begin with a price initially set below the equilibrium ($P_1 < \overline{P}$). The excess quantity demanded, equal to $Q_1^d - Q_1^s$, is indicated by the line segment F_1G_1. Reflecting the shortage, the price rises, and in so doing, reduces the quantity demanded (see the movement back along the demand curve from G_1 to E_0) and increases the quantity supplied (from F_1 to E_0 along the supply curve). The price continues to rise until reaching $\overline{P}$, where the excess quantity demanded is eliminated.

In Figure 1.7, the initial price is above the market-clearing level. The surplus (or negative excess quantity demanded) is equal to $Q_2^s - Q_2^d$ and is indicated by the line segment G_2F_2. Consequently the market price falls, increasing the quantity demanded (from G_2 to E_0) and decreasing the quantity supplied (from F_2 to E_0) until $\overline{P}$ is restored and the surplus is eliminated. Thus, the standard case of a perfectly competitive market with a downward-sloping demand curve and an upward-sloping supply curve is statically Walrasian stable.

What if the market price were restricted and not able to adjust to eliminate excess quantities demanded or supplied? To conclude this chapter, we address price ceilings and price floors.

PRICE CEILINGS AND PRICE FLOORS

In some cases, the government might deem that the market-clearing price is socially undesirable or unfair. For instance, in wartime, shortages abound as resources are

---

[5]Leon Walras (1834 to 1910) was a French economist who developed a competitive general equilibrium model where prices adjust to equilibrate or clear the markets.

FIGURE 1.6 WALRASIAN STABILITY: SHORTAGE

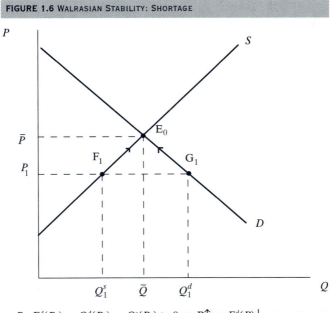

at P_1: $E^d(P_1) = Q^d(P_1) - Q^s(P_1) > 0$; so $P\uparrow \rightarrow E^d(P)\downarrow$

FIGURE 1.7 WALRASIAN STABILITY: SURPLUS

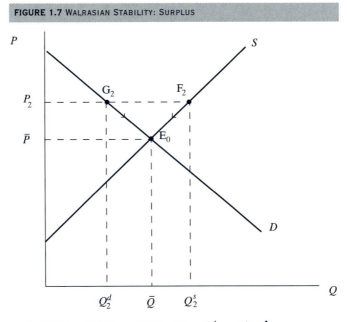

at P_2: $E^d(P_2) = Q^d(P_2) - Q^s(P_2) < 0$; so $P\downarrow \rightarrow E^d(P)\uparrow$

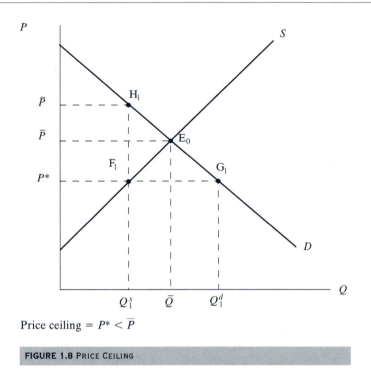

Price ceiling $= P^* < \bar{P}$

FIGURE 1.8 PRICE CEILING

devoted to national defense. The supplies of basic consumer goods, like home heating oil, may decrease sharply, driving up the market equilibrium prices. In order to reduce the burden on low-income households and distribute the sacrifice more equitably, the government might impose a **price ceiling**, which is a legally set maximum price above which no transactions should take place.

Refer to Figure 1.8 and suppose that a price ceiling of P^* has been instituted in the market for the commodity. Note, to be binding, a price ceiling must be set below the market equilibrium price ($P^* < \bar{P}$). At P^*, there is an excess quantity demanded equal to $Q_1^d - Q_1^s$, indicated also by the line segment F_1G_1; but the market price is not allowed to rise to eliminate the shortage. A method for allocating the quantity supplied of Q_1^s must be found.

That is, under a binding price ceiling, the quantity transacted is determined by the quantity supplied. Mathematically, in our linear model:

$$\bar{Q}^* = Q^s(P^*) = s_0 + s_1 P^*$$

See Q_1^s in Figure 1.8.

With first come–first served, individual demanders queue up for the scarce commodity, resulting in long lines or waiting lists. An example of this method of allocation would be concert tickets for a popular band, where there is an excess quantity of tickets demanded at the set admission price. A second method is known as sellers' preference. Here the suppliers arbitrarily choose which demanders are allowed to purchase the commodity—a practice that may discriminate against certain types of individuals. For instance, when a Major League baseball team makes the World Series, season ticketholders receive preference in the purchase of tickets. Note that these two examples of allocating a scarce commodity do not reflect a government-imposed price ceiling, but the more common occurence of suppliers with market power, for example, concert promoters and Major League baseball teams, charging fixed prices for events. If the set price is below the market-clearing level, then there will be an excess quantity demanded. In such cases, ticket-scalping is likely to take place where individuals who have purchased tickets offer to resell them for a higher price.

The third option for allocation under a price ceiling is for the government to ration the scarce commodity. Ration coupons would be distributed permitting Q_1^s units to be purchased. That is, in order to buy a unit of the commodity, individuals would need to surrender a ration coupon as well as pay the price of P^*. The government needs to determine criteria for distributing the ration coupons, and then administer the system to prevent counterfeiting.

Regardless of the method selected, under a binding price ceiling, a **black market** or **parallel market** is likely to arise, where transactions occur at prices greater than the legal maximum of P^*. In Figure 1.8, with the market demand curve, D, if Q_1^s were the quantity available, then the black market-clearing price would be $\tilde{P}$ (read P tilde).

Mathematically, the black market-clearing price of $\tilde{P}$ is found by equating the quantity demanded at that price, $Q^d(\tilde{P}) = d_0 + d_1\tilde{P}$, with the quantity supplied at the price ceiling, $Q^s(P^*) = \overline{Q}^*$. That is,

$$Q^d(\tilde{P}) = d_0 + d_1\tilde{P} = s_0 + s_1P^* = \overline{Q}^*$$

Solving for $\tilde{P}$, we have

$$d_0 + d_1\tilde{P} = s_0 + s_1P^*$$

$$\tilde{P} = \frac{s_0 - d_0 + s_1P^*}{d_1}$$

If the entire quantity supplied were sold on the black market, the illegal revenue on each unit sold would be $\tilde{P} - P^*$. In sum, under a price ceiling imposed by the government or a fixed price set by a supplier that results in a shortage, some frustrated demanders would be willing to pay a premium for the scarce commodity.

A **price floor**, in contrast, is a legally set minimum price below which no market transaction is to take place. The best example of a price floor might be the minimum wage. If the government believes that the market-clearing wage for unskilled labor is too low and reflects an exploitation of workers, a price floor for wages might be established. Refer to Figure 1.9, where the commodity represents the services of unskilled labor. The market equilibrium wage rate is $\overline{P}$. If the government sets a minimum wage of P^* (which, to be binding, must be above the market equilibrium wage), then the quantity of labor hired is Q_2^d, (which is less than the market equilibrium quantity of $\overline{Q}$).

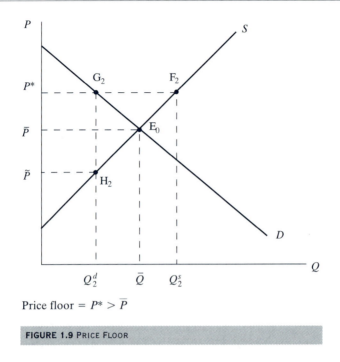

Price floor = $P^* > \overline{P}$

FIGURE 1.9 PRICE FLOOR

That is, under a binding price floor, the quantity transacted is determined by the quantity demanded. Mathematically, in our linear model:

$$\overline{Q}^* = Q^d(P^*) = d_0 + d_1 P^*$$

See Q_2^d in Figure 1.9.

At the price floor of P^*, there is an excess quantity supplied of $Q_2^s - Q_2^d$, indicated also by the line segment $G_2 F_2$. The price is not allowed to fall to eliminate this surplus.

As with a price ceiling, illegal transactions may occur under a price floor. In the case of the minimum wage, examples include the use of illegal immigrant labor to harvest crops or manufacture goods in sweatshops, where workers are paid wages below the minimum allowed. In Figure 1.9, given the demand and supply curves of D and S and the quantity of labor demanded at the price floor, Q_2^d, the illegal market-clearing price would be $\tilde{P}$. That is, the quantity supplied at $\tilde{P}$ would be equal to Q_2^d, which is the quantity demanded at P^*.

Mathematically, the illegal market-clearing price of $\tilde{P}$ is found by equating the quantity supplied at that price, $Q^s(\tilde{P}) = s_0 + s_1 \tilde{P}$, with the quantity demanded at the price floor, $Q^d(P^*) = \overline{Q}^*$. That is,

$$Q^s(\tilde{P}) = s_0 + s_1 \tilde{P} = d_0 + d_1 P^* = \overline{Q}^*$$

Solving for $\tilde{P}$, we have

$$s_0 + s_1 \tilde{P} = d_0 + d_1 P^*$$

$$\tilde{P} = \frac{d_0 - s_0 + d_1 P^*}{s_1}$$

In sum, with binding legislated prices like price ceilings and price floors, a market would not legally attain a competitive equilibrium, where the quantity demanded equals the quantity supplied at a market-clearing price. Instead, an institutional equilibrium would be imposed, and with the frustrated buyers or sellers, a parallel market of illegal transactions would likely develop.

PRACTICE PROBLEM 1.2

Given the linear demand and supply equations for a commodity:

$$Q^d = 250 - 8P \quad \text{and} \quad Q^s = -50 + 12P$$

a) Determine the market equilibrium price and quantity transacted.
b) Determine the quantity transacted under a price ceiling of $P^* = 12$.
c) Determine the quantity transacted under a price floor of $P^* = 17$.

(The answers are at the end of the chapter.)

In Chapter 3, we will extend the static analysis of competitive markets and express the Walrasian stability condition in terms of the slopes of the demand and supply curves. We also examine a type of market system where quantity, instead of price, serves as the adjustment mechanism. First, however, in Chapter 2, we review some basic mathematical concepts that are important not only for the static analysis of competitive markets, but also for economic models in general.

❖ KEY TERMS

Economics

- black market (parallel market) (p. 15)
- economic model (p. 2)
- excess quantity demanded (p. 5)

- law of demand (p. 4)
- law of supply (p. 4)
- perfectly competitive market (p. 3)
- price ceiling (p. 14)

- price floor (p. 15)
- shortage (p. 7)
- surplus (p. 7)
- Walrasian stability (p. 12)
- Walrasian system (p. 12)

Mathematics

- behavioral equation (p. 2)
- dynamic analysis (p. 3)
- endogenous variable (p. 2)
- equilibrium (p. 3)
- equilibrium condition (p. 2)
- existence of equilibrium (p. 3)

- exogenous variable (p. 2)
- flow variable (p. 4)
- identity (p. 2)
- inconsistent equations (p. 9)
- parameter (p. 6)
- reduced-form equation (p. 9)

- stability of equilibrium (p. 3)
- static analysis (p. 3)
- stock variable (p. 4)
- structural equation (p. 9)
- uniqueness of equilibrium (p. 3)

❖ PROBLEMS

1. Given the demand and supply schedules for a commodity in a perfectly competitive market:

$$Q^d = 15 - 2P$$

$$Q^s = -3 + 4P$$

$$Q^d \overset{e}{=} Q^s$$

a) Plot the demand and supply curves and solve graphically for the equilibrium price and quantity transacted.
b) Determine the slopes of the demand and supply curves.
c) Solve algebraically for the equilibrium price and quantity transacted.
d) Derive and plot the excess demand curve.
e) Suppose the government set a price ceiling of $P^* = 2.5$. Discuss the consequences for this market.
f) Suppose the government set a price floor of $P^* = 3.5$. Discuss the consequences for this market.

2. Given the demand and supply schedules for a commodity in a perfectly competitive market:

$$Q^d = 20 - 4P$$

$$Q^s = -4 + 2P$$

$$Q^d \overset{e}{=} Q^s$$

Repeat steps a) through d) in problem 1.
e) Suppose the government set a price ceiling of $P^* = 3.5$. Discuss the consequences for this market.
f) Suppose the government set a price floor of $P^* = 3.0$. Discuss the consequences for this market.

3. Given the demand and supply schedules for a commodity in a perfectly competitive market:

$$Q^d = 6 - 3P$$

$$Q^s = -9 + 2P$$

$$Q^d \overset{e}{=} Q^s$$

Determine the market equilibrium price and quantity transacted. What do you conclude?

4. Given the demand and supply schedules for a commodity in a perfectly competitive market:

$$Q^d = 50 + d_1P \qquad (d_1 < 0)$$

$$Q^s = -10 + 5P$$

$$Q^d \overset{e}{=} Q^s$$

Solve for the market equilibrium price and quantity transacted (both will be in terms of the parameter d_1). What, if any, additional restrictions must be placed on d_1 to ensure a positive equilibrium price and a positive quantity transacted?

5. Given the demand and supply schedules for a commodity in a perfectly competitive market:

$$Q^d = 80 - 8P$$

$$Q^s = s_0 + 2P$$

$$Q^d \stackrel{e}{=} Q^s$$

Solve for the market equilibrium price and quantity transacted (both will be in terms of the parameter s_0). What restrictions, if any, must be placed on s_0 to ensure a positive equilibrium price and a positive quantity transacted?

6. Given the demand and supply schedules for a commodity in a perfectly competitive market:

$$Q^d = d_0 + d_1P \quad (d_0 > 0, d_1 < 0)$$

$$Q^s = s_0 + s_1P \quad (s_0 < 0, s_1 > 0)$$

a) Determine the market equilibrium price and quantity transacted.
b) Suppose that the government wanted to reduce the quantity transacted of this commodity to 80% of the current market quantity transacted, that is, set $Q^* = .8\overline{Q}$. Expressed in terms of the parameters of the model, what legal price would the government have to impose to reduce the quantity transacted to $Q^* = .8\overline{Q}$ using:
   i) a price ceiling
   ii) a price floor

7. Given the demand and supply schedules for a commodity in a perfectly competitive market:

$$Q^d = 45 - 5P \quad \text{and} \quad Q^s = -11 + 3P$$

a) Determine the market equilibrium price and quantity transacted.
b) Suppose that the government wanted to reduce the quantity transacted to $Q^* = 8$. What legal price would the government have to impose using:
   i) a price ceiling
   ii) a price floor.
c) If over time the demand for this commodity were expected to increase relative to the supply, which of the legally imposed prices would become less of a market distortion? Why?

❖ ANSWERS TO PRACTICE PROBLEMS

1.1 a) The slopes of the demand and supply curves are equal to $-1/6$ and $1/5$, respectively.
   b) The market equilibrium price and quantity transacted are: $\overline{P} = 4$ and $\overline{Q} = 16$.

c) The excess demand equation is $E^d(P) = 44 - 11P$. At $\overline{P} = 4$, $E^d(\overline{P}) = 44 - 11(4) = 0$.

1.2   a) The market equilibrium price and quantity transacted are: $\overline{P} = 15$ and $\overline{Q} = 130$.

      b) The quantity transacted under the price ceiling is $\overline{Q}^* = 94$.

      c) The quantity transacted under the price floor is $\overline{Q}^* = 114$.

A Review of Some Basic Mathematics

Before we extend our analysis of perfectly competitive markets, we will review some basic mathematical concepts, namely, sets, derivatives, and integrals. Throughout the text we will be solving economic models, determining sets of solution values for the included endogenous variables. So too, we will see numerous applications of differentiation. Some of the more familiar are: marginal revenue (derived from total revenue); marginal cost (derived from total cost); marginal product of labor (derived from production functions); and the marginal propensity to consume and autonomous expenditure multipliers (derived from macroeconomic models). We will use integration to find the areas under curves (e.g., calculating consumers' surplus) and in the solution of dynamic models. We begin our review with sets.

SETS

A *set* is a well-defined collection of elements, which may be numbers, variables, functions or objects. For example, the integers between 7 and 12 constitute a set; and the current members of the United States Senate constitute another set.

There may be zero, one, two, several, many, or an infinite number of elements in a set. At one extreme is a set with no elements, known as the *null set,* and designated by Ø. An example would be the set of all individuals who are taller than 10 feet. We illustrate the other possibilities below with sets $S_1, S_2, S_3, S_4,$ and S_5.

$S_1 = \{5\}$. The set S_1 contains the highest score possible on an Advanced Placement (AP) test.

$S_2 = \{4, 5\}$. The set S_2 contains the qualifying scores on the AP tests in microeconomics and macroeconomics required for Davidson College credit for Economics 101, the economic principles course.

$S_3 = \{1, 2, 3, 5, 7\}$. The set S_3 consists of the positive prime numbers less than 11. (Recall, *prime numbers* are only divisible by 1 and the numbers themselves.)

$S_4 = \{x|x$ is an integer, $5 \leq x \leq 100\}$. The set S_4 consists of the 96 integers between 5 and 100, inclusive. The above notation is read "S_4 is the set of numbers x that are the integers from five to one hundred." (Recall, *integers* are the negative and positive whole numbers and zero: $\ldots -3, -2, -1, 0, 1, 2, 3 \ldots$.)

$S_5 = \{x|x$ is a real number$\}$. S_5 is an infinite set containing all the real numbers. We may designate the set of real numbers by the symbol $\mathbb{R}$. *Real numbers* consist of both rational numbers and irrational numbers.

Rational numbers are numbers that can be expressed as a ratio of two integers and as repeating decimals, for example, $5 = 10/2 = 5/1 = 5.\overline{0}$, or $1/3 = .333333 \ldots = .\overline{3}$, where the bar over the last number indicates that number is repeating. *Irrational numbers* are numbers that cannot be expressed as the ratio of two integers and as repeating decimals. Examples include $\sqrt{3}$ and Π, *pi*, which is the ratio of the circumference of a circle to its diameter. Not included as real numbers are *imaginary numbers,* consisting of the squares of negative numbers and designated by the symbol i, for example, $i = \sqrt{-1}$ and $2i = \sqrt{-4}$.

SET NOTATION

To indicate that an element, say x, is a member of a set, S, we use the symbol $\in$, and write $x \in S$. Conversely, the symbol $\notin$ indicates that an element is not a member of a particular set. Consider two sets from above: $S_2 = \{4, 5\}$ and $S_3 = \{1, 2, 3, 5, 7\}$. We can see that: $4 \in S_2$, but $4 \notin S_3$.

A *subset* of a set includes one, some, or all of the members of the set. A subset is thus "contained in" a set, indicated by the symbol $\supset$. For example, if $S_4 = \{x|x$ is an integer and $5 \leq x \leq 100\}$ and $S_5 = \{x|x$ is a real number$\}$, then $S_4 \supset S_5$. Note that the null set, $\emptyset$, with no members, is considered to be a subset of every set.

The *union* of two sets, say S_2 and S_3, indicated by the symbol $\cup$, and written as, $S_2 \cup S_3$, is the set formed by all the elements contained in either of the sets. The *intersection* of two sets, S_2 and S_3, indicated by the symbol $\cap$, and written as $S_2 \cap S_3$, is the set formed by all the elements contained in both sets, that is, all the elements common to both sets. From $S_2 = \{4, 5\}$ and $S_3 = \{1, 2, 3, 5, 7\}$, we have: $S_2 \cup S_3 = \{\{1, 2, 3, 4, 5, 7\}$ and $S_2 \cap S_3 = \{5\}$. Also, we note that: $S_3 \cup \emptyset = S_3$ (the union of any set, S_3, and the null set is the set itself) and $S_3 \cap \emptyset = \emptyset$ (the intersection of any set, S_3, and the null set is the null set.

A *universal set* consists of all the possible elements that could be included in the set, according to some specified criteria. Given a subset, S_1, of a universal set, S, i.e., $S_1 \supset S$, then the *complement set,* written as $\widetilde{S}_1$, consists of those elements in the universal set, S, that are not in the subset, S_1. For example, given $S_1 = \{5\}$ and $S = \{1, 2, 3, 5, 7\}$, where the universal set contains the positive prime numbers less than 11, then $\widetilde{S}_1 = \{1, 2, 3, 7\}$.

For an example from economics, consider a household with a budgeted income of I that is available for spending on two goods, x and y, with unit prices, P_x and P_y, respectively. The universal set might be all the combinations of the two goods that the household could afford: $S = \{(x, y)|P_x x + P_y y \leq I\}$, where x and y indicate the quantities of the two goods. A subset, S_1, would consist of all the combinations of the two goods that exactly expend the budgeted income: $S_1 = \{(x, y)|P_x\, x + P_y\, y = I\}$. Note, here the elements of the sets are ordered pairs (x, y). The complement set, $\tilde{S}_1$, would consist of all the combinations of the two goods that are affordable, but do not require all of the budgeted income: $\tilde{S}_1 = \{(x, y)|P_x\, x + P_y\, y < I\}$. Here $S_1 \supset S$, $\tilde{S}_1 \supset S$, and $S_1 \cup \tilde{S}_1 = S$, while $S_1 \cap \tilde{S}_1 = \emptyset$. In Chapter 12, which deals with constrained optimization, we will set forth a model to determine the optimal or utility-maximizing combination of the two goods, given the budgeted income, unit prices, and tastes and preferences of the household.

In general, as we solve economic models, we should ensure that the solution values for the endogenous variables included (e.g., the quantities of the two goods, x and y, the household consumes) are mathematically viable (e.g., division by zero is not allowed) and economically feasible (e.g., nonnegative quantities of the two goods). Consequently, the final set of solution values may be a subset of the universal set of possible solution values. Moreover, as we will see, additional restrictions (second-order conditions to assess critical points in optimization problems) may rule out some solution values.

PRACTICE PROBLEM 2.1

Given the three sets: $S_1 = \{1, 2, 5, 7\}$; $S_2 = \{2, 3, 5, 8, 10\}$; and $S = \{1, 2, 3, 5, 7, 8, 10\}$:
a) Find $S_1 \cup S_2$.
b) Find $S_1 \cap S_2$.
c) If S is the universal set, then find:
    i) $\tilde{S}_1$ ii) $\tilde{S}_2$ iii) $\tilde{S}_1 \cup \tilde{S}_2$ iv) $\tilde{S}_1 \cap \tilde{S}_2$

(The answers are at the end of the chapter.)

FUNCTIONS

Before reviewing derivatives, we should be clear on the concept of a function. A *function* is a correspondence between two sets of variables, such that for each element in one of the sets of variables, there is an associated unique element in the other set of variables. Consider a simple function with a dependent variable, y, and one independent variable, x; that is, $y = f(x)$, read as "y is a function of x." For the variable y to be a function of the variable x means that for each value in the *domain* of x (i.e., for each value that the variable x can assume), there is a unique value in the *range* of y (i.e., a unique value for y among the values that the variable y can assume). If there is not a unique value for the variable y (i.e., if there is more than one possible value for y) for every value of the variable x, then there is a *relation* between the variables y and x; but y is not a function of x.

For examples of functions, recall the linear demand and supply equations for a commodity in a perfectly competitive market introduced in Chapter 1: $Q^d = d_0 + d_1 P$ and $Q^s = s_0 + s_1 P$. Another example would be the combinations of the goods x and y that exactly exhaust the budgeted income of a household, given by the equation:

$P_x\, x + P_y\, y = I$; or rewritten to indicate the quantities of good y that could be purchased with the income remaining after the household's expenditures on good x: $y = I/P_y - (P_x/P_y)x$.

An example of a relation would be the combinations of the goods x and y that do not require all of the household's budgeted income: $P_x\, x + P_y\, y < I$, which can be written as $y < I/P_y - (P_x/P_y)x$. For any quantity of the good x, there may be more than one quantity of the good y that could be purchased.

To illustrate, let the unit prices of the goods x and y be $P_x = \$5$ and $P_y = \$2$, and the budgeted income of the household be $I = \$60$. The combinations of goods x and y that are affordable but leave some of the budgeted income unspent are: $5x + 2y < 60$, or $y < 30 - (5/2)x$. If the household purchases 10 units of x, that is, $x = 10$, then $y < 5$; for example, $0, 1, 2, 3$, or 4 units of y could be purchased. As noted, the budget line itself, here $5x + 2y = 60$ or $y = 30 - (5/2)x$, represents a function. If the household were to purchase 10 units of x, then exactly 5 units of y could be afforded using all of the budgeted income.

Multivariate functions, or functions of more than one independent variable, will be addressed later in the chapter.

THE DERIVATIVE

A *derivative* is a measure of the rate of change of a function. To begin, consider a function of one independent variable, $y = f(x)$. The derivative of y with respect to x, written as "dy/dx," is the instantaneous change in y that results from an infinitesimal change in x. Notationally, using the symbol d for the derivative operator, we can write:

$$dy/dx = f'(x) = \lim_{\Delta x \to 0} (\Delta y/\Delta x)$$

where the prime $'$ affixed to the function of x, read "f prime of x," indicates a first derivative. The notation, $\lim_{\Delta x \to 0} (\Delta y/\Delta x)$, means the limit (or final value) that is approached by the ratio of the change in y to the change in x ($\Delta y/\Delta x$), as the change in x approaches zero (or becomes arbitrarily small). Later in the chapter we will discuss limits and derivatives more formally. Our intent now, however, is to review the essential intuition underlying the concept of the derivative. We do note here, however, that for a function to be *differentiable* (i.e., to have a derivative), it must be *smooth* (i.e., there must be no sharp points in the graph of the function) and *continuous* (i.e., there must be no gaps or breaks in the graph of the function). Intuitively, you would be able to graph a continuous function without ever lifting the pencil from the paper.

Graphically, the derivative of a function at a point is given by the value of the slope of the line tangent to the curve $y = f(x)$ at that point. Refer to Figure 2.1, where we illustrate for linear functions. In the case of a *constant function*, $y = b + 0x = b$ (where b is a constant), the value of y is unchanged regardless of the value of x. The graph is

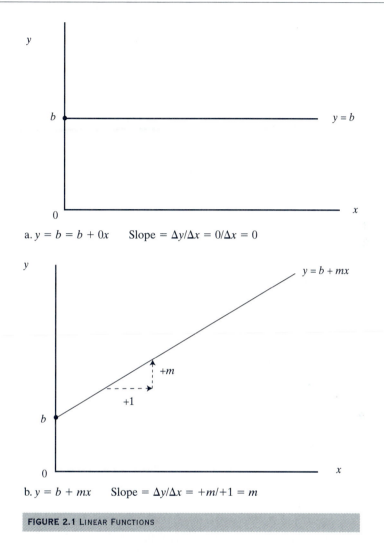

a. $y = b = b + 0x$ Slope $= \Delta y/\Delta x = 0/\Delta x = 0$

b. $y = b + mx$ Slope $= \Delta y/\Delta x = +m/+1 = m$

FIGURE 2.1 LINEAR FUNCTIONS

a line parallel to the x-axis and cutting the y-axis at $y = b$. Clearly, here the ratio $\Delta y/\Delta x$ equals zero, which is the value of the slope of the line.

In Figure 2.1b the general equation represented is $y = b + mx$ (where b and m are constants). Here we can see that every time x increases by one unit, the value of y increases by m units. The slope of the line equals m. In the case of linear functions the derivative is constant—as is the slope of the line. In general, if $y = b + mx$, then $dy/dx = m$.

For nonlinear functions, however, the derivative (and slope of the function) will not be constant. Refer to Figure 2.2 and the graph of a general function $y = f(x)$, where y is a positive, but decreasing, function of x. The slope of the curve at any point is given by the slope of the line tangent to the curve at that point. Consider the point e, with coordinates (x_e, y_e). The derivative of the function, $y = f(x)$, at point e, is equal to the

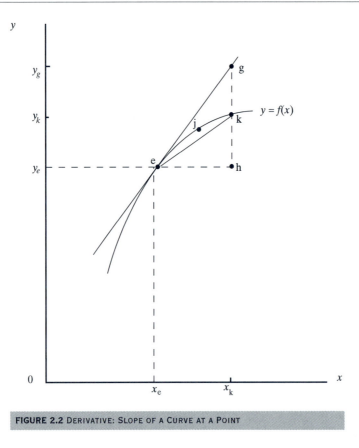

FIGURE 2.2 DERIVATIVE: SLOPE OF A CURVE AT A POINT

slope of the line tangent to the curve at point e. (See the line passing through points e and g.) The slope of the line segment $\overline{eg}$ is equal to the ratio of the line segments $\overline{gh}$ and $\overline{eh}$: the slope of $\overline{eg} = \overline{gh}/\overline{eh}$.

We can approximate the slope of the function at point e by finding the slope of a line segment between point e and another point on the curve, say point k. In this example, the slope of the line segment $\overline{ek}$, given by the ratio of the line segments $\overline{kh}$ and $\overline{eh}$ (slope of $\overline{ek} = \overline{kh}/\overline{eh}$), understates the slope of the curve at point e: that is, $\overline{gh}/\overline{eh} > \overline{kh}/\overline{eh}$. As point k moves down the curve closer to point e (or as Δx approaches zero and x_k approaches x_e), the approximation given by the slope of the line segment $\overline{ek}$ gets closer to the slope of the tangent line $\overline{eg}$. In other words, at point j (between points e and k on the curve), the line segment $\overline{ej}$ better approximates the slope of the curve at point e than does the line segment $\overline{ek}$.

BASIC RULES FOR DERIVATIVES OF FUNCTIONS WITH ONE INDEPENDENT VARIABLE

The formula for the derivative of a general power function of the form $y = ax^n$, where a and n are constants, is $dy/dx = nax^{n-1}$. Note, if $n = 0$, then the function reduces to $y = ax^0 = a$, since $x^0 = 1$. For the addition, subtraction, multiplication, or division of two functions of the same independent variable, say $y = f(x)$ and $z = g(x)$, the following basic rules apply.

Addition: If $q = q(x) = y + z = f(x) + g(x)$, then $dq/dx = dy/dx + dz/dx = f'(x) + g'(x) = q'(x)$

The derivative of the sum of two functions is equal to the sum of the derivatives of two functions.

Example: Let $y = f(x) = 3 + 5x^2$ and $z = g(x) = 6x - x^2 + x^3$

$$q(x) = f(x) + g(x) = (3 + 5x^2) + (6x - x^2 + x^3) = 3 + 6x + 4x^2 + x^3$$

$$dq/dx = f'(x) + g'(x) = (10x) + (6 - 2x + 3x^2) = 6 + 8x + 3x^2 = q'(x)$$

Subtraction: If $q = q(x) = y - z = f(x) - g(x)$, then $dq/dx = dy/dx - dz/dx = f'(x) - g'(x) = q'(x)$

The derivative of the difference of two functions is equal to the difference of the derivatives of the two functions.

Example: Let $y = f(x) = 3 + 5x^2$ and $z = g(x) = 6x - x^2 + x^3$

$$q(x) = f(x) - g(x) = (3 + 5x^2) - (6x - x^2 + x^3) = 3 - 6x + 6x^2 - x^3$$

$$dq/dx = f'(x) - g'(x) = (10x) - (6 - 2x + 3x^2) = -6 + 12x - 3x^2 = q'(x)$$

Multiplication (Product Rule): If $q = q(x) = y \cdot z = f(x) \cdot g(x)$ then $dq/dx = (dy/dx) \cdot z + y \cdot (dz/dx) = f'(x) \cdot g(x) + f(x) \cdot g'(x)$

The derivative of the product of two functions is equal to the derivative of the first function times the second function plus the first function times the derivative of the second function.

Example: $y = f(x) = 3 + 5x^2$ and $z = g(x) = 6x - x^2 + x^3$

$$q(x) = f(x) \cdot g(x) = (3 + 5x^2)(6x - x^2 + x^3) = 18x - 3x^2 + 33x^3 - 5x^4 + 5x^5$$

$$dq/dx = f'(x) \cdot g(x) + f(x) \cdot g'(x)$$

$$= (10x)(6x - x^2 + x^3) + (3 + 5x^2)(6 - 2x + 3x^2)$$

$$= 18 - 6x + 99x^2 - 20x^3 + 25x^4$$

$$= q'(x)$$

Division (Quotient Rule): If $q = q(x) = y/z = f(x)/g(x)$ then

$$dq/dx = \frac{(dy/dx) \cdot z - y \cdot (dz/dx)}{z^2} = \frac{f'(x) \cdot g(x) - f(x) \cdot g'(x)}{[g(x)]^2}$$

The derivative of the quotient of two functions is equal to the derivative of the numerator function times the denominator function less the numerator function times the derivative of the denominator function all divided by the square of the denominator function.

> ***Example:*** $y = f(x) = 3 + 5x^2$ and $z = g(x) = 6x - x^2 + x^3$
>
> $q = f(x)/g(x) = (3 + 5x^2)/(6x - x^2 + x^3)$
>
> $$dq/dx = \frac{f'(x) \cdot g(x) - f(x) \cdot g'(x)}{[g(x)]^2}$$
>
> $$= \frac{(10x)(6x - x^2 + x^3) - (3 + 5x^2)(6 - 2x + 3x^2)}{(6x - x^2 + x^3)^2}$$
>
> $$= \frac{-18 + 6x + 21x^2 - 5x^4}{(6x - x^2 + x^3)^2} = q'(x)$$

These basic rules clearly are useful (especially the product and quotient rules), since we can directly find the derivative of a function made up of the sum, difference, product, or quotient of two or more functions, without first adding, subtracting, multiplying or dividing the functions involved. An important rule for the differentiation of more complex functions of one variable is the chain rule.

THE CHAIN RULE

The *chain rule* is used to differentiate functions within functions. For example, if a variable z is a function of a second variable, y, which, itself, is a function of a third variable, x, then the variable z is ultimately a function of the variable x. Consequently, we can differentiate z with respect to x. Formally, given $z = z(y)$ and $y = y(x)$, then we can write $z = z(y(x))$, and according to the chain rule, $dz/dx = (dz/dy)(dy/dx) = z'(y) \cdot y'(x)$.

An example is: $z = 2y^2 - 5y + 1$, where $y = 4x + 3$. Here we can easily substitute x for y in the z function: $z = 2(4x + 3)^2 - 5(4x + 3) + 1 = 32x^2 + 28x + 4$. Directly differentiating z with respect to x gives: $dz/dx = 64x + 28$.

Instead, using the chain rule, we have: $dz/dx = (dz/dy)(dy/dx) = (4y - 5)(4) = 16y - 20$, and, substituting in for y, we get $dz/dx = 16(4x + 3) - 20 = 64x + 28$.

For an economic example, consider the total revenue and short-run production functions for a firm, written in general form as $R = R(Q)$ and $Q = Q(L)$. That is, total revenues (R) depend on the firm's output (Q) sold; and in the short run, the output available for sale depends on the labor (L) used by the firm. Thus, $R = R(Q(L))$. The derivative of revenues with respect to labor, known as the **marginal revenue product of labor**, MRP_L, is, using the chain rule,

$$dR/dL = (dR/dQ)(dQ/dL) = MR \cdot MP_L = MRP_L$$

The marginal revenue product of labor, which is the additional revenue earned by the firm from using another unit of labor, equals the product of the marginal revenue of output (MR) and the marginal (physical) product of labor, MP_L. Intuitively, using more labor increases the firm's output (MP_L), and this additional output generates more revenue for the firm (MR).

An example of the marginal revenue product of labor for a firm facing a linear demand function might help. Given a linear demand schedule for the firm's product, $Q^d = d_0 - d_1 P$, or alternatively, $P = (d_0/d_1) - (1/d_1)Q^d$, where $d_0 > 0$ and $d_1 > 0$, then the associated total revenue function for the firm is: $R(Q) = P \cdot Q = (d_0/d_1)Q - (1/d_1)Q^2$. Substituting in for Q, the quantity demanded of the firm's output, $Q(L)$, the general expression for the firm's short-run production function, where L is the labor used by the firm, the total revenue function becomes:

$$R(Q(L)) = (d_0/d_1)[Q(L)] - (1/d_1)[Q(L)]^2.$$

To find the marginal revenue product, we differentiate the total revenue function with respect to labor.

$$dR(Q(L))/dL = (dR/dQ)(dQ/dL) = (d_0/d_1)(dQ/dL) - (2/d_1)[Q(L)](dQ/dL)$$

$$MRP_L = MR \cdot MP_L = [(d_0/d_1) - (2/d_1)Q(L)] \, (dQ/dL)$$

since $MR = dR/dQ = (d_0/d_1) - (2/d_1)Q(L)$ and $MP_L = dQ/dL$.

Other rules for derivatives (e.g., for logarithmic and exponential functions) will be reviewed as the need arises. Partial derivatives for functions with more than two independent variables will be addressed later in this chapter. We now turn to a more formal treatment of limits.

PRACTICE PROBLEM 2.2

For each of the following functions, $y = f(x)$, find the derivative, $dy/dx = f'(x)$.
a) $y = 2x^2 - 5x^3$
b) $y = (2x - 1)/(3x + 2)$
c) $y = (2x - 1)^2(x + 1)^3$
d) $y = 3(5x - 4)^4 + 6/x^2$

(The answers are at the end of the chapter.)

LIMITS AND DERIVATIVES

The concept of a limit, referred to above, is important for establishing the continuity condition for the differentiability of a function. Given a dependent variable, y, a function of a second variable, x, that is, $y = f(x)$, the *limit* is the value that y converges to as x approaches a specific value, x_0.

The *left-hand limit*, written as, $\lim_{x \to x_0^-} y = \lim_{x \to x_0^-} f(x)$, refers to the value that y converges to as the variable x approaches a specific value, x_0, from the negative side, that is, $x < x_0$.

The *right-hand limit*, written as $\lim_{x \to x_0^+} y = \lim_{x \to x_0^+} f(x)$, refers to the value that y converges to as the variable x approaches a specific value, x_0, from the positive side, that is, $x > x_0$.

The limit of $y = f(x)$ exists at x_0, a specific value of the variable x, and is equal to L, a finite number, when both the left-hand limit and right-hand limit equal L. That is, the limit of y exists at $x = x_0$ when:

$$\lim_{x \to x_0} f(x) = L = \lim_{x \to x_0^-} f(x) = \lim_{x \to x_0^+} f(x)$$

Strictly speaking, when x approaches some arbitrary value, x_0, the value of the function, $y = f(x)$, becomes arbitrarily close to the magnitude L. When the limit of the function, $y = f(x)$, exists as x approaches x_0 and equals the value of the function at x_0, that is, $\lim_{x \to x_0} f(x) = L = f(x_0)$, then the function is said to be *continuous* at $x = x_0$. We illustrate the concept of continuity initially with two examples of discontinuous functions. Consider first the function:

$$y = f(x) = -1 \text{ if } x < 0$$

$$= 0 \text{ if } x = 0$$

$$= +1 \text{ if } x > 0.$$

The graph of the function is given in Figure 2.3a. We can see that, even though the variable x is defined for all real numbers, the function is discontinuous at $x_0 = 0$. As x approaches $x_0 = 0$, the left-hand limit is not equal to the right-hand limit.

$$\lim_{x \to 0^-} f(x) = -1 \neq +1 = \lim_{x \to 0^+} f(x)$$

The value of the function at $x = 0$, however, is equal to 0, that is, $f(0) = 0$, which is equal to neither the left-hand nor the right-hand limits.

Consider now the function: $y = 2/(x - 1)$. Here the variable x is not defined for all real numbers. In particular, $x \neq 1$. Figure 2.3b illustrates this point. The left-hand limit is $\lim_{x \to 1^-} 2/(x - 1) = -\infty$, since as x approaches 1 from below, the value of the function, $y = 2/(x - 1)$, decreases without limit. For example, for $x = .5, .95$, and $.995$, the corresponding values of y are $-4, -40$, and -400, respectively. The right-hand limit is $\lim_{x \to 1^+} 2/(x - 1) = +\infty$, since as x approaches 1 from above, the value of the function, $y = 2/(x - 1)$, increases without limit. For example, for $x = 1.5, 1.05$, and 1.005, the values of y are 4, 40, and 400, respectively. Note, the fact that $\lim_{x \to -\infty} 2/(x - 1) = \lim_{x \to +\infty} 2/(x - 1) = 0$ does not alter the discontinuity of the function.

A function, $y = f(x)$, is said to be differentiable at a point, $x = x_0$, that is, the derivative dy/dx exists at the point $x = x_0$, only if the function is continuous at the point $x = x_0$. The continuity of a function, however, is a necessary, but not sufficient, condition for differentiability. For a function, $y = f(x)$, to be differentiable at a point, $x = x_0$, it must be continuous and smooth. *Smooth* means that the function has no sharp points or sudden changes in direction.

Consider the following function, which is illustrated in Figure 2.4.

$$y = f(x) = x \quad \text{if } x \leq 5$$

$$= 10 - x \quad \text{if } x > 5$$

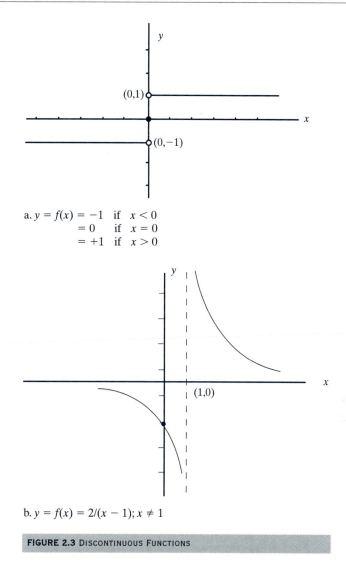

a. $y = f(x) = -1$ if $x < 0$
$ = 0$ if $x = 0$
$ = +1$ if $x > 0$

b. $y = f(x) = 2/(x - 1); x \neq 1$

FIGURE 2.3 DISCONTINUOUS FUNCTIONS

The function is continuous. In particular, the left-hand limit equals the right-hand limit at $x = 5$. See point A, with coordinates (5,5).

$$\lim_{x \to 5-} f(x) = 5 = \lim_{x \to 5+} f(x) = \lim_{x \to 5} f(x)$$

The function, however, is not differentiable at $x = 5$. Graphically, at point A, the sharp point in the graph of the function, we can see that there is no unique tangent line to the function. The derivative of $y = f(x) = x$ (for $x \leq 5$) is $dy/dx = 1$. The derivative of $y = f(x) = 10 - x$ (for $x > 5$) is $dy/dx = -1$. Clearly, the function takes a sudden change in direction at point A, where $x = 5$.

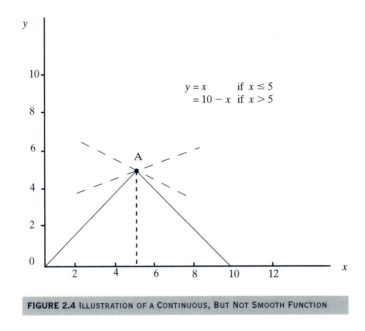

$$y = x \quad \text{if } x \leq 5$$
$$= 10 - x \quad \text{if } x > 5$$

FIGURE 2.4 ILLUSTRATION OF A CONTINUOUS, BUT NOT SMOOTH FUNCTION

In sum, a function that is continuous, need not be differentiable. A function that is smooth and continuous, however, is differentiable.

PRACTICE PROBLEM 2.3

For each of the following functions, calculate the left-hand and right-hand limits and determine whether the function is differentiable at the given value of x, here x_0.

a) $y = 1/(x + 3); x_0 = -3$

b) $y = x^2; x_0 = 0$

c) $y = |x|; x_0 = 0$ (Note: $|x|$ indicates the absolute value of x.)

(The answers are at the end of the chapter.)

DIFFERENTIALS AND DERIVATIVES

Given a function of two or more variables, the *total differential,* represents all of the possible sources of change in the dependent variable. For example, if $y = f(x_1, x_2, \ldots x_n)$, then the total differential of y, written as dy, equals

$$dy = f_1 \, dx_1 + f_2 \, dx_2 + \cdots + f_n \, dx_n$$

where f_i is the *partial derivative* of y with respect to the ith independent variable, $f_i = \delta y / \delta x_i, i = 1 \ldots n$.

Therefore, given a multivariate function, $y = f(x_1, x_2, \ldots x_n)$, we can assess the instantaneous effect on the dependent variable, y, of an infinitesimal change in any *one* of the n independent variables, x_i, $(i = 1 \ldots n)$, *holding constant the values of the other*

$n - 1$ *independent variables,* by taking the partial derivative with respect to the selected independent variable. We denote the partial derivative operator with the symbol, δ. Formally, the partial derivative of the dependent variable y with respect to the independent variable x_i is given by

$$\delta y / \delta x_i = f_i = \lim_{\Delta x_i \to 0} \Delta y / \Delta x_i$$

The term on the right-hand side of the equation is read "the limit of the ratio of the change in the dependent variable, y, to the change in the ith independent variables, x_i, as the change in that ith independent variable approaches zero."

With partial differentiation we isolate the effects from a change in one of the independent variables. Partial equilibrium analysis, the economist's version of a controlled experiment, is often indicated verbally by the Latin expression *ceteris paribus,* meaning "other things being equal." The "other things" are the other independent variables in the model that are held constant when the effects of a change in the selected independent variable of interest are evaluated. We will do numerous partial equilibrium exercises throughout the text, beginning in Chapter 3 with our analysis of perfectly competitive markets.

Geometrically, the partial derivative is the slope of the line tangent to a hypersurface at a point. (By *hypersurface,* we mean the n-dimensional surface representing the graph of a multivariate function. For more than three dimensions ($n > 3$), of course, a hypersurface is not possible to graph.) The tangent line is a function of the independent variable allowed to change.

Some numerical examples may help to illustrate.

Example 1: $y = 2x_1^2 x_2 - 3x_1 x_2^3 + 4$

Here y is a function of two independent variables x_1 and x_2. When we take the partial derivative with respect to x_1, we regard the independent variable, x_2, as a constant.

$$\delta y / \delta x_1 = 4x_1 x_2 - 3x_2^3$$

Similarly, when we take the partial derivative of the function with respect to x_2, we regard the independent variable, x_1, as a constant.

$$\delta y / \delta x_2 = 2x_1^2 - 9x_1 x_2^2$$

Example 2: $y = 3x_1^2 / x_2$

$$\delta y / \delta x_1 = 6x_1 / x_2$$
$$\delta y / \delta x_2 = -3x_1^2 / x_2^2$$

Example 3: $y = -7x_2 + (3x_3^4 + x_1)^{-2}$
$$\delta y / \delta x_1 = -2(3x_3^4 + x_1)^{-3}$$
$$\delta y / \delta x_2 = -7$$
$$\delta y / \delta x_3 = -2(3x_3^4 + x_1)^{-3} (3)(4x_3^3) = -24x_3^3 (3x_3^4 + x_1)^{-3}$$

Partial Differentials Isolating a change in one of the independent variables in a function, $y = f(x_1, x_2, \ldots x_n)$, say dx_i, $(i = 1 \ldots n)$ and holding constant all of the other independent variables, $dx_j = 0$ (where $j = 1 \ldots n$, and $j \neq i$) gives a *partial differential*. Formally, an instantaneous change in the dependent variable, y, due to an infinitesimal change in the ith independent variable, x_i, *ceteris paribus*, is the partial differential of y with respect to x_i. Here $dy = (\delta y/\delta x_i)dx_i = f_i \, dx_i$, $(i = 1 \ldots n$, and $dx_j = 0, j = 1 \ldots n$, and $j \neq i)$ is the partial differential of y with respect to the ith independent variable, x_i.

For example, if $y = x_1^4 + 8x_1 x_2 + 3x_2^3$, then $dy = (4x_1^3 + 8x_2) \, dx_1 + (8x_1 + 9x_2^2) \, dx_2$, with the partial differentials:

$$\text{for } x_1: dy = (4x_1^3 + 8x_2) \, dx_1 \qquad (\text{with } dx_2 = 0)$$

$$\text{for } x_2: dy = (8x_1 + 9x_2^2) \, dx_2 \qquad (\text{with } dx_1 = 0)$$

The associated partial derivates can easily be derived by dividing through by the change in the independent variable in question, and realizing that the other independent variable(s) are held constant, converting to the partial derivative notation.

$$(dy/dx_1)|_{dx_2=0} = \delta y/\delta x_1 = 4x_1^3 + 8x_2$$

Here we use the notation $|_{dx_2=0}$ after (dy/dx_1) to emphasize that the other independent variable (x_2) is held constant.

$$(dy/dx_2)|_{dx_1=0} = \delta y/\delta x_2 = 8x_1 + 9x_2^2$$

An example from economics comes from the analysis of the firm in the long run, where there are no fixed factors of production. Using the simple two-factor production function, $Q = Q(K, L)$, the firm can vary both capital (K) and labor (L) in producing the desired level of output (Q). (Note that in Chapter 10 we will develop the firm's decision rule for selecting the cost-minimizing (profit-maximizing) combination of capital and labor.) The total differential of output is:

$$dQ = (\delta Q/\delta K) \, dK + (\delta Q/\delta L) \, dL$$
where $\delta Q/\delta K = Q_K = MP_K = $ marginal product of capital
and $\delta Q/\delta L = Q_L = MP_L = $ marginal product of labor

The partial differentials of output with respect to capital and labor are:

$$dQ = (\delta Q/\delta K) \, dK \qquad (\text{with } dL = 0)$$
and $$dQ = (\delta Q/\delta L) \, dL \qquad (\text{with } dK = 0).$$

Total Derivatives *Total derivatives* measure the instantaneous change in a dependent variable with respect to infinitesimal changes in the exogenous variables in the model. A derivative can be interpreted as the ratio of two differentials. For example, consider the following system of equations: $z = z(y)$, $y = y(u, v)$, and $u = u(c)$. In words, the variable z is a function of the variable y, which is a function of the variables u and v; and the variable u is a function of the variable c. The exogenous variables in the system are v and c. We can illustrate the model with a flow chart, where the exogenous variables are enclosed in squares, the endogenous variables are enclosed in circles, and arrows indicate the lines of causality.

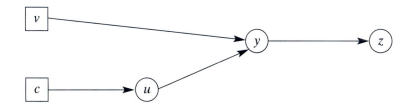

The total differential of z is found by totally differentiating the equation, $z = z[y(u(c), v)]$. Using the chain rule, we have

$$dz = (dz/dy)[(\delta y/\delta u)(du/dc)dc + (\delta y/\delta v)dv]$$

That is, the possible sources of change in the dependent variable z are:

- a change in the exogenous variable v, which affects the variable y, which affects the variable z,

$$(dz/dy)(\delta y/\delta v)dv$$

and

- a change in the exogenous variable c, which affects the variable u, which affects the variable y, which affects the variable z

$$(dz/dy)(\delta y/\delta u)(du/dc)dc.$$

Recall that a partial derivative isolates the change in one of the exogenous variables, holding constant all of the other exogenous variables. Sometimes, an exogenous variable will influence an endogenous variable indirectly or in more than one way. To capture the influence of such an exogenous variable on the endogenous variable of interest (here the dependent variable of the single equation), we should take the *total derivative* with respect to that exogenous variable. Because we are holding the other exogenous variable(s) constant, we are still taking a partial derivative (albeit one that is more involved) and we will still use the notation for partial derivatives.

In the example above, where $z = z[y(u(c), v)]$, we can find the total derivatives of the dependent variable, z, with respect to the exogenous variables, c and v. The derivative of z with respect to the exogenous variable c, dz/dc, equals

$$\delta z/\delta c = dz/dc \, |_{dv = 0} = (dz/dy)[(\delta y/\delta u)(du/dc)]$$

To emphasize that the other exogenous variable, here v, is being held constant, we use the notation $dz/dc \, |_{dv = 0}$.

The total derivative of z with respect to the exogenous variable v, dz/dv, equals

$$\delta z/\delta v = dz/dv \, |_{dc = 0} = (dz/dy)(\delta y/\delta v)$$

Given the total differential of a function of more than one exogenous variable, we can obtain the total or partial derivatives by dividing through the relevant partial differentials by the change in the exogenous variable of interest. From the partial differential with respect to the independent variable c,

$$dz = (dz/dy)[(\delta y/\delta u)(du/dc)\ dc] \qquad (dv = 0)$$

we find the total derivative, $\delta z/\delta c$, by dividing through dz by dc and converting to the partial derivate notation, $\delta z/\delta c$.

$$\delta z/\delta c = (dz/dy)[(\delta y/\delta u)(du/dc)].$$

Consider a simple economic model of the labor supply decision of a self-employed individual. Let

L = number of hours of labor supplied by the individual each month
W = wage rate per hour earned by the individual
I = labor income earned by the individual each month
E = education (in years) of the individual
Z = financial wealth of the individual (at the beginning of the month)

We hypothesize that $L = L(W(E), I(W(E)), Z)$, where $\delta L/\delta W > 0$, $\delta L/\delta I < 0$, $\delta L/\delta Z < 0$, $dI/dW > 0$, and $dW/dE > 0$. That is, the labor hours worked are directly related to the wage rate per hour, but inversely related to the income earned (assuming leisure is a normal good) and financial wealth. The income earned is positively related to the wage rate, which is a positive function of the individual's education. We illustrate below with a flow chart. The independent variables are education and financial wealth. The plus "+" or minus "−" over an arrow linking two variables indicates whether the hypothesized influence is direct or indirect.

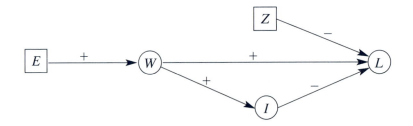

The total differential for labor supply is:

$$dL = (\delta L/\delta W)(dW/dE)\ dE + (\delta L/\delta I)(dI/dW)(dW/dE)\ dE + (\delta L/\delta Z)\ dZ$$

The total derivative of labor supply with respect to education is:

$$dL/dE\ \big|_{\ dZ = 0} = (\delta L/\delta W)(dW/dE) + (\delta L/\delta I)(dI/dW)(dW/dE)$$

$$= \delta L/\delta E \qquad (\text{since } dZ/dE = 0)$$

The total derivative of labor supply with respect to financial wealth is:

$$dL/dZ \,|_{\,dE\,=\,0} = \delta L/\delta Z \qquad (\text{since } dE/dZ = 0)$$

PRACTICE PROBLEMS 2.4 AND 2.5

2.4   For each of the following functions, find the indicated partial derivatives.

a) $y = 5x_1^3 + 2x_1^2x_2 + 3x_1x_2^2 - x_2^3 + 4$
   i) $\delta y/\delta x_1$ ii) $\delta y/\delta x_2$

b) $y = -7(x_1 + 2x_2)^5$
   i) $\delta y/\delta x_1$ ii) $\delta y/\delta x_2$

c) $y = 6x^2 - 2x + 5$ where $x = (3u + 4v)$
   i) $\delta y/\delta u$ ii) $\delta y/\delta v$

2.5   Given the following function, $e = e(a, b, c(b))$, where $\delta e/\delta a > 0$, $\delta e/\delta b < 0$, $\delta e/\delta c < 0$, and $dc/db > 0$:

a) Find the total differential, de.

b) Find the partial differentials of e with respect to:
   i) a ii) b

c) Find the partial derivatives of e with respect to
   i) a ii) b.

(The answers are at the end of the chapter.)

INTEGRATION

The procedure of integration is the reverse of that of differentiation. For a given function, $y = f(x)$, we can find the derivative, $dy/dx = f'(x)$. With integration, we begin with a derivative function, $f'(x)$, and work backward to find an original function, $y = f(x)$, called the *antiderivative* or the *integral* of the function $f'(x)$.

For example, if we have a total variable cost function, taking the derivative gives the associated marginal cost function. If we start with the marginal cost function, taking the integral yields the total variable cost function. (Recall, the short-run total cost is the sum of the total variable cost and total fixed cost, the latter being independent of the level of output.)

Graphically, if the derivative measures the slope of a curve, the integral measures the area under a curve.

NOTATION AND TERMINOLOGY

Let $y = f(x)$ be a function, assumed to be continuous, with a derivative of $dy/dx = f'(x)$. Then the integral of $f'(x)$ with respect to x can be written as $\int f'(x)\,dx = f(x) + C$, where $\int$ is the symbol for the *integral sign,* the counterpart in differentiation being the derivative operator, d. The *integrand,* or the function to be integrated is $f'(x)$. The variable of interest in the integration, here x, is indicated by dx. If there are no limits on the range of values for the variable of interest over which the integral is to be evaluated, then we say we have an *indefinite integral*. The *constant of integration* is C. If we know the initial conditions (the value of the derivative function when the independent variable in question equals zero), C can be determined. Otherwise, the constant of integration is arbitrary. We elaborate below.

Since the derivative of the constant of integration (or any constant term) equals zero, an indefinite integral yields a set of functions (differing only by an arbitrary constant of integration) whereby differentiating any one of these functions would give the integrand of the indefinite integral. For example, as noted above, the integral of a marginal cost function gives a total variable cost function plus a constant of integration. If we are given the initial conditions, we could determine the total fixed costs and, by adding the total fixed costs to the total variable cost function, derive the short run total cost function. The marginal cost function (the integrand) is associated with a set of short-run total cost functions that, for the derived total variable cost function, differ on the basis of the total fixed costs.

The procedure of integration tends to be more difficult than differentiation. While there are techniques for integration applicable in certain cases and tables for complex integrals, the standard formulas we set out for operations with derivatives are of limited use. We will restrict our analysis, however, to relatively simple integrals—ones that can be easily checked through the reverse procedure of differentiation. One general rule that we will use is for the integral of the power function, $y = ax^n$.

$$\int ax^n \, dx = a \int x^n \, dx = ax^{n+1}/(n + 1) + C$$

Some examples follow:

Example 1: $\int (x^3 + 2x)dx = \int x^3 \, dx + \int 2x \, dx = \int x^3 \, dx + 2\int x \, dx = (x^4/4 + C_1) + (2x^2/2 + C_2) = x^4/4 + x^2 + C$

Note here that we split up the integral of a sum into the sum of integrals and we brought the constant coefficient "2" outside the second integral ($\int 2x \, dx = 2 \int x \, dx$). We combined the two constants of integration to have an overall constant of integration for the integral ($C = C_1 + C_2$). We can check our work by differentiating the result.

$$\frac{d(x^4/4 + x^2 + C)}{dx} = x^3 + 2x$$

To illustrate the earlier point about the arbitrary constant of integration, C, we can see that differentiating ($x^4/4 + x^2 + C$) with respect to x would yield the integrand ($x^3 + 2x$) regardless of the value of the constant C, (e.g., $C = -5, .01, 100$, or any real number), since $dC/dx = 0$.

Example 2: $\int (2x^2 + 5x^5) \, dx = 2 \int x^2 \, dx + 5 \int x^5 \, dx = [(2/3)x^3 + C_1] + [5(2/3)x^{1.5} + C_2] = (2/3)x^3 + (10/3)x^{1.5} + C$

Check: $\dfrac{d[(2/3)x^3 + (10/3)x^{1.5} + C]}{dx} = 2x^2 + 5x^5$

Example 3: $\int(x^{-3} - 2)\, dx = \int x^{-3}\, dx - 2\int dx = (-(1/2)x^{-2} + C_1) + (-2x + C_2)$
$= -(1/2)x^{-2} - 2x + C$

Check: $\dfrac{d[(-1/2)x^{-2} - 2x + C]}{dx} = x^{-3} - 2$

Before addressing definite integrals, we will note one technique of integration that may be useful. This is the method of substitution, which reflects the chain rule used in differentiation. Examples 4 and 5 illustrate.

Example 4: Given $\int 2x\,(x^2 + 1)^3\, dx$
If we let $u(x) = x^2 + 1$, then we have $du = 2x\, dx$. Since $2x\,(x^2 + 1)^3\, dx = (x^2 + 1)^3\, 2x\, dx = u^3\, du$, we can rewrite the original integral in terms of the variable u. Doing so gives $\int u^3\, du$, which is easily integrated as $u^4/4 + C$. Now, substituting back into the original variable x, we can write: $\int 2x\,(x^2 + 1)^3\, dx = (1/4)(x^2 + 1)^4 + C$.

Check: $\dfrac{d[(1/4)(x^2 + 1)^4 + C]}{dx} = 2x(x^2 + 1)^3$

Example 5: Given $\int 6x^2\,(x^3 - 1)^2\, dx$
Let $u(x) = (x^3 - 1)$, so $du = 3x^2\, dx$, and we can write: $\int 6x^2\,(x^3 - 1)^2\, dx = 2\int 3x^2\,(x^3 - 1)^2\, dx = 2\int u^2\, du = 2\,(u^3/3) + C = (2/3)\,(x^3 - 1)^3 + C$.

Check: $\dfrac{d[(2/3)(x^3 - 1)^3 + C]}{dx} = 2(x^3 - 1)^2(3x^2) = 6x^2(x^3 - 1)^2$

As the above examples illustrate, when the substitution technique can be applied, the integration becomes simpler.

DEFINITE INTEGRALS

Definite integrals have limits of integration and specific values. In general, given a function, $f'(x)$, that is continuous over the interval, $a \le x \le b$, we can write

$$\int_a^b f'(x)\, dx = f(x)]_a^b = f(b) - f(a)$$

where a and b are, respectively, the lower and upper *limits of integration,* indicating the specific values in the domain of the variable x over which the integral is to be evaluated. The term, $f(x)]_a^b$, indicates that the function, $f(x)$, which is the integral of $f'(x)$, is to be evaluated at $x = a$ and $x = b$, and the difference, $f(b) - f(a)$, is to be taken. This result, $\int_a^b f'(x)\, dx = f(b) - f(a)$, is known as the *fundamental theorem of calculus.*

The difference between the function $f(x)$ evaluated at $x = b$ and at $x = a$ gives the value of the definite integral over this interval and, as we will see, the area under the curve $f(x)$ between these two points in the domain. First we will illustrate with selected upper and lower limits of integration for three earlier examples.

Example 1′: $\displaystyle\int_0^1 (x^3 + 2x)\,dx = (x^4/4 + x^2)\Big]_0^1 = (1/4 + 1) - (0 + 0) = 5/4$

Example 2': $\int_1^4 (2x^2 + 5x^{.5})dx = [(2/3)x^3 + (10/3)x^{1.5})]\Big|_1^4$

$$= [(128/3) + (80/3)] - [(2/3) + 10/3)] = 196/3$$

Example 3':

$$\int_{.5}^1 (x^{-3} - 2)dx = [(-1/2)x^{-2} - 2x]\Big|_{.5}^1 = [(-1/2)(1) - 2] - [(-1/2)(4) - 1] = 1/2$$

We should note that if the technique of substitution is used in the evaluation of definite integrals, then, if we calculate the value of the integral using the substituted variable, we must change the limits of integration correspondingly. Return to the examples 4 and 5 from the previous section that are now written as definite integrals.

Example 4': $\int_0^2 2x(x^2 + 1)^3 dx = \int_1^5 u^3 du$ where $u(x) = (x^2 + 1)$

The original limits of integration, 0 and 2, have been changed to 1 and 5, respectively, to conform to the substitution of the variable u for the original variable x. That is,

$$u(0) = (0^2 + 1) = 1 \text{ and } u(2) = (2^2 + 1) = 5$$

While we can evaluate either definite integral, we need to remember to keep the limits of integration consistent.

$$\int_0^2 2x(x^2 + 1)dx = (1/4)(x^2 + 1)^4\Big|_0^2 = (1/4)[(2)^2 + 1]^4 - (1/4)[(0)^2 + 1]^4$$

$$= 625/4 - 1/4 = 156$$

$$\int_1^5 u^3 du = u^4/4\Big|_1^5 = (1/4)(5)^4 - (1/4)(1)^4 = 625/4 - 1/4 = 156$$

Example 5': $\int_1^2 6x^2(x^3 - 1)^2 dx = 2\int_0^7 u^2 du$ where $u(x) = (x^3 - 1)$

Here the limits of integration have been switched from 1 and 2 to 0 and 7, since

$$u(1) = (1^3 - 1) = 0 \quad \text{and} \quad u(2) = (2^3 - 1) = 7.$$

$$\int_1^2 6x^2(x^3 - 1)^2 dx = (2/3)(x^3 - 1)^3\Big|_1^2 = (2/3)[(2)^3 - 1]^3 - (2/3)[(1)^3 - 1]^3 = 686/3$$

$$2\int_0^7 u^2 du = (2/3)u^3\Big|_0^7 = (2/3)[(7)^3 - (0)^3] = (2/3)(343) = 686/3$$

2.6   Find the following integrals:

a) $\int (x^3 + 2x^2 + 1)\, dx$

b) $\int (-3x + 5)\, dx$

c) $\int 10x\, (x^2 - 4)^2\, dx$

2.7   Evaluate the following definite integrals:

a) $\int_0^3 (x^3 + 2x^2 + 1)\, dx$

b) $\int_{-2}^2 (-3x + 5)\, dx$

c) $\int_1^3 10x(x^2 - 4)^2\, dx$

(The answers are at the end of the chapter.)

MEASURING THE AREA UNDER A CURVE

Given a continuous function, $y = f(x)$, illustrated in Figure 2.5, suppose we want to find the area under the curve bounded by the interval on the x-axis from $x_1 = a$ to $x_4 = b$. The area of this region, labelled $x_1 e_1 e_4 x_4$, we denote as A. We could approximate this area by finding the area of the large rectangle under the curve formed by $x_1 e_1 h x_4$, which is equal to the product of the height of the rectangle ($y_1 = f(x_1)$ or the value of the function at $x = x_1$) and the length of the base ($x_4 - x_1$ or the line segment $e_1 h$). Here the area of the rectangle underestimates the area under the curve by the area of the pie-shaped wedge $e_1 e_4 h$.

If we divide up the selected interval on the x-axis and use more (thinner) rectangles we can better approximate the area under the curve. For example, using three rectangles, where, for simplicity, we assume the same width for the bases ($\Delta x = x_4 - x_3 = x_3 - x_2 = x_2 - x_1$), and, for consistency we always take the minimum value of the function over the subinterval i as the height of the rectangle, $f(x_i)$, we can sum the areas of the rectangles to approximate the area A.[1]

The area of the three rectangles, call it $\underline{A}$, is equal to

$$\underline{A} = \sum_{i=1}^{3} f(x_i)\, \Delta x_i = f(x_1)\, (x_2 - x_1) + f(x_2)\, (x_3 - x_2) + f(x_3)\, (x_4 - x_3)$$

where $\Delta x_i = x_{i+1} - x_i$ is the length of subinterval i.[2] This approximation of the area under the curve is more accurate, since our underestimation is reduced to the sum of

---

[1] Note, with our example of a monotonically increasing function over the interval of interest (i.e., the values of y rise continuously with the values of x), the minimum value of the function over any subinterval always occurs at the left-hand side (or minimum value of x) of the subinterval.

[2] The symbol Σ indicates a summation, where the lower and upper limits of summation are given by the values at the bottom and top of the symbol. For example,

$$\sum_{i=1}^{n} i = 1 + 2 + 3 + \cdots + n \quad \text{and} \quad \sum_{i=1}^{n} x_i = x_1 + x_2 + x_3 + \cdots + x_n$$

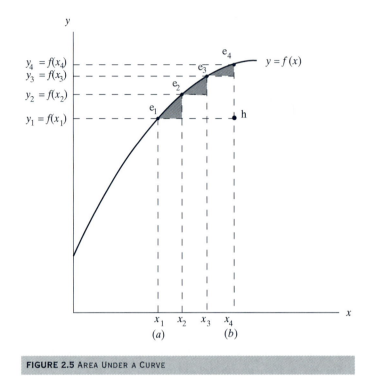

FIGURE 2.5 AREA UNDER A CURVE

the three shaded areas. As the number of rectangles (n) defined over the interval increases, the approximation of the area A obtained by summing the areas of the rectangles improves. In the limit we have

$$\lim_{n \to \infty} \sum_{i=1}^{n} f(x_i)\Delta x_i = A$$

That is, as the number of rectangles defined increases toward infinity, the base of any subinterval, Δx_i approaches zero (i.e., the rectangles become thinner). We state, without proof, that the area A under the curve defined for the interval from $x_1 = a$ to $x_4 = b$ is equal to the definite integral

$$A = \int_a^b f(x)\,dx$$

Note, in this limiting case, we have "substituted" the integral sign $\int$ for the summation sign Σ; the continuous function $f(x)$ for the minimum value of the function over the subinterval $f(x_i)$; and the infinitesimal change dx for the discrete change Δx_i.

To illustrate the geometric difference between the derivative and integral, refer to Figure 2.6, where the curve $y = x^2 + 3$ is plotted for positive values of x. The derivative of the function, $dy/dx = f'(x) = 2x$, gives the slope of the curve, which as we can see varies continuously along the curve. For example, at $x = 2$, the derivative is equal to 4, which is the slope of the tangent line to the curve at $x = 2$. (See point e_2.) The integral of the function is $\int (x^2 + 3)\,dx = (1/3)x^3 + 3x + C$. To find the area under the curve between

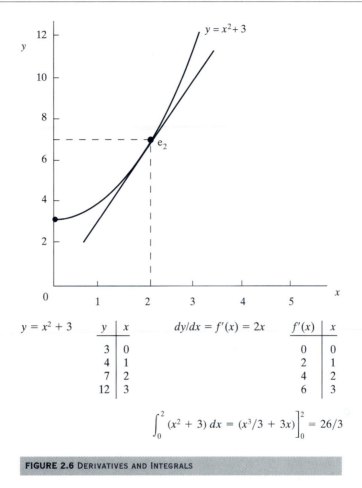

FIGURE 2.6 DERIVATIVES AND INTEGRALS

two values in the domain of x, for example, from $x = 0$ to $x = 2$, we find the value of the definite integral with lower and upper limits of integration of 0 and 2, respectively.

$$\int_0^2 (x^2 + 3)dx = (x^3/3 + 3x)\Big]_0^2 = [(8/3) + 6] - [0 + 0] = 26/3$$

Thus, the area under the curve over the interval on the x-axis from $x = 0$ to $x = 2$ is equal to 26/3.

With this mathematical review, we are ready to continue our analysis of perfectly competitive markets in Chapter 3, where we will apply the techniques of differentiation and integration.

❖ KEY TERMS

Economics

- marginal revenue product of labor (p. 28)

Mathematics

- antiderivative (integral) (p. 37)
- chain rule (p. 28)
- complement set (p. 22)
- constant of integration (p. 38)
- constant function (p. 24)
- continuous (p. 24)
- derivative (p. 24)
- definite integral (p. 39)
- differentiable (p. 24)
- domain (p. 23)
- function (p. 23)
- fundamental theorem of calculus (p. 39)
- hypersurface (p. 33)
- imaginary number (p. 22)
- indefinite integral (p. 38)
- integer (p. 22)
- integral sign (p. 37)
- integrand (p. 37)
- intersection (p. 22)
- irrational number (p. 22)
- left-hand limit (p. 29)
- limit (p. 29)
- limits of integration (p. 39)
- null set (p. 21)
- partial derivative (p. 32)
- partial differential (p. 34)
- prime number (p. 21)
- range (p. 23)
- rational number (p. 22)
- real number (p. 22)
- relation (p. 23)
- right-hand limit (p. 29)
- set (p. 21)
- smooth (p. 24)
- subset (p. 22)
- total derivative (p. 34)
- total differential (p. 32)
- union (p. 22)
- universal set (p. 22)

❖ PROBLEMS

1. Given the three sets: $S_1 = \{-1, 0, 1\}$; $S_2 = \{x | x$ is an integer and $0 < x < 10\}$; and $S_3 = \{4, 5, 6, 7\}$:
   a) Find $S_1 \cup S_2$.
   b) Find $S_1 \cap S_2$.
   c) Find $(S_1 \cap S_2) \cup S_3$
   d) If S_2 is regarded as the universal set, then find $\tilde{S}_3$.

2. Given the following sets:

   $A = \{x | x$ is a rational number$\}$

   $I = \{x | x$ is an irrational number$\}$

   $P = \{x | x$ is a prime number$\}$

   $N = \{x | x$ is an integer$\}$

   $R = \{x | x \in \mathbb{R}\}$

   Determine whether the following statements are true or false.
   a) $A \cup I = R$ b) $A \cap I = \emptyset$ c) $I \cup P = \emptyset$
   d) $3i \in R$ e) $P \cap N = P$ f) $A \supset N$

3. For each of the following functions, $y = f(x)$, find the derivative, $dy/dx = f'(x)$.
   a) $y = 3$ b) $y = 7x^2$
   c) $y = -8/x$ d) $y = 4x^{-3}$
   e) $y = (1/4)x^4 + 3x^2 - 7x$ f) $y = 1/(2x + 1)^2$
   g) $y = (3x^2 - 2x + 1)^5$ h) $y = -2u^3 + 3u$ where $u = (5x - 1)$
   i) $y = -1/u^2$ where $u = (5x^2 + 1)^3$

4. For each of the following functions: sketch the graph, then calculate the left-hand and right-hand limits and determine whether the function is differentiable at the given value of x, here x_0.
   a) $y = 3/(x - 4)$; $x_0 = 4$.
   b) $y = 2x - 1$ if $x \le 5$
      $y = 2x + 1$ if $x > 5$; $x_0 = 5$.
   c) $y = (x^2 - 4)/(x - 2)$; $x_0 = 2$.
   d) $y = |x + 2|$; $x_0 = -2$.

5. For each of the following functions, find the indicated partial derivatives:
   a) $y = x_1^2 + 2x_1 x_2 + x_2^2$
      i) $\delta y/\delta x_1$ ii) $\delta y/\delta x_2$
   b) $y = -3x_1/x_2$
      i) $\delta y/\delta x_1$ ii) $\delta y/\delta x_2$
   c) $y = -4x_1^3 + 2x_1^2 x_2 - x_1 x_3 + x_3^2 + 5$
      i) $\delta y/\delta x_1$ ii) $\delta y/\delta x_2$ iii) $\delta y/\delta x_3$
   d) $y = (x_1^2 - 5x_2)^3 + x_3$
      i) $\delta y/\delta x_1$ ii) $\delta y/\delta x_2$ iii) $\delta y/\delta x_3$

6. Given the following function: $z = z[y(u), x(u, v), v]$:
   a) Find the total differential, dz.
   b) Find the partial differentials of z with respect to:
      i) u ii) v
   c) Find the partial derivatives of z with respect to:
      i) u ii) v

7. Suppose that the birth rate in a country (B) were:
   - inversely related to the average level of education of women in the country (E);
   - directly related to the infant mortality rate in the country (M), which, in turn, is inversely related to the average level of income in the country (I);
   - directly related to the average level of income in the country (I).
   a) Set up the general equation for the birth rate (B), and then find the total differential, dB.
   b) Find the partial derivatives of the birth rate (B) with respect to:
      i) the average level of female education (E)
      ii) the average income (I)
   c) Discuss the effect that the average level of income has on the birth rate. In particular, based on this model, can you say that increases in the average level of income would lower the birth rate?

8. Find the following integrals:
   a) $\int (3x^4 - 2x + 1)\, dx$ b) $\int x^{-2}\, dx$
   c) $\int 5x^{1.5}\, dx$ d) $\int 6x\, (x^2 - 1)^3\, dx$

9. Evaluate the following definite integrals:

a) $\int_{-1}^{1} (3x^4 - 2x + 1)dx$ b) $\int_{2}^{5} x^{-2} dx$

c) $\int_{1}^{4} 5x^{1.5} dx$ d) $\int_{0}^{2} 6x(x^2 - 1)^3 dx$

10. Given the following function: $y = x^3 + 1$
    a) Plot the curve.
    b) Find the area under the curve from:
       i) $x = 0$ to $x = 1$ ii) $x = 1$ to $x = 2$.
    c) Find the slope of the curve at:
       i) $x = 0$ ii) $x = 1$ iii) $x = 2$

11. Find the area between the two curves given by the functions: $y_1 = x^3 + 1$ and $y_2 = x^2 + 1$ from $x = 1$ to $x = 2$.

❖ ANSWERS TO PRACTICE PROBLEMS

2.1 a) $S_1 \cup S_2 = \{1, 2, 3, 5, 7, 8, 10\}$
     b) $S_1 \cap S_2 = \{2, 5\}$
     c)   i) $\tilde{S}_1 = \{3, 8, 10\}$
         ii) $\tilde{S}_2 = \{1, 7\}$
         iii) $\tilde{S}_1 \cup \tilde{S}_2 = \{1, 3, 7, 8, 10\}$
         iv) $\tilde{S}_1 \cap \tilde{S}_2 = \varnothing$

2.2 a) $dy/dx = 4x - 15x^2$
     b) $dy/dx = 7/(3x + 2)^2$
     c) $dy/dx = 4(2x - 1)(x + 1)^3 + 3(2x - 1)^2 (x + 1)^2$
     d) $dy/dx = 60(5x - 4)^3 - 12/x^3$

2.3 a) $\lim_{x \to -3-} [1/(x + 3)] = -\infty$; $\lim_{x \to -3+} [1/(x + 3)] = +\infty$; function is not differentiable at $x_0 = -3$.

     b) $\lim_{x \to 0-} x^2 = 0$; $\lim_{x \to 0+} x^2 = 0$; function is differentiable at $x_0 = 0$.

     c) $\lim_{x \to 0-} |x| = 0$; $\lim_{x \to 0+} |x| = 0$; function is not differentiable at $x_0 = 0$ due to a sharp point.

2.4 a)   i) $\delta y/\delta x_1 = 15x_1^2 + 4x_1 x_2 + 3x_2^2$
         ii) $\delta y/\delta x_2 = 2x_1^2 + 6x_1 x_2 - 3x_2^2$
     b)   i) $\delta y/\delta x_1 = -35(x_1 + 2x_2)^4$
         ii) $\delta y/\delta x_2 = -70(x_1 + 2x_2)^4$

   c)　i)　$\delta y/\delta u = 108u + 144v - 6$
      ii)　$\delta y/\delta v = 144u + 192v - 8$

2.5　a)　$de = (\delta e/\delta a)da + (\delta e/\delta b)db + (\delta e/\delta c)(dc/db)db$
    b)　i)　$de = (\delta e/\delta a)da$ (with $db = 0$)
      ii)　$de = (\delta e/\delta b)db + (\delta e/\delta c)(dc/db)db$ (with $da = 0$)
    c)　i)　$\delta e/\delta a = \delta e/\delta a$
      ii)　$\delta e/\delta b = \delta e/\delta b + (\delta e/\delta c)(dc/db)$

2.6　a)　$x^4/4 + 2x^3/3 + x + C$
    b)　$-3x^2/2 + 5x + C$
    c)　$(5/3)(x^2 - 4)^3 + C$

2.7　a)　41.25
    b)　20
    c)　760/3

CHAPTER

3

PERFECTLY COMPETITIVE MARKETS: STATIC ANALYSIS

In this chapter, aided by the mathematics of differentiation and integration, we extend the static analysis of a perfectly competitive market. A Walrasian model, where price is the adjustment mechanism, is compared with a Marshallian model, with quantity as the adjustment mechanism. Departures from the usual case of negatively sloped demand and positively sloped supply curves are examined, as well as the existence of more than one equilibrium. We will see how the static stability of a given market equilibrium may be sensitive to the adjustment mechanism specified.

Derivatives will be used to express the Walrasian and Marshallian stability conditions and for the comparative static analysis, where the effects of changes in the exogenous variables of the model on the market equilibrium are evaluated. Other features of market equilibrium, in particular, total expenditures by consumers, total revenues of sellers, consumers' surplus, and producers' surplus are identified. Integral calculus is used to measure the relevant areas on the graphs of the market equilibrium.

We begin with the Walrasian model of a perfectly competitive market that was introduced in Chapter 1.

WALRASIAN STABILITY REVISITED

The three equations of the model are rewritten below, where we assume the usual case (i.e., negatively sloped demand and positively sloped supply curves) and a linear specification.

$$Q^d = d_0 + d_1 P \qquad (d_0 > 0, d_1 < 0)$$

$$Q^s = s_0 + s_1 P \qquad (s_0 < 0, s_1 > 0)$$

$$Q^d(P) \stackrel{e}{=} Q^s(P) \qquad \text{or} \qquad E^d(P) = Q^d(P) - Q^s(P) \stackrel{e}{=} 0$$

Recall from Chapter 1 that for Walrasian stability, a rise in price would decrease excess quantity demanded. Conversely, a fall in price would increase excess quantity demanded (or decrease excess quantity supplied). We can write this condition in terms of derivatives. For Walrasian static stability, we need

$$\frac{dE^d(P)}{dP} = \frac{dQ^d(P)}{dP} - \frac{dQ^s(P)}{dP} < 0$$

Substituting in the relevant derivatives from the linear demand and supply equations:

$$dQ^d(P)/dP = d_1 \quad \text{and} \quad dQ^s(P)/dP = s_1$$

we have

$$\frac{dE^d(P)}{dP} = d_1 - s_1 < 0 \ (\text{or } d_1 < s_1)$$

Note that in the normal case of a downward-sloping demand curve ($d_1 < 0$) and an upward-sloping supply curve ($s_1 > 0$), the Walrasian condition for static stability is met—regardless of the magnitudes of these derivatives.

We can express the stability condition in terms of the slopes of the demand and supply curves. We must be careful, however, when we use the Walrasian specification because of the convention in economics of placing the price on the vertical axis and quantity on the horizontal axis. The slope of the demand schedule is given by: $dP/dQ^d = 1/d_1$, and the slope of the supply schedule by: $dP/dQ^s = 1/s_1$. Thus, the Walrasian stability condition can be written as

$$\frac{dE^d(P)}{dP} = d_1 - s_1 < 0$$

$$= \frac{1}{(1/d_1)} - \frac{1}{(1/s_1)} < 0$$

$$= \frac{1}{\text{demand slope}} - \frac{1}{\text{supply slope}} < 0$$

or

$$\frac{1}{\text{demand slope}} < \frac{1}{\text{supply slope}}$$

Again, in the normal case the Walrasian stability condition holds regardless of the magnitudes of the slopes (or the relative steepness of the demand and supply curves). We illustrate with a numerical example. Suppose

$$Q^d = 40 - 8P$$

$$Q^s = -4 + 3P$$

$$Q^d(P) \overset{e}{=} Q^s(P)$$

Solving we find an equilibrium price of $\overline{P} = 4$ and quantity transacted of $\overline{Q} = 8$.

$$Q^d = 40 - 8P = -4 + 3P = Q^s$$

$$44 = 11P$$

$$\overline{P} = 4$$

$$\overline{Q} = \overline{Q^d} = 40 - 8(4) = 8 = -4 + 3(4) = \overline{Q^s}$$

If we started, however, out of equilibrium, say with an initial price of $P_1 = 3.5$ (below the market-clearing level), we would have an excess quantity demanded of 5.5 units (i.e., a shortage of 5.5 units): $E^d(3.5) = Q^d(3.5) - Q^s(3.5) = 12 - 6.5 = 5.5$. The market price is bid up by frustrated buyers seeking the desired quantities demanded. If the price rises to 3.6, the excess quantity demanded would decrease to 4.4 units in each period. The price would continue to rise until $\overline{P} = 4$ were reached, at which point the market would clear in every period. The market appears to be Walrasian stable. Here, in this linear model, every .10 increase in the market price reduces the excess quantity demanded by 1.1 units—as the quantity demanded decreases by .8 units and the quantity supplied increases by .3 units.

Indeed, the condition for Walrasian stability is satisfied. The excess demand schedule is

$$E^d(P) = Q^d(P) - Q^s(P) = (40 - 8P) - (-4 + 3P) = 44 - 11P$$

and

$$\frac{dE^d(P)}{dP} = -8 - 3 = -11 < 0$$

Conversely, an initial price above the market-clearing level, resulting in a negative excess quantity demanded, (i.e., an excess quantity supplied or surplus), should induce a drop in price, as suppliers attempt to reduce their accumulating inventories. Recall, however, the discussion of price ceilings and price floors in Chapter 1. A market may be inherently Walrasian stable, but institutional rigidities, such as legislated price limits, may prevent adjustment to eliminate a disequilibrium situation.

MARSHALLIAN SYSTEM

In a Walrasian market system price is the adjustment mechanism—with an excess quantity demanded inducing a price increase and an excess quantity supplied inducing a price decrease. The quantities demanded and supplied respond to the changes in the unit price.

Another type of adjustment occurs through changes in quantity. In a **Marshallian market system** the demand and supply equations are written in terms of the demand price and supply price.[1] Below we write a general Marshallian version of a perfectly competitive market for a commodity.

$$P^d = P^d(\bar{Q})$$

$$P^s = P^s(\overset{+}{Q})$$

$$P^d(Q) \overset{e}{=} P^s(Q)$$

where P^d = demand price for the commodity
$\quad\quad P^s$ = supply price for the commodity
$\quad\quad Q$ = quantity of the commodity on the market

The **demand price** is the unit price that buyers are willing to pay for a given quantity of the commodity. Here, consistent with the usual case, we assume that a rise in the quantity would lower the demand price. The **supply price** is the unit price that sellers are willing to accept for a given quantity of the commodity. We assume that a rise in the quantity available on the market would increase the supply price.[2] In equilibrium, the quantity available on the market must be such that the demand price matches the supply price. See Figure 3.1 for a general depiction. Note the graphical orientation (with P, the dependent variable on the vertical axis) is now consistent with the mathematical formulation. The equilibrium quantity is $\bar{Q}$, where $\bar{P} = \bar{P}^d = \bar{P}^s$.

Equivalently, we define the **excess demand price** as: $E^d(Q) \equiv P^d(Q) - P^s(Q)$. The equilibrium quantity, $\bar{Q}$, is where the excess demand price is zero: $E^d(\bar{Q}) = P^d(\bar{Q}) - P^s(\bar{Q}) = 0$.

In the Marshallian market, an excess demand price, $P^d(Q) > P^s(Q)$, should increase the quantity on the market—as the willingness of buyers to pay a higher price than sellers are prepared to accept prompts an increase in the quantity available. If the greater quantity on the market then reduces the excess demand price, the market is said to be Marshallian stable. Conversely, an excess supply price, $P^s(Q) > P^d(Q)$, should reduce the quantity on the market—as sellers require a higher unit price than the buyers are willing to pay for the given quantity. For **Marshallian stability** the drop in the quantity should increase the negative excess demand price (i.e., decrease the excess supply price).

---

[1] Alfred Marshall (1842 to 1924) was an English economist whose work laid much of the theoretical foundation for microeconomic theory.

[2] The underlying support for these relationships is from microeconomic theory. From the theory of consumer behavior we hypothesize that marginal utility diminishes as additional units of a commodity are consumed. Thus the demand price would be inversely related to the quantity of the commodity purchased. From the theory of the firm we expect that the short run marginal costs of firms eventually rise with output due to diminishing returns to labor (the variable factor). In fact, the short-run supply curve of the perfectly competitive firm is the positively-sloped portion of the short run marginal cost curve rising beyond the minimum of the short run average variable cost curve. The short run industry supply curve is the summation of the perfectly competitive firms' supply curves. Consequently, with rising marginal costs, firms would require higher supply prices to produce more output. The theories of consumer and firm behavior will be addressed formally in subsequent chapters.

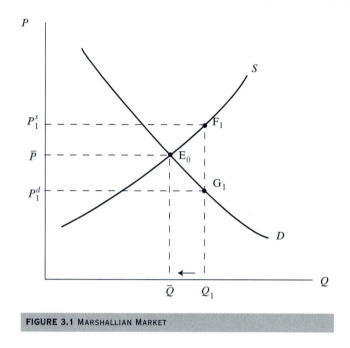

FIGURE 3.1 MARSHALLIAN MARKET

We illustrate for the usual case shown in Figure 3.1. At Q_1, there is an excess supply price of $P_1^s - P_1^d$. Consequently the quantity on the market is reduced, which does decrease the supply price (from F_1 to E_0 along the supply curve) and increase the demand price (from G_1 to E_0 along the demand curve) until $\overline{Q}$ is attained. As an exercise you should illustrate and discuss the adjustment for an initial quantity, Q_2, that is below the market-equilibrium level of $\overline{Q}$.

In sum, the condition for Marshallian stability is that the derivative of the excess demand price with respect to quantity must be negative.

$$\frac{dE^d(Q)}{dQ} = \frac{dP^d(Q)}{dQ} - \frac{dP^s(Q)}{dQ} < 0$$

In words, an increase (decrease) in quantity should decrease (increase) an excess demand price.

The particular institutional context will determine whether the Walrasian price adjustment or Marshallian quantity adjustment is the more relevant. For example, in markets for primary commodities like wheat or for trading in assets like shares of corporate stocks, prices may adjust quickly to equilibrate supply and demand. On the other hand, in some labor markets, wages may be set by contract or by implicit agreement so that employment (the quantity of labor) may bear the brunt of adjustment in the short run. In oligopolistic markets, large firms may seek to avoid costly price competition and, as a result, we find greater fluctuations in inventories and production than in prices. In Chapter 9 we will address oligopolies.

You might have noticed that, at least graphically, the demand and supply curves of the Walrasian and Marshallian systems appear indistinguishable. In fact, in the case of linear demand and supply equations we can show that the Walrasian and Marshallian formulations are examples of inverse functions.

INVERSE FUNCTIONS

Recall that to say that a variable y is a function of a variable x, written as $y = f(x)$, means that for each value in the domain of x there is a unique value in the range of y. If, in addition, for each value of y, there is a unique value of x, then an *inverse function* exists for the function $y = f(x)$, which can be written as $x = f^{-1}(y)$. In other words, for inverse functions there is a 1 to 1 mapping between the variables x and y.

Graphically, inverse functions are said to be monotonic—either continuously increasing or decreasing—so the slopes of inverse functions do not change signs. Furthermore, the derivative of the original function equals the reciprocal of the derivative of its inverse function. That is, if $y = f(x)$ and $x = f^{-1}(y)$ are inverse functions, then $dy/dx = 1/(dx/dy)$.

We will illustrate with the linear specification of the Walrasian model for a perfectly competitive market. The corresponding inverse functions yield the Marshallian model. That is, we can rewrite the demand equation to isolate the price (now referred to as the demand price) on the left-hand side. Similarly, we rewrite the supply equation in terms of the supply price. Below the equations of the two systems are listed.

Walrasian (linear)	*Marshallian* (linear)

$$Q^d = d_0 + d_1 P \qquad\qquad P^d = -d_0/d_1 + (1/d_1)Q$$

$$Q^s = s_0 + s_1 P \qquad\qquad P^s = -s_0/s_1 + (1/s_1)Q$$

$$Q^d(P) \overset{e}{=} Q^s(P) \qquad\qquad P^d(Q) \overset{e}{=} P^s(Q)$$

slope of demand curve: $dP^d/dQ = 1/d_1 = 1/(dQ^d/dP)$

slope of supply curve: $dP^s/dQ = 1/s_1 = 1/(dQ^s/dP)$

Stability conditions:

Walrasian: $dE^d(P)/dP = dQ^d/dP - dQ^s/dP = d_1 - s_1 < 0$

Marshallian: $dE^d(Q)/dQ = dP^d/dQ - dP^s/dQ = 1/d_1 - 1/s_1 < 0$

We can explain now the apparent confusion between the mathematical and graphical representations favored by economists. In analyzing most competitive markets, economists have tended to assume as more realistic the Walrasian mathematical formulation (with price as the adjustment mechanism), but used a graphical orientation consistent with the Marshallian version (with price on the vertical axis). The main drawback from this practice is in deriving the slopes of the demand and supply curves from the Walrasian demand and supply schedules. We need to use the reciprocals of dQ^d/dP and dQ^s/dP to obtain the slopes.

PRACTICE PROBLEM 3.1

Given the following Walrasian model of a perfectly competitive market:

$$Q^d = 20 - 4P$$

$$Q^s = -1 + 2P$$

$$Q^d(P) \overset{e}{=} Q^s(P)$$

a) Solve for the equilibrium price, $\overline{P}$, and quantity transacted, $\overline{Q}$.
b) Show that the condition for Walrasian stability is satisfied.
c) Convert the model to a Marshallian system and solve for the equilibrium market quantity, $\overline{Q}$, and price, $\overline{P}$.
d) Show that the condition for Marshallian stability is satisfied.
e) If the market price initially were $P_1 = 4$, what type of disequilibrium would exist and how would the market adjust?
f) If the market quantity initially were $Q_2 = 7$, what type of disequilibrium would exist and how would the market adjust?

(The answers are at the end of the chapter.)

DEPARTURES FROM THE USUAL CASE

As we have seen in the usual case of downward-sloping demand and upward-sloping supply curves that the market is stable in both the Walrasian and Marshallian senses. We now discuss some unusual cases where, despite the same demand and supply curves, the market is not stable in both senses. Consider first the case of an upward-sloping demand curve ($d_1 > 0$).

Positively Sloped Demand Curves   From microeconomic theory you might recall the theoretical possibility of a **Giffen good**, that is, an inferior good with such a strong income effect that an increase (decrease) in the unit price of the good would increase (decrease) the quantity demanded, yielding a positively sloped demand curve. Giffen goods, if they exist (and the evidence is not clear), would be inferior goods, (with an inverse relationship between the income of demanders and the demand for the commodity), that constitute a substantial portion of the consumer's budget. An example might be cassava, a staple for very poor families in the tropics.

At the other end of the spectrum, would be **status goods**, such as designer handbags or greens fees at an exclusive golf club, where the more expensive is the commodity, the greater is the quantity demanded—at least for those individuals deriving satisfaction from being able to afford these goods. Indeed, status goods may have an insignificant income effect for these individuals. Given that the market demand for the commodity is dominated by such individuals, the demand curve would be upward-sloping.

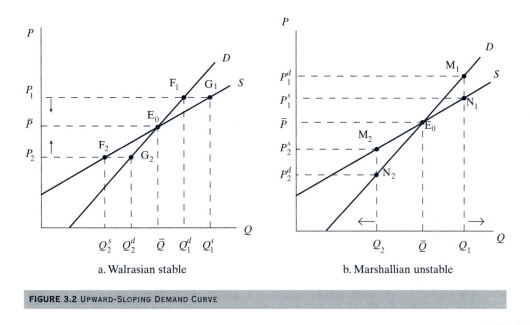

a. Walrasian stable   b. Marshallian unstable

FIGURE 3.2 UPWARD-SLOPING DEMAND CURVE

In Figure 3.2 we illustrate upward-sloping demand curves, that are, in this example, steeper or less price elastic than the supply curves.[3] If price is the adjustment mechanism, as in the Walrasian model, the market is statically stable. See Figure 3.2a and select a disequilibrium price, say $P_1 > \bar{P}$. At this above-market equilibrium price there is an excess quantity supplied, equal to $Q_1^s - Q_1^d$, and indicated by the line segment F_1G_1. The surplus drives down the unit price toward $\bar{P}$. As the market price falls, the excess quantity supplied decreases. Here with the price decrease, the quantity supplied declines faster (from G_1 to E_0) than the quantity demanded (from F_1 to E_0).

Similarly, an initial price below the market-equilibrium level, for example, $P_2 < \bar{P}$, would yield a shortage. The excess quantity demanded would drive the price up until the shortage was eliminated. We can verify mathematically that the market is Walrasian stable.

$$dE^d(P)/dP = dQ^d(P)/dP - dQ^s(P)/dP = d_1 - s_1 < 0.$$

Here, d_1 is positive, but less than s_1 ($0 < d_1 < s_1$). That is, even with an upward-sloping demand curve, the market will be Walrasian stable if the quantity demanded is less sensitive to price than is the quantity supplied.

---

[3]The **price elasticity of demand** (**price elasticity of supply**) is the ratio of the percentage change in the quantity demanded (quantity supplied) of a commodity to the percentage change in the price of the commodity. The demand is less elastic than the supply if a given change in the price induces a smaller percentage change (in absolute value) in the quantity demanded than the quantity supplied. Given two intersecting curves with positive (or negative) slopes graphed with price on the vertical axis and quantity on the horizontal axis, we can say that the steeper curve is the less price elastic. In Chapter 7 we discuss the price elasticity of demand in greater detail.

The same demand and supply curves produce a statically unstable situation in the Marshallian system. See Figure 3.2b. Begin with a quantity that is above the market-clearing level of $\overline{Q}$, say Q_1. For this quantity on the market there is an excess demand price of $P_1^d - P_1^s$, indicated by the line segment M_1N_1. With buyers willing to pay a higher price than sellers require, the quantity on the market increases. The greater quantity, however, increases the excess demand price and moves the system away from the equilibrium. The market is Marshallian unstable. Similarly, you can show that for an initial quantity that is below the equilibrium, for example, $Q_2 < \overline{Q}$, the resulting excess supply price reduces the quantity on the market, exacerbating the disequilibrium. See the arrow pointing left from the quantity Q_2.

We can confirm that the market does not satisfy the condition for Marshallian stability: $dE^d(Q)/dQ < 0$. Here, $dE^d(Q)/dQ = dP^d(Q)/dQ - dP^s(Q)/dQ = 1/d_1 - 1/s_1 > 0$, since $1/d_1 > 1/s_1 > 0$, that is, the demand curve is steeper than the supply curve, or the demand price is more sensitive than the supply price to changes in quantity.

As an exercise investigate the case of an upward-sloping demand curve that is flatter, or more price-elastic, than the upward-sloping supply curve. Would the market be Walrasian stable, or Marshallian stable, or both?

Negatively Sloped Supply Curves   Consider now the case of a downward-sloping supply curve. One possibility is a **decreasing cost industry**. The increased output that accompanies the expansion of the industry allows the suppliers of inputs to achieve economies of scale in production as they move to the right and down their long run average cost curves. The decrease in the unit costs and market prices of the inputs, in turn, shifts down the long run average cost curves of the firms in the decreasing-cost

FIGURE 3.3 DOWNWARD-SLOPING SUPPLY CURVE

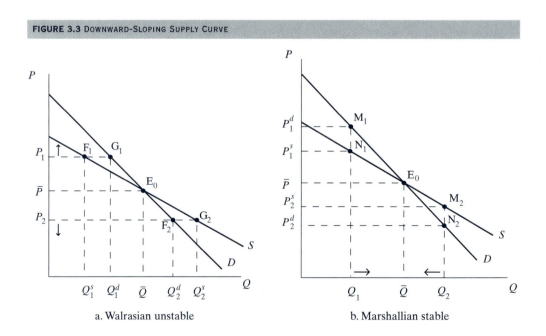

a. Walrasian unstable   b. Marshallian stable

industry. Consequently the long-run market supply curve is negatively sloped, that is, in the long run as the quantity supplied in the market rises, the unit price of the commodity falls. Personal computers may be an example of a decreasing-cost industry.

A different example comes from the market for foreign exchange (foreign currencies). If the foreign demand for the goods and services of a nation is price inelastic (i.e., the magnitude of the percentage change in the quantity demanded of the nation's exports is less than the magnitude of the percentage change in the foreign currency price of the exported goods and services), then the supply curve of foreign currency to the nation would be downward-sloping. A fall in the price of the foreign currency (i.e., an appreciation of the nation's currency) would be associated with an increase in the quantity supplied of the foreign currency to purchase the nation's exports of goods and services.[4]

To illustrate the implications of a downward-sloping supply curve for static stability, refer to Figure 3.3. Here we examine a supply curve that is more price elastic than the demand curve. (As an exercise, you should illustrate and discuss a negatively sloped supply curve that is steeper or less price elastic than the negatively sloped demand curve.) Begin with the Walrasian system in Figure 3.3a. Suppose the initial price is P_1, above the market-equilibrium price of $\bar{P}$. At P_1 there is an excess quantity demanded. The shortage prompts a rise in price, which actually increases the shortage and moves the market further away from the equilibrium. The market is Walrasian unstable.

Mathematically we can see that the condition for Walrasian stability is not met, since

$$dE^d(P)/dP = dQ^d(P)/dP - dQ^s(P)/dP = d_1 - s_1 > 0$$

Here, with the quantity supplied more responsive to a change in price than the quantity demanded, we have $|s_1| > |d_1|$; however, with the downward-sloping demand and supply curves, this means $s_1 < d_1 < 0$. Consequently, $d_1 - s_1 > 0$.

You can show that an initial price below the market equilibrium, for example, $P_2 < \bar{P}$, would generate an excess quantity supplied which, in turn, drives the market price down and further from the equilibrium.

-----

[4]For a nation that relies on exports of a commodity with a fairly price inelastic demand, the supply curve of foreign exchange may be downward-sloping. A numerical example might help. Consider Saudi Arabia, with its currency, the riyal, and let the U.S. dollar ($) represent foreign exchange. Suppose that the initial exchange rate is 4 riyal = $1.00 and that the world is importing 10 million barrels of Saudi oil each day. If the Saudi price of a barrel of oil is 72 riyal, then the dollar price would be $18, and the quantity of dollars supplied to Saudi Arabia for its oil exports would be $180 million a day. Assume that the price elasticity of the foreign demand for Saudi oil equals $-.5$. If the Saudi currency were to appreciate in value, so that only 3.6 riyal = $1.00 (here the riyal price of the dollar has decreased), then the dollar price of a 72-riyal barrel of oil rises from $18 to $20 (a 11.1% increase). The foreign quantity demanded of Saudi oil, however, would decline by only 5.5% (from 10 million barrels a day to 9.44 million barrels a day). At the new dollar price, the quantity supplied of dollars to Saudi Arabia rises from $180 million to $188.9 million a day—in response to a fall in the price of foreign exchange (from 4 riyal to 3.6 riyal per dollar). Thus, the supply curve of foreign exhange (dollars) to Saudi Arabia would be downward-sloping. For most nations, however, the supply curve of foreign exchange is likely to be upward-sloping, indicating a price-elastic foreign demand for it's exports of goods and services.

In Figure 3.3b we illustrate the Marshallian system with the identical demand and supply curves. Begin with a quantity, for example, Q_1, which is less than the market equilibrium of $\overline{Q}$. At Q_1 there is an excess demand price of $P_1^d - P_1^s$. The market quantity would rise and in doing so reduce the excess demand price (to zero). The market is Marshallian stable. Checking the condition for Marshallian stability, we find:

$$dE^d(Q)/dQ = dP^d(Q)/dQ - dP^s(Q)/dQ = 1/d_1 - 1/s_1 < 0$$

Here the demand curve is more elastic with respect to quantity than the supply—reflecting the assumption that the demand price is more responsive to quantity than is the supply price: $|1/d_1| > |1/s_1|$. And, since both curves are negatively sloped, we have: $1/d_1 < 1/s_1 < 0$.

We can see that an initial quantity above the equilibrium, for example, $Q_2 > \overline{Q}$, would produce an excess supply price ($P_2^s > P_2^d$), which triggers a decrease in the quantity on the market back to equilibrium. As the quantity is reduced, the demand price rises faster than the supply price, eliminating the discrepancy.

We illustrate with a numerical example. The Walrasian and Marshallian versions are given below, and in Figure 3.4, the accompanying demand and supply curves are plotted.

Walrasian	*Marshallian*
$Q^d = 35 - 5P$	$P^d = 7 - (1/5)Q$
$Q^s = 50 - 10P$	$P^s = 5 - (1/10)Q$
$Q^d(P) \overset{e}{=} Q^s(P)$	$P^d(Q) \overset{e}{=} P^s(Q)$

You can confirm that the demand equations in the two versions are inverse functions—as are the supply equations. The equilibrium price found in the Walrasian system is 3, at which the quantity demanded equals the quantity supplied of 20 units. The equilibrium quantity found in the Marshallian system is 20 units, at which the demand price equals the supply price of 3. Checking the conditions for static stability, we find:

Walrasian stability:

$$dE^d(P)/dP = dQ^d/dP - dQ^s/dP = (-5) - (-10) = 5 > 0 \text{ (unstable)}$$

Marshallian stability:

$$dE^d(Q)/dQ = dP^d/dQ - dP^s/dQ = (-1/5) - (-1/10) = -1/10 < 0 \text{ (stable)}$$

We see again that with negatively sloped demand and supply curves, the static stability of the market depends on the relative magnitudes of the slopes. Here the quantity demanded is less sensitive to price than is the quantity supplied (the demand curve is steeper than the supply curve) and the market is Walrasian unstable. This means, however, that the demand price is more sensitive to quantity than is the supply price. Consequently, the market is Marshallian stable.

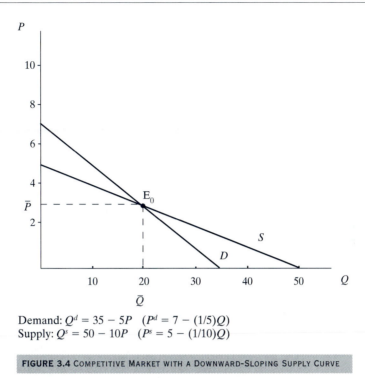

Demand: $Q^d = 35 - 5P$ $(P^d = 7 - (1/5)Q)$
Supply: $Q^s = 50 - 10P$ $(P^s = 5 - (1/10)Q)$

FIGURE 3.4 COMPETITIVE MARKET WITH A DOWNWARD-SLOPING SUPPLY CURVE

A final note: do not try to memorize the various situations for demand and supply. Rather, seek to develop the ability to analyze the particular case under investigation so that you can determine the stability properties.

PRACTICE PROBLEM 3.2

Given the demand and supply schedules for a commodity in a perfectly competitive market:

Walrasian	Marshallian
$Q^d = 30 - 3P$	$P^d = 10 - (1/3)Q$
$Q^s = 25 - 2P$	$P^s = 12.5 - (1/2)Q$
$Q^d(P) \stackrel{e}{=} Q^s(P)$	$P^d(Q) \stackrel{e}{=} P^s(Q)$

a) Find the market equilibrium price, $\overline{P}$, and quantity transacted, $\overline{Q}$.
b) Determine whether the market is Walrasian stable.
c) Determine whether the market is Marshallian stable.

(The answers are at the end of the chapter.)

MULTIPLE EQUILIBRIA

Up to now we have confined our analysis to market equilibria that existed (and made sense economically) and that were unique. In part, the limited scope reflected our use of linear demand and supply equations. With nonlinear demand or supply equations and slopes that change direction, the possibility of multiple equilibria arises.

For example, in a competitive labor market we expect to find an upward-sloping supply curve for labor, representing the positive relationship between the quantity of labor supplied (number of labor hours per period) and the unit price of labor (the hourly wage rate). For individuals, a rise in the wage rate indicates a rise in the opportunity cost of an hour of leisure. Thus, individuals would tend to substitute away from leisure and increase the quantity of labor hours supplied—the **substitution effect**. Given that leisure is a normal good, we need to consider the opposing income effect. A higher wage would, for a given quantity of hours worked, increase income and the ability to purchase or consume more leisure—the **income effect**. Usually we assume that the substitution effect dominates in the labor market so that the labor supply curve is upward-sloping. (In Chapter 12 we will formally model an individual's labor-leisure decision.) In Figure 3.5, however, we illustrate a labor market where, for a range of wage rates (between w_a and w_b), the income effect overwhelms the substitution effect and the labor supply curve is negatively-sloped. We can see that for the given labor demand curve there are three equilibria. The implications for stability are interesting.

We will restrict our analysis in this example to a Walrasian system—since for each wage there is a unique quantity of labor supplied (and a unique quantity of labor demanded); however, for each quantity of labor there is not a unique supply price of labor. Of the equilibrium wages, two are stable: w_1 and w_3. For wages below w_1 there is an excess demand for labor, pushing the wage rate back up to w_1. For wages between

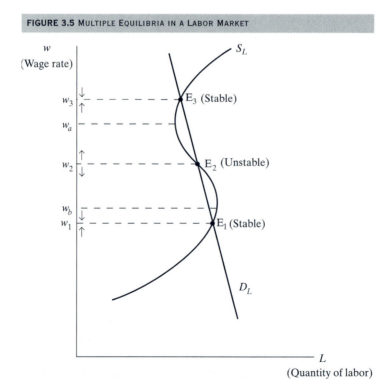

FIGURE 3.5 MULTIPLE EQUILIBRIA IN A LABOR MARKET

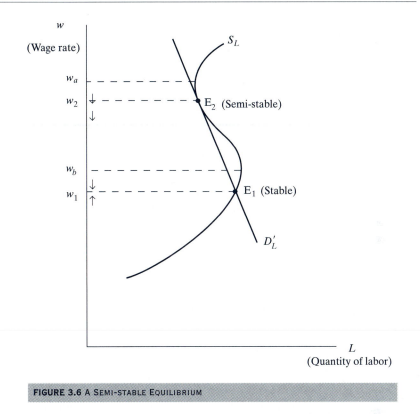

FIGURE 3.6 A SEMI-STABLE EQUILIBRIUM

w_1 and w_2, an excess supply of labor would exist, pulling the market wage back down to w_1. If the initial wage were between w_2 and w_3, an excess demand for labor would again occur, and the wage would rise to w_3. Finally, any wage greater than w_3 would be reduced back to w_3, due to the excess supply of labor.[5] While such an unusual labor market may be hard to identify in practice, the theoretical possibility should be noted. Moreover, with multiple equilibria in a market we would not expect to find adjacent equilibria (e.g., E_1 and E_2, or E_2 and E_3) either both stable or both unstable. Why not?

Before leaving this subject we illustrate an interesting variation on this labor market. Suppose the demand for labor decreased so that the new demand curve, D_L', was just tangent to the downward-sloping portion of the supply curve while also cutting the lower upward-sloping portion of the supply curve. See Figure 3.6. The equilibrium represented by E_1 is stable. For wages below w_1, the excess demand for labor would push the market wage back up to w_1. For wages between w_1 and w_2, the excess supply of labor would pull the wage back down to w_1. For wages above w_2, however, the excess supply

---

[5]At the wage rates of w_a and w_b, the labor supply curve is vertical. As the wage falls from w_2 to w_b, the excess supply of labor initially increases (i.e., the negative excess quantity demanded of labor decreases, becoming more negative). From w_b to w_1, however, declines in the wage rate reduce the excess supply of labor—consistent with Walrasian stability. Conversely, as the wage rate rises from w_2 to w_a, the excess demand for labor initially increases. From w_a to w_3, however, a rise in the wage rate reduces the excess demand for labor—consistent with Walrasian stability. Thus, the downward-sloping portion of the labor supply curve and wages between w_a and w_b produce the Walrasian instability in this labor market.

of labor would reduce the wage back to w_2. We might label the equilibrium represented by E_2 as *semi-stable,* or stable only for wages higher than the equilibrium wage of w_2. Note that with the exception of the equilibrium wage, w_2, for any wage greater than w_1, there is an excess supply of labor with downward pressure on the market wage.

To sum up our discussion of static stability, we might note that we do find large movements in prices and quantities in one direction. In particular, on occasion, we observe prices either collapsing toward zero (e.g., the stock price of a speculative company that has fallen out of favor with investors) or accelerating seemingly without limit (e.g., money prices in a nation experiencing hyperinflation). Do these movements in prices and quantities reflect statically unstable markets—in either the Walrasian or Marshallian senses? Or might these movements reflect frequent and reinforcing shifts in the underlying demand and supply curves of the commodities in question? To explore the latter possibility, we will turn to comparative static analysis. First, we discuss some other important measures associated with a static market equilibrium.

ADDITIONAL FEATURES OF MARKET EQUILIBRIUM

We have examined equilibrium solutions in a perfectly competitive market and determined the conditions under which the equilibrium exists, is unique, and is statically stable. There are other features of market equilibrium of interest.

For example, **total expenditures** (TE) and **total revenues** (TR) refer, respectively, to the values of the expenditures made by buyers and the revenues received by sellers for the quantity transacted in the market. Absent of market distortions, such as excise taxes, total expenditures would equal total revenues—both being the product of the market equilibrium price and quantity transacted.

Consumers' surplus (CS) refers to the difference between the value placed by the demanders on a given quantity of a commodity (read off the market demand curve) and the unit price that must be paid to purchase the commodity. In a perfectly competitive market, the price paid by all buyers, as well as the price received by all sellers, would be equal to the market equilibrium price. Consumers' surplus enhances the welfare of consumers, since it indicates the "savings" to consumers of being able to purchase the commodity for a price that is lower than they would have been willing to pay.

For example, suppose you are willing to pay up to $10 to see the latest James Bond movie. The cost of the movie ticket, however, is only $7. You would then pay the $7, and regard the "savings" of $3 as your consumer's surplus on this transaction.

Producers' surplus (PS) refers to the difference between the price received for a given quantity of the commodity and the price sellers would be willing to accept to supply that quantity (read off the market supply curve). Producers' surplus increases the profits of producers, since it indicates the additional revenues gained by selling the commodity for a higher price than the minimum prices acceptable.

To continue the earlier example, suppose the proprietor of the movie theater would be actually willing to sell a ticket for $5, but charges the market price of $7. The producers' surplus on the ticket sold to you is $2.

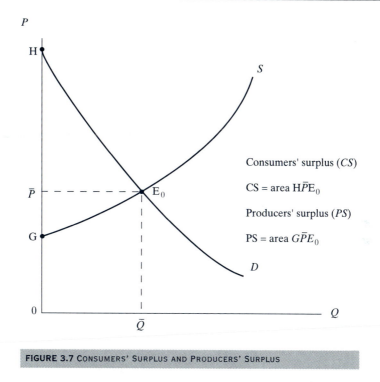

FIGURE 3.7 CONSUMERS' SURPLUS AND PRODUCERS' SURPLUS

We illustrate this concept in Figure 3.7. The market equilibrium price and quantity transacted give total expenditures and total revenues of $\bar{P} \cdot \bar{Q}$, or the area represented by the rectangle $O\bar{P}E_0\bar{Q}$. The greatest per unit consumers' surplus is "nearly" $H\bar{P}$. Per unit consumers' surplus declines with additional units purchased.[6] The total consumers' surplus is given by the area $H\bar{P}E_0$, which indicates the total value placed by the demanders on the $\bar{Q}$ units purchased less the total expenditures made. Per unit producers' surplus, greatest at "nearly" $G\bar{P}$, also declines as the quantity sold rises. The total producers' surplus is given by the area $G\bar{P}E_0$, which indicates the difference between the total revenues received for the $\bar{Q}$ units sold and the total variable costs of production. At $\bar{Q}$, where the demand price equals the supply price, the consumers' surplus and producers' surplus on the last unit transacted equal zero.

In a perfectly competitive market, the sum of the total consumers' surplus and producers' surplus is maximized—compared to other types of market structures like monopoly. (This result will be illustrated in Chapter 8 when monopolies are addressed.) Intuitively, if on the last unit sold during the period there is no additional consumers' surplus or producers' surplus to be realized, that is, on that last unit the market equilibrium price equals the (highest) price consumers are willing to pay and

---

[6]We say "nearly," since the demand and supply curves are really "step-functions," where the quantities demanded and supplied are in discrete units. Technically, points H and G are not included on the demand and supply curves, respectively, and should be indicated graphically by open dots. Thus, the first unit demanded has a consumers' surplus that is "slightly" less than $H\bar{P}$, and the first unit supplied has a producers' surplus that is "slightly" less than $G\bar{P}$.

the (lowest) price sellers are willing to accept, then the sum of consumers' and producers' surpluses must be maximized.

Economists attempt to measure consumers' surplus and producers' surplus in order to assess the impacts on consumers and producers of given policies. For instance, with barriers to trade (e.g., import tariffs and quotas) that raise the prices of the imported commodities to domestic consumers, there are losses in consumers' surplus that can be compared with the gains in domestic producers' surplus to assess the distributional impact of the protection. There are also deadweight losses in consumers' surplus and producers' surplus that reflect the losses in consumer welfare and producer efficiency as domestic producers increase their home market share at the expense of more efficient foreign producers.

Finding the consumers' surplus and producers' surplus is straightforward with linear demand and supply equations. We can use the formula for the area of a triangle (one-half the product of the base and the height). If the market demand and supply curves, however, are not linear, then we need to use integral calculus to find the areas.

MEASURING CONSUMERS' SURPLUS AND PRODUCERS' SURPLUS

We set forth general procedures for finding consumers' surplus and producers' surplus in a perfectly competitive market. Writing the Walrasian and Marshallian versions of the model below, we assume that the demand equations (d and d^{-1}) and supply equations (s and s^{-1}) are inverse functions, although not necessarily linear. We also assume the normal case of an upward-sloping supply curve and a downward-sloping demand curve.

Walrasian	*Marshallian*
$Q^d = d\,(P)$	$P^d = d^{-1}\,(Q)$
$Q^s = s\,(P)$	$P^s = s^{-1}\,(Q)$
$Q^d \overset{e}{=} Q^s$	$P^d \overset{e}{=} P^s$

Refer back to Figure 3.7 for an illustration. To find consumers' surplus (CS) we need to subtract the total expenditures of consumers ($\overline{P} \cdot \overline{Q}$) from the area under the demand curve up to the quantity transacted. Note that if we integrate with respect to the quantity variable, we must use the Marshallian formulation.

$$CS = \text{area } H\overline{P}E_0 = \int_0^{\overline{Q}} d^{-1}\,(Q)\,dQ - (\overline{P} \cdot \overline{Q})$$

Alternatively, we could find consumers' surplus by integrating with respect to the price variable.

$$CS = \text{area } H\overline{P}E_0 = \int_{\overline{P}}^{H} d\,(P)\,dP$$

Here the interval of interest is along the price axis from the equilibrium price $\overline{P}$ to the maximum demand price of H.

To find producers' surplus (PS) we need to subtract from the total revenues received, ($\overline{P} \cdot \overline{Q}$), the area under the supply curve up to the quantity transacted $\overline{Q}$.

$$PS = \text{area } G\overline{P}E_0 = (\overline{P} \cdot \overline{Q}) - \int_0^{\overline{Q}} s^{-1}(Q)\, dQ$$

Alternatively, we could find the producers' surplus directly by integrating with respect to the price variable.

$$PS = \text{area } G\overline{P}E_0 = \int_G^{\overline{P}} s(P)\, dP$$

Here the interval of interest along the price axis is from the minimum supply price of G up to the market-equilibrium price of $\overline{P}$.

We illustrate with a numerical example, using a linear demand schedule and non-linear supply schedule.

Walrasian	*Marshallian*
$Q^d = 7 - P$	$P^d = 7 - Q$
$Q^s = (-1 + P)^{.5}$	$P^s = 1 + Q^2$
$Q^d \overset{e}{=} Q^s$	$P^d \overset{e}{=} P^s$

Note here that $P > 1$ is the minimum supply price and we restrict our solutions to non-negative prices and quantities. Using the Walrasian equilibrium condition to solve for the market-clearing price we find that

$$7 - P = (-1 + P)^{.5}$$

Squaring both sides gives

$$49 - 14P + P^2 = -1 + P$$

$$50 - 15P + P^2 = 0$$

We can use the quadratic formula to solve for the equilibrium price(s).[7]

$$\overline{P} = \frac{-(-15) \pm [(-15)^2 - 4(1)(50)]^{.5}}{2(1)} = \frac{15 \pm 5}{2} = 10 \text{ and } 5$$

Alternatively, this quadratic equation can be factored into

$$P^2 - 15P + 50 = (P - 10)(P - 5) = 0 \qquad \text{Thus } \overline{P} = 10, 5$$

---

[7]Given a general quadratic equation of the form $ax^2 + bx + c = 0$, the *quadratic formula* for the solution for x is: $x = \dfrac{-b \pm \sqrt{b^2 - 4ac}}{2a}$.

Mathematically the equilibrium prices are 10 and 5. If the unit price were 10, however, the quantity demanded would equal -3. Thus, we can eliminate 10 as a market-equilibrium price and select $\bar{P} = 5$. The quantity transacted is $\bar{Q} = 2$. Total expenditures (TE) and total revenues (TR) are equal to 10: $TE = \bar{P} \cdot \bar{Q} = (5)(2) = 10 = TR$. Refer to Figure 3.8.

To find consumers' surplus we can use:

$$CS = \int_0^2 (7 - Q)\, dQ - TE = (7Q - Q^2/2)\Big]_0^2 - (5)(2)$$

$$= [7(2) - 4/2] - [7(0) - 0/2] - (5)(2) = 2$$

Note that the limits of integration here are from 0 (the origin) to 2 (the equilibrium quantity transacted). Or we can use

$$CS = \int_5^7 (7 - P)\, dP = (7P - P^2/2)\Big]_5^7 = [7(7) - 49/2] - [(7)(5) - (25)/2] = 2$$

The limits of integration here are from 5 (the market equilibrium price) to 7 (the maximum demand price). The value of 2 for consumers' surplus indicates the "savings" in

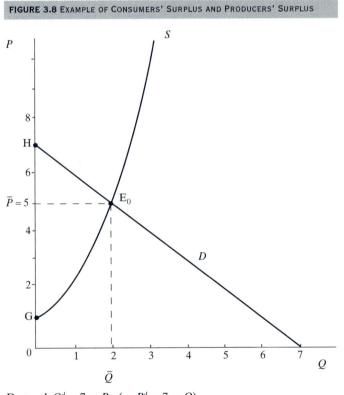

FIGURE 3.8 EXAMPLE OF CONSUMERS' SURPLUS AND PRODUCERS' SURPLUS

Demand: $Q^d = 7 - P$ (or $P^d = 7 - Q$)
Supply: $Q^s = (-1 + P)^5$ (or $P^s = 1 + Q^2$)

total expenditures to consumers from being able to purchase the commodity at the market equilibrium price, which is lower (up until the $\overline{Q}$th unit purchased) than the demand prices consumers would have been willing to pay.

To find producers surplus we can use:

$$PS = TR - \int_0^2 (1 + Q^2) \, dQ = (\overline{P} \cdot \overline{Q}) - (Q + Q^3/3) \Big]_0^2$$

$$= (5)(2) - [2 + (8/3)] - [0 + 0] = 16/3$$

or

$$PS = \int_1^5 (-1 + P)^{.5} \, dP = (2/3)(-1 + P)^{3/2} \Big]_1^5$$

$$= (2/3)[(-1 + 5)^{3/2} - (-1 + 1)^{3/2}] = 16/3$$

The limits of integration are from 1 (the minimum supply price) to 5 (the market equilibrium price). The value of 16/3 for producers' surplus indicates the gain in total revenues to producers from selling the commodity at the market equilibrium price, which is higher (up until the $\overline{Q}$th unit sold) than the supply prices producers would have accepted.

To conclude this chapter, we turn to comparative statics, an analysis that illustrates another use of the derivative.

PRACTICE PROBLEM 3.3

Given the demand and supply equations for a commodity in a perfectly competitive market:

$$Q^d = (20 - 4P)^{.5}$$

$$Q^s = -2 + 1P$$

$$Q^d(P) \overset{e}{=} Q^s(P)$$

a) Find the market equilibrium price $(\overline{P})$ and quantity transacted $(\overline{Q})$.
b) Find the consumers' surplus (CS) and producers' surplus (PS) associated with this equilibrium.

(The answers are at the end of the chapter.)

COMPARATIVE STATICS

Why do market prices and quantities transacted change? Even if a market were statically stable, and an equilibrium price and quantity had been attained, that price and quantity would likely change at some point. There are eight possible combinations of change in the market equilibrium: 1 through 3) a rise in the market price along with either a rise, fall, or no change in the quantity transacted; 4 through 6) a fall in the market price along with either a rise, fall, or no change in the quantity transacted; and 7 through 8) no change in the market price along with either a rise or fall in the quantity transacted. To understand these changes in a static market equilibrium, we turn to comparative static analysis.

Comparative statics is the comparison of different equilibrium states of a model that are associated with different sets of values for the exogenous variables in the model. Recall from Chapter 1 that the equilibrium or solution values for the endogenous variables in a model can be expressed as functions of the exogenous variables. A change in any one of the exogenous variables will disturb an equilibrium and induce adjustments in the endogenous variables. Given that the model is statically stable, a new equilibrium will be reached. We then contrast the new equilibrium values of the endogenous variables with the initial equilibrium values, attributing the differences to the change in that exogenous variable.

Comparative static analysis can be either qualitative, where only the direction of change is determined, or quantitative, where both the direction and magnitude of change are determined. Figuratively, with comparative statics we have snapshots of two different equilibrium states of a model. In dynamic analysis, the subject of Chapter 4, we are concerned with the time paths of adjustment for the endogenous variables, as with a motion picture.

The relevant mathematical concept in comparative static analysis is the derivative. If there are two or more independent or exogenous variables in the model, however, we need to use partial derivatives and the comparative static analysis is referred to as *partial equilibrium analysis.*

COMPARATIVE STATIC ANALYSIS IN A COMPETITIVE MARKET

We will use a Walrasian (price adjustment) model of a perfectly competitive market for a commodity and assume the normal case of a downward-sloping demand curve and an upward-sloping supply curve. We will include an explicit exogenous variable in each of the demand and supply equations. Furthermore, we will use a linear model in order to solve exactly for the equilibrium price and quantity transacted.

A common determinant of the demand for a commodity is income, in particular, the average income of the demanders of the commodity.[8] An increase in average income would increase the purchasing power of the demanders and for a **normal good** increase the quantity demanded at any unit price of the good. Graphically, a rise in average income shifts the demand curve for a normal good to the right. For an **inferior good** the income effect is negative: a rise in the average income of the demanders, *ceteris paribus*, reduces the demand for the good.

---

[8]As noted in Chapter 1, other common determinants of the demand for a commodity are: the number of prospective demanders (buyers) in the market; tastes and preferences; and the prices of substitute and complement commodities. To illustrate comparative static analysis, we will include one independent variable in the demand equation, here the average income of the demanders.

The exogenous variable specifically included in the supply equation for the commodity is the cost of the inputs used to produce each unit of the commodity.[9] An increase in the input cost would decrease the quantity supplied for any unit price of the commodity. Graphically the supply curve of the commodity would shift left with a rise in the unit cost of the inputs.

We write the equations for the market for the commodity below.

$$Q^d = d_0 + d_1 P + d_2 I \qquad d_0 > 0, d_1 < 0, d_2 > 0 \text{ (normal good)}$$

$$d_2 < 0 \text{ (inferior good)}$$

$$Q^s = s_0 + s_1 P + s_2 C \qquad s_0 < 0, s_1 > 0, s_2 < 0$$

$$Q^d(P) \stackrel{e}{=} Q^s(P)$$

where, in addition to the usual variables,

$$I = \text{average income of the demanders of the commodity}$$

$$C = \text{unit cost of the inputs used to produce the commodity}$$

In the model there are now three endogenous variables (Q^d, Q^s, and P) and eight exogenous variables: two independent variables I and C; and six parameters (d_0, d_1, d_2, s_0, s_1, and s_2). Setting the demand and supply equations equal we solve for the equilibrium price.

$$d_0 + d_1 P + d_2 I = s_0 + s_1 P + s_2 C$$

$$(d_1 - s_1) P = (s_0 - d_0) + s_2 C - d_2 I$$

$$\overline{P} = \frac{s_0 - d_0}{d_1 - s_1} + \frac{s_2}{d_1 - s_1} C - \frac{d_2}{d_1 - s_1} I \qquad \{1\}$$

The market equilibrium price is expressed entirely in terms of the independent variables and parameters of the model. To solve for the quantity transacted we substitute this expression for $\overline{P}$ into either the demand or supply equation and simplify. We find:

$$\overline{Q} = \frac{d_1 s_0 - d_0 s_1}{d_1 - s_1} + \frac{d_1 s_2}{d_1 - s_1} C - \frac{d_2 s_1}{d_1 - s_1} I \qquad \{2\}$$

We illustrate in Figure 3.9. Note the familiar restriction for an equilibrium to exist: that $d_1 \neq s_1$, or the reciprocals of the slopes of the demand and supply equations cannot be equal. In the usual case ($d_1 < 0$ and $s_1 > 0$), this condition is satisfied regardless of the relative magnitudes of the sensitivities of the quantities demanded and supplied to the unit price of the commodity. Note also that the independent variables in this model, I and C, affect the quantity intercepts for the demand and supply curves.

---

[9]Also, recall from Chapter 1 that there are other common determinants of supply, including the number of suppliers (sellers) in the market; the technology of production; and government regulations and taxes assessed on the suppliers of the commodity in question.

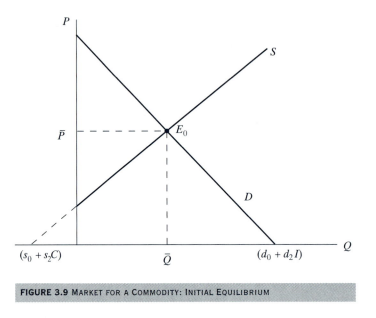

FIGURE 3.9 MARKET FOR A COMMODITY: INITIAL EQUILIBRIUM

Changes in average income and input cost will shift the demand and supply curves, respectively, in a parallel fashion; the slopes of the curves, however, will not be affected.

Changes in Income   The market equilibrium state of $\bar{P}$ and $\bar{Q}$ would prevail given the values of the independent variables and parameters of the model. If any exogenous variable changes, however, the equilibrium will be upset and adjustments in the market price and quantity transacted will occur. We will focus on changes in the independent variables of average income and input cost.

Consider first the consequences of a change in the average income of the demanders of the commodity on the equilibrium price and quantity transacted. From the equilibrium expressions (the reduced-form equations {1} and {2} for $\bar{P}$ and $\bar{Q}$), we take the partial derivatives with respect to average income.

$$\delta\bar{P}/\delta I = -d_2/(d_1 - s_1)$$

and

$$\delta\bar{Q}/\delta I = -d_2 s_1/(d_1 - s_1)$$

Signing the partial derivatives as positive or negative will allow us to determine the direction of the income effect on the market equilibrium price and quantity transacted. Recall that we have assumed $d_1 < 0$ and $s_1 > 0$, so the denominators of the partials are clearly negative. The signs of the partials therefore depend on whether the commodity is a normal good ($d_2 > 0$) or an inferior good ($d_2 < 0$).

For a normal good, $\delta\bar{P}/\delta I > 0$ and $\delta\bar{Q}/\delta I > 0$, since the numerators ($-d_2$ and $-d_2 s_1$) are also negative. In general, we can state: *Ceteris paribus*, an increase (decrease) in the average income of the demanders of a normal good would increase (decrease) the market equilibrium price and quantity transacted of the good. In the case of an inferior good, an increase (decrease) in the average income of the demanders would decrease (increase) the market equilibrium price and quantity transacted. Moreover, we can see that quantitatively the effect on price from a change in income ($|\delta \overline{P}/\delta I|$) depends directly on the magnitude of the parameter d_2. The effect on the quantity transacted ($|\delta \overline{Q}/\delta I|$) is directly related also to the price responsiveness of the quantity supplied (the s_1 parameter).

We illustrate these concepts in Figure 3.10. For a normal good (e.g., color television sets) an increase in average income would shift the linear demand curve to the right in a parallel fashion by the amount $d_2 \Delta I$ (where $\Delta I = I' - I$ is the increase in average income). At the initial equilibrium price of $\overline{P}$, there is now an excess quantity demanded (represented by the line segment $E_0 F$). The market price rises, reducing the quantity demanded (from F to E_0' along the new demand curve, D', corresponding to the higher income of I') and increasing the quantity supplied (from E to E_0' along the supply curve, S) until the shortage is eliminated. In the new equilibrium associated with the greater income of the demanders the market-clearing price and quantity transacted are higher.

For an inferior good (e.g., black and white television sets) the increase in demand from D to D' would be consistent with a fall in the average income of the demanders

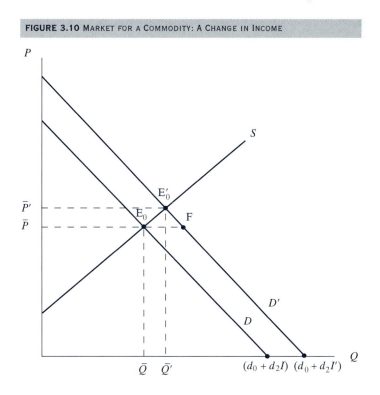

FIGURE 3.10 MARKET FOR A COMMODITY: A CHANGE IN INCOME

of the commodity. Nevertheless, the same adjustments to the new equilibrium would occur with the resulting shortage.

Changes in the Input Cost Consider now a change originating on the supply-side of the market; in particular, an increase in the input cost of producing a unit of a commodity (say the wages paid to the labor used to assemble color television sets have risen). As above, we will illustrate mathematically by taking the partial derivatives and graphically by shifting the affected curve.

Returning to the reduced form equations {1} and {2} for $\bar{P}$ and $\bar{Q}$, respectively, the operative partial derivatives are:

$$\delta \bar{P}/\delta C = s_2/(d_1 - s_1)$$

and

$$\delta \bar{Q}/\delta C = d_1 s_2/(d_1 - s_1)$$

Here with our assumptions about the parameters, namely, $d_1 < 0$, $s_1 > 0$, and $s_2 < 0$, these partials can be unambiguously signed $\delta \bar{P}/\delta C > 0$ and $\delta \bar{Q}/\delta C < 0$. That is, an increase (decrease) in the cost of the inputs used will increase (decrease) the market equilibrium price and decrease (increase) the quantity transacted of the commodity. Quantitatively, the effect on price ($|\delta \bar{P}/\delta C|$) is directly related to the magnitude of the parameter s_2; while the effect on the quantity transacted ($|\delta \bar{Q}/\delta C|$) also depends directly on the price sensitivity of the quantity demanded $|d_1|$.

Graphically, refer to Figure 3.11. The increase in input cost to C' shifts the supply curve for the commodity in a parallel fashion by the amount $s_2 \Delta C$ (where $\Delta C = C' - C$, and $s_2 < 0$). At the initial equilibrium price of $\bar{P}$ there is now an excess quantity

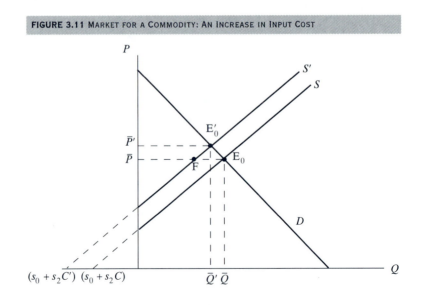

FIGURE 3.11 MARKET FOR A COMMODITY: AN INCREASE IN INPUT COST

demanded (indicated by the line segment FE_0). The shortage in the market drives up the price. As the price rises the quantity demanded is reduced (from E_0 to E_0' along the demand curve D), while the quantity supplied rises (from F to E_0' along the new supply curve S' reflecting the higher input cost). The model is statically stable so a new equilibrium is attained at E_0' with a higher price $\overline{P}'$ and lower quantity transacted $\overline{Q}'$.

PRACTICE PROBLEM 3.4

Given the demand and supply schedules for a commodity in a perfectly competitive market:

$$Q^d = 30 - 8P + .5I$$

$$Q^s = -5 + 2P - 1C$$

$$Q^d(P) \overset{e}{=} Q^s(P)$$

where I = average income of the demanders of the commodity: $I = 500$

C = unit cost of the inputs used to produce the commodity: $C = 10$

a) Find the initial equilibrium price $(\overline{P})$ and quantity transacted $(\overline{Q})$.
b) Find the effect on the initial market equilibrium price and quantity transacted of a decrease in the average income to $I' = 450$.
c) Find the effect on the initial market equilibrium price and quantity transacted of a decrease in the unit cost of the inputs used to produce the commodity to $C' = 9$.

(The answers are at the end of the chapter.)

We have illustrated comparative statics with a linear model of a perfectly competitive market. The technique of partial equilibrium analysis, however, also applies to nonlinear systems and more complex economic models. Indeed, throughout this text we will have numerous occasions to apply comparative statics. So too, we will use derivatives and integrals in different economic contexts. In Chapter 4 we extend our analysis of a competitive market to dynamic models.

❖ KEY TERMS

Economics

- consumers' surplus (p. 62)
- decreasing cost industry (p. 56)
- demand price (p. 51)
- excess demand price (p. 51)
- Giffen good (p. 54)
- income effect (p. 60)
- inferior good (p. 68)

- Marshallian market system (p. 50)
- Marshallian stability (p. 51)
- normal good (p. 68)
- price elasticity of demand (p. 55)
- price elasticity of supply (p. 55)

- producers' surplus (p. 62)
- status good (p. 54)
- substitution effect (p. 60)
- supply price (p. 51)
- total expenditures (p. 62)
- total revenues (p. 62)

Mathematics

- comparative statics (p. 68)
- inverse function (p. 53)

- partial equilibrium analysis (p. 68)

- quadratic formula (p. 65)
- semi-stable (p. 62)

❖ PROBLEMS

1. Given the demand and supply schedules for a commodity in a perfectly competitive market:

$$Q^d = 36 - 4P$$

$$Q^s = -6 + 3P$$

$$Q^d \overset{e}{=} Q^s$$

   a) Plot the demand and supply curves and solve graphically for the equilibrium price and quantity transacted.
   b) Solve algebraically for the equilibrium price and quantity transacted.
   c) Convert the above Walrasian system to a Marshallian system by deriving the schedules for the demand price and supply price.
   d) Solve algebraically for the equilibrium quantity and market price.
   e) Determine whether the market is Walrasian stable.
   f) Determine whether the market is Marshallian stable.

2. Given the demand and supply schedules for a commodity in a perfectly competitive market:

$$Q^d = 16 + 2P$$

$$Q^s = -20 + 5P$$

$$Q^d \overset{e}{=} Q^s$$

Repeat steps a) through f) of problem 1.

3. Given the demand and supply schedules for a commodity in a perfectly competitive market:

$$Q^d = d_0 + d_1 P$$

$$Q^s = s_0 + s_1 P$$

$$Q^d \overset{e}{=} Q^s \qquad \text{(Walrasian)}$$

$$P^d \overset{e}{=} P^s \qquad \text{(Marshallian)}$$

where $d_0 > 0, d_1 < 0, s_0 > 0$, and $s_1 < 0$.

Determine the conditions under which the market will exhibit Marshallian stability but not Walrasian stability. Illustrate your answer with a graph.

4. Given the demand and supply schedules for a commodity in a perfectly competitive market:

$$Q^d = 70 - 10P + .2I$$

$$Q^s = -12 + 5P - .6C$$

$$Q^d \overset{e}{=} Q^s$$

where $I = 100$ (average income of the demanders of the commodity)

$C = 5$ (unit cost of the inputs used to produce the commodity)

a) Plot the demand and supply curves and solve graphically for the equilibrium price and quantity transacted.
b) Solve algebraically for the equilibrium price and quantity transacted.
c) Calculate the total expenditures and total revenues.
d) Using integral calculus determine the consumers' surplus and producers' surplus.
e) Find the effects of an increase in the average income of 10 ($\Delta I = +10$ so that $I' = 110$) on the market equilibrium price and quantity transacted, total expenditures, consumers' surplus, and producers' surplus.
f) Find the effects of an increase in the unit cost of the inputs of 2 ($\Delta C = +2$ so that $C' = 7$) on the market equilibrium price and quantity transacted, total expenditures, consumers' surplus, and producers' surplus.

5. Given the demand and supply schedules for a commodity in a perfectly competitive market:

$$Q^d = 25 - P^2$$

$$Q^s = -3 + 3P$$

$$Q^d \overset{e}{=} Q^s$$

a) Plot the demand and supply schedules and solve graphically for the equilibrium price and quantity transacted.
b) Solve algebraically for the equilibrium price and quantity transacted.
c) Using integral calculus determine the consumers' surplus and producers' surplus.

6. Given the demand and supply schedules for a commodity in a perfectly competitive market:

$$Q^d = d_0 + d_1 P + d_2 P_c \qquad (d_0 > 0, d_1 < 0, d_2 < 0)$$

$$Q^s = s_0 + s_1 P + s_2 Z \qquad (s_0 < 0, s_1 > 0, s_2 > 0)$$

$$Q^d(P) \overset{e}{=} Q^s(P)$$

where P_c = exogenous unit price of a complement commodity
  Z = exogenous index of the technology used to produce the commodity

a) Solve for the equilibrium price and quantity transacted.
b) Find and determine the sign of the following comparative statics. Discuss whether your results make sense.
   i) $\delta \overline{P}/\delta P_c$ ii) $\delta \overline{Q}/\delta P_c$ iii) $\delta \overline{P}/\delta Z$ iv) $\delta \overline{Q}/\delta Z$

❖ ANSWERS TO PRACTICE PROBLEMS

3.1 a) The equilibrium price and quantity transacted are: $\overline{P} = 3.5$ and $\overline{Q} = 6$.

   b) $dE^d(P)/dP = dQ^d(P)/dP - dQ^s(P)/dP = -4 - 2 = -6 < 0$.

   c) $P^d = 5 - (1/4)Q$
       $P^s = 1/2 + (1/2)Q$
       $P^d(Q) \overset{e}{=} P^s(Q)$
       The equilibrium market quantity and price are: $\overline{Q} = 6$ and $\overline{P} = 3.5$.

   d) $dE^d(Q)/dQ = dP^d(Q)/dQ - dP^s(Q)/dQ = -(1/4) - (1/2) = -3/4 < 0$

   e) If $P_1 = 4$, there would be an excess quantity supplied of 3 units. The market price would fall until the surplus was eliminated.

   f) If $Q_1 = 7$, there would be an excess supply price of .75. The market quantity would fall until the excess supply price was eliminated.

3.2 a) The equilibrium price and quantity transacted are: $\overline{P} = 5$ and $\overline{Q} = 15$.

   b) The market is Walrasian stable: $dE^d(P)/dP = dQ^d(P)/dP - dQ^s(P)/dP = -3 - (-2) = -1 < 0$.

   c) The market is Marshallian unstable: $dE^d(Q)/dQ = dP^d(Q)/dQ - dP^s(Q)/dQ = -(1/3) - (-1/2) = 1/6 > 0$

3.3 a) The market equilibrium price and quantity transacted are: $\overline{P} = 4$ and $\overline{Q} = 2$.

   b) The consumers' surplus and producers' surplus are: $CS = 4/3$ and $PS = 2$.

3.4 a) The initial market equilibrium price and quantity transacted are: $\overline{P} = 29.5$ and $\overline{Q} = 44$.

   b) With the decrease in average income, the new market equilibrium price and quantity transacted are: $\overline{P}' = 27$ and $\overline{Q}' = 39$.

   c) With the decrease in the unit cost of the inputs, the new market equilibrium price and quantity transacted are: $\overline{P}' = 29.4$ and $\overline{Q}' = 44.8$.

CHAPTER

4

Perfectly Competitive Markets: Dynamic Analysis

So far we have addressed static models of a perfectly competitive market. In particular, we examined the conditions under which a market equilibrium would exist (both mathematically and economically), would be unique, and would be statically stable. Then with comparative statics we contrasted different equilibrium positions associated with different values of the exogenous variables of the model. Time did not enter explicitly into the analysis—all the variables were defined over the same time period.

We now introduce dynamic models of a perfectly competitive market. Here the endogenous variables of price and quantity are defined for different points in time. In fact, the values of the endogenous variables are functions of time. In dynamic analysis we are interested in the time paths of the endogenous variables, that is, not only the direction of adjustment, but also the speed of adjustment of these endogenous variables when in disequilibrium.

We will cover two basic types of dynamic analysis: discrete time and continuous time. When the endogenous variables in the model are assumed to change in finite amounts and only at distinct points in time (such as the end of intervals of a given duration), then *period analysis* is appropriate and *difference equations* are used. In economics, the data for many variables are recorded for uniformly spaced periods. For example, national output, income, and expenditure data are reported on a quarterly basis. The unemployment rate and the consumer price index are reported on a monthly basis. Annual money wages set in labor contracts may be automatically adjusted for the previous year's inflation rate. Also, Social Security benefits are periodically adjusted for cost of living increases. If, on the other hand, the endogenous variables in the model are assumed to change continuously (i.e., the length of the time period of analysis approaches zero and we have instantaneous adjustments), then *differential equations* are used. In asset markets like foreign exchange, stocks, and bonds, market prices are constantly changing according to the current demand and supply conditions.

In this chapter we begin with period analysis and the most basic form of difference equations. We discuss two well-known dynamic models of a competitive market. The conditions for dynamic stability are established and contrasted with those for static stability. Then, as necessary background to continuous time analysis and differential equations, we review exponential and logarithmic functions. As with difference equations, we will deal with only the most basic form of differential equations, using the example of a perfectly competitive market to illustrate the solution and dynamic stability of a continuous time model.

FIRST-ORDER DIFFERENCE EQUATIONS

With difference equations we use distinct periods of time. That is, the endogenous variables are assumed to retain their values over time periods of a given duration and change only at the beginning of the next time period. An example would be a 1-year time deposit on which the interest is added only at the end of the year. Assuming simple annual compounding at 5%, a given sum of money (say $1,000) placed on deposit on the first day of the year would not increase (to $1,050) until the beginning of the next year (which coincides with the end of the current year).

The *order* of a difference equation is the maximum difference between the time periods over which the endogenous variables are defined. Here we are concerned only with first-order difference equations, so only a one-period difference between the values of the endogenous variable is modeled.

For y, an endogenous variable, the *first difference* of y can be written as:

$$\Delta y / \Delta t = \Delta y_t = y_{t+1} - y_t = y_t - y_{t-1} = y_{t-1} - y_{t-2}, \text{ etc.}$$

The Δ operator indicates discrete time, where the duration of the time periods of analysis is finite and constant and the values of time (t) are integers only. In each case, the difference is between consecutive values of y. The continuous time analogue, used for differential equations, is the derivative operator d, or here, dy/dt.

Furthermore, we will restrict our attention to linear, first-order difference equations; that is, the endogenous variable, y, is not raised to any power (other than one), nor is itself multiplied by any difference expression, for example, $(y_t) \cdot (\Delta y_t)$.

SOLUTION TO A LINEAR, FIRST-ORDER DIFFERENCE EQUATION

In general, a linear, first-order difference equation takes the form, $y_t - ay_{t-1} = b$, where a and b are given constants. The solution consists of the sum of two parts. The first, known as the *particular solution, $\bar{y}$*, is obtained by solving the static version of the model. The particular solution represents the intertemporal equilibrium of the dynamic model. To find the particular solution, we convert to a static model by assuming that $y_t = y_{t-1}$, or that the endogenous variable is dated only for one time period. The equation then reduces to $y_t - ay_t = b$. We can easily solve:

$$(1 - a)y_t = b$$

$$y_t = b/(1 - a) = \bar{y}$$

We restrict the constant a to not equal one, that is, $a \neq 1$. [Later we will consider the special case where $a = 1$.]

The second part of the solution is known as the *complementary function, y_c*. Here we set the right-hand side of the first-order difference equation equal to zero, that is, $b = 0$.

$$y_t - ay_{t-1} = 0$$

Isolating y_t on the left-hand side gives $y_t = ay_{t-1}$. Using iteration by substituting in positive integer values for t ($t = 1, 2, 3 \ldots$), we can establish a pattern over successive periods:

$$\text{for} \quad t = 1: y_1 = ay_0$$

$$t = 2: y_2 = ay_1 = a(ay_0) = (a)^2 y_0$$

$$t = 3: y_3 = ay_2 = a(a)^2 y_0 = (a)^3 y_0.$$

or, in general, we can write: $y_t = (a)^t y_0$

Since the complementary function is only part of the solution, we are not yet able to initialize, or establish the initial conditions for the model. Therefore, we need to replace the y_0 here with a general term, A, that serves like a constant of integration. (Recall the discussion of integration in Chapter 2.) The complementary function can be written as: $y_c = (a)^t A$.

Adding together the particular solution and the complementary function we obtain the *general solution* to the first-order difference equation, $y_t - ay_{t-1} = b$

$$y_t = \bar{y} + y_c$$

$$y_t = b/(1 - a) + (a)^t A$$

To find the *definite solution*, which will incorporate the initial condition, we need to "solve" for A. Let $t = 0$, then

$$y_0 = b/(1 - a) + (a)^0 A$$

$$A = y_0 - b/(1 - a) = y_0 - \bar{y}$$

The definite solution is given by

$$y_t = b/(1 - a) + [y_0 - b/(1 - a)](a)^t$$

$$y_t = \bar{y} + [y_0 - \bar{y}](a)^t \quad \text{where } \bar{y} = b/(1 - a) \text{ and } a \neq 1$$

The definite solution consists of the sum of the intertemporal equilibrium ($\bar{y}$) and deviations from the intertemporal equilibrium over time $[y_0 - \bar{y}](a)^t$. Note that the definite solution for the endogenous variable, y, is expressed in terms of time (t) and the exogenous variables of the model: the parameters, a and b, and y_0, the given initial value for y. If we do not begin in intertemporal equilibrium, that is, if $y_0 \neq b/(1 - a)$, then the value of y will vary over time according to the term $(a)^t$.

DYNAMIC STABILITY

For the dynamic stability of this first-order linear difference equation, we need the value of the endogenous variable, y_t, over time to approach the intertemporal equilibrium, $\bar{y}$. From the definite solution, we can see that the deviations from intertemporal equilibrium must diminish (approach zero) over time. Given that $y_0 \neq b/(1 - a)$, the dynamic stability of the model hinges on the term $(a)^t$. Recall that the values of t, indicating time periods, are integers. For the term $(a)^t$ to converge to zero as t increases requires that the absolute value of a be less than unity: $|a| < 1$.

Thus, we can state that the linear, first-order linear difference equation, $y_t - ay_{t-1} = b$, with a definite solution of $y_t = b/(1 - a) + [y_0 - b/(1 - a)](a)^t$, where $a \neq 1$, is dynamically stable if $|a| < 1$. Note, while y_t would converge to $\bar{y}$ over time if the equation is dynamically stable; y_t would never actually reach $\bar{y}$, since a^t only approaches zero when $|a| < 1$ and t increases.

If, however, $|a| > 1$ and $y_0 \neq b/(1 - a)$, then over time the value of the endogenous variable y will depart increasingly from the intertemporal equilibrium, that is, the time path of y_t is divergent and the model is dynamically unstable.

While the dynamic stability of the model depends on the magnitude of the parameter, a, the type of time path depends on the sign of a. If a is positive, $a > 0$, then the time path of y_t is *monotonic*, meaning y_t converges to $\bar{y}$ (if $0 < a < 1$) or diverges from $\bar{y}$ (if $a > 1$) in the same direction. If a is negative, $a < 0$, then the time path of y_t is *oscillatory*, meaning y_t fluctuates around the intertemporal equilibrium, overshooting and undershooting in successive periods. Specifically, if $-1 < a < 0$, then the time path is oscillatory and convergent, with the fluctuations around the intertemporal equilibrium diminishing over time. If $a < -1$, then the time path is oscillatory and divergent, with increasing fluctuations around the intertemporal equilibrium.

Special Cases   Three special cases are when the parameter, a, equals $-1, 0$, or $+1$. If $a = -1$, then the time path of y_t is oscillatory and uniform—neither convergent nor divergent—since $(-1)^t$ will alternate between -1 and $+1$ according to whether t is an odd or even integer. Since y_t does not approach the intertemporal equilibrium over time, we consider the model to be dynamically unstable.

If $a = 0$, then we do not have a difference equation, since $y_t - ay_{t-1} = b$ reduces to $y_t = b$, which is a constant function.

If $a = +1$, then the difference equation becomes $y_t - 1y_{t-1} = b$ and there is no intertemporal equilibrium; since for $y_t = y_{t-1}$ (as in the static version of the model), we would have $y_t - y_t = b$ or $0 = b$. We solve the system $y_t - y_{t-1} = b$ as follows. Isolating y_t on the left-hand side and then using iteration we find

$$y_t - y_{t-1} = b$$

$$y_t = y_{t-1} + b$$

$$\text{for}\quad t = 1:\quad y_1 = y_0 + b$$

$$t = 2:\quad y_2 = y_1 + b = (y_0 + b) + b = y_0 + 2b$$

$$t = 3:\quad y_3 = y_2 + b = (y_0 + 2b) + b = y_0 + 3b$$

and, in general, $y_t = y_0 + tb$.

Thus, when $a = 1$, we have a moving equilibrium. The equilibrium value of the endogenous variable is changing with each period.

An example might be found in a type of foreign exchange rate system known as a "crawling peg." Here, a nation that has experienced relatively high and chronic inflation, may regularly increase the official domestic currency price of foreign currency (e.g., pesos per U.S. dollar) according to a set time schedule (e.g., x pesos per dollar per month).

Numerical Example   To illustrate the solution and stability properties of a linear, first-order difference equation, consider the following numerical example.

$$y_t - 3y_{t-1} = 12 \quad \text{and} \quad y_0 = -2$$

The particular solution is obtained by converting to a static model (assuming $y_t = y_{t-1}$) and then solving the resulting linear equation for the intertemporal equilibrium.

$$y_t - 3y_t = 12$$

$$-2y_t = 12$$

$$\bar{y} = -6$$

For the complementary function we set the right-hand side of the equation equal to zero and then solve by iteration.

$$y_t - 3y_{t-1} = 0$$

$$y_t = 3y_{t-1}$$

$$\text{for}\quad t = 1:\quad y_1 = 3y_0$$

$$t = 2:\quad y_2 = 3y_1 = 3(3y_0) = (3)^2 y_0$$

$$t = 3:\quad y_3 = 3y_2 = 3(3)^2 y_0 = (3)^3 y_0$$

or, in general: $y_t = (3)^t y_0$

Since the complementary function is only part of the solution we cannot initialize yet. Replacing y_0 with A, a constant to be solved for later, we have the complementary function: $y_c = (3)^t A$.

Adding the complementary function to the particular solution gives the general solution.

$$y_t = \bar{y} + y_c$$

$$y_t = -6 + (3)^t A$$

To derive the definite solution we set $t = 0$ and solve for A.

$$y_0 = -6 + (3)^0 A$$

$$A = y_0 + 6$$

In this example we are given the initial value for y: $y_0 = -2$. Thus

$$A = -2 + 6 = 4$$

We now have the definite solution to the first-order difference equation, $y_t - 3y_{t-1} = 12$,

$$y_t = -6 + 4(3)^t$$

We can check this answer. Substituting in $t = 0$ and $t = 1$ gives

$$y_0 = -6 + 4(3)^0 = -2 \text{ (It checks.)}$$

$$y_1 = -6 + 4(3)^1 = 6$$

Plugging into the difference equation, $y_t - 3y_{t-1} = 12$

$$y_1 - 3y_0 = 12$$

$$6 - 3(-2) = 12 \text{ (It checks)}$$

Moreover, we can establish that the model is dynamically unstable, with y_t diverging monotonically over time from $\bar{y} = -6$, the intertemporal equilibrium. From the definite solution $y_t = -6 + 4(3)^t$, observe the values for y in the first three periods.

$$t = 0: y_0 = -2$$

$$t = 1: y_1 = 6$$

$$t = 2: y_2 = 30$$

$$t = 3: y_3 = 102$$

PRACTICE PROBLEM 4.1

Find the definite solution to each of the following linear first order difference equations and determine whether the time path for y is dynamically stable.

a) $y_t - 2y_{t-1} = 1 \ (y_0 = 3)$
b) $3y_t + y_{t-1} = 4 \ (y_0 = -1)$
c) $5y_t + 2y_{t-1} = 0 \ (y_0 = 1)$
d) $3y_t - 3y_{t-1} = 6 \ (y_0 = -2)$

(The answers are at the end of the chapter.)

COBWEB MODEL

One model of a competitive commodity market that can be reduced to a first order difference equation is known as the **cobweb model**, for reasons that will become evident when we illustrate the time path of adjustment for the market price. We assume a linear Walrasian model. The quantity supplied in period t, Q_t^s, however, is a function of the market-clearing price of the previous period, P_{t-1}.

Agriculture offers an example of such a lagged supply response. In nature there is a significant time lapse between the initiation of production (planting the crops) and the sale of the output (after harvesting the crops). At the beginning of the season farmers base their decisions on the amounts and types of crops to plant on the prices expected to be received at the time of sale. Without perfect foresight, and in the absence of comprehensive futures markets (with contracts for future delivery of given quantities of the crops at set prices), farmers might simply use the known market-clearing prices of the last season as the expected prices to be received at the end of the current season. Note, this is the simplest form of the **adaptive expectations hypothesis**, which postulates that the recent past (e.g., the previous period's price) can be a useful guide to the future (e.g., the price expected to prevail in the market).

The system of equations for the cobweb model is given below. In every period the market is assumed to clear with zero excess quantity demanded (the equilibrium condition). While the quantity supplied in period t is based on the market equilibrium price in period $t - 1$, the current market price adjusts so that the quantity demanded equals the available quantity supplied. Note that the subscripts in dynamic analysis refer to the time period (t). Note also that we have made no assumptions about the parameters d_0, d_1, s_0, and s_1 in order to allow for the most general analysis.

$$Q_t^d = d_0 + d_1 P_t$$

$$Q_t^s = s_0 + s_1 P_{t-1}$$

$$Q_t^d \overset{\text{e}}{=} Q_t^s$$

Collapsing the system of three equations in three unknowns (Q_t^d, Q_t^s, and P_t) into the equilibrium condition gives:

$$Q_t^d = d_0 + d_1 P_t = s_0 + s_1 P_{t-1} = Q_t^s$$

Rearranging, we have a first-order difference equation,

$$d_1 P_t - s_1 P_{t-1} = s_0 - d_0$$

For the particular solution we assume $P_t = P_{t-1}$ and solve for the intertemporal equilibrium price $\overline{P}$:

$$d_1 P_t - s_1 P_t = s_0 - d_0$$
$$(d_1 - s_1) P_t = s_0 - d_0$$
$$\overline{P} = (s_0 - d_0)/(d_1 - s_1)$$

Checking back to Chapter 3 confirms that the particular solution is the equilibrium price for the static model. And, as in the static model, we must restrict $d_1 \neq s_1$, or equivalently, the demand and supply equations cannot have the same slopes ($1/d_1 \neq 1/s_1$).

For the complementary function, we set the right-hand side of the first-order difference equation equal to zero and solve by iteration.

$$d_1 P_t - s_1 P_{t-1} = 0$$
$$P_t = (s_1/d_1) P_{t-1}$$
$$\text{for} \quad t = 1: P_1 = (s_1/d_1) P_0$$
$$t = 2: P_2 = (s_1/d_1) P_1 = (s_1/d_1)(s_1/d_1) P_0 = (s_1/d_1)^2 \, P_0$$
$$t = 3: P_3 = (s_1/d_1) P_2 = (s_1/d_1)(s_1/d_1)^2 \, P_0 = (s_1/d_1)^3 \, P_0$$
$$\text{or, in general:} \ P_t = (s_1/d_1)^t \, P_0$$

Replacing the initial price, P_0, with the constant, A, we obtain the complementary function P_c.

$$P_c = (s_1/d_1)^t \, A$$

The general solution for P_t is the sum of the particular solution and the complementary function.

$$P_t = \overline{P} + P_c$$
$$P_t = (s_0 - d_0)/(d_1 - s_1) + (s_1/d_1)^t \, A$$

To derive the definite solution we initialize by setting $t = 0$ and solving for A.

$$P_0 = \overline{P} + (s_1/d_1)^0 A$$

Thus

$$A = P_0 - \overline{P}.$$

The definite solution is then

$$P_t = \overline{P} + (s_1/d_1)^t \, (P_0 - \overline{P}) \qquad \text{where } \overline{P} = (s_0 - d_0)/(d_1 - s_1).$$

Dynamic stability, where $(s_1/d_1)^t$ approaches zero and P_t approaches $\overline{P}$ over time, requires $|s_1/d_1| < 1$. For this condition to be met, we must have $|s_1| < |d_1|$ or $|dQ_t^s/dP_{t-1}|$

$< |dQ_t^d/dP_t|$. In words, the sensitivity of the quantity supplied in period t to the market price in period $t - 1$ must be less in absolute value than the sensitivity of the quantity demanded in period t to the market price in period t. If the magnitude of the supply response to the lagged price exceeds the magnitude of the demand response to the current price, the cobweb model is dynamically unstable.

Given that $P_0 \neq \overline{P}$, or that we begin out of the intertemporal equilibrium, the time path of adjustment depends on the signs of the slopes of the demand and supply curves. In the normal case of an upward-sloping supply curve $(s_1 > 0)$ and a downward-sloping demand curve $(d_1 < 0)$, the time path for P_t will oscillate around $\overline{P}$. If the demand and supply curves have slopes of the same sign, then the time path for the market price will be monotonic.

We illustrate with a numerical example.

$$Q_t^d = 18 - 3P_t$$

$$Q_t^s = -3 + 4P_{t-1}$$

$$Q_t^d \overset{e}{=} Q_t^s$$

The system reduces to a first-order difference equation.

$$18 - 3P_t = -3 + 4P_{t-1}$$

$$-3P_t - 4P_{t-1} = -21$$

$$P_t + (4/3)P_{t-1} = 7$$

The particular solution is: $\overline{P} = 3$.

$$P_t + (4/3)P_t = 7$$

$$(7/3)P_t = 7$$

$$\overline{P} = 3$$

The complementary function is: $P_c = (-4/3)^t A$

$$P_t + (4/3)P_{t-1} = 0$$

$$P_t = (-4/3)P_{t-1}$$

$$P_t = (-4/3)^t P_0$$

$$P_c = (-4/3)^t A$$

The general solution is: $P_t = \overline{P} + P_c = 3 + (-4/3)^t A$
Setting $t = 0$, gives $P_0 = 3 + (-4/3)^t A$ and $A = P_0 - 3$.
The definite solution is: $P_t = 3 + (-4/3)^t (P_0 - 3)$.

We can see that this model is dynamically unstable (since $|-4/3| > 1$). The market price would diverge from the intertemporal equilibrium price over time in an oscillatory fashion (since the signs of the slopes of the demand and supply curves are opposites).

To illustrate, suppose we are given an initial price, P_0, that is not equal to the intertemporal equilibrium price of $\overline{P} = 3$. In particular, let $P_0 = 2.5$. From the definite solution we can find the sequence of market-clearing prices in the first four periods.

$$P_1 = 3 + (-4/3)^1\,(2.5 - 3) = 3.6\overline{6}$$

$$P_2 = 3 + (-4/3)^2\,(2.5 - 3) = 2.1\overline{1}$$

$$P_3 = 3 + (-4/3)^3\,(2.5 - 3) = 4.19$$

$$P_4 = 3 + (-4/3)^4\,(2.5 - 3) = 1.42$$

In Figure 4.1 we illustrate the oscillating and divergent time path for the market-clearing prices. Recall that in period analysis the values of an endogenous variable are constant until the period changes. In the graph for the time path for P_t, see the open dots at the ends of the flat line segments of varying heights indicating the values for the market price.

In Figure 4.2 the demand and supply equations are plotted and we can trace out the time path of the market equilibria. The intertemporal equilibrium is represented by point E, with a price of $\overline{P} = 3$ and a quantity transacted of $\overline{Q} = 9$. Given the initial price of $P_0 = 2.5$, the quantity supplied in period one would be 7. $Q_1^s = -3 + 4P_0 = -3 + 4(2.5)$. At P_0 there is an excess quantity demanded. In order for the market to clear, the price has to rise in order to reduce the quantity demanded to the 7 units that are supplied. Setting the quantity demanded in period one equal to 7 and solving for the market equilibrium price gives:

FIGURE 4.1 OSCILLATING AND DIVERGENT TIME PATH FOR THE MARKET EQUILIBRIUM PRICE

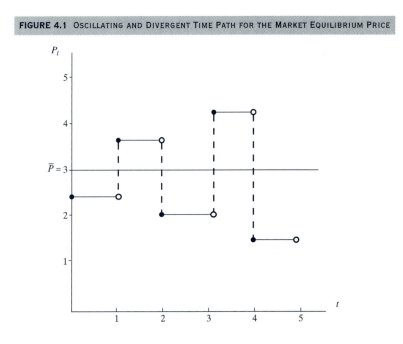

$$Q_1^d = 18 - 3P_1 = 7$$

$$-3P_1 = -11$$

$$P_1 = 3.6\overline{6} \text{ (See point 1 in Figure 4.2.)}$$

In period two the quantity supplied rises to 11.66. $Q_2^s = -3 + 4(3.6\overline{6}) = 11.6\overline{6}$. At the price of $P_1 = 3.6\overline{6}$, however, there is now a surplus, so that the market price falls until the quantity demanded in period two equals the $11.6\overline{6}$ units supplied. The market-clearing price in period two is $2.1\overline{1}$.

$$Q_2^d = 18 - 3P_2 = 11.6\overline{6}$$

$$-3P_2 = -6.3\overline{3}$$

$$P_2 = 2.1\overline{1} \text{ (See point 2 in Figure 4.2.)}$$

You should be able to confirm that the market equilibrium price and quantity transacted in period three are 4.19 and $5.4\overline{4}$ units, respectively. (See point 3 in Figure 4.2.)

The time path in Figure 4.2 does resemble a cobweb—here one that is becoming increasingly larger as the market is "spinning out of control." The market-clearing prices and quantities transacted for the first four periods are labeled on the demand curve by the numbers 1, 2, 3, and 4. Mathematically we find that the condition for dynamic stability in the market does not hold. Here $|dQ_t^s/dP_{t-1}| = 4 > 3 = |dQ_t^d/dP_t|$. That is, the quantity supplied is more sensitive to the lagged price than is the quantity demanded to the current price. Graphically the demand curve is steeper than the supply curve.

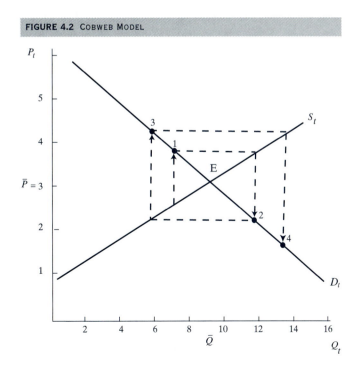

FIGURE 4.2 COBWEB MODEL

Note, in this example we can show that the quantity supplied would be negative in the seventh period, based on a market-clearing price of $\overline{P}_6 = .19$ in the sixth period. In effect then, the market would cease to operate, *ceteris paribus*. The "disappearance" of this market, however, assumes that the parameters underlying the demand and supply equations do not change over time.

While markets do cease to operate, on occasion, it is more likely due to shifts in the demand and supply curves (e.g., with changes in tastes or sharply higher input costs) that yield what would be a negative equilibrium quantity transacted—rather than a market spinning out of control over time with unchanging demand and supply curves, as in this dynamically unstable cobweb model. Indeed, previously unstable markets may become stable with changes in the demand and supply curves. Nevertheless, the cobweb model, as well as the inventory model to follow, may provide insight into the movement of equilibrium prices and quantities over time.

In the problems at the end of the chapter, there are other examples of the cobweb model, including some unusual cases where the slopes of the demand and supply curves have the same sign. One final note before we move on to the next dynamic model: in this numerical example the static Walrasian version of the model is stable, while the dynamic (cobweb) version is not. In short, the static stability or instability of a market need not imply anything about the dynamic stability or instability. Can a model of a competitive market be statically unstable, but dynamically stable? (*Hint:* Think of an unusual case where the slopes of the demand and supply curves have the same sign.)

Recall the condition for Walrasian static stability is:

$$dE^d(P_t)/dP_t = dQ_t^d/dP_t - dQ_t^s/dP_t < 0$$

or

$$dQ_t^d/dP_t < dQ_t^s/dP_t$$

where the subscript t refers to the period, which in static analysis is the same for all the endogenous variables. The condition for dynamic stability in this cobweb model is

$$|dQ^d(P_t)/dP_t| > |dQ_t^s(P_{t-1})/dP_{t-1}|.$$

We now turn to another dynamic model of a competitive market, one in which the market does not clear in every period.

PRACTICE PROBLEM 4.2

Given the following demand and supply schedules for a commodity in a perfectly competitive market:

$$Q_t^d = 24 - 4P_t$$
$$Q_t^s = -6 + 2P_{t-1}$$
$$Q_t^d \stackrel{\text{e}}{=} Q_t^s$$

a) Find the time path for the market price, that is, the definite solution for P_t.
b) Determine whether the market is dynamically stable.

c) Find the market-clearing prices and quantities transacted for the first two periods, given that $P_0 = 4.0$.

(The answers are at the end of the chapter.)

INVENTORY MODEL

In the cobweb model, price adjusts in every period to equilibrate the quantity demanded with the available quantity supplied. Such a model may be relevant for perishable goods (e.g., many agricultural products) that cannot be stored as inventories. In contrast, in the **inventory model**, the market price in each period is assumed to be set based on the previous period's price, adjusted for any change in inventories that took place.

If, in the previous period, the market price had been set too high, an excess quantity supplied would have resulted, with the unsold surplus of the good added to the firms' inventories. In the current period then, to reduce the stocks of inventories, firms would lower the market price from the level of the previous period.

Conversely, if in the previous period there had been a decrease in inventories to meet an excess quantity demanded that resulted from a price set too low, firms would raise the price in the current period. In the inventory model the market price is set at the beginning of the period. The quantity transacted is determined by the quantity demanded at that set price. A change in inventories fills the gap between the quantity supplied and the quantity demanded. The inventory model may be relevant for manufactured goods that can be stored.

Linear equations for the inventory model are given below.

$$Q_t^d = d_0 + d_1 P_t$$

$$Q_t^s = s_0 + s_1 P_t$$

$$P_t = P_{t-1} - v \cdot (Q_{t-1}^s - Q_{t-1}^d) \qquad (v > 0)$$

The new variable is v, an **inventory adjustment coefficient**. Note that in this model there is no explicit equilibrium condition. The market is not assumed to clear in every period. The price in the current period is set based on the previous period's outcome. The quantity transacted equals the quantity demanded. An excess quantity demanded (resulting in a decrease in inventories) induces a price increase in the following period. An excess quantity supplied (resulting in an increase in inventories) induces a price decrease in the following period. The parameter v indicates the responsiveness of the current price to the change in inventories in the previous period. Note, if the market cleared in the previous period, with the quantity demanded equalling the quantity supplied and no change in inventories, then the price would not change.

To solve the model we lag the demand and supply equations by one period and then substitute into the price equation.

$$Q^d_{t-1} = d_0 + d_1 P_{t-1}$$

$$Q^s_{t-1} = s_0 + s_1 P_{t-1}$$

and

$$P_t = P_{t-1} - v \cdot (s_0 + s_1 P_{t-1} - d_0 - d_1 P_{t-1})$$

Simplifying by combining like terms gives

$$P_t = [1 - v \cdot (s_1 - d_1)] P_{t-1} - v \cdot (s_0 - d_0)$$

$$P_t - [1 - v \cdot (s_1 - d_1)] P_{t-1} = -v \cdot (s_0 - d_0)$$

For convenience, let $m = 1 - v \cdot (s_1 - d_1)$ and $n = -v \cdot (s_0 - d_0)$.
The system then can be written as: $P_t - mP_{t-1} = n$.
The particular solution is: $\overline{P} = n/(1 - m)$, where $m \neq 1$.
The complementary function is: $P_c = (m)^t A$.
The general solution is: $P_t = \overline{P} + P_c = \overline{P} + (m)^t A$.
The definite solution is: $P_t = \overline{P} + (m)^t (P_0 - \overline{P})$.

　　Substituting in the original parameters we have the definite solution of the inventory model.

$$P_t = \overline{P} + [1 - v \cdot (s_1 - d_1)]^t (P_0 - \overline{P}) \quad \text{where} \quad \overline{P} = (s_0 - d_0)/(d_1 - s_1).$$

Note that the intertemporal equilibrium price, $\overline{P}$, the solution to the static version of the model (with the familiar restriction that $d_1 \neq s_1$), does not include the inventory adjustment coefficient v, which defines this dynamic model.

　　The model is dynamically stable if $|1 - v \cdot (s_1 - d_1)| < 1$, or $-1 < 1 - v \cdot (s_1 - d_1) < 1$. Subtracting 1 from each of the terms in the inequality, we obtain $-2 < v \cdot (s_1 - d_1) < 0$. Multiplying through by -1, which reverses the inequality signs, gives the condition for dynamic stability in this inventory model: $0 < v \cdot (s_1 - d_1) < 2$.

　　In words, the inventory model is dynamically stable if the product of the inventory adjustment coefficient and the difference between the price sensitivities of the quantity supplied and the quantity demanded is positive but less than two. The time path of adjustment for the market price depends on the sign of the term, $[1 - v \cdot (s_1 - d_1)]$.

　　If $1 - v \cdot (s_1 - d_1) < 0$, or $v \cdot (s_1 - d_1) > 1$, then the time path is oscillatory.

　　If $1 - v \cdot (s_1 - d_1) > 0$, or $v \cdot (s_1 - d_1) < 1$, then the time path is monotonic.

Clearly, the magnitude of the inventory adjustment coefficient is crucial for the stability of the model, as well as for the type of time path.

　　To illustrate, consider the following numerical example of an inventory model where we assume the normal case (downwardly sloping demand curve and upwardly sloping supply curve), but do not fix the value of the inventory adjustment coefficient.

$$Q^d_t = 10 - 2P_t$$

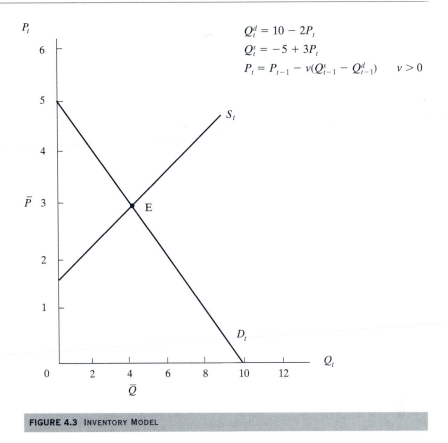

FIGURE 4.3 INVENTORY MODEL

$$Q_t^s = -5 + 3P_t$$
$$P_t = P_{t-1} - v \cdot (Q_{t-1}^s - Q_{t-1}^d)$$

In Figure 4.3 we plot the demand and supply curves. The market is statically stable, since an excess quantity demanded would induce a price increase that, in turn, reduces the shortage. Similarly, an excess quantity supplied would induce a price decrease that works to eliminate the surplus. Whether the associated inventory model is dynamically stable depends on the value of the inventory adjustment coefficient.

Solving the dynamic model by first substituting the lagged demand and supply equations into the price equation gives:

$$P_t = P_{t-1} - v \cdot (-5 + 3P_{t-1} - 10 + 2P_{t-1})$$
$$P_t = P_{t-1} - v \cdot (-15 + 5P_{t-1})$$
$$P_t = (1 - 5v)P_{t-1} + 15v$$
$$P_t - (1 - 5v)P_{t-1} = 15v \quad \text{(a first-order difference equation)}$$

The particular solution is: $\overline{P} = 3$.

$$P_t - (1 - 5v)P_t = 15v$$

$$5vP_t = 15v$$

$$P_t = 3 = \overline{P}$$

The complementary function is: $P_c = (1 - 5v)^t A$.

$$P_t - (1 - 5v)P_{t-1} = 0$$

$$P_t = (1 - 5v)P_{t-1}$$

$$P_t = (1 - 5v)^t P_0$$

$$P_c = (1 - 5v)^t A$$

The general solution is: $P_t = \overline{P} + P_c = 3 + (1 - 5v)^t A$.
The definite solution is: $P_t = 3 + (1 - 5v)^t (P_0 - 3)$.

We can determine the values of the inventory adjustment coefficient ($v > 0$) for which this model is dynamically stable (and unstable). If $0 < v < 2/5$, then the inventory model is dynamically stable since for the term $(1 - 5v)^t$ to approach zero over time we need for

$$-1 < 1 - 5v < 1$$

or

$$-2 < -5v < 0$$

or

$$2/5 > v > 0$$

It follows that, for $v \geq 2/5$, the model is dynamically unstable.

For the type of time path for the price, we need to determine the sign of $1 - 5v$. If $1 - 5v < 0$, or $v > 1/5$, then the time path is oscillatory. If $1 - 5v > 0$, or $v < 1/5$, then the time path is monotonic. Note that, if $v = 1/5$, we are in intertemporal equilibrium, since $(1 - 5v) = 0$, and $P_t = \overline{P} = 3$.

As an example, let $v = .1$ and suppose that $P_0 = 2.4$. The definite solution becomes

$$P_t = 3 + (1 - 5v)^t (P_0 - 3) = 3 + (1 - .5)^t (2.4 - 3)$$

$$P_t = 3 + (.5)^t (-.6)$$

The sequence of market prices over time would converge in a monotonic fashion to $\overline{P} = 3$.

$$P_1 = 3 + (.5)^1 (-.6) = 2.70$$

$$P_2 = 3 + (.5)^2 (-.6) = 2.85$$

$$P_3 = 3 + (.5)^3 (-.6) = 2.925 \text{ etc.}$$

To elaborate, with the given initial price of $P_0 = 2.4$, below the market-clearing price of $\overline{P} = 3$, there would be an excess quantity demanded equal to 3: ($Q_0^d = 10 - 2(2.4)$

$= 5.2$ and $Q_0^s = -5 + 3(2.4) = 2.2$). The quantity transacted would equal the quantity demanded of 5.2 units, which is met by the quantity supplied of 2.2 units and the release of 3 units from inventories. With the assumed inventory adjustment coefficient of .1, the price adjustment for period one would equal $-.1(-3) = .3$, or 10% of the excess quantity demanded of 3. The shortage has induced a price increase of .3 to establish a set price of 2.7 for period one.

$$P_1 = P_0 - v\,(Q_0^s - Q_0^d) = 2.4 - .1\,(-3) = 2.7$$

In period one, however, there would still be an excess quantity demanded, albeit diminished from the previous period: $Q_1^d = 10 - 2(2.7) = 4.6$ and $Q_1^s = -5 + 3(2.7) = 3.1$. Now the quantity demanded and transacted, reduced to 4.6 units, is met by an increased quantity supplied of 3.1 units and a smaller reduction in inventories of 1.5 units. The shortage of 1.5 units induces another price increase, now equal to $-.1(-1.5) = .15$ and the market price set for period 2 becomes 2.85 (or $2.7 + .15$). We can see that the market price is converging monotonically. Note that after three periods, the market price has adjusted 87.5% of the way toward the market-clearing price level of $\overline{P} = 3$ [that is, $.875 = (2.925 - 2.4)/(3 - 2.4)$].

As an exercise, we can confirm, using the same demand and supply equations and initial price of $P_0 = 2.4$, that if the inventory adjustment coefficient were equal to $v' = .5$, the model would be dynamically unstable. The definite solution to this inventory model would be

$$P_t = \overline{P} + [1 - v' \cdot (s_1 - d_1)]^t\,(P_0 - \overline{P})$$

$$P_t = 3 + [1 - .5(3 - (-2))]^t\,(2.4 - 3)$$

$$P_t = 3 + (-1.5)^t\,(-.6)$$

The oscillatory and divergent time path for this dynamically unstable inventory model would begin:

$$P_1 = 3 + (-1.5)^1\,(-.6) = 3.9$$

$$P_2 = 3 + (-1.5)^2\,(-.6) = 1.65$$

$$P_3 = 3 + (-1.5)^3\,(-.6) = 5.025 \text{ etc.}$$

In short, here the dynamic instability results from an overreaction in price setting to any change in inventories.

PRACTICE PROBLEM 4.3

Given the following demand and supply schedules for a commodity and the price adjustment equation:

$$Q_t^d = 40 - 5P_t$$

$$Q_t^s = -10 + 3P_t$$

$$P_t = P_{t-1} - .15(Q_{t-1}^s - Q_{t-1}^d)$$

a) Find the time path for the market price, that is, the definite solution for P_t.
b) Determine whether this market is dynamically stable.
c) Find the market price, quantity transacted, and change in inventories for the first two periods, given that $P_0 = 7$.

(The answers are at the end of the chapter.)

EXPONENTIAL AND LOGARITHMIC FUNCTIONS

Before discussing first-order differential equations, we should review exponential and logarithmic functions. In particular, natural exponential and natural logarithmic functions will be used in the solution of the differential equations and continuous time models of the competitive market that follow.

In general, an exponential function can be written as: $y = ab^x$, where

y = dependent variable

x = independent variable

b = constant base $(b > 0, b \neq 1)$

a = constant coefficient.

Note that, in contrast to a power function of the form, $y = ax^n$, where the base x is the independent variable and the exponent n is the constant, with an exponential function the base b is a constant and the exponent x is the independent variable. The base b is restricted to positive real numbers, eliminating the possibility of imaginary numbers such as $(-4)^{.5}$, or the square root of negative four, which is equal to $2i$, where $i = \sqrt{-1}$.[1] If the base were equal to zero, $y = a(0)^x = 0$, or one, $y = a(1)^x = a$, then we no longer would have an exponential function, but a constant function.

The graph of a general exponential function, $y = ab^x$, is illustrated in Figure 4.4. The curve is smooth (i.e., it has no sharp points) and continuous (i.e., there are no breaks in the graph), with a y-intercept of $(0, a)$. Note that while the exponent x can be any real number, the value of y is restricted to positive or negative real numbers— depending on the sign of the coefficient a. For $a > 0$ (see Figure 4.4a), the slope of the curve $y = ab^x$ is positive and increasing. For $a < 0$ (see Figure 4.4b), the slope of the curve $y = ab^x$ is negative and decreasing. If the base (b) of the function increases, the curve rotates about the intercept $(0, a)$: in a counterclockwise direction for $a > 0$ and in a clockwise direction for $a < 0$. Examples of exponential functions are $y = 2^x$ (here $a = 1$ and $b = 2$) and $y = -3(.5)^x$ (here $a = -3$ and $b = .5$).

---

[1]Recall that imaginary numbers involve the square root of negative numbers and are denoted by the symbol i. *Complex numbers* have a real component and an imaginary component, for example, $8 - 2i$.

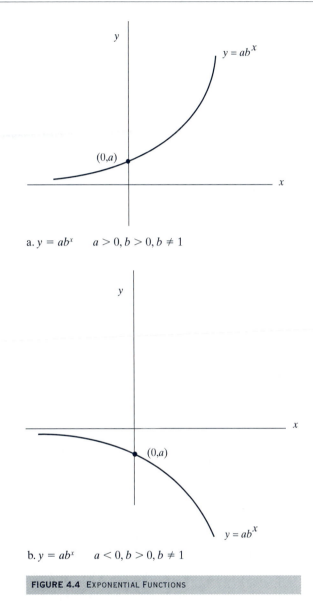

a. $y = ab^x$ $a > 0, b > 0, b \neq 1$

b. $y = ab^x$ $a < 0, b > 0, b \neq 1$

FIGURE 4.4 EXPONENTIAL FUNCTIONS

If an *exponent* is the power to which a given base is to be raised, then a *logarithm* is the power to which a given base must be raised to obtain a particular number. In general, given the exponential function $y = ab^x$ (where x is the exponent), the corresponding logarithmic function is $x = \log_b (y/a)$, where x is the logarithm. These exponential and logarithmic functions are inverse functions. To illustrate

Example 1. exponential: $y = (1/3)(2^x)$ logarithmic: $\log_2 (3y) = x \ (y > 0)$
Example 2. exponential: $y = -5(3^{-x})$ logarithmic: $\log_3 (-y/5) = -x \ (y < 0)$

The base for the *common logarithm* is 10. For example:

logarithmic: $\log_{10} 10 = 1$ exponential: $10^1 = 10$

$\log_{10} .01 = -2$ $10^{-2} = .01$

$\log_{10} 1{,}000 = 3$ $10^3 = 1{,}000$

Any nonnegative number can be expressed as a common logarithm.[2] For example: $\log_{10} 2 = .3010$, since $10^{.3010} = 2$. In mathematics texts, there are often tables for the values of common logarithms and the laws of logarithms can be used to extend these tables. Using the laws of addition and subtraction we can show that:

$\log_{10} 20 = \log_{10} (2)(10) = \log_{10} 2 + \log_{10} 10 = .3010 + 1 = 1.3010$, since $10^{1.3010} = 20$

and

$\log_{10} .2 = \log_{10} (2/10) = \log_{10} 2 - \log_{10} 10 = .3010 - 1 = -.6090$, since $10^{-.6090} = .2$.

Furthermore, logarithms to other bases can easily be converted to common logarithms. Most pocket calculators, however, are capable of calculating logarithms, so reliance on logarithmic tables and conversion formulas has been greatly reduced.

More widely used in economics than the common logarithm is the *natural logarithm*, with the irrational number e as the base. We will develop the natural logarithmic and natural exponential functions through the example of compound interest.

COMPOUND INTEREST

Earlier in our discussion of discrete time we used an example of a time deposit and simple annual compounding, where the interest on a given sum of money is calculated at the end of the year. Formally, let

S_0 = initial sum of money (at the beginning of the year)

S_t = value of the initial sum of money at time t

i = annual rate of interest.

With iteration we can express the future value, S_t, in terms of the initial value, S_0, the annual rate of interest, i, and the elapsed time, t. At the end of:

year 1: $S_1 = S_0 (1 + i)$

year 2: $S_2 = S_1 (1 + i) = S_0 (1 + i)(1 + i) = S_0 (1 + i)^2$

year 3: $S_3 = S_2 (1 + i) = S_0 (1 + i)^2 (1 + i) = S_0 (1 + i)^3$ etc . . .

---

[2]We should be clear on the distinction between nonnegative and nonpositive numbers. Given a universal set of real numbers, $R = \{x | x \in \mathbb{R}\}$: the subset of negative numbers, N, is given by $N = \{x | x < 0\}$; the subset of positive numbers, P, is given by $P = \{x | x > 0\}$; the subset of nonnegative numbers, $\tilde{N}$, is given by $\tilde{N} = \{x | x \geq 0\}$; and the subset of nonpositive numbers, $\tilde{P}$, is given by $\tilde{P} = \{x | x \leq 0\}$, where $\tilde{N}$ and $\tilde{P}$ are the complement sets to N and P, respectively.

Generalizing, for year t we have: $S_t = S_0 (1 + i)^t$.

That is, with simple annual compounding the value of any sum of money at the beginning of a year increases by the multiple $(1 + i)$ at the end of the year.

If we allow compounding m times a year, then, given the annual interest rate of i, the value of the initial sum of money at time t is equal to $S_t = S_0 (1 + i/m)^{mt}$

where m = number of times the interest is compounded during the year,

so i/m = the interest rate used for each compounding,

and mt = the total number of compoundings over t years.

Thus, with multiple compounding, each of the m times in the year that the interest is calculated, the rate i/m is used.

For example, suppose: $S_0 = \$1,000$, $i = .05$, and $t = 1$ (1 year maturity).

for $m = 1$ (annual compounding): $S_1 = \$1,000 (1 + .05)^1 = \$1,050$.

for $m = 2$ (semiannual compunding): $S_1 = \$1,000 (1 + .05/2)^2 = \$1,050.625$.

for $m = 4$ (quarterly compounding): $S_1 = \$1,000 (1 + .05/4)^4 = \$1,050.945$.

We can see that for a given **nominal interest rate**, i, the **effective interest rate**, i^*, is directly related to the number of interest compoundings in a year. Intuitively, the more compoundings of interest, albeit at proportionally lower interest rates, the greater will be the growth of an initial sum of money, since interest is being earned on interest more often. For example, with quarterly compounding (at 3-month intervals), the effective annual interest rate is 5.0945% for a nominal annual interest rate of 5.0%.

We can directly solve for the effective interest rate, i^*. Given an annual nominal interest rate of i, for t years, compounded m times a year, an initial sum of S_0 would increase to a future sum of S_t, where: $S_t = S_0 (1 + i/m)^{mt}$. To achieve the same future sum, the effective interest rate under annual compounding would be: $S_t = S_0 (1 + i^*)^t$. Setting the two future sums equal to each other and solving for i^* gives:

$$S_t = S_0 (1 + i/m)^{mt} = S_0 (1 + i^*)^t$$

Dividing through by S_0, and taking the tth root of both sides, we have:

$$(1 + i/m)^m = (1 + i^*)$$

Solving for the effective interest rate,

$$i^* = (1 + i/m)^m - 1.$$

With **continuous compounding**, as the term suggests, interest is compounded continuously. The number of compoundings of interest during the year approaches infinity as the time interval between compoundings approaches zero. To illustrate we begin with the formula for compound interest: $S_t = S_0 (1 + i/m)^{mt}$, and take the special case of $S_0 = \$1$, $i = 1.0$ (or 100%), and $t = 1$ (1 year). That is, we begin with one dollar which is to be compounded at an nominal annual interest rate of 100% for 1 year. We then see the convergence of the values for this sum of money at the end of 1 year as the number of compoundings within the year increases. Thus, in our example we have: $S_1 = 1 (1 + 1/m)^m$.

for $m = 1$: $S_1 = 1 (1 + 1/1)^1 = 2$ ($1 doubles to $2 under simple compounding.)

$\quad m = 2$: $S_1 = 1 (1 + 1/2)^2 = 2.25$

$\quad m = 3$: $S_1 = 1 (1 + 1/3)^3 = 2.3707$

$\qquad\qquad$ etc.

$\quad m = 100$: $S_1 = 1 (1 + 1/100)^{100} = 2.7048$

$\qquad\qquad$ etc.

$\quad m = 1,000$: $S_1 = 1 (1 + 1/1,000)^{1,000} = 2.7169$

$\qquad\qquad$ etc.

$\quad m = 10,000$: $S_1 = 1 (1 + 1/10,000)^{10,000} = 2.7182$

$\qquad\qquad$ etc.

Taking the limit as the number of compoundings approaches infinity, we get

$$\lim_{m\to\infty} (1 + 1/m)^m = e = 2.71828\ldots$$

In words, $1 would double in 1 year under simple annual compounding at a nominal interest rate of 100%. Under continuous compounding $1 would grow to slightly more than $2.718 at a nominal interest rate of 100%. The number e, an irrational number, is the base of the natural exponential function, $y = e^x$, and the natural logarithmic function, which we can write as $x = \log_e y$ or $x = \ln y$ (where ln stands for logarithm natural).

Generalizing, we state that an initial sum of money, S_0, will grow to a sum of S_t, after t years of continuous compounding at an annual nominal interest rate of i, where

$$S_t = S_0 \left[\lim_{m\to\infty} (1 + i/m)^{mt}\right] = S_0 e^{it}$$

and

$$e = 2.71828\ldots$$

The effective interest rate under continuous compounding is $i^* = e^i - 1$, where i is the annual nominal interest rate. To show this, we set $S_t = S_0 e^{it} = S_0 (1 + i^*)^t$. Dividing through by S_0 and taking the tth root of both sides, we get: $e^i = 1 + i^*$. Subtracting 1 from both sides gives: $i^* = e^i - 1$. For example, if $i = .05$, the effective interest rate under continuous compounding would be: $i^* = e^{.05} - 1 = 1.0513 - 1 = .0513$.

PRACTICE PROBLEM 4.4

Find the effective interest rate, i^*, given an annual nominal interest rate, i, equal to 8% when compounded:

a) semiannually
b) quarterly
c) continuously

(The answers are at the end of the chapter.)

As we will see below, the above formula applies not only to interest compounded continuously, but to any magnitude that is increasing or decreasing at a continuous rate, such as population growth or decline.

DERIVATIVES OF NATURAL EXPONENTIAL AND NATURAL LOGARITHMIC FUNCTIONS

If we have the natural exponential function, $y = e^x$ $(y > 0)$, then the inverse natural logarithmic function is $x = \ln y$ $(y > 0)$. One of the attractive features of the natural exponential function is that its derivative can be easily determined. We state, without proof, that for $y = e^x$, the derivative is $dy/dx = e^x$.

More generally, if $x = x(t)$, that is, the variable x is itself a function of another variable t, then for $y = e^{x(t)}$, the derivative is $dy/dt = e^{x(t)} (dx/dt) = x'(t) e^{x(t)}$. In words, the derivative of the natural exponential function is equal to the original function times the derivative of the exponent.

Example 1: $y = e^{t^2-1}$ and $dy/dt = 2te^{t^2-1}$

Example 2: $y = 3e^{-t}$ and $dy/dt = -3e^{-t}$

For the natural logarithmic function $x = \ln y$, the derivative is $dx/dy = 1/y$. Recall that the derivatives of inverse functions are reciprocals. Thus, we have for

$$\text{exponential function, } y = e^x;\ dy/dx = e^x = y$$

$$\text{logarithmic function, } x = \ln y;\ dx/dy = 1/y = 1/(dy/dx)$$

More generally, if $y = y(t)$, then for $x = \ln y(t)$, the derivative dx/dt is given by

$$dx/dt = (dx/dy)(dy/dt) = (1/y)\, y'(t) = y'(t)/y(t)$$

Example 1: $x = \ln 6t^2,\ dx/dt = (1/6t^2)(12t) = 2/t$

Example 2: $x = \ln (-6/t);\ dx/dt = (1/(-6/t))\, (6/t^2) = -1/t$

Conversion into Natural Exponential and Natural Logarithmic Functions   We have focused on natural exponential and natural logarithmic functions not only because of their more frequent applications in economics and their relative ease of differentiation, but due to our ability to convert exponential and logarithmic functions of any base into their natural counterparts.

Conversion of Exponential Function   Begin with the exponential function of the base b, $y = ab^{f(t)}$, which we want to transform into an exponential function of the form $y = ae^{x(t)}$. Setting

$$y = ab^{f(t)} = ae^{x(t)} \quad \text{or} \quad b^{f(t)} = e^{x(t)} \text{ (after dividing through by } a)$$

and taking the natural logarithm of both sides, gives

$$\ln b^{f(t)} = \ln e^{x(t)} = x(t) \text{ [since } \ln e^{x(t)} = x(t)]$$

Thus, we have $f(t) \ln b = x(t) = (\ln b) f(t)$ [since $\ln b^{f(t)} = f(t) \ln b = (\ln b) f(t)$]. Substituting in $(\ln b) f(t)$ for $x(t)$, we can write $y = ab^{f(t)} = ae^{x(t)} = ae^{(\ln b) f(t)}$

Example: $y = .4 (2^{5t}) = ae^{x(t)}$, so

$$a = .4 \text{ and } 2^{5t} = e^{x(t)}$$

$$\ln 2^{5t} = x(t)$$

$$5t (\ln 2) = x(t)$$

and

$$y = .4 (2^{5t}) = .4e^{(\ln 2) 5t} = .4^{(.693)5t} = .4e^{3.465t} \text{ (since } \ln 2 = .693)$$

Conversion of Logarithmic Function We can convert a logarithm of base b, for example, $x = \log_b f(t)$, to a natural logarithm, $x = \ln y(t)$ as follows. Writing $x = \log_b f(t)$ in exponential form, we have $b^x = f(t)$. Taking the natural logarithm of both sides of the equation gives

$$\ln b^x = \ln f(t)$$

or

$$x (\ln b) = \ln f(t)$$

Solving for x: $x = \ln f(t)/\ln b$
Therefore $x = \log_b f(t) = (1/\ln b) \ln f(t)$.

Example: $x = \log_b (2t^2 + 1)$

$$b^x = 2t^2 + 1$$

$$\ln b^x = \ln (2t^2 + 1)$$

$$x (\ln b) = \ln (2t^2 + 1)$$

$$x = \ln (2t^2 + 1)/ \ln b$$

and

$$x = \log_b (2t^2 + 1) = (1/\ln b) \ln (2t^2 + 1)$$

We can now differentiate exponential and logarithmic functions to the base b after converting to their natural exponential and natural logarithmic counterpart functions. For example, given $x = \log_b (2t^2 + 1)$, to find dx/dt we would first convert $x = \log_b (2t^2 + 1)$ to $(1/\ln b) \ln (2t^2 + 1)$. Then differentiating, $dx/dt = (1/\ln b)[1/(2t^2 + 1)](4t) = 4t/(\ln b)(2t^2 + 1)$.

Later we will use natural exponential and natural logarithmic functions in other contexts, including growth rates and elasticities. For now, this overview is sufficient to allow us to discuss first-order differential equations.

PRACTICE PROBLEMS 4.5 AND 4.6

4.5   a) Convert the following exponential functions to logarithmic functions:
    i) $y = 4^x$ ii) $y = -3e^x$ iii) $y = 2(.5)^x$
    b) Convert the following logarithmic functions to exponential functions and solve for x:
    i) $x = \log_2 8$ ii) $x = \log_{25} 5$ iii) $\ln x = 2$

4.6   Find the derivative, dy/dt, of each of the following:
    i) $y = e^{-3t}$ ii) $y = \ln t^3$ iii) $y = (1/4) \ln (2t)$
    iv) $y = 3^{2t}$ v) $y = \log_2 (3t)$

(The answers are at the end of the chapter.)

FIRST-ORDER DIFFERENTIAL EQUATIONS

Differential equations are the continuous time counterparts to difference equations. Changes in the values of the endogenous variables in the model occur continuously with time—not in discrete amounts at the ends of periods of a given duration. Whereas the Δ operator indicates discrete time (e.g., Δt), the derivative operator d indicates continuous time (e.g., dt). As with difference equations, however, the solutions to differential equations set forth time paths for the endogenous variables.

Differential equations involve derivatives with respect to time. Similar to our treatment of difference equations, we discuss only the most basic form of differential equations. This means linear, first-order differential equations with a constant coefficient and a constant term of the form:

$$dy/dt + ay = b$$

where y = dependent variable

t = independent variable (time)

and a and b are the constant coefficient and constant term, respectively. This differential equation is *first order*, since no higher differentials are present, for example, a second-order differential, d^2y/dt^2. Not raising the endogenous variable, y, to any power other than one and not multiplying the endogenous variable by its derivative, for example, $(y)(dy/dt)$, makes this a *linear* first-order differential equation.

We will derive the solution and the conditions for the dynamic stability of this type of linear, first-order differential equation and then we will illustrate with an example of a perfectly competitive commodity market.

SOLUTION TO A CONSTANT COEFFICIENT-CONSTANT TERM, LINEAR, FIRST-ORDER DIFFERENTIAL EQUATION

The procedure for the solution is similar to that for linear, first-order difference equations. The solution has two parts: the particular solution (also known as the *particular integral* in the case of differential equations) and the complementary function.

Given a linear first-order differential equation: $dy/dt + ay = b$, the particular solution represents the intertemporal equilibrium or the solution to the static version of the model. Here we assume that the endogenous variable y is independent of time, that is, $dy/dt = 0$. The equation reduces to $ay = b$. Solving for y gives the particular solution, $\bar{y} = b/a$, where we restrict $a \neq 0$. (Later we will examine the case where the constant coefficient a is equal to zero.)

For the complementary function, we set the right-hand side of the differential equation equal to zero: $dy/dt + ay = 0$.

Then dividing through by y and subtracting the constant coefficient a from both sides of the equation we find:

$$(1/y)dy/dt + a = 0$$

$$(1/y)dy/dt = -a$$

Integrating both sides of this equation with respect to time (t), we have:

$$\int (1/y)(dy/dt)\ dt = -\int a\ dt$$

and

$$\ln y + c_1 = -at + c_2$$

or

$$\ln y = -at + C \qquad \text{where } C = c_2 - c_1, \text{ the constant of integration}$$

Writing the equation in exponential form gives

$$e^{-at+C} = e^{-at}e^C = y$$

The complementary function, y_c, can be written as

$$y_c = Ae^{-at} \qquad \text{where} \qquad A = e^C, \text{ a constant term which will be defined later.}$$

The general solution to this linear, first-order differential equation equals the sum of the particular solution and the complementary function.

$$y(t) = \bar{y} + y_c = b/a + Ae^{-at}$$

To obtain the definite solution and solve for the constant A, we set $t = 0$.

$$y(0) = b/a + Ae^0 = b/a + A$$

Thus

$$A = y(0) - b/a = y(0) - \bar{y}$$

The definite solution is then:

$$y(t) = \bar{y} + [y(0) - \bar{y}]e^{-at} = b/a + [y(0) - b/a]e^{-at} \ (a \neq 0)$$

The similarity to the definite solution to a linear, first-order difference equation is apparent. The time path of the dependent variable is a function of the parameters of the model (here the constant coefficient a and the constant term b), the initial condition, $y(0)$, and time, t. The term, $(y(0) - b/a)e^{-at}$, represents the deviations over time from the intertemporal equilibrium of $\bar{y} = b/a$.

Special Case: Constant Coefficient Equals Zero   Before establishing the conditions for dynamic stability, we will examine the case where the constant coefficient, a, is equal to zero. The linear, first-order differential equation, $dy/dt + ay = b$, then becomes $dy/dt + 0 = b$, or simply $dy/dt = b$. With $a = 0$, there is no particular solution or intertemporal equilibrium. We solve for the time path by integrating both sides of the equation with respect to time.

$$\int (dy/dt)\,dt = \int b\,dt$$

$$y + c_1 = bt + c_2$$

or

$$y = bt + C \quad \text{where } C = c_2 - c_1 \text{ (constant of integration).}$$

From this general solution $y(t) = bt + C$, we derive the definite solution, as usual, by setting $t = 0$.

$$y(0) = (b)(0) + C = C$$

The definite solution to the linear first-order differential equation $dy/dt = b$ is: $y(t) = bt + y(0)$, which represents a moving equilibrium. Here the value of the endogenous variable at time t is equal to the sum of the initial value $y(0)$ and a term, bt, that is a linear function of time. An example might be a family planning program, where a woman who adopts effective contraception receives an initial sum of money, $y(0)$, plus a variable amount that depends on the time she does not become pregnant, bt.

DYNAMIC STABILITY

We have shown that the definite solution to the linear, first-order differential equation, $dy/dt + ay = b$, $(a \neq 0)$, is equal to: $y(t) = b/a + [y(0) - b/a]e^{-at}$. For dynamic stability the value of the endogenous variable, $y(t)$, must approach the intertemporal equilibrium, $\bar{y} = b/a$, over time. Given that the system is not already in intertemporal equilibrium, $y(0) \neq b/a$, then dynamic stability requires that the deviations from intertemporal equilibrium diminish with time. The term e^{-at} determines the dynamic stability of the system. For $a > 0$, the system is dynamically stable, since as t increases, $e^{-at} = 1/e^{at}$ decreases toward zero. For $a < 0$, however, the system is dynamically unstable, since as t increases, $e^{|-at|}$ increases exponentially.

Note that in contrast to the general linear, first-order difference equation studied in the first part of this chapter, dynamic stability does not depend on the magnitude of the coefficient a, only on its sign. Furthermore, the term e^{-at} will always be positive; thus the time path of the endogenous variable, $y(t)$, will be monotonic—converging monotonically to the intertemporal equilibrium if $a > 0$, but diverging monotonically from the intertemporal equilibrium if $a < 0$.

We illustrate with a numerical example. Given the linear first-order differential equation 2 $dy/dt + 4y = -7$ and $y(0) = -1$, as the initial condition, we first divide through by 2 to normalize the derivative expression: $dy/dt + 2y = -7/2$.

For the particular solution we assume $dy/dt = 0$ and then solve for y.

$$0 + 2y = -7/2$$

$$\bar{y} = -7/4$$

For the complementary function we begin by setting the right-hand side equal to zero:

$$dy/dt + 2y = 0$$

Dividing through by y and then subtracting 2 from both sides gives:

$$(1/y)dy/dt + 2 = 0$$

$$(1/y)dy/dt = -2$$

Integrating both sides with respect to time, we have:

$$\int (1/y)(dy/dt) \, dt = -\int 2 \, dt$$

$$\ln y + c_1 = -2t + c_2$$

$$\ln y = -2t + C \qquad (C = c_2 - c_1)$$

Expressed in exponential form, the complementary function becomes: $y_c = e^{-2t+C} = e^{-2t}e^C = Ae^{-2t}$ where $A = e^C$.

The general solution is: $y(t) = \bar{y} + y_c = -7/4 + Ae^{-2t}$.

Setting $t = 0$ and using the inital condition, $y(0) = -1$, we solve for A and derive the definite solution.

$$y(0) = -7/4 + Ae^{-2(0)} = -7/4 + A = -1$$

Thus,

$$A = 3/4.$$

The definite solution to the differential equation $2dy/dt + 4y = -7$, given $y(0) = -1$, is:

$$y(t) = -7/4 + (3/4)e^{-2t}$$

To check, we can differentiate the definite solution to get: $dy/dt = -2(3/4)e^{-2t} = -(3/2)e^{-2t}$. Substituting this derivative and the definite solution for $y(t)$ back into the original differential equation we have:

$$2 \, dy/dt + 4y = -7$$

$$2(-3/2)e^{-2t} + 4[-7/4 + (3/4)e^{-2t}] = -7$$

$$-3e^{-2t} - 7 + 3e^{-2t} = -7$$

$$-7 = -7 \text{ (It checks.)}$$

Note that the initial condition $y(0) = -1$ is also satisfied since $y(0) = -7/4 + (3/4)e^{-2(0)} = -1$.

Moreover, the system is dynamically stable. Referring back to the definite solution, $y(t) = -7/4 + (3/4)e^{-2t}$, confirms that over time the value for y approaches the

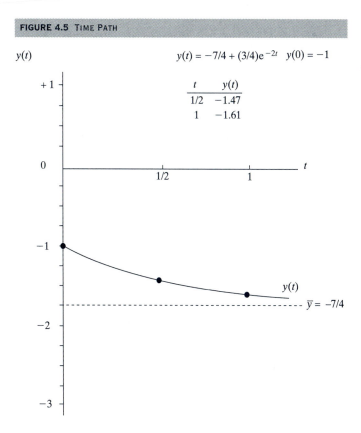

FIGURE 4.5 TIME PATH

$y(t)$

$y(t) = -7/4 + (3/4)e^{-2t}$ $y(0) = -1$

t	$y(t)$
1/2	−1.47
1	−1.61

$\bar{y} = -7/4$

intertemporal equilibrium. We note that the endogenous variable, y, while converging to the particular solution (here $\bar{y} = -7/4 = -1.75$), in this dynamically stable equation, never actually attains the particular solution. In this example, however, at time $t = 1$, the adjustment of y to the intertemporal equilibrium, $\bar{y} = -1.75$, is 81.3% complete; that is, since $y(1) = -1.61$ and $[y(1) - y(0)]/[\bar{y} - y(0)] = [-1.61 - (-1)]/[-1.75 - (-1)] = -.61/-.75 = .813$). An example might be a pollution abatement program with an ideal goal of reducing the air pollution caused by the emissions from a particular factory to zero.

In Figure 4.5 we illustrate the time path for y, which is smooth, continuous, and monotonically decreasing as it converges to the intertemporal equilibrium. If $y(0) < \bar{y}$, say $y(0) = -3$, then the convergence of the time path would be monotonically increasing.

PRACTICE PROBLEM 4.7

Find the definite solutions for the following linear first-order differential equations. Determine if the time path $y(t)$ is dynamically stable.
a) $dy/dt - 3y = 9; y(0) = -2$
b) $2\, dy/dt + y = 4; y(0) = 1$

(The answers are at the end of the chapter.)

APPLICATION TO A PERFECTLY COMPETITIVE MARKET

To illustrate an economics application of linear, first-order differential equations we return to a perfectly competitive market for a commodity. We assume a Walrasian system of price adjustment. The equations are given below, where the subscript t refers to continuous time and, *a priori*, we make no assumptions about the signs of the parameters d_0, d_1, s_0, and s_1.

$$Q_t^d = d_0 + d_1 P_t$$

$$Q_t^s = s_0 + s_1 P_t$$

$$dP_t/dt = u \cdot (Q_t^d - Q_t^s) \qquad u > 0$$

In this dynamic model of a market, like in the inventory model discussed earlier, there is no equilibrium condition. In particular, the market is not assumed to clear continuously or at each point in time. Rather, we postulate how the market price changes. The parameter u indicates the responsiveness of the change in the market price to shortages and surpluses. If there is an excess quantity demanded

$(Q_t^d - Q_t^s > 0)$, the market price would rise $(dP_t/dt > 0)$. Conversely, an excess quantity supplied $(Q_t^d - Q_t^s < 0)$ would induce a decrease in the market price $(dP_t/dt < 0)$.

To solve, we incorporate the demand and supply equations into the dynamic price equation.

$$dP_t/dt = u \cdot (d_0 + d_1 P_t - s_0 - s_1 P_t)$$

Simplifying, we obtain the linear, first-order differential equation

$$dP_t/dt - u \cdot (d_1 - s_1)P_t = u \cdot (d_0 - s_0)$$

For the particular solution we assume $dP_t/dt = 0$ and solve for P_t.

$$0 - u \cdot (d_1 - s_1)P_t = u \cdot (d_0 - s_0)$$

$$P_t = -u \cdot (d_0 - s_0)/u \cdot (d_1 - s_1) = (s_0 - d_0)/(d_1 - s_1) = \overline{P} \qquad (d_1 \neq s_1)$$

where $\overline{P}$, the familiar solution to the static version of the model, represents the intertemporal equilibrium.

For the complementary function we set the right-hand side of the differential equation equal to zero,

$$dP_t/dt - u \cdot (d_1 - s_1)P_t = 0$$

divide through by P_t, and then add the term, $u \cdot (d_1 - s_1)$, to both sides of the equation.

$$(1/P_t)(dP_t/dt) - u \cdot (d_1 - s_1) = 0$$

$$(1/P_t)(dP_t/dt) = u \cdot (d_1 - s_1)$$

Integrating both sides with respect to time, we find

$$\int (1/P_t)(dP_t/dt)\, dt = \int u \cdot (d_1 - s_1)\, dt$$

and

$$\ln P_t + c_1 = u \cdot (d_1 - s_1)t + c_2$$

or

$$\ln P_t = u \cdot (d_1 - s_1)t + C \qquad \text{where } C = c_2 - c_1.$$

Converting to exponential form we have

$$P_t = e^{u(d_1 - s_1)t}\, e^C = A e^{u(d_1 - s_1)t} \qquad \text{where } A = e^C$$

The complementary function is equal to:

$$P_c = A e^{u(d_1 - s_1)t}$$

For the general solution, we add the particular solution and complementary function.

$$P(t) = \overline{P} + P_c = \overline{P} + Ae^{u(d_1 - s_1)t}$$

Setting $t = 0$, we can solve for A.

$$P(0) = \overline{P} + Ae^0 = \overline{P} + A$$

Therefore, $A = P(0) - \overline{P}$.

The definite solution to this dynamic, continuous-time model of a competitive commodity market is:

$$P(t) = \overline{P} + (P(0) - \overline{P})e^{u(d_1 - s_1)t} \quad \text{where } \overline{P} = (s_0 - d_0)/(d_1 - s_1) \quad d_1 \neq s_1$$

Dynamic stability requires that the deviations from the intertemporal equilibrium price must diminish over time. Here the term $u \cdot (d_1 - s_1)$ must be negative. Given that the price adjustment parameter u is positive, the condition for dynamic stability reduces to $d_1 - s_1 < 0$ or $dQ_t^d/dP_t - dQ_t^s/dP_t < 0$, which is the identical condition for Walrasian static stability. (Refer back to Chapter 3.) The additional insight from a dynamic model compared to a static model comes from the representation of the time path of adjustment.

Knowledge of the time path of adjustment can be important in monitoring progress toward a goal. Return to the earlier example of pollution abatement. While it may be impossible to reduce the harmful emissions of a factory to zero, we may nevertheless want to know how fast a particular program of abatement would work to reduce the emissions to a tolerable level. We note again that assessing the dynamic stability for a market (like static stability) assumes given parameters and independent variables underlying the demand and supply curves. In reality, market demand and supply curves are likely to be changing over time, rendering any assessment of stability more difficult.

PRACTICE PROBLEM 4.8

Given the following demand and supply schedules and price adjustment equation:

$$Q_t^d = 60 - 5P_t$$

$$Q_t^s = -10 + 2P_t$$

$$dP/dt = .5(Q_t^d - Q_t^s)$$

Determine the time path for the market price, $P(t)$, and assess the dynamic stability of the model. Assume $P(0) = 9$.

(The answers are at the end of the chapter.)

In concluding this chapter, we might also remember that we have kept the mathematics of difference and differential equations fairly simple—in order to concentrate on the utility of these basic techniques for the dynamic modeling of competitive markets. Coverage of more complex types of difference and differential equations can be found in advanced mathematics texts. Moreover, up to this point we have restricted our attention to single markets. In the next chapter we use matrix algebra to analyze two or more related markets and models of general competitive equilibrium.

❖ KEY TERMS

Economics

- adaptive expectations hypothesis (p. 83)
- cobweb model (p. 83)
- continuous compounding (p. 97)

- effective interest rate (p. 97)
- inventory adjustment coefficient (p. 89)

- inventory model (p. 89)
- nominal interest rate (p. 97)

Mathematics

- common logarithm (p. 96)
- complementary function (p. 79)
- complex number (p. 94)
- definite solution (p. 79)
- difference equation (p. 77)
- differential equation (p. 77)
- exponent (p. 95)

- first difference (p. 78)
- first order (p. 101)
- general solution (p. 79)
- linear (p. 101)
- logarithm (p. 95)
- monotonic (p. 80)
- natural logarithm (p. 96)

- order (p. 78)
- particular integral (p. 102)
- particular solution (p. 78)
- period analysis (p. 77)
- oscillatory (p. 80)

❖ PROBLEMS

1. Given the demand and supply schedules for a commodity in a perfectly competitive market, where the subscript t indicates the time period:

$$Q_t^d = 32 - 4P_t$$
$$Q_t^s = -4 + 2P_{t-1}$$
$$Q_t^d \overset{e}{=} Q_t^s$$

   a) Derive the first-order difference equation associated with this system.
   b) Find the definite solution and determine whether the market is dynamically stable.
   c) Given $P_0 = 5$, determine the market prices and quantities transacted in the first three periods ($t = 1, t = 2$, and $t = 3$). Illustrate graphically the time path for the market price.

2. Given the demand and supply schedules for a commodity in a perfectly competitive market, where the subscript t indicates the time period:

$$Q_t^d = 32 - 4P_t$$
$$Q_t^s = 42 - 6P_{t-1}$$
$$Q_t^d \overset{e}{=} Q_t^s$$

   a) Derive the first-order difference equation associated with this system.

b) Find the definite solution and determine whether the market is dynamically stable.

c) Given $P_0 = 4$, determine the market prices and quantities transacted in the first three periods ($t = 1, t = 2$, and $t = 3$). Illustrate graphically the time path for the market price.

3. Given the demand and supply schedules for a commodity in a perfectly competitive market, where the subscript t indicates the time period.

$$Q_t^d = 32 - 4P_t$$

$$Q_t^s = -4 + 2P_t$$

$$P_t = P_{t-1} - .25(Q_{t-1}^s - Q_{t-1}^d)$$

a) Derive the first-order difference equation associated with this system.

b) Find the definite solution and determine whether the market is dynamically stable.

c) Given $P_0 = 5$, determine the market prices and quantities transacted in the first three periods ($t = 1, t = 2$, and $t = 3$). Illustrate graphically the time path for the market price.

d) Repeat steps a) through c) if suppliers instead set the current price according to:

$$P_t = P_{t-1} - .5(Q_{t-1}^s - Q_{t-1}^d)$$

e) Determine the range of values for the inventory adjustment coefficient for which the market is:

i)   dynamically stable in an oscillatory fashion.
ii) dynamically stable in a monotonic fashion.
iii) dynamically unstable in an oscillatory fashion.
iv) dynamically unstable in a monotonic fashion.

4. Given an initial sum of $10,000 and a nominal annual interest rate of $i = .06$, determine the effective annual interest rate under:

a) annual compounding
b) semiannual compounding
c) quarterly compounding
d) continuous compounding.

5. Find the derivative (dy/dt) of the following functions:
   a) $y = e^{4t-2}$ b) $y = 3(4)^{t^2}$ c) $y = \ln(5t + 1)$
   d) $y = \log_4 t^3$ e) $y = -2\log_2(3t)$ f) $y = -2(5)^{t^5}$

6. Given the demand and supply schedules for a commodity in a perfectly competitive market, where the subscript t indicates time:

$$Q_t^d = 32 - 4P_t$$

$$Q_t^s = -4 + 2P_t$$

$$dP_t/dt = .5\,(Q_t^d - Q_t^s)$$

a) Derive the first-order differential equation associated with this system.
b) Find the definite solution and determine whether the market is dynamically stable.
c) Given $P_0 = 5$, illustrate graphically the time path for the market price.

7. Given the demand and supply schedules for a commodity in a perfectly competitive market, where the subscript t indicates time.

$$Q_t^d = 32 - 4P_t$$
$$Q_t^s = 42 - 6P_t$$
$$dP_t/dt = .5\,(Q_t^d - Q_t^s)$$

a) Derive the first-order differential equation associated with the system.
b) Find the definite solution and determine whether the market is dynamically stable.
c) Given $P_0 = 4$, illustrate graphically the time path for the market price.

❖ ANSWERS TO PRACTICE PROBLEMS

4.1 a) The definite solution is: $y_t = 4(2)^t - 1$. The time path is dynamically unstable in a monotonic fashion.
b) The definite solution is: $y_t = -2(-1/3)^t + 1$. The time path is dynamically stable in an oscillatory fashion.
c) The definite solution is: $y_t = (-2/5)^t + 0$. The time path is dynamically stable in an oscillatory fashion.
d) The definite solution is: $y_t = 2t - 2$. The time path is a moving equilibrium.

4.2 a) The definite solution is: $P_t = (P_0 - 5)(-.5)^t + 5$.
b) The market is dynamically stable in an oscillatory fashion.
c) The market-clearing prices and quantities transacted for the first two periods are:

$P_1 = 5.5$ and $Q_1 = 2$ (period 1); $P_2 = 4.75$ and $Q_2 = 5$ (period 2).

4.3 a) The definite solution is: $P_t = (P_0 - 6.25)(-.2)^t + 6.25$.
b) The market is dynamically stable in an oscillatory fashion.
c) The market prices, quantities transacted, and inventory changes for the first two periods are: $P_1 = 6.10$, $Q_1 = 9.5$, and inventory change $= -1.2$. (period 1) $P_2 = 6.28$, $Q_2 = 8.6$, and inventory change $= +.24$. (period 2).

4.4 a) $i^* = .0816$ (under semiannual compounding)
b) $i^* = .0824$ (under quarterly compounding)
c) $i^* = .0833$. (under continuous compounding)

4.5 a) i) $x = \log_4 y$ ii) $x = -\ln(y/3)$ iii) $x = \log_{.5}(y/2)$
     b) i) $2^x = 8; x = 3$ ii) $25^x = 5; x = .5$ iii) $e^2 = x; x = 7.389$

4.6 a) $dy/dt = -3e^{-3t}$ b) $dy/dt = 3/t$ c) $dy/dt = 1/2t$
     d) $dy/dt = 2 \ln 3 \, (3)^{2t}$ e) $dy/dt = (1/\ln 2)(1/t)$

4.7 a) The definite solution is: $y(t) = -3 + e^{3t}$. The time path is dynamically unstable.
     b) The definite solution is: $y(t) = -3e^{-.5t} + 4$. The time path is dynamically stable.

4.8 The definite solution is: $P(t) = -e^{-3.5t} + 10$. The model is dynamically stable in a monotonic fashion.

SYSTEMS OF LINEAR EQUATIONS AND GENERAL EQUILIBRIUM

We have studied the characteristics of perfectly competitive individual markets—progressing from static, to comparative static, to dynamic analysis. While the prices of related commodities [substitutes, like beef and pork; and complements, like TV sets and videocassette recorders (VCRs)] were determinants of the market demand, and the prices of inputs (e.g., grain feed for livestock and plastic for VCRs) were determinants of the market supply of the commodity in question, we did not explicitly link together markets. In this chapter we address general equilibrium models, where we analyze systems of two or more competitive markets. We will retain, for now, the linear specification for the equations of the models.

We begin with a linear system of two related commodity markets, where we solve for the equilibrium set of market prices. We then move to a linear system of n markets and set forth the characteristics of a general equilibrium. To solve systems of linear equations we will use matrix algebra. A review of vectors will precede the discussion of matrix algebra.

A MODEL OF TWO PERFECTLY COMPETITIVE MARKETS

Consider two related commodities, 1 and 2, sold in perfectly competitive markets. The assumed linear demand and supply schedules are given below.

$$Q_1^d = d_{10} + d_{11}P_1 + d_{12}P_2$$

$$Q_1^s = s_{10} + s_{11}P_1 + s_{12}P_2$$

$$Q_1^d(P_1, P_2) \stackrel{e}{=} Q_1^s(P_1, P_2)$$

$$Q_2^d = d_{20} + d_{21}P_1 + d_{22}P_2$$

$$Q_2^s = s_{20} + s_{21}P_1 + s_{22}P_2$$

$$Q_2^d(P_1, P_2) \overset{e}{=} Q_2^s(P_1, P_2)$$

where the dual subscripts for the parameters d and s indicate the involved markets. Here, d_{10} and s_{10} (d_{20} and s_{20}) are the demand- and supply-quantity intercepts for market 1 (market 2). The own price sensitivities for the quantities demanded and supplied for commodity 1 (commodity 2) are represented by d_{11} and s_{11} (d_{22} and s_{22}), respectively. In the usual case (negatively sloped demand and positively sloped supply curves), $d_{11} < 0, d_{22} < 0$, and $s_{11} > 0, s_{22} > 0$.

The sensitivities of the quantities demanded and supplied of commodity 1 (commodity 2) to the unit price of commodity 2 (commodity 1) are given by d_{12} and s_{12} (d_{21} and s_{21}), respectively. If commodities 1 and 2 are substitutes (complements) in consumption, then $d_{12} > 0$ and $d_{21} > 0$ ($d_{12} < 0$ and $d_{21} < 0$). If the two commodities are unrelated in consumption, then $d_{12} = d_{21} = 0$. If commodity 2 (commodity 1) is an input used in the production of commodity 1 (commodity 2), then $s_{12} < 0$ ($s_{21} < 0$). If the two commodities are unrelated in production then $s_{12} = s_{21} = 0$.

We solve this system of six equations in six unknowns (the endogenous variables, $Q_1^d, Q_1^s, P_1, Q_2^d, Q_2^s$, and P_2), by first substituting the demand and supply equations into the equilibrium conditions and reducing the model to two equations in two unknowns (P_1 and P_2). Intuitively, we need to find a combination of unit prices, P_1 and P_2, such that both markets simultaneously clear, with zero excess quantities demanded.

1) $d_{10} + d_{11} P_1 + d_{12} P_2 \overset{e}{=} s_{10} + s_{11} P_1 + s_{12} P_2$

2) $d_{20} + d_{21} P_1 + d_{22} P_2 \overset{e}{=} s_{20} + s_{21} P_1 + s_{22} P_2$

Rewriting these equilibrium conditions in terms of the excess quantities demanded equaling zero gives:

1') $(d_{10} - s_{10}) + (d_{11} - s_{11}) P_1 + (d_{12} - s_{12}) P_2 \overset{e}{=} 0$

2') $(d_{20} - s_{20}) + (d_{21} - s_{21}) P_1 + (d_{22} - s_{22}) P_2 \overset{e}{=} 0$

Using the method of substitution we can isolate P_1 in equation 1').

$$1'') \ P_1 = \frac{s_{10} - d_{10}}{d_{11} - s_{11}} + \frac{s_{12} - d_{12}}{d_{11} - s_{11}} P_2 \qquad (\text{where } d_{11} \neq s_{11})$$

and then substituting for P_1 into equation 2')

$$2'') \ (d_{20} - s_{20}) + (d_{21} - s_{21}) \left[\frac{s_{10} - d_{10}}{d_{11} - s_{11}} + \frac{s_{12} - d_{12}}{d_{11} - s_{11}} P_2 \right] + (d_{22} - s_{22}) P_2 = 0$$

We now have reduced the system to one equation in one unknown, P_2, which we can solve to obtain the equilibrium value for $\overline{P}_2$. Multiplying through by $(d_{11} - s_{11})$ and simplifying we find:

$$\overline{P}_2 = \frac{(d_{20} - s_{20})(d_{11} - s_{11}) + (s_{10} - d_{10})(d_{21} - s_{21})}{(s_{22} - d_{22})(d_{11} - s_{11}) - (s_{12} - d_{12})(d_{21} - s_{21})}$$

Then, substituting this equilibrium value for P_2 into equation 1″) we can solve for $\overline{P}_1$.

$$\overline{P}_1 = \frac{(d_{20} - s_{20})(s_{12} - d_{12}) + (d_{10} - s_{10})(d_{22} - s_{22})}{(s_{22} - d_{22})(d_{11} - s_{11}) - (s_{12} - d_{12})(d_{21} - s_{21})}$$

Having solved for the equilibrium prices, we can find the quantities transacted in the two markets by substituting $\overline{P}_1$ and $\overline{P}_2$ into the demand (or supply) equations for commodities 1 and 2. Clearly, even with just two markets, the algebra is tedious. A more efficient method, especially as the number of markets in the model increases, is provided by matrix algebra.

Nevertheless, at this point, we should note some important properties of the equilibrium. First, the equilibrium values for the endogenous variables ($\overline{P}_1, \overline{P}_2$, as well as $\overline{Q}_1^d, \overline{Q}_1^s, \overline{Q}_2^d$, and $\overline{Q}_2^s$) are expressed entirely in terms of the parameters or exogenous variables of the model. Second, in order for a unique equilibrium to exist, we must impose some restrictions on the parameters. Mathematically, to avoid division by zero we must have $d_{11} \neq s_{11}$ and $d_{22} \neq s_{22}$, as well as $(s_{22} - d_{22})(d_{11} - s_{11}) \neq (s_{12} - d_{12})(d_{21} - s_{21})$. Further restrictions (including the same signs for the numerators and denominators) are needed to ensure positive equilibrium prices and quantities transacted. Third, given the values of the exogenous variables, the equilibrium prices and quantities transacted would persist. Consequently, changes in the equilibrium values would be due to changes in the values of the underlying exogenous variables. Indeed, we could do comparative static experiments, although without *a priori* assumptions about the signs and relative magnitudes of the parameters of the model, we may not be able to sign the partial derivatives.

To illustrate, consider the effect of an increase in the value of d_{10} (an increase in the market demand for commodity 1) on the market equilibrium price of commodity 2. The relevant partial derivative is $\delta \overline{P}_2 / \delta d_{10}$. Differentiating the expression for the equilibrium value for the unit price of commodity 2 with respect to the parameter d_{10} we have:

$$\delta \overline{P}_2 / \delta d_{10} = \frac{-(d_{21} - s_{21})[(s_{22} - d_{22})(d_{11} - s_{11}) - (s_{12} - d_{12})(d_{21} - s_{21})]}{[(s_{22} - d_{22})(d_{11} - s_{11}) - (s_{12} - d_{12})(d_{21} - s_{21})]^2}$$

$$\delta \overline{P}_2 / \delta d_{10} = \frac{-(d_{21} - s_{21})}{(s_{22} - d_{22})(d_{11} - s_{11}) - (s_{12} - d_{12})(d_{21} - s_{21})}$$

This comparative static result generally cannot be signed—even if we make specific assumptions about the signs of the parameters. For example, if we assume the usual case of negatively sloped demand curves ($d_{11} < 0$ and $d_{22} < 0$) and positively sloped supply curves ($s_{11} > 0$ and $s_{22} > 0$); and if we assume that commodities 1 and 2 are unrelated in production ($s_{12} = 0$ and $s_{21} = 0$), but are substitutes in consumption ($d_{12} > 0$ and $d_{21} > 0$); then the partial derivative reduces to:

$$\delta \overline{P}_2 / \delta d_{10} = \frac{-d_{21}}{(s_{22} - d_{22})(d_{11} - s_{11}) + (d_{12})(d_{21})}$$

While the numerator is now unambiguously negative, the denominator cannot be signed. If we assume, however, that $| (s_{22} - d_{22})(d_{11} - s_{11}) | > | (d_{12})(d_{21}) |$, the denominator would be negative. A sufficient condition for the denominator of this partial derivative to be negative is that $|(d_{22})(d_{11})| > |(d_{12})(d_{21})|$, that is, the direct effects of price changes (represented by $d_{22} = \delta Q_2^d / \delta P_2$ and $d_{11} = \delta Q_1^d / \delta P_1$) dominate the indirect effects (represented by $d_{12} = \delta Q_1^d / \delta P_2$ and $d_{21} = \delta Q_2^d / \delta P_1$). If this is so, as might be expected, then the denominator of the partial derivative is negative and the comparative static result can be signed as $\delta \overline{P}_2 / \delta d_{10} > 0$.

Thus, in the usual case, and assuming commodities 1 and 2 are substitutes in consumption (e.g., coffee and tea), but unrelated in production, an increase in the demand for commodity 1 (represented by a rise in the parameter d_{10}) would increase the market equilibrium price for commodity 2. To elaborate, the increase in the demand for commodity 1 (here a parallel shift right in the demand curve) disturbs the initial equilibrium in market 1, increasing the market price and quantity transacted of commodity 1. The rise in the market price for commodity 1 increases the demand for the substitute commodity 2, throwing market 2 out of equilibrium and raising the market price and quantity transacted of commodity 2. The rise in the market price of commodity 2 reverberates back to market 1, causing additional, albeit smaller, increases in the market demand and price for commodity 1, which again feeds back into market 2, leading to additional (and smaller) increases in the market demand and price for commodity 2. The simultaneous adjustments continue until a general equilibrium is reached—where both markets clear with zero excess quantities demanded at higher equilibrium prices.

In sum, in a system of related markets, assuming static stability in each market, a general equilibrium is not restored, after an initial disturbance in one market, until all of the markets simultaneously attain equilibrium.

PRACTICE PROBLEM 5.1

Given the following demand and supply schedules for commodities 1 and 2 that are complements in consumption and sold in perfectly competitive markets:

$$Q_1^d = 50 - 6P_1 - 2P_2$$

$$Q_1^s = -4 + 2P_1$$

$$Q_1^d(P_1, P_2) \overset{e}{=} Q_1^s(P_1)$$

$$Q_2^d = 32 - P_1 - 7P_2$$

$$Q_2^s = -4 + 3P_2$$

$$Q_2^d(P_1, P_2) \overset{e}{=} Q_2^s(P_2)$$

Find the market equilibrium prices and quantities transacted for the two commodities.

(The answers are at the end of the chapter.)

GENERAL COMPETITIVE EQUILIBRIUM

We can extend the model to n commodity markets. The n demand equations, n supply equations, and n equilibrium conditions are presented below.

$$Q_i^d = d_{i\,0} + d_{i\,1} P_1 + d_{i\,2} P_2 + \; \dots \; + d_{in} P_n \qquad (i = 1 \dots n)$$

$$Q_i^s = s_{i\,0} + s_{i\,1} P_1 + s_{i\,2} P_2 + \; \dots \; + s_{in} P_n$$

$$Q_i^d (P_1, P_2, \dots P_n) \overset{\text{e}}{=} Q_i^s(P_1, P_2, \dots P_n)$$

where

$$d_{ij} = \text{coefficient of } P_j \text{ in the } i\text{th demand equation: } d_{ij} = \delta Q_i^d / \delta P_j$$

$$(i = 1 \dots n; j = 1 \dots n)$$

and

$$s_{ij} = \text{coefficient of } P_j \text{ in the } i\text{th supply equation: } s_{ij} = \delta Q_i^s / \delta P_j$$

$$(i = 1 \dots n; j = 1 \dots n).$$

This system of $3n$ equations in $3n$ unknowns (the endogenous variables P_i, Q_i^d, and Q_i^s) can be collapsed into n simultaneous equations (the n equilibrium conditions) in n unknowns (the market prices P_i). Writing the n equilibrium conditions in terms of the excess quantities demanded we have:

$$E_i^d (P_1, P_2, \dots P_n) = Q_i^d (P_1, P_2, \dots P_n) - Q_i^s (P_1, P_2, \dots P_n) \overset{\text{e}}{=} 0$$

A solution, if existing, will express the n equilibrium prices in terms of the parameters of the system. In general,

$$\overline{P}_i = f_i (d_{10}, \dots d_{n\,0}, d_{ij}, s_{10}, \dots s_{n\,0}, s_{ij}) \qquad (i = 1 \dots n; j = 1 \dots n)$$

Once we find the equilibrium set of market prices, whereby every one of the n markets simultaneously clears with a zero excess quantity demanded, we can substitute the $\overline{P}_i$ values back into the demand or supply equations to determine the quantities transacted. Before we proceed further with our analysis of linear systems of equations, we need to understand the basics of matrix algebra.

A REVIEW OF VECTORS

An understanding of vectors provides the foundation for matrix algebra. A *vector* is a directed line segment, which can be represented as a ray from the origin of a set of axes. That is, a vector represents a point in n-dimensional space and is characterized by a given magnitude (its length) and a given direction. Here we will restrict the elements of a vector, known as its *coordinates,* to be real numbers.

The number of coordinates determines the space over which the vector is defined. For 2-space, indicated by R^2, the vector **v** is an ordered pair of real numbers: **v** = (a_1, a_2), or more familiarly, **v** = (x, y). Examples in the two-dimensional Cartesian coordinate plane (i.e., the perpendicular x- and y-axes) are $\mathbf{v}_1 = (3, -2)$, $\mathbf{v}_2 = (4, 6)$, and $\mathbf{v}_3 = (-2, -5)$. See Figure 5.1 for a plot of these three vectors. Defined over 3-space, R^3, a vector is an ordered triple, **v** = (a_1, a_2, a_3). While we cannot graph in more than three dimensions, a vector defined over 4-space, $\mathbf{R}^4$, represents an ordered quadruple, **v** = (a_1, a_2, a_3, a_4); and, in general, a vector defined over n-space is an ordered n-tuple, **v** = $(a_1, a_2, \ldots, a_n)$. Note that a vector defined over 1-space is simply a real number or a *scalar*—having a magnitude but not a direction.

OPERATIONS WITH VECTORS

Two vectors are *conformable* if they have the same number of elements, that is, if both are defined over the same space. For example, **v** = $(a_1, a_2, \ldots, a_n)$ and **w** = $(b_1, b_2, \ldots, b_n)$, are conformable vectors since each has n elements and so is defined over n-space.

Two vectors are equal if they are conformable and if their corresponding elements are equal. For example, if **v** = $(a_1, a_2, \ldots, a_n)$ and **w** = $(b_1, b_2, \ldots, b_n)$, then **v** = **w,** if,

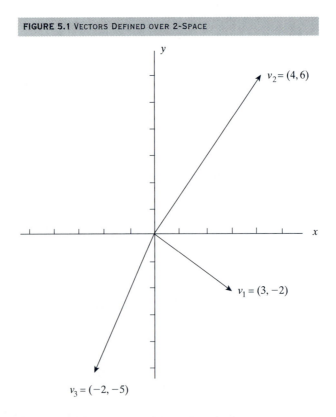

FIGURE 5.1 VECTORS DEFINED OVER 2-SPACE

$v_2 = (4, 6)$

$v_1 = (3, -2)$

$v_3 = (-2, -5)$

and only if, $a_i = b_i$ (for $i = 1 \ldots n$). The two vectors, $\mathbf{v} = (-3, 2)$ and $\mathbf{w} = (4, 5)$, are conformable, but clearly are not equal.

The product of a vector $\mathbf{v} = (a_1, a_2, \ldots, a_n)$ and a scalar k is the vector obtained by multiplying each element of the vector by the scalar: $k\mathbf{v} = (ka_1, ka_2, \ldots, ka_n)$. Multiplying a vector by a scalar k will shorten the vector (if $|k| < 1$) or lengthen the vector (if $|k| > 1$). Multiplying a vector by a negative scalar will reverse the direction of the vector. Again, illustrating with 2-space, if $\mathbf{v} = (-3, 2)$, then $2\mathbf{v} = (-6, 4)$ and $-.5\mathbf{v} = (1.5, -1)$. See Figure 5.2 for the graphs.

Only conformable vectors can be added, subtracted, or multiplied together. Vectors cannot be divided into each other. To add (subtract) two conformable vectors, we simply add (subtract) the corresponding elements. Given $\mathbf{v} = (a_1, a_2, \ldots, a_n)$ and $\mathbf{w} = (b_1, b_2, \ldots, b_n)$ then:

$$\mathbf{v} + \mathbf{w} = (a_1 + b_1, a_2 + b_2, \ldots, a_n + b_n)$$

$$\mathbf{v} - \mathbf{w} = (a_1 - b_1, a_2 - b_2, \ldots, a_n - b_n)$$

For example, if $\mathbf{v} = (-3, 2)$ and $\mathbf{w} = (4, 5)$, then

$$\mathbf{v} + \mathbf{w} = (-3 + 4, 2 + 5) = (1, 7)$$

$$\mathbf{v} - \mathbf{w} = (-3 - 4, 2 - 5) = (-7, -3)$$

FIGURE 5.2 SCALAR MULTIPLICATION OF A VECTOR

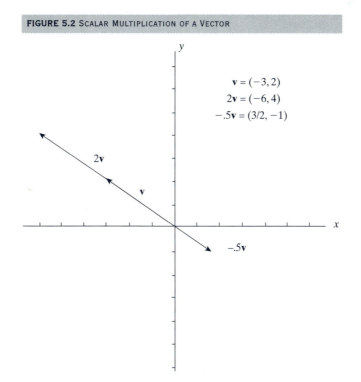

Note that while it does not matter in which order you add two or more conformable vectors, that is, $\mathbf{v} + \mathbf{w} = \mathbf{w} + \mathbf{v}$, the order of subtraction is important.[1] In general, $\mathbf{v} - \mathbf{w} \neq \mathbf{w} - \mathbf{v}$, unless $\mathbf{v} = \mathbf{w}$. From the example above:

$$\mathbf{v} - \mathbf{w} = (-3 - 4, 2 - 5) = (-7, -3) \neq (7, 3) = (4 - (-3), 5 - 2) = \mathbf{w} - \mathbf{v}$$

Graphically we can add two vectors using the parallelogram method, adding head to toe (see Figure 5.3). Subtraction of two vectors is similar, since subtracting a vector is equivalent to adding the negative of the vector: $\mathbf{v} - \mathbf{w} = \mathbf{v} + (-\mathbf{w})$. Here, we have:

$$\mathbf{v} - \mathbf{w} = (-3 - 4, 2 - 5) = (-7, -3) = (-3 + (-4), 2 + (-5)) = \mathbf{v} + (-\mathbf{w})$$

The multiplication of two conformable vectors, known as the *dot product* or the *inner product* of the two vectors, yields a scalar. If $\mathbf{v} = (a_1, a_2, \ldots, a_n)$ and $\mathbf{w} = (b_1, b_2, \ldots, b_n)$, then to find the inner product, $\mathbf{v} \cdot \mathbf{w}$, we multiply the corresponding elements and sum.

$$\mathbf{v} \cdot \mathbf{w} = a_1 b_1 + a_2 b_2 + \cdots + a_n b_n = c \text{ (a scalar)}$$

From the earlier simple example, where $\mathbf{v} = (-3, 2)$ and $\mathbf{w} = (4, 5)$, the inner product is:

$$\mathbf{v} \cdot \mathbf{w} = (-3)(4) + (2)(5) = -2$$

Note that, like vector addition, the order in vector multiplication does not matter: $\mathbf{v} \cdot \mathbf{w} = \mathbf{w} \cdot \mathbf{v}$.[2]

$$\mathbf{v} \cdot \mathbf{w} = (-3)(4) + (2)(5) = -2 = (4)(-3) + (5)(2) = \mathbf{w} \cdot \mathbf{v}$$

To illustrate with an economics example, suppose that a firm requires 4 units of input A, 2 units of input B, 5 units of input C, and 10 units of input D, to produce each unit of output of commodity j. The input quantity vector is $\mathbf{q} = (4, 2, 5, 10)$. If the unit prices of the inputs are \$1.00 for input A, \$3.50 for input B, \$4.00 for input C, and \$.20 for input D, then the input price vector can be written as $\mathbf{p} = (1.00, 3.50, 4.00, .20)$. The unit cost of producing commodity j, C_j, is given by the inner product of the input price and quantity vectors: $C_j = \mathbf{p} \cdot \mathbf{q} = (1.00)(4) + (3.50)(2) + (4.00)(5) + (.20)(10) = 14.40 = \mathbf{q} \cdot \mathbf{p} = (4)(1.00) + (2)(3.50) + (5)(4.00) + (10)(.20)$.

If the inner product of two conformable vectors is equal to zero, the two vectors are *orthogonal* or perpendicular to each other. For example, $\mathbf{v} = (-3, 4)$ and $\mathbf{w} = (6, 4.5)$ are orthogonal vectors defined over 2-space, since $\mathbf{v} \cdot \mathbf{w} = (-3)(6) + (4)(4.5) = 0$. You should plot these two vectors to confirm that they are perpendicular.

The *norm* or length of a vector, $\mathbf{v} = (a_1, a_2, \ldots, a_n)$, written as $\|\mathbf{v}\|$, is equal to the square root of the inner product of the vector with itself.

$$\|\mathbf{v}\| = \sqrt{(a_1^2 + a_2^2 + \cdots + a_n^2)}$$

---

[1] Formally, given conformable vectors, $\mathbf{v}$, $\mathbf{w}$, and $\mathbf{u}$, vector addition is commutative: $\mathbf{v} + \mathbf{w} = \mathbf{w} + \mathbf{v}$; and associative: $\mathbf{u} + (\mathbf{v} + \mathbf{w}) = (\mathbf{u} + \mathbf{v}) + \mathbf{w}$.

[2] In addition to this commutative property, for vector multiplication, the distributive property holds. That is, given $\mathbf{v}$, $\mathbf{w}$, and $\mathbf{u}$ are conformable vectors, then $(\mathbf{v} + \mathbf{w}) \cdot \mathbf{u} = \mathbf{v} \cdot \mathbf{u} + \mathbf{w} \cdot \mathbf{u}$.

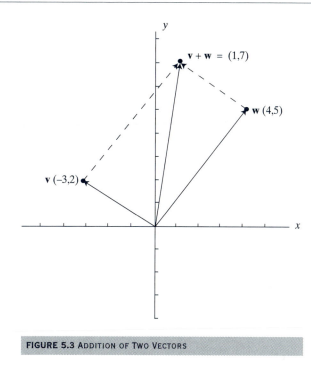

FIGURE 5.3 ADDITION OF TWO VECTORS

In 2-space, the norm of a vector is found using the Pythagorean theorem: the length of the hypotenuse of a right triangle is equal to the square root of the sum of the squares of the lengths of the sides of the right triangle. To illustrate, let $\mathbf{v} = (3, -2)$, then $\|\mathbf{v}\| = \sqrt{(3)^2 + (-2)^2} = \sqrt{13}$. See Figure 5.4a.

The distance between two vectors, $\mathbf{v} = (a_1, a_2, \ldots, a_n)$ and $\mathbf{w} = (b_1, b_2, \ldots, b_n)$, written as $d(\mathbf{v}, \mathbf{w})$ or $d(\mathbf{w}, \mathbf{v})$, is equal to the square root of the sum of the squares of the differences between the corresponding elements of the two vectors.

$$d(\mathbf{v}, \mathbf{w}) = \sqrt{(a_1 - b_1)^2 + (a_2 - b_2)^2 + \cdots + (a_n - b_n)^2}$$
$$= \sqrt{(b_1 - a_1)^2 + (b_2 - a_2)^2 + \cdots + (b_n - a_n)^2} = d(\mathbf{w}, \mathbf{v})$$

Again, taking an example in R^2, let $\mathbf{v} = (3, -2)$ and $\mathbf{w} = (5, 4)$. The distance between $\mathbf{v}$ and $\mathbf{w}$ is equal to $d(\mathbf{v}, \mathbf{w}) = \sqrt{(3 - 5)^2 + (-2 - 4)^2} = \sqrt{40} = \sqrt{(5 - 3)^2 + (4 - (-2))^2} = d(\mathbf{w}, \mathbf{v})$. See Figure 5.4b, where drawing on the Pythagorean theorem the distance between the vector $\mathbf{v}$ and the vector $\mathbf{w}$ can be represented by the hypotenuse of a right triangle.

PRACTICE PROBLEM 5.2

Given the two vectors, $\mathbf{u} = (-1, 4)$ and $\mathbf{v} = (2, 5)$, find:

a) $\mathbf{u} + \mathbf{v}$ b) $\mathbf{u} - \mathbf{v}$ c) $\mathbf{v} - \mathbf{u}$ d) $\mathbf{u} \cdot \mathbf{v}$ e) $\mathbf{v} \cdot \mathbf{u}$ f) $\|\mathbf{v}\|$ g) $d(\mathbf{u}, \mathbf{v})$

(The answers are at the end of the chapter.)

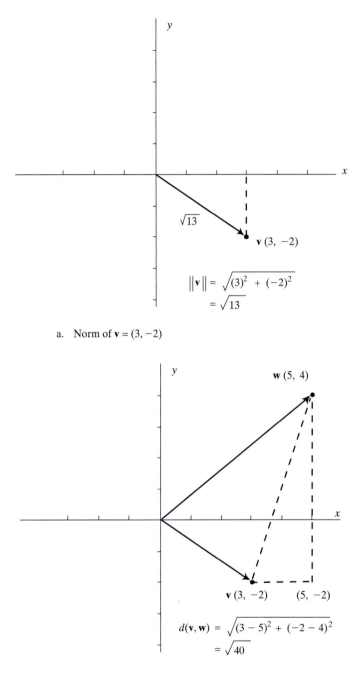

a. Norm of $\mathbf{v} = (3, -2)$

b. Distance between $\mathbf{v}$ and $\mathbf{w}$

FIGURE 5.4 NORMS OF VECTORS AND DISTANCES BETWEEN VECTORS

LINEAR DEPENDENCE AND INDEPENDENCE OF VECTORS

Given a set of n vectors, $\mathbf{v}_1, \mathbf{v}_2, \ldots, \mathbf{v}_n$, defined over m-space, meaning that each of the n vectors has m elements, that is, $\mathbf{v}_i = (a_{i\,1}, a_{i\,2}, \ldots, a_{im}), i = 1 \ldots n$, then a linear combination of the vectors is the vector resulting from the sum of the n scalar products of the vectors:

$$\sum_{i=1}^{n} k_i\,\mathbf{v}_i = k_1\mathbf{v}_1 + k_2\mathbf{v}_2 + \cdots + k_n\mathbf{v}_n, \qquad \text{where } k_i\,(i = 1 \ldots n) \text{ is a set of scalars.}$$

For example, consider the three vectors defined over 2-space: $\mathbf{v}_1 = (3, -2)$, $\mathbf{v}_2 = (5, 4)$, and $\mathbf{v}_3 = (-1, -6)$. One linear combination of these three vectors, arbitrarily setting $k_1 = 1$, $k_2 = -1$, and $k_3 = 4$, is: $\mathbf{v}_4 = 1\mathbf{v}_1 - 1\mathbf{v}_2 + 4\mathbf{v}_3 = 1(3, -2) - 1(5, 4) + 4(-1, -6) = (-6, -30)$.

A set of n conformable vectors is *linearly dependent* if one of the vectors can be expressed as a linear combination of the other $n - 1$ vectors. That is, given $\mathbf{v}_j$ is a vector in the set of n vectors, and the $\mathbf{v}_i, (i = 1 \ldots n - 1)$, refer to the other $n - 1$ vectors in the set, then the n vectors are linearly dependent if:

$$\mathbf{v}_j = \sum_{i=1}^{n-1} k_i\,\mathbf{v}_i$$

(where $j \neq i$, meaning that vector j is not one of the other $n - 1$ vectors).

Equivalently, if for a set of n vectors defined over m-space, a linear combination of the vectors equals the zero vector, when at least one of the scalars, k_i, is nonzero, that is,

$$\text{if} \quad \sum_{i=1}^{n} k_i\,\mathbf{v}_i = (a_1, a_2, \ldots, a_m) = (0, 0, \ldots 0), \text{ and at least one } k_i \neq 0,$$

then the vectors $\mathbf{v}_1, \mathbf{v}_2, \ldots, \mathbf{v}_n$ are linearly dependent.

If instead, none of the vectors can be expressed as a linear combination of the other $n - 1$ vectors in the set, or if a linear combination of the n vectors equals the zero vector only when all of the k_i scalars are equal to zero, that is,

$$\text{if} \quad \mathbf{v}_j \neq \sum_{i=1}^{n-1} k_i\,\mathbf{v}_i \qquad (j \neq i)$$

$$\text{or if} \quad \sum_{i=1}^{n} k_i\,\mathbf{v}_i = (a_1, a_2, \ldots, a_m) = (0, 0, \ldots, 0) \text{ only if } k_i = 0 \text{ for } i = 1 \ldots n$$

then the vectors $\mathbf{v}_1, \mathbf{v}_2, \ldots, \mathbf{v}_n$ are *linearly independent*.

We state, without proof, that in m-space, R^m, there can be at most m linearly independent vectors. Thus, if the n vectors are defined, as above, over m-space, $(n > m)$ only m of the n vectors could be linearly independent.

For example, in R^2, given two linearly independent vectors, $\mathbf{v}_1 = (x_1, y_1)$ and $\mathbf{v}_2 = (x_2, y_2)$, where $\mathbf{v}_1 \neq k_2\mathbf{v}_2$, any third vector $\mathbf{v}_3 = (x_3, y_3)$ could be written as a linear combination of v_1 and v_2. That is, we could find scalars k_1 and k_2 (not both equal to zero) such that $v_3 = k_1 v_1 + k_2 v_2$.

To illustrate, consider the three vectors, v_1, v_2, and v_3, defined over 2-space, where $v_1 = (3, -2)$, $v_2 = (5, 4)$, and $v_3 = (-1, -6)$. We can show that for any two of these vectors that are linearly independent, the third vector will be linearly dependent. The vectors v_1 and v_2 are linearly independent, since there is no scalar k_2 that could be multiplied with the vector v_2 to obtain the vector v_1. In order for $v_1 = k_2 v_2$, we would need to have $(3, -2) = k_2 (5, 4)$. Setting the corresponding elements equal gives $3 = 5k_2$ and $-2 = 4k_2$. The first equation requires that $k_2 = 3/5$; while the second equation would require that $k_2 = -1/2$. Thus, v_1 and v_2 are linearly independent.

Similarly, we could show that v_1 and v_3 are linearly independent and that v_2 and v_3 are linearly independent. Taking the linearly independent vectors v_1 and v_2 defined over R^2, however, we can find scalars k_1 and k_2 (not both equal to zero) such that $v_3 = k_1 v_1 + k_2 v_2$.

Beginning with $(-1, -6) = k_1 (3, -2) + k_2 (5, 4)$, and setting the corresponding elements equal gives two equations in two unknowns:

$$-1 = 3k_1 + 5k_2$$

$$-6 = -2k_1 + 4k_2$$

Solving simultaneously for k_1 and k_2 we find $k_1 = 13/11$ and $k_2 = -10/11$. Thus,

$$v_3 = (13/11)v_1 + (-10/11)v_2$$

Checking, we have

$$(-1, -6) = (13/11)(3, -2) + (-10/11)(5, 4)$$

$$(-1, -6) = (39/11, -26/11) + (-50/11, -40/11)$$

$$(-1, -6) = (-11/11, -66/11)$$

Equivalently, we can show that $\sum_{i=1}^{3} k_i v_i = (0, 0)$ where not all $k_i = 0$.

Here: $k_1 = 13/11$, $k_2 = -10/11$, $k_3 = -1$, and $(13/11)v_1 + (-10/11)v_2 + (-1)v_3 = (0,0)$. Checking, we have:

$$(13/11)(3, -2) + (-10/11)(5,4) + (-1)(-1, -6)$$

$$= (39/11, -26/11) + (-50/11, -40/11) + (1, 6)$$

$$= (0, 0)$$

which establishes v_1, v_2, and v_3 as linearly dependent vectors.

A set of n linearly independent vectors defined over n-space is said to *span* n-space and to constitute a *basis* for n-space. For example, the vectors $v_1 = (3, -2)$ and $v_2 = (5,4)$ span 2-space and form a basis for 2-space. There are, in fact, an infinite number of sets of two vectors that form a basis for 2-space. Other linearly independent vector pairs are: $(5,4)$ and $(-1, -6)$; $(1,0)$ and $(0,1)$; and $(-1, 0)$ and $(0, 1)$. As an exercise, determine whether or not the vectors, $\mathbf{v}_1 = (-1, 3)$ and $\mathbf{v}_2 = (2, -6)$, span R^2. With this review of vectors, we are ready for the basics of matrix algebra.

PRACTICE PROBLEM 5.3

Given the three vectors, $\mathbf{u} = (-1, 4)$, $\mathbf{v} = (2, 5)$, and $\mathbf{w} = (3, -1)$:
a) Show that $\mathbf{u}$ and $\mathbf{v}$ are linearly independent.
b) Show that $\mathbf{v}$ and $\mathbf{w}$ are linearly independent.
c) Show that $\mathbf{w}$ can be written as a linear combination of $\mathbf{u}$ and $\mathbf{v}$.

(The answers are at the end of the chapter.)

AN INTRODUCTION TO MATRIX ALGEBRA

A *matrix* is a rectangular array of elements that represent numbers, variables, or even functions. A matrix can also be viewed as a stack of conformable vectors. The location of each element in a matrix is given by its dual subscripts; with the first subscript indicating the row and the second subscript indicating the column of the element. The element a_{ij} would be found in the ith row and jth column.

A matrix $\mathbf{A}$ with m rows and n columns is said to have dimension $m \times n$ (read "m by n"). The general representation of this matrix is:

$$A_{m \times n} = \begin{bmatrix} a_{11} & a_{12} & \cdots & a_{1n} \\ a_{21} & a_{22} & \cdots & a_{2n} \\ \cdot & & & \\ \cdot & & & \\ a_{m1} & a_{m2} & \cdots & a_{mn} \end{bmatrix}$$

Vectors are matrices consisting of either one row or one column. For example, the ith row vector, $[a_{i1}\ a_{i2} \ldots a_{in}]$ is a matrix of dimension $1 \times n$.

The jth column vector, $\begin{bmatrix} a_{1j} \\ a_{2j} \\ \cdot \\ \cdot \\ a_{mj} \end{bmatrix}$, is a matrix of dimension $m \times 1$.

Matrix Terminology We need to be familiar with the vocabulary of matrices. Listed below are some of the common terms.

Two matrices are *conformable* if they have the same dimension. For example, $\mathbf{A}_{m \times n}$ and $\mathbf{B}_{m \times n}$ are conformable matrices, since each has m rows and n columns.

A *square matrix* has the same number of rows as columns, that is, $m = n$. The matrix $\mathbf{A}_{n \times n}$ is a square matrix, with n rows and n columns.

$$\mathbf{A}_{n\times n} = \begin{bmatrix} a_{11} & a_{12} & \cdots & a_{1n} \\ a_{21} & a_{22} & \cdots & a_{2n} \\ . & & & \\ . & & & \\ a_{n1} & a_{n2} & \cdots & a_{nn} \end{bmatrix}$$

All the elements of a *zero matrix* are zero. Below, the matrix $\mathbf{A}_{n\times n}$ is an example of a square zero matrix. The matrix $\mathbf{B}_{2\times 3}$ is also an example of a zero matrix, with dimension 2×3.

$$\mathbf{A}_{n\times n} = \begin{bmatrix} 0 & 0 & \cdots & 0 \\ 0 & 0 & \cdots & 0 \\ . & & & \\ . & & & \\ 0 & 0 & \cdots & 0 \end{bmatrix}, \mathbf{B}_{2\times 3} = \begin{bmatrix} 0 & 0 & 0 \\ 0 & 0 & 0 \end{bmatrix}$$

The *main diagonal* of a matrix consists of all of the elements for which the row subscript (i) equals the column subscript (j). The elements on the main diagonal of the above matrix $\mathbf{A}$ are $a_{11}, a_{22}, a_{33}, \ldots$ etc. Below, the elements of the main diagonal of the 3×4 matrix $\mathbf{A}$, are underlined.

$$\mathbf{A}_{3\times 4} = \begin{bmatrix} \underline{5} & 7 & -1 & 0 \\ 2 & \underline{-3} & 4 & 1 \\ 6 & 8 & \underline{-4} & 9 \end{bmatrix}$$

The *identity matrix* is a square matrix with ones on the main diagonal and zeros everywhere else. The identity matrix of dimension $n \times n$, written as $\mathbf{I}_n$, is written below.

$$\mathbf{I}_n = \begin{bmatrix} 1 & 0 & \cdots & 0 \\ 0 & 1 & \cdots & 0 \\ . & & & \\ . & & & \\ 0 & 0 & \cdots & 1 \end{bmatrix}$$

The *transpose* of a matrix is formed by interchanging the rows and columns. The transpose of $\mathbf{A}$, written as $\mathbf{A}'$ or $\mathbf{A}^T$, is

$$\mathbf{A}' = \begin{bmatrix} a_{11} & a_{21} & \cdots & a_{m1} \\ a_{12} & a_{22} & \cdots & a_{m2} \\ . & & & \\ . & & & \\ a_{1n} & a_{2n} & \cdots & a_{mn} \end{bmatrix} \text{ given } \mathbf{A} = \begin{bmatrix} a_{11} & a_{12} & \cdots & a_{1n} \\ a_{21} & a_{22} & \cdots & a_{2n} \\ . & & & \\ . & & & \\ a_{m1} & a_{m2} & \cdots & a_{mn} \end{bmatrix}$$

Note that, if the dimension of the matrix $\mathbf{A}$ is $m \times n$, the dimension of the transpose matrix $\mathbf{A}'$ is $n \times m$.

Consider the following matrix $\mathbf{A}$ with 2 rows and 3 columns:

$$\mathbf{A} = \begin{bmatrix} 3 & -7 & 2 \\ 0 & 1 & 8 \end{bmatrix}$$

The transpose of **A** is: $\mathbf{A}' = \begin{bmatrix} 3 & 0 \\ -7 & 1 \\ 2 & 8 \end{bmatrix}$

The transpose of a column vector is a row vector, and vice versa. For example, if $\mathbf{v} = \begin{bmatrix} 3 \\ -7 \\ 2 \end{bmatrix}$, then $\mathbf{v}' = [3 \ -7 \ 2]$.

OPERATIONS WITH MATRICES

The rules for the basic operations of the addition, subtraction, and multiplication of matrices are given below. Division of matrices is not allowed.

Addition and Subtraction Matrices that are conformable can be added (or subtracted) by adding (or subtracting) the corresponding elements. In general, given two conformable matrices **A** and **B**,

$$\mathbf{A}_{m \times n} = \begin{bmatrix} a_{11} & a_{12} & \ldots & a_{1n} \\ a_{21} & a_{22} & \ldots & a_{2n} \\ & \cdot & & \\ & \cdot & & \\ a_{m1} & a_{m2} & \ldots & a_{mn} \end{bmatrix} = [a_{ij}]_{(m, n)}$$

$$\mathbf{B}_{m \times n} = \begin{bmatrix} b_{11} & b_{12} & \ldots & b_{1n} \\ b_{21} & b_{22} & \ldots & b_{2n} \\ & \cdot & & \\ & \cdot & & \\ b_{m1} & b_{m2} & \ldots & b_{mn} \end{bmatrix} = [b_{ij}]_{(m, n)}$$

then $\quad \mathbf{A}_{m \times n} + \mathbf{B}_{m \times n} = \mathbf{C}_{m \times n} = [c_{ij}]_{(m, n)} \quad$ where $c_{ij} = a_{ij} + b_{ij} \quad (i = 1 \ldots m)$
$$(j = 1 \ldots n)$$

and $\quad \mathbf{A}_{m \times n} - \mathbf{B}_{m \times n} = \mathbf{D}_{m \times n} = [d_{ij}]_{(m, n)} \quad$ where $d_{ij} = a_{ij} - b_{ij} \quad (i = 1 \ldots m)$
$$(j = 1 \ldots n)$$

Examples

$$\mathbf{A} = \begin{bmatrix} 3 & -7 & 2 \\ 0 & 1 & 8 \end{bmatrix} \text{ and } \mathbf{B} = \begin{bmatrix} 4 & 0 & 1 \\ 2 & -3 & 0 \end{bmatrix}$$

$$\mathbf{A} + \mathbf{B} = \begin{bmatrix} 7 & -7 & 3 \\ 2 & -2 & 8 \end{bmatrix} = \mathbf{B} + \mathbf{A}$$

$$\mathbf{A} - \mathbf{B} = \begin{bmatrix} -1 & -7 & 1 \\ -2 & 4 & 8 \end{bmatrix} \neq \mathbf{B} - \mathbf{A} = \begin{bmatrix} 1 & 7 & -1 \\ 2 & -4 & -8 \end{bmatrix}$$

As the examples illustrate, for conformable matrices, the order of addition does not matter ($\mathbf{A} + \mathbf{B} = \mathbf{B} + \mathbf{A}$); however, the order of subtraction does matter (in general, $\mathbf{A} - \mathbf{B} \neq \mathbf{B} - \mathbf{A}$).

Scalar Multiplication of a Matrix   We can multiply a matrix by a scalar k by multiplying each element of the matrix by the scalar:

$$k\mathbf{A}_{(m,n)} = [ka_{ij}]_{(m,n)} \; (i = 1 \ldots m)$$

$$(j = 1 \ldots n)$$

Example

$$\mathbf{A} = \begin{bmatrix} 3 & -7 & 2 \\ 0 & 1 & 8 \end{bmatrix} \quad k = -2$$

$$k\mathbf{A} = -2 \begin{bmatrix} 3 & -7 & 2 \\ 0 & 1 & 8 \end{bmatrix} = \begin{bmatrix} -6 & 14 & -4 \\ 0 & -2 & -16 \end{bmatrix}$$

Matrix Multiplication   Matrix multiplication is possible only when the number of columns of the first (lead) matrix (e.g., $\mathbf{A}_{m \times n}$, with m rows and n columns) is equal to the number of rows of the second (lag) matrix (e.g., $\mathbf{B}_{n \times p}$, with n rows and p columns). Given this dimensional requirement, the product matrix, $\mathbf{C} = \mathbf{AB}$ will have dimension m by p (the number of rows of the lead matrix and the number of columns of the lag matrix). The elements of the product matrix are derived by taking the inner products of the row vectors of the lead matrix with the column vectors of the lag matrix—hence the dimensional requirement for matrix multiplication. Given

$$\mathbf{A}_{m \times n} = [a_{ij}]_{(m,n)} \quad \text{and} \quad \mathbf{B}_{n \times p} = [b_{jk}]_{(n,p)} \quad (i = 1 \ldots m)$$

$$(j = 1 \ldots n)$$

$$(k = 1 \ldots p)$$

then

$$\mathbf{AB} = \mathbf{C}_{m \times p} = [c_{ik}]_{(m,p)}$$

where

$$c_{ik} = a_{i1}b_{1k} + a_{i2}b_{2k} + \cdots + a_{ij}b_{jk} + \cdots + a_{in}b_{nk}$$

or, written in summation notation:

$$c_{ik} = \sum_{j=1}^{n} a_{ij}b_{jk} \quad (i = 1 \ldots m)$$

$$(k = 1 \ldots p)$$

That is, the element, c_{ik}, located in the ith row and kth column of the product matrix, **C**, is given by the inner product of the ith row of the lead matrix, $\mathbf{A}_{m \times n}$, and the kth column of the lag matrix, $\mathbf{B}_{n \times p}$.

Examples. The element in the first row and first column of the product matrix **C** is c_{11}

$$c_{11} = a_{11} b_{11} + a_{12} b_{21} + \cdots + a_{1j}b_{j1} + \cdots + a_{1n} b_{n1}$$

The element in the third row and second column of the product matrix **C** is c_{32}

$$c_{32} = a_{31} b_{12} + a_{32} b_{22} + \cdots + a_{3j} b_{j2} + \cdots + a_{3n} b_{n2}$$

Notice how the inner subscripts of the terms in each summation match, reflecting the number of the column of the lead matrix and row of the lag matrix. While we can multiply $\mathbf{A}_{m \times n} \mathbf{B}_{n \times p} = \mathbf{C}_{m \times p}$, we could not reverse the order and multiply $\mathbf{B}_{n \times p} \mathbf{A}_{m \times n}$ unless $p = m$.

Example

$$\mathbf{A} = \begin{bmatrix} 3 & -7 & 2 \\ 0 & 1 & 8 \end{bmatrix} \quad \mathbf{B} \begin{bmatrix} 5 & 0 & 1 & -2 \\ 0 & -1 & 3 & 1 \\ -2 & 1 & 0 & 0 \end{bmatrix}$$

The dimensions of the **A** and **B** matrices are 2×3 and 3×4, respectively. We can find the product matrix **C = AB**, since the lead matrix has 3 columns and the lag matrix has 3 rows. The product matrix **C** has dimension 2×4.

$$\mathbf{AB} = \begin{bmatrix} 3 & -7 & 2 \\ 0 & 1 & 8 \end{bmatrix} \begin{bmatrix} 5 & 0 & 1 & -2 \\ 0 & -1 & 3 & 1 \\ -2 & 1 & 0 & 0 \end{bmatrix} = \begin{bmatrix} 11 & 9 & -18 & -13 \\ -16 & 7 & 3 & 1 \end{bmatrix} = \mathbf{C}$$

Here we cannot multiply **BA**; however, we can find the product of the transpose matrices in reverse order, $\mathbf{B'A'} = \mathbf{C'}$.

$$\mathbf{B'A'} = \begin{bmatrix} 5 & 0 & -2 \\ 0 & -1 & 1 \\ 1 & 3 & 0 \\ -2 & 1 & 0 \end{bmatrix} \begin{bmatrix} 3 & 0 \\ -7 & 1 \\ 2 & 8 \end{bmatrix} = \begin{bmatrix} 11 & -16 \\ 9 & 7 \\ -18 & 3 \\ -13 & 1 \end{bmatrix} = \mathbf{C'}$$

If **A** and **B** are conformable square matrices, then both products **AB** and **BA** can be found; but, in general, $\mathbf{AB} \neq \mathbf{BA}$. Formally, matrix multiplication is not commutative. An exception would be for multiplication with an identity matrix. $\mathbf{AI} = \mathbf{IA} = \mathbf{A}$.

Examples

$$\mathbf{A} = \begin{bmatrix} 5 & 2 & 1 \\ 0 & -1 & 0 \\ 3 & 0 & -3 \end{bmatrix} \mathbf{B} = \begin{bmatrix} -1 & 0 & 2 \\ 3 & 1 & -2 \\ 0 & 0 & 4 \end{bmatrix} \mathbf{I} = \begin{bmatrix} 1 & 0 & 0 \\ 0 & 1 & 0 \\ 0 & 0 & 1 \end{bmatrix}$$

$$\mathbf{AB} = \begin{bmatrix} 1 & 2 & 10 \\ -3 & -1 & 2 \\ -3 & 0 & -6 \end{bmatrix} \neq \begin{bmatrix} 1 & -2 & -7 \\ 9 & 5 & 9 \\ 12 & 0 & -12 \end{bmatrix} = \mathbf{BA}$$

$$\mathbf{AI} = \begin{bmatrix} 5 & 2 & 1 \\ 0 & -1 & 0 \\ 3 & 0 & -3 \end{bmatrix} = \mathbf{IA} = \mathbf{A}$$

Unlike the multiplication of two scalars, x and y, where if $xy = 0$, then either $x = 0, y = 0$, or both $x = 0$ and $y = 0$, if the product of two matrices is a zero matrix ($\mathbf{AB} = \mathbf{0}$), then it is not necessarily the case that either one of the two matrices is itself the zero matrix.

Example

$$\mathbf{A} = \begin{bmatrix} 1 & 2 & 0 \\ 1 & 1 & 0 \\ -1 & 4 & 0 \end{bmatrix} \qquad \mathbf{B} = \begin{bmatrix} 0 & 0 \\ 0 & 0 \\ 1 & 5 \end{bmatrix}$$

$$\mathbf{AB} = \begin{bmatrix} 0 & 0 \\ 0 & 0 \\ 0 & 0 \end{bmatrix} = \mathbf{0}_{(3,2)}$$

The following properties for matrix multiplication also hold.

1. Matrix multiplication is associative.

Given $\mathbf{A}_{m \times n}$, $\mathbf{B}_{n \times p}$, and $\mathbf{C}_{p \times q}$, then $(\mathbf{AB})\mathbf{C} = \mathbf{D}_{m \times q} = \mathbf{A}(\mathbf{BC})$

Example

$$\text{Let } \mathbf{A} = \begin{bmatrix} -1 & 0 & 7 \\ 2 & 3 & -4 \\ 1 & 0 & 1 \end{bmatrix}, \mathbf{B} = \begin{bmatrix} 5 \\ -1 \\ -1 \end{bmatrix}, \text{ and } \mathbf{C} = [2 \ -3]$$

$$\begin{bmatrix} -1 & 0 & 7 \\ 2 & 3 & -4 \\ 1 & 0 & 1 \end{bmatrix}\begin{bmatrix} 5 \\ -1 \\ -1 \end{bmatrix} [2 \ -3] = \begin{bmatrix} -12 \\ 11 \\ 4 \end{bmatrix} [2 \ -3] = \begin{bmatrix} -24 & 36 \\ 22 & -33 \\ 8 & -12 \end{bmatrix}$$

$$\mathbf{ABC} \qquad = \qquad (\mathbf{AB})\mathbf{C} \qquad = \qquad \mathbf{D}$$

$$= \begin{bmatrix} -1 & 0 & 7 \\ 2 & 3 & -4 \\ 1 & 0 & 1 \end{bmatrix}\begin{bmatrix} 10 & -15 \\ -2 & 3 \\ -2 & 3 \end{bmatrix}$$

$$= \qquad \mathbf{A}(\mathbf{BC})$$

2. Matrix multiplication is distributive.

Given $\mathbf{A}_{m \times n}$, $\mathbf{B}_{n \times p}$, and $\mathbf{C}_{n \times p}$, then $\mathbf{A}(\mathbf{B} + \mathbf{C}) = \mathbf{D}_{m \times p} = \mathbf{AB} + \mathbf{BC}$

Example Let $\mathbf{C} = \begin{bmatrix} -2 \\ 3 \\ 0 \end{bmatrix}$ now, while $\mathbf{A}$ and $\mathbf{B}$ are the same as in the previous example.

$$\begin{bmatrix} -1 & 0 & 7 \\ 2 & 3 & -4 \\ 1 & 0 & 1 \end{bmatrix} \left(\begin{bmatrix} 5 \\ -1 \\ -1 \end{bmatrix} + \begin{bmatrix} -2 \\ 3 \\ 0 \end{bmatrix} \right) = \begin{bmatrix} -10 \\ 16 \\ 2 \end{bmatrix}$$

$$\mathbf{A\,(B + C)} \qquad\qquad = \qquad \mathbf{D}$$

$$= \begin{bmatrix} -1 & 0 & 7 \\ 2 & 3 & -4 \\ 1 & 0 & 1 \end{bmatrix} \begin{bmatrix} 5 \\ -1 \\ -1 \end{bmatrix} + \begin{bmatrix} -1 & 0 & 7 \\ 2 & 3 & -4 \\ 1 & 0 & 1 \end{bmatrix} \begin{bmatrix} -2 \\ 3 \\ 0 \end{bmatrix}$$

$$= \qquad\qquad\qquad \mathbf{AB + AC}$$

3. The transpose of the product of two matrices is the product of the transposes in reverse order. Given $\mathbf{A}_{m \times n}$ and $\mathbf{B}_{n \times p}$, with transposes $\mathbf{A}'_{n \times m}$ and $\mathbf{B}'_{p \times n}$, then $(\mathbf{AB})' = \mathbf{D}_{p \times m} = \mathbf{B}'\mathbf{A}'$

Note that this property was illustrated in an earlier example.

Matrix Division   While we can add and subtract conformable matrices, and we can multiply matrices that meet the dimensional requirement (i.e., the number of columns of the lead matrix must equal the number of rows of the lag matrix); we are not able to divide two matrices. That is, the quotient of two matrices is not defined. Nevertheless, we know that for scalars, dividing one scalar by a second (nonzero) scalar is equivalent to multiplying the first scalar by the reciprocal of the second scalar, for example, $a/b = a\,(1/b)$, where $b \neq 0$. Analogous to the reciprocal of a scalar might be the inverse of a matrix.

We will see that, in solving a system of linear equations, we will use the inverse of the associated coefficient matrix. Note that only square matrices can have inverses, and not all square matrices have inverses. If a square matrix, $\mathbf{A}$, does have an inverse, written as $\mathbf{A}^{-1}$, then the product of the matrix and its inverse is the identity matrix: $\mathbf{A}\,\mathbf{A}^{-1} = \mathbf{I}$. To derive the inverse of a square matrix, we need to find the determinant of that matrix.

PRACTICE PROBLEM 5.4

Given the three matrices:

$$\mathbf{A} = \begin{bmatrix} -4 & 0 & 1 \\ 2 & -1 & 3 \\ 0 & 1 & 2 \end{bmatrix}, \quad \mathbf{B} = \begin{bmatrix} 5 & -1 & 0 \\ 0 & 1 & -3 \\ 7 & 12 & 4 \end{bmatrix}, \quad \mathbf{C} = \begin{bmatrix} 0 & 1 \\ 2 & -1 \\ 5 & 3 \end{bmatrix}$$

Find:

a) $\mathbf{A + B}$ b) $\mathbf{A - B}$ c) $\mathbf{B - A}$ d) $\mathbf{AB}$

e) $\mathbf{A}' + \mathbf{B}'$ f) $\mathbf{BC}$ g) $\mathbf{C}'\mathbf{A}$

(The answers are at the end of the chapter.)

THE DETERMINANT OF A MATRIX

Associated with any square matrix, $\mathbf{A}_{n \times n}$, is a number, the *determinant* of $\mathbf{A}$, indicated by $\det(\mathbf{A})$ or $|\mathbf{A}|$. As suggested above, the determinant is used in finding the solution to a system of linear equations. We begin with the calculation of the determinant.

For a general 2×2 matrix,

$$\mathbf{A} = \begin{bmatrix} a_{11} & a_{12} \\ a_{21} & a_{22} \end{bmatrix}$$

the determinant of $\mathbf{A}$ is given by the difference between the product of the elements on the main diagonal and the product of the off-diagonal elements. $|\mathbf{A}| = a_{11} a_{22} - a_{21} a_{12}$. For example, for

$$\mathbf{A} = \begin{bmatrix} 3 & 5 \\ -1 & 2 \end{bmatrix}, \text{ we have } |\mathbf{A}| = \begin{vmatrix} 3 & 5 \\ -1 & 2 \end{vmatrix} = 6 - (-5) = 11.$$

For square matrices of higher dimension, the calculation of the determinant is more complicated and involves the concepts of minors and cofactors. The *minor* of the (i, j)th element, $|M_{ij}|$, in an $n \times n$ matrix $\mathbf{A}$ ($n \geq 2$) is the determinant of the submatrix of dimension $(n - 1) \times (n - 1)$ formed by deleting the ith row and jth column of $\mathbf{A}$. For example, if we have a 4×4 matrix,

$$\begin{bmatrix} a_{11} & a_{12} & a_{13} & a_{14} \\ a_{21} & a_{22} & a_{23} & a_{24} \\ a_{31} & a_{32} & a_{33} & a_{34} \\ a_{41} & a_{42} & a_{43} & a_{44} \end{bmatrix}$$

the minors of the elements in the first row and third column ($|M_{13}|$) and third row and second column ($|M_{32}|$) are the determinants:

$$|M_{13}| = \begin{vmatrix} a_{21} & a_{22} & a_{24} \\ a_{31} & a_{32} & a_{34} \\ a_{41} & a_{42} & a_{44} \end{vmatrix} \quad \text{and} \quad |M_{32}| = \begin{vmatrix} a_{11} & a_{13} & a_{14} \\ a_{21} & a_{23} & a_{24} \\ a_{41} & a_{43} & a_{44} \end{vmatrix}$$

The *cofactor,* $|C_{ij}|$, of the (i, j)th element in an $n \times n$ matrix $\mathbf{A}$ ($n \geq 2$) is the associated signed minor: $|C_{ij}| = (-1)^{i+j} |M_{ij}|$. For elements with the subscripts i and j summing to an even number, the cofactor equals the minor. For elements with the subscripts i and j summing to an odd number, the cofactor equals the negative of the minor: $|C_{13}| = (-1)^{1+3} |M_{13}| = |M_{13}|$; and $|C_{32}| = (-1)^{3+2} |M_{32}| = -|M_{32}|$.

To evaluate a determinant $|\mathbf{A}|$ of order n (i.e., for a square matrix of dimension $n \times n$), we use a method called *Laplace expansion*. Although we can expand along any row or column of the determinant, we usually choose the row or column containing the most zeros, since this reduces the number of calculations required.

If we expand along the ith row, then $|\mathbf{A}| = \sum_{j=1}^{n} a_{ij} |C_{ij}|$

If we expand along the jth column, then $|\mathbf{A}| = \sum_{i=1}^{n} a_{ij} |C_{ij}|$

Note that the only difference in the expansions is the summations. The columns vary $(j = 1 \ldots n)$ when we expand along a row i. The rows vary $(i = 1 \ldots n)$ when we expand along a column j.

Returning to the example of the general 4×4 matrix, expanding along the third row gives

$$|\mathbf{A}| = a_{31} |C_{31}| + a_{32} |C_{32}| + a_{33} |C_{33}| + a_{34} |C_{34}|$$

$$= a_{31} |M_{31}| - a_{32} |M_{32}| + a_{33} |M_{33}| - a_{34} |M_{34}|$$

Expanding along the fourth column we have

$$|\mathbf{A}| = a_{14} |C_{14}| + a_{24} |C_{24}| + a_{34} |C_{34}| + a_{44} |C_{44}|$$

$$= -a_{14} |M_{14}| + a_{24} |M_{24}| - a_{34} |M_{34}| + a_{44} |M_{44}|$$

For any expansion, once we reduce the calculations to evaluating third-order determinants, we can use the rule for second-order determinants. For example, in the above expansion along the third row for the determinant of order 4, the term $-a_{32} |M_{32}|$ can be broken down to:

$$-a_{32} |M_{32}| = -a_{32} \begin{vmatrix} a_{11} & a_{13} & a_{14} \\ a_{21} & a_{23} & a_{24} \\ a_{41} & a_{43} & a_{44} \end{vmatrix}$$

and expanding along row 1 of this determinant of order 3 gives:

$$-a_{32} |M_{32}| = -a_{32} \left[a_{11} \begin{vmatrix} a_{23} & a_{24} \\ a_{43} & a_{44} \end{vmatrix} + a_{13} \begin{vmatrix} a_{21} & a_{24} \\ a_{41} & a_{44} \end{vmatrix} - a_{14} \begin{vmatrix} a_{21} & a_{23} \\ a_{41} & a_{43} \end{vmatrix} \right]$$

$$= -a_{32}[a_{11}(a_{23} a_{44} - a_{43} a_{24}) + a_{13}(a_{21} a_{44} - a_{41} a_{24}) - a_{14}(a_{21} a_{43} - a_{41} a_{23})]$$

Example Find the third-order determinant $|\mathbf{A}| = \begin{vmatrix} 1 & 5 & -2 \\ 3 & 7 & 0 \\ 0 & 1 & -4 \end{vmatrix}$

Either the third row or third column, each containing a zero element, would be good choices for expansion. We might choose the third row which also contains a 1. Along the third row:

$$|\mathbf{A}| = 0 \begin{vmatrix} 5 & -2 \\ 7 & 0 \end{vmatrix} - 1 \begin{vmatrix} 1 & -2 \\ 3 & 0 \end{vmatrix} - 4 \begin{vmatrix} 1 & 5 \\ 3 & 7 \end{vmatrix}$$

$$= 0 - 1 (6) - 4 (-8) = 26$$

We can check our work by expanding along the third column:

$$|\mathbf{A}| = -2 \begin{vmatrix} 3 & 7 \\ 0 & 1 \end{vmatrix} - 0 \begin{vmatrix} 1 & 5 \\ 0 & 1 \end{vmatrix} - 4 \begin{vmatrix} 1 & 5 \\ 3 & 7 \end{vmatrix}$$

$$= -2 (3) - 0 - 4 (-8) = 26$$

Properties of Determinants Some useful properties of determinants include:

1. Multiplying every element in a row (column) by a constant, k, multiplies the determinant by that constant.

Example

$$k \begin{vmatrix} a_{11} & a_{12} \\ a_{21} & a_{22} \end{vmatrix} = \begin{vmatrix} ka_{11} & ka_{12} \\ a_{21} & a_{22} \end{vmatrix} = \begin{vmatrix} ka_{11} & a_{12} \\ ka_{21} & a_{22} \end{vmatrix} = ka_{11}a_{22} - ka_{21}a_{12} = k\left(a_{11}a_{22} - a_{21}a_{12} \right)$$

$$3 \begin{vmatrix} 5 & -1 \\ 6 & 2 \end{vmatrix} = \begin{vmatrix} 15 & -3 \\ 6 & 2 \end{vmatrix} = \begin{vmatrix} 15 & -1 \\ 18 & 2 \end{vmatrix} = 30 - (-18) = 48$$

2. Interchanging two rows (columns) in a determinant changes the sign of the determinant.

Example

$$\begin{vmatrix} a_{11} & a_{12} \\ a_{21} & a_{22} \end{vmatrix} = - \begin{vmatrix} a_{21} & a_{22} \\ a_{11} & a_{12} \end{vmatrix} = -a_{21}a_{12} - (-a_{11}a_{22}) = a_{11}a_{22} - a_{21}a_{12}$$

$$\begin{vmatrix} 5 & -1 \\ 6 & 2 \end{vmatrix} = 10 - (6) = 16 = - \begin{vmatrix} 6 & 2 \\ 5 & -1 \end{vmatrix} = -(-6 - 10) = 16$$

3. The determinant of the transpose of a matrix is equal to the determinant of the matrix.

Example: $|\mathbf{A}'| = |\mathbf{A}|$

$$\begin{vmatrix} a_{11} & a_{21} \\ a_{12} & a_{22} \end{vmatrix} = \begin{vmatrix} a_{11} & a_{12} \\ a_{21} & a_{22} \end{vmatrix} = a_{11}a_{22} - a_{21}a_{12}$$

$$\begin{vmatrix} 5 & 6 \\ -1 & 2 \end{vmatrix} = \begin{vmatrix} 5 & -1 \\ 6 & 2 \end{vmatrix} = 10 - (-6) = 16$$

4. Multiplying any row (column) of a determinant by a constant k and adding the result to any other row (column) of the determinant does not change the value of the determinant.

Example

$$\begin{vmatrix} a_{11} & a_{12} \\ a_{21} & a_{22} \end{vmatrix} = \begin{vmatrix} a_{11} & a_{12} \\ a_{21} + ka_{11} & a_{22} + ka_{12} \end{vmatrix} = a_{11}a_{22} + k a_{11}a_{12} - a_{12}a_{21} - k a_{11}a_{12}$$

$$= a_{11}a_{22} - a_{12}a_{21}$$

Below, we multiply row 1 of the determinant by $k = 3$, and then add the result to row 2 of the determinant, which leaves the value of the determinant unchanged.

$$\begin{vmatrix} 5 & 6 \\ -1 & 2 \end{vmatrix} = \begin{vmatrix} 5 & 6 \\ 14 & 20 \end{vmatrix} = (5)(20) - (14)(6) = 16$$

This last property can be helpful in evaluating large determinants. We can use row (column) manipulation to obtain zeros in the column (row) we select for expansion. For example, consider the following fourth-order determinant.

$$|\mathbf{A}| = \begin{vmatrix} 4 & -3 & 1 & 0 \\ 0 & 1 & 2 & 3 \\ -2 & 5 & 4 & -1 \\ 1 & -1 & 0 & 2 \end{vmatrix}$$

and suppose that we select the first column for expansion. While the first column already contains one zero, we can obtain two more zeros through row manipulation (using the above fourth property of determinants). First, add -4 times row 4 to row 1 to get a zero in the $(1,1)$ position.

$$|\mathbf{A}| = \begin{vmatrix} 0 & 1 & 1 & -8 \\ 0 & 1 & 2 & 3 \\ -2 & 5 & 4 & -1 \\ 1 & -1 & 0 & 2 \end{vmatrix}$$

Next, add 2 times row 4 to row 3 to get a zero in the $(3,1)$ position.

$$|\mathbf{A}| = \begin{vmatrix} 0 & 1 & 1 & -8 \\ 0 & 1 & 2 & 3 \\ 0 & 3 & 4 & 3 \\ 1 & -1 & 0 & 2 \end{vmatrix}$$

We can now expand along column 1 of this determinant of order 4, and then along row 1 of the resulting determinant of order 3.

$$|\mathbf{A}| = -1 \begin{vmatrix} 1 & 1 & -8 \\ 1 & 2 & 3 \\ 3 & 4 & 3 \end{vmatrix} = -1 \left[1 \begin{vmatrix} 2 & 3 \\ 4 & 3 \end{vmatrix} - 1 \begin{vmatrix} 1 & 3 \\ 3 & 3 \end{vmatrix} - 8 \begin{vmatrix} 1 & 2 \\ 3 & 4 \end{vmatrix} \right]$$

$$= -1 \left[1(-6) - 1(-6) - 8(-2) \right] = -16$$

PRACTICE PROBLEM 5.5

Find the following determinants.

a) $|\mathbf{A}| = \begin{vmatrix} 3 & -2 \\ 4 & 1 \end{vmatrix}$ b) $|\mathbf{B}| = \begin{vmatrix} 5 & -1 & 2 \\ 0 & 7 & -3 \\ -4 & 1 & 1 \end{vmatrix}$ c) $|\mathbf{C}| = \begin{vmatrix} 1 & 0 & 2 & 3 \\ -1 & 4 & 0 & 5 \\ 2 & 7 & -1 & 2 \\ 0 & 1 & -1 & -3 \end{vmatrix}$

(The answers are at the end of the chapter.)

THE INVERSE OF A MATRIX

As noted above, the determinant is used to find the inverse of a square matrix. For a square matrix $\mathbf{A}_{n \times n}$,

$$\mathbf{A} = \begin{bmatrix} a_{11} & a_{12} & \cdots & a_{1n} \\ a_{21} & a_{22} & \cdots & a_{2n} \\ . \\ . \\ a_{n1} & a_{n2} & \cdots & a_{nn} \end{bmatrix}$$

we define the *cofactor matrix,* $\mathbf{C}_{n \times n}$, to be the matrix formed by replacing every element a_{ij} $(i = 1 \ldots n; j = 1 \ldots n)$ of $\mathbf{A}$ by its cofactor, $|C_{ij}|$.

$$\mathbf{C} = \begin{bmatrix} |C_{11}| & |C_{12}| & \cdots & |C_{1n}| \\ |C_{21}| & |C_{22}| & \cdots & |C_{2n}| \\ . \\ . \\ |C_{n1}| & |C_{n2}| & \cdots & |C_{nn}| \end{bmatrix}$$

If we then take the transpose of the cofactor matrix, we obtain the *adjoint matrix,* **Adj(A)**.

$$\mathbf{Adj(A)} = \mathbf{C}' = \begin{bmatrix} |C_{11}| & |C_{21}| & \cdots & |C_{n1}| \\ |C_{12}| & |C_{22}| & \cdots & |C_{n2}| \\ . \\ . \\ |C_{1n}| & |C_{2n}| & \cdots & |C_{nn}| \end{bmatrix}$$

The inverse of the square matrix, $\mathbf{A}$, written as $\mathbf{A}^{-1}$, is given by

$$\mathbf{A}^{-1} = \frac{1}{|\mathbf{A}|} \mathbf{Adj(A)} \qquad (\text{where } |\mathbf{A}| \neq 0)$$

We should emphasize that, like determinants, inverses are defined only for square matrices. Moreover, only for those square matrices where the determinant is not equal to zero will the inverse matrix be defined. If a square matrix has an inverse, then it is said to be *nonsingular.* If a square matrix does not have an inverse, then it is *singular.*

    Example Given

$$\mathbf{A} = \begin{bmatrix} 2 & 3 & -1 \\ 0 & 1 & 2 \\ 5 & -3 & 4 \end{bmatrix}, \text{find } \mathbf{A}^{-1}$$

First we should calculate $|\mathbf{A}|$, since if $|\mathbf{A}| = 0$, the inverse is not defined. Expanding along column 1, we have:

$$|\mathbf{A}| = 2 \begin{vmatrix} 1 & 2 \\ -3 & 4 \end{vmatrix} + 5 \begin{vmatrix} 3 & -1 \\ 1 & 2 \end{vmatrix} = 2(10) + 5(7) = 55 \qquad (\text{Thus, } \mathbf{A}^{-1} \text{ exists.})$$

The cofactor matrix is obtained by replacing each element of $\mathbf{A}$ by its cofactor.

$$\mathbf{C} = \begin{bmatrix} 10 & 10 & -5 \\ -9 & 13 & 21 \\ 7 & -4 & 2 \end{bmatrix}$$

For the adjoint matrix we take the transpose of the cofactor matrix.

$$\mathbf{Adj(A)} = \mathbf{C'} = \begin{bmatrix} 10 & -9 & 7 \\ 10 & 13 & -4 \\ -5 & 21 & 2 \end{bmatrix}$$

Thus, the inverse of **A** is equal to

$$\mathbf{A}^{-1} = \frac{1}{55} \begin{bmatrix} 10 & -9 & 7 \\ 10 & 13 & -4 \\ -5 & 21 & 2 \end{bmatrix}$$

To check, we multiply $\mathbf{AA}^{-1}$ to get an identity matrix, **I**.

$$\mathbf{AA}^{-1} = \frac{1}{55} \begin{bmatrix} 2 & 3 & -1 \\ 0 & 1 & 2 \\ 5 & -3 & 4 \end{bmatrix} \begin{bmatrix} 10 & -9 & 7 \\ 10 & 13 & -4 \\ -5 & 21 & 2 \end{bmatrix} = \frac{1}{55} \begin{bmatrix} 55 & 0 & 0 \\ 0 & 55 & 0 \\ 0 & 0 & 55 \end{bmatrix} = \begin{bmatrix} 1 & 0 & 0 \\ 0 & 1 & 0 \\ 0 & 0 & 1 \end{bmatrix} = \mathbf{I}$$

Properties of Inverses   We state the following properties of inverses, given that **A** and **B** are conformable, nonsingular matrices.

1. The product of a matrix and its inverse is the identity matrix. $\mathbf{AA}^{-1} = \mathbf{I} = \mathbf{A}^{-1}\mathbf{A}$

Note, here is another instance where matrix multiplication is commutative.

2. The inverse of the inverse of a matrix is the matrix itself. $(\mathbf{A}^{-1})^{-1} = \mathbf{A}$.
3. The inverse of the product of two matrices is the product of the inverses of the matrices in reverse order. $(\mathbf{AB})^{-1} = \mathbf{B}^{-1}\mathbf{A}^{-1}$
4. The inverse of the transpose of a matrix is the transpose of the inverse of the matrix. $(\mathbf{A'})^{-1} = (\mathbf{A}^{-1})'$

PRACTICE PROBLEM 5.6

Find the inverses of the following matrices:

a) $\mathbf{A} = \begin{bmatrix} 2 & -1 \\ 5 & 0 \end{bmatrix}$ b) $\mathbf{B} = \begin{bmatrix} 1 & 7 & 0 \\ -1 & 2 & 3 \\ -2 & 0 & 4 \end{bmatrix}$ c) $\mathbf{C} = \begin{bmatrix} 2 & 5 & -1 \\ 0 & -2 & -3 \\ -2 & -7 & -2 \end{bmatrix}$

(The answers are at the end of the chapter.)

SOLVING A SYSTEM OF LINEAR EQUATIONS

Matrix algebra provides a compact way of writing a system of linear equations, testing for the existence of a solution, and then finding the solution (if existing) to the system of linear equations. To begin, a system of linear equations

$$a_{11} x_1 + a_{12} x_2 + \cdots + a_{1n} x_n = d_1$$

$$a_{21} x_1 + a_{22} x_2 + \cdots + a_{2n} x_n = d_2$$

$$\cdot$$
$$\cdot$$

$$a_{n1} x_1 + a_{n2} x_2 + \cdots + a_{nn} x_n = d_n$$

can be concisely written in matrix notation as $\mathbf{Ax} = \mathbf{d}$, where

$$\mathbf{A} = \begin{bmatrix} a_{11} & a_{12} & \cdots & a_{1n} \\ a_{21} & a_{22} & \cdots & a_{2n} \\ \cdot & & & \\ \cdot & & & \\ a_{n1} & a_{n2} & \cdots & a_{nn} \end{bmatrix}$$ is an $n \times n$ matrix of exogenous coefficients

$$\mathbf{x} = \begin{bmatrix} x_1 \\ x_2 \\ \cdot \\ \cdot \\ x_n \end{bmatrix}$$ is an $n \times 1$ matrix (vector) of endogenous variables

and

$$\mathbf{d} = \begin{bmatrix} d_1 \\ d_2 \\ \cdot \\ \cdot \\ d_n \end{bmatrix}$$ is an $n \times 1$ matrix (vector) of exogenous constants.

The solution to this system of linear equations, $\mathbf{Ax} = \mathbf{d}$, can be found as follows. Recall that we cannot simply divide through by the coefficient matrix, $\mathbf{A}$, since matrix division is not defined. Instead we premultiply both sides of $\mathbf{Ax} = \mathbf{d}$ by $\mathbf{A}^{-1}$ to get

$$\mathbf{A}^{-1}\mathbf{Ax} = \mathbf{A}^{-1}\mathbf{d}.$$

Since $\mathbf{A}^{-1}\mathbf{A} = \mathbf{I}$, we have

$$\mathbf{Ix} = \mathbf{A}^{-1}\mathbf{d}$$

or

$$\bar{\mathbf{x}} = \begin{bmatrix} \bar{x}_1 \\ \bar{x}_2 \\ \cdot \\ \cdot \\ \bar{x}_n \end{bmatrix} = \mathbf{A}^{-1}\mathbf{d} = \frac{1}{|\mathbf{A}|} \mathbf{Adj(A)} \, \mathbf{d}$$

where $|\mathbf{A}| \neq 0$ and $\mathbf{Adj(A)}$ is the adjoint matrix associated with $\mathbf{A}$.

We note, as always, that the solution values of the endogenous variables, $\bar{\mathbf{x}}$, are expressed solely in terms of the exogenous variables of the model (the a_{ij} elements in the $\mathbf{A}^{-1}$ matrix and the d_i constant terms, $i = 1 \ldots n, j = 1 \ldots n$). Note also that a necessary condition for the existence of a solution to a system of linear equations is that the coefficient matrix be nonsingular, $|\mathbf{A}| \neq 0$. In fact, we can state that, given a system of linear equations, $\mathbf{Ax} = \mathbf{d}$, the solution $\bar{\mathbf{x}} = \dfrac{1}{|\mathbf{A}|} \mathbf{Adj(A)}\, \mathbf{d}$ exists and is unique if $|\mathbf{A}| \neq 0$.

Nonsingularity of the Coefficient Matrix The key question to address now is when will the coefficient matrix $\mathbf{A}$ be nonsingular. A square matrix, $\mathbf{A}$, is nonsingular, that is, $|\mathbf{A}| \neq 0$ and $\mathbf{A}^{-1}$ exists, when the rows (columns) of $\mathbf{A}$ are linearly independent. The row vectors (column vectors) of the matrix $\mathbf{A}$ are linearly independent if none of the row vectors (column vectors) can be written as a linear combination of the other row vectors (column vectors). We will illustrate with linear systems of two equations, where we do not assume specific numerical values for the constants, d_1 and d_2.

Example 1. The system of linear equations

$$7x_1 + 5x_2 = d_1$$

$$-2x_1 + 8x_2 = d_2$$

can be written in matrix notation as

$$\begin{bmatrix} 7 & 5 \\ -2 & 8 \end{bmatrix} \begin{bmatrix} x_1 \\ x_2 \end{bmatrix} = \begin{bmatrix} d_1 \\ d_2 \end{bmatrix}$$

Evaluating the determinant of the coefficient matrix we find

$$\begin{bmatrix} 7 & 5 \\ -2 & 8 \end{bmatrix} = 66 \neq 0$$

Thus, the coefficient matrix $\mathbf{A}$ is nonsingular and its inverse $\mathbf{A}^{-1}$ exists. We can confirm that the rows (columns) of $\mathbf{A}$ are linearly independent. Let $\mathbf{v}_1 = (7, 5)$ and $\mathbf{v}_2 = (-2, 8)$ be the row vectors of $\mathbf{A}$. $\mathbf{v}_1 \neq k_2\, \mathbf{v}_2$ for any k_2, since

$$(7, 5) = k_2\,(-2, 8) \quad \text{implies} \quad 7 = -2k_2 \quad \text{so} \quad k_2 = -7/2$$

$$\text{and} \quad 5 = 8k_2 \quad \text{so} \quad k_2 = 5/8 \neq -7/2$$

Figure 5.5a illustrates that the vectors $\mathbf{v}_1 = (7, 5)$ and $\mathbf{v}_2 = (-2, 8)$ span $\mathbf{R}^2$ and form a basis for 2-space.

The solution to this system of linear equations exists and is unique.

$$\begin{bmatrix} \bar{x}_1 \\ \bar{x}_2 \end{bmatrix} = \frac{1}{66} \begin{bmatrix} 8 & -5 \\ 2 & 7 \end{bmatrix} \begin{bmatrix} d_1 \\ d_2 \end{bmatrix} \qquad \text{where} \qquad \frac{1}{66} \begin{bmatrix} 8 & -5 \\ 2 & 7 \end{bmatrix} \text{ is the inverse of } \begin{bmatrix} 7 & 5 \\ -2 & 8 \end{bmatrix}$$

or

$$\bar{x}_1 = (8/66)d_1 - (5/66)d_2$$

$$\bar{x}_2 = (2/66)d_1 + (7/66)d_2$$

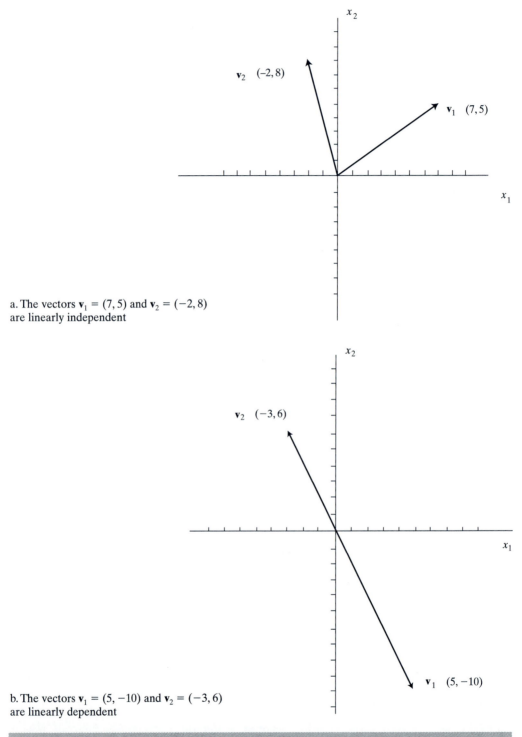

a. The vectors $\mathbf{v}_1 = (7, 5)$ and $\mathbf{v}_2 = (-2, 8)$
are linearly independent

b. The vectors $\mathbf{v}_1 = (5, -10)$ and $\mathbf{v}_2 = (-3, 6)$
are linearly dependent

FIGURE 5.5 LINEAR INDEPENDENCE AND LINEAR DEPENDENCE OF VECTORS

Example 2. The system of linear equations

$$5x_1 - 10x_2 = d_1$$

$$-3x_1 + 6x_2 = d_2$$

can be written in matrix notation as

$$\begin{bmatrix} 5 & -10 \\ -3 & 6 \end{bmatrix} \begin{bmatrix} x_1 \\ x_2 \end{bmatrix} = \begin{bmatrix} d_1 \\ d_2 \end{bmatrix}$$

Evaluating the determinant of the coefficient matrix we find

$$\begin{vmatrix} 5 & -10 \\ -3 & 6 \end{vmatrix} = 0$$

The coefficient matrix is singular, so the inverse, $\mathbf{A}^{-1}$ does not exist. The rows (columns) of $\mathbf{A}$ are linearly dependent. Let $\mathbf{v}_1 = (5, -10)$ and $\mathbf{v}_2 = (-3, 6)$. We can show that $\mathbf{v}_1 = k_2 \mathbf{v}_2$, since

$$(5 - 10) = k_2 (-3, 6) \quad \text{implies} \quad 5 = -3k_2 \quad \text{so } k_2 = -5/3$$

$$\text{and} \quad -10 = 6k_2 \quad \text{so } k_2 = -10/6 = -5/3.$$

Therefore, $\mathbf{v}_1 = (-5/3) \mathbf{v}_2$.

Figure 5.5b illustrates the linear dependence of the vectors $\mathbf{v}_1 = (5, -10)$ and $\mathbf{v}_2 = (-3, 6)$. Having exactly opposite directions, these two vectors do not span $\mathbf{R}^2$ and do not form a basis for 2-space.

Singularity of the Coefficient Matrix   With the singularity of the coefficient matrix, there are two possibilities for this system of equations.

CASE I. $d_1 = (-5/3) d_2$
The two equations are:

$$\text{1) } 5x_1 - 10x_2 = d_1 = (-5/3)d_2$$

$$\text{2) } -3x_1 + 6x_2 = d_2$$

If we multiply equation 2) by $-5/3$, we get equation 2′)

$$\text{2′) } 5x_1 - 10x_2 = (-5/3)d_2$$

which is identical to equation 1). The system consists of one equation, either 2′) or 1), in two unknowns, x_1 and x_2, yielding an infinite number of solutions. That is, there is an infinite number of ordered pairs $(\bar{x}_1, \bar{x}_2)$ that satisfy the equation $5x_1 - 10x_2 = (-5/3)d_2$.

CASE II. $d_1 \neq (-5/3)d_2$
The two equations are

$$\text{1) } 5x_1 - 10x_2 = d_1 \neq (-5/3)d_2$$

$$\text{2) } -3x_1 + 6x_2 = d_2$$

If, as before, we multiply equation 2) by $(-5/3)$ we get equation 2')

$$2') \; 5x_1 - 10x_2 = (-5/3)d_2$$

which is inconsistent with equation 1) $5x_1 - 10x_2 \neq (-5/3)d_2$. With *inconsistent equations*, there is no solution. That is, there is no ordered pair $(\bar{x}_1, \bar{x}_2)$ that simultaneously satisfies the inconsistent equations: 1) $5x_1 - 10x_2 \neq (-5/3)d_2$ and 2') $5x_1 - 10x_2 = (-5/3)d_2$.

In sum, given a system of linear equations, $\mathbf{Ax} = \mathbf{d}$,

if $|\mathbf{A}| \neq 0$, then a unique solution exists: $\mathbf{x} = \mathbf{A}^{-1}\mathbf{d}$ where $\mathbf{A}^{-1} = \dfrac{1}{|\mathbf{A}|} \mathbf{Adj(A)}$

if $|\mathbf{A}| = 0$, then either i) the equations are functionally dependent and there is an infinite number of solutions (i.e., more endogenous variables than independent equations) or ii) the equations are inconsistent and there is no solution.

PRACTICE PROBLEM 5.7

Using matrix algebra, find the solutions, if they exist, to the following systems of equations:

a) $\quad 5x_1 - 2x_2 = 7$
$\quad\;\; -x_1 + 3x_2 = 2$

b) $\quad 2x_1 + 3x_2 = 10$
$\quad\;\; -4x_1 - 6x_2 = 12$

c) $\quad -x_1 + 5x_2 = 10$
$\quad\;\; 3x_1 - 15x_2 = -30$

(The answers are at the end of the chapter.)

Systems of Homogeneous Equations When the vector of constants consists entirely of zeros, the system of linear equations is said to be *homogeneous*. That is, given $\mathbf{Ax} = \mathbf{d}$, and $d_i = 0$ for $i = 1 \ldots n$,

$$\mathbf{A} = \begin{bmatrix} a_{11} & a_{12} & \cdots & a_{1n} \\ a_{21} & a_{22} & \cdots & a_{2n} \\ \cdot & & & \\ \cdot & & & \\ a_{n1} & a_{n2} & \cdots & a_{nn} \end{bmatrix}, \quad \mathbf{x} = \begin{bmatrix} x_1 \\ x_2 \\ \cdot \\ \cdot \\ x_n \end{bmatrix}, \quad \text{and} \quad \mathbf{d} = \begin{bmatrix} d_1 \\ d_2 \\ \cdot \\ \cdot \\ d_n \end{bmatrix} = \begin{bmatrix} 0 \\ 0 \\ \cdot \\ \cdot \\ 0 \end{bmatrix}$$

If the coefficient matrix is nonsingular, $|\mathbf{A}| \neq 0$, then the solution to this system of homogeneous equations is said to be trivial: $\bar{x}_1 = \bar{x}_2 = \ldots = \bar{x}_n = 0$.

$$\bar{\mathbf{x}} = \mathbf{A}^{-1}\mathbf{d} = \mathbf{0} = \begin{bmatrix} 0 \\ 0 \\ \cdot \\ \cdot \\ 0 \end{bmatrix}$$

If the coefficient matrix is singular, $|\mathbf{A}| = 0$, then the equations are functionally dependent (i.e., at least one of the equations is a multiple of the other equations in the system). In this case, there are an infinite number of solutions for $\bar{\mathbf{x}}$.

Example. Solve for the following system of three homogeneous linear equations.

$$1)\ 3x_1 + 2x_2 - x_3 = 0$$

$$2)\ 6x_1 + x_2 - x_3 = 0$$

$$3)\ 3x_1 + 5x_2 - 2x_3 = 0$$

Written in matrix notation, the system is

$$\begin{bmatrix} 3 & 2 & -1 \\ 6 & 1 & -1 \\ 3 & 5 & -2 \end{bmatrix} \begin{bmatrix} x_1 \\ x_2 \\ x_3 \end{bmatrix} = \begin{bmatrix} 0 \\ 0 \\ 0 \end{bmatrix}$$

Evaluating the determinant of the coefficient matrix, we find $|\mathbf{A}| = 0$.

$$\begin{vmatrix} 3 & 2 & -1 \\ 6 & 1 & -1 \\ 3 & 5 & -2 \end{vmatrix} = 0$$

Thus, the system has an infinite number of solutions.

We can confirm this by solving the system using elimination and substitution. Multiply equation 1) by -2 and add to equation 2), we have

$$1')\ -6x_1 - 4x_2 + 2x_3 = 0$$

$$2)\ \underline{\quad 6x_1 + x_2 - x_3 = 0 \quad}$$

$$-3x_2 + x_3 = 0 \qquad \text{or} \quad x_3 = 3x_2$$

Substituting $x_3 = 3x_2$ into equation 3), we find

$$3')\ 3x_1 + 5x_2 - 2(3x_2) = 0$$

$$3x_1 - x_2 = 0 \qquad \text{or} \quad x_2 = 3x_1$$

Therefore, we have established that $x_3 = 3x_2 = 9x_1$. There are an infinite number of ordered triples $(\bar{x}_1, \bar{x}_2, \bar{x}_3)$ that satisfy this condition. In fact, we could show that:

$$3(\text{equation 1}) - 1(\text{equation 2}) = (\text{equation 3}).$$

CRAMER'S RULE

As we know, solving a system of linear equations involves finding the inverse of the coefficient matrix (if nonsingular). To review, given a system of linear equations, $\mathbf{Ax} = \mathbf{d}$, where

$$\mathbf{A} = n \times n \text{ matrix of exogenous coefficients}$$

$$\mathbf{x} = n \times 1 \text{ matrix of endogenous variables}$$

$$\mathbf{d} = n \times 1 \text{ matrix of exogenous constants,}$$

provided $|\mathbf{A}| \neq 0$, the solution is $\bar{\mathbf{x}} = \mathbf{A}^{-1}\mathbf{d} = \dfrac{1}{|\mathbf{A}|}\,\mathbf{Adj(A)}\,\mathbf{d}$.

This procedure can be tedious. There is an alternative method for finding the solution to a system of linear equations, one that is especially useful when the solution of only a subset of the endogenous variables is of interest. This method, known as *Cramer's rule*, is demonstrated below.

We begin by writing the solution, $\bar{\mathbf{x}} = \mathbf{A}^{-1}\mathbf{d} = \dfrac{1}{|\mathbf{A}|}\,\mathbf{Adj(A)}\,\mathbf{d}$, out in matrix notation.

$$
\begin{bmatrix} \bar{x}_1 \\ \bar{x}_2 \\ \cdot \\ \cdot \\ \bar{x}_n \end{bmatrix} = \frac{1}{|\mathbf{A}|}
\begin{bmatrix} |C_{11}| & |C_{21}| & \cdots & |C_{n1}| \\ |C_{12}| & |C_{22}| & \cdots & |C_{n2}| \\ \cdot & & & \\ \cdot & & & \\ |C_{1n}| & |C_{2n}| & \cdots & |C_{nn}| \end{bmatrix}
\begin{bmatrix} d_1 \\ d_2 \\ \cdot \\ \cdot \\ d_n \end{bmatrix} = \frac{1}{|\mathbf{A}|}
\begin{bmatrix} |C_{11}|\,d_1 + |C_{21}|\,d_2 + \cdots + |C_{n1}|\,d_n \\ |C_{12}|\,d_1 + |C_{22}|\,d_2 + \cdots + |C_{n2}|\,d_n \\ \cdot \\ \cdot \\ |C_{1n}|\,d_1 + |C_{2n}|\,d_2 + \cdots + |C_{nn}|\,d_n \end{bmatrix}
$$

$$
\begin{bmatrix} \bar{x}_1 \\ \bar{x}_2 \\ \cdot \\ \cdot \\ \bar{x}_n \end{bmatrix} = \frac{1}{|\mathbf{A}|}
\begin{bmatrix} \sum_{i=1}^{n} d_i\,|C_{i1}| \\ \sum_{i=1}^{n} d_i\,|C_{i2}| \\ \cdot \\ \cdot \\ \sum_{i=1}^{n} d_i\,|C_{in}| \end{bmatrix}
$$

or, in general, $\bar{x}_j = \dfrac{1}{|\mathbf{A}|}\displaystyle\sum_{i=1}^{n} d_i\,|C_{ij}| \qquad j = 1\ldots n$

Recall, in evaluating the determinant of the coefficient matrix, $|\mathbf{A}|$, expanding along the jth column gave $|\mathbf{A}| = \displaystyle\sum_{i=1}^{n} a_{ij}\,|C_{ij}| = a_{1j}\,|C_{1j}| + a_{2j}\,|C_{2j}| + \cdots + a_{nj}\,|C_{nj}|$.

The solution for $\bar{x}_j$ is similar to this expansion for $|\mathbf{A}|$, except that the cofactors $|C_{ij}|$ are multiplied by the exogenous constants, d_i, instead of the coefficients, a_{ij}. Let $|\mathbf{A}_j|$ indicate the determinant associated with the matrix $\mathbf{A}$ when the jth column of $\mathbf{A}$,

$$
\begin{bmatrix} a_{1j} \\ a_{2j} \\ \cdot \\ \cdot \\ a_{nj} \end{bmatrix}
$$

is replaced by the column of constant terms,

$$
\mathbf{d} = \begin{bmatrix} d_1 \\ d_2 \\ \cdot \\ \cdot \\ d_n \end{bmatrix}
$$

We can then write the solution to the jth endogenous variable, $\bar{x}_j$, $(j = 1 \ldots n)$ as

$$
\bar{x}_j = \frac{|\mathbf{A}_j|}{|\mathbf{A}|} = \frac{1}{|\mathbf{A}|} \begin{vmatrix} a_{11} & a_{12} & \ldots & d_1 & \ldots & a_{1n} \\ a_{21} & a_{22} & \ldots & d_2 & \ldots & a_{2n} \\ \cdot & & & & & \\ \cdot & & & & & \\ a_{n1} & a_{n2} & \ldots & d_n & \ldots & a_{nn} \\ & & & \uparrow & & \end{vmatrix}
$$

jth column

This is Cramer's rule. In other words, we do not have to calculate the inverse of the coefficient matrix to solve for a system of linear equations. To find the solution to any one of the endogenous variables, say x_j, we take the ratio of $|\mathbf{A}_j|$, the determinant formed by replacing the jth column of $\mathbf{A}$ by the vector of constants, to $|\mathbf{A}|$, the determinant of the coefficient matrix. As suggested above, Cramer's rule is useful when finding $\mathbf{A}^{-1}$ is onerous or when we are interested in the solution for just one or a few of the endogenous variables.

To illustrate with a numerical example, consider the following system of linear equations.

$$2x_1 + 3x_2 - x_3 = 40$$

$$x_1 - 2x_2 + x_3 = 100$$

$$4x_1 - x_2 + 2x_3 = 60$$

Written in matrix notation, the system is:

$$
\begin{bmatrix} 2 & 3 & -1 \\ 1 & -2 & 1 \\ 4 & -1 & 2 \end{bmatrix} \begin{bmatrix} x_1 \\ x_2 \\ x_3 \end{bmatrix} = \begin{bmatrix} 40 \\ 100 \\ 60 \end{bmatrix}
$$

The coefficient matrix is nonsingular, indicating that the solution exists and is unique.

$$
\begin{vmatrix} 2 & 3 & -1 \\ 1 & -2 & 1 \\ 4 & -1 & 2 \end{vmatrix} = -7 \neq 0
$$

Proceeding, we can solve for x_1, x_2, and x_3 using Cramer's rule. For x_1, we take the ratio of the determinant of the modified coefficient matrix (where we replace the first column of the coefficient matrix with the column of constants) to the determinant of the coefficient matrix (here equal to -7).

$$
\bar{x}_1 = \frac{\begin{vmatrix} 40 & 3 & -1 \\ 100 & -2 & 1 \\ 60 & -1 & 2 \end{vmatrix}}{-7} = \frac{-560}{-7} = 80
$$

Similarly, solving for x_2 and x_3 by replacing the second and third columns, respectively, of the determinant of the coefficient matrix by the column of constants, we find

$$\bar{x}_2 = \frac{\begin{vmatrix} 2 & 40 & -1 \\ 1 & 100 & 1 \\ 4 & 60 & 2 \end{vmatrix}}{-7} = \frac{700}{-7} = -100$$

$$\bar{x}_3 = \frac{\begin{vmatrix} 2 & 3 & 40 \\ 1 & -2 & 100 \\ 4 & -1 & 60 \end{vmatrix}}{-7} = \frac{1{,}260}{-7} = -180$$

To check, we substitute the equilibrium values back into the equations of the model.

$$2\bar{x}_1 + 3\bar{x}_2 - \bar{x}_3 = 2(80) + 3(-100) - (-180) = 40$$

$$\bar{x}_1 - 2\bar{x}_2 + \bar{x}_3 = (80) - 2(-100) + (-180) = 100$$

$$4\bar{x}_1 - \bar{x}_2 + 2\bar{x}_3 = 4(80) - (-100) + 2(-180) = 60$$

PRACTICE PROBLEM 5.8

Given the following system of linear equations, solve for $x_1, x_2,$ and x_3 using Cramer's rule.

$$-x_1 + 2x_2 + 4x_3 = 20$$

$$2x_1 - 5x_2 + x_3 = 30$$

$$x_1 - x_2 + 2x_3 = 15$$

(The answers are at the end of the chapter.)

GENERAL COMPETITIVE EQUILIBRIUM IN MATRIX NOTATION

With our knowledge of matrix algebra, we can revisit the general competitive equilibrium model. Recall, with n perfectly competitive markets, there are n demand equations, n supply equations, and n equilibrium conditions.

$$Q_i^d = d_{i0} + d_{i1} P_1 + d_{i2} P_2 + \cdots + d_{in} P_n \qquad i = 1 \ldots n$$

$$Q_i^s = s_{i0} + s_{i1} P_1 + s_{i2} P_2 + \cdots + s_{in} P_n$$

$$E_i^d (P_1, P_2, \ldots, P_n) = Q_i^d (P_1, P_2, \ldots, P_n) - Q_i^s (P_1, P_2, \ldots, P_n) \overset{e}{=} 0$$

Collapsing the system of $3n$ equations in $3n$ unknowns (P_i, Q_i^d, Q_i^s) into n equations in n unknowns (P_i) by substituting the demand and supply equations into the equilibrium conditions, we get:

$$E_i^d (P_1, P_2, \ldots, P_n) = (d_{i0} - s_{i0}) + (d_{i1} - s_{i1}) P_1 + (d_{i2} - s_{i2}) P_2 + \cdots + (d_{in} - s_{in}) P_n \overset{e}{=} 0$$

For general equilibrium we need to find a price vector $\overline{\mathbf{P}}' = (\overline{P}_1, \overline{P}_2, \ldots, \overline{P}_n)$ such that simultaneously each market clears with zero excess quantity demanded. We can write this reduced system in matrix notation as $\mathbf{AP} = \mathbf{d}$ where

$$
\mathbf{A} = \begin{bmatrix} (d_{11} - s_{11}) & (d_{12} - s_{12}) & \ldots & (d_{1n} - s_{1n}) \\ (d_{21} - s_{21}) & (d_{22} - s_{22}) & \ldots & (d_{2n} - s_{2n}) \\ . \\ . \\ (d_{n1} - s_{n1}) & (d_{n2} - s_{n2}) & \ldots & (d_{nn} - s_{nn}) \end{bmatrix}
$$
$n \times n$ matrix of exogenous demand and supply price coefficients

$$
\mathbf{P} = \begin{bmatrix} P_1 \\ P_2 \\ . \\ . \\ P_n \end{bmatrix}
$$
$n \times 1$ matrix of endogenous prices

and

$$
\mathbf{d} = \begin{bmatrix} s_{10} - d_{10} \\ s_{20} - d_{20} \\ . \\ . \\ s_{n0} - d_{n0} \end{bmatrix}
$$
$n \times 1$ matrix of exogenous demand and supply quantity intercepts.

The general solution is $\overline{\mathbf{P}} = \mathbf{A}^{-1} \mathbf{d} = \dfrac{1}{|\mathbf{A}|} \mathbf{Adj(A)} \, \mathbf{d}$ $(|\mathbf{A}| \neq 0)$

Again we note that the equilibrium prices are expressed entirely in terms of the exogenous variables of the model. We can find the equilibrium quantities transacted by substituting the equilibrium prices back into the demand or supply equations. Using Cramer's rule, however, we can find the equilibrium price in any market, say $\overline{P}_j$, as $\overline{P}_j = |\mathbf{A}_j| / |\mathbf{A}|$.

EXAMPLE OF A GENERAL EQUILIBRIUM: THREE RELATED, COMPETITIVE MARKETS

Given the equilibrium conditions in three related markets: $E_j^d \, (P_1, P_2, P_3) \overset{e}{=} 0, (j = 1, 2, 3)$. For general equilibrium we need to find a price vector, $\overline{\mathbf{P}}$, such that all three markets simultaneously clear with zero excess quantities demanded. In particular, assume that:

$$
E_1^d = -11P_1 + P_2 + P_3 + 31 = 0
$$

$$
E_2^d = P_1 - 6P_2 + 2P_3 + 26 = 0
$$

$$
E_3^d = P_1 + 2P_2 - 7P_3 + 24 = 0
$$

Note that this is not a system of homogeneous equations, since we can rewrite these equations as:

$$11P_1 - P_2 - P_3 = 31$$

$$-P_1 + 6P_2 - 2P_3 = 26$$

$$-P_1 - 2P_2 + 7P_3 = 24$$

or, in matrix notation as:

$$\begin{bmatrix} 11 & -1 & -1 \\ -1 & 6 & -2 \\ -1 & -2 & 7 \end{bmatrix} \begin{bmatrix} P_1 \\ P_2 \\ P_3 \end{bmatrix} = \begin{bmatrix} 31 \\ 26 \\ 24 \end{bmatrix}$$

Since

$$|\mathbf{A}| = \begin{vmatrix} 11 & -1 & -1 \\ -1 & 6 & -2 \\ -1 & -2 & 7 \end{vmatrix} = 401 \neq 0,$$

that is, the coefficient matrix is nonsingular, we know that a unique solution exists. First, solving with the matrix inversion method, we would find,

$$\overline{\mathbf{P}} = \mathbf{A}^{-1}\mathbf{d}$$

$$\overline{\mathbf{P}} = \begin{bmatrix} \overline{P}_1 \\ \overline{P}_2 \\ \overline{P}_3 \end{bmatrix} = \frac{1}{401} \begin{bmatrix} 38 & 9 & 8 \\ 9 & 76 & 23 \\ 8 & 23 & 65 \end{bmatrix} \begin{bmatrix} 31 \\ 26 \\ 24 \end{bmatrix} = \frac{1}{401} \begin{bmatrix} 1{,}178 + & 234 + & 192 \\ 279 + & 1{,}976 + & 552 \\ 248 + & 598 + & 1{,}560 \end{bmatrix}$$

$$= \begin{bmatrix} 4 \\ 7 \\ 6 \end{bmatrix}$$

We can check by confirming that:

$$E_1^d(\overline{P}_1, \overline{P}_2, \overline{P}_3) = 11\overline{P}_1 - \overline{P}_2 - \overline{P}_3 - 31 = 11(4) - (7) - (6) - 31 = 0 \text{ (It checks.)}$$

$$E_2^d(\overline{P}_1, \overline{P}_2, \overline{P}_3) = -\overline{P}_1 + 6\overline{P}_2 - 2\overline{P}_3 - 26 = -(4) + 6(7) - 2(6) - 26 = 0 \text{ (It checks.)}$$

$$E_3^d(\overline{P}_1, \overline{P}_2, \overline{P}_3) = -\overline{P}_1 - 2\overline{P}_2 + 7\overline{P}_3 - 24 = -(4) - 2(7) + 7(6) - 24 = 0 \text{ (It checks.)}$$

Solving with Cramer's rule, we use $\overline{P}_j = \dfrac{|\mathbf{A}_j|}{|\mathbf{A}|}$

$$\overline{P}_1 = \frac{1}{401} \begin{vmatrix} 31 & -1 & -1 \\ 26 & 6 & -2 \\ 24 & -2 & 7 \end{vmatrix} = \frac{1{,}604}{401} = 4$$

$$\overline{P}_2 = \frac{1}{401} \begin{vmatrix} 11 & 31 & -1 \\ -1 & 26 & -2 \\ -1 & 24 & 7 \end{vmatrix} = \frac{2{,}807}{401} = 7$$

$$\overline{P}_3 = \frac{1}{401} \begin{vmatrix} 11 & -1 & 31 \\ -1 & 6 & 26 \\ -1 & -2 & 24 \end{vmatrix} = \frac{2,406}{401} = 6$$

In this text, we will use matrix algebra frequently, including: to find the solution to a system of linear equations; to determine the type of extremum in optimization problems; to conduct comparative static analysis when we cannot explicitly solve for the endogenous variables in terms of the exogenous variables of the model; and to evaluate input-output models.

We now begin the second part of the text: Optimization. First, in Chapter 6, we review some basic concepts for the firm and establish general decision rules for profit maximization in the short run. Then, in Chapter 7, we continue our discussion of competitive markets by modeling the perfectly competitive firm and, in comparison, the monopolistically competitive firm. Subsequently, we analyze monopolies and monopsonies (in Chapter 8) and duopolies and oligopolies (in Chapter 9).

❖ KEY TERMS

Mathematics

- adjoint matrix (p. 136)
- basis (p. 124)
- cofactor (p. 132)
- cofactor matrix (p. 136)
- conformable (p. 118)
- coordinates (p. 118)
- Cramer's rule (p. 144)
- determinant (p. 132)
- dot product (inner product) (p. 120)

- homogeneous (p. 142)
- identity matrix (p. 126)
- inconsistent equations (p. 142)
- Laplace expansion (p. 132)
- linearly dependent (p. 123)
- linearly independent (p. 123)
- main diagonal (p. 126)
- matrix (p. 125)
- minor (p. 132)

- nonsingular (p. 136)
- norm (p. 120)
- orthogonal (p. 120)
- scalar (p. 118)
- singular (p. 136)
- span (p. 124)
- square matrix (p. 125)
- transpose (p. 126)
- vector (p. 117)
- zero matrix (p. 126)

❖ PROBLEMS

1. Given the two matrices below:

$$\mathbf{A} = \begin{bmatrix} 4 & -2 & 0 \\ 1 & 7 & -1 \\ 0 & 2 & 1 \end{bmatrix} \quad \mathbf{B} = \begin{bmatrix} -1 & 0 & 3 \\ 3 & 5 & -5 \\ 1 & 5 & 1 \end{bmatrix}$$

   a) Find $\mathbf{A} + \mathbf{B}$ and $\mathbf{A} - \mathbf{B}$.
   b) Find $\mathbf{AB}$ and $\mathbf{BA}$.
   c) Find $\mathbf{A}^{-1}$ and $\mathbf{B}^{-1}$.
   d) Confirm that $(\mathbf{A}')^{-1} = (\mathbf{A}^{-1})'$.

2. Given the demand and supply schedules for commodities 1 and 2 in two related perfectly competitive markets:

$$Q_1^d = 40 - 5P_1 + 2P_2$$

$$Q_1^s = -10 + 4P_1$$

$$Q_1^d(P_1, P_2) \overset{\text{e}}{=} Q_1^s(P_1)$$

$$Q_2^d = 25 + P_1 - 4P_2$$

$$Q_2^s = -7 + 2P_2$$

$$Q_2^s(P_1, P_2) \overset{\text{e}}{=} Q_2^s(P_2)$$

a) Reduce this system of six equations in six unknowns to a system of two equations (the equilibrium conditions) in two unknowns (the unit prices, P_1 and P_2).
b) Find the market equilibrium prices and quantities transacted using either the method of elimination or the method of substitution.
c) Find the consequences on the market equilibrium prices and quantities transacted of a decrease in the demand for commodity 1 to $Q_1^{d'} = 34.8 - 5P_1 + 2P_2$.
d) Repeat parts a) and b) using matrix algebra and Cramer's rule.

3. Given the following system of equations describing the demand and supply schedules in three related, perfectly competitive markets:

$$Q_1^d = 20 - 3P_1 + P_2 - P_3 \qquad Q_1^s = -5 + 2P_1 \qquad Q_1^d \overset{\text{e}}{=} Q_1^s$$

$$Q_2^d = 24 + 2P_1 - 4P_2 + P_3 \qquad Q_2^s = -8 + P_2 \qquad Q_2^d \overset{\text{e}}{=} Q_2^s$$

$$Q_3^d = 10 - P_1 + P_2 - 2P_3 \qquad Q_3^s = -2 + 3P_3 \qquad Q_3^d \overset{\text{e}}{=} Q_3^s$$

a) Solve for the equilibrium price vector $\mathbf{P'} = (\overline{P}_1, \overline{P}_2, \overline{P}_3)$ using both:

i) the matrix inversion method
ii) Cramer's rule
Note: Round off the final price calculations to the nearest hundredth.
b) Find the equilibrium quantities transacted from the supply schedules.

4. Given the following system of equations describing the demand and supply schedules for labor in three related, perfectly competitive labor markets:

$$Q_1^d = 20 - 3w_1 \qquad Q_1^s = -5 + 2w_1 - w_2 - w_3 \qquad Q_1^d \overset{\text{e}}{=} Q_1^s$$

$$Q_2^d = 24 - 4w_2 \qquad Q_2^s = -11 - 2w_1 + 5w_2 - w_3 \qquad Q_2^d \overset{\text{e}}{=} Q_2^s$$

$$Q_3^d = 10 - 2w_3 \qquad Q_3^s = 70 - 3w_1 - 8w_2 \qquad Q_3^d \overset{\text{e}}{=} Q_3^s$$

where Q_i^d and Q_i^s ($i = 1, 2, 3$) are the quantities demanded and supplied of labor in market i and w_i is the market wage rate.
a) Explain what is required for general equilibrium in the system.
b) Collapse the system into three equations and write the system in matrix notation.
c) Solve for $\overline{w}_2$ using Cramer's rule. What do you conclude?

❖ ANSWERS TO PRACTICE PROBLEMS

5.1 The market equilibrium prices and quantities transacted for commodities 1 and 2 are: $\overline{P}_1 = 6$ and $\overline{Q}_1 = 8$; $\overline{P}_2 = 3$ and $\overline{Q}_2 = 5$.

5.2 a) $\mathbf{u} + \mathbf{v} = (1, 9)$ b) $\mathbf{u} - \mathbf{v} = (-3, -1)$ c) $\mathbf{v} - \mathbf{u} = (3, 1)$ d) $\mathbf{u} \cdot \mathbf{v} = 18$
e) $\mathbf{v} \cdot \mathbf{u} = 18$ f) $\|\mathbf{v}\| = \sqrt{29}$ g) $d(\mathbf{u}, \mathbf{v}) = \sqrt{10}$

5.3 a) $\mathbf{u} = (-1, 4) \neq k\mathbf{v} = k(2, 5)$, since $-1 = 2k$ implies $k = -.5$; while $4 = 5k$ implies $k = .8$.

   b) $\mathbf{v} = (2, 5) \neq k\mathbf{w} = k(3, -1)$, since $2 = 3k$ implies $k = 2/3$; while $5 = -1k$ implies $k = -5$.

   c) $k_1 \mathbf{u} + k_2 \mathbf{v} = \mathbf{w}$, where $k_1 = -17/13$ and $k_2 = 11/13$; so $\mathbf{w}$ is a linear combination of $\mathbf{u}$ and $\mathbf{v}$.

5.4 a) $\mathbf{A} + \mathbf{B} = \begin{bmatrix} 1 & -1 & 1 \\ 2 & 0 & 0 \\ 7 & 13 & 6 \end{bmatrix}$ b) $\mathbf{A} - \mathbf{B} = \begin{bmatrix} -9 & 1 & 1 \\ 2 & -2 & 6 \\ -7 & -11 & -2 \end{bmatrix}$

   c) $\mathbf{B} - \mathbf{A} = \begin{bmatrix} 9 & -1 & -1 \\ -2 & 2 & -6 \\ 7 & 11 & 2 \end{bmatrix}$ d) $\mathbf{AB} = \begin{bmatrix} -13 & 16 & 4 \\ 31 & 33 & 15 \\ 14 & 25 & 5 \end{bmatrix}$

   e) $\mathbf{A}' + \mathbf{B}' = \begin{bmatrix} 1 & 2 & 7 \\ -1 & 0 & 13 \\ 1 & 0 & 6 \end{bmatrix}$ f) $\mathbf{BC} = \begin{bmatrix} -2 & 6 \\ -13 & -10 \\ 44 & 7 \end{bmatrix}$

   g) $\mathbf{C}'\mathbf{A} = \begin{bmatrix} 4 & 3 & 16 \\ -6 & 4 & 4 \end{bmatrix}$

5.5 a) $|\mathbf{A}| = 11$ b) $|\mathbf{B}| = 94$ c) $|\mathbf{C}| = 62$

5.6 a) $\mathbf{A}^{-1} = (1/5) \begin{bmatrix} 0 & 1 \\ -5 & 2 \end{bmatrix}$ b) $\mathbf{B}^{-1} = (-1/6) \begin{bmatrix} 8 & -28 & 21 \\ -2 & 4 & -3 \\ 4 & -14 & 9 \end{bmatrix}$

   c) $\mathbf{C}$ is singular, $|\mathbf{C}| = 0$, so $\mathbf{C}$ does not have an inverse.

5.7 a) $\bar{x}_1 = 25/13$ and $\bar{x}_2 = 17/13$.

   b) There is no solution. The equations are inconsistent: $2x_1 + 3x_2 = 10$ and $2x_1 + 3x_2 = -6$.

   c) There are an infinite number of solutions: $x_1 = 5x_2 - 10$.

5.8 $\bar{x}_1 = -6, \bar{x}_2 = -7,$ and $\bar{x}_3 = 7$.

CHAPTER

6

THEORY OF THE FIRM: SHORT-RUN DECISION RULES

In Part I of the text our focus was on perfectly competitive markets, characterized by the interaction of many buyers and many sellers of a standardized product, with no single buyer or seller exerting any significant influence over the market outcomes. We discussed the attainment of equilibrium, whereby the market clears at a price that equates the quantity demanded of the good or service by the buyers with the quantity supplied by the sellers over some given period of time. Furthermore, the conditions under which a market equilibrium exists, is unique, and is stable, were defined.

In Part II of the text we look behind the market outcomes to the behavior of households and firms. For consumer goods and services, households constitute the demand and firms constitute the supply. In factor markets, like labor and financial capital, the roles are reversed: households supply the factors demanded by firms.

We assume that the primary economic objective of a household, as the basic unit of consumption, is the maximization of utility. That is, households seek the maximum satisfaction from their expenditures on goods and services. In Chapter 12 we formally model the theory of consumer behavior.

We assume that the primary objective of firms is the maximization of profits, or the difference between total revenues and total costs. In Chapter 6 we derive common decision rules for firms in selecting their profit-maximizing outputs and employments in the short run. The behavior of a firm in setting prices and engaging in nonprice competition, such as advertising, however, depends on the market structure in which the firm operates. In Chapter 7 we address competition among many firms. Here, the perfectly competitive firm is compared with the monopolistically competitive firm. In Chapter 8 we shift to the other extreme where there is only one firm in the market—either on the supply-side as a monopolist (a single seller) or on the demand-side as a monopsonist (a single buyer). Then in Chapter 9 competition among the few is examined with models of duopoly and oligopoly.

In Chapters 10 and 11 the analysis of the firm is extended to long-run decision making, where all the factors of production are variable and the firm seeks the least-cost combinations of factors for producing a selected level of output.

When we study questions of optimizing behavior, such as profit maximization by firms and utility maximization by households, the mathematical technique of differentiation is used. Thus, in this first chapter in Part II, we start with an overview of unconstrained optimization for functions of one independent variable. Understanding the calculus of functions of one variable is important for our work with a firm's short run cost and revenue curves. In particular, the derivation of the firm's short-run decision rules for profit maximization are illustrated graphically using these curves. Chapter 6 concludes with a discussion of implicit functions, a concept that significantly expands our ability to do comparative statics. Then, in the following chapters, parallel with our analysis of more complex market structures, will be a progression to more advanced mathematics, including unconstrained optimization for functions with two or more independent variables and constrained optimization.

UNCONSTRAINED OPTIMIZATION FOR FUNCTIONS WITH ONE INDEPENDENT VARIABLE

With optimization, we seek a *goal equilibrium*, or an equilibrium that is desirable. An *objective function* specifies the relationship between the dependent variable of interest, say y, whose value is to be optimized (i.e., minimized or maximized), and the independent variable(s), also known as the *choice variable(s)* or *decision variable(s)*, that can be altered to achieve the desired optimum.

An objective function with one independent variable, say x, can be written in general form as $y = f(x)$. Examples of linear, quadratic (including a squared term for the independent variable), and cubic (including a term where the independent variable is raised to the third power) functions are illustrated in Figure 6.1. In these graphs, the objective functions illustrated are differentiable. Recall, this means that the functions are smooth (no sharp points in the graphs of the functions) and continuous (no breaks in the graphs of the functions).

For these functions depicted, the domain of the independent variable, x, is all real numbers. In Figures 6.1b, 6.1d, and 6.1e, the range for y is also all real numbers. For the constant function in Figure 6.1a, the range of y is restricted to one value, a_0. For the quadratic function in Figure 6.1c, the range is $y \geq a_0$.

Recall that an inverse function would exist if there were one-to-one relationships between the values of the independent variable in the domain and the values of the dependent variable in the range of the original function. Referring back to Figure 6.1, unless the domain of the variable x were restricted (for example, $x \leq a_2$ for the quadratic in Figure 6.1c, or $x \geq 0$ for the cubic in Figure 6.1e), an inverse function would only exist for the linear function, $y = a_0 + a_1 x$ (in Figure 6.1b) and the cubic function (illustrated in Figure 6.1d).

Note the two examples of cubic functions. In Figure 6.1d, the cubic function is monotonic, here y is directly related to x (since $a_1 > 0$). In contrast, the cubic function in Figure 6.1e is not monotonic, but changes direction twice: positively sloped for $x < x_m$; negatively sloped between $x_m < x < x_n$; and then positively sloped for $x > x_n$. The difference between the two cubic functions is that the monotonic function (in Figure 6.1d) can be written $y = a_0 + a_1(x - a_2)^3$. The function illustrated in Figure 6.1e, however, is not similarly factorable, and assumes the general form, $y = a_0 + a_1x + a_2x^2 + a_3x^3$, where a_2 and a_3 have opposite signs (here $a_2 < 0$ and $a_3 > 0$).

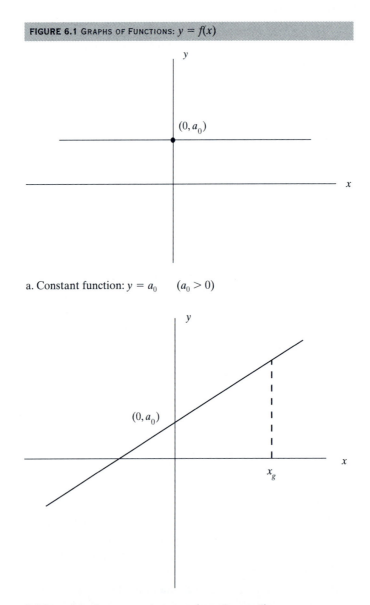

FIGURE 6.1 GRAPHS OF FUNCTIONS: $y = f(x)$

a. Constant function: $y = a_0$ $(a_0 > 0)$

b. Linear function: $y = a_0 + a_1x$ $(a_0 > 0, a_1 > 0)$

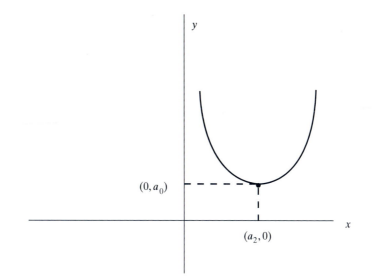

c. Quadratic function: $y = a_0 + a_1(x - a_2)^2$ $(a_0 > 0, a_1 > 0, a_2 > 0)$

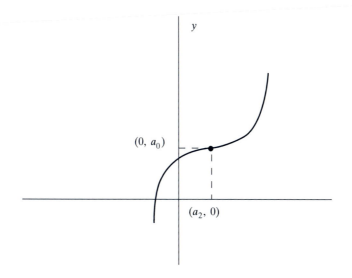

d. Cubic function: $y = a_0 + a_1(x - a_2)^3$ $(a_0 > 0, a_1 > 0, a_2 > 0)$

FIGURE 6.1 (CONTINUED)

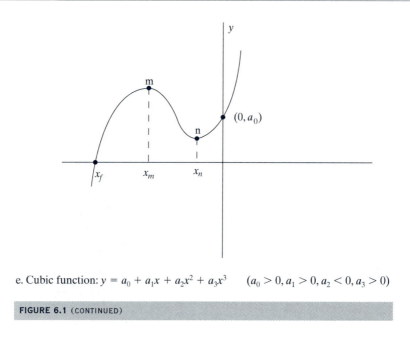

e. Cubic function: $y = a_0 + a_1x + a_2x^2 + a_3x^3$ $(a_0 > 0, a_1 > 0, a_2 < 0, a_3 > 0)$

FIGURE 6.1 (CONTINUED)

RELATIVE EXTREMA

A *relative extremum* is found when the dependent variable achieves a maximum or minimum value over any open subset (that is, not inclusive of the endpoints) of the domain of the independent variable, say for x defined over $x_g < x < x_h$. An *absolute extremum* is found when the dependent variable achieves a maximum or minimum value over the entire domain of the independent variable (inclusive of the endpoints), for example, for x defined over all real numbers, or for x defined over a closed subset of real numbers, $x_g \le x \le x_h$. A relative extremum may also be, but is not necessarily, an absolute extremum. In Figure 6.1c, the relative minimum occurring at the point (a_2, a_0) is also an absolute minimum. Unless the domain were restricted, there is no absolute maximum for this quadratic function.

In Figure 6.1e, there is a relative maximum, (at the point labeled m) and a relative minimum (at the point labeled n), but neither is an absolute maximum or minimum unless the domain of x were limited. For example, for this cubic function, if the domain of x were limited to nonpositive real numbers greater than x_f, $x_f \le x \le 0$, then the absolute maximum would occur at the point labeled m (here also a relative maximum), and the absolute minimum would occur at the point $(x_f, 0)$. Other restrictions on the domain could yield other absolute maxima.

Similarly, for the linear function depicted in Figure 6.1b, there are no extrema unless the domain of the function is limited. For example, if $0 \le x \le x_g$, the absolute minimum occurs where $x = 0$, and the absolute maximum is where $x = x_g$. Finally, for the constant function shown in Figure 6.1a, there are no extrema—relative or absolute—even when the domain of the independent variable is restricted.

Graphically, we can see that a necessary condition for relative extrema to occur is when the slope of the function equals zero (figuratively, at the top of a two-dimensional hill for a maximum and at the bottom of a two-dimensional valley for a minimum). Mathematically, when the slope equals zero, the *first derivative* of the function evaluated at that point equals zero. Thus, to find the relative extrema of a function, also known as the *critical points*, we set the first derivative equal to zero and solve for the critical values of the independent variable.

Note, if the slope of a function is zero at a particular point, that point need not be a critical point. Consider any point in the domain of the constant function, $y = a_0$. In Figure 6.1d, the cubic function, $y = a_0 + a_1(x - a_2)^3$, has a slope equal to zero at $x = a_2$, but (a_2, a_0) is not a critical point.[1]

Formally, given a function, $y = f(x)$ and its first derivative, $dy/dx = f'(x)$, a necessary, but not a sufficient, condition for a relative extremum at a point in the domain of the function, x_0, is that the first derivative of the function, evaluated at this critical value of x, is equal to zero, that is, $f'(x_0) = 0$. This is the *first-order condition* for a relative extremum.

Graphing Nonlinear Functions   Often we can use this first-order condition to aid in the graphing of nonlinear functions. Consider the cubic function, $y = -2x^3 + 9x^2 - 12x + 12$. Taking the first derivative and setting it equal to zero gives: $dy/dx = f'(x) = -6x^2 + 18x - 12 = 0$. Solving for the critical values of x, we have:

$$-x^2 + 3x - 2 = 0$$

$$(-x + 1)(x - 2) = 0$$

so, $x = 1, 2$. Thus, it appears that we have two critical points, where $x = 1$ and $x = 2$, since the first derivative of the function evaluated at these points equals zero; $f'(1) = 0$ and $f'(2) = 0$. The coordinates of the critical points are found by substituting these values of x back into the original function, $y = f(x)$.

$$f(1) = -2(1)^3 + 9(1)^2 - 12(1) + 12 = 7$$

$$f(2) = -2(2)^3 + 9(2)^2 - 12(2) + 12 = 8$$

Graphically, we know that the slope of the curve equals zero at the points (1,7) and (2,8). Finding the coordinates for only two more points could give us a rough sketch of the function.

For a value of x less than the first critical value, $(x = 1)$, we could take the y-intercept, which can be found easily enough by setting x equal to zero: $f(0) = 12$. For a value of x greater than the second critical value, $(x = 2)$, we select $x = 3$, and find $f(3) = -2(3)^3 + 9(3)^2 - 12(3) + 12 = 3$. Plotting the four ordered pairs, (0,12), (1,7),

---

[1] Actually, the point (a_2, a_0) represents an inflection point, which will be formally defined later in the chapter.

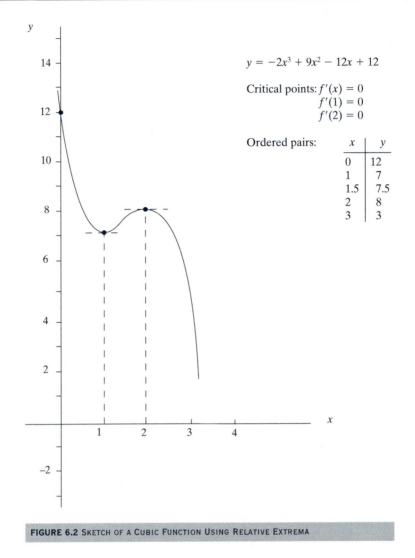

$$y = -2x^3 + 9x^2 - 12x + 12$$

Critical points: $f'(x) = 0$
$f'(1) = 0$
$f'(2) = 0$

Ordered pairs:

x	y
0	12
1	7
1.5	7.5
2	8
3	3

FIGURE 6.2 SKETCH OF A CUBIC FUNCTION USING RELATIVE EXTREMA

(2,8), and (3,3), allows us to sketch the curve, as shown in Figure 6.2. We can clearly see that the function achieves a relative minimum when $x = 1$, at the point (1,7), and a relative maximum when $x = 2$, at the point (2,8). For a domain of all real numbers, this function has no absolute minimum or absolute maximum.

Concavity and Convexity   While the first derivative measures the rate of change of a function, or the slope of a function, the *second derivative* gives the curvature of the function, or the rate of change of the slope of the function. For the general function, $y = f(x)$, the second derivative can be denoted by

$$\frac{d(dy/dx)}{dx} = \frac{d^2y}{dx^2} = f''(x)$$

For a linear function, the second derivative is zero, since the slope of the function is constant. In Figure 6.3, we illustrate the four cases for nonlinear, monotonically increasing or decreasing, functions.

If the second derivative is positive, then the slope is increasing as x, the independent variable, increases in value. Here, either a positive slope is becoming steeper, that is, more positive, (as in Figure 6.3a), or a negative slope is becoming flatter, that is, less negative (as in Figure 6.3c). If the second derivative is always positive, then the function is said to be *strictly convex*. Graphically, a line segment between any two points on a strictly convex curve would lie entirely above the portion of the curve connecting those two points.

If the second derivative is negative, then the slope is decreasing as x, the independent variable, increases in value. Here, either a positive slope is becoming flatter, that is, less positive, (as in Figure 6.3b), or a negative slope is becoming steeper, that is, more negative, (as in Figure 6.3d). If the second derivative is always negative, then the function is said to be *strictly concave*. Graphically, a line segment between any two points on a strictly concave curve would lie entirely below the portion of the curve connecting these two points.

If we relax these conditions and allow for weak inequalities, we can see that strictly convex and strictly concave functions are subsets of convex and concave functions, respectively. That is, given the function, $y = f(x)$, if the second derivative is nonnegative, $f''(x) \geq 0$, then the function is *convex*. The slope of a convex function is not decreasing. A line segment between any two points on the curve would either lie above or coincide with the curve. A convex curve can contain linear segments. See Figure 6.4a. The convex curve extending through points M and N′ contains a linear segment on which points M and N lie. Thus, a line segment connecting points M and N coincides with the curve. A line segment between points M and N′ (or between N and N′) lies above the portion of the curve between these points.

For a *concave* function, $y = f(x)$, the second derivative is nonpositive, $f''(x) \leq 0$. The slope of a concave function is not increasing. A line segment between any two points on the curve would either lie below or coincide with the curve between these points. A concave function can also contain linear segments. See Figure 6.4b. The concave curve extending through points R and S′ contains a linear segment on which points R and S lie. Thus, a line segment connecting points R and S coincides with the curve. A line segment between points R and S′ (or between points S and S′) lies below the curve.

Note that since either a concave or convex curve can contain linear segments, a straight line can be considered to be both concave and convex. Formally, given $y = f(x) = ax$, then $dy/dx = f'(x) = a$, and $d^2y/dx^2 = f''(x) = 0$. The zero second derivative satisfies the weak inequality conditions for both concavity and convexity.

To establish the type of relative extremum, we check the second derivative evaluated at the critical point in question. Given a function, $y = f(x)$, and a critical point at x_0, where $f'(x_0) = 0$, if the second derivative of the function evaluated at x_0 is negative, $f''(x_0) < 0$, then that critical point is a relative maximum. Graphically, for any infini-

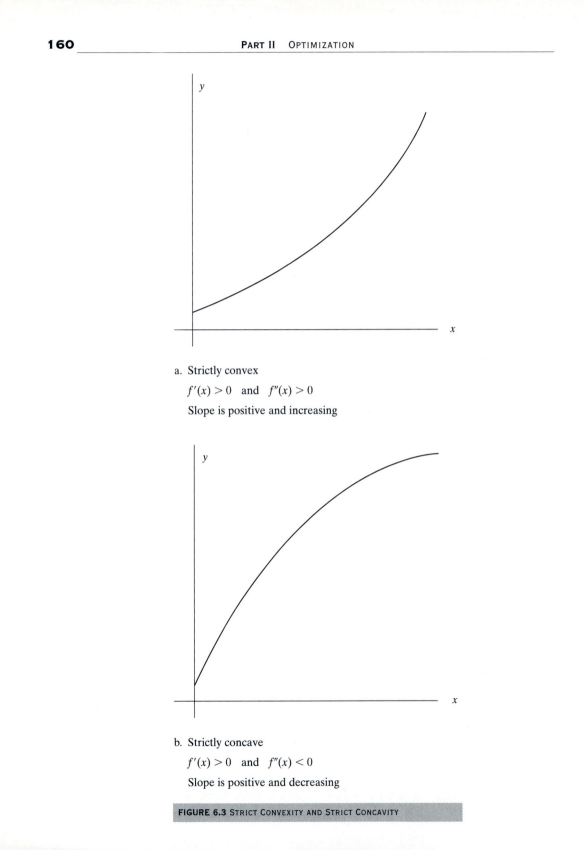

a. Strictly convex

$f'(x) > 0$ and $f''(x) > 0$

Slope is positive and increasing

b. Strictly concave

$f'(x) > 0$ and $f''(x) < 0$

Slope is positive and decreasing

FIGURE 6.3 STRICT CONVEXITY AND STRICT CONCAVITY

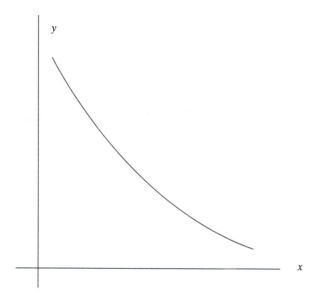

c. Strictly convex

$f'(x) < 0$ and $f''(x) > 0$

Slope is negative and increasing

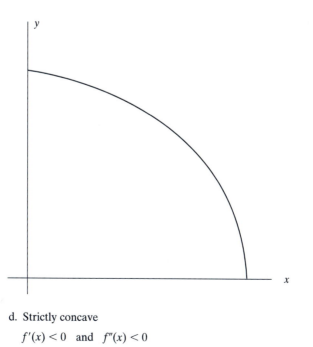

d. Strictly concave

$f'(x) < 0$ and $f''(x) < 0$

Slope is negative and decreasing

FIGURE 6.3 (CONTINUED)

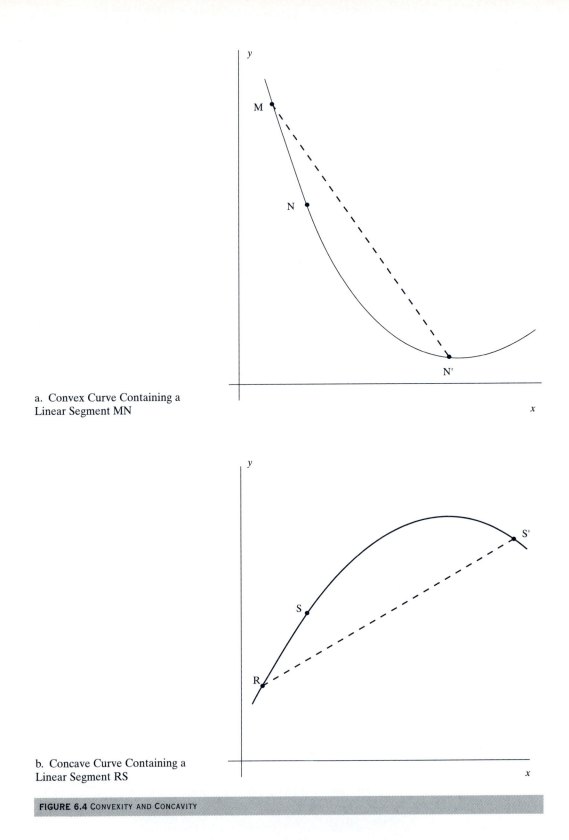

a. Convex Curve Containing a
Linear Segment MN

b. Concave Curve Containing a
Linear Segment RS

FIGURE 6.4 CONVEXITY AND CONCAVITY

tesimal positive (negative) change in x from x_0, the slope of the function is decreasing (increasing) from zero. Thus, in either case, the ratio $d(dy/dx)/dx$ is negative. Visually, picture the top of a hill on a roller coaster.

If the second derivative evaluated at the critical point, x_0, is positive, $f''(x_0) > 0$, then we have a relative minimum. For any infinitesimal positive (negative) change in x from x_0, the slope of the function is increasing (decreasing) from zero. Picture the bottom of a dip on a roller coaster.

For the function, $y = -2x^3 + 9x^2 - 12x + 12$, setting the first derivative equal to zero and solving for x identifies the critical points at $x = 1$ and $x = 2$.

$$f'(x) = -6x^2 + 18x - 12 = 0 \quad \text{and} \quad f'(1) = 0, f'(2) = 0.$$

Evaluating the second derivative at the critical points establishes the types of relative extrema.

$$f''(x) = -12x + 18$$

and

$$f''(1) = -12(1) + 18 = 6 > 0, \text{ so at } x = 1, \text{ there is a relative minimum: } f(1) = 7$$

$$f''(2) = -12(2) + 18 = -6 < 0, \text{ so at } x = 2, \text{ there is a relative maximum: } f(2) = 8.$$

Inflection Points   An *inflection point* occurs where the second derivative of a function changes sign. Graphically, at an inflection point, the curvature changes from strictly convex to strictly concave (the second derivative changes from positive to negative) or the curvature changes from strictly concave to strictly convex (the second derivative changes from negative to positive). It follows that the second derivative evaluated at an inflection point, say x_i, equals zero: $f''(x_i) = 0$. Note that the slope of a function at an inflection point does not need to equal zero. Refer to Figure 6.5 for illustrations of inflection points.

In Figure 6.5a, point P is an inflection point: to the left of point P, the curve is strictly convex ($f''(x) \geq 0$); and to the right of point P, the curve is strictly concave ($f''(x) \leq 0$). We can see that for a line segment through the inflection point P that connects the points M and N on the curve, the line segment MP lies above the curve and the line segment PN lies below the curve.

In Figure 6.5b, the point T is an inflection point. To the left of point T, the curve is strictly concave ($f''(x) < 0$); and to the right of point T, the curve is strictly convex ($f''(x) > 0$). For the line segment RS passing through point T, the line segment RT lies below the curve between R and T; and the line segment TS lies above the curve between T and S.

Note that the second derivative evaluated at a point, say x_i, equaling zero is a necessary, but not a sufficient, condition for an inflection point. The second derivative can equal zero at points on a curve that are not inflection points. In addition to the linear function, $y = a_0 + a_1 x$, where the second derivative is zero for all x, an example would be the function $y = x^4$. (The graph of $y = x^4$ is a parabola with a relative and absolute

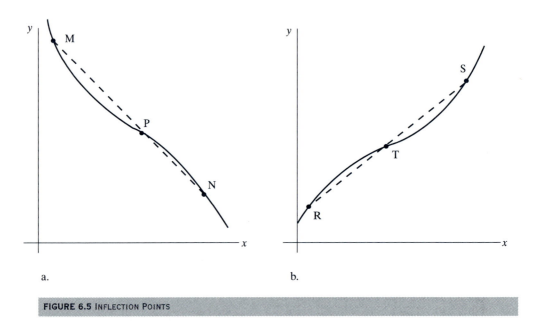

a.   b.

FIGURE 6.5 INFLECTION POINTS

minimum at the origin.) Here $f'(x) = 4x^3$; $f''(x) = 12x^2$, and $f''(0) = 0$, implying that there may be an inflection point at $x = 0$. A sufficient condition for an inflection point to occur at x_i, given that $f''(x_i) = 0$, is that the third derivative, $f'''(x)$, evaluated at that point is not equal to zero: $f'''(x_i) \neq 0$. For $y = x^4$, we have $f'''(0) = 24x$ and evaluated at the point where $x = 0, f'''(0) = 0$. Thus, there is no inflection point at $x = 0$ for the function $y = x^4$. As an exercise, determine whether the function, $y = -x^3$, has an inflection point at the origin.

Return once again to the function, $y = -2x^3 + 9x^2 - 12x + 12$, sketched in Figure 6.2. With a relative minimum at $x = 1$ and a relative maximum at $x = 2$, we know there is an inflection point—since in the neighborhood of the relative minimum (i.e., the graph of the function in the area immediately surrounding this point) the curve is strictly convex; and in the neighborhood of the relative maximum, the curve is strictly concave. To determine where the inflection point is, we set the second derivative equal to zero and solve for x.

$$f'(x) = -6x^2 + 18x - 12$$

$$f''(x) = -12x + 18 = 0, \text{ and } x = 1.5, \text{ since } f''(1.5) = 0.$$

For $x = 1.5$, the value of the function is $f(1.5) = -2(1.5)^3 + 9(1.5)^2 - 12(1.5) + 12 = 7.5$. To confirm that the point $(1.5, 7.5)$ is indeed an inflection point, we apply the third derivative test: $f'''(1.5) = -12 \neq 0$. Thus, the function does have an inflection point where $x = 1.5$. Note, you can confirm that the slope of the function at the inflection point, $x = 1.5$, is not equal to zero.

In sum, for a differentiable function, $y = f(x)$: the necessary first order condition to establish a critical point at $x = x_0$ is that $f'(x_0) = 0$. The second-order condition to establish the type of relative extremum is that $f''(x_0) > 0$, for a relative minimum, and $f''(x_0) < 0$, for a relative maximum.

PRACTICE PROBLEM 6.1

For each of the following functions, find the critical points and determine whether the critical points are relative minima or relative maxima. Identify any inflection points that may exist.

a) $y = x^2 - 1$ b) $y = x^3 - 3x^2 - 24x + 12$ c) $y = -x^3 + 7.5x^2 - 12x - 4$
d) $y = x^3 - 1$ e) $y = -(x - 1)^3 + 4$

(The answers are at the end of the chapter.)

SHORT-RUN PRODUCT AND COST CURVES

As stated at the outset of this chapter, the firm's primary objective is to maximize its profits. The profits of a firm are equal to the difference between its total revenues and total costs. So, we begin the analysis of the firm by illustrating the properties of the short-run revenue and cost curves. We proceed to derive the decision rule for a firm's selection of the profit-maximizing level of output in the short run.

In the **short run,** at least one factor of production is fixed—in the sense that a set amount of that factor is available to the firm for use in production. The basic two-factor production function for a firm can be written as $Q = Q(K, L)$ where

$$Q = \text{output of the firm over the period}$$

$$K = \text{physical capital stock of the firm over the period}$$

$$L = \text{labor employed by the firm over the period.}$$

Typically, physical capital is assumed to be the fixed factor and labor assumed to be the variable factor of production. That is, in the short run, the firm has a given amount of plant, equipment, and machinery on hand, and to vary its output, the firm adjusts the amount of labor it uses.

LABOR PRODUCTIVITY

Two measures of labor productivity are commonly used. The **average product of labor,** AP_L, is the ouput per unit of labor and is given by the ratio of output to labor, $AP_L = Q/L$. The **marginal product of labor,** MP_L, is the change in output associated with a change in labor, $MP_L = \Delta Q/\Delta L$. For infinitesimal changes in labor, the marginal product of labor is given by the derivative, $MP_L = dQ/dL$.

For a given capital stock, output varies directly, but not necessarily proportionally, with the employment of labor. Indeed, initially we might find the marginal and average products of labor increasing as more labor is employed and the firm realizes effi-ciencies in the utilization of the given capital stock. That is, as labor is added, there may be increasing gains in output from the division of labor. Eventually, the **law of diminishing returns** would kick in and the marginal product of labor would decrease as more labor is used. Here, the spreading of the capital stock over more labor diminishes the gains in output achieved with each unit increase in labor. In any case, a profit-maximizing firm would not use additional labor if the marginal product of labor were zero (additional output were not produced) or if the marginal product of labor were negative (the production of output began to decline).

Figure 6.6a, a short-run production function with this hypothesized relationship between output and labor is illustrated. To remind us that the production function is drawn for a given physical capital stock, we write the capital variable with a subscript, "0". The slope of the short-run production function is given by the marginal product of labor. As labor increases up to L_a, the MP_L is rising. Each additional unit of labor is increasingly adding to the output produced—as the labor is allocated such that the existing capital stock is being used more productively. Beyond L_a, the MP_L is declin-ing. Now, the gains in output with each additional unit of labor are diminishing. It fol-lows that the MP_L is maximized at the level of employment corresponding to L_a, the point at which diminishing returns to labor begin.

Put differently, the short-run production function of the firm is strictly convex up to the point, L_a, $dMP_L/dL = d^2Q/dL^2 > 0$; after which the short-run production func-tion is strictly concave, $dMP_L/dL < 0$. At the quantity of labor of L_a, there is an inflec-tion point in the short-run production function.

Graphically, the average product of labor can be found by taking the slope of a ray from the origin to the curve of the short-run production function. The AP_L is maxi-mized when it equals the MP_L, here at the level of employment, L_b, where a ray from the origin is tangent to the curve. See point B in Figure 6.6a.

Figure 6.6b illustrates the associated marginal and average product of labor curves. For employment between L_a and L_b, the AP_L is rising even though the MP_L is declin-ing. The AP_L will increase with labor as long as the marginal product of labor is greater than the average product of labor. Beyond L_b, $MP_L < AP_L$, so the AP_L is decreasing.

Consider a simple numerical example of a short-run production function, given by $Q = 72L + 15L^2 - L^3$, and illustrated in Table 6.1, with a partial listing of the units of labor (L) and the associated units of output (Q). Note, the units of output may be thou-sands per day, and the units of labor may be thousands of workers per day. Conditional on the given physical capital stock (K_0) and the technology defining this short-run pro-duction function, the associated marginal and average product of labor schedules are: $MP_L = 72 + 30L - 3L^2$ and $AP_L = 72 + 15L - L^2$. The maximum MP_L and AP_L occur at 5 units and 7.5 units of labor, respectively.

Diminishing returns to labor set in after the fifth unit of labor, since the MP_L declines from 147.00 to 146.97 additional units of output. Although the MP_L is declin-ing, as long as the MP_L exceeds the AP_L, the AP_L will be rising—here until the 7.5th unit of labor. When the MP_L is less than the AP_L (after the 7.5th unit of labor), the AP_L

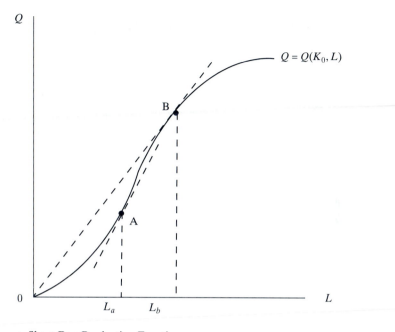

a. Short-Run Production Function

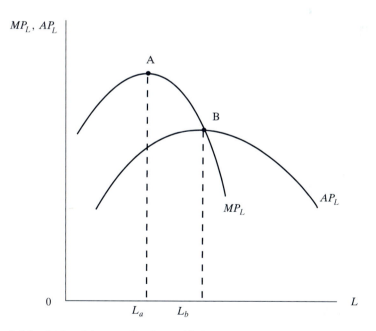

b. Marginal and Average Products of Labor

FIGURE 6.6 SHORT-RUN PRODUCTION FUNCTION AND PRODUCT CURVES FOR A FIRM

TABLE 6.1	Selected Combinations of Labor and Output for $Q = 72L + 15L^2 - L^3$		
L *(units)*	**Q** *(units)*	**AP_L** *(Q/L)*	**MP_L** *($\Delta Q/\Delta L$)*
.	.	.	.
.	.	.	.
.	.	.	.
4.8	580.608	120.96	146.88
4.9	595.301	121.49	146.97
5.0	610.000	122.00	147.00
5.1	624.699	122.49	146.97
.	.	.	.
.	.	.	.
7.4	948.976	128.24	129.72
7.5	961.875	128.25	128.25
7.6	974.624	128.24	126.72
.	.	.	.

begins to decline. At the 7.5th unit of labor, the AP_L is maximized and equal to the MP_L of 128.25 units of output.

This relationship between marginal and average is general, and applies to other variables besides labor productivity. That is, whenever the marginal exceeds the average, the average will rise. Whenever the marginal is less than the average, the average will fall.

An increase in the capital stock or technological progress that enhances the productivity of labor would rotate the short-run production function in a counterclockwise fashion from the origin and shift upward the MP_L and AP_L curves. That is, with more physical capital or improved technology, each unit of labor should be able to produce more output. As we will see, the product functions for the firm are important for generating its revenue and cost functions.

PRACTICE PROBLEM 6.2

Given the short-run production function, $Q = 30L + 6L^2 - .1L^3$:
a) Find the level of employment where diminishing returns to labor begin.
b) Find the level of employment where the average product of labor (AP_L) is maximized. What is the maximum value of the AP_L?

(The answers are at the end of the chapter.)

SHORT-RUN COSTS

Given the unit prices of capital and labor, we can derive the firm's short-run cost curves from its short-run production function. First, we need to identify the types of short-run costs.

The **short-run total costs** (*STC*) of a firm can be divided into the **total variable costs** (*TVC*) and the **total fixed costs** (*TFC*). Let the wage rate paid by the firm, w, represent the user cost of a unit of labor to the firm. The rental rate, r, represents the user cost of a unit of physical capital to the firm. The total variable costs are the costs associated with the variable factor(s) of production. Here, with labor as the variable factor, $TVC = wL$. The total fixed costs are the costs associated with the fixed factor(s) of production. Here, $TFC = rK_0$. Short-run total costs are the sum: $STC = TVC + TFC$.

In Figure 6.7a, we sketch the total cost curves. Unlike the product curves, where output is measured on the vertical axis and labor on the horizontal axis; for the cost curves, output is on the horizontal axis and costs, measured in dollars or some other monetary unit, are on the vertical axis. These cost curves reflect the short-run production function and are drawn for a given physical capital stock, technology, and user costs of labor and capital.

Total fixed costs (TFC) are constant and do not vary with output. Total variable costs (TVC) rise with output, initially at a diminishing rate, up to the output Q_a, and then at an increasing rate. The same holds for the short-run total cost curve, STC, which can be found graphically by vertically adding the TFC curve to the TVC curve.

The **marginal cost** of production, MC, is the change in the total costs associated with a change in output. For discrete changes in output, $MC = \Delta STC/\Delta Q = \Delta TVC/\Delta Q$. For infinitesimal changes in output, $MC = dSTC/dQ = dTVC/dQ$. Graphically, the slope of the STC and TVC curves is given by the marginal cost. In Figure 6.7b, we illustrate the MC curve. For outputs up to Q_a, the marginal cost is declining; correspondingly, the STC and TVC curves are strictly concave. As output rises beyond Q_a, the marginal cost is increasing, and the STC and TVC curves are strictly convex. The minimum of the MC curve occurs at Q_a, the output associated with the inflection points of the TVC and STC curves.

From the total costs we can find the average costs by dividing by output. The average fixed cost, AFC, equals the total fixed cost per unit of ouput: $AFC = TFC/Q$. Similarly, average variable cost, AVC, is total variable cost per unit of output: $AVC = TVC/Q$. Average total cost, ATC, can be found either by dividing total cost by output (STC/Q), or by adding average fixed cost and average variable cost: $ATC = AFC + AVC$.

Graphically, to derive average variable cost or average total cost, we find the slopes of rays from the origin to the total variable cost curve or short-run total cost curve, respectively. At the output where a ray from the origin is tangent to the total variable cost curve (short-run total cost curve), the marginal cost equals the average variable cost (average total cost).

The average cost curves are illustrated in Figure 6.7b. We can see that $MC = AVC$ at Q_b and $MC = ATC$ at Q_c. The marginal cost curve cuts the average variable and average total cost curves at their respective minimums. The minimum of the short run average total cost curve corresponds to the **capacity output** of the firm. Note, here the capacity output does not connote an upper limit on production, rather it identifies the output with the minimum average total cost.

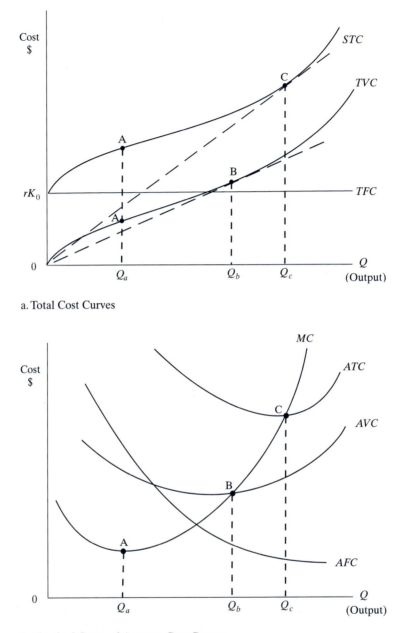

a. Total Cost Curves

b. Marginal Cost and Average Cost Curves

FIGURE 6.7 SHORT-RUN COST CURVES OF THE FIRM

Average fixed cost declines with output, as the firm spreads its constant fixed costs over a rising output. Indeed, the AFC curve is a *rectangular hyperbola*. The rectangular areas formed by dropping perpendiculars from any point on the AFC curve to the axes are equal and given by the total fixed cost: $TFC = (AFC) \cdot (Q)$.

Graphically, the distance between the ATC and AVC curves is given by the AFC. The AVC curve will be decreasing as long as the $MC < AVC$ (up to the output Q_b in Figure 6.7b). Similarly, the ATC is decreasing as long as the $MC < ATC$ (up to the output Q_c). For outputs between the minimums of the AVC and ATC curves, $Q_b < Q < Q_c$, the declining AFC dominates the rising AVC, so the ATC continues to fall. The ATC curve rises with output beyond Q_c, the capacity output of the firm.

The Marginal Product of Labor and the Marginal Cost of Output   We can relate the marginal cost of output to the marginal product of labor for the firm as follows. The marginal cost is the ratio of the change in total variable cost to the change in output, $MC = \Delta TVC/\Delta Q$. The change in total variable cost is given by the product of the user cost of labor, w, and the change in labor, $\Delta TVC = w\Delta L$. (*Note:* We are assuming here that the user cost of labor is constant and exogenous to the firm.) Thus, the MC is equal to the ratio of the user cost of labor to the marginal product of labor. $MC = w\Delta L/\Delta Q = w/MP_L$.

Thus, for a given user cost of labor, when the marginal product of labor is rising (up to L_a in Figure 6.6b), the marginal cost of output is falling (up to the output Q_a in Figure 6.7b). The output where the MC is minimized corresponds to the employment of labor where the MP_L is maximized, $Q_a = Q(K_0, L_a)$. As the MP_L declines with diminishing returns to labor, the MC of output rises.

To illustrate, we can extend Table 6.1 and add variable and marginal costs to the hypothetical short-run production function illustrated. Assume that the wage rate is $100 per unit of labor ($w = \$100$). Three columns, representing the total variable cost (TVC), average variable cost (AVC), and marginal cost (MC) are added.

We see that the minimum marginal cost ($MC = \$.6803 = 100/147.00$) occurs at the output ($Q = 610.000$) where the marginal product of labor reaches a maximum ($MP_L = 147.00$ units of output). As the marginal product of labor begins to decline, then for a given user cost of labor, the marginal cost of output will begin to rise.

Similarly, the average variable cost (AVC) is inversely related to the average product of labor (AP_L). $AVC = TVC/Q = w \cdot L/Q = w/AP_L$. Consequently, for a given user cost of labor, the average variable cost of output will be declining as long as the average product of labor is rising. The minimum of the average variable cost will occur at an output (see Q_b in Figure 6.7b) corresponding to the maximum of the average product of labor (see L_b in Figure 6.6b, where L_b is the amount of labor required in the short run to produce the output, Q_b). As the use of labor is increased beyond L_b, the AP_L declines and the AVC of output rises.

In Table 6.2, the minimum average variable cost ($AVC = \$.7797 = \$100/128.25$) occurs at an output ($Q = 961.875$), where the average product of labor is maximized ($AP_L = 128.25$ units of output). Beyond this output, the average product of labor begins to decline, and the average cost of output begins to rise.

TABLE 6.2 Selected Output and Variable Cost Combinations for $Q = 72L + 15L^2 - L^3$

L (units)	Q (units)	AP_L (Q/L)	MP_L ($\Delta Q/\Delta L$)	TVC (wL)	AVC (TVC/Q = w/AP_L)	MC ($\Delta TVC/\Delta Q = w/MP_L$)
.	.	.	.	.	.	.
.	.	.	.	.	.	.
4.8	580.608	120.96	146.88	$480	$.8267	$.6808
4.9	595.301	121.49	146.97	$490	$.8231	$.6804
5.0	610.000	122.00	147.00	$500	$.8197	$.6803*
5.1	624.699	122.49	146.97	$510	$.8164	$.6804
.	.	.	.	.	.	.
.	.	.	.	.	.	.
7.4	948.976	128.24	129.72	$740	$.7798	$.7709
7.5	961.875	128.25	128.25	$750	$.7797	$.7797
7.6	974.624	128.24	126.72	$760	$.7798	$.7891
.	.	.	.	.	.	.

*The minimum of the MC.

The short-run cost curves, like the short run product curves, are drawn for a given capital stock and technology (reflected in the production function). In addition, the short-run cost curves are conditional on given user costs of labor and capital. For example, an increase in the user cost of labor to the firm, for given marginal and average product of labor curves, would shift up the marginal cost, average variable cost, and average total cost curves.

PRACTICE PROBLEM 6.3

For the short run production function, $Q = 30L + 6L^2 - .1L^3$, and a wage rate of $w = \$15$:
a) Find the level of output where the marginal cost, $MC(Q)$, is minimized.
b) Find the level of output where the average variable cost, $AVC(Q)$, is minimized.
    Determine the minimum value of the $AVC(Q)$.

(The answers are at the end of the chapter.)

SHORT-RUN COST FUNCTIONS

Below we illustrate some general equations for short-run total cost functions. In each case, we derive the associated marginal cost and average cost functions.

A general cubic equation for short-run total costs that exhibits a declining, then increasing marginal cost, such as illustrated in Figure 6.7, can be written as

$$STC = c_3Q^3 - c_2Q^2 + c_1Q + c_0$$

where the parameters c_3, c_2, c_1, and c_0 are positive and Q is the output of the firm. As we will see below, in order for the minimum of the AVC curve to occur at a positive output, the quadratic term, c_2Q^2, in the expression for the cubic short-run total cost curve, STC, should be subtracted.

The marginal and average cost functions associated with the short-run total cost function, $STC = c_3Q^3 - c_2Q^2 + c_1Q + c_0$, are derived as follows:

$$MC = dSTC/dQ = 3c_3Q^2 - 2c_2Q + c_1$$

$$ATC = STC/Q = c_3Q^2 - c_2Q + c_1 + c_0/Q$$

where $AVC = c_3Q^2 - c_2Q + c_1$ and $AFC = c_0/Q$

To ensure that the marginal and average variable costs are positive, consistent with economic theory, additional restrictions must be placed on the positive coefficients c_1, c_2, and c_3. In particular, for the marginal cost curve, given by the equation, $MC = 3c_3Q^2 - 2c_2Q + c_1$, we could use the quadratic formula to find the values of output for which the marginal cost equals zero. Here, $Q = [2c_2 \pm \sqrt{4c_2^2 - 12c_3c_1}]/6c_3$. For a U-shaped marginal cost curve with a positive minimum marginal cost occuring at a positive output, we need for there to be no real roots in the above quadratic equation. (Recall that, the square root of a negative real number is an imaginary number.) In this case, the marginal cost curve would not intersect, but lie entirely above, the quantity axis. Thus, we need for $4c_2^2 - 12c_3c_1 < 0$, or $0 < c_2 < \sqrt{3c_3c_1}$). Given that the minimum of the marginal cost occurs at a lower level of output than the minimum of the average variable cost, and that the rising marginal cost equals the average variable cost at the output where the average variable cost is minimized; the restriction that $0 < c_2 < \sqrt{3c_3c_1}$ is sufficient also to guarantee that the average variable cost (and average total cost) is always positive.

We can easily find the minimums of the marginal and average variable cost curves. $dMC/dQ = 6c_3Q - 2c_2 = 0$, and $Q = c_2/3c_3$ is the output where the marginal cost is minimized, since $d^2MC/dQ^2 = 6c_3 > 0$.

$dAVC/dQ = 2c_3Q - c_2 = 0$, and $Q = c_2/2c_3$ is the output where the average variable cost is minimized, since $d^2AVC/dQ^2 = 2c_3 > 0$.

Determining the minimum of the average total cost curve, however, is more difficult. We would have to solve for the output where the declining slope of the AFC curve (given by $-c_0/Q^2$) just offsets the rising slope of the AVC curve (given by $2c_3Q - c_2$).

We can demonstrate that the marginal cost equals the average variable cost at the minimum of the latter. The marginal cost evaluated at the output where the AVC is minimized is equal to $-c_2^2/4c_3 + c_1 > 0$.

$$MC(c_2/2c_3) = 3c_3(c_2/2c_3)^2 - 2c_2 (c_2/2c_3) + c_1 = -c_2^2/4c_3 + c_1$$

The minimum average variable cost is also equal to $-c_2^2/4c_3 + c_1$.

$$AVC(c_2/2c_3) = c_3 (c_2/2c_3)^2 - c_2 (c_2/2c_3) + c_1 = -c_2^2/4c_3 + c_1.$$

A numerical example may help to illustrate. Assume a short-run total cost curve given by

$$STC = Q^3 - 2Q^2 + 6Q + 10,$$

where Q is the firm's output, measured in hundreds of units per day, and costs are measured in dollars. Note, we can confirm that this cubic cost function has positive marginal costs and average variable costs since the condition $c_2 < \sqrt{3c_3c_1}$ is met: here,

$c_3 = 1, c_2 = 2$, and $c_1 = 6$, so $2 < \sqrt{3(1)(6)} = 4.24$. The associated marginal, average variable, average fixed, and average total cost curves are:

$$MC = 3Q^2 - 4Q + 6$$

$$AVC = Q^2 - 2Q + 6$$

$$AFC = 10/Q$$

$$ATC = Q^2 - 2Q + 6 + 10/Q$$

The minimums of the marginal cost and average variable cost are found at outputs of .67 and 1, respectively.

$$dMC/dQ = 6Q - 4 = 0, \quad \text{and } Q = .67 \text{ (hundred units per day)}$$

$$dAVC/dQ = 2Q - 2 = 0, \quad \text{and } Q = 1.0 \text{ (hundred units per day)}$$

The minimum marginal cost is $4.67.

$$MC(.67) = 3(.67)^2 - 4(.67) + 6 = 4.67$$

The minimum average variable cost is $5.

$$AVC(1) = (1)^2 - 2(1) + 6 = 5$$

Marginal cost equals average variable cost when average variable cost is minimized.

$$MC(1) = 3(1)^2 - 4(1) + 6 = 5 = AVC(1)$$

Quadratic and Linear Short-Run Total Cost Equations   A general equation for a short-run total cost curve where diminishing returns to the variable factor, labor, set in immediately, is given by the quadratic, $STC = c_2Q^2 + c_0$, where c_0 and c_2 are positive parameters. The associated marginal and average cost functions are: $MC = 2c_2Q$; $AVC = c_2Q$; $AFC = c_0/Q$; and $ATC = c_2Q + c_0/Q$.

The quadratic short-run total cost curve is strictly convex, beginning at the level of fixed cost, c_0, and rising with output, with a slope equal to the increasing marginal cost, $2c_2Q$. The marginal and average variable cost curves are linear, with slopes equal to $2c_2$ and c_2, respectively. Figure 6.8 illustrates this situation.

Finally, a very simple, short-run total cost curve is given by the linear equation, $STC = c_1Q + c_0$, where c_0 and c_1 are positive parameters. Here the marginal cost and average variable cost are constant and equal to c_1. $MC = c_1$, $AVC = c_1$, $AFC = c_0/Q$, and $ATC = c_1 + c_0/Q$. In Figure 6.9 the cost curves associated with this linear short-run total cost function are illustrated. Note that the average total cost curve has the same shape as the average fixed cost curve. There are no diminishing returns to the variable factor and there is no capacity output in the case of a linear short run total cost function.

PRACTICE PROBLEMS 6.4 AND 6.5

6.4 For the following short-run total cost functions, find the associated marginal cost (MC), average variable cost (AVC) and average total cost (ATC) functions.

a) $STC(Q) = .2Q^3 - 6Q^2 + 90Q + 100$

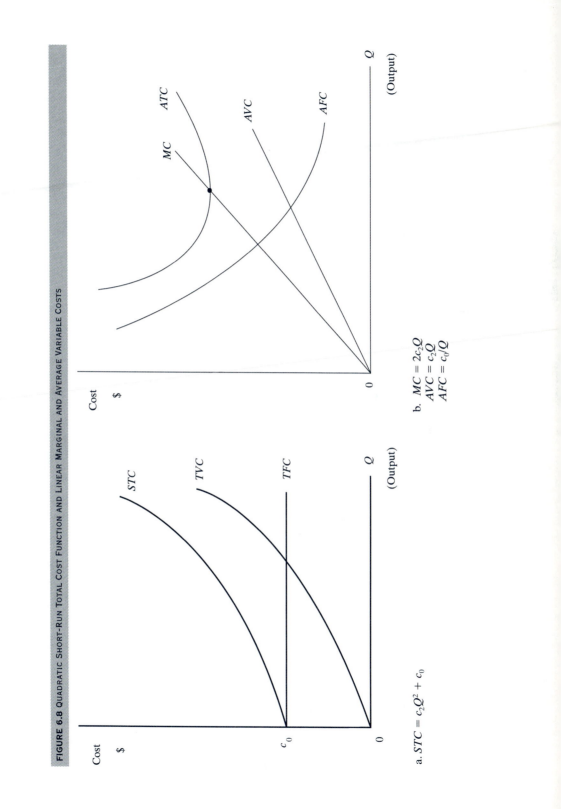

FIGURE 6.8 QUADRATIC SHORT-RUN TOTAL COST FUNCTION AND LINEAR MARGINAL AND AVERAGE VARIABLE COSTS

a. $STC = c_2Q^2 + c_0$

b. $MC = 2c_2Q$
$AVC = c_2Q$
$AFC = c_0/Q$

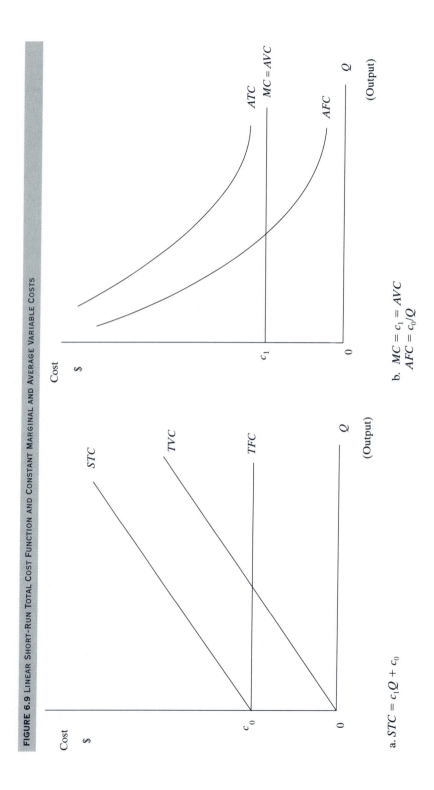

FIGURE 6.9 Linear Short-Run Total Cost Function and Constant Marginal and Average Variable Costs

a. $STC = c_1 Q + c_0$

b. $MC = c_1 = AVC$
$AFC = c_0/Q$

   b) $STC(Q) = Q^2 + 100$
   c) $STC(Q) = 3Q + 100$

6.5 For the short-run total cost function, $STC(Q) = .2Q^3 - 6Q^2 + 90Q + 100$, determine the outputs where the MC and AVC are minimized and find the minimum values for the MC and AVC. Confirm that $MC = AVC$ at the minimum of the AVC.

(The answers are at the end of the chapter.)

SHORT-RUN DECISION RULES FOR A FIRM

In this section we derive the general decision rules in the short run for a firm selecting its profit-maximizing levels of output and employment of the variable factor, presumed to be labor. We will then apply these decision rules to the case of a perfectly competitive firm.

SELECTION OF THE PROFIT-MAXIMIZING OUTPUT

Given a short run production function, $Q = Q(K_0, L)$, the output of the firm, Q, depends on the amount of labor, L, used. The firm's physical capital stock, K, is constant at K_0. The firm's short-run total costs (C) and total revenues (R) are functions of output: $C = C(Q)$, where $dC/dQ = C'(Q) > 0$, and $R = R(Q)$, where $dR/dQ = R'(Q) > 0$. That is, both marginal cost, $MC = C'(Q)$, and marginal revenue, $MR = R'(Q)$, are positive; since producing additional units of output would increase the total cost of the firm, and a profit-maximizing firm would sell additional units of output only if its total revenues increased.

The firm's profits, Π, are equal to the difference between its total revenues and total costs, $\Pi(Q) = R(Q) - C(Q)$. Recall that economists are concerned with **economic profits**, which incorporate, in addition to the accounting costs, the opportunity costs of the owners' funds invested in the firm's physical capital stock (that is, the firm's plant, equipment, and machinery).[2] For example, suppose that the owners of the firm could have earned as much as 8% on their funds if they had invested not in the physical capital of the firm, but in another venture. In calculating economic profits then, we would also deduct from total revenues 8% of the capital invested as part of the total costs. When a firm earns positive (negative) economic profits, its total revenues are greater (less) than its total costs, inclusive of the opportunity costs of the owners' capital invested.

To find the profit-maximizing level of output, we differentiate the profit function with respect to output, set the resulting derivative equal to zero, and solve for the crit-

---

[2]Also incorporated in the calculation of economic profits would be the opportunity cost of the owners' labor. For example, if the owners are also employees of the firm and receive wages, then the difference between the wages that they could have earned if employed elsewhere and the wages received would be subtracted from the accounting profits to obtain the firm's economic profits. We will focus, however, on the opportunity cost of the funds invested in the firm's physical capital.

ical level of output. (*Note:* Here, with no specific functional forms assumed, we cannot solve explicitly for output.) The first-order condition for profit-maximization is:

$$d\Pi/dQ = \Pi'(Q) = dR/dQ - dC/dQ = R'(Q) - C'(Q) = 0$$

or

$$R'(Q) = C'(Q).$$

Thus, to maximize profits, the firm would select the level of output where marginal revenue, $R'(Q)$, equals marginal cost, $C'(Q)$. Intuitively, as long as the next unit of output increases revenues more than costs, $R'(Q) > C'(Q)$, profits would be rising and the firm would continue to increase production and sales. Conversely, the firm would cut back on output if the costs saved exceeded the revenues lost, that is, if $C'(Q) > R'(Q)$. It follows that $MR = MC$ is a necessary condition for profit maximization.

We should check the second-order condition, however, to establish that the relative extremum is indeed a maximum. For a relative maximum we need $\Pi''(Q) < 0$, where

$$\Pi''(Q) = \frac{d(d\Pi/dQ)}{dQ} = \frac{d^2\Pi}{dQ^2} = \frac{d(dR/dQ)}{dQ} - \frac{d(dC/dQ)}{dQ} = \frac{d^2R}{dQ^2} - \frac{d^2C}{dQ^2}$$

$$\Pi''(Q) = R''(Q) - C''(Q) < 0$$

or

$$R''(Q) < C''(Q)$$

In words, for the output, where marginal revenue equals marginal cost, to be a profit-maximizing level of output, the slope of the marginal revenue curve, $d(dR/dQ)/dQ = R''(Q)$, must be less than the slope of the marginal cost curve, $d(dC/dQ)/dQ = C''(Q)$.

Note: As we will demonstrate later, the slope of the marginal revenue curve is either zero (for a perfectly competitive firm) or negative (for a price-setting firm). Therefore, the second order condition will be satisfied if the intersection of the marginal revenue and marginal cost curves occurs on the rising portion of the marginal cost curve. If the intersection occurs on the declining portion of the marginal cost curve, the second-order condition requires that the marginal revenue curve be steeper (more negative) than the marginal cost curve.

Shut-Down Rule   Satisfaction of the first- and second-order conditions will establish the profit-maximizing level of output; however, the associated profits may be negative. That is, the firm may incur economic losses. In the short run, the firm will always have its fixed costs of production, regardless of the level of output produced. If at the profit-maximizing, or in this case, loss-minimizing, level of output, the firm's total variable costs exceed its total revenues, the firm would actually minimize its losses by ceasing production. While producing zero output will not generate any revenues for the firm, the losses would be held to the fixed costs, which would be less than losses equal to the total fixed costs plus the excess of total variable costs over total revenues.

Consider a simple numerical example. Suppose, at the profit-maximizing output of $Q = 50$ units, the firm's price (P) is \$20 per unit and its average variable cost (AVC) is \$22 per unit. Further, suppose that the total fixed costs (TFC) of the firm equal \$300. If the firm produces at $Q = 50$, then its profits are equal to: $\Pi(50) = TR - TVC - TFC = P \cdot Q - AVC \cdot Q - TFC = \$20\,(50) - \$22\,(50) - \$300 = -\$400$. That is, the firm's losses are equal to its total fixed costs of \$300 plus the excess of its total variable costs ($TVC = \$1100$) over its total revenues ($TR = \$1000$). The firm would minimize its losses by shutting down and producing no output in the short run ($Q = 0$). By ceasing production, the firm's losses are reduced to its fixed costs of \$300: $\Pi(0) = TR - TVC - TFC = 0 - 0 - \$300 = -\$300$.

Therefore, to the firm's decision rules for the profit-maximizing level of output (produce where $MR = MC$, provided that the slope of the MR curve is less than the slope of the MC curve), we add a **shut-down rule**. To minimize its losses, a firm would cease production in the short run, if, at the loss-minimizing level of output, total variable costs are greater than total revenues. Stated differently, a profit-maximizing firm would produce in the short run only if its total revenues exceed its total variable costs.

Note that by dividing total revenues and total variable costs by the output of the firm, we obtain average revenue, $AR = R/Q$, and average variable cost, $AVC = TVC/Q$. Since average revenue is equal to the unit price charged by the firm, $AR = R/Q = (P \cdot Q)/Q = P$, the shut-down rule can also be expressed as follows: A profit-maximizing firm would cease production in the short run if the unit price of its output (P) were less than its average variable cost of production (AVC).

To illustrate the determination of the profit-maximizing level of output with a numerical example, assume that a firm's total revenue and short-run total cost functions are, respectively:

$$R(Q) = 15Q - (1/2)Q^2 \quad \text{and} \quad STC(Q) = Q^3 - 13.5Q^2 + 50Q + 40$$

The profit function is: $\Pi(Q) = R(Q) - STC(Q)$

$$= 15Q - (1/2)Q^2 - (Q^3 - 13.5Q^2 + 50Q + 40)$$

$$= -Q^3 + 13Q^2 - 35Q - 40$$

To find the profit-maximizing output, we differentiate the profit function with respect to output, set the result equal to zero, and solve for the critical levels of output. That is, we are finding the critical point or points of the objective function.

$$d\Pi(Q)/dQ = -3Q^2 + 26Q - 35 = 0$$

$$(-3Q + 5)(Q - 7) = 0$$

$$Q = 5/3, 7$$

The critical outputs are $Q = 5/3$ and $Q = 7$.

Note that we could have also solved for the output levels using the quadratic formula. From $-3Q^2 + 26Q - 35 = 0$, we have

$$Q = \frac{-26 \pm \sqrt{(26)^2 - 4(-3)(-35)}}{2(-3)} = \frac{-26 \pm 16}{-6} = 5/3, 7$$

Also, we could have directly applied the short-run decision rule for the profit-maximizing level of output by setting marginal revenue (*MR*) equal to marginal cost (*MC*) and solving for output.

Differentiating the total revenue function with respect to output gives the marginal revenue function: $dR(Q)/dQ = MR(Q) = 15 - Q$.

Differentiating the short-run total cost function with respect to output gives the marginal cost function: $dSTC(Q)/dQ = MC(Q) = 3Q^2 - 27Q + 50$.

Setting $MR = MC$, we have: $15 - Q = 3Q^2 - 27Q + 50$ or $-3Q^2 + 26Q - 35 = 0$, which is the same objective function that we derived above.

Continuing, with two levels of output satisfying the first-order condition for profit maximization, we need to check the second-order conditions to determine which critical point constitutes the maximum. Differentiating the profit function a second time with respect to output,

$$d^2\Pi(Q)/dQ^2 = \frac{d(d\Pi/dQ)}{dQ} = \Pi''(Q) = -6Q + 26$$

Evaluating the second-order derivative at the critical outputs, we find:

$$\Pi''(5/3) = -6(5/3) + 26 = 16 > 0 \text{ (relative minimum)}$$

$$\Pi''(7) = -6(7) + 26 = -16 < 0 \text{ (relative maximum)}$$

Thus, $\overline{Q} = 7$ is the profit-maximizing level of output, yielding a level of profits of 9:

$$\Pi(7) = -(7)^3 + 13(7)^2 - 35(7) - 40 = -343 + 637 - 245 - 40 = 9$$

Note that the output, $Q = 5/3$, is the profit-minimizing level of output.

PRACTICE PROBLEM 6.6

Given the total revenue function, $R(Q)$, and short-run total cost function, $STC(Q)$, for a firm:

$$R(Q) = 25Q - Q^2 \quad \text{and} \quad STC(Q) = Q^3 - 9Q^2 + 30Q + 20$$

a) Find the firm's profit-maximizing level of output. Check the second-order condition.
b) Find the associated level of profits.

(The answers are at the end of the chapter.)

SELECTION OF THE PROFIT-MAXIMIZING LEVEL OF EMPLOYMENT

We begin again with the short run production function of the firm, $Q = Q(K_0, L)$, but now we write the revenue and cost functions explicitly in terms of the variable and fixed factors of production, labor, and capital, respectively. The total revenue function is: $R = R(Q(K_0, L))$ and the total cost function is: $C = C(Q(K_0, L))$. The profit function to be maximized becomes:

$$\Pi(Q(K_0, L)) = R(Q(K_0, L)) - C(Q(K_0, L))$$

Totally differentiating profits with respect to labor and setting the result equal to zero, we obtain the first-order condition

$$d\Pi/dL = (dR/dQ)[(\delta Q/\delta K_0)(dK_0/dL) + (\delta Q/\delta L)(dL/dL)]$$

$$- (dC/dQ)[(\delta Q/\delta K_0)(dK_0/dL) + (\delta Q/\delta L)(dL/dL)]$$

Since $dL/dL = 1$, and in the short run, $dK_0 = 0$, we have

$$d\Pi/dL = (dR/dQ)(\delta Q/\delta L) - (dC/dQ)(\delta Q/\delta L) = 0$$

Recall that multiplying the marginal revenue of output (MR) and the marginal product of labor (MP_L) yields the marginal revenue product of labor (MRP_L).

$$MRP_L = MR \cdot MP_L = (dR/dQ)(\delta Q/\delta L) = (dR/dQ)(dQ/dL) = dR/dL$$

since $(\delta Q/\delta L) = (dQ/dL)$ in the short run, given $dK_0 = 0$. The marginal revenue product of labor indicates the change in total revenues associated with a change in the labor employed.

The term $(dC/dQ)(\delta Q/\delta L)$ represents the **marginal factor cost of labor**, MFC_L. Multiplying the marginal cost of output (MC) and the marginal product of labor (MP_L) gives the change in total cost associated with a change in labor employed.

$$MFC_L = MC \cdot MP_L = (dC/dQ)(\delta Q/\delta L) = (dC/dQ)(dQ/dL) = dC/dL$$

Therefore, the profit-maximizing level of employment of labor in the short run is found where the marginal revenue product of labor equals the marginal factor cost of labor.

$$d\Pi/dL = (dR/dQ)(dQ/dL) - (dC/dQ)(dQ/dL) = 0$$

$$= MRP_L - MFC_L = 0$$

or

$$MRP_L = MFC_L$$

Note that dividing through by the marginal product of labor, we obtain the first order condition for the profit-maximizing level of output of the firm: $MR = MC$. This makes sense. In the short run, the level of output that maximizes profits would be the same level of output that is produced at the profit-maximizing level of employment.

Checking the second-order condition for a profit-maximization, we need $d^2\Pi/dL^2 < 0$.

$$\frac{d(d\Pi/dL)}{dL} = \frac{d^2\Pi}{dL^2} = \frac{d(dR/dL)}{dL} - \frac{d(dC/dL)}{dL} = \frac{d^2R}{dL^2} - \frac{d^2C}{dL^2} < 0$$

The terms in the inequality indicate the slopes of the marginal revenue product of labor curve, $d(dR/dL)/dL$, and the marginal factor cost of labor curve, $d(dC/dL)/dL$, respectively. The second-order condition reduces to:

$$\frac{d(dR/dL)}{dL} < \frac{d(dC/dL)}{dL}$$

Thus, given that the first-order condition, $MRP_L = MFC_L$, is satisfied, for a profit-maximizing level of employment, the slope of the MRP_L curve must be less than the slope of the MFC_L curve. This requirement also parallels the second-order condition for the profit-maximizing level of output. In the next chapter, we will illustrate graphically these decision rules for a firm that is a perfect competitor in both the product and labor markets.

Shut-Down Rule for Labor   Finally, the firm's shut-down rule for labor can be derived from the shut-down rule for output. Recall, if at the critical level of output, (where $MC = MR$), average variable cost exceeds average revenue ($AVC > AR$), the firm would minimize losses in the short run by ceasing production. Correspondingly, we can show that, if at the critical level of employment of labor (where $MFC_L = MRP_L$), the wage paid by the firm, w, exceeds the **average revenue product of labor** (ARP_L), the firm would minimize losses by not hiring any labor and ceasing production.

With labor as the variable factor of production, the average variable cost of the firm is equal to the wage rate divided by the average product of labor:

$$AVC = TVC/Q = (w \cdot L)/Q = w/AP_L.$$

From the output shut-down rule, the firm would cease production when

$$AVC > AR \quad \text{or} \quad w/AP_L > AR$$

Multiplying through by the average product of labor, we obtain:

$$w > AR \cdot AP_L \quad \text{or} \quad w > ARP_L$$

The average revenue product of labor (ARP_L) is equal to the average revenue or unit price received by the firm ($AR = P$) times the average product of labor (AP_L). The average revenue product of labor measures the total revenue of the firm per unit of labor employed.

$$ARP_L = AR \cdot AP_L = P \cdot Q/L = TR/L$$

In sum, the output shut-down rule for the firm, when the average variable cost of production exceeds the unit price of output ($AVC > P$), is equivalent to the employment shut-down rule, when the wage exceeds the average revenue product of labor ($w > ARP_L$). Intuitively, if the wage paid by the firm were greater than the value of output produced per unit of labor, the firm would not employ any labor or produce any output.

To illustrate with a numerical problem, consider a firm with a short-run production function, which we write in general form as $Q = Q(L)$; a total revenue function, $R(Q) = 33Q - Q^2$; and a total cost function, $STC(Q) = Q^3 - 6Q^2 + 20Q + 80$. To find the profit-maximizing level of output, and from this, the associated level of employment, we set up the profit function:

$$\Pi[Q(L)] = R[Q(L)] - STC[Q(L)]$$

$$= 33Q(L) - [Q(L)]^2 - [Q(L)]^3 + 6[Q(L)]^2 - 20Q(L) - 80.$$

Differentiating with respect to labor using the chain rule and setting the result equal to zero, the first-order condition for profit-maximization is:

$$d\Pi/dL = (d\Pi/dQ)(dQ/dL)$$

$$= 33\,(dQ/dL) - 2\,Q(L)\,(dQ/dL) - 3\,[Q(L)]^2\,(dQ/dL)$$

$$+ 12\,Q(L)\,(dQ/dL) - 20\,(dQ/dL) = 0$$

Dividing through by the marginal product of labor, dQ/dL, and simplifying, gives:

$$-3Q^2 + 10Q + 13 = 0$$

Using the quadratic formula to solve for output,

$$Q = \frac{-10 \pm \sqrt{(10)^2 - 4(-3)(13)}}{2(-3)} = \frac{-10 \pm 16}{-6} = -1, 4.\overline{3}$$

Rejecting the negative quantity, the profit-maximizing output is $\overline{Q} = 4.\overline{3}$. To confirm, we check the second-order condition. Here, consistent with a maximum, we have:

$$d^2\Pi/dQ^2 = \Pi''(Q) = -6Q + 10$$

and

$$\Pi''(4.\overline{3}) = -6(4.\overline{3}) + 10 = -15.9 < 0$$

If we had a specific short-run production function, $Q = Q(L)$, we could determine the required level of labor to produce the profit-maximizing level of output. The associated level of profits are:

$$\Pi(4.\overline{3}) = R(4.\overline{3}) - STC(4.\overline{3})$$

$$= 33(4.\overline{3}) - (4.\overline{3})^2 - [(4.\overline{3})^3 - 6(4.\overline{3})^2 + 20(4.\overline{3}) + 80]$$

$$= 124.2 - 135.3$$

$$= -11.1$$

In this example, the firm has negative economic profits in the short run. The firm, however, would not cease production, since its total revenues, $R(4.\overline{3}) = 124.2$, exceed its total variable costs, $TVC(4.\overline{3}) = 55.3$, and at least some of its fixed costs of 80 are being covered. If the firm did shut down, its losses would equal its total fixed costs of 80. Thus, the profit-maximizing output of $Q = 4.\overline{3}$ is better regarded here as the loss-minimizing level of output. While the profit-maximizing firm would continue producing in the short run, it would not replace its physical capital when worn out as long as all of its fixed costs were not covered. If the firm ever reached the point where its total revenues fell short of its total variable costs, then it would shut down and cease production.

PRACTICAL CONSIDERATIONS

Before concluding this chapter with a discussion of implicit functions, several points about firm behavior might be made. First, remember that the analysis is in terms of economic profits, or the difference between the firm's total revenues and its total costs, inclusive of the opportunity costs of the funds invested in the firm's physical capital stock (that is, the firm's plant, equipment, and machinery). Zero economic profits imply that a firm is earning a normal rate of return on its invested capital. Assuming there are other options for the funds invested in the firm's physical capital, for example, the interest that could be earned on a government bond, the opportunity cost of capital to the firm is positive. Therefore, zero economic profits imply positive accounting profits. Indeed, negative economic profits may coexist with positive accounting profits.

Consider a simple example of a business earning a 4% return on its capital investment, that is, its profits are equal to 4% of the value of its physical capital stock. If the owners of the firm, however, could earn 6% on a government bond, then while the firm's rate of accounting profits is 4%, its rate of economic profits is −2%. So, while a firm may be earning negative economic profits and have an incentive to reduce its investment in the business, it may nevertheless continue to replace its physical capital stock when worn out—perhaps satisfied with its present rate of accounting profits and hoping for future improvement. The firm, however, would not be currently maximizing its economic profits.

Similarly, according to the shut-down rule, a firm in the short run would stop production if its average variable cost exceeded its average revenue (or its total variable costs exceeded its total revenues). Given the uncertainty about the future and the difficulty of hiring back labor to restart production, a firm may continue to operate in the short run—for a while at least—even when not all of its variable costs of production are covered by its revenues. Again, while understandable behavior, the firm would not be maximizing its economic profits or, more appropriately here, minimizing its economic losses, in the short run.

These practical considerations do not diminish the insights gained from economic analysis. As economists, we should be cognizant that human behavior is not always driven by optimal decision rules based on perfect information. Furthermore, behavioral models in the social sciences are abstractions from reality. For example, throughout this text we simplify our production function to include explicitly only two factors of production, physical capital and labor. We understand, of course, that there are other inputs, such as raw materials and intermediate goods, which contribute to the firm's output and costs. Indeed, we realize that the units of capital and labor are likely to be differentiated by quality or inherent productivity. Nevertheless, graphically we are constrained to at most three dimensions—and in practice, usually two dimensions. The enhanced ability to analyze simpler and more manageable models compensates for the loss in "reality."

In any case, it is important to keep a healthy perspective when working with economic models—balancing the rigor of the mathematical analysis against the impreciseness or, for lack of a better word, humanness, of human behavior. We should be sensitive to our assumptions, for example, the objective functions to be optimized, and to our methods of analysis, for example, differential calculus. And, we should remember that our theories and techniques are not ends in themselves, but means to an end—a better understanding.

One of the more powerful tools at our disposal is comparative static analysis, used to explain changes in systems. Before we apply this technique to the behavior of firms in the following chapters, we need to present the Implicit Function Theorem.

IMPLICIT FUNCTIONS

A function, $y = f(x)$, where a dependent variable, y, is explicitly expressed as a function of an independent variable, x, can also be written as $y - f(x) = 0$. If we begin, however, with an equation, $y - f(x) = 0$, can we say that a function $y = f(x)$ is implicitly defined? For example, we know that the equation, $y - x^2 + 4 = 0$, implicitly defines a function, $y = x^2 - 4$; since y can be written explicitly as a function of x.[3] What about the equation, $4x^2 + y^2 - 100 = 0$? Does this define an implicit function of the form, $y = f(x)$?

In general, we would like to know when an equation of the form, $F(y; x_1, x_2, \ldots x_m) = 0$, defines an *implicit function*, $y = f(x_1, x_2, \ldots x_m)$. The *Implicit Function Theorem*, stated below, establishes the conditions.

IMPLICIT FUNCTION THEOREM

If an equation, $F(y; x_1, x_2, \ldots x_m) = 0$ has continuous partial derivatives, $F_y, F_1, \ldots F_m$, and at any point, $(y_0; x_{10}, x_{20}, \ldots x_{m0})$, satisfying the equation, $F(y; x_1, x_2, \ldots x_m) = 0$, the partial derivative, $F_y \neq 0$, then in the m-dimensional neighborhood of that point, y is an implicitly defined function of the variables, $x_1, x_2, \ldots x_m$. In addition, the implicit function, $y = f(x_1, x_2, \ldots x_m)$, is continuous and has continuous partial derivatives.

Let's consider whether the following equation, $F(y; x) = 4x^2 + y^2 - 100 = 0$, defines an implicit function, $y = f(x)$. In this example, we can easily solve for y: here $y = \pm\sqrt{100 - 4x^2}$. The equation does not define an implicit function—even though we can solve for y explicitly in terms of x—unless we impose some restriction. If we restrict y to be positive, $y > 0$, however, then an implicit function is defined, $y = +\sqrt{100 - 4x^2}$. Note that the domain of x is restricted to $-5 < x < +5$.[4] (See Figure 6.10 for a graph of this equation.)

To see that the conditions of the Implicit Function Theorem are satisfied, we take the partial derivatives of the equation, $F(y; x) = 4x^2 + y^2 - 100 = 0$.

---

[3]We should not confuse *implicit functions* with inverse functions, which were introduced in Chapter 3. Recall for inverse functions, there is a one-to-one relationship between the dependent and independent variables. If $y = f(x)$ and $x = f^{-1}(y)$ are both functions, then they are inverse functions. In the example with $y - x^2 + 4 = 0$, where an implicit function, $y = x^2 - 4$, is defined, the graph of the function is a U-shaped parabola, with a vertical intercept of -4. The function $y = x^2 - 4$, however, does not have an inverse function unless we restrict the domain of x. For instance, if $x \geq 0$, then $x = +(y + 4)^{.5}$, where $y \geq -4$, is the inverse function for $y = x^2 - 4$, where $x \geq 0$.

[4]Note also that the function, $y = \sqrt{100 - 4x^2}$, does not have an inverse, since for each positive value of y there is more than one value of x.

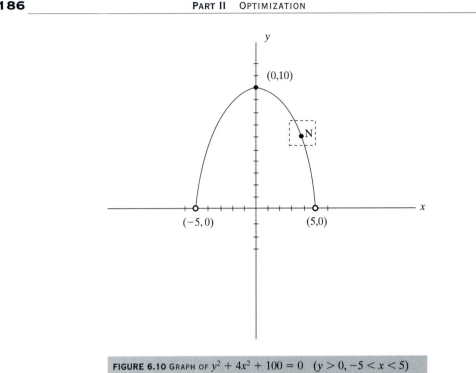

FIGURE 6.10 GRAPH OF $y^2 + 4x^2 + 100 = 0$ $(y > 0, -5 < x < 5)$

$$\delta F/\delta y = F_y = 2y$$

$$\delta F/\delta x = F_x = 8x$$

Both F_y and F_x are continuous. Moreover, the partial derivative, F_y, does not equal zero when we restrict the variable y to be positive (graphically restricting the function to the upper half of the ellipse). See the open dots for the x-intercepts in Figure 6.10, indicating that the domain of x is the open subset, $-5 < x < 5$, that is, exclusive of the endpoints.

Therefore, for any ordered pair, $(y; x)$, satisfying the equation, $4x^2 + y^2 - 100 = 0$, where $y > 0$, in the neighborhood of that plotted point, an implicit function is defined. That is, for every value of x in the domain, there is a unique value of y, which is given by $y = \sqrt{100 - 4x^2}$. For example, the ordered pair, $y = 6$ and $x = 4$, satisfies the equation, $4x^2 + y^2 - 100 = 0$. In an arbitrary neighborhood around the point corresponding to this ordered pair we have a function. (See the dashed rectangle around the point labeled N in Figure 6.10.) Indeed, for either the upper half or the lower half of the ellipse, the Implicit Function Theorem holds.[5]

Implicit Function Rule   The *Implicit Function Rule* establishes the derivatives of an implicit function. To demonstrate: Totally differentiating an equation, $F(y; x_1, x_2, \ldots x_m) = 0$, that defines an implicit function, $y = f(x_1, x_2, \ldots x_m)$, we have

---

[5]As y approaches zero, the arbitrary neighborhoods around the relevant points on the curve, $4x^2 + y^2 - 100 = 0$, would become tighter, in order to satisfy the restriction that $y > 0$.

$$F_y \, dy + F_1 \, dx_1 + F_2 \, dx_2 + \cdots + F_i \, dx_i + \cdots + F_m \, dx_m = 0$$

If we hold constant all of the independent variables except one, x_i, that is, we assume that $dx_j = 0$, for $j = 1 \ldots m$ and $j \neq i$, the total differential reduces to

$$F_y \, dy + F_i \, dx_i = 0$$

or

$$F_y \, dy = -F_i \, dx_i$$

Solving for dy/dx, which is actually the partial derivative, $\delta y/\delta x_i$ (since $dx_j = 0, j \neq i$), we obtain

$$dy/dx_i \,|_{dx_j = 0} = \delta y/\delta x_i = -F_i/F_y \qquad (F_y \neq 0)$$

Recall that $F_y \neq 0$ is one of the key conditions of the Implicit Function Theorem.

Concisely stated, the Implicit Function Rule is: Given an equation, $F(y; x_1, x_2, \ldots x_m) = 0$ that defines an implicit function, $y = f(x_1, x_2, \ldots x_m)$, the partial derivatives of the implicit function are: $\delta y/\delta x_i = -F_i/F_y$, $(i = 1 \ldots m)$.

The Implicit Function Theorem and Implicit Function Rule allow us to find the partial derivatives of an implicit function, when we cannot solve for the dependent variable, y, explicitly in terms of the independent variables, $x_1, x_2, \ldots x_m$. We use the partial derivatives of the underlying equation, $F(y; x_1, x_2, \ldots x_m)$ to obtain the partial derivatives of the implicit function.

Return to our example, $F(y; x) = 4x^2 + y^2 - 100 = 0$, which defines an implicit function, $y = f(x)$. Here, we can actually solve explicitly for y in terms of x: $y = \sqrt{100 - 4x^2}$, where $y > 0$, so it is straightforward to find the derivative dy/dx. First, we will apply the Implicit Function Rule, which in this case with only one independent variable is: $dy/dx = -F_x/F_y = -8x/2y = -4x/y$. Recall that given our restriction, $y > 0$ (the upper half of the ellipse), $F_y = 2y \neq 0$.

If, instead, we write the implicit function explicitly and then diffentiate directly, we get the same result:

$$y = \sqrt{100 - 4x^2} = (100 - 4x^2)^{.5}$$

$$dy/dx = .5(100 - 4x^2)^{-.5} \, (-8x) = -4x/(100 - 4x^2)^{.5} = -4x/y. \text{ (It checks.)}$$

Now consider an example with two independent variables, where we cannot easily solve for the dependent variable or plot the curve (in three dimensions). Given the equation:

$$F(y; x_1, x_2) = x_1^2 + 3x_1 x_2 + 2x_2 y + x_2^2 + y^2 - 11 = 0$$

we will determine whether an implicit function, $y = f(x_1, x_2)$ is defined around the point $y = 0$, $x_1 = 1$, and $x_2 = 2$. If so, then we will use the Implicit Function Rule to find the partial derivatives, $\delta y/\delta x_1$ and $\delta y/\delta x_2$.

We begin by checking to see if the equation, $F(y; x_1, x_2) = 0$, has continuous partial derivatives, F_y, F_1, and F_2.

$$F_y = 2x_2 + 2y$$

$$F_1 = 2x_1 + 3x_2$$

$$F_2 = 3x_1 + 2y + 2x_2$$

The partial derivatives do exist and are continuous.

Second, the point in question, $y_0 = 0$, $x_{10} = 1$, and $x_{20} = 2$, does satisfy the equation.

$$F(y; x_1, x_2) = x_1^2 + 3x_1 x_2 + 2x_2 y + x_2^2 + y^2 - 11 = 0$$

$$F(0; 1, 2) = (1)^2 + 3(1)(2) + 2(2)(0) + (2)^2 + (0)^2 - 11 = 0$$

Moreover, the partial derivative with respect to the dependent variable, F_y, does not equal zero when evaluated at this point.

$$F_y(y_0; x_{10}, x_{20}) = F_y(0; 1, 2) = 2(2) + 2(0) = 4 \neq 0.$$

Therefore, we can say that an implicit function, $y = f(x_1, x_2)$, is defined about the point $(0, 1, 2)$.

Now, we use the Implicit Function Rule to find the partial derivatives, $\delta y/\delta x_1$ and $\delta y/\delta x_2$, since we can't solve explicitly for y in terms of x_1 and x_2.

$$\delta y/\delta x_1 = -F_1/F_y = \frac{-(2x_1 + 3x_2)}{2x_2 + 2y}$$

$$\delta y/\delta x_2 = -F_2/F_y = \frac{-(3x_1 + 2y + 2x_2)}{2x_2 + 2y}$$

Finally, the partial derivatives evaluated at the point in question ($y_0 = 0$, $x_{10} = 1$, and $x_{20} = 2$) equal:

$$\delta y/\delta x_1(0, 1, 2) = \frac{-(2(1) + 3(2))}{2(2) + 2(0)} = -8/4 = -2$$

$$\delta y/\delta x_2(0, 1, 2) = \frac{-(3(1) + 2(0) + 2(2))}{2(2) + 2(0)} = -7/4$$

PRACTICE PROBLEM 6.7

Given the equation, $F(y; x_1, x_2) = x_1^3 + 2x_1^2 x_2 + x_1 x_2 y + x_2^3 y - y^3 + 4 = 0$:

a) Determine whether an implicit function, $y = f(x_1, x_2)$ is defined around the point $(y_0; x_{10}, x_{20}) = (-1; -2, 3)$ satisfying the function.

b) If an implicit function is defined around this point, then find and evaluate the following partial derivatives at this point: $\delta y/\delta x_1$ and $\delta y/\delta x_2$.

(The answers are at the end of the chapter.)

The Implicit Function Theorem and Implicit Function Rule provide a powerful technique of analysis. When a dependent variable cannot be solved explicitly in terms of the exogenous variable(s) in a model; then—if the Implicit Function Theorem holds—we can still do comparative statics and assess the effects of changes in the exogenous variable(s) on the equilibrium value of the dependent variable. Moreover, we will see in the models to follow that the variables assumed to be exogenous differ. For example, in the next chapter, a perfectly competitive firm is a price-taker, regarding the price of its output as exogenously determined by the interaction of market demand and supply. In contrast, a monopolistically competitive firm is a price-setter. The price charged is endogenously determined by the firm. In later chapters we will extend the Implicit Function Theorem to a system of equations.

❖ KEY TERMS

Economics

- average product of labor (p. 165)
- average revenue product of labor (p. 182)
- capacity output (p. 169)
- economic profits (p. 177)
- law of diminishing returns (p. 166)

- marginal cost (p. 169)
- marginal factor cost of labor (p. 181)
- marginal product of labor (p. 165)

- short run (p. 165)
- short-run total cost (p. 168)
- shut-down rule (p. 179)
- total fixed cost (p. 168)
- total variable cost (p. 168)

Mathematics

- absolute extremum (p. 156)
- choice variable (p. 153)
- concave (p. 159)
- convex (p. 159)
- critical point (p. 157)
- decision variable (p. 153)
- first derivative (p. 157)
- first-order condition (p. 157)

- goal equilibrium (p. 153)
- implicit function (p. 185)
- Implicit Function Theorem (p. 185)
- Implicit Function Rule (p. 186)
- inflection point (p. 163)

- objective function (p. 153)
- rectangular hyperbola (p. 171)
- relative extremum (p. 156)
- second derivative (p. 158)
- strictly concave (p. 159)
- strictly convex (p. 159)

❖ PROBLEMS

1. For each of the following equations:
   a) Find the critical points (if any) and determine the type of relative extrema (maximum or minimum).
   b) Find the inflection point (if any).
   c) By plotting five or fewer, carefully chosen, ordered pairs, sketch the curve.
      i) $y = 2x^3 + 3x^2 - 36x + 40$
      ii) $y = x^3 - 8$
      iii) $y = (1/3)x^3 - 2x^2 + 3x + 10$
      iv) $y = x^3 - 6x^2 + 12x - 8$
      v) $y = (x-2)^2 + 5$

2. Given the following short-run production functions:
   a) Find the level of employment where diminishing returns to labor begin.

b) Find the level of employment where the average product of labor (AP_L) is maximized. What is the maximum value of the average product of labor?
  i) $Q = 40L + 5L^2 - .2L^3$
  ii) $Q = 30L - L^2$
  iii) $Q = 10L + 2L^2 - L^3$

3. Given a wage rate of $w = \$200$, for each of the following short-run production functions:
  a) Find the level of output where the marginal cost of output (MC) is minimized.
  b) Find the level of output where the average variable cost (AVC) is minimized. What is the minimum value of the average variable cost?
  i) $Q = 40L + 5L^2 - .2L^3$
  ii) $Q = 30L - L^2$
  iii) $Q = 10L + 2L^2 - L^3$

4. Given the following short-run total cost (STC) functions, in each case:
  a) Determine the inflection points in the STC and total variable cost (TVC) curves.
  b) Find the equations for the associated marginal cost (MC), average variable cost (AVC), and average total cost (ATC) curves.
  c) Determine the outputs where the MC and AVC are minimized and the minimum values of the MC and AVC. Confirm that $MC = AVC$ at the minimum of AVC.
  i) $STC(Q) = Q^3 - 6Q^2 + 20Q + 30$
  ii) $STC(Q) = Q^3 - 12Q^2 + 6Q + 50$
  iii) $STC(Q) = (1/6)Q^3 - 3Q^2 + 30Q + 60$
  iv) $STC(Q) = .2Q^3 - 3Q^2 + 20Q + 30$

5. Given a firm's total revenue function, $R(Q)$, and short-run total cost function, $STC(Q)$:
  a) Find the firm's profit-maximizing level of output.
  b) Check the second-order condition.
  c) Find the associated level of profits.
  i) $R(Q) = 41Q - Q^2$ and $STC(Q) = Q^3 - 12Q^2 + 60Q + 40$
  ii) $R(Q) = 33.75Q - Q^2$ and $STC(Q) = Q^3 - 12Q^2 + 60Q + 40$
  iii) $R(Q) = 25Q - Q^2$ and $STC(Q) = Q^3 - 12Q^2 + 60Q + 40$

6. For each of the following equations of the form, $F(y; x) = 0$:
  a) Determine whether an implicit function, $y = f(x)$, is defined around the given point $(y_0; x_0)$.
  b) If so, find and evaluate dy/dx at this point.
  i) $F(y; x) = x^2 + 3y^2 - 27 = 0$, $(y_0; x_0) = (3; 0)$
  ii) $F(y; x) = x/(y-1)^2 + xy - 1 = 0$, $(y_0; x_0) = (0; 1)$

7. For each of the following equations of the form, $F(y; x_1, x_2) = 0$:

a) Determine whether an implicit function, $y = f(x_1, x_2)$ is defined around the given point $(y_0; x_{10}, x_{20})$.

b) If so, find and evaluate $\delta y/\delta x_1$ and $\delta y/\delta x_2$ at this point.

  i) $F(y; x_1, x_2) = x_1^2 y + x_1 x_2 + x_2 y^3 - 2 = 0$; $(y_0; x_{10}, x_{20}) = (1; 0, 2)$

  ii) $F(y; x_1, x_2) = x_1^3 + x_1^2 y + x_2^2 y + y^2 + 8 = 0$; $(y_0; x_{10}, x_{20}) = (-1; 1, 3)$

❖ ANSWERS TO PRACTICE PROBLEMS

6.1 a) The point $(0, -1)$ is a relative (and absolute) minimum. There are no inflection points.

b) The point $(4, -68)$ is a relative minimum. The point $(-2, 40)$ is a relative maximum. The point $(1, -14)$ is an inflection point.

c) The point $(4, 4)$ is a relative maximum. The point $(1, -9.5)$ is a relative minimum. The point $(2.5, -2.75)$ is an inflection point.

d) There are no critical points. The point $(0, -1)$ is an inflection point.

e) There are no critical points. The point $(1, 4)$ is an inflection point.

6.2 a) The point of diminishing returns occurs after the marginal product of labor is maximized, here $L = 20$.

b) The average product of labor reaches a maximum of 120 when $L = 30$.

6.3 a) The minimum marginal cost occurs at an output of $Q = 2200$, which equals the output produced by the labor when the marginal product of labor is maximized (at $L = 20$).

b) The minimum average variable cost equals $\$.125$ and occurs at an output of $Q = 3600$, which equals the output produced by the labor when the average product of labor is maximized (at $L = 30$).

6.4 a) $MC(Q) = .6Q^2 - 12Q + 90$
$AVC(Q) = .2Q^2 - 6Q + 90$
$ATC(Q) = .2Q^2 - 6Q + 90 + 100/Q$

b) $MC(Q) = 2Q$
$AVC(Q) = Q$
$ATC(Q) = Q + 100/Q$

c) $MC(Q) = 3$
$AVC(Q) = 3$
$ATC(Q) = 3 + 100/Q$

6.5 The minimum marginal cost equals 30 and occurs at an output of $Q = 10$. The minimum average variable cost equals 45 and occurs at an output of $Q = 15$. $MC(15) = 45 = AVC(15)$.

6.6 a) The profit-maximizing level of output is $\overline{Q} = 5$. The second-order condition for a maximum is satisfied: $\Pi''(5) = -14 < 0$.

b) Profits are: $\Pi(5) = 30$.

6.7 a) An implicit function, $y = f(x_1, x_2)$ is defined around the point $(y_0; x_{10}, x_{20}) = (-1; -2, 3)$. This point satisfies the function $F(y; x_1, x_2) = x_1^3 + 2x_1^2 x_2 + x_1 x_2 y + x_2^3 y - y^3 + 4 = 0$, since $F(-1; -2, 3) = (-2)^3 + 2(-2)^2(3) + (-2)(3)(-1) + (3)^3(-1) - (-1)^3 + 4 = 0$; and $F(y; x_1, x_2)$ has continuous partial derivatives: $F_y = x_1 x_2 + x_2^3 - 3y^2$; $F_1 = 3x_1^2 + 4x_1 x_2 + x_2 y$; and $F_2 = 2x_1^2 + x_1 y + 3x_2^2 y$, with $F_y(-1; -2, 3) = 18 \neq 0$.

b) $\delta y / \delta x_1 = -F_1/F_y = \dfrac{-(3x_1^2 + 4x_1 x_2 + x_2 y)}{x_1 x_2 + x_2^3 - 3y^2}$ and $\delta y / \delta x_1 (-1; -2, 3) = 15/18 = 5/6$.

$\delta y / \delta x_2 = -F_2/F_y = \dfrac{-(2x_1^2 + x_1 y + 3x_2^2 y)}{x_1 x_2 + x_2^3 - 3y^2}$ and $\delta y / \delta x_2 (-1; -2, 3) = 17/18$.

COMPETITION AMONG MANY: PERFECTLY COMPETITIVE AND MONOPOLISTICALLY COMPETITIVE FIRMS

In this chapter we illustrate the short-run decision rules for profit-maximization for firms in perfectly competitive and monopolistically competitive markets. In both cases, there are many firms in the market.

The major difference between these two types of market structure is product differentiation. Perfectly competitive firms sell a homogeneous or identical product, while monopolistically competitive firms sell slightly differentiated versions of a product. An example of perfect competition would be the market for fresh shrimp in a coastal city: the shrimp caught are indistinguishable across the suppliers. An example of monopolistic competition would be the seafood restaurants in this coastal city; these restaurants may be differentiated by the preparation of the shrimp dishes and the service, as well as the setting. As such, perfectly competitive firms are price-takers, accepting the market price (e.g., dollars per pound of fresh shrimp) as given. Monopolistically competitive firms, in contrast, are price-setters, for example, the price of a shrimp dinner likely varies somewhat across the seafood restaurants.

A common feature of perfect competition and monopolistic competition, however, is the freedom of entry and exit of firms. Consequently, long-run equilibrium is characterized by zero economic profits.

We begin the chapter analyzing the perfectly competitive firm, both in the product or output market and in the labor market. In the former, we illustrate the selection of the profit-maximizing output and discuss the adjustment to long-run equilibrium. For a perfectly competitive firm in the labor market (a wage-taker), we depict the selection of the profit-maximizing level of employment. Using the Implicit Function Theorem, we do comparative statics on a firm in each of the markets.

Before shifting the analysis to a monopolistically competitive firm in the output market, we formally discuss the concept of the price elasticity of demand. As a price-taker, a perfectly competitive firm faces a perfectly elastic (horizontal) demand curve for its output set at the market equilibrium price. As a price-setter, a monopolistically competitive firm faces a highly—but not perfectly—elastic demand curve for its differentiated product. This essential difference has repercussions for the long-run equilibrium prices and outputs of the perfectly competitive and monopolistically competitive firms—even if the firms have identical cost curves.

While there are no new mathematical techniques introduced, the calculus of optimization of functions of one variable and the Implicit Function Theorem are applied throughout the chapter.

PERFECTLY COMPETITIVE FIRMS

In perfect competition, there are many demanders and many suppliers of a homogeneous good or service. Each market participant is a price-taker, accepting the market equilibrium price as given for all transactions. Moreover, freedom of entry and exit characterizes perfectly competitive markets. No potential demanders or suppliers are hindered from participating in the market, nor are there any restrictions on leaving the market. It may seem ironic, but perfectly competitive firms don't actually compete against each other. Examples that approach perfect competition are the market for unskilled labor and the markets for farm produce.

A firm may be a perfect competitor in a product market, a factor market, both types of markets, or not at all. We begin with a product market.

PRODUCT MARKET

In a product or output market, a perfectly competitive firm assumes that it can sell all of its output at the going market price. In essence, the demand curve for the output of the firm is perfectly elastic at the market-clearing price. See Figure 7.1, where the output of the market, Q, is expressed in thousands of units per period, and the output of perfectly competitive firm i, Q_i, a very small fraction of the market output, is expressed in units per period.

The demand curve facing firm i, D_i, is horizontal at the market equilibrium price, P_0. Intuitively, since the outputs of the firms are identical, no firm could charge a price above the market equilibrium. Attempting to charge a higher price than P_0 would reduce a firm's sales to zero. Conversely, a perfectly competitive firm does not have to lower its price to sell additional units of its output. Thus, exogenous to the perfectly competitive firm is the market equilibrium price, which is identical to the firm's average revenue, AR_i. The market price also sets the firm's marginal revenue, $P_0 = MR_i$, since the change in the firm's total revenues (R_i) associated with a one unit change in output (and sales) is equal to the market price received.

Formally, the total revenue, average revenue, and marginal revenue of a perfectly competitive firm i are given by:

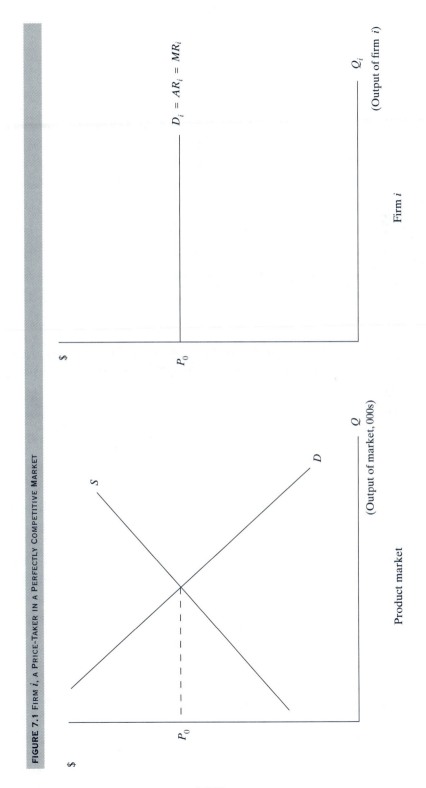

FIGURE 7.1 FIRM i, A PRICE-TAKER IN A PERFECTLY COMPETITIVE MARKET

$D_i = AR_i = MR_i$

P_0

Q_i
(Output of firm i)

Firm i

S

D

Q
(Output of market, 000s)

P_0

Product market

$$R_i = P_0 \cdot Q_i$$

$$AR_i = R_i/Q_i = P_0$$

$$MR_i = dR_i/dQ_i = P_0$$

Selection of the Profit-Maximizing Output   For given total revenue and short-run total cost functions of a perfectly competitive firm, $R_i = R(Q_i) = P_0 \cdot Q_i$ and $STC_i = STC(Q_i)$, respectively, the profit function is: $\Pi_i = \Pi(Q_i) = R_i - STC_i = P_0 \cdot Q_i - STC(Q_i)$. To determine the profit-maximizing level of output, the firm sets the derivative of profits with respect to output equal to zero, and then solves for the critical output.

$$d\Pi_i/dQ_i = P_0 - dSTC_i/dQ_i = 0$$

or

$$P_0 = STC'(Q_i)$$

Therefore, a perfectly competitive firm will maximize its short run profits at the output where its marginal cost of production, $STC'(Q_i) = dSTC_i/dQ_i$, is equal to the market equilibrium price. Note, this is a special case of the more general first-order condition for profit maximization, where marginal cost is set equal to marginal revenue — since, for a perfectly competitive firm, marginal revenue equals the market price.

Checking the second-order condition, for a maximum we need, $d^2\Pi_i/dQ_i^2 = \Pi''(Q_i) < 0$.

$$\frac{d(d\Pi_i/dQ_i)}{dQ_i} = d^2\Pi_i/dQ_i^2 = \frac{-d(dSTC_i/dQ_i)}{dQ_i} = -d^2STC_i/dQ_i^2 < 0$$

or

$$\Pi''(Q_i) = -STC''(Q_i) < 0 \qquad \text{(since } dP_0/dQ_i = 0\text{)}$$

At the critical level of output, for a maximization of profits (or a minimization of losses), the slope of the marginal cost curve, $STC''(Q_i) = d(dSTC_i/dQ_i)/dQ_i$, must be positive.

If we denote the critical or optimal level of output by $\overline{Q}_{i0}$, we can determine the level of maximum profits (or minimum losses) by substituting into the profit function.

$$\overline{\Pi}_i = \Pi(\overline{Q}_{i0}) = P_0 \cdot \overline{Q}_{i0} - STC(\overline{Q}_{i0})$$

Note, we need to ensure that, in the case of losses, the firm would not be better off in the short run by ceasing production altogether. Recall that if at the optimal level of output the firm's average variable cost exceeds its average revenue (the market price here), the firm would minimize its losses by shutting down its production.

We illustrate graphically in Figure 7.2, where the firm's demand curve, D_i, perfectly elastic at the given market price, P_0, is superimposed on the firm's short-run marginal and average cost curves. To simplify the graph, we do not include the firm's average fixed cost curve, AFC_i. Nevertheless, at any output the average fixed cost is represented by the vertical distance between the average total cost (ATC_i) and average vari-

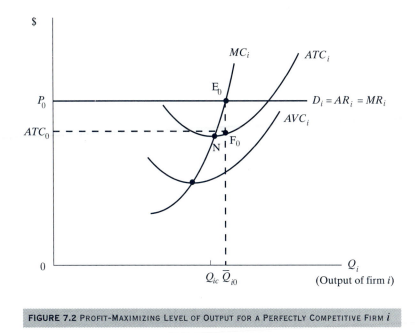

FIGURE 7.2 PROFIT-MAXIMIZING LEVEL OF OUTPUT FOR A PERFECTLY COMPETITIVE FIRM i

able cost (AVC_i) curves. The profit-maximizing level of output, $\overline{Q}_{i0}$, is found where $MC_i = P_0 = MR_i$. (See point E_0, the intersection of the marginal cost and marginal revenue curves.) The second-order condition is satisfied—since the profit-maximizing level of output occurs along the upward-sloping portion of the marginal cost curve.

Note that, in the short run, the profit-maximizing firm does not necessarily produce at capacity output, here Q_{ic}, where the average total cost of the firm is minimized. In this example, the profit-maximizing level of output exceeds the capacity output, $\overline{Q}_{i0} > Q_{ic}$.

The profits of the firm can be found graphically as the difference between the areas representing the total revenues and total costs. The rectangle $P_0 E_0 \overline{Q}_{i0}\, 0$ represents the total revenues of the firm and is equal to the product of the market price, P_0, and the firm's output, $\overline{Q}_{i0}$. Total costs of the firm, equal to the product of the average total cost and output, $(ATC_0) \cdot (\overline{Q}_{i0})$, are represented by the area of the rectangle, $ATC_0 F_0 \overline{Q}_{i0}\, 0$. The profits are the product of the per unit profit ($P_0 - ATC_0$) and the quantity of output, $\overline{Q}_{i0}$. The area of the rectangle, $P_0 E_0 F_0\, ATC_0$, represents the profits of the firm. In this example, the firm is earning positive economic profits, or above normal returns on the capital invested.

To illustrate with a numerical example, suppose the market demand and supply schedules for a commodity sold in a perfectly competitive market are:

$$Q^d = 156 - 8P \quad \text{and} \quad Q^s = -24 + 4P$$

where Q^d and Q^s are the market quantities demanded and supplied (in thousands of units per day) and P is the dollar price per unit. The market equilibrium price and quantity transacted are: $P_0 = \$15$ and $Q_0 = 36$ (thousand units per day)

$$Q^d = 156 - 8P = -24 + 4P = Q^s$$

$$180 = 12P$$

$$P_0 = 15$$

$$Q_0 = 156 - 8(15) = 36 = -24 + 4(15)$$

Firm i, a perfect competitor in this market, has a short-run total cost function given by: $STC_i = STC(Q_i) = Q_i^3 - 5Q_i^2 + 10Q_i + 30$, where Q_i is the output of firm i (in hundred units per day). To find the profit-maximizing output and associated profits, we set up the profit function:

$$\Pi_i = \Pi(Q_i) = R(Q_i) - STC(Q_i) = P_0 \cdot Q_{i0} - STC(Q_i)$$

$$= 15Q_i - (Q_i^3 - 5Q_i^2 + 10Q_i + 30)$$

Note that the total revenue function for the firm, $R(Q_i)$, is given by the product of the market price, $P_0 = 15$ (regarded as exogenous by the firm), and the firm's output, Q_i. The first-order condition for profit maximization is:

$$d\Pi_i/dQ_i = 15 - (3Q_i^2 - 10Q_i + 10) = 0$$

or

$$-3Q_i^2 + 10Q_i + 5 = 0$$

Using the quadratic formula to solve for Q_i, we get,

$$Q_i = \frac{-10 \pm \sqrt{(10)^2 - (4)(-3)(5)}}{2(-3)} = \frac{-10 \pm \sqrt{160}}{-6} = \frac{-10 \pm 12.65}{-6} = -.44, 3.78$$

Firm i's profit-maximizing output is $\overline{Q}_{i0} = 3.78$ (hundred units per day). Note that the firm's output is a small fraction of the market output of 36 (thousand units per day), which is characteristic of perfectly competitive markets.

To confirm, we check the second-order condition for a maximum:

$$\frac{d(d\Pi_i/dQ_i)}{dQ_i} = \Pi''(\overline{Q}_{i0}) = -6\overline{Q}_{i0} + 10$$

$$= \Pi_i''(3.78) = -22.68 + 10 = -12.68 < 0.$$

The firm's profits are:

$$\Pi(3.78) = (15)(3.78) - [(3.78)^3 - 5(3.78)^2 + 10(3.78) + 30]$$

$$= 56.70 - 50.37$$

$$= 6.33 \text{ (hundred dollars per day)}$$

The firm has positive economic profits.

Adjustment with Economic Profits   With freedom of entry to the market, positive economic profits would attract new firms. Moreover, existing firms enjoying positive economic profits may invest in additional physical capital—if not already operating at the minimum of their long-run average cost curves. The resulting increase in the market supply would drive down the market price until zero economic profits prevailed. In the long run, perfectly competitive firms will earn zero economic profits or normal returns on the capital invested. In long-run equilibrium, the market price, P, will equal the average total cost of production, ATC.

We turn now to a situation where the initial market equilibrium price is between the firm's average total cost and average variable cost at the optimal level of output. Refer to Figure 7.3 and the given market price of P_1. At the optimal level of output, $\overline{Q}_{i1}$, the firm incurs economic losses equal to $(ATC_1 - P_1) \cdot \overline{Q}_{i1}$, represented by the rectangle $ATC_1F_1E_1P_1$. The second-order condition is satisfied, as the slope of the marginal cost curve is positive at $\overline{Q}_{i1}$. Moreover, even though experiencing economic losses, the firm would still produce, since the price exceeds the average variable cost of production ($P_1 > AVC_1$). If the firm were to cease production, its losses would be equal to its fixed costs of production, given by the difference between its total costs $(ATC_1) \cdot (\overline{Q}_{i1})$ and its total variable costs $(AVC_1) \cdot (\overline{Q}_{i1})$. In Figure 7.3, the total fixed costs are indicated by the area of the rectangle $ATC_1F_1G_1AVC_1$. Continuing to operate at $\overline{Q}_{i1}$ allows the firm to minimize its losses, because its total revenues exceed its total variable costs. Therefore, at least some of its total fixed costs are being covered (here the amount $P_1E_1G_1AVC_1$).

Nevertheless, over time, in order to reduce its fixed costs, the firm would not replace its worn-out physical capital. As its capital stock was reduced, the firm's short-run cost curves would shift left. If the market price ever fell below the firm's average variable cost, the firm would cease production and, in effect, exit from the market.

FIGURE 7.3 ECONOMIC LOSSES FOR A PERFECTLY COMPETITIVE FIRM i

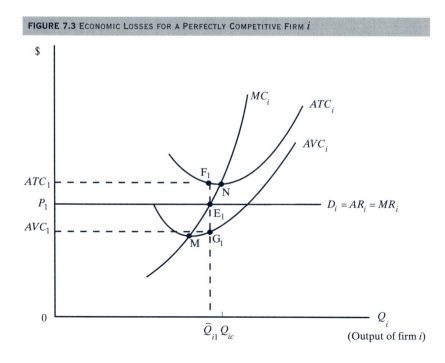

With economic losses and firms' short run cost curves shifting left, and perhaps even some firms exiting the market, the market supply curve shifts left. Consequently, the market price is driven up until zero economic profits are attained. As discussed in the previous example, in long-run equilibrium under perfect competition, the market price will just equal the average total cost for the typical or representative firm i.

To illustrate, return to the earlier numerical example, and suppose that the market demand declined to: $Q^{d'} = 120 - 8P$ (from $Q^d = 156 - 8P$), perhaps due to a change in tastes and preferences away from the product. With the market supply of $Q^s = -24 + 4P$, the new market equilibrium price and quantity transacted are: $P_1 = 12$ and $Q_1 = 24$ (thousand units per day).

Firm i, with its short-run total cost curve, $STC_i = STC(Q_i) = Q_i^3 - 5Q_i^2 + 10Q_i + 30$, would find its profit maximizing output decline with the fall in the market demand and market price:

$$\Pi_i = \Pi(Q_i) = P_1 \cdot Q_i - STC_i$$

$$= 12Q_i - (Q_i^3 - 5Q_i^2 + 10Q_i + 30)$$

The first-order condition is:

$$d\Pi_i/dQ_i = 12 - (3Q_i^2 - 10Q_i + 10) = 0$$

or

$$-3Q_i^2 + 10Q_i + 2 = 0$$

Solving, we have

$$Q_i = \frac{-10 \pm \sqrt{(10)^2 - (4)(-3)(2)}}{2(-3)} = \frac{-10 \pm \sqrt{124}}{-6} = \frac{-10 \pm 11.14}{-6} = -.19, 3.52$$

Checking the second-order condition for the positive output, $\overline{Q}_{i1} = 3.52$ (hundred units per day) we find: $\Pi''(\overline{Q}_{i1}) = -6\overline{Q}_{i1} + 10$

$$\Pi''(3.52) = -6(3.52) + 10 = -11.12 < 0 \text{ (consistent with a maximum).}$$

The firm's profits are:

$$\Pi(3.52) = (12)(3.52) - [(3.52)^3 - 5(3.52)^2 + 10(3.52) + 30]$$

$$= 42.24 - (46.86)$$

$$= -4.62 \text{ (hundred dollars per day).}$$

The firm has negative economic profits. It would still produce, however, since its total revenues, $R(3.52) = 42.24$, exceed its total variable costs, $TVC(3.52) = 16.86$. Yet, as long as not all of its fixed costs of 30 are being covered, firm i would tend not to replace its capital when worn out.

PRACTICE PROBLEM 7.1

Given the market demand and supply schedules in a perfectly competitive market:

$$Q^d = 50 - 4P \quad \text{and} \quad Q^s = -6 + 3P$$

where Q^d and Q^s are the market quantities demanded and supplied (in thousands of units per day) and P is the unit price (in dollars), and given the short run total cost function for firm i, $STC_i = STC(Q_i) = .5Q_i^3 - 4Q_i^2 + 12Q_i + 20$, where Q_i is the output of firm i (in hundreds of units per day):

  a) Determine the profit maximizing output and level of profits for firm i. Check the second-order condition.
  b) If the market demand increased to $Q^{d'} = 57 - 4P$, *ceteris paribus*, determine the new profit-maximizing output and profits. Check the second-order condition.

(The answers are at the end of the chapter.)

In Chapters 10 and 11 we will examine the behavior of the firm in the long run, when there are no fixed factors and the firm seeks the least-cost combination of capital and labor for producing the desired level of output. At this point, however, some observations on perfectly competitive firms in both the short run and long run should be made.

Short-Run Supply Curves   First, the short-run supply curve of the perfectly competitive firm is the positively sloped portion of its marginal cost curve that rises above its average variable cost curve. This makes sense. The short-run supply curve depicts the relationship between the price received by the firm (the market price in perfect competition) and the quantity of output supplied by the firm. Since the firm sets its marginal cost equal to the given market price in determining its profit-maximizing level of output, the quantity of output supplied by the firm can be read off its marginal cost curve. According to the shut-down rule, however, the firm would not produce (reducing its quantity supplied to zero) if the market price fell below its average variable cost. The minimum of the average variable cost curve, where $MC = AVC$, indicates the shut-down price for the firm. (See point M in Figure 7.3.).

Second, the market supply curve is derived from the horizontal summation of the individual firms' supply curves, that is, their marginal cost curves rising above their average variable cost curves. Anything that causes a shift in the firms' marginal cost curves, for example, a change in the firms' capital stocks, technological change, or a change in factor prices, would cause a shift in the market supply curve. As noted, if positive economic profits prevailed in an industry, then firms might invest in additional physical capital—if not already at the minimums of their long-run average cost curves—and new firms may enter the market. Increases in the capital stocks of firms would shift those firms' short run cost curves to the right. The entrance of new firms would increase the number of short-run supply curves in the market. Both of these changes would increase the market supply, which would drive down the market price until a long-run equilibrium of zero economic profits was reached.

Long-Run Equilibrium   In the short run, a profit-maximizing firm need not produce at economic capacity, the output where average total cost is minimized. (In Figure 7.3, see the output Q_{ic} and point N, where the MC_i curve cuts the ATC_i curve.) Operating beyond economic capacity, $\overline{Q}_{i0} > Q_{ic}$, is consistent with positive economic profits.

Conversely, a firm in the short run that is operating below capacity, $\overline{Q}_{i0} < Q_{ic}$, would be earning negative economic profits.

In a long-run equilibrium, however, a perfectly competitive firm would produce with the optimal amount of capital and labor (at the minimum of its long-run average cost curve) and its profit-maximizing output will coincide with its capacity output (the minimum of its selected short-run average total cost curve). Since the perfectly competitive firm is a price-taker, then, in the long run, maximizing its profits is consistent with minimizing its average cost. Due to freedom of entry and exit, in long-run equilibrium, the firm would be earning zero economic profits, that is, normal returns on the capital invested.

In Figure 7.4 we illustrate a long run equilibrium for a perfectly competitive firm i. The firm will be producing $\overline{Q}_{i0}^*$, on a short-run average total cost curve, ATC_i^*, that reflects the optimal amount of physical capital invested by the firm. This short-run average total cost curve is tangent to the firm's long run average cost curve ($LRAC_i$) and to the firm's demand curve, D_i^*, which is perfectly elastic at the long-run equilibrium market price, P_0^*. The long-run average cost curve represents the lowest unit cost of production for each rate of output, when the firm is free to vary its use of all of the factors of production. At this equilibrium level of output, the first-order condition for profit-maximization is met: $MC_i^* = P_0^* = MR_i^*$. The second-order condition of a positively sloped marginal cost curve in the neighborhood of the optimal output is also satisfied. The firm is earning zero economic profits in the short run ($P_0^* = ATC_i^*$) and also in the long run ($P_0^* = LRAC_i$). Moreover, in long-run equilibrium, a perfectly competitive firm will produce its profit-maximizing output for the lowest unit cost in both the

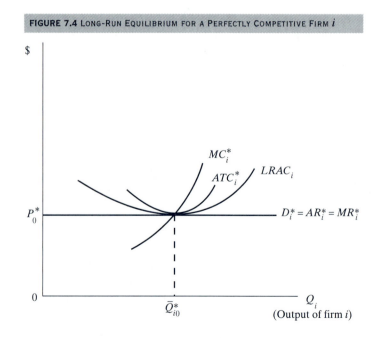

FIGURE 7.4 LONG-RUN EQUILIBRIUM FOR A PERFECTLY COMPETITIVE FIRM i

current short run (at its capacity output) and in the long run (at the minimum of its *LRAC* curve).

Intuitively, a perfectly competitive firm assumes that it can sell all of its output produced at the given market-clearing price. Consequently, maximizing its profits is consistent with minimizing its long-run average cost. The perfectly competitive firm therefore would invest in the amount of physical capital that corresponds to an output at the minimum of its long-run average cost curve (Q_{i0}^*) in Figure 7.4.

LABOR MARKET

A firm that is a perfect competitor in a labor market is a wage-taker. That is, the firm accepts the market equilibrium wage as given and assumes that it can hire all the labor it wants at this wage rate. Formally, the supply curve of labor to the firm is perfectly elastic (horizontal) at the market equilibrium wage.

We illustrate in Figure 7.5, where the quantity of labor in the market, L, is measured in thousands of units per period, for example, thousands of labor hours per day, and the quantity of labor for firm i, L_i, is measured in units per period, for example, labor hours per day. The wage rate, w, is measured in dollars per hour.

Recall from Chapter 6 that we defined the marginal factor cost of labor, MFC_L, as the change in total cost associated with a change in the labor employed. With our assumption of a two-factor production function, $Q_i = Q(K_i, L_i)$, where physical capital is the fixed factor in the short run ($K_i = K_{i0}$) and labor is the variable factor, the marginal factor cost of labor for a firm that is a perfect competitor in the labor market is the market wage. To demonstrate, for firm i, the **total factor cost of labor**, $(TFC_L)_i$, **average factor cost of labor**, $(AFC_L)_i$, and **marginal factor cost of labor**, $(MFC_L)_i$, are given by:

$$(TFC_L)_i = w_0 \cdot L_i$$

$$(AFC_L)_i = (TFC_L)_i/L_i = w_0$$

$$(MFC_L)_i = d(TFC_L)_i/dL_i = w_0$$

where L_i is the quantity of labor hired by firm i and w_0 is the given market wage rate. Note, with labor as the single variable factor of production, the total factor cost of labor is equal to the total variable cost of the firm.

Selection of the Profit-Maximizing Employment To set up the profit function for firm i, Π_i, we subtract the total cost function from the total revenue function, both expressed in terms of the labor employed by firm i. The total cost function is: $C_i = r_0 \cdot K_{i0} + w_0 \cdot L_{i0}$, where K_{i0} is the fixed capital stock of firm i; r_0 is the given user cost of capital (that is, the dollar cost of using a unit of physical capital); and w_0 is the market equilibrium wage rate. The total revenue function is: $R_i = R[Q(K_{i0}, L_i)]$. The profit function can be written as: $\Pi_i = \Pi[Q(K_{i0}, L_i)] = R[Q(K_{i0}, L_i)] - r_0 \cdot K_{i0} - w_0 \cdot L_i$.

Setting the first derivative of profits with respect to labor equal to zero, we can derive the condition for the profit-maximizing level of employment for firm i.

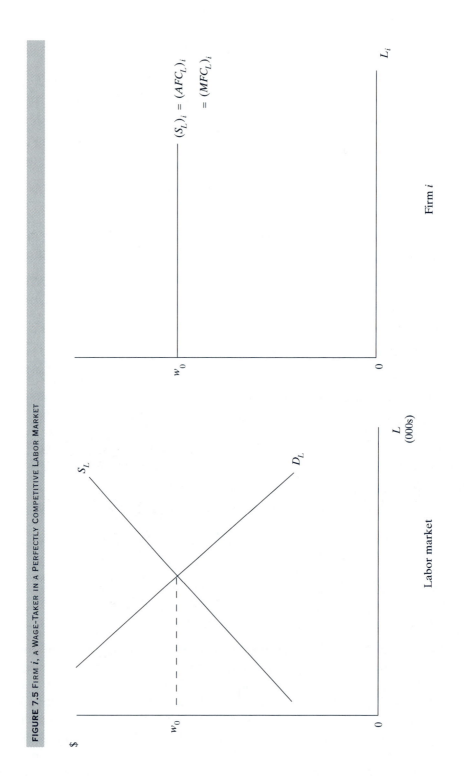

FIGURE 7.5 Firm i, a Wage-Taker in a Perfectly Competitive Labor Market

$\$$

S_L

D_L

w_0

L
(000s)

Labor market

w_0

$(S_L)_i = (AFC_L)_i$

$= (MFC_L)_i$

L_i

Firm i

$$d\Pi_i/dL_i = (dR_i/dQ_i)(dQ_i/dL_i) - w_0 = 0$$

since, in the short run, $dK_{i0} = 0$. Adding w_0 to both sides gives:

$$(dR_i/dQ_i)(dQ_i/dL_i) = w_0$$

The term on the left-hand side of the equation is the marginal revenue product of labor for firm i, $(MRP_L)_i$, equal to the marginal revenue of the firm, $dR_i/dQ_i = MR_i$, times the marginal product of labor of the firm, $dQ_i/dL_i = (MP_L)_i$. Thus, to maximize its profits, the perfectly competitive firm should employ labor up to the point where its marginal revenue product of labor equals the market wage. Intuitively, the marginal revenue product of labor represents the contribution to the firm's revenues of employing another unit of labor, while the market wage is the cost to the firm of employing another unit of labor. If there were a discrepancy between the two, the firm would benefit from adjusting its level of employment.

If the firm were also a perfect competitor in the product market, that is, a price-taker, where its marginal revenue (MR_i) equalled the market price of its output (P_0), then the firm's marginal revenue product of labor is known as its **value of marginal product of labor**, $(VMP_L)_i$. The condition for the profit-maximizing level of employment becomes: $(VMP_L)_i = P_0 \cdot (MP_L)_i = w_0$.

The second-order condition for a maximum requires that $d^2\Pi_i/dL_i^2 < 0$.

$$d^2\Pi_i/dL_i^2 = \frac{d(d\Pi_i/dL_i)}{dL_i} = \frac{d(dR_i/dL_i)}{dL_i} = d^2R_i/dL_i^2 < 0$$

That is, the slope of the marginal revenue product of labor curve should be negative.

We should also state the shut-down rule in terms of employment. Perfectly competitive firm i would cease production and employ no labor if the market wage were greater than its average revenue product of labor. Recall that the average revenue product of labor, $(ARP_L)_i$, equal to the price of the firm's output (that is, its average revenue, AR_i) times its average product of labor $(AP_L)_i$, indicates the revenue per unit of labor for the firm. If the market wage exceeds the firm's average revenue product of labor, then the total variable costs of the firm exceed its total revenues. Consequently, the firm would minimize its losses by shutting down production.

We illustrate the profit-maximizing employment decision of a perfectly competitive firm in Figure 7.6. The average revenue product and marginal revenue product of labor curves are drawn conditional on the firm's capital stock and technology, (which determine the firm's average and marginal products of labor), as well as on the demand for the firm's output (which determines the firm's average and marginal revenues). We can ignore the positively sloped portion of the $(MRP_L)_i$ curve, since the second-order condition for profit-maximization requires a negatively sloped $(MRP_L)_i$ curve at the critical level of employment. The $(MRP_L)_i$ curve cuts the $(ARP_L)_i$ curve at the maximum of the latter. This point of intersection, (labeled M in Figure 7.6), corresponds to the shut-down point for the perfectly competitive firm. If the market wage were greater than the maximum of the $(ARP_L)_i$, firm i would minimize its losses in the short run by ceasing production and not hiring any labor.

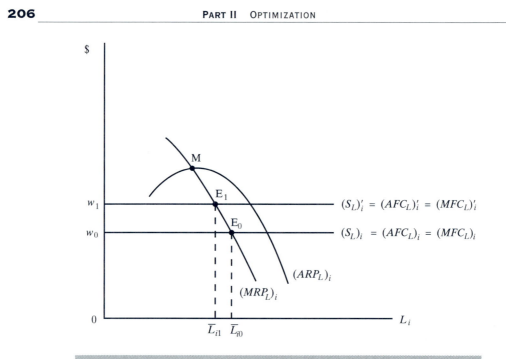

FIGURE 7.6 PROFIT-MAXIMIZING LEVEL OF EMPLOYMENT FOR PERFECTLY COMPETITIVE FIRM *i*

For the market wage of w_0, which sets the marginal factor cost of labor to perfectly competitive firm i, $\overline{L}_{i0}$ units of labor would be employed, where $(MRP_L)_i = (MFC_L)_i = w_0$. If the market wage were higher, say w_1, the firm would reduce the quantity of labor employed to $\overline{L}_{i1}$. As expected, an increase in the market wage, *ceteris paribus*, reduces the quantity of labor demanded by the firm. In fact, the demand curve for the perfectly competitive firm is the negatively-sloped portion of its MRP_L curve that falls below its ARP_L curve.

To illustrate with a numerical example, suppose that firm i is a perfect competitor in the product market, that is, a price-taker, and a perfect competitor in the labor market, a wage-taker. Let

$$Q^d = 68 - 7P \quad \text{and} \quad Q^s = -4 + 5P$$

be the market demand and supply schedules for the product, where Q^d and Q^s are the market quantities demanded and supplied (in thousands of units per day) and P is the unit price (in dollars) of the product. The market equilibrium price, P_0, and quantity transacted, Q_0, are \$6 and 26 thousand units, respectively.

$$Q^d = 68 - 7P = -4 + 5P = Q^s$$

$$12P = 72$$

$$P_0 = 6$$

$$Q_0 = 68 - 7(6) = 26 = -4 + 5(6)$$

Let the market demand and supply schedules for labor be:

$$L^d = 6200 - 40w \quad \text{and} \quad L^s = -1000 + 20w$$

where L^d and L^s are the market quantities demanded and supplied of labor (in workers per day) and w is the daily wage rate or user cost of labor per 8-hour day. The market equilibrium wage, w_0, and employment, L_0, are \$120 per day and 1,400 workers per day, respectively.

$$L^d = 6,200 - 40w = -1,000 + 20w = L^s$$

$$60\,w = 7,200$$

$$w_0 = 120$$

$$L_0 = 6,200 - 40(120) = 1,400 = -1,000 + 20(120)$$

Suppose the firm's short-run production function is: $Q_i = -L_i^3 + 10L_i^2 + 15L_i$ where Q_i is the output of the firm (in units per day) and L_i is the labor employed by firm i (in workers per day). The firm's marginal product of labor $(MP_L)_i$ and average product of labor $(AP_L)_i$ schedules are:

$$(MP_L)_i = dQ_i/dL_i = -3L_i^2 + 20L_i + 15$$

$$(AP_L)_i = Q_i/L_i = -L_i^2 + 10L_i + 15$$

To find the firm's profit-maximizing employment, we can use the decision rule, whereby the firm hires labor up to the point where the marginal revenue product of labor equals the marginal factor cost of labor. (Note that if we knew the total fixed costs of the firm, we could set up the firm's profit function and directly find the optimal level of employment.)

The marginal revenue product of labor schedule, $(MRP_L)_i$, for the perfectly competitive firm i, also known as the value of marginal product of labor schedule, $(VMP_L)_i$, is obtained by multiplying the marginal product of labor schedule by the market equilibrium price for the firm's output, $P_0 = \$6$.

$$(MRP_L)_i = P_0 \cdot (MP_L)_i = 6\,(-3L_i^2 + 20L_i + 15) = -18L_i^2 + 120L_i + 90$$

The marginal factor cost of labor to a perfectly competitive firm in the labor market is the market equilibrium wage rate, here $w_0 = \$120$. Setting the firm's marginal revenue product of labor equal to its marginal factor cost of labor and solving for the level of employment we have:

$$(MRP_L)_i = -18L_i^2 + 120L_i + 90 = 120 = (MFC_L)_i$$

$$-18L_i^2 + 120L_i - 30 = 0$$

$$-3L_i^2 + 20L_i - 5 = 0$$

Using the quadratic formula, we find

$$L_i = \frac{-20 \pm \sqrt{(20)^2 - (4)(-3)(-5)}}{(2)(-3)} = \frac{-20 \pm 18.4}{-6} = .4, 6.4$$

The employment of $L_i = .4$ occurs along the positively-sloped portion of the marginal revenue product of labor and so corresponds to a profit-minimizing level of labor for the firm. The profit-maximizing level of employment is $\overline{L}_{i0} = 6.4$ workers per day. Note, the .4 worker here may represent a part-time employee, working an average of 3.2 hours (out of 8 hours) per day. From the short-run production function, the associated output is $\overline{Q}_{i0} = 243.5$ units per day.

$$\overline{Q}_{i0} = -(\overline{L}_{i0})^3 + 10(\overline{L}_{i0})^2 + 15\,\overline{L}_{i0}$$

$$= -(6.4)^3 + 10(6.4)^2 + 15(6.4) = -262.1 + 409.6 + 96$$

$$= 243.5$$

We should check that the firm's total revenues (R_i) exceed its total variable costs (TVC_i), ensuring that the firm would actually produce this level of output and not shut down.

$$R_i = P_0 \cdot \overline{Q}_{i0} = (\$6)(243.5) = \$1461 \text{ per day}$$

$$TVC_i = w_0 \cdot \overline{L}_{i0} = (\$120)(6.4) = \$768 \text{ per day}$$

Since $R(\overline{Q}_{i0}) > TVC(\overline{Q}_{i0})$, the firm would produce $\overline{Q}_{i0} = 243.5$ units per day, its profit-maximizing output corresponding to its optimal employment of labor of $\overline{L}_{i0} = 6.4$ workers per day. Moreover, if the firm's total fixed costs are less than (more than) $693 per day, the firm would earn positive (negative) economic profits. Either situation would result in adjustments in the long run until zero economic profits prevailed.

We note that each firm's profit-maximizing output of 243.5 units per day is just a small fraction of the market output of 26,000 units per day. So too, this firm's profit-maximizing level of employment of 6.4 workers per day is a small fraction of the 1400 workers per day employed in the labor market.

If instead the market wage were $w_1 = \$110$ (per day), then we can show that this firm would increase its level of employment to 6.5 workers per day, *ceteris paribus*.[1] That is, setting the firm's marginal revenue product of labor schedule, $(MRP_L)_i = -18L_i^2 + 120L_i + 90$, equal to the new marginal factor cost of labor, given by the lower market wage of $w_1 = \$110$, and solving, we have:

$$-18L_i^2 + 120L_i + 90 = 110$$

$$-18L_i^2 + 120L_i - 20 = 0$$

$$-9L_i^2 + 60L_i - 10 = 0$$

$$L_i = \frac{-60 \pm \sqrt{(60)^2 - (4)(-9)(-10)}}{(2)(-9)} = \frac{-60 \pm 59.9}{-18} = .2, 6.5$$

---

[1] Note that we are assuming that the lower market wage rate does not affect the market supply curve for the output and thus has no effect on the market equilibrium price and the firm's marginal revenue product of labor curve. If the lower market wage rate did increase the market supply of the product, then the market equilibrium price would fall and the firm's marginal revenue product of labor curve would shift down, which would reduce the increase in the quantity of labor employed by the firm.

So, with the fall in the market wage, the profit-maximizing employment is $\overline{L}_{i1} = 6.5$ workers per day.

PRACTICE PROBLEM 7.2

Given a firm i that is a perfect competitor in both the product market and labor market, where:

$$Q^d = 100 - 12P \quad \text{and} \quad Q^s = -5 + 3P$$

are the market demand and supply schedules for the product, with Q^d and Q^s being the market quantities demanded and supplied (in thousands of units per day) and P is the market price per unit (in dollars); and

$$L^d = 7,200 - 80w \quad \text{and} \quad L^s = -800 + 20w$$

are the market demand and supply schedules for labor, with L^d and L^s as the market quantities demanded and supplied of labor (in workers per day) and w is the market wage rate (in dollars per 8-hour day); assume the firm's short-run production function is:

$$Q_i = -L_i^3 + 11L_i^2 + 6L_i,$$

with Q_i as the quantity of output produced by firm i (in units per day) and L_i as the quantity of labor employed by firm i (in workers per day):
a) Find the profit-maximizing level of employment and output for firm i.
b) Check to see that firm i would produce this output, rather than ceasing production.

(The answers are at the end of the chapter.)

COMPARATIVE STATICS FOR A PERFECTLY COMPETITIVE FIRM

Recall that for firm i, assumed to be a perfect competitor in a product market, the short-run profit function can be written as $\Pi(Q_i) = P_0 \cdot Q_i - STC(Q_i)$, where the total revenue of the firm is equal to the product of the market price, P_0, and the firm's output, Q_i, and $STC(Q_i)$ represents the firm's short-run total cost function. The first-order condition for profit maximization is: $d\Pi/dQ_i = P_0 - STC'(Q_i) = 0$. From the first-order condition, we obtained the firm's profit-maximizing output decision rule of setting the marginal cost of production, $STC'(Q_i)$ equal to the market price.

Changes in Market Price Here, without a specific functional form for the cost function, we are not able to solve explicitly for the optimal level of output. Nevertheless, if we can apply the Implicit Function Theorem, we can still do comparative static analysis.

We regard the first-order condition, $P_0 - STC'(Q_i) = 0$, as an equation of the form, $F(Q_i; P_0) = 0$, where the output of the firm, Q_i, is the dependent variable and the market price, P_0, is the independent variable. If this equation has continuous partial derivatives, F_{Q_i} and F_{P_0}; and, if at the critical point, $(\overline{Q}_{i0}, P_0)$, the partial derivative, $F_{Q_i} \neq 0$, then an implicit function, $\overline{Q}_{i0} = Q(P_0)$, is defined, continuous, and has continuous partial derivatives.

We can show that these conditions are met. The partial derivatives, F_{Q_i} and F_{P_0}, exist and are continuous.

$$F_{Q_i} = \delta F/\delta Q_i = -STC''(Q_i)$$

$$F_{P_0} = \delta F/\delta P_0 = 1$$

In particular, the partial, $F_{Q_i} = -STC''(Q_i)$, equals the negative of the slope of the marginal cost curve. Recall that the second-order condition for profit maximization requires that the slope of the marginal cost curve at the critical level of output be positive. Moreover, a perfectly competitive firm's supply curve is the rising portion of its marginal cost curve above its average variable cost curve. Therefore, at the critical level of output, $\overline{Q}_{i0}$, we can say that $F_{Q_i} \neq 0$.

To do the comparative static analysis, we totally differentiate the first-order condition, evaluated at the critical level of output. Differentiating the equation, $P_0 - STC'(\overline{Q}_{i0}) = 0$, we get

$$dP_0 - STC''(\overline{Q}_{i0})\, d\overline{Q}_i = 0$$

The term, $STC''(\overline{Q}_{i0})$, indicates the slope of the marginal cost curve at the profit-maximizing level of output:

$$STC''(\overline{Q}_{i0}) = \frac{d(STC'(\overline{Q}_{i0}))}{d\overline{Q}_i} > 0$$

With one independent variable, P_0, the only comparative static result we have is $d\overline{Q}_i/dP_0$. We can solve the equation, $dP_0 - STC''(\overline{Q}_{i0})\, d\overline{Q}_i = 0$, for this derivative. Dividing through by dP_0, and then isolating $d\overline{Q}_i/dP_0$, we obtain:

$$d\overline{Q}_i/dP_0 = \frac{1}{STC''(\overline{Q}_{i0})} > 0$$

Thus, consistent with expectations, the instantaneous effect on the firm's optimal output of an infinitesimal change in the market price is positive. More simply, in the short run, a rise (fall) in the market price, *ceteris paribus,* would induce an increase (decrease) in the profit-maximizing level of output for a perfectly competitive firm.

Return to the earlier numerical example of a perfectly competitive firm i facing a market equilibrium price of $P_0 = \$15$ and producing a profit-maximizing output of $Q_i = 378$ units per day. A fall in the market equilibrium price to $P_1 = \$12$ reduced the firm's profit-maximizing output to 352 units a day.

Changes in Market Wage   Now consider a firm i, that is a perfect competitor in a labor market. The firm's short-run profit function is: $\Pi_i = \Pi[Q(K_{i0}, L_i)] = R[Q(K_{i0}, L_i)] - r_0 \cdot K_{i0} - w_0 \cdot L_{i0}$; where K_{i0} is the firm's fixed capital stock, r_0 is the given user cost of capital, and w_0 is the market equilibrium wage rate. To maximize profits, firm i would employ labor, L_i, up to the point where the marginal revenue product of labor, $(MRP_L)_i = dR_i/dL_i$, equals the market wage, w_0, which is the firm's marginal factor cost of labor, $(MFC_L)_i = dSTC_i/dL_i$. Recall that this decision rule follows from the first-order condition:

$$d\Pi_i/dL_i = (dR_i/dQ_i)(dQ_i/dL_i) - w_0 = 0$$

and

$$(dR_i/dQ_i)(dQ_i/dL_i) = w_0$$

$$dR_i/dL_i = w_0$$

If we regard the first-order condition as an equation of the form, $F(L_i; w_0) = 0$, where L_i, the labor employed by firm i, is the dependent variable and w_0, the market wage, is the independent variable, then we may be able to apply the Implicit Function Theorem. To check, the equation, $dR_i/dL_i - w_0 = 0$, does have continuous partial derivatives:

$$F_{L_i} = \delta F/\delta L_i = \frac{d(dR_i/dL_i)}{dL_i} = \frac{d^2 R_i}{dL_i^2} = R''(L_i)$$

$$F_{w_0} = \delta F/\delta w_0 = -1$$

In addition, at the critical point, (here, the profit-maximizing level of labor, $\overline{L}_{i0}$, where $R'(\overline{L}_{i0}) = w_0$), the partial derivative, $F_{L_i} \neq 0$. In fact, the second-order condition for a profit maximization requires that the slope of the marginal revenue product of labor curve is negative at the optimal level of employment, that is,

$$\frac{d^2 R_i(\overline{L}_{i0})}{dL_i^2} = R''(\overline{L}_{i0}) < 0.$$

In addition, the perfectly competitive firm's demand curve for labor is the declining portion of its marginal revenue product of labor curve that falls below its average revenue product of labor curve. Therefore, the conditions of the Implicit Function Theorem are satisfied, and we can assume that the implicit function, $\overline{L}_i = L(w_0)$, is defined. Note that, as in the previous example of a perfectly competitive firm in a product market, in this short-run model we only have one independent variable, the market wage.

To find the effect of a change in the market wage on the optimal level of labor, we totally differentiate the first-order condition, evaluated at the profit maximizing level of employment, $\overline{L}_{i0}$, and then solve for $d\overline{L}_i/dw_0$. Proceeding, we write the first-order condition as: $R'(\overline{L}_{i0}) - w_0 = 0$. Totally differentiating, we have

$$R''(\overline{L}_{i0}) \, d\overline{L}_i - dw_0 = 0$$

where $R''(\overline{L}_{i0})$ is the value of the slope of the marginal revenue product of labor curve at the profit maximizing level of employment:

$$R''(\overline{L}_{i0}) = \frac{d(R'(\overline{L}_{i0}))}{dL_i} < 0$$

Solving for $d\bar{L}_i/dw_0$, the comparative static result we seek, gives

$$d\bar{L}_i/dw_0 = \frac{1}{R''(\bar{L}_{i0})} < 0$$

In words, the instantaneous effect on the firm's optimal level of employment in the short run of an infinitesimal change in the market wage, is negative. That is, a rise (fall) in the market wage, *ceteris paribus,* would decrease (increase) the profit-maximizing level of employment for a perfectly competitive firm in a labor market.

Return to the earlier numerical example where a perfectly competitive firm *i* hired 6.4 workers per day when the daily market wage was $120. *Ceteris paribus*, if the market wage declined to $110, the firm would hire 6.5 workers per day.

We could also analyze a firm that is a perfect competitor in both a product market and a labor market — assessing the effects of a change in the market wage or a change in the market price of the firm's output on the firm's profit-maximizing level of employment in the short run. We leave this exercise as an end-of-chapter problem.

A final observation, we have set forth a model of the perfectly competitive firm. Actually, we may be hard pressed to find "real-world" examples of perfect competition. Even the competitive market for unskilled labor may be restricted by minimum wage legislation. Nevertheless, the model of perfect competition provides a useful frame of reference for the more common forms of imperfect competition. Next, we turn to monopolistically competitive firms.

MONOPOLISTICALLY COMPETITIVE FIRMS

As noted at the outset of the chapter, in **monopolistic competition** there are a large number of sellers of slightly differentiated products — as opposed to perfect competition where the outputs of the firms are identical. This characteristic of product differentiation means that each firm is a price-setter (not a price-taker) and faces a highly elastic or price-sensitive (but not horizontal) demand curve for its output. Examples of monopolistically competitive markets include fast food restaurants, gasoline stations, and convenience stores. Each firm, while supplying essentially the same goods or services, engages in both price competition (lowering its price to increase the quantity demanded of its output) and nonprice competition (advertising, salesmanship, and service to increase the demand for its output).

In monopolistic competition, with many suppliers, no one firm has any significant market influence. Firms are free to enter and exit the market. Positive economic profits would attract new firms and perhaps lead to the expansion of existing firms. Conversely, negative economic profits may result in the contraction of existing firms, and even the exit of firms from the market. Therefore, just as in perfect competition, zero economic profits prevail in long-run equilibrium.

The Firm's Marginal Revenue Schedule As noted earlier, monopolistically competitive firms set their own prices. *Ceteris paribus*, facing a negatively sloped demand curve, a monopolistically competitive firm i has to lower its price in order to increase its sales over any given period of time. Since the price charged by firm i, P_i, is inversely related to the quantity of its output demanded and sold, Q_i, we can write $P_i = P(Q_i)$, where $dP_i/dQ_i < 0$.

Since firm i is a price-setter, its total revenue, R_i, is not a linear function of its output. Moreover, the firm's marginal revenue, MR_i, is less than the price it charges, P_i, which equals its average revenue, AR_i. Formally, the total revenue, average revenue, and marginal revenue of a monopolistically competitive firm i are:

$$R_i = P(Q_i) \cdot Q_i$$

$$AR_i = R_i/Q_i = P_i$$

$$MR_i = dR_i/dQ_i = (dP_i/dQ_i) \cdot Q_i + P_i \quad \text{(with } MR_i < P_i, \text{ since } dP_i/dQ_i < 0\text{)}$$

We illustrate in Figure 7.7 for a monopolistically competitive firm i, facing a linear demand schedule for its output: $Q_i^d = Q^d(P_i) = d_0 - d_1 P_i$, where $d_0 > 0$ and $d_1 > 0$. First, we will take the inverse of the demand schedule, and solve for the price in order to correspond better with the graphical orientation (with price on the vertical axis). The demand schedule is rewritten as: $P_i = (d_0/d_1) - (1/d_1)Q_i$. The revenue functions are:

$$R_i = (P_i)(Q_i) = (d_0/d_1)Q_i - (1/d_1)Q_i^2$$

$$AR_i = R_i/Q_i = P_i = (d_0/d_1) - (1/d_1)Q_i$$

$$MR_i = dR_i/dQ_i = (d_0/d_1) - (2/d_1)Q_i$$

As is true for any firm, the monopolistically competitive firm's average revenue curve is identical to its demand curve (see $AR_i = D_i$ in Figure 7.7). Plotting the firm's average revenue against the quantity demanded of its output is equivalent to plotting the price charged against the quantity demanded.

The linear marginal revenue curve has the same vertical intercept, but twice the slope of the linear demand curve: $dMR_i/dQ_i = -2/d_1 = 2(dP_i/dQ_i) = 2(-1/d_1)$.[2] For a price-setting firm i, $MR_i < P_i$ for any output sold, since its marginal revenue curve lies below its demand curve. Marginal revenue is less than price due to the loss in revenue on units that could have been sold during the period at a higher price if the firm had not reduced its price to increase sales. Marginal revenue equals zero when the quantity demanded equals $d_0/2$; that is, the marginal revenue curve cuts the quantity axis at the midpoint of the demand curve intercept.

For a linear demand equation, the graph of the total revenue function is a parabola. For output (sales) up to the amount, $d_0/2$, total revenue is rising, since mar-

---

[2]Technically, marginal revenue (MR) is not defined for an output of zero, so the vertical intercept of the demand curve is not included on the marginal revenue curve.

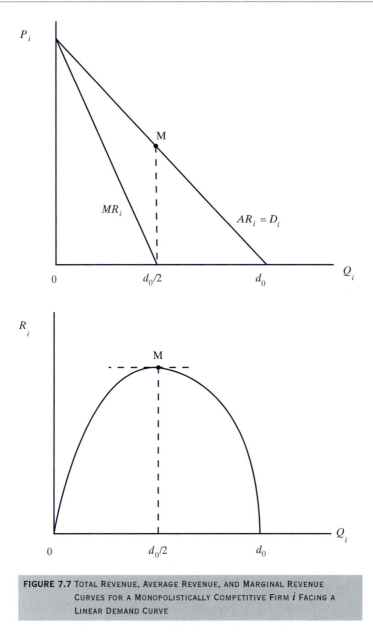

FIGURE 7.7 TOTAL REVENUE, AVERAGE REVENUE, AND MARGINAL REVENUE
CURVES FOR A MONOPOLISTICALLY COMPETITIVE FIRM *i* FACING A
LINEAR DEMAND CURVE

ginal revenue is positive. Beyond this level of output (sales), total revenue is declining since marginal revenue is negative. Total revenue is maximized when marginal revenue equals zero: $dR_i/dQ_i = MR(Q_i) = 0$ when $Q_i = d_0/2$.

To illustrate with a numerical example, consider the linear demand schedule for a monopolistically competitive firm i: $Q_i^d = 30 - 6P_i$.

Rewriting in terms of the firm's price, we have: $P_i = 5 - (1/6)Q_i$

The total revenue schedule for the firm is: $R_i = (P_i) \cdot (Q_i) = [5 - (1/6)Q_i]Q_i = 5Q_i - (1/6)Q_i^2$.

The average revenue and marginal revenue schedules are:

$$AR_i = R_i/Q_i^2 = 5 - (1/6)Q_i = P_i$$

$$MR_i = dR_i/dQ_i = 5 - (1/3)Q_i$$

Note that marginal revenue is less than price for positive quantities:

$$MR_i = 5 - (1/3)Q_i < 5 - (1/6)Q_i = P_i$$

To find the output where total revenues are maximized, we set marginal revenue equal to zero.

$$dR_i/dQ_i = MR_i = 5 - (1/3)Q_i = 0$$

Solving for output, we have $Q_i = 15$.

For output up to $Q_i = 15$, the marginal revenue is positive and total revenues are increasing. For output beyond $Q_i = 15$, the marginal revenue is negative and total revenue is decreasing.

PRICE ELASTICITY OF DEMAND

Elasticity provides a standardized measure of the responsiveness of one variable to a change in a related variable. By standardized, we mean that the magnitude of the elasticity is independent of the units of measurement for the involved variables. In general, for a function, $y = f(x)$, the elasticity of the variable y with respect to the variable x, evaluated at any ordered pair, (x,y), that satisfies the function, is given by:

$$\epsilon_{y,x} = \frac{dy/y}{dx/x} = \frac{dy/dx}{y/x}.$$

The ratio of the differential of y, (dy), divided by y, to the differential of x, (dx), divided by x, is the ratio of the instantaneous growth rate of y, (dy/y), to the instantaneous growth rate of x, (dx/x). Rearranging, the elasticity of y with respect to x can also be expressed as the ratio of the derivative of y with respect to x, (dy/dx), to the quotient of the two variables, (y/x).

If we allow for discrete changes in the variables, Δx and Δy, as opposed to infinitesimal changes, dx and dy, then the elasticity of y with respect to x is the ratio of the percentage change in y to the percentage change in x:

$$\epsilon_{y,x} = \frac{\Delta y/y}{\Delta x/x} = \frac{\% \text{ change in } y}{\% \text{ change in } x}$$

Relevant to our discussion here is the **price elasticity of demand**, ϵ_p^d, which measures the responsiveness of the quantity demanded of a commodity to a change in its price.

$$\epsilon_p^d = \frac{(dQ^d/Q^d)}{(dP/P)} = \frac{(dQ^d/dP)}{(Q^d/P)}$$

For the usual case of a downward-sloping demand curve, $dQ^d/dP < 0$, the price elasticity of demand is negative, so we can focus on the magnitude or absolute value of the elasticity.

If the price elasticity of demand is less than negative one, $\epsilon_p^d < -1$ or $|\epsilon_p^d| > 1$, then the demand is price elastic. The quantity demanded is fairly sensitive to changes in price: $|dQ^d/Q^d| > |dP/P|$.

If the price elasticity of demand equals negative one, $\epsilon_p^d = -1$ or $|\epsilon_p^d| = 1$, then the demand is unitary elastic. Here $|dQ^d/Q^d| = |dP/P|$.

Finally, if the price elasticity of demand is greater than negative one, but less than zero, $-1 < \epsilon_p^d < 0$ or $|\epsilon_p^d| < 1$, then the demand is price inelastic. The quantity demanded is not very sensitive to changes in price: $|dQ^d/Q^d| < |dP/P|$.

The Price Elasticity of Demand and Total Revenues   The price elasticity of demand is systematically related to the changes in total expenditures associated with price changes for a commodity. Note that total expenditures are equal to total revenues when there are no market "distortions," such as excise taxes. Consequently, we focus on the total revenues of the firm.

For a price elastic demand, total revenues, R, vary inversely with price changes. That is, a rise in price decreases the total revenues and a fall in price increases total revenues. For $|\epsilon_p^d| > 1$: if $P \uparrow$ then $R \downarrow$; if $P \downarrow$ then $R \uparrow$.

For unitary price elasticity of demand, total revenues are invariant to price changes. A $r\%$ rise (fall) in the unit price of a commodity will be exactly offset by an $r\%$ decrease (increase) in the quantity demanded, leaving total revenues unchanged.

For a price inelastic demand, total revenues, R, vary directly with price changes. A rise in price increases the total revenues. A fall in price decreases the total revenues. For $|\epsilon_p^d| < 1$: if $P \uparrow$ then $R \uparrow$; if $P \downarrow$ then $R \downarrow$.

The price elasticity of demand varies along a negatively sloped, linear demand curve from elastic (the upper half of the curve) to inelastic (the lower half of the curve). Refer back to Figure 7.7. For output below $d_0/2$, a decrease in price would increase total revenues—since $MR > 0$ and the demand is price elastic. Beyond the output $d_0/2$, decreases in price reduce total revenues—since $MR < 0$ and the demand is price inelastic. Total revenues are maximized when $MR = 0$ and the demand is unitary price elastic. (See point M at the output $d_0/2$). Thus, in general, for a given demand curve for a commodity, the value of the price elasticity of demand depends on the particular price-quantity combination under consideration.

We demonstrate for the linear demand equation, $Q^d = d_0 - d_1 P$, or alternatively, $P = (d_0/d_1) - (1/d_1)Q$, where $d_0, d_1 > 0$. The price elasticity of demand is:

$$\epsilon_p^d = \frac{dQ^d/dP}{Q^d/P} = \frac{-d_1}{Q/[(d_0/d_1) - (1/d_1)Q]} = \frac{Q - d_0}{Q} = 1 - (d_0/Q)$$

For $0 < Q < d_0/2$, the demand is price elastic, $\epsilon_p^d < -1$.
For $Q = d_0/2$, the demand is unitary price elastic, $\epsilon_p^d = -1$.
For $d_0/2 < Q < d_0$, the demand is price inelastic, $-1 < \epsilon_p^d < 0$.

Recall the earlier numerical example, where the firm's demand curve was: $Q_i^d = 30 - 6P_i$ or $P_i = 5 - (1/6)Q_i$. We showed that total revenues would rise with quantity (sales) up to $Q_i = 15$. The price elasticity of demand for this schedule is given by:

$$\epsilon_p^d = \frac{Q_i - d_0}{Q_i} = \frac{Q_i - 30}{Q_i} \qquad \text{where } d_0 = 30$$

For $0 < Q_i < 15$, or the upper half of the demand curve, $\epsilon_p^d < -1$, and the demand is price elastic. For $Q_i = 15$, the midpoint of the demand curve, $\epsilon_p^d = -1$, and the demand is unitary elastic. For $15 < Q_i < 30$, or the lower half of the demand curve, $-1 < \epsilon_p^d < 0$, and the demand is price inelastic.

PRACTICE PROBLEM 7.3

For the following demand schedule for firm i, $Q_i^d = 40 - 5P_i$:
a) Determine the level of output that maximizes the firm's total revenues. What is the price elasticity of demand at this output?
b) Determine the ranges of output that correspond to the price elastic and price inelastic regions of the demand curve.
c) Determine the price elasticity of demand when the firm's output is:
   i) $Q_i = 15$ ii) $Q_i = 25$.

(The answers are at the end of the chapter.)

Note that a profit-maximizing, price-setting firm, like a monopolistic competitor, would not push sales into the price inelastic region of its demand curve. Here, with a demand curve given by $Q_i = d_0 - d_1P$, a firm would not lower its price such that the quantity demanded increased beyond $Q = d_0/2$. To maximize profits, a firm sets $MC = MR$, and given that marginal cost is always positive, the firm would restrict output (and sales) to the upper half or price elastic region of its demand curve (where $MR > 0$). Put another way, as output increases beyond $d_0/2$, not only would the total cost be rising, but the total revenue would also be falling.

There are two cases of linear demand curves where the price elasticity of demand is constant. See Figure 7.8. The vertical demand curve represents a perfectly price inelastic demand: the quantity demanded is invariant to price changes, so $\epsilon_p^d = 0$. Examples that might approach this extreme case would be the demand for life-saving medical procedures (for example, heart transplants) and the demand of addicted individuals for illicit drugs. Here total revenue varies directly with price. The horizontal demand curve represents a perfectly elastic demand: the quantity demanded is infinitely sensitive to price changes, so $\epsilon_p^d = -\infty$. Recall, a perfectly competitive firm faces a perfectly elastic demand curve, assuming that it can sell any quantity it produces at the market-clearing price. Here, total revenues vary directly with the quantity sold.

An important determinant of the price elasticity of demand for a commodity is the availability of close substitutes. In perfect competition, the outputs of the firms are perfect substitutes. In monopolistic competition, the outputs of the firms are somewhat differentiated, for example, the different varieties of grilled chicken sandwiches

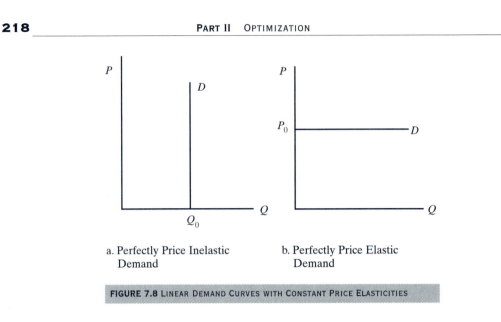

a. Perfectly Price Inelastic
Demand

b. Perfectly Price Elastic
Demand

FIGURE 7.8 LINEAR DEMAND CURVES WITH CONSTANT PRICE ELASTICITIES

offered by fast food outlets. Consequently, the demand curve facing each firm would be fairly elastic.

Before leaving this subject, we should note a nonlinear case of a constant price elasticity of demand. The demand equation, $Q^d = k/P$, where $k > 0$ represents a constant, has unitary price elasticity.

$$\epsilon_p^d = \frac{dQ/dP}{Q/P} = \frac{-k/P^2}{(k/P)/P} = -1$$

The graph of this demand equation, illustrated in Figure 7.9, is a rectangular hyperbola. Any change in price induces an offsetting change in quantity demanded such that total revenue is unchanged. For all price-quantity combinations on the demand curve, D, the areas formed by dropping perpendiculars to the axes are equal to k, for example, $(P_1) \cdot (Q_1) = (P_2) \cdot (Q_2) = k$. In fact, $k = (P) \cdot (Q) = (P) \cdot (k/P) = k$.

We now turn to the determination of the profit-maximizing output and price for a monopolistically competitive firm.

PROFIT MAXIMIZATION FOR A MONOPOLISTICALLY COMPETITIVE FIRM

The profit function to be maximized by firm i is $\Pi_i = \Pi(Q_i) = R_i - STC_i = P(Q_i) \cdot Q_i - STC(Q_i)$. The firm's total revenue, R_i, is equal to the product of the unit price, P_i, and the quantity of output, Q_i. The price charged by the firm, however, depends inversely on the quantity sold ($dP_i/dQ_i < 0$). The short-run total cost of the firm, STC_i, is a positive function of the output produced.

To determine the profit-maximizing level of output, we set the derivative of profits with respect to output equal to zero. Rearranging this first-order condition reveals the optimal decision rule.

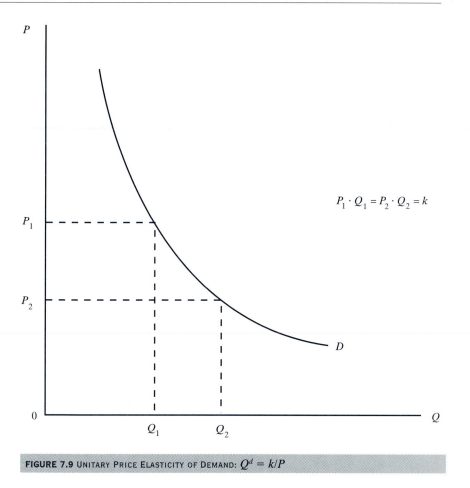

$$P_1 \cdot Q_1 = P_2 \cdot Q_2 = k$$

FIGURE 7.9 UNITARY PRICE ELASTICITY OF DEMAND: $Q^d = k/P$

$$d\Pi_i/dQ_i = dR_i/dQ_i - dSTC_i/dQ_i = 0$$
$$= (dP_i/dQ_i) \cdot Q_i + P_i - dSTC_i/dQ_i = 0$$
$$P'(Q_i) \cdot Q_i + P(Q_i) = STC'(Q_i)$$
$$MR(\overline{Q}_i) = MC(\overline{Q}_i)$$

To maximize profits, monopolistically competitive firm i would select the level of output, $\overline{Q}_i$, where the marginal revenue, $MR(\overline{Q}_i) = P'(\overline{Q}_i) \cdot \overline{Q}_i + P(\overline{Q}_i)$, equals the marginal cost of production, $MC(\overline{Q}_i) = STC'(\overline{Q}_i)$. Recall, this is the general profit-maximizing rule for any firm.

For a maximum, the second-order condition requires, at the critical level of output, $\overline{Q}_i$:

$$\frac{d(d\Pi_i/dQ_i)}{dQ_i} = \frac{d^2\Pi_i}{dQ_i^2} = \frac{d\,(dR_i/dQ_i)}{dQ_i} - \frac{d\,(dSTC_i/dQ_i)}{dQ_i} = \frac{dMR_i}{dQ_i} - \frac{dMC_i}{dQ_i} < 0$$

That is, at the profit-maximizing level of output, the slope of the marginal revenue curve,

$$\frac{d(MR(\overline{Q}_i))}{dQ_i} = R''(\overline{Q}_i),$$

must be less than the slope of the marginal cost curve,

$$\frac{d(MC\,(\overline{Q}_i))}{dQ_i} = STC''(\overline{Q}_i).$$

Moreover, the shut-down rule still applies. To minimize losses, monopolistically competitive firm i would cease production in the short run if its average variable cost exceeds its price.

Being a price-setter, a monopolistically competitive firm will charge the highest price it can for the output produced. If $\overline{Q}_i$ is the profit-maximizing output, the price is derived from the firm's demand curve: $\overline{P}_i = P(\overline{Q}_i)$. For example, if the firm's demand equation were linear, $Q_i^d = d_0 - d_1 P_i$, then solving for the price gives the inverse function, $P_i = (d_0/d_1) - (1/d_1)Q_i$. At the optimal output, the price set is $\overline{P}_i = (d_0/d_1) - (1/d_1)\overline{Q}_i$.

We illustrate in Figure 7.10 for a monopolistically competitive firm i. Given the demand and short run cost functions, firm i's profit-maximizing output is $\overline{Q}_{i0}$, where its marginal revenue and marginal cost curves intersect. The second order condition is clearly satisfied at this point by the negative slope of the marginal revenue curve and the positive slope of the marginal cost curve. Given the output, $\overline{Q}_{i0}$, firm i will charge the price, $\overline{P}_{i0}$, read off its demand curve. In other words, at the price, $\overline{P}_{i0}$, the quantity demanded of the firm's output equals the profit-maximizing level of output produced by the firm. In this example, the firm is earning positive economic profits equal to $(\overline{P}_{i0} - ATC_0) \cdot \overline{Q}_{i0}$, and represented by the area of the rectangle, $\overline{P}_{i0}E_0F_0ATC_0$.

Long-Run Equilibrium   With freedom of entry and exit, new firms would be attracted to the market by the above normal returns on invested capital. The demand and marginal revenue curves for firm i would shift left. With more competitors in the market, firm i's share of the market demand would be reduced. Firm i, however, earning positive economic profits, may expand by investing in additional capital. If so, its short run cost curves would shift right. In the market, new firms enter and existing firms expand until zero economic profits prevail.

Recall, with zero economic profits, total revenue just covers total cost, including the opportunity cost of the funds invested in the physical capital stock. With zero economic profits, there is no incentive for a firm to either increase or decrease the amount invested in physical capital. Nor is any incentive provided for new firms to enter the market.

In Figure 7.11 we illustrate a situation where the monopolistically competitive firm is earning negative economic profits. At the profit-maximizing output, $\overline{Q}_{i1}$, economic

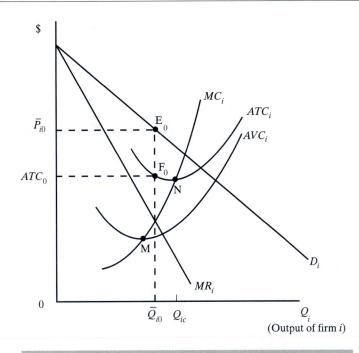

FIGURE 7.10 PROFIT-MAXIMIZING LEVEL OF OUTPUT FOR A MONOPOLISTICALLY
COMPETITIVE FIRM i

FIGURE 7.11 ECONOMIC LOSSES FOR A MONOPOLISTICALLY COMPETITIVE FIRM i

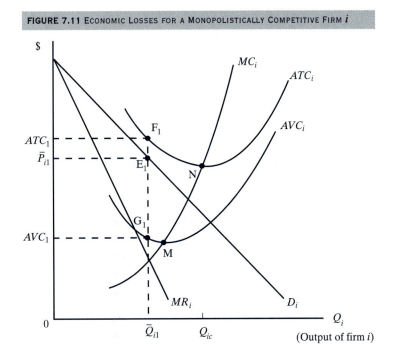

losses equal $(ATC_1 - \overline{P}_{i1}) \cdot \overline{Q}_{i1}$ and are represented by the area of the rectangle, $ATC_1F_1E_1\overline{P}_{i1}$. The firm would keep producing, however, since its price exceeds its average variable cost $(\overline{P}_{i1} > AVC_1)$, so all of its variable costs and at least some of its fixed costs are being covered. To elaborate, $\overline{P}_{i1}E_1G_1AVC_1$ of its total fixed costs of $ATC_1F_1G_1AVC_1$ are covered by the firm's total revenue of $\overline{P}_{i1}E_1\overline{Q}_{i1} 0$.

Nevertheless, with a below-normal return on its capital invested, the owners of the firm would begin to reduce their investment by not replacing the worn-out physical capital. As the capital stock declines, the firm's short run cost curves shift left. If other firms exit the market—because their average variable costs exceed the prices they can charge—then firm i (and any other remaining firms) would find their demand and marginal revenue curves shifting right, reflecting less competition in the market. These adjustments continue until a long run equilibrium of zero economic profits is reached.

To illustrate with a numerical problem, suppose firm i, a monopolistic competitor, faces a demand schedule for its product given by, $Q_i^d = 16 - 2P_i$, where Q_i is the quantity demanded (in hundreds of units per day) and P_i is the price set by the firm. The firm's short-run total cost function is: $STC(Q_i) = Q_i^3 - 5Q_i^2 + 10Q_i + 12$. To find the firm's profit-maximizing output we could either set up the profit function, $\Pi_i = \Pi(Q_i)$ $= R(Q_i) - STC(Q_i) = P(Q_i) \cdot Q_i - STC(Q_i)$; or we could apply the decision rule, setting the firm's marginal revenue (MR_i) equal to its marginal cost (MC_i). Let's do the latter.

The firm's total revenue function is obtained by multiplying the firm's price, P_i, by the output demanded and sold, Q_i. Rewriting the demand schedule as: $P_i = 8 - (1/2)Q_i$, the total revenue schedule is: $R_i = R(Q_i) = P_i \cdot Q_i = 8Q_i - (1/2)Q_i^2$. The marginal revenue schedule is then: $MR_i = dR(Q_i)/dQ_i = 8 - Q_i$.

The marginal cost schedule, as we know, is derived from the short-run total cost schedule: $MC_i = dSTC(Q_i)/dQ_i = 3Q_i^2 - 10Q_i + 10$. Setting marginal revenue equal to marginal cost and solving for the profit-maximizing output, we find:

$$8 - Q_i = 3Q_i^2 - 10Q_i + 10$$

$$3Q_i^2 - 9Q_i + 2 = 0$$

$$Q_i = \frac{-(-9) \pm \sqrt{(9)^2 - 4(3)(2)}}{2(3)} = \frac{9 \pm \sqrt{81 - 24}}{6} = \frac{9 \pm 7.55}{6} = .24, 2.76$$

The second-order condition for profit maximization is that the slope of the marginal revenue curve, $dMR(Q_i)/dQ_i = MR'(Q_i)$, is less than the slope of the marginal cost curve, $dMC(Q_i)/dQ_i = MC'(Q_i)$, at the critical output. We can show that this condition is not met for the lower critical output of $Q_i = .24$.

$$MR'(.24) = -1$$

$$MC'(.24) = 6Q_i - 10 = 6(.24) - 10 = -8.56.$$

So, here $MC'(.24) < MR'(.24)$, and $Q_i = .24$ is actually the profit-minimizing level of output.

The critical output $Q_i = 2.76$, however, does meet the second-order condition for a profit maximization.

$$MR'(2.76) = -1$$

$$MC'(2.76) = 6Q_i - 10 = 6(2.76) - 10 = 6.56.$$

Since $MC'(\overline{Q}_i) > MR'(\overline{Q}_i)$, then $\overline{Q}_{i0} = 2.76$ (hundred units per day) is the firm's profit-maximizing output.

At this output, the firm would set the price from its demand schedule: $\overline{P}_{i0} = 8 - (1/2)\overline{Q}_{i0} = 8 - (1/2)(2.76) = \$6.62$. Consequently, the firm's total revenues are: $R(\overline{Q}_{i0}) = \overline{P}_{i0} \cdot \overline{Q}_{i0} = (6.62)(2.76) = \$18.27$ (hundred per day). The firm's total costs are: $STC(\overline{Q}_{i0}) = \overline{Q}_{i0}^3 - 5\overline{Q}_{i0}^2 + 10\overline{Q}_{i0} + 12 = (2.76)^3 - 5(2.76)^2 + 10(2.76) + 12 = \$22.53$ (hundred per day). The firm is earning negative economic profits of $4.26 (hundred per day).

$$\Pi(\overline{Q}_{i0}) = \Pi(2.76) = 18.27 - 22.53 = -4.26$$

Nevertheless, since its revenues, $18.27, exceed its total variable costs, $10.53 (i.e., $STC - TFC = 22.53 - 12$), the firm would continue to produce in the short run. Though, as long as some of its fixed costs were uncovered, the firm would not replace its physical capital when worn out (resulting in leftward shifts in the firm's short-run average and marginal cost curves). The firm would hope that other firms might exit the market, which would shift its demand curve to the right. As discussed earlier, in long-run equilibrium, the monopolistically competitive firm would earn zero economic profits.

Two observations should be made before leaving this numerical example. First, at its profit-maximizing output, the monopolistically competitive firm's price exceeds its marginal cost—in contrast to a perfectly competitive firm, where the price (set by the market) is equal to the firm's marginal cost of output when profits are maximized. Here, $\overline{P}_{i0} = \$6.62$ and the marginal cost at $\overline{Q}_{i0}$ is $MC(\overline{Q}_{i0}) = 3\overline{Q}_{i0}^2 - 10\overline{Q}_{i0} + 10 = 3(2.76)^2 - 10(2.76) + 10 = \$5.25$.

Second, for a price-setting firm, the profit-maximizing output will be in the price-elastic range of its demand curve. Here, the price elasticity of demand at $\overline{Q}_{i0} = 2.76$ equals:

$$\epsilon_p^d = \frac{dQ_i^d/dP_i}{Q_{i0}/P_{i0}} = \frac{-2}{(2.76)/(6.62)} = -4.80$$

Consistent with the availability of close substitutes found in monopolistic competition, the firm's price elasticity of demand at its profit-maximizing output is high.

PRACTICE PROBLEM 7.4

Given a monopolistically competitive firm i, facing a demand schedule, $Q_i^d = 14 - 2P_i$, where Q_i^d is the quantity demanded of the firm's output (in hundred units per day) and P_i is the unit price set by the firm (in dollars), and given the firm's short run total cost function, $STC(Q_i) = Q_i^3 - 6Q_i^2 + 8Q_i + 20$.

a) Find the firm's profit-maximizing level of output and price charged. Check the second-order condition.
b) Determine the level of profits for firm i.
c) Determine the price elasticity of demand at this profit-maximizing level of output.

(The answers are at the end of the chapter.)

An illustration of long run equilibrium for a monopolistic competitor is given in Figure 7.12. See point E* and the tangency of the firm's demand curve, short-run average total cost curve, and long-run average cost curve at the profit-maximizing level of output, Q_{i0}^*, where marginal revenue equals marginal cost. The firm is earning zero economic profits, since $P_{i0}^* = ATC_0^* = LRAC$. In long-run equilibrium, in contrast to a perfectly competitive firm, a monopolistically competitive firm will produce at less than its economic capacity $(Q_{i0}^* < Q_{ic})$ and on the declining portion of its long-run average cost curve. The additional unit cost above the minimum $(ATC_0^* > ATC_c)$ reflects the product differentiation in monopolistic competition, or the "price" consumers pay for product variety and choice.

Labor Employment Recall that to maximize profits in the short run, a firm i would hire labor up to the point where its marginal revenue product of labor $(MRP_L)_i$ equals its mar-

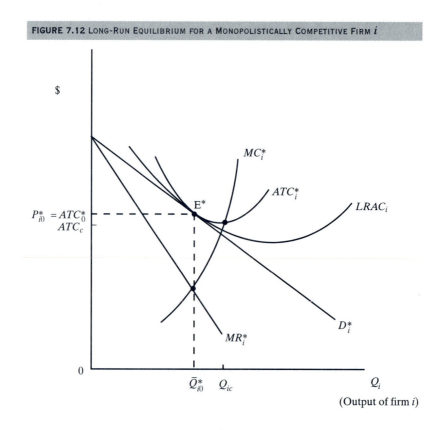

FIGURE 7.12 LONG-RUN EQUILIBRIUM FOR A MONOPOLISTICALLY COMPETITIVE FIRM i

ginal factor cost of labor $(MFC_L)_i$. A firm's marginal revenue product of labor is equal to its marginal revenue of output (MR_i) times its marginal product of labor $(MP_L)_i$.

For a perfectly competitive firm in an output market, its marginal revenue of output is constant and equal to the given market price, P_0. As noted earlier, the marginal revenue product of labor for a perfectly competitive firm in an output market is known as its value of marginal product of labor: $(VMP_L)_i = P_0 \cdot (MP_L)_i$.

For a monopolistic competitor, its marginal revenue of output is less than the price it sets, P_i. Consequently, its marginal revenue product of labor decreases as more labor is used, not only due to diminishing returns to labor, but also with the decrease in marginal revenue as its output rises.

For identical marginal product of labor curves and unit prices received by the firms, the marginal revenue product of labor curve for a monopolistic competitor would lie to the left of the value of marginal product of labor curve for a perfect competitor. Thus, for any given market wage, the monopolistically competitive firm's employment of less labor than the perfectly competitive firm is consistent with the monopolistically competitive firm's production of less output in long run equilibrium than the perfectly competitive firm.

From competition among many firms, we move to the other extreme for market structure. In Chapter 8 we discuss markets where there is only one firm—either as a single seller or as a single buyer.

❖ KEY TERMS

Economics

- average factor cost of labor (p. 203)
- marginal factor cost of labor (p. 203)

- monopolistic competition (p. 212)
- price elasticity of demand (p. 215)

- total factor cost of labor (p. 203)
- value of marginal product of labor (p. 205)

❖ PROBLEMS

1. Given firm i, a perfect competitor in a product market, with a short-run total cost function of $STC_i = STC(Q_i) = Q_i^3 - 8Q_i^2 + 20Q_i + 40$,

   where Q_i is the output of firm i (in hundreds of units per day).

   The market demand and supply schedules for the product are:

   $$Q^d = 600 - 20P \quad \text{and} \quad Q^s = -150 + 30P$$

   where Q^d and Q^s are the quantities demanded and supplied in the market (in hundreds of thousands of units per day) and P is the market price (in dollars per unit).
   a) Find the profit-maximizing level of output for firm i. Check the second order condition.
   b) Calculate the level of profits (losses).

c) Given the level of economic profits, discuss the long-run adjustment in the market and for this firm.

d) Repeat parts a, b, and c for a market demand curve of $Q^{d'} = 287.5 - 20P$.

2. Given firm i, a perfect competitor in a labor market and in an output market, with a short-run production function, $Q_i = -L_i^3 + 6L_i^2 + 2L_i$ where Q_i is the firm's output (in hundreds of units per day) and L_i is the labor employed by the firm (in hundreds of labor-hours per day).

Assume that the market demand and supply schedules of labor are:

$$L^d = 770 - 40w \quad \text{and} \quad L^s = -100 + 20w$$

where L^d and L^s are the market quantities of labor demanded and supplied (in hundreds of thousands of labor-hours per day) and w is the market wage (dollars per hour).

Assume that the market demand and supply schedules for the product are:

$$Q^d = 50 - 20P \quad \text{and} \quad Q^s = -20 + 15P$$

where Q^d and Q^s are the market quantities of output demanded and supplied (in hundreds of thousands of units per day) and P is the market price of the output (dollars per unit).

a) Derive the firm's average product of labor $(AP_L)_i$ and marginal product of labor $(MP_L)_i$ schedules.

b) Find the level of employment where diminishing returns to labor first set in for firm i.

c) Show that $(MP_L)_i = (AP_L)_i$ at the maximum of $(AP_L)_i$.

d) Determine the profit-maximizing level of employment for firm i in the short run and the level of output produced by the firm.

e) Suppose the market supply of labor fell to: $L^{s'} = -310 + 20w$. Determine the new profit-maximizing level of employment for firm i and the level of output produced by the firm.

f) Suppose, instead, the market demand for the output produced by firm i increased to:

$$Q^{d'} = 85 - 20P.$$

Determine the new profit-maximizing level of employment for firm i and the level of output produced by the firm.

3. Given a firm i, a perfect competitor in both its labor market and its product market, where w_0 is the given market wage and P_0 is the given market price for the output of the firm. The firm's short-run production function is $Q_i = Q(K_{i0}, L_i)$, where Q_i is the firm's output, K_{i0} is the firm's fixed capital stock, and L_i is the labor employed by the firm. Regard the user cost of capital, r_0, as given:

a) Write out the firm's short-run profit function.

b) Derive the conditions for the firm's profit-maximizing level of employment, $\overline{L}_{i0}$.

c) Verify that the Implicit Function Theorem holds for the above first-order condition evaluated at the profit-maximizing level of employment, $\overline{L}_{i0}$.

d) Find and determine the signs of the following comparative statics.

    i) $\delta \overline{L}_i / \delta w_0$

    ii) $\delta \overline{L}_i / \delta P_0$

4. Given the short-run total cost (STC) function of firm i, a monopolistic competitor in an output market, $STC_i = STC(Q_i) = Q_i^3 - 8Q_i^2 + 20Q_i + 21$, where Q_i is the output of firm i (in hundreds of units per day), and the demand schedule facing firm i of $Q_i^d = (32/3) - (2/3)P_i$:

a) Find the firm's total revenue and marginal revenue schedules. Find the output that maximizes the firm's total revenues.

b) Determine the firm's profit-maximizing level of output and the level of profits (losses).

c) Calculate the price elasticity of demand at this profit-maximizing level of output.

d) Given the level of economic profits, discuss the long run adjustment in the market and for this firm.

e) Repeat parts a, b, c, and d if firm i's demand schedule were instead: $Q_i^{d'} = 9 - (5/9)P_i$.

5. Show that for any price, the demand schedule, $Q^{d'} = 2d_0 - d_1 P$, is less price elastic than the demand schedule, $Q^d = d_0 - d_1 P$.

❖ ANSWERS TO PRACTICE PROBLEMS

7.1 a) The profit-maximizing output for firm i is $\overline{Q}_{i0} = 4.77$ (hundred units per day). The profits are: $\Pi_i = -\$2.34$ (hundred per day). $\Pi''(4.77) = -6.31 < 0$, which is consistent with a maximum.

b) The new profit-maximizing output for firm i is $\overline{Q}_{i1} = 4.93$ (hundred units per day). The profits are $\Pi_i = \$2.52$ (hundred per day). $\Pi''(4.93) = -6.79 < 0$, which is consistent with a maximum.

7.2 a) The profit-maximizing employment and output are: $\overline{L}_{i0} = 7.1$ (workers per day) and $\overline{Q}_{i0} = 239.2$ (units per day).

b) The total revenues of $R_i = \$1,674.4$ per day exceed the total variable costs of $TVC_i = \$568$ per day, so the firm would produce the profit-maximizing output of 239.2 units per day.

7.3 a) The firm's total revenue is maximized at an output of $Q_i = 20$. The price elasticity of demand at this output equals $\epsilon_p^d = -1$.

b) The demand is price elastic for outputs less than 20: $0 < Q_i < 20$. The demand is price inelastic for outputs between 20 and 40: $20 < Q_i < 40$.

c) The price elasticity of demand equals $\epsilon_p^d = -5/3$ when the firm's output is $Q_i = 15$. The price elasticity of demand equals $\epsilon_p^d = -3/5$ when the firm's output is $Q_i = 25$.

7.4 a) The firm's profit-maximizing output is $\overline{Q}_{i0} = 3.57$ (hundred units per day). The price set by the firm is $\overline{P}_{i0} = \$5.21$. The second order condition is satisfied since: $MR'(3.57) = -1$ and $MC'(3.57) = 9.42$, so $MC'(\overline{Q}_{i0}) > MR'(\overline{Q}_{i0})$.

b) The profits of firm i are $\Pi_i(\overline{Q}_{i0}) = \$1.03$ (hundred per day).

c) The price elasticity of demand at this profit-maximizing output is $\epsilon_p^d = -2.92$.

MONOPOLIES AND MONOPSONIES

At the other extreme from perfect competition is a market with only one firm—either as a single supplier (a monopoly) or as a single demander (monopsony). The primary objective of the sole firm is still assumed to be the maximization of profits. Moreover, with barriers to the entry of competitors, positive economic profits may be maintained over time.

In this chapter we examine a monopolist in an output market, where the firm in setting its profit-maximizing output and price is able to capture some of the consumers' surplus that would have been realized by the demanders of the commodity under perfect competition. Moreover, we will see that a monopolist may be able to enhance its profits through price discrimination.

We will also model the behavior of a monopsonist in the labor market, that in setting its profit-maximizing level of employment and wage is able to capture some of the economic rent that would have been realized by the workers in a perfectly competitive situation. We will also see how a labor union may be able to turn a monopsonist into a wage-taker and increase the wages and employment of labor.

As the economic models of the firm are extended to explain behavior such as price discrimination, so too more advanced mathematics must be used. We begin this chapter with a discussion of optimization of functions of two or more independent or choice variables. Next we apply this mathematical technique to a firm seeking to maximize its profits with the optimal allocation of production over two or more plants. Then our analyses of monopolies and monopsonies follow.

UNCONSTRAINED OPTIMIZATION FOR MULTIVARIATE FUNCTIONS

We have illustrated cases of unconstrained optimization for objective functions of a single independent or choice variable; in particular, a firm's selection of the profit-maximizing level of output in the short run. We now address unconstrained optimization for objective functions of two independent variables, which will then be extended to functions of n independent variables. The first- and second-order conditions for the optimization of these objective functions are derived.

RELATIVE EXTREMA

Consider an objective function with two independent variables, $z = z(x, y)$, which is assumed to be smooth and continuous, hence differentiable. Totally differentiating the objective function, we obtain

$$dz = z_x \, dx + z_y \, dy$$

where $z_x = \delta z/\delta x$ and $z_y = \delta z/\delta y$ are the partial derivatives of the objective function with respect to the independent variables, x and y, respectively. The necessary, but not sufficient, first-order condition for a relative extremum at a point (x_0, y_0, z_0) satisfying the function is that: $dz = z_x \, dx + z_y \, dy = 0$. This, in turn, implies that $z_x = z_y = 0$, since dx and dy represent any arbitrary variations (although presumably infinitesimal) in the independent variables.

   Graphically, the first-order partials equaling zero means that lines tangent to the surface of $z = z(x, y)$ at the point (x_0, y_0, z_0), that are parallel to the xz plane (for $dy = 0$) and yz plane (for $dx = 0$), have zero slopes. For an absolute maximum (absolute minimum), picture two strings perpendicular to the sides of a box that are tangent to the top half (bottom half) of a beachball that is sitting in the box.

Second-Order Condition   For the second-order condition, which is needed to determine the type of relative extremum, we must evaluate $d(dz) = d^2z$, the differential of the differential of the function, $z = z(x, y)$. With our general function of two independent variables and three-dimensional graph, we are evaluating the curvature of the surface as we move away from a relative extremum. If in every direction the surface curls upward, that is, the change in the slope of the function is positive, $d(dz) > 0$ for any dx and dy, then we have a *relative minimum.* In the earlier illustration of an absolute minimum, imagine moving along the surface away from the bottom of the lower half of the beachball. Alternatively, picture leaving the bottom of a crater, where in any direction, you would walk up.

   Conversely, if the surface of $z = z(x, y)$ curls downward in every direction from a relative extremum, that is, the change in the slope of the function is negative, $d(dz) < 0$ for any dx and dy, then we have a *relative maximum.* In the case of the beachball in the box, coming off the top of the upper half of the ball, the slope of a line tangent to the surface is declining. Picture descending from the top of a hill.

   To obtain the second-order total differential associated with $z = z(x, y)$, we totally differentiate the first-order total differential, $dz = z_x \, dx + z_y \, dy$.

$$d(dz) = d^2z = \frac{\delta(dz)}{\delta x} \, dx + \frac{\delta(dz)}{\delta y} \, dy$$

$$= \frac{\delta(z_x\, dx + z_y\, dy)}{\delta x} + \frac{\delta(z_x\, dx + z_y\, dy)}{\delta y}$$

$$= (z_{xx}\, dx + z_{xy}\, dy)\, dx + (z_{yx}\, dx + z_{yy}\, dy)\, dy$$

$$d^2 z = z_{xx}\,(dx)^2 + z_{xy}\, dx\, dy + z_{yx}\, dx\, dy + z_{yy}\,(dy)^2$$

z_{xx} is the second-order partial derivative of the function with respect to x—meaning that the function, $z = z(x, y)$, has been partially differentiated twice with respect to x (with $dy = 0$).

$$z_{xx} = \frac{\delta(z_x)}{\delta x} = \frac{\delta(\delta z/\delta x)}{\delta x} = \frac{\delta^2 z}{\delta x^2}$$

z_{yy} is the second-order partial derivative of the function with respect to y—meaning that the function, $z = z(x, y)$, has been partially differentiated twice with respect to y (with $dx = 0$).

$$z_{yy} = \frac{\delta(z_y)}{\delta y} = \frac{\delta(\delta z/\delta y)}{\delta y} = \frac{\delta^2 z}{\delta y^2}$$

z_{xy} is the cross-partial derivative—meaning that the function, $z = z(x, y)$, has been partially differentiated with respect to y (with $dx = 0$), and then partially differentiated with respect to x (with $dy = 0$).

$$z_{xy} = \frac{\delta(z_y)}{\delta x} = \frac{\delta(\delta z/\delta y)}{\delta x} = \frac{\delta^2 z}{\delta x \delta y}$$

z_{yx} is the cross-partial derivative—meaning that the function, $z = z(x, y)$, has been partially differentiated with respect to x (with $dy = 0$), and then partially differentiated with respect to y (with $dx = 0$).

$$z_{yx} = \frac{\delta(z_x)}{\delta y} = \frac{\delta(\delta z/\delta x)}{\delta y} = \frac{\delta^2 z}{\delta y \delta x}$$

Note that, given that the cross-partial derivatives are continuous, we can show that they are also equal to each other: $z_{xy} = z_{yx}$. This equality of the cross-partials, z_{xy} and z_{yx}, is known as Young's theorem. Thus, we can write the second-order total differential, d^2z, as

$$d^2 z = z_{xx}\,(dx)^2 + 2\, z_{xy}\, dx\, dy + z_{yy}\,(dy)^2$$

Equivalently, since $(dx)^2 = dx^2$ and $(dy)^2 = dy^2$, we have

$$d^2 z = z_{xx}\, dx^2 + 2\, z_{xy}\, dx\, dy + z_{yy}\, dy^2$$

Note that $dx^2 \neq d^2x$ and $dy^2 \neq d^2y$. That is, d^2x and d^2y are second-order differentials:

$$d^2 x = d(dx) \text{ and } d^2 y = d(dy); \text{ while } dx^2 = (dx)\cdot(dx) \text{ and } dy^2 = (dy)\cdot(dy).$$

Consider the following examples.

Example 1.   Given the function in two independent variables, $z = 7x^3 + 10x^2y + 5xy^2 + 14y^3$

$$z_x = \delta z/\delta x = 21x^2 + 20xy + 5y^2$$

$$z_y = \delta z/\delta y = 10x^2 + 10xy + 42y^2$$

and

$$dz = z_x \, dx + z_y \, dy = (21x^2 + 20xy + 5y^2) \, dx + (10x^2 + 10xy + 42y^2) \, dy$$

$$z_{xx} = \frac{\delta(z_x)}{\delta x} = 42x + 20y$$

$$z_{yy} = \frac{\delta(z_y)}{\delta y} = 10x + 84y$$

$$z_{xy} = \frac{\delta(z_y)}{\delta x} = 20x + 10y = \frac{\delta(z_x)}{\delta y} = z_{yx}$$

and

$$d^2z = z_{xx} \, dx^2 + 2 \, z_{xy} \, dx \, dy + z_{yy} \, dy^2$$

$$= (42x + 20y) \, dx^2 + (40x + 20y) \, dx \, dy + (10x + 84y) \, dy^2$$

Example 2.   Consider the long-run production function, $Q = Q(K, L) = K^a L^b$, with $0 < a < 1$ and $0 < b < 1$, and where Q = output, K = physical capital stock, and L = labor. (*Note:* This is an example of a Cobb-Douglas production function. In Chapter 10, the properties of production functions will be addressed in greater detail.) Partially differentiating output with respect to capital and labor, we have:

$$Q_K = \delta Q/\delta K = aK^{a-1} L^b > 0 \qquad \text{(The marginal product of capital is positive.)}$$

$$Q_L = \delta Q/\delta L = bK^a L^{b-1} > 0 \qquad \text{(The marginal product of labor is positive.)}$$

The total differential for output is: $dQ = Q_K \, dK + Q_L \, dL = aK^{a-1} L^b \, dK + bK^a L^{b-1} \, dL$.
Now, differentiating the marginal products with respect to capital and labor, we find

$$Q_{KK} = \frac{\delta(Q_K)}{\delta K} = (a-1)aK^{a-2} L^b < 0 \qquad \text{(given that } 0 < a < 1)$$

$$Q_{LL} = \frac{\delta(Q_L)}{\delta L} = (b-1)bK^a L^{b-2} < 0 \qquad \text{(given that } 0 < b < 1)$$

Note $Q_{KK} < 0$ and $Q_{LL} < 0$ reflect the law of diminishing returns applied to capital and labor, respectively. That is, for a given amount of labor (capital), increasing the use of capital (labor) will reduce the marginal product of capital (labor).

$$Q_{KL} = \frac{\delta(Q_L)}{\delta K} = abK^{a-1} L^{b-1} > 0$$

$$Q_{LK} = \frac{\delta(Q_K)}{\delta L} = abK^{a-1} L^{b-1} > 0$$

The cross-partials indicate the effects of changes in the use of one factor on the marginal product of the other. For example, an increase in the use of capital (labor), *ceteris paribus,* will increase the marginal product of labor (capital).

The second-order total differential, d^2Q, is equal to

$$d^2Q = Q_{KK} \, dK^2 + 2Q_{KL} \, dK \, dL + Q_{LL} \, dL^2$$

$$d^2Q = (a - 1)aK^{a-2} L^b \, dK^2 + 2 \, abK^{a-1} L^{b-1} \, dK \, dL + (b - 1)bK^a L^{b-2} \, dL^2$$

PRACTICE PROBLEM 8.1

Find the second-order total differentials, d^2z, of the following functions:

a) $z = 3x^4 + 2x^2y^2 - 4y^3$

b) $z = x^a + (xy)^b - y$

(The answers are at the end of the chapter.)

Signing the Second-Order Total Differential   In order to establish the type of relative extremum, we need to sign the second-order total differential: $d^2z > 0$ for a relative minimum, and $d^2z < 0$ for a relative maximum. Note that if $d^2z = 0$ at a critical point (i.e., given $dz = 0$ for any dx and dy, not both equal to zero), then we may have a saddle point. With a *saddle point,* from one perspective (e.g., for arbitrary dx, where $dy = 0$), the critical point appears to be a relative maximum; while from the other perspective (e.g., for arbitrary dy, where $dx = 0$), the critical point appears to be a relative minimum.

Visualize a saddle on a horse. Viewing the horse from the side, the saddle seat appears to be a relative minimum, since moving off center, the saddle slopes upwards to either the pommel (front of the saddle) or the cantle (back of the saddle). Viewing the saddle from behind the horse, a rider is sitting on the saddle, so the saddle would look like a relative maximum, since moving off center the saddle slopes down the sides of the horse.

So, to sign $d^2z = z_{xx} \, (dx)^2 + 2z_{xy} \, dx \, dy + z_{yy} \, (dy)^2$, and establish the type of relative extremum, we note that

$$z_{xx} \, (dx)^2 + 2 \, z_{xy} \, dx \, dy + \frac{(z_{xy})^2}{z_{xx}} \, (dy)^2 = z_{xx} \left[(dx) + \frac{(z_{xy})}{z_{xx}} \, (dy) \right]^2$$

Thus, we can write

$$d^2z = z_{xx} \left[(dx) + \frac{(z_{xy})}{z_{xx}} \, (dy) \right]^2 + (z_{yy})(dy)^2 - \frac{(z_{xy})^2}{z_{xx}} \, (dy)^2$$

where we added and subtracted the term, $\dfrac{(z_{xy})^2}{z_{xx}} (dy)^2$, from the d^2z expression.[1]
Consequently,

$$d^2z = z_{xx}\left[(dx) + \frac{(z_{xy})}{z_{xx}}(dy)\right]^2 + \left[z_{yy} - \frac{(z_{xy})^2}{z_{xx}}\right](dy)^2$$

and since the squared terms are positive, that is, $\left[(dx) + \dfrac{(z_{xy})}{z_{xx}}(dy)\right]^2 > 0$ and $(dy)^2 > 0$, the sign of the second-order total differential, d^2z, depends on the signs of z_{xx} and $\left[z_{yy} - \dfrac{(z_{xy})^2}{z_{xx}}\right]$.

We can say that $d^2z > 0$ and *positive definite* if $z_{xx} > 0$ and $\left[z_{yy} - \dfrac{(z_{xy})^2}{z_{xx}}\right] > 0$.

Moreover, $\left[z_{yy} - \dfrac{(z_{xy})^2}{z_{xx}}\right] > 0$ implies, for $z_{xx} > 0$, that $z_{xx}\,z_{yy} > (z_{xy})^2$ and $z_{yy} > 0$, since the product of z_{xx} and z_{yy} must be positive and greater than $(z_{xy})^2$.

We can say that $d^2z < 0$ and *negative definite* if $z_{xx} < 0$ and $\left[z_{yy} - \dfrac{(z_{xy})^2}{z_{xx}}\right] < 0$. For $z_{xx} < 0$, $\left[z_{yy} - \dfrac{(z_{xy})^2}{z_{xx}}\right] < 0$ implies that $z_{xx}z_{yy} - (z_{xy})^2 > 0$ and $z_{yy} < 0$. Note that multiplying through by $z_{xx} < 0$ reverses the sign of the inequality. Therefore, we also require for a negative definite the condition: $z_{xx}z_{yy} > (z_{xy})^2$.

In summary, given $z = z(x, y)$, a differentiable function:

1. $z_x = z_y = 0$ is a necessary condition for a relative extremum.
2. a. $z_{xx} > 0$ and $z_{xx}z_{yy} - (z_{xy})^2 > 0$ are sufficient conditions for the relative extremum to be a minimum (d^2z is positive definite).
   b. $z_{xx} < 0$ and $z_{xx}z_{yy} - (z_{xy})^2 > 0$ are sufficient conditions for the relative extremum to be a maximum (d^2z is negative definite).
   c. If $z_{xx}z_{yy} - (z_{xy})^2 < 0$, then the sign of d^2z is indefinite, and given the first-order condition is satisfied, we have a saddle point.
   d. If $z_{xx}z_{yy} - (z_{xy})^2 = 0$, then the second-order test is indeterminate. Further examination of points in the neighborhood of the critical point is required.

Hessians   We can also write the second-order total differential for $z = z(x, y)$ in matrix notation as:

$$d^2z = z_{xx}(dx)^2 + 2\,z_{xy}\,dx\,dy + z_{yy}(dy)^2$$

$$= [dx\ dy]\begin{bmatrix} z_{xx} & z_{xy} \\ z_{yx} & z_{yy} \end{bmatrix}\begin{bmatrix} dx \\ dy \end{bmatrix}$$

---

[1]Here we are using the technique of "completing the square," by adding and subtracting the term, $[(z_{xy})^2/z_{xx}]\,(dy)^2$, to the expression. In general, given a quadratic equation, $y = ax^2 + bx + c$, we can add and subtract the term, $b^2/4a$, which allows us to write: $y = a(x + b/2a)^2 + (c - b^2/4a)$. Now the sign of y depends on the signs of the coefficient a and the term $(c - b^2/4a)$, since $(x + b/2a)^2 > 0$.

The determinant of the matrix of second-order partial derivatives, arranged with the second-order direct partials on the principal diagonal, is called the *Hessian,* and is written as:

$$|H| = \begin{vmatrix} z_{xx} & z_{xy} \\ z_{yx} & z_{yy} \end{vmatrix}.$$

The first principal minor of the Hessian, written as $|H_1|$, is the subdeterminant formed by the first element in the principal diagonal. Here $|H_1| = |z_{xx}|$. The second principal minor of the Hessian, $|H_2|$, is the subdeterminant of dimension 2×2, formed by the first two elements along the principal diagonal. Here

$$|H_2| = \begin{vmatrix} z_{xx} & z_{xy} \\ z_{yx} & z_{yy} \end{vmatrix}.$$

Note: In our example with only two independent variables, the second principal minor of the Hessian is identical to the Hessian itself: $|H_2| = |H|$.

We can express the second-order conditions for a relative extremum in terms of the principal minors of the Hessian. Given a function, $z = z(x, y)$ and that $dz = 0$, that is, the first-order condition is satisfied with $z_x = z_y = 0$, then a sufficient condition:

for a relative minimum, $d^2z > 0$, is that the Hessian, $|H|$, is positive definite,

$$|H_1| > 0 \text{ and } |H_2| > 0;$$

for a relative maximum, $d^2z < 0$, is that the Hessian, $|H|$, is negative definite,

$$|H_1| < 0 \text{ and } |H_2| > 0$$

where $|H_1| = z_{xx}$ and $|H_2| = |H| = z_{xx}z_{yy} - (z_{xy})^2$

If the necessary first-order conditions are met, and if $|H_2| = |H| = z_{xx}z_{yy} - (z_{xy})^2 < 0$, then the critical point is a saddle point. If z_{xx} and z_{yy} have opposite signs, then the surface of the function will bend upward in one direction and downward in another direction. We will provide an example of this below. And, as noted earlier, if $|H_2| = 0$, the second-order test is inconclusive.

Consider the following function, $z = z(x, y) = 6x^2 - 9x - 3xy - 7y + 5y^2$. The first-order conditions to establish the critical points are:

$$z_x = 12x - 9 - 3y = 0$$

and

$$z_y = -3x - 7 + 10y = 0$$

This system of two equations in two unknowns can be solved as follows:

$$\begin{bmatrix} 12 & -3 \\ -3 & 10 \end{bmatrix} \begin{bmatrix} x \\ y \end{bmatrix} = \begin{bmatrix} 9 \\ 7 \end{bmatrix}$$

Note: We know that a solution exists and is unique since $\begin{vmatrix} 12 & -3 \\ -3 & 10 \end{vmatrix} = 111 \neq 0$

Using Cramer's rule, we solve

$$\bar{x}_0 = \frac{\begin{vmatrix} 9 & -3 \\ 7 & 10 \end{vmatrix}}{\begin{vmatrix} 12 & -3 \\ -3 & 10 \end{vmatrix}} = \frac{111}{111} = 1 \qquad \bar{y}_0 = \frac{\begin{vmatrix} 12 & 9 \\ -3 & 7 \end{vmatrix}}{\begin{vmatrix} 12 & -3 \\ -3 & 10 \end{vmatrix}} = \frac{111}{111} = 1$$

The optimal value of the dependent variable, $\bar{z}_0$, when $\bar{x}_0 = 1$ and $\bar{y}_0 = 1$, is -8.

$$\bar{z}_0 = 6(1)^2 - 9(1) - 3(1)(1) - 7(1) + 5(1)^2 = -8$$

Therefore, the critical point is $(\bar{x}_0, \bar{y}_0, \bar{z}_0) = (1, 1, -8)$.

Setting up the Hessian to evaluate the second-order conditions, we have

$$|H| = \begin{vmatrix} z_{xx} & z_{xy} \\ z_{yx} & z_{yy} \end{vmatrix} = \begin{vmatrix} 12 & -3 \\ -3 & 10 \end{vmatrix}$$

and

$$|H_1| = 12 > 0, \qquad |H_2| = |H| = (12)(10) - (-3)(-3) = 120 - 9 = 111 > 0.$$

The critical point, $(1, 1, -8)$ is a relative minimum.

As another example, consider the function, $z = z(x, y) = 4x^2 + 2xy - y^2 + 20y$. The first-order conditions are

$$z_x = 8x + 2y = 0$$

$$z_y = 2x - 2y + 20 = 0$$

Writing this system in matrix notation and using Cramer's rule to solve, we have

$$\begin{bmatrix} 8 & 2 \\ 2 & -2 \end{bmatrix} \begin{bmatrix} x \\ y \end{bmatrix} = \begin{bmatrix} 0 \\ -20 \end{bmatrix}$$

Note: Since the coefficient matrix is nonsingular, that is, $\begin{vmatrix} 8 & 2 \\ 2 & -2 \end{vmatrix} = -20 \neq 0$, this system has a unique solution.

$$\bar{x} = \frac{\begin{vmatrix} 0 & 2 \\ -20 & -2 \end{vmatrix}}{-20} = \frac{40}{-20} = -2$$

$$\bar{y} = \frac{\begin{vmatrix} 8 & 0 \\ 2 & -20 \end{vmatrix}}{-20} = \frac{-160}{-20} = 8$$

The value of the function at this critical point is

$$\bar{z}(\bar{x}_0, \bar{y}_0) = z(-2, 8) = 4(-2)^2 + 2(-2)(8) - (8)^2 + 20(8) = 80$$

The critical point to be evaluated is $(\bar{x}_0, \bar{y}_0, \bar{z}_0) = (-2, 8, 80)$.

Setting up the Hessian to assess the second-order conditions:

$$|H| = \begin{vmatrix} z_{xx} & z_{xy} \\ z_{yx} & z_{yy} \end{vmatrix} = \begin{vmatrix} 8 & 2 \\ 2 & -2 \end{vmatrix}$$

Here, $|H_1| = 8 > 0$ and $|H_2| = |H| = -20 < 0$. While $|H_1| > 0$ is consistent with a relative minimum, $|H_2| < 0$ indicates that the critical point $(-2, 8, 80)$ is a saddle point. Note, if we were to write the Hessian as $|H| = \begin{vmatrix} z_{yy} & z_{yx} \\ z_{xy} & z_{xx} \end{vmatrix} = \begin{vmatrix} z_{xx} & z_{xy} \\ z_{yx} & z_{yy} \end{vmatrix} = z_{yy} \, z_{xx} - (z_{xy})^2$

We would have:

$$|H| = \begin{vmatrix} -2 & 2 \\ 2 & 8 \end{vmatrix}, \text{ with } |H_1| = -2 < 0, \text{ which is consistent with a relative maximum,}$$

but $|H_2| = |H| = -20 < 0$, which establishes a saddle point.[2]

Since $z_{xx} = 8$ and $z_{yy} = -2$ have different signs, then from one direction, for example, holding the variable y constant ($dy = 0$) and evaluating the slope of a line tangent to the surface of the function as x increases from the critical point, we would find the slope increasing (i.e., the surface bends upward, as for a minimum). From the other direction, here holding the variable x constant ($dx = 0$) and evaluating the slope of a line tangent to the surface of the function as y increases from the critical point, we would find the slope decreasing (that is, the surface bends downward, as for a maximum).

To elaborate, the value of the function at the critical point, $(x_0, y_0) = (-2, 8)$, is $z_0 = 80$, that is, $z(-2, 8) = 80$. If we increase the variable x only, say to $x_1 = -1$, that is, $\Delta x = +1$, while holding y constant, $dy = 0$, then the value of the function evaluated at $(x_1, y_0) = (-1, 8)$ increases to $z_1 = 84$, $\Delta z = +4$; implying, from this perspective, that the critical point is a minimum. Now, if we hold x constant, $dx = 0$, and move in the perpendicular direction by allowing only the variable y to increase, say to $y_2 = 9$, ($\Delta y = +1$) then the value of the function evaluated at (x_0, y_2) decreases to $z_2 = 79$, that is, $z(-2, 9) = 79$ and $\Delta z = -1$; implying, from this perspective, that the critical point is a maximum. (*Note:* We are using discrete changes in the variables, Δx and Δy, here to illustrate. As we know, the differentials, dx and dy, theoretically refer to infinitesimal changes.)

Similarly, evaluating the slopes of the perpendicular lines that are tangent to the surface of the function at this critical point, we find

$$z_x \, (x_0, y_0) = z_x \, (-2, 8) = 8x_0 + 2y_0 = 8(-2) + 2(8) = 0$$

$$z_y \, (x_0, y_0) = z_y \, (-2, 8) = 2x_0 - 2y_0 + 20 = 2(-2) - 2(8) + 20 = 0$$

As expected, the slopes of the lines tangent to the surface of the function at the critical point (and perpendicular to the y-z plane and x-z plane, respectively given by the

---

[2]Recall from Chapter 5 that interchanging the rows (or columns) of a 2×2 determinant changes the sign, but not the absolute value, of the determinant. Therefore, interchanging the two rows and then the two columns does not alter the value of the determinant.

z_x and z_y equations) equal zero. Now, allowing for an increase in the variable x, $dx > 0$, while holding y constant, $dy = 0$, and evaluating the slope of the surface of the function $z(x, y)$ as we move from the critical point out from the y-z plane, we would expect the slope to increase, consistent with moving from a relative minimum. As before, let x increase from $x_0 = -2$ to $x_1 = -1$, we find that

$$z_x (x_1, y_0) = z_x (-1, 8) = 8x_1 + 2y_0 = 8(-1) + 2(8) = +8$$

So, for $\Delta x = +1$, we find $\Delta z_x = +8$. Roughly approximating the change in the curvature of the surface of the function as we move from the critical point with the variable x only changing, that is, the second-order differential, $d^2z/dx^2 = d(z_x)/dx$, with Δz_x and $\Delta x = +1$, we find the slope of the function increasing. Similarly, allowing the variable y to increase from $y_0 = 8$ to $y_2 = 9$, holding the variable x constant, $dx = 0$, that is, approximating the second-order differential $d^2z/dy^2 = d(z_y)/dy$, we find the slope of the function as we move from the critical point out from the x-z plane:

$$z_y (x_0, y_2) = z_y (-2, 9) = 2x_0 - 2y_2 + 20 = 2(-2) - 2(9) + 20 = -2$$

So, for $\Delta y = +1$, we find $\Delta z_y = -2$, and the slope of the function is decreasing, consistent with moving from a relative maximum. In short, the point, $(x_0, y_0, z_0) = (-2, 8, 80)$ defines a saddle point — a relative minimum from one perspective (dx, with $dy = 0$) and a relative maximum from the other perspective (dy, with $dx = 0$).

PRACTICE PROBLEM 8.2

For each of the following functions, $z = z(x, y)$, find the critical point and then evaluate the second-order conditions to determine the type of relative extremum.

a) $z(x, y) = -x^2 + 5x + xy - 10y - y^2$
b) $z(x, y) = x^2 + 5x + xy - 10y + y^2$
c) $z(x, y) = x^2 + 5x + xy - 10y - y^2$

(The answers are at the end of the chapter.)

UNCONSTRAINED OPTIMIZATION FOR FUNCTIONS OF N INDEPENDENT VARIABLES

The conditions for establishing relative extrema for an objective function with n choice or independent variables follow from the case with two independent variables. Below, we state these conditions.

Given a differentiable function, $z = z(x_1, x_2, \ldots x_n)$, the first-order conditions necessary for a relative extremum are that the first-order partial derivatives equal zero at that critical point. Totally differentiating the objective function, we get

$$dz = z_1 dx_1 + z_2 dx_2 + \cdots + z_n dx_n$$

where $z_i = \delta z/\delta x_i$ ($i = 1 \ldots n$). Finding critical points requires that $dz = 0$. So, for arbitrary, and theoretically infinitesimal, changes in the independent variables, (e.g., dx_1, dx_2, $\ldots dx_n$, not all equal to zero), the first-order partials must each equal zero: $z_1 = z_2 = \cdots = z_n = 0$.

To evaluate the type of relative extremum that exists at the critical point established by the first-order conditions, we set up the Hessian. The Hessian can be obtained by differentiating the n first-order conditions, $z_i = 0$ $(i = 1 \ldots n)$, with respect to the n independent variables, $x_1, x_2, \ldots x_n$.

$$|H| = \begin{vmatrix} z_{11} & z_{12} & \cdots & z_{1n} \\ z_{21} & z_{22} & \cdots & z_{2n} \\ \cdot & & & \\ \cdot & & & \\ z_{n1} & z_{n2} & \cdots & z_{nn} \end{vmatrix} \qquad \text{where } z_{ij} = \frac{\delta(\delta z/\delta x_j)}{\delta x_i} \qquad i = 1 \ldots n, j = 1 \ldots n$$

If the principal minors of the Hessian are all positive:

$$|H_1| > 0, |H_2| > 0, |H_3| > 0, |H_4| > 0, \ldots \text{etc.},$$

then the Hessian is positive definite, $d^2z > 0$, and we have sufficient conditions to establish the critical point as a relative minimum.

If, on the other hand, the principal minors of the Hessian follow the sequence:

$$|H_1| < 0, |H_2| > 0, |H_3| < 0, |H_4| > 0, \ldots \text{etc., alternating in sign,}$$

then the Hessian is negative definite, $d^2z < 0$, and we have sufficient conditions to establish the critical point as a relative maximum.

If neither of these patterns pertain, then the second-order conditions are inconclusive and further examination of points in the neighborhood of the critical points is required.

CONCAVITY AND CONVEXITY OF AN OBJECTIVE FUNCTION

Sometimes in economics, theory may impose structure on an objective function. For example, if diminishing returns to labor hold from the outset, then a short-run production function is strictly concave. If we have prior knowledge about the objective function, namely, that the function is strictly concave or strictly convex, then we do not need to check the second-order conditions upon finding a relative extremum.

To see this, return to the simple case of an objective function with only one independent variable, $y = f(x)$. The first-order condition for a relative extremum or critical point at $x = x_0$, is that the slope of the line tangent to the curve at this point equals zero, $f'(x_0) = 0$. The second-order condition identifies the curvature of the function around the critical point.

Recall from Chapter 6 that if $f''(x) < 0$ for all values of x, then the function is strictly concave. That is, the rate of change of the slope of a line tangent to the curve of the function is decreasing (increasing) as the value of the independent variable, x, increases (decreases). See Figure 8.1a. As x increases up to the critical point, x_0, the slope of a tangent line to the curve is decreasing (becoming less positive); at $x = x_0$, a tangent line has a slope equal to zero; and as x increases beyond x_0, the slope of a tan-

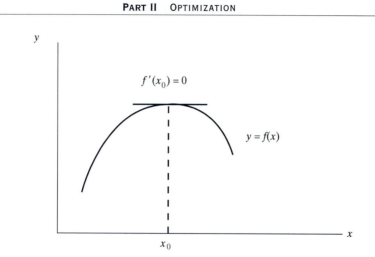

a. $y = f(x)$ is strictly concave: $f''(x) < 0$; x_0 is a unique absolute maximum

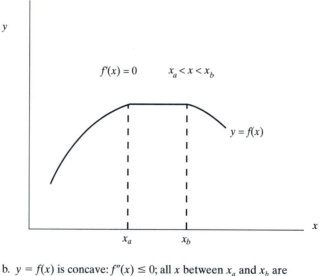

b. $y = f(x)$ is concave: $f''(x) \leq 0$; all x between x_a and x_b are absolute maxima

FIGURE 8.1   RELATIVE EXTREMA AND CONCAVE FUNCTIONS

gent line is decreasing (becoming more negative). Thus, if we know that the function, $y = f(x)$ is strictly concave, then finding a critical point will establish not only a relative maximum, but the absolute maximum. If the function is concave, $f''(x) \leq 0$, and includes a horizontal linear segment, as in Figure 8.1b, then the critical points, $x_a < x < x_b$, are absolute maxima, although we no longer have a unique maximum.

If $f''(x) > 0$ for all values of x, then the function is strictly convex. The rate of change of the slope of a line tangent to the curve of the function is increasing (decreasing) as the value of the independent variable, x, increases (decreases). For an objective function that is strictly convex, finding a relative extremum at $x = x_0$ will establish an absolute minimum that is unique. See Figure 8.2a, where the slope of a line tangent to the curve is continuously increasing as x increases, becoming less negative as x approaches x_0 from the left, and more positive as x increases above x_0. If the objective function is convex and contains a horizontal line segment, as in Figure 8.2b, then the critical points, $x_c < x < x_d$, are absolute minima, but there is not a unique minimum.

We can generalize to an objective function with n independent variables. Knowledge that an objective function, $z = z(x_1, x_2, \ldots x_n)$ is strictly concave allows us

FIGURE 8.2 RELATIVE EXTREMA AND CONVEX FUNCTIONS

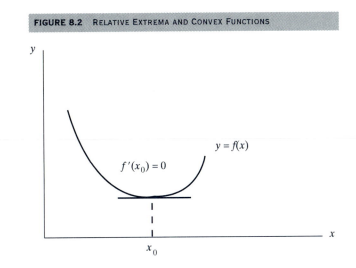

a. $y = f(x)$ is strictly convex: $f''(x) > 0$; x_0 is a unique absolute minimum

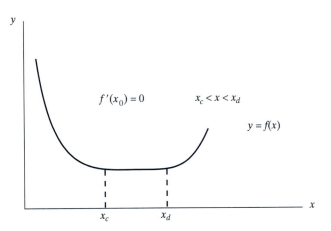

b. $y = f(x)$ is convex: $f''(x) \geq 0$; all x between x_c and x_d are absolute minima.

to assert that the associated Hessian, $|H|$, is negative definite, $d^2z < 0$, and the critical point, $(x_{10}, x_{20}, \ldots x_{n0})$, is the absolute maximum.

Conversely, if we know that an objective function, $z = z(x_1, x_2, \ldots x_n)$ is strictly convex, then we can say that the associated Hessian, $|H|$, is positive definite, $d^2z > 0$, and the critical point, $(x_{10}, x_{20}, \ldots x_{n0})$, is the absolute minimum.

Before discussing the optimal allocation of production for a firm with more than one plant, we present a test for the functional independence of a system of equations. Afterward, the behavior of monopolists and monopsonists will be examined.

JACOBIANS AND FUNCTIONAL INDEPENDENCE

In Chapter 1, we highlighted three possible characteristics or attributes of equilibrium in a market: existence, uniqueness, and stability. Chapters 3 and 4 focused on the question of stability. In Chapter 5, we examined the conditions under which a system of linear equations had a unique solution—in particular, a price vector that simultaneously cleared the n commodity markets in a general equilibrium model. Now, in Chapter 8, we discuss a test for determining whether a system of equations—not necessarily linear—has a unique solution.

Recall from Chapter 5 that a system of linear equations

$$a_{11} x_1 + a_{12} x_2 + \cdots + a_{1n} x_n = d_1$$

$$a_{21} x_1 + a_{22} x_2 + \cdots + a_{2n} x_n = d_2$$

$$\vdots$$

$$a_{n1} x_1 + a_{n2} x_2 + \cdots + a_{nn} x_n = d_n$$

can be concisely written in matrix notation as $\mathbf{Ax} = \mathbf{d}$, where

$$\mathbf{A} = n \times n \text{ matrix of coefficients}$$

$$\mathbf{x} = n \times 1 \text{ matrix (vector) of endogenous variables}$$

and $\mathbf{d} = n \times 1$ matrix (vector) of exogenous constants

$$\mathbf{A} = \begin{bmatrix} a_{11} & a_{12} & \cdots & a_{1n} \\ a_{21} & a_{22} & \cdots & a_{2n} \\ \vdots & & & \\ a_{n1} & a_{n2} & \cdots & a_{nn} \end{bmatrix} \qquad \mathbf{x} = \begin{bmatrix} x_1 \\ x_2 \\ \vdots \\ x_n \end{bmatrix} \quad \text{and} \quad \mathbf{d} = \begin{bmatrix} d_1 \\ d_2 \\ \vdots \\ d_n \end{bmatrix}$$

We can test to see whether a solution exists and is unique. If the determinant of the coefficient matrix, $\mathbf{A}$, is nonsingular, that is, if $|\mathbf{A}| \neq 0$, then the rows (columns) of the coefficient matrix are linearly independent and a unique solution to the system of linear equations exists and is equal to

$$\bar{\mathbf{x}} = \mathbf{A}^{-1} \mathbf{d} = \frac{1}{|\mathbf{A}|} \text{Adj}(\mathbf{A}) \, \mathbf{d}$$

where $\mathbf{A}^{-1}$ and $\mathbf{Adj(A)}$ are the inverse and adjoint matrices of the coefficient matrix $\mathbf{A}$, respectively.

A *Jacobian determinant* permits testing for the functional independence of a system of equations—both linear and nonlinear. A Jacobian determinant, written as $|J|$, is composed of all the first-order partial derivatives of a system of equations. To elaborate, given a system of n differentiable functions, $f^1, f^2, \ldots f^n$, in n endogenous variables, $x_1, x_2, \ldots x_n$,

$$y_1 = f^1(x_1, x_2, \ldots x_n)$$
$$y_2 = f^2(x_1, x_2, \ldots x_n)$$
$$\vdots$$
$$y_n = f^n(x_1, x_2, \ldots x_n)$$

the Jacobian, $|J|$, is defined to be the determinant formed by partially differentiating the n functions with respect to the n endogenous variables.

$$|J| = \left| \frac{\delta(y_1, y_2, \ldots y_n)}{\delta(x_1, x_2, \ldots x_n)} \right| = \begin{vmatrix} \delta y_1/\delta x_1 & \delta y_1/\delta x_2 & \cdots & \delta y_1/\delta x_n \\ \delta y_2/\delta x_1 & \delta y_2/\delta x_2 & \cdots & \delta y_2/\delta x_n \\ \vdots & & & \\ \delta y_n/\delta x_1 & \delta y_n/\delta x_2 & \cdots & \delta y_n/\delta x_n \end{vmatrix}$$

If $|J| \neq 0$, then the equations, $f^1, f^2, \ldots f^n$, are functionally independent and a unique solution to the system of equations exists.

If $|J| = 0$, then the equations, $f^1, f^2, \ldots f^n$, are functionally dependent and a unique solution to the system of equations does not exist.

We can see that a system of linear equations, $\mathbf{Ax} = \mathbf{d}$, is a special case, where the Jacobian is equal to the determinant of the coefficient matrix, $|J| = |\mathbf{A}|$.

To illustrate, consider the following system of equations:

$$y_1 = x_1 x_3 - 3x_2$$
$$y_2 = x_1^2 + 2 x_1 x_3 + x_3^2$$
$$y_3 = x_1^2 + x_1 x_3 + 3x_2 + x_3^2$$

The Jacobian is

$$|J| = \begin{vmatrix} \delta y_1/\delta x_1 & \delta y_1/\delta x_2 & \delta y_1/\delta x_3 \\ \delta y_2/\delta x_1 & \delta y_2/\delta x_2 & \delta y_2/\delta x_3 \\ \delta y_3/\delta x_1 & \delta y_3/\delta x_2 & \delta y_3/\delta x_3 \end{vmatrix} = \begin{vmatrix} x_3 & -3 & x_1 \\ 2x_1 + 2x_3 & 0 & 2x_1 + 2x_3 \\ 2x_1 + x_3 & 3 & x_1 + 2x_3 \end{vmatrix}$$

We may simplify the task of evaluating this determinant by row manipulation. Recall that multiplying any row (column) of a determinant by a constant k and adding the result to any other row (column) of the determinant does not change the value of the determinant.

Proceeding, we add row 3 to row 1 to get

$$|J| = \begin{vmatrix} 2x_1 + 2x_3 & 0 & 2x_1 + 2x_3 \\ 2x_1 + 2x_3 & 0 & 2x_1 + 2x_3 \\ 2x_1 + x_3 & 3 & x_1 + 2x_3 \end{vmatrix}$$

Now, subtracting row 2 from row 1, we have

$$|J| = \begin{vmatrix} 0 & 0 & 0 \\ 2x_1 + 2x_3 & 0 & 2x_1 + 2x_3 \\ 2x_1 + x_3 & 3 & x_1 + 2x_3 \end{vmatrix}$$

Clearly, expanding along the first row, $|J| = 0$; so this system of equations is functionally dependent and there is no unique solution. In fact, we can show that $y_3 = y_2 - y_1$, or $y_3 - y_2 + y_1 = 0$.

$$y_3 = x_1^2 + x_1x_3 + 3x_2 + x_3^2 = (x_1^2 + 2x_1x_3 + x_3^2) - (x_1x_3 - 3x_2) = y_2 - y_1$$

or

$$y_3 - y_2 + y_1 = (x_1^2 + x_1x_3 + 3x_2 + x_3^2) - (x_1^2 + 2x_1x_3 + x_3^2) + (x_1x_3 - 3x_2) = 0$$

As a second example, consider now the system of equations:

$$y_1 = x_1^2 + x_2$$

$$y_2 = x_1 - x_2x_3$$

$$y_3 = x_3^2 + x_3$$

Forming the Jacobian by partially differentiating each of the three equations with respect to the endogenous variables, x_1, x_2, and x_3, we have

$$|J| = \begin{vmatrix} \delta y_1/\delta x_1 & \delta y_1/\delta x_2 & \delta y_1/\delta x_3 \\ \delta y_2/\delta x_1 & \delta y_2/\delta x_2 & \delta y_2/\delta x_3 \\ \delta y_3/\delta x_1 & \delta y_3/\delta x_2 & \delta y_3/\delta x_3 \end{vmatrix} = \begin{vmatrix} 2x_1 & 1 & 0 \\ 1 & -x_3 & -x_2 \\ 0 & 3x_2^2 & 1 \end{vmatrix}$$

Expanding along row 1, we find

$$|J| = 2x_1 \begin{vmatrix} -x_3 & -x_2 \\ 3x_2^2 & 1 \end{vmatrix} - 1 \begin{vmatrix} 1 & -x_2 \\ 0 & 1 \end{vmatrix} = 2x_1(3x_2^3 - x_3) - 1$$

If $|J| \neq 0$, then the equations y_1, y_2, and y_3 are functionally independent.

PRACTICE PROBLEM 8.3

For each set of equations, form the Jacobian and assess the functional dependence.

a) $y_1 = 2x_1 + x_2$
   $y_2 = 3x_1 - x_2$
b) $y_1 = x_1^2 - 2x_2$
   $y_2 = x_1 + x_2^2 x_3$
   $y_3 = x_2^3 - x_3$

(The answers are at the end of the chapter.)

Frequently we will use Jacobians to test for the functional independence of a system of equations. In fact, we will see a correspondence between the Hessian (used in the second-order conditions for optimization problems) and the Jacobian. We can now address the case of the optimal allocation of production for a firm with more than one plant or factory.

PROFIT MAXIMIZATION FOR A FIRM WITH TWO PLANTS

To simplify the analysis, we will consider a firm with two plants or factories available for producing its output. The analysis can easily be extended to a multiplant firm. Assume that plant 2, the newer plant, incorporates a more advanced technology than does plant 1. This advantage is reflected in plant 2's lower marginal cost of production for any rate of output—compared to plant 1. The firm, however, would not necessarily shut down the older, less efficient plant. The firm seeks the optimal allocation of production of its profit-maximizing output over the two plants.

Let Q_1 = quantity of output produced in plant 1

Q_2 = quantity of output produced in plant 2

Q = total quantity of output produced by the firm: $Q = Q_1 + Q_2$

The short-run total cost function of the firm is: $STC = C_1 (Q_1) + C_2 (Q_2)$ where

$C_1 (Q_1)$ = total cost of producing an output of Q_1 in plant 1

$C_2 (Q_2)$ = total cost of producing an output of Q_2 in plant 2

The total revenue function of the firm is: $R = R(Q)$. In this model we will assume that the firm is a price-setter, like a monopolistic competitor, and faces negatively sloped demand and marginal revenue curves for its output.

The firm's profit function is: $\Pi(Q_1, Q_2) = R(Q) - C_1(Q_1) - C_2 (Q_2)$. The first-order conditions for profit maximization are

$$\Pi_1 = \delta\Pi/\delta Q_1 = (dR/dQ)(\delta Q/\delta Q_1) - (dC_1/dQ_1) = R' - C_1' = 0$$

$$\Pi_2 = \delta\Pi/\delta Q_2 = (dR/dQ)(\delta Q/\delta Q_2) - (dC_2/dQ_2) = R' - C_2' = 0$$

where $R' = dR/dQ = MR$ is the marginal revenue of output; $dC_1/dQ_1 = C_1' = MC_1$ and $dC_2/dQ_2 = C_2' = MC_2$ are the marginal costs of production in plants 1 and 2, respectively. Since $\delta Q/\delta Q_1 = \delta Q/\delta Q_2 = 1$, we can rewrite the first-order conditions as

$$MR - MC_1 = 0$$

$$MR - MC_2 = 0$$

and combining, we have: $MR = MC_1 = MC_2$.

Therefore, to maximize profits, the firm should allocate its production across the two plants such that the marginal cost of production in each plant equals the marginal revenue of the total output.[3] The more advanced plant, here plant 2, would produce the greater output.

We illustrate in Figure 8.3. The firm's overall marginal cost (MC) curve, shown in panel c, is equal to the horizontal summation of the marginal cost curves in plants 1 and 2: $MC = \sum_{p=1}^{2} MC_p = MC_1 + MC_2$, where MC_p is the marginal cost curve in plant p ($p = 1,2$).[4] The profit-maximizing output is $\overline{Q}$, where $MC = MR$, with $\overline{Q}_1$ and $\overline{Q}_2$ produced in plants 1 and 2, respectively, and $MR = MC_1 = MC_2$. If, for example, the firm were to find that $MC_1 > MC_2$, then it could reduce its costs and increase its profits by reallocating production from plant 1 to plant 2 until $MC_1 = MC_2 = MR$ again.

We need to check the second-order conditions for the critical point to be a maximum. To do this, we partially differentiate the first-order conditions with respect to the choice variables, Q_1 and Q_2, and form the Hessian.

$$\Pi_{11} = \frac{\delta(\delta\Pi/\delta Q_1)}{\delta Q_1} = \frac{\delta(dR/dQ)}{\delta Q_1} - \frac{\delta(dC_1/dQ_1)}{\delta Q_1} = \frac{d^2R}{dQ^2}(\delta Q/\delta Q_1) - \frac{d^2C_1}{dQ_1^2} = R'' - C_1''$$

$$\Pi_{12} = \frac{\delta(\delta\Pi/\delta Q_2)}{\delta Q_1} = \frac{\delta(dR/dQ)}{\delta Q_1} - \frac{\delta(dC_2/dQ_2)}{\delta Q_1} = \frac{d^2R}{dQ^2}(\delta Q/\delta Q_1) - 0 = R''$$

$$\Pi_{21} = \frac{\delta(\delta\Pi/\delta Q_1)}{\delta Q_2} = \frac{\delta(dR/dQ)}{\delta Q_2} - \frac{\delta(dC_1/dQ_1)}{\delta Q_2} = \frac{d^2R}{dQ^2}(\delta Q/\delta Q_2) - 0 = R''$$

$$\Pi_{22} = \frac{\delta(\delta\Pi/\delta Q_2)}{\delta Q_2} = \frac{\delta(dR/dQ)}{\delta Q_2} - \frac{\delta(dC_2/dQ_2)}{\delta Q_2} = \frac{d^2R}{dQ^2}(\delta Q/\delta Q_2) - \frac{d^2C_2}{dQ_2^2} = R'' - C_2''$$

Note that

$$\frac{\delta(dC_1/dQ_1)}{\delta Q_2} = \frac{\delta(dC_2/dQ_2)}{\delta Q_1} = 0,$$

since changes in the output of one plant should not affect the marginal cost of production in the other. Also, note that $\delta Q/\delta Q_1 = \delta Q/\delta Q_2 = 1$.

Forming the Hessian, we get

$$|H| = \begin{vmatrix} \Pi_{11} & \Pi_{12} \\ \Pi_{21} & \Pi_{22} \end{vmatrix} = \begin{vmatrix} R'' - C_1'' & R'' \\ R'' & R'' - C_2'' \end{vmatrix}$$

where

$R'' = d^2R/dQ^2$ indicates the slope of the firm's marginal revenue curve ($R'' < 0$)

---

[3]If the firm were a perfect competitor in its output market, then its marginal revenue would be given by the market price (P_0). The perfectly competitive firm would then equate the marginal cost of production in each plant to this market price: $MC_1 = MC_2 = P_0$.

[4]Note: Graphically the horizontal summation of the marginal cost curves corresponds algebraically to the summation of the inverses of the marginal cost functions, $\sum_{p=1}^{2} MC_p^{-1}(Q_p)$. That is, for each marginal cost, the outputs produced by the plants are added.

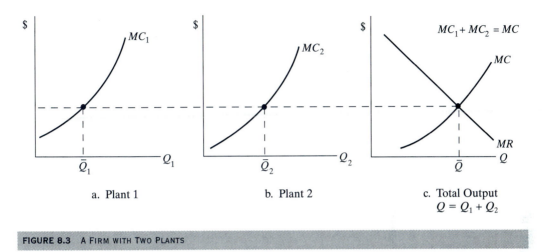

a. Plant 1   b. Plant 2   c. Total Output
$$Q = Q_1 + Q_2$$

FIGURE 8.3   A FIRM WITH TWO PLANTS

$C_1'' = d^2C_1/dQ_1^2$ indicates the slope of the firm's marginal cost curve for plant 1

and

$C_2'' = d^2C_2/dQ_2^2$ indicates the slope of the firm's marginal cost curve for plant 2.

Note that if we regard the first-order conditions as a set of differentiable equations, then in forming the Hessian, $|H|$, we are also forming the Jacobian, $|J|$. Furthermore, if the second-order conditions for a maximum hold, in particular, $|H| > 0$, then $|H| = |J| \neq 0$, and the first-order conditions are functionally independent equations, with a unique solution $(\overline{Q}_1, \overline{Q}_2)$.

For a maximum, the second-order conditions require that: $|H_1| = R'' - C_1'' < 0$ and $|H_2| = |H| = (R'' - C_1'')(R'' - C_2'') - R''R'' > 0$. Recall the second-order condition for a firm with a single plant. At the profit-maximizing level of output, the slope of the marginal revenue curve must be less than the slope of the marginal cost curve, that is, $R'' < C''$. For a firm with two plants, this condition is modified. For $|H_1| = R'' - C_1'' < 0$, the slope of the marginal revenue curve at the optimal level of total output, $R''(\overline{Q})$, must be less than the slope of the marginal cost curve at the optimal plant levels of output, $C_1''(\overline{Q}_1)$ and $C_2''(\overline{Q}_2)$, since it is arbitrary which plant (newer or older) is designated as plant 1. As drawn in Figure 8.3, this condition is clearly met with the positively-sloped marginal cost curves.[5]

With respect to the requirement that $|H_2| > 0$, we can simplify the determinant as follows:

$$|H_2| = (R'' - C_1'')(R'' - C_2'') - R''R'' > 0$$

$$= -R''C_1'' - R''C_2'' + C_1''C_2'' > 0$$

---

[5]The second-order conditions are met for a perfectly competitive firm in the output market since its short-run supply curve is the positively sloped portion of its marginal cost curve rising above its average variable cost curve and the slope of its marginal revenue curve is zero.

Again, if at the optimal plant levels of output, the marginal cost curves are positively sloped, the second-order conditions would be satisfied. Even if the firm were operating on the negatively sloped portions of its plant marginal cost curves, the second-order condition may still be satisfied. Specific functional forms for the revenue and cost schedules, rather than the general model analyzed here, may allow us to determine whether the second-order conditions for profit maximization hold.

Nevertheless, even with the general model, we are able to derive the profit-maximizing condition for a firm with more than one plant. To maximize profits, a firm should allocate production across its plants such that the marginal cost of output in each plant equals the marginal revenue of the last unit of total output produced. This decision rule holds for all types of firms, including a monopolist, which is the next type of market structure examined in this chapter. Before turning to monopolies, however, we will illustrate the selection of the profit-maximizing levels of output for a firm with two plants.

Suppose a firm faces a demand curve for its product given by: $Q^d = 40 - 4P$ (or written in terms of price, $P = 10 - (1/4)Q$), where Q is the total output of the firm (in hundreds of units per day) and P is the unit price (in dollars) of the output. The firm has two plants in operation producing its output, with short-run total cost curves given by

$$STC_1 = C_1(Q_1) = .10Q_1^2 + 50 \text{ (plant 1)}$$

$$STC_2 = C_2(Q_2) = .05Q_2^2 + 25 \text{ (plant 2)}$$

where

Q_1 = total output produced in plant 1 (in hundreds of units per day)

Q_2 = total output produced in plant 2 (in hundreds of units per day)

and

$$Q = Q_1 + Q_2.$$

Plant 2, the newer plant with the improved technology, has the lower unit costs for any rate of output.

Note that this firm is a price-setter, facing a downward-sloping demand curve for its product. The total revenue schedule for the firm is given by: $R = R(Q) = P \cdot Q = [10 - (1/4)Q] \cdot Q = 10Q - (1/4)Q^2$. The derived marginal revenue schedule is: $MR(Q) = dR/dQ = 10 - (1/2)Q$.

The short-run total cost curves in each plant are quadratic, indicating that diminishing returns to labor set in from the outset. The associated marginal cost functions are linear, with the marginal cost function for the newer plant 2 lying to the right (or below) the marginal cost function for plant 1. The marginal cost functions are:

$$MC_1 = dSTC_1/dQ_1 = C_1' (Q_1) = .2Q_1$$

$$MC_2 = dSTC_2/dQ_2 = C_2' (Q_2) = .1Q_2$$

To get the firm's aggregate marginal cost we sum the individual plant's marginal cost schedules. First we need to write the respective marginal costs in terms of the outputs.

For plant 1: $MC_1 = .2Q_1$, so $Q_1 = 5MC_1 = 5MC$

For plant 2: $MC_2 = .1Q_2$, so $Q_2 = 10MC_2 = 10MC$

The firm's marginal cost function is given by: $Q = Q_1 + Q_2 = 5MC + 10MC = 15MC$, or $MC = (1/15)Q = .06\overline{Q}$.

Figure 8.4 illustrates this result. The marginal cost curves of the two plants are horizontally summed to obtain the firm's marginal cost curve.

To find the profit-maximizing outputs of the firm's two plants, we set up the profit function:

$$\Pi(Q_1, Q_2) = R(Q) - C_1(Q_1) - C_2(Q_2)$$

$$= 10(Q_1 + Q_2) - (1/4)(Q_1 + Q_2)^2 - .10Q_1^2 - 50 - .05Q_2^2 - 25$$

The first-order conditions are

$$\delta\Pi/\delta Q_1 = 10 - (1/2)(Q_1 + Q_2) - .2Q_1 = 0$$

$$\delta\Pi/\delta Q_2 = 10 - (1/2)(Q_1 + Q_2) - .1Q_2 = 0$$

Note that these first-order conditions can be rewritten as

FIGURE 8.4 PROFIT-MAXIMIZING OUTPUT FOR A FIRM WITH TWO PLANTS

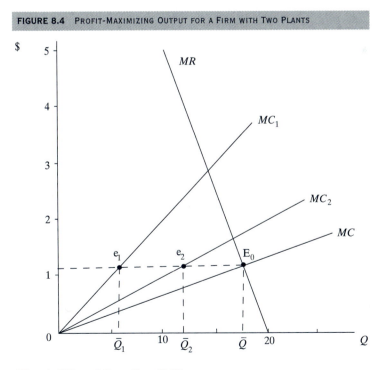

Plant 1: $MC_1 = .2Q_1$ or $Q_1 = 5MC_1$
Plant 2: $MC_2 = .1Q_2$ or $Q_2 = 10MC_2$
Firm: $MC = (1/15)Q = .0\overline{6}Q$ or $Q = 15MC$

$$MR = 10 - (1/2)(Q_1 + Q_2) = .2Q_1 = MC_1$$

$$MR = 10 - (1/2)(Q_1 + Q_2) = .1Q_2 = MC_2$$

Thus, to maximize profits the firm sets the marginal revenue equal to the marginal cost of output in each plant. See Figure 8.4 for the illustration where the optimal outputs in the two plants are $\overline{Q}_1$ and $\overline{Q}_2$. The profit-maximizing output of the firm is $\overline{Q} = \overline{Q}_1 + \overline{Q}_2$, where the firm's marginal revenue ($MR = 10 - (1/2)\overline{Q}$) equals the marginal cost ($MC = .06\,\overline{Q}$). See point E_0.

Simplifying the first-order conditions and writing them in matrix notation, we can solve for the profit-maximizing output in each plant using Cramer's rule.

$$10 - (1/2)Q_1 - (1/2)Q_2 - .2Q_1 = 0$$

$$10 - (1/2)Q_1 - (1/2)Q_2 - .1Q_2 = 0$$

or

$$.7Q_1 + .5Q_2 = 10$$

$$.5Q_1 + .6Q_2 = 10$$

$$\begin{bmatrix} .7 & .5 \\ .5 & .6 \end{bmatrix} \begin{bmatrix} Q_1 \\ Q_2 \end{bmatrix} = \begin{bmatrix} 10 \\ 10 \end{bmatrix}$$

$$\overline{Q}_1 = \frac{\begin{vmatrix} 10 & .5 \\ 10 & .6 \end{vmatrix}}{\begin{vmatrix} .7 & .5 \\ .5 & .6 \end{vmatrix}} = \frac{1}{.17} = 5.88 \text{ (hundred units per day)}$$

$$\overline{Q}_2 = \frac{\begin{vmatrix} .7 & 10 \\ .5 & 10 \end{vmatrix}}{\begin{vmatrix} .7 & .5 \\ .5 & .6 \end{vmatrix}} = \frac{2}{.17} = 11.76 \text{ (hundred units per day)}$$

The profit-maximizing output for the firm is: $\overline{Q} = \overline{Q}_1 + \overline{Q}_2 = 5.88 + 11.76 = 17.64$ (hundred units per day). The price charged by the firm is: $\overline{P} = 10 - (1/4)\overline{Q} = 10 - (1/4)17.64 = \$5.59$. The firm's total revenues are: $R = \overline{P} \cdot \overline{Q} = (\$5.59)(17.64) = \$98.61$ (hundred per day). The short-run total costs are:

$$STC_1 = C_1(\overline{Q}_1) = .10(5.88)^2 + 50 = 53.46$$

$$STC_2 = C_2(\overline{Q}_2) = .05(11.76)^2 + 25 = 31.91.$$

$$STC(\overline{Q}) = C_1(\overline{Q}_1) + C_2(\overline{Q}_2) = \$85.37 \text{ (hundred per day)}$$

The firm is earning positive economic profits equal to: $\Pi(\overline{Q}) = R(\overline{Q}) - STC(\overline{Q}) = 98.61 - 85.37 = \$13.24$ (hundred per day).

We can verify that the second-order conditions hold. Setting up the Hessian, we have

$$|H| = \begin{vmatrix} \Pi_{11} & \Pi_{12} \\ \Pi_{21} & \Pi_{22} \end{vmatrix} = \begin{vmatrix} -.7 & -.5 \\ -.5 & -.6 \end{vmatrix}$$

since

$$\Pi_{11} = \frac{\delta(\delta\Pi/\delta Q_1)}{\delta Q_1} = -.7$$

$$\Pi_{12} = \frac{\delta(\delta\Pi/\delta Q_2)}{\delta Q_1} = \frac{\delta(\delta\Pi/\delta Q_1)}{\delta Q_2} = \Pi_{21} = -.5$$

$$\Pi_{22} = \frac{\delta(\delta\Pi/\delta Q_2)}{\delta Q_2} = -.6$$

We find $|H_1| = -.7 < 0$ and $|H_2| = |H| = .17 > 0$, which are consistent with a maximum.

We note that the slope of the marginal revenue (here $\dfrac{d(dR/dQ)}{dQ} = -.5$) is less than the slope of the marginal cost for each plant at the profit-maximizing output (here $\dfrac{d(dC_1/dQ_1)}{dQ_1} = .2$ and $\dfrac{d(dC_2/dQ_2)}{dQ_2} = .1$) and the marginal cost for the firm $\left(\dfrac{d(dC/dQ)}{dQ} = .0\overline{6}\right)$. Actually, with the positively sloped marginal cost curves, the second-order conditions are clearly satisfied.

Finally, we can confirm that the condition for profit maximization for this two-plant firm is met:

$$MR = MC_1 = MC_2 = MC$$

$$MR(\overline{Q}) = MR(17.64) = 10 - (1/2)17.64 = 1.18$$

$$MC_1(\overline{Q_1}) = MC_1(5.88) = .2(5.88) = 1.18$$

$$MC_2(\overline{Q_2}) = MC_2(11.76) = .1(11.76) = 1.18$$

$$MC(\overline{Q}) = MC(17.64) = .0\overline{6}(17.64) = 1.18$$

PRACTICE PROBLEM 8.4

Given a firm facing a demand curve for its product, $Q^d = 25 - 5P$, where Q^d is the quantity demanded of the firm's output (in hundreds of units per day) and P is the unit price (in dollars) and with two plants for producing its output with short-run total costs,

$$STC_1 = C_1(Q_1) = .4Q_1^2 + 10 \quad \text{(plant 1)}$$

$$STC_2 = C_2(Q_2) = .3Q_2^2 + 6 \quad \text{(plant 2)}$$

where Q_1 and Q_2 are the outputs produced in plants 1 and 2, respectively (in hundreds of units per day).

a) Determine the firm's profit-maximizing level of output, the price charged, the level of profits, and the output produced in each plant.

b) Confirm that the marginal cost at the profit-maximizing output for each plant equals the marginal revenue at the profit-maximizing level of output.

(The answers are at the end of the chapter.)

MONOPOLIES

If perfect competition represents one end of the theoretical spectrum of market structures, monopoly is at the other end. A **monopoly** exists when there is a single supplier or seller in a market. Thus, the market demand for the good or service is the actual demand facing the monopolist. Like a monopolistically competitive firm, a monopolist is a price-setter. Unlike a monopolistically competitive firm, a monopolist can earn positive economic profits in the long run — provided that other firms can be prevented from entering the market.

Some barriers to entry are legal. A firm may have a patent, giving it exclusive rights to a specific product or process for a period of time. Pharmaceutical companies obtain patents on promising new drugs. Copyrights on original works also give monopoly power, for example, Mickey Mouse, copyrighted by Disney. The government may grant monopoly power, as in the case of the U.S. Postal Service and first-class mail or the single gasoline station and restaurant at public rest areas along interstate highways.

Alternatively, a firm may own a scarce resource, such as prime real estate around a picturesque lake used as a vacation resort or a snowy mountain used for a ski lodge. The National Parks in the United States are examples of publicly owned monopolies.

Significant **economies of scale** may render competition in a market infeasible, as has historically been the case with public utilities like water, power, and natural gas. Usually these **natural monopolies** have been regulated by government-appointed commissions.[6]

A monopoly may arise simply because a market initially is too small to support more than one firm, for example, a movie theater serving an isolated town. As the market demand grows, the monopolist may be able to discourage competition with aggressive price cutting against any firm that attempts to enter the market. Such predatory behavior is illegal in the United States; however, the threat of significant price discounting by a monopolist may be enough to deter the entry of potential competitors.

---

[6]Economies of scale refer to the decrease in the long-run average cost of production that may be experienced by a firm as its output rises. Scale economies may reflect indivisibilities in production or the sunk costs necessary to begin production, for example, the research and development costs of design and the minimum amount of basic infrastructure that must be in place before an automobile manufacturer can produce even one car. Scale economies may also result from the division of labor (the principle behind the assembly line) and the substitution of capital for labor (e.g., specialized equipment whose expense are justified when the volume of production is high). In sum, when the output of a firm increases faster than its long-run costs, long-run average cost declines and the firm experiences economies of scale.

When economies of scale are exhausted at a low rate of output relative to the market demand, then many firms can be cost competitive and barriers to entry in the market are low. In natural monopolies like the water company, the minimum initial investment in infrastructure (e.g., reservoirs, treatment plants, and transmission pipes) necessary before any service is provided is substantial and may be most efficiently provided by one firm, resulting in a natural monopoly. That is, where scale economics are large relative to the market demand, competition between firms may be not feasible, since sharing the market would require each firm to charge much higher prices in order to cover their long-run average cost of production.

THE ALLOCATIVE INEFFICIENCY OF A MONOPOLY

Whatever the underlying reason, a monopolist, by definition, exercises market power, that in the short run may be at the expense of consumer welfare. To illustrate, consider the following hypothetical scenario. Suppose a market is initially characterized by perfect competition. Refer to Figure 8.5, where the market demand and market supply curves intersect to yield a market-clearing price of $\bar{P}_c$ and quantity transacted of $\bar{Q}_c$. For simplicity, we will assume a linear market demand curve, D. In perfect competition the market supply, S, is the horizontal summation of all the individual firms' supply curves. Recall that the short-run supply curve of a perfectly competitive firm i is the rising portion of its marginal cost curve above its average variable cost curve, which we indicate here by $\underline{MC_i}$. Thus, we denote the market supply curve as: $S = \sum_{i=1}^{n} \underline{MC_i}$, where n is the number of firms in the market.

Perfect competition is characterized by **allocative efficiency**. On the last unit transacted in any period, (the $\bar{Q}_c$ unit), the price consumers are willing to pay, (the market-clearing price, $\bar{P}_c$), equals the marginal cost of production, $[MC(\bar{Q}_c)]$. Moreover, in perfect competition, the sum of consumers' surplus (given by the area $H\bar{P}_cE_c$ in Figure 8.5) and producers' surplus (given by the area $G\bar{P}_cE_c$) is maximized. Indeed, on the last unit sold, there is no more consumers' surplus or producers' surplus to be realized.

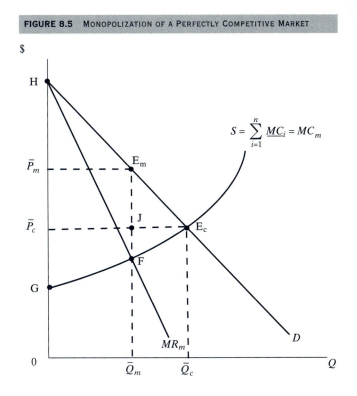

FIGURE 8.5 MONOPOLIZATION OF A PERFECTLY COMPETITIVE MARKET

Now suppose that a wealthy private investor purchases all of the n firms or perhaps the government nationalizes all of the firms—in either case, turning a perfectly competitive market into a monopoly. Since there is no change in the cost curves of the individual firms, only a change in ownership, the market supply curve can be regarded as the marginal cost curve of the monopolist. See MC_m in Figure 8.5. In effect, we have a multiplant monopolist. To maximize profits, the monopolist sets marginal cost equal to marginal revenue. Recall, the marginal revenue curve has the same vertical intercept but twice the slope of the associated linear demand curve. The profit-maximizing output is $\overline{Q}_m$, less than the market quantity transacted under perfect competition. With the lower output, the monopolist can set a higher price, $\overline{P}_m$.

With the monopolization of the market, consumers' surplus is reduced to the area $H\overline{P}_mE_m$. On net, producers' surplus increases to the area $\overline{P}_mE_mFG$. Part of the loss in consumers' surplus is gained by the monopolist as producer surplus (the area $\overline{P}_mE_mJ\overline{P}_c$). The area E_mJE_c is the **deadweight loss** in consumers' surplus, and the area JE_cF is the deadweight loss in producer surplus. A monopoly is allocatively inefficient. On the last unit sold, the $\overline{Q}_m$ unit, the price, $\overline{P}_m$, exceeds the marginal cost of production, $MC(\overline{Q}_m)$. That is, the value consumers place on the last unit purchased is greater than the opportunity cost of producing that unit. Compared to perfect competition then, a monopoly produces too little at too high a price. A measure of the allocative inefficiency of the monopolist is the sum of the deadweight losses—in Figure 8.5, the area E_mE_cF.[7]

To illustrate, consider a perfectly competitive market with a demand schedule given by

$$Q^d = 90 - 10P \quad \text{or} \quad P = 9 - .1Q$$

where Q is the quantity (in thousands of units per day) and P is the unit price (in dollars). Assume that the market supply schedule is given by

$$Q^s = (500P - 1{,}000)^{.5} \quad \text{or} \quad P = 2 + .002Q^2$$

Recall that in perfect competition, the market supply is the aggregation of all of the individual firm supply curves, which are the portions of their marginal cost curves rising above their average variable cost curves.

To find the market equilibrium price and quantity transacted, we set the market demand equal to the market supply and solve.

$$Q^d = 90 - 10P = (500P - 1{,}000)^{.5} = Q^s$$

$$(90 - 10P)^2 = 500P - 1{,}000$$

---

[7]We can use integral calculus to measure the sum of the deadweight losses. If the market demand schedule is $Q^d = D(P)$, or inversely, $P = D^{-1}(Q)$, and the market supply schedule is $Q^s = S(P)$, or inversely, $P = S^{-1}(Q)$, then the area E_mE_cF is given by the definite integral

$$\int_{\overline{Q}_m}^{\overline{Q}_c} [D^{-1}(Q) - S^{-1}(Q)]\, dQ.$$

Simplifying, we have: $P^2 - 23P + 91 = 0$

Using the quadratic formula, we find:

$$P = \frac{-(-23) \pm \sqrt{(23)^2 - 4(1)(91)}}{2(1)} = 5.08, 17.93$$

We reject the higher price of 17.93, since this exceeds the maximum demand price of 9. So, the perfectly competitive market equilibrium price is $\bar{P}_c = \$5.08$. The quantity transacted can be found with the demand schedule as: $\bar{Q}_c = 90 - 10\bar{P}_c = 90 - 10(5.08) = 39.2$ (thousand units per day).

The consumers' surplus, CS_c, given by the area $H\bar{P}_cE_c$ in Figure 8.6, is equal to

$$CS_c = \int_0^{39.2} (9 - .1Q)\, dQ - \bar{P}_c \cdot \bar{Q}_c = (9Q - .05Q^2)\Big]_0^{39.2} - (5.08)(39.2)$$

$$= 9(39.2) - .05(39.2)^2 - 199.14$$

$$= \$76.83 \text{ (thousand per day)}$$

The producers' surplus, PS_c, given by the area $G\bar{P}_cE_c$ in Figure 8.6, is equal to:

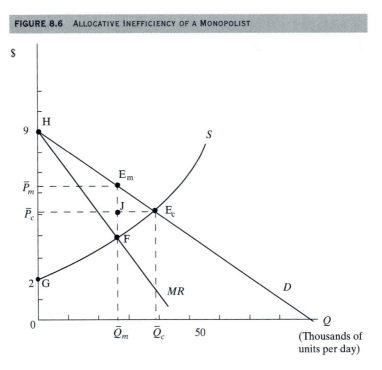

FIGURE 8.6 ALLOCATIVE INEFFICIENCY OF A MONOPOLIST

Market Demand: $Q^d = 90 - 10P$ or $P = 9 - .1Q$

Market Supply: $Q^s = (500P - 1,000)^{.5}$ or $P = 2 + .002Q^2$

Perfect Competition: $\bar{P}_c = \$5.08$ and $\bar{Q}_c = 39.2$

Monopoly: $\bar{P}_m = \$6.25$ and $\bar{Q}_m = 27.5$

$$PS_c = \bar{P}_c \cdot \bar{Q}_c - \int_0^{39.2} (2 + .002Q^2)\, dQ = (5.08)(39.2) - (2Q + .000\bar{6}Q^3) \Big|_0^{39.2}$$

$$= 199.14 - 2(39.2) - .000\bar{6}(39.2)^3$$

$$= \$80.38 \text{ (thousand per day)}$$

Suppose instead that the market were a monopoly and that the market supply schedule is the monopolist's marginal cost schedule. The monopolist would set its profit-maximizing output where its marginal revenue equals its marginal cost. The marginal revenue schedule, MR, associated with the market demand of $Q^d = 90 - 10P$ or $P = 9 - .1Q$ is: $MR = 9 - .2Q$. Setting marginal revenue equal to marginal cost and solving for output, we find

$$MR = 9 - .2Q = 2 + .002Q^2 = MC$$

Simplifying gives

$$.002Q^2 + .2Q - 7 = 0$$

Using the quadratic formula:

$$Q = \frac{-.2 \pm \sqrt{(.2)^2 - 4(.002)(-7)}}{2(.002)} = -127.5, 27.5$$

The profit-maximizing output for the monopolist is $\bar{Q}_m = 27.5$ (thousand units per day). The price charged by the monopolist, $\bar{P}_m$, is the demand price at this profit-maximizing output

$$\bar{P}_m = 9 - .1\bar{Q}_m = 9 - .1(27.5) = \$6.25$$

As expected, compared to a perfectly competitive market with the same demand and supply schedules, a monopolist would sell a lesser quantity at a higher price.

The consumers' surplus under the monopoly, CS_m, indicated by the area $H\bar{P}_m E_m$, in Figure 8.6, is equal to

$$CS_m = \int_0^{27.5} (9 - .1Q)\, dQ - \bar{P}_m \cdot \bar{Q}_m = (9Q - .05Q^2) \Big|_0^{27.5} - (6.25)(27.5)$$

$$= 9(27.5) - .05(27.5)^2 - 171.88$$

$$= \$37.8 \text{ (thousand per day)}$$

The producers' surplus under the monopoly, PS_m, indicated by the area $\bar{P}_m E_m FG$ in Figure 8.6, is equal to

$$PS_m = \bar{P}_m \cdot \bar{Q}_m - \int_0^{27.5} (2 + .002Q^2)\, dQ = (6.25)(27.5) - (2Q + .000\bar{6}Q^3) \Big|_0^{27.5}$$

$$= 171.88 - 2(27.5) - .000\bar{6}\,(27.5)^3$$

$$= \$102.95 \text{ (thousand per day)}$$

We see that the consumers' surplus is reduced from \$76.83 to \$37.81 (thousand per day) and the producers' surplus is increased from \$80.38 to \$102.95 (thousand per day) with the monopolization of the perfectly competitive market. The difference between the sums of the consumers' and producers' surpluses under perfectly competition $(76.83 + 80.38 = 157.21)$ and monopoly $(37.81 + 102.95 = 140.76)$ is accounted for by the deadweight losses $157.21 - 140.76 = 16.45)$. These losses, represented by the areas $E_m JE_c$ and JE_cF in Figure 8.6, measure the allocative inefficiency of a monopoly — since over this range of output (from $\overline{Q}_m = 27.5$ to $\overline{Q}_c = 39.2$), the prices consumers are willing to pay exceed the marginal costs of production.

To calculate directly the sum of the deadweight losses, we take the difference between the area under the demand curve and the area under the supply curve over the range of output from the quantities transacted under the monopoly and perfect competition.

$$\text{Sum of the deadweight losses} = \int_{27.5}^{39.2} (9 - .1Q)\, dQ - \int_{27.5}^{39.2} (2 + .002Q^2)\, dQ$$

$$= \int_{27.5}^{39.2} (7 - .1Q - .002Q^2)\, dQ$$

$$= (7Q - .05Q^2 - .00\overline{6}Q^3)\Big]_{27.5}^{39.2}$$

$$= 7(39.2) - .05(39.2)^2 - .000\overline{6}(39.2)^3$$

$$- 7(27.5) + .05(27.5)^2 + .000\overline{6}(27.5)^3$$

$$= \$16.45 \text{ (thousand per day)}$$

PRACTICE PROBLEM 8.5

Consider a perfectly competitive market with a demand schedule given by: $Q^d = 50 - 8P$, where Q is the quantity (in thousands of units per day) and P is the unit price (in dollars). Assume the market supply schedule is given by: $Q^s = (200P - 300)^{.5}$.

a) Find the market equilibrium price and quantity transacted. Calculate the consumers' surplus (CS_c) and producers' surplus (PS_c).

Now suppose a monopolist buys all of the perfectly competitive firms so that the market supply becomes the marginal cost schedule of the monopolist.

b) Find the quantity sold and price charged by the monopolist. Calculate the consumers' surplus (CS_m) and producers' surplus (PS_m) under the monopoly.

c) Calculate the sum of the deadweight losses in consumers' surplus and producers' surplus due to the allocative inefficiency of the monopoly.

(The answers are at the end of the chapter.)

Monopolist's Profits In order to determine the level of the monopolist's economic profits, we need the short-run average cost curves — in particular, the average total cost (ATC) curve. If at the profit-maximizing output, the monopolist's price exceeds its average total cost, then positive economic profits are earned. Moreover, as noted, positive economic profits may persist if there are sufficient barriers to entry to new firms. If firms do enter the market, the monopolist's demand curve would shift left. In fact, we would no longer have a monopoly. In the next chapter we will examine competition among two firms (duopolies) and a few firms (oligopolies).

If at the profit-maximizing level of output, the monopolist's price is between its average variable cost (*AVC*) and average total cost, then negative economic profits, or economic losses, result. The monopolist would have an incentive not to replace its worn out physical capital.

Finally, if the demand curve of the monopolist falls below its average variable cost curve, such that its price is less than its average variable cost, the monopolist may cease production.

In any case, a monopolist is not guaranteed to earn positive economic profits. The profitability of any monopolist depends on the demand for its product (and the substitutes for the monopolist's product) and the strength of the barriers to entry. Patents run out and demands shift with changes in tastes and preferences, population, and income. Also, cost conditions may change. For example, an increase in input costs, *ceteris paribus*, would reduce profits.

In some markets, a monopolist may find it profitable to engage in price discrimination. Below, we model this behavior.

Price Discrimination   **Price discrimination** occurs when a firm charges different unit prices to different buyers for the same commodity for reasons that are not due to differences in unit costs. Examples of price discrimination would include senior citizen discounts on movie tickets, reduced student subscription rates for magazines, and the higher tuition charged by public universities to out-of-state students. Also, special introductory rates for health clubs and book-of-the-month clubs, where the initial units are discounted and subsequent units are priced much higher, constitute price discrimination—here to the same buyer.

An individual who buys a jumbo-sized box of breakfast cereal may pay less per ounce of cereal if economies of scale in advertising or packaging reduce the unit cost of the cereal. This is not an example of price discrimination. Nor is an individual receiving a discount at the gasoline pump when paying cash rather than using a credit card, since the gasoline station incurs the direct commission fees from the credit card company, as well as the opportunity cost of waiting to be paid for the charged purchase (the interest lost).

A monopolist can practice price discrimination if a) submarkets or groups of buyers can be distinguished based on their willingness to pay for the product and b) secondary transactions can be prevented. That is, the firm must be able to prevent individuals purchasing the product in the lower-priced submarket from reselling in the higher-priced submarket.

Suppose a monopolist can identify two groups of buyers for its product, for example, adults and adolescents. The total revenue functions in submarkets 1 and 2 are, respectively, $R_1(Q_1)$ and $R_2(Q_2)$, where Q_1 and Q_2 refer to the quantities sold in the two submarkets. The total revenue function for the monopolist is: $R = R(Q) = R_1(Q_1) + R_2(Q_2)$.

The monopolist's total cost function is: $STC = C(Q)$, where Q is the total quantity produced and sold ($Q = Q_1 + Q_2$). Note, there is no difference in the cost of production for the commodity based on the submarket in which it is sold.

The monopolist seeks to maximize the profits from the total sales of its product. The profit function is $\Pi = \Pi(Q_1, Q_2) = R_1(Q_1) + R_2(Q_2) - C(Q)$. The first-order conditions are

$$\Pi_1 = \delta\Pi/\delta Q_1 = dR_1/dQ_1 - (dC/dQ)(\delta Q/\delta Q_1) = R_1' - C' = 0$$

$$\Pi_2 = \delta\Pi/\delta Q_2 = dR_2/dQ_2 - (dC/dQ)(\delta Q/\delta Q_2) = R_2' - C' = 0$$

where

$R_1' = dR_1/dQ_1 = MR_1$ is the marginal revenue in submarket 1

$R_2' = dR_2/dQ_2 = MR_2$ is the marginal revenue in submarket 2

and

$C' = dC/dQ = MC$ is the marginal cost of production.

Since $\delta Q/\delta Q_1 = \delta Q/\delta Q_2 = 1$, we can write the first-order conditions as

$$MR_1 - MC = 0$$

$$MR_2 - MC = 0$$

and combining, we have: $MR_1 = MR_2 = MC$. Therefore, to maximize profits the price-discriminating monopolist should equate the marginal revenue in each submarket to the overall marginal cost of production. If, for example, $MR_1 > MR_2$, the monopolist could increase total revenues and profits by reallocating its output and sales from submarket 2 to submarket 1 until the marginal revenues were again equal.

We illustrate the first-order conditions in Figure 8.7. In panel c, the intersection of the aggregate marginal revenue curve, MR (the horizontal summation of the marginal

FIGURE 8.7   PRICE-DISCRIMINATING MONOPOLIST

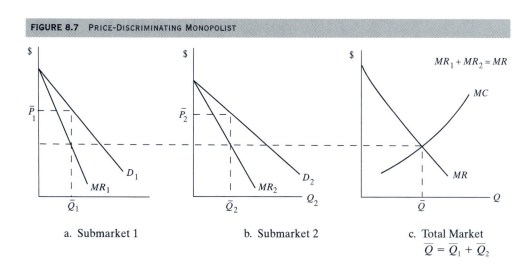

a. Submarket 1   b. Submarket 2   c. Total Market
$\overline{Q} = \overline{Q}_1 + \overline{Q}_2$

revenue curves in the two submarkets, MR_1 and MR_2), with the marginal cost curve, MC, sets the overall profit-maximizing level of output, $\overline{Q}$, and the sales in the two submarkets, $\overline{Q}_1$ and $\overline{Q}_2$, where $\overline{Q}_1 + \overline{Q}_2 = \overline{Q}$. In each submarket the unit price is read off the respective demand curve. See $\overline{P}_1$ from demand curve, D_1, and $\overline{P}_2$ from demand curve, D_2.

We can establish a relationship between the unit prices charged in the submarkets and the underlying price elasticities of demand. For example, for the marginal revenue in submarket 1, we have

$$MR_1 = dR_1/dQ_1 = \frac{d(P_1(Q_1)\cdot Q_1)}{dQ_1} = (dP_1/dQ_1)\cdot Q_1 + P_1$$

Factoring out P_1 gives

$$MR_1 = P_1\,[(dP_1/dQ_1)\cdot(Q_1/P_1) + 1] = P_1\,[1/(\epsilon_p^d)_1 + 1]$$

where $(\epsilon_p^d)_1$ is the price elasticity of demand in submarket 1.

$$(\epsilon_p^d)_1 = \frac{dQ_1/dP_1}{Q_1/P_1} = \frac{dQ_1/Q_1}{dP_1/P_1}$$

From the law of demand (the expected inverse relationship between the quantity demanded and unit price of a commodity that is captured by a negatively sloped demand curve), we know that $(\epsilon_p^d)_1 < 0$, so we can write: $1/(\epsilon_p^d)_1 = -1/|(\epsilon_p^d)_1|$. Thus, we express the marginal revenue in submarket 1 as

$$MR_1 = P_1\,[1 - 1/|(\epsilon_p^d)_1|]$$

Similarly, the marginal revenue in submarket 2 can be expressed as

$$MR_2 = P_2\,[1 - 1/|(\epsilon_p^d)_2|]$$

where $(\epsilon_p^d)_2$ is the price elasticity of demand in submarket 2.

$$(\epsilon_p^d)_2 = \frac{dQ_2/dP_2}{Q_2/P_2} = \frac{dQ_2/Q_2}{dP_2/P_2}$$

Remember that in each submarket, the profit-maximizing monopolist will be operating in the price-elastic region of the demand curve. Now, from the first-order condition for profit maximization, $MR_1 = MR_2 = MC$, we substitute the derived expressions for the marginal revenues.

$$MR_1 = P_1\,[1 - 1/|(\epsilon_p^d)_1|] = P_2\,[1 - 1/|(\epsilon_p^d)_2|] = MR_2 = MC$$

We can see that if demand is more price elastic in submarket 2, $|(\epsilon_p^d)_2| > |(\epsilon_p^d)_1|$, then the price-discriminating monopolist would charge a lower price in submarket 2, $P_2 < P_1$.

For example, suppose at the profit-maximizing output levels in the two submarkets, the price elasticities of demand are: $(\epsilon_p^d)_1 = -2$ and $(\epsilon_p^d)_2 = -3$. The corresponding ratio of prices can then be calculated.

$$P_1 [1 - 1/|(\epsilon_p^d)_1|] = P_1 [1 - 1/2] = P_2 [1 - 1/3] = P_2 [1 - 1/|(\epsilon_p^d)_2|]$$

$$(1/2)P_1 = (2/3)P_2$$

$$P_1 = (4/3)P_2$$

As expected, the higher price is set in the submarket with the less elastic demand. This result is intuitive. In submarket 1, the lower price elasticity of demand suggests a greater willingness of those consumers to pay for the product than for the consumers in submarket 2. Consequently, total revenues and profits would be increased by raising the unit price in submarket 1 and lowering the unit price in submarket 2—compared to charging a common price to all demanders—until the marginal revenue in each submarket equals the marginal cost of production.

Finally, we should check the second-order conditions for a maximum. Partially differentiating the first-order conditions and setting up the Hessian gives

$$\Pi_{11} = \frac{\delta(\delta\Pi/\delta Q_1)}{\delta Q_1} = \frac{\delta(dR_1/dQ_1)}{\delta Q_1} - \frac{\delta(dC/dQ)}{\delta Q_1}(\delta Q/\delta Q_1) = R_1'' - C''$$

$$\Pi_{12} = \frac{\delta(\delta\Pi/\delta Q_2)}{\delta Q_1} = \frac{\delta(dR_2/dQ_2)}{\delta Q_1} - \frac{\delta(dC/dQ)}{\delta Q_1}(\delta Q/\delta Q_1) = -C''$$

$$\Pi_{21} = \frac{\delta(\delta\Pi/\delta Q_1)}{\delta Q_2} = \frac{\delta(dR_1/dQ_1)}{\delta Q_2} - \frac{\delta(dC/dQ)}{\delta Q_2}(\delta Q/\delta Q_2) = -C''$$

$$\Pi_{21} = \frac{\delta(\delta\Pi/\delta Q_2)}{\delta Q_2} = \frac{\delta(dR_2/dQ_2)}{\delta Q_2} - \frac{\delta(dC/dQ)}{\delta Q_2}(\delta Q/\delta Q_2) = R_2'' - C''$$

Note that

$$\frac{\delta(dR_1/dQ_1)}{\delta Q_2} = \frac{\delta(dR_2/dQ_2)}{\delta Q_1} = 0.$$

Changes in the quantities sold in one submarket should not affect the marginal revenue in the other submarket.

The Hessian is

$$|H| = \begin{vmatrix} \Pi_{11} & \Pi_{12} \\ \Pi_{21} & \Pi_{22} \end{vmatrix} = \begin{vmatrix} R_1'' - C'' & -C'' \\ -C'' & R_2'' - C'' \end{vmatrix}$$

For a maximum, we need $|H_1| < 0$ and $|H_2| > 0$. $|H_1| = R_1'' - C''$, where R_1'' represents the slope of the marginal revenue curve in submarket 1, $(R_1'' < 0)$, and C'' represents the slope of the marginal cost curve. For profit maximization, the slope of the marginal revenue curve at the optimal level of sales in each submarket must be less than the slope of the marginal cost curve at the overall optimal level of output. If $R_1'' < C''$ and $R_2'' < C''$ then $|H_1| > 0$.

$$|H_2| = |H| = (R_1'' - C'')(R_2'' - C'') - C''C'' = R_1''R_2'' - R_1''C'' - R_2''C''.$$

If we had specific functional forms for the marginal revenue and marginal cost equations we might be able to confirm that the second-order conditions for a maximum are met. Even if we knew that the slope of the marginal cost curve at the optimal level of output is positive, $C'' > 0$, then both second-order conditions would clearly be satisfied. This is the case illustrated in Figure 8.7.

To illustrate with a numerical example, suppose a monopolist has identified two submarkets or groups of buyers for its product with demand curves given by

$$\text{Group 1: } Q_1^d = 50 - 5P_1 \quad \text{or} \quad P_1 = 10 - (1/5)Q_1$$

$$\text{Group 2: } Q_2^d = 30 - 2P_2 \quad \text{or} \quad P_2 = 15 - (1/2)Q_2$$

The total market demand for the monopolist is: $Q^d = Q_1^d + Q_2^d = 80 - 7P$ (for $P \leq 10$), where Q_1 and Q_2 are the quantities in submarkets 1 and 2 (in thousands of units per day) and P_1 and P_2 are the unit prices of the monopolist's product in the submarkets (in dollars). Note, if the monopolist set its price at \$10 (\$15) or higher, the quantity demanded in submarket 1 (2) would fall to zero.

Assume the short-run total cost curve of the monopolist is given by $STC = C(Q) = .1Q^2 + 120$, where $Q = Q_1 + Q_2$. That is, the cost of the output produced is not affected by which submarket the output is sold. Note, we are assuming a relatively simple short-run total cost function, where diminishing returns to labor set in immediately and the marginal cost is linear, in order to highlight the demand-side of the market. The total revenue functions associated with the submarkets are

$$R_1 = R(Q_1) = 10Q_1 - (1/5)Q_1^2$$

$$R_2 = R(Q_2) = 15Q_2 - (1/2)Q_2^2$$

The profit function for the price-discriminating monopolist is

$$\Pi(Q_1, Q_2) = R(Q_1) + R(Q_2) - C(Q)$$

$$= 10Q_1 - (1/5)Q_1^2 + 15Q_2 - (1/2)Q_2^2 - .1(Q_1 + Q_2)^2 - 120$$

The first-order conditions are

$$\delta\Pi/\delta Q_1 = 10 - (2/5)Q_1 - .2(Q_1 + Q_2) = 0$$

$$\delta\Pi/\delta Q_2 = 15 - Q_2 - .2(Q_1 + Q_2) = 0$$

We should note that the first-order conditions yield the profit-maximizing decision rule for a price-discriminating monopolist: $MR_1 = 10 - (2/5)Q_1 = MR_2 = 15 - Q_2 = MC = .2(Q_1 + Q_2) = .2Q$

Rewriting the first-order conditions, we have

$$-.6Q_1 - .2Q_2 = -10$$

$$-.2Q_1 - 1.2Q_2 = -15$$

or, in matrix notation

$$\begin{bmatrix} -.6 & -.2 \\ -.2 & -1.2 \end{bmatrix} \begin{bmatrix} Q_1 \\ Q_2 \end{bmatrix} = \begin{bmatrix} -10 \\ -15 \end{bmatrix}$$

Using Cramer's rule, we solve

$$\overline{Q}_1 = \frac{\begin{vmatrix} -10 & -.2 \\ -15 & -1.2 \end{vmatrix}}{\begin{vmatrix} -.6 & -.2 \\ -.2 & -1.2 \end{vmatrix}} = \frac{9}{.68} = 13.24 \text{ (thousand units per day)}$$

$$\overline{Q}_2 = \frac{\begin{vmatrix} -.6 & -10 \\ -.2 & -15 \end{vmatrix}}{\begin{vmatrix} -.6 & -.2 \\ -.2 & -1.2 \end{vmatrix}} = \frac{7}{.68} = 10.29 \text{ (thousand units per day)}$$

The prices charged to each group of buyers are found from the demand curves.

Submarket 1: $\overline{P}_1 = 10 - (1/5)\overline{Q}_1 = 10 - (1/5)(13.24) = \$7.35$

Submarket 2: $\overline{P}_2 = 15 - (1/2)\overline{Q}_2 = 15 - (1/2)(10.29) = \$9.85$.

The total revenues are:

$$R = R_1 + R_2 = P_1 \cdot Q_1 + P_2 \cdot Q_2 = (\$7.35)(13.24) + (\$9.85)(10.29)$$

$$R = \$97.31 + \$101.36 = \$198.67 \text{ (thousand per day)}$$

The total costs are:

$$STC = .1(Q_1 + Q_2)^2 + 10 = .1(13.24 + 10.29)^2 + 120$$

$$STC = 55.37 + 120 = \$175.37 \text{ (thousand per day)}$$

The monopolist's profits are: $\Pi = R - STC = \$198.67 - \$175.37 = \$23.30$ (thousand per day).

To check the second-order conditions, we set up the Hessian.

$$|H| = \begin{vmatrix} \Pi_{11} & \Pi_{12} \\ \Pi_{21} & \Pi_{22} \end{vmatrix} = \begin{vmatrix} -.6 & -.2 \\ -.2 & -1.2 \end{vmatrix}$$

We find: $|H_1| = -.6 < 0$ and $|H_2| = |H| = .68 > 0$, consistent with a maximum.

We confirm that the monopolist would charge the higher price in the submarket with the less price elastic demand (here submarket 2).

$$(\epsilon_p^d)_1 = \frac{(dQ_1^d/dP_1)}{(\overline{Q}_1/\overline{P}_1)} = \frac{-5}{(13.24)/(7.35)} = -2.78$$

$$(\epsilon^d)_2 = \frac{(dQ_2^d/dP_2)}{(\overline{Q}_2/\overline{P}_2)} = \frac{-2}{(10.29)/(9.85)} = -1.92$$

Finally, we can show that the monopolist's profits would be lower if it does not practice price discrimination. Regarding the market demand as a whole, $Q^d = 80 - 7P$, or $P = (80/7) - (1/7)Q$, the total revenue function is: $R = R(Q) = (80/7)Q - (1/7)Q^2$. Combining with the short-run total cost function, $STC = C(Q) = .1Q^2 + 120$, we write the profit function.

$$\Pi(Q) = (80/7)Q - (1/7)Q^2 - .1Q^2 - 120.$$

To find the profit-maximizing output, we differentiate profits with respect to output, set the result equal to zero, and solve

$$\delta\Pi/dQ = (80/7) - (2/7)Q - .2Q = 0$$

$$80 - 2Q - 1.4Q = 0$$

$$3.4Q = 80$$

$$\overline{Q} = 23.53 \text{ (thousand units per day)}$$

Note that the total output of the monopolist is the same as under price discrimination. Recall that with price discrimination the quantities sold in the submarkets are: $\overline{Q}_1 = 13.24$ and $\overline{Q}_2 = 10.29$, and $\overline{Q}_1 + \overline{Q}_2 = 13.24 + 10.29 = 23.53 = \overline{Q}$. Consequently, the total costs are the same. Without price discrimination, however, the monopolist charges the same price to all buyers. Here, the common price is: $\overline{P} = (80/7) - (1/7)\overline{Q} = (80/7) - (1/7)(23.53) = 8.07$. The total revenues are less: $\overline{R}(Q) = \overline{P} \cdot \overline{Q} = (\$8.07)(23.53) = \$189.89$ (thousand per day) and the total profits are less: $\Pi(\overline{Q}) = R(Q) - C(\overline{Q}) = \$189.89 - \$175.37 = \$14.52$ (thousand per day).

In sum, with price discrimination, a monopolist can enhance its profits. Here, profits with price discrimination ($23.30 thousand per day) exceed profits without price discrimination ($14.52 thousand per day). Of course, to realize the extra profits the monopolist must be able to distinguish the two submarkets and prevent secondary transactions (buyers in the lower-priced submarket from reselling the product to demanders in the higher-priced submarket).

PRACTICE PROBLEM 8.6

Given a monopolist who has identified two submarkets or groups of buyers for its product with demand schedules:

$$\text{Group 1: } Q_1^d = 40 - 5P_1$$

$$\text{Group 2: } Q_2^d = 60 - 10P_2$$

The short-run total cost curve of the monopolist is: $STC = C(Q) = .025Q^2 + 120$, where $Q = Q_1 + Q_2$, with Q_1 and Q_2 as the quantities in submarkets 1 and 2 respectively. P_1 and P_2 are the units prices (in dollars) in submarkets 1 and 2.

a) Determine the profit-maximizing outputs and prices in the two submarkets and the total profits of the monopolist under price discrimination. Check the second-order conditions and calculate the price elasticity of demand in each submarket at the profit-maximizing output.
b) Determine the profit-maximizing output, price charged, and total profits if the monopolist does not practice price discrimination.

(The answers are at the end of the chapter.)

To conclude this chapter, we examine monopsony. In particular, we will contrast a monopsonistic firm with a perfectly competitive firm in the labor market.

MONOPSONIES

Whereas a monopoly is a single supplier or seller in a market, a **monopsony** is a single demander or buyer in a market. As such, the relevant supply curve facing the monopsonistic firm is the market supply; and there may be one, a few, or many suppliers of the good or service in question. The case of one supplier and one demander is known as a **bilateral monopoly**. An example might be the individual who is a first-round draft pick and the professional sports team that owns the rights to that individual. Examples of a monopsony in an output market include the U.S. Navy's demand for nuclear submarines or National Aeronautics and Space Administration's (NASA's) demand for precision parts for a space shuttle. In each case there may be only a few firms with the technical expertise to supply the goods. Monopolies in the output market may translate into monopsonies in the input market. For instance, Americans desiring to become nuclear submarine officers must work for the U.S. Navy. Umpires seeking to work in the big leagues must be hired by Major League baseball. Here there are potentially many suppliers of the labor services to a single buyer.

In this chapter we model a monopsony in a labor market. Examples would be the police department or a single hospital in a city. Individuals living in the area who want to be police officers or surgical nurses would deal with employers with monopsonistic power. Often in such circumstances, labor unions are formed to represent the interests of the workers.

MONOPSONY IN THE LABOR MARKET

Consider firm i, with a short-run production function, $Q_i = Q(K_{i0}, L_i)$, where K_{i0} is the firm's fixed capital stock and L_i is the variable labor. As a monopsonist in a labor market, firm i faces an upward-sloping labor supply curve, $L_i^s = L^s(w_i)$, where w_i is the wage paid by firm i and $dL_i^s/dw_i > 0$. Firm i is a wage-setter. We can express this relationship by taking the inverse of the labor supply function, $w_i = w(L_i)$, where $dw_i/dL_i > 0$. In order to hire more labor, firm i has to raise the wage it pays—not only for the new labor employed, but also for all the labor previously employed at the lower wage. Consequently, for a monopsonistic firm, the marginal factor cost of labor exceeds the wage paid.

Formally, the total factor cost of labor $(TFC_L)_i$, average factor cost of labor $(AFC_L)_i$, and marginal factor cost of labor $(MFC_L)_i$ for a monopsonistic firm i are

$$(TFC_L)_i = (w_i) \cdot (L_i)$$
$$(AFC_L)_i = (TFC_L)_i/L_i = w_i$$

$$(MFC_L)_i = d(TFC_L)_i/dL_i = (dw_i/dL_i) \cdot L_i + w_i$$

We can see that the average factor cost of labor is the wage rate, w_i; and the labor supply curve for firm i is equivalently the $(AFC_L)_i$ curve. The $(MFC_L)_i$ curve rises above the $(AFC_L)_i$ curve, since the $(MFC_L)_i$ includes the additional wages that must be paid to all workers in order to increase employment. This difference is indicated by $(dw_i/dL_i) \cdot L_i$ in the equation for the $(MFC_L)_i$. Two simple examples may help to illustrate.

Suppose a monopsonistic firm i employs 19 workers at \$5 per hour. Thus, $(TFC_L)_i = \$95$ per hour and $(AFC_L)_i = \$95$ per hour/19 workers = \$5 per hour = w_i. Facing an upward-sloping supply curve of labor, assume that the firm has to increase the wage rate to \$5.10 per hour in order to hire a 20th worker. The new total and average factor costs of labor are: $(TFC_L)'_i = \$102$ per hour and $(AFC_L)'_i = \$102$ per hour/20 workers = \$5.10 per hour = w'_i. The marginal factor cost of the 20th worker is \$7 per hour: $(\Delta TFC_L)_i/\Delta L_i = (\$102 - \$95)/1 = \$7$. The marginal factor cost exceeds the new wage of \$5.10 by \$1.90, which reflects the extra \$.10 per hour that must be paid to the other 19 workers after the new worker is hired.

We can also illustrate with a linear supply curve for labor facing firm i. Given

$$L_i^s = L_i = -h_0 + h_1 w_i \quad \text{where } h_0 > 0 \text{ and } h_1 = dL_i/dw_i > 0$$

Rewriting the firm's labor supply curve in terms of the wage it pays (the inverse function), we have

$$w_i = (h_0/h_1) + (1/h_1) L_i \quad \text{where } dw_i/dL_i = 1/h_1 > 0.$$

Firm i's total factor cost of labor, average factor cost of labor, and marginal factor cost of labor are

$$(TFC_L)_i = (w_i)(L_i) = (h_0/h_1)L_i + (1/h_1)L_i^2$$

$$(AFC_L)_i = (TFC_L)_i/L_i = (h_0/h_1) + (1/h_1) L_i = w_i$$

$$(MFC_L)_i = d(TFC_L)_i/dL_i = (h_0/h_1) + (2/h_1) L_i$$

The graphs of the firm's labor supply and marginal factor cost of labor curves are given in Figure 8.8. Note that the $(MFC_L)_i$ curve has the same vertical intercept (h_0/h_1), but twice the slope of the linear labor supply curve: $d(MFC_L)_i/dL_i = 2/h_1 = 2 (1/h_1) = 2 (dw_i/dL_i)$. The vertical intercept of the labor supply curve indicates the **reservation wage** of labor, or the minimum supply price of labor that must be paid before any quantity of labor would be supplied.

To illustrate, suppose firm i, a monopsonist in a labor market, faces a labor supply schedule given by:

$$L_i^s = -50 + 6w_i \quad \text{or} \quad w_i = 50/6 + (1/6)L_i,$$

where

$$L_i = \text{quantity of labor for firm } i \text{ (in thousands of workers) and}$$

$$w_i = \text{wage rate per hour (in dollars)}$$

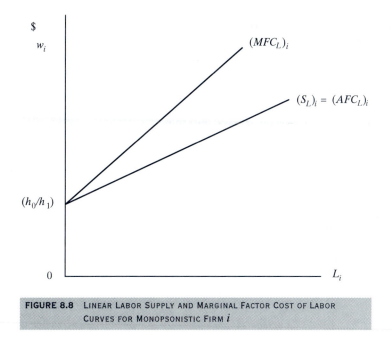

FIGURE 8.8 LINEAR LABOR SUPPLY AND MARGINAL FACTOR COST OF LABOR CURVES FOR MONOPSONISTIC FIRM i

The total, average, and marginal factor costs of labor are, respectively,

$$(TFC_L)_i = w_i \cdot L_i = (50/6)L_i + (1/6)L_i^2$$

$$(AFC_L)_i = (TFC_L)_i/L_i = 50/6 + (1/6)L_i = w_i$$

$$(MFC_L)_i = d(TFC_L)_i/dL_i = 50/6 + (1/3)L_i$$

We see that the marginal factor cost of labor schedule has a slope, $d(MFC_L)_i/dL_i = 1/3$, that is twice the slope of the labor supply schedule, which is identical to the average factor cost of labor schedule $(dw_i/dL_i = d(AFC_L)_i/dL_i = 1/6)$. The reservation wage is $(50/6) = \$8.33$ per hour.

PRACTICE PROBLEM 8.7

Given the labor supply schedule for a monopsonistic firm i: $L_i^s = -60 + 10w_i$,

where L_i = quantity of labor for firm i (in thousands of workers)

and w_i = wage rate per hour (in dollars)

a) Find the average factor cost of labor $(AFC_L)_i$ and marginal factor cost of labor $(MFC_L)_i$ schedules.

b) Find the reservation wage.

(The answers are at the end of the chapter.)

MONOPSONIST'S PROFIT-MAXIMIZING EMPLOYMENT AND WAGE

Like a monopolist, a monopsonist will take advantage of its market power. To illustrate, consider a monopsonistic firm i, facing a labor supply curve given by $w_i = w(L_i)$, where $dw_i/dL_i > 0$. That is, unlike a perfectly competitive firm in a labor market, a monopsonist sets the wage it pays; and this wage varies directly with the level of labor it employs.

The short-run profit function for monopsonistic firm i is

$$\Pi_i = \Pi[Q(K_{i0}, L_i)] = R[Q(K_{i0}, L_i)] - r_0 \cdot K_{i0} - w_i(L_i) \cdot L_i.$$

The first-order condition for the profit-maximizing level of employment is

$$d\Pi_i/dL_i = (dR_i/dQ_i)(dQ_i/dL_i) - (dw_i/dL_i) \cdot L_i - w_i = 0$$

or

$$(dR_i/dQ_i)(dQ_i/dL_i) = (dw_i/dL_i) \cdot L_i + w_i$$

Thus, like any firm, to maximize profits the monopsonist would hire labor up to the point where the marginal revenue product of labor, $(MRP_L)_i = (dR_i/dQ_i)(dQ_i/dL_i) = dR_i/dL_i$, equals the marginal factor cost of labor, $(MFC_L)_i = (dw_i/dL_i) \cdot L_i + w_i$. The monopsonist, however, would not pay a wage higher than necessary to secure the optimal quantity of labor, $\overline{L}_{i0}$. The wage paid is derived from the labor supply curve facing the firm: $\overline{w}_{i0} = w_i(\overline{L}_{i0})$.

Figure 8.9 illustrates. For simplicity, we will assume a linear labor supply curve, $(S_L)_i$. Consequently, the $(MFC_L)_i$ curve has the same vertical intercept, but twice the slope of the labor supply curve. The firm's marginal revenue product of labor curve, $(MRP_L)_i$, is also drawn. The profit-maximizing level of employment is $\overline{L}_{i0}$, where the $(MRP_L)_i$ and $(MFC_L)_i$ curves intersect. The wage would only have to be $\overline{w}_{i0}$ to generate the required quantity of labor to be supplied. With a monopsony, the wage received by labor is less than the marginal revenue product of labor. (See the gap represented by the line segment F_0E_0 in Figure 8.9.) Is labor being exploited? Could a labor union organize workers and force a higher wage?

Before addressing these questions, we should note that the total payments to labor can be disaggregated into transfer earnings and economic rent. The total wages received by the $\overline{L}_{i0}$ units of labor employed are equal to $(\overline{w}_{i0}) \cdot (\overline{L}_{i0})$ and are represented by the area $\overline{w}_{i0}E_0\overline{L}_{i0}0$ in Figure 8.9. **Transfer earnings** refer to the wage receipts necessary to have the quantity of labor supplied. The transfer earnings for the $\overline{L}_{i0}$ units of labor are represented by the area under the labor supply curve, $0G_0E_0\overline{L}_{i0}$. **Economic rent**, any wage payment above transfer earnings, is indicated by the area, $\overline{w}_{i0}E_0G_0$. Note that on the last unit of labor employed there is no economic rent—the wage paid, $\overline{w}_{i0}$, is just sufficient to employ the $\overline{L}_{i0}$ unit of labor. A labor union can gain some of the economic rent that is captured by a monopsonist.

A Labor Union in a Monopsonistic Labor Market Suppose that a union were successful in organizing the labor employed by the monopsonist. If powerful enough, the

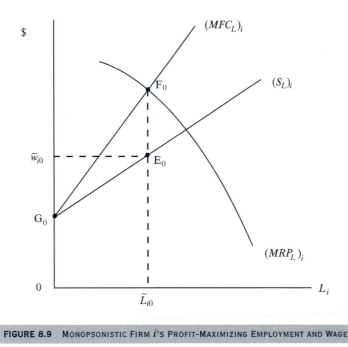

FIGURE 8.9   MONOPSONISTIC FIRM i'S PROFIT-MAXIMIZING EMPLOYMENT AND WAGE

union could turn the monopsonist into a wage-taker. If the union presents a wage, below which no labor is willing to work, then the marginal factor cost of labor to the firm becomes this union wage. (*Note:* A binding minimum wage would have the same effect.)

Refer to Figure 8.10, where the profit-maximizing level of employment and wage for the monopsonist are $\overline{L}_{i0}$ and $\overline{w}_{i0}$. The maximum wage that the union could demand, while maintaining the level of employment of $\overline{L}_{i0}$, is w_1. In this case, the total wages paid to labor rise to $(w_1) \cdot (\overline{L}_{i0})$, with the entire increase being additional economic rent (the area $w_1F_0E_0\overline{w}_{i0}$). Members of the union, however, pay union dues, so the net increase in wages would be less. Moreover, the union must be able to prevent the firm from hiring nonunion labor. At the wage, w_1, the quantity of labor supplied, L_1^s, exceeds the quantity hired ($\overline{L}_{i0}$). The surplus job seekers (unemployed) may exert downward pressure on the union wage.

The union could set a wage as low as w_2 and "force" the firm not only to pay a higher wage, $w_2 > \overline{w}_{i0}$, but employ more workers, $L_2 > \overline{L}_{i0}$. In this case, the total wages received by labor increase to $(w_2) \cdot (L_2)$. Transfer earnings rise by the area $E_0F_2L_2\overline{L}_{i0}$, reflecting the additional labor hired. Economic rent increases by the area $w_2F_2E_0\overline{w}_{i0}$. Furthermore, at the wage, w_2, there are no surplus job seekers.

In the case of a bilateral monopoly, here a labor union versus a monopsonist, the actual outcome, that is, the union wage and employment, will depend on relative bargaining strength. The more aggressive is a union in setting the wage, the greater the incentive for the monopsonist to replace labor with capital in the long run, or, even to shift operations out of the country.

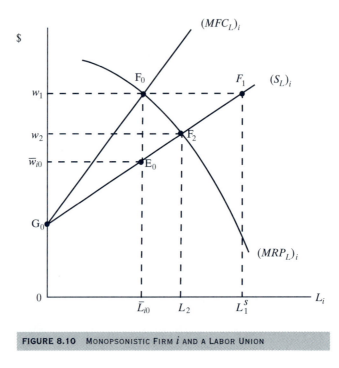

FIGURE 8.10   MONOPSONISTIC FIRM *i* AND A LABOR UNION

To illustrate with a numerical example, consider firm i, a monoposonist, facing a labor supply schedule given by:

$$L_i^s = -30 + 5w_i \quad \text{or} \quad w_i = 6 + .2L_i$$

where

L_i = quantity of labor for firm i (in thousands of workers)

and w_i = wage rate per hour (in dollars)

Suppose the firm's short-run production function is: $Q_i = -.04L_i^3 + .25L_i^2 + 10L_i$ where

Q_i = output of firm i (in thousands of units per hour).

Further, assume that the unit price of firm i's output is $P_i = \$2.00$. For example, firm i might be a perfect competitor in its output market and $2.00 is the market equilibrium price. Or, more likely, firm i may be an oligopolist, who, uncertain of the demand for its product, sets its unit price as a percentage mark-up over its average total cost of production. In the next chapter we will model oligopoly behavior.

To find the profit-maximizing employment for firm i, we use the decision rule:

$$(MRP_L)_i = (MFC_L)_i$$

The revenue function for the firm is: $R_i = R(Q_i) = P_i \cdot Q_i = 2(-.04L_i^3 + .25L_i^2 + 10L_i) = -.08L_i^3 + .50L_i^2 + 20L_i$. The marginal revenue product of labor schedule is easily derived.

$$(MRP_L)_i = dR_i/dL_i = -.24L_i^2 + 1.0L_i + 20$$

The total factor cost of labor for firm i is: $(TFC_L)_i = w_i \cdot L_i = (6 + .2L_i) \cdot L_i = 6L_i + .2L_i^2$. The marginal factor cost of labor schedule is then

$$(MFC_L)_i = d(TFC_L)_i/dL_i = 6 + .4L_i$$

Setting the marginal revenue product of labor equal to the marginal factor cost of labor and solving for the critical level of employment, we find

$$-.24L_i^2 + 1.0L_i + 20 = 6 + .4L_i$$

$$-.24L_i^2 + .6L_i + 14 = 0$$

Using the quadratic formula, we find:

$$L_i = \frac{-.6 \pm \sqrt{(.6)^2 - 4(-.24)(14)}}{2(-.24)} = \frac{-.6 \pm 3.71}{-.48} = -6.48, 8.98$$

Thus, the profit-maximizing employment for firm i is: $\overline{L}_i = 8.98$ (thousand workers)

The monopsonist will set the wage as low as possible. This wage is found from the labor supply schedule facing the monopsonist evaluated at $\overline{L}_i = 8.98$.

$$\overline{w}_i = 6 + .2L_i = 6 + .2(8.98) = \$7.80 \text{ (per hour)}$$

Note that the wage set by the monopsonist is less than the marginal revenue product and marginal factor cost of labor at the profit-maximizing level of employment.

$$[MFC_L(\overline{L}_i)] = 6 + .4(8.98) = \$9.59 = [MRP_L(\overline{L}_i)]$$

The economic rent for the labor employed by the monopsonist is equal to the difference between the total wages received, here $\overline{w}_i \cdot \overline{L}_i = (7.80)(8.98) = \$70.04$ (thousand per hour) and the transfer earnings (measured by the area under the labor supply curve up to the level of employment). That is,

$$\text{Economic rent} = 70.04 - \int_0^{8.98} (6 + .2L_i) \, dL_i = 70.04 - (6L_i + .1L_i^2) \Big]_0^{8.98}$$

$$= 70.04 - 53.88 - 8.06$$

$$= \$8.10 \text{ (thousand per hour)}$$

Suppose now that a union enters and successfully organizes the employees of the firm. The lowest wage the union would demand would be $7.90, which corresponds to the equilibrium wage if this labor market were characterized by perfect competition, that is, with no union or monopsonistic employer. To demonstrate, regard the monopsonist's marginal revenue product of labor schedule, $(MRP_L) =$

$-.24L^2 + 1.0L + 20$, as the market demand for labor. Setting the labor demand equal to the labor supply schedule, $w = 6 + .2L$, and solving for the equilibrium level of employment, we have

$$-.24L^2 + 1.0L + 20 = 6 + .2L$$

$$-.24L^2 + .8L + 14 = 0$$

$$L = \frac{-.8 \pm \sqrt{(.8)^2 - 4(-.24)(14)}}{2(-.24)} = \frac{-.8 \pm 3.75}{-.48} = -6.15, 9.48$$

With a perfectly competitive labor market, the level of employment would be $L_c = 9.48$ (thousand workers), which exceeds the profit-maximizing employment of the monoposonist of $\overline{L}_i = 8.98$ (thousand workers). The market-clearing wage is $w_c = 6 + .2L_c = 6 + .2(9.48) = 7.90$ or \$7.90 per hour, which is higher than the wage paid by the monopsonist, $\overline{w}_i = \$7.80$.

To avoid reducing employment below the monopsonist's level, the union would demand a wage no higher than \$9.59. Recall, the marginal revenue product of labor and marginal factor cost of labor equaled \$9.59 at the monopsonist's profit-maximizing employment of $\overline{L}_i = 8.98$.

Let's say the union sets the wage at $w_u = \$9.00$. The union seeks to turn the monopsonist into a wage-taker, so the union wage would become the marginal factor cost of labor to the firm. To maximize profits now, the monopsonist would set its marginal revenue product equal to the union wage.

$$(MRP_L)_i = -.24L_i^2 + 1.0L_i + 20 = 9 = w_u$$

Solving for the profit-maximizing employment under the union wage, we have

$$-.24L_i^2 + 1.0L_i + 11 = 0$$

$$L_i = \frac{-1.0 \pm \sqrt{(1.0)^2 - 4(-.24)(11)}}{2(-.24)} = \frac{-1 \pm 3.40}{-.48} = -5.0, 9.1\overline{6}$$

The profit-maximizing level of employment for the firm given the union wage of $w_u = \$9.00$ is: $(\overline{L}_i)_u = 9.1\overline{6}$ (thousand workers).

Thus, the union may be able to raise both the wage paid and the level of employment of the monopsonist. The economic rent of labor increases for both of these reasons.

$$\text{Economic rent} = w_u \cdot (\overline{L}_i)_u - \int_0^{9.16} (6 + .2L_i)\, dL_i = (9)(9.1\overline{6}) - \left(6L_i + .1L_i^2\right)\Big|_0^{9.16}$$

$$= 82.50 - 55.00 - 8.40$$

$$= \$19.10 \text{ (thousand per hour)}$$

The union, in this example, more than doubles the economic rent of labor (\$19.10 vs. \$8.10 thousand per hour), although some of labor's gain in wages would go for union dues.

In practice, the union may not be able to dictate a wage to the monopsonist, as illustrated in this example. The bilateral monopoly of the union (the supplier of labor) and the firm (the demander of labor) would likely result in collective bargaining. That is, the union wage and employment would be a matter of negotiation.

Moreover, the strength of the union depends in large part on its ability to organize labor and prevent the monopsonist from hiring non-union workers. Here, at the union wage of $w_u = \$9.00$, the quantity of labor supplied is: $L^s = -30 + 5(9.00) = 15$ (thousand workers), while the quantity of labor demanded and employed is $(L_i)_u = 9.1\overline{6}$ (thousand workers). In sum, compared to the initial monopsony, where 8.98 thousand workers were hired at a wage of $7.80 per hour and there was no surplus labor seeking employment; with the union the monopsonist employs $9.1\overline{6}$ thousand workers at a wage of $9.00 per hour, and there is an excess quantity supplied of 5.83 thousand workers.

PRACTICE PROBLEM 8.8

Given a firm i, a monopsonist facing a labor supply schedule, $L_i^s = -40 + 4w_i$

where L_i = quantity of labor for firm i (in thousands of workers)

and w_i = wage rate per hour (in dollars);

and with a short-run production function, $Q_i = -.03L_i^3 + .15L_i^2 + 5L_i$

where Q_i = output of firm i (in thousands of units per hour);

and assuming that the unit price of the firm's output is $P_i = \$3.00$:

a) Find the profit-maximizing employment and wage paid by the monopsonistic firm i. Calculate the economic rent of labor under the monopsony.
b) Now suppose a union enters and sets a union wage of $w_u = \$12.00$. Determine the new profit-maximizing employment for the firm under the union. Calculate the economic rent of labor with the union.

(The answers are at the end of the chapter.)

In these last two chapters, we have dealt with perfectly and monopolistically competitive firms, monopolists, and monopsonists. In each case we could model the typical or representative firm. With perfect and monopolistic competition, the presence of many firms means that no one firm has any market power; and, with freedom of entry and exit, zero economic profits will prevail in long-run equilibrium. In fact, in these market structures, individual firms do not really compete against each other. With monopolies and monopsonies, there is no competition if barriers to entry are sufficiently high. Natural monopolies may be regulated, however, and unions may form to counter the monopsonist in the labor market. In Chapter 9, we address competition among the few, where firms are aware of their interdependence and act accordingly. We will see that modeling the behavior of these firms is more difficult.

❖ KEY TERMS

Economics

- allocative efficiency (p. 253)
- bilateral monopoly (p. 265)
- deadweight loss (p. 254)
- economic rent (p. 268)

- economies of scale (p. 252)
- monopoly (p. 252)
- monopsony (p. 265)
- natural monopolies (p. 252)

- price discrimination (p. 258)
- reservation wage (p. 266)
- transfer earnings (p. 268)

Mathematics

- Hessian (p. 235)
- Jacobian determinant (p. 243)

- positive definite (p. 234)
- negative definite (p. 234)
- relative maximum (p. 230)

- relative minimum (p. 230)
- saddle point (p. 233)

❖ PROBLEMS

1. For each of the following functions, $z = z(x, y)$, find the critical point(s) and evaluate the second-order conditions to determine the type of relative extremum.
   a) $z(x, y) = -4x^2 - 12x + 2xy - 3y^2$
   b) $z(x, y) = -4x^2 - 12x + 2xy + 3y^2$
   c) $z(x, y) = x^3 - x + xy + y^2$

2. The demand schedule for a firm's product is $Q^d = 60 - 10P$, and the firm has two plants producing the commodity with the following short-run total cost functions:

$$STC_1 = C_1(Q_1) = .1Q_1^2 + 20 \quad \text{(Plant 1)}$$

$$STC_2 = C_2(Q_2) = .25Q_2^2 + 15 \quad \text{(Plant 2)}$$

   a) Set up the objective function. Determine the firm's profit-maximizing level of output, the selling price of the product, the level of profits, and the output produced in each of the two plants.
   b) Find the value of the marginal cost at the profit-maximizing output for each plant and compare with the value of the marginal revenue at the profit-maximizing level of output. Check the second-order conditions.

3. Given the market demand and market supply schedules for a perfectly competitive industry:

$$Q^d = 10 - 2P \quad \text{and} \quad Q^s = -2 + 2P^{.5}$$

   a) Find the market equilibrium price and quantity transacted.
   b) Find the values of consumers' surplus and producers' surplus associated with the perfectly competitive market equilibrium.
   c) Find the price elasticity of demand at this equilibrium.

   Now suppose that one firm purchases all of the other firms. The industry becomes a monopoly, with no changes in the cost curves for the individual firms, so that the market supply can be regarded as the monopolist's marginal cost function.
   d) Determine the profit-maximizing output and price for the monopolist.

e) Find the new values of consumers' surplus and producers' surplus with the monopoly.

f) Calculate the sum of the deadweight losses in consumers' surplus and producers' surplus due to the monopolization of this perfectly competitive industry.

g) Find the price elasticity of demand at the monopolist's equilibrium.

4. Given the marginal cost function of a monopolistic firm, $MC = MC(Q) = 3Q^2 - 17Q + 27$, where Q is the firm's level of output and the firm's fixed cost is equal to 4:

a) Derive the firm's short-run total cost function.

b) Given the marginal revenue function of the monopolist, $MR = MR(Q) = 35 - 7Q$, find the price at which total revenues are maximized.

c) Find the profit-maximizing level of output and price for the monopolist. Determine the level of profits. Could this situation persist in the long run? Discuss.

d) Check the second-order conditions.

5. A monopolist sells a product to both residential (r) and commercial (c) consumers. The demand schedules in these two distinct submarkets are

$$Q_r^d = 23 - (1/6)P_r \qquad \text{(residential)}$$

$$Q_c^d = 55 - (1/2)P_c \qquad \text{(commercial)}$$

The short-run total cost function of the monopolist is: $STC = C(Q) = 18Q + 750$, where $Q = Q_r + Q_c$. Q_r and Q_c are the quantities sold in the submarkets and Q is the total output of the monopolist. If the monopolist practices price discrimination:

a) Determine the profit-maximizing output and price charged by the monopolist in each submarket. Find the level of total profits.

b) Determine the price elasticity of demand in each submarket at the profit-maximizing level of output.

c) Check the second-order conditions.

d) Find the profit-maximizing output, price charged, and profits if the monopolist does not practice price discrimination.

6. Given a monopolist who has identified two submarkets or groups of buyers for its product:

$$\text{Group 1: } Q_1^d = 30 - 4P_1$$

$$\text{Group 2: } Q_2^d = 26 - 3P_2$$

The monopolist's short-run total cost function is: $STC = C(Q) = .0013Q^3 + 2Q + 50$, where $Q = Q_1 + Q_2$, with Q_1 and Q_2 as the quantities in the two submarkets (in thousands of units per day). P_1 and P_2 are the unit prices in the submarkets (in dollars).

a) Determine the profit-maximizing output, price, and profits if the monopolist does not practice price discrimination. Check the second order condition.

b) Determine the profit-maximizing outputs and prices in the two submarkets if the monopolist practices price discrimination. Calculate the total profits of the monopolist. Check the second-order conditions and calculate the price elasticity of demand at the profit-maximizing output in each submarket.

7. Given a firm that is a monopsonist in the local labor market. The firm's marginal revenue product of labor schedule is: $MRP_L = 20 - .02L$. The supply of labor schedule for the monopsonist is: $L^s = L = -600 + 200w$, where L is the quantity of labor (in workers) and w is the hourly wage.
   a) Determine the profit-maximizing level of employment and wage paid by the monopsonist. Calculate the transfer earnings and economic rent.
   b) Suppose a union successfully organizes the workers and turns the monopsonist into a wage-taker. The union demands a union wage of $7 per hour. Find the new level of employment under the union. Calculate the new transfer earnings and economic rent. Determine the excess supply of labor at the union wage.

8. Given a firm i, a monopsonist, facing a labor supply schedule: $L_i^s = -25 + 5w_i$,

   where L_i = quantity of labor for firm i (in thousands of workers)

   and w_i = wage rate per hour (in dollars).

   The firm's short-run production function is: $Q_i = -.02L_i^3 + .16L_i^2 + 8L_i$.

   The total fixed costs of the firm are $200 (thousand) per hour.

   The unit price of the firm's output is: $P_i = \$4.00$.

   a) Find the profit-maximizing employment and wage paid for the monopsonistic firm i. Calculate the firm's profits and the economic rent of labor.
   b) If a union organizes the workers and demands a union wage of $w_u = \$9.00$ per hour, find the new profit-maximizing level of employment for the firm. Calculate the firm's profits and the economic rent of labor under the union.

❖ **ANSWERS TO PRACTICE PROBLEMS**

8.1 a) $d^2z = (36x^2 + 4y^2)\, dx^2 + 16xy\, dx\, dy + (4x^2 - 24y)\, dy^2$
   b) $d^2z = [(a - 1)ax^{a-2} + (b - 1)bx^{b-2}\, y^b]\, dx^2 + 2b^2x^{b-1}y^{b-1}\, dxdy + [(b - 1)bx^by^{b-2}]\, dy^2$

8.2 a) The critical point is $(\bar{x}_0, \bar{y}_0, \bar{z}_0) = (0, -5, 25)$. Since $|H_1| = -2 < 0$ and $|H_2| = 3 > 0$, the critical point is a relative maximum.
   b) The critical point is $(\bar{x}_0, \bar{y}_0, \bar{z}_0) = (-20/3, 25/3, -525/9)$. Since $|H_1| = 2 > 0$ and $|H_2| = 3 > 0$, the critical point is a relative minimum.
   c) The critical point is $(\bar{x}_0, \bar{y}_0, \bar{z}_0) = (0, -5, 25)$. $|H_1| = 2 > 0$, but $|H_2| = -5 < 0$, so the critical point is a saddle point.

8.3 a) $|J| = -5 \neq 0$, so the two equations are functionally independent.

b) $|J| = -4x_1x_2x_3 - 6x_1x_2^4 - 2$. If $|J| \neq 0$, the three equations are functionally independent.

8.4 a) The profit-maximizing output is $\overline{Q} = 6.73$ (hundred units per day). The price charged is $\overline{P} = \$3.65$. The profits are $\Pi = \$.79$ (hundred per day). The outputs produced in the two plants are: $\overline{Q}_1 = 2.88$ and $\overline{Q}_2 = 3.85$ (hundred units per day).

b) $MC_1(\overline{Q}_1) = MC_2(\overline{Q}_2) = MR(\overline{Q}) = 2.31$.

8.5 a) The market equilibrium price and quantity transacted are: $\overline{P}_c = \$3.65$ and $\overline{Q}_c = 20.8$ (thousand units per day). Consumers' surplus equals: $CS_c = \$27.04$ (thousand per day) and $PS_c = \$29.69$ (thousand per day).

b) The quantity sold and price charged by the monopolist are $\overline{Q}_m = 15.0$ (thousand units per day) and $\overline{P}_m = \$4.38$. Consumers' surplus equals: $CS_m = \$13.99$ (thousand per day). Producers' surplus equals: $PS_m = \$37.56$ (thousand per day).

c) The sum of the deadweight losses in consumers' surplus and producers' surplus equals $\$5.18$ (thousand per day).

8.6 a) The profit-maximizing outputs (in thousand units per day) and prices in the two submarkets are: $\overline{Q}_1 = 15.45$ and $\overline{Q}_2 = 20.91$; $\overline{P}_1 = \$4.91$ and $\overline{P}_2 = \$3.91$. Total profits are: $\Pi = \$4.57$ (thousand per day). The second-order conditions for a maximum are satisfied: $|H_1| = -.45 < 0$ and $|H_2| = |H| = .11 > 0$. The price elasticities of demand equal: $(\epsilon_P^d)_1 = -1.59$ and $(\epsilon_P^d)_2 = -1.87$.

b) If the monopolist does not practice price discrimination, then the profit-maximizing output and price are: $\overline{Q} = 36.36$ (thousand per day) and $\overline{P} = \$4.24$. The profits of the monopolist are: $\Pi = \$1.12$ (thousand per day)

8.7 a) $(AFC_L)_i = 6 + .1L_i$; $(MFC_L)_i = 6 + .2L_i$.

b) The reservation wage is $\$6.00$ per hour.

8.8 a) The profit-maximizing employment and wage paid by the monopsonist are: $\overline{L}_i = 5.11$ (thousand workers) and $\overline{w}_i = \$11.28$ per hour. The economic rent of labor equals $\$3.28$ (thousand per hour).

b) With a union wage of $w_u = \$12.00$ per hour, the profit-maximizing employment for the monopsonist is $(\overline{L}_i)_u = 5.38$ (thousand workers). The new economic rent of labor equals $\$7.15$ (thousand per hour).

CHAPTER

9

DUOPOLIES AND OLIGOPOLIES

Between the theoretical extremes of perfect competition (many sellers of a homogeneous product) and monopoly (one seller) are forms of imperfect competition. In Chapter 7 we began with perfect competition, then we addressed monopolistic competition (many sellers of a slightly differentiated product). In Chapter 8 we discussed monopolies. In the present chapter, we study models of competition among a few firms, loosely defined as more than one firm but less than many firms. In particular, we begin with a simple model of duopoly (a market with two firms), then move to an examination of oligopoly (a market dominated by a small number of firms).

We will continue to assume that the primary motivation of a firm—regardless of market structure—is the maximization of profits. Recall that in perfect competition, firms do not actually compete against each other, since the price is set by the market, and nonprice competition, such as advertising, makes no sense for a homogeneous product. In a pure monopoly, by definition, there is no actual competition; although the threat of entry of potential rival firms or the possible loss of monopoly status (e.g., the expiration of a patent), may modify the short-run profit-maximizing behavior of the firm. In monopolistic competition, firms are price setters (like monopolists); however, freedom of entry and exit yields a long-run equilibrium of zero economic profits (like perfect competition). In each case (perfect competition, monopoly, and monopolistic competition), there is a standard theoretical model based on the behavior of a representative firm. Not so for duopoly and oligopoly, where firms are aware of their interdependence and act accordingly. Indeed, to model competition among the few, consistent behavioral assumptions or "rules of the game" have to be imposed. As we will see, these behavioral assumptions are often fairly simplistic, which limit the model's relevance.

Oligopolies are the most prevalent form of market structure in modern economies and efforts to understand better their behavior continue. The task is complex, since oligopolies may differ according to: whether the product is homogeneous or differentiated (e.g., steel vs. automobiles); the degree of government regulation (e.g., airlines versus breakfast cereals); the importance of technological change (e.g., personal computers vs. baseball gloves); and the extent of tacit collusion (which may not only vary across industries, but within any industry over time). To model the interdependence of firms, where the actions—both actual and anticipated—of any firm in the market affect the behavior of the other firms, economists have used game theory. We conclude this chapter with an introduction to basic game theory applied to oligopolistic firms. We begin, however, with a classic example of duopoly, the most basic type of oligopoly, to illustrate different assumptions about firm behavior.

DUOPOLY

In a **duopoly**, two firms constitute the market supply of the product. If they were to collude, the duopoly would become, in effect, a monopoly. A classic model of a duopoly is the Cournot "mineral springs" example. We will illustrate this model and discuss two variants, with a simple numerical example.[1]

Assume there are two mineral springs (or artesian wells) situated side by side. The mineral water, while reknowned for its purity and purported health benefits, is identical for the two springs. There are no marginal costs of supplying the mineral water. Buyers of the water bring their own gallon containers to fill themselves. (Perhaps a more familiar example would be two strawberry fields situated together where customers "pick their own.") The only costs to the owners, firms A and B, are the fixed costs of tapping the springs (or sinking the wells). Finally, assume that firm A is the first to open for business, and temporarily is a monopolist, before firm B enters the market.

The market demand schedule is given by

$$Q = 30 - 5P \quad \text{or} \quad P = 6 - (1/5)Q$$

where Q = quantity of mineral water demanded (in hundreds of gallons per day)

P = unit price of mineral water (dollars per gallon)

To model this market we need to impose some consistent rules of behavior on the firms.

COURNOT CASE

Cournot, the originator of this model, assumes that each firm regards its rival's output, once set, as fixed.[2] That is, firm B assumes that firm A will not change its output and firm A assumes that firm B's output will not change. With these rules of the game, we begin with firm A opening first.

---

[1]For the presentation of the Cournot, Edgeworth, and Chamberlin versions of the mineral springs example, from which our discussion is drawn, see "Theories of Price in Oligopoly Markets," pages 302–315 in C. E. Ferguson, *Microeconomic Theory*, Homewood, Illinois: Richard D. Irwin, 1969.

[2]Augustin Cournot (1801 to 1877) was a French mathematician and economist.

To maximize profits, firm A would select the output where marginal revenue equals marginal cost, and set its price from the demand schedule. As a temporary monopolist, the demand schedule facing firm A is the market demand. (Recall for a price-setting firm, the marginal revenue curve lies below the negatively-sloped demand curve.) To derive the marginal revenue schedule facing firm A, MR_A, we differentiate its total revenue schedule, TR_A. Letting Q_A and P_A denote the output and unit price for firm A, we have

$$TR_A = P_A \cdot Q_A = [6 - (1/5)Q_A]Q_A = 6Q_A - (1/5)Q_A^2$$

and

$$MR_A = dTR_A/dQ_A = 6 - (2/5)Q_A$$

Note that with the assumption of zero marginal costs, maximizing profits is equivalent to maximizing total revenues, which occurs when marginal revenue equals zero. Setting the marginal revenue equal to zero and solving for output, we find that firm A, as a monopolist, would maximize profits with an output of $(Q_A)_1 = 15$, and a price of $(P_A)_1 = \$3.00$. See point A_1 in Figure 9.1.

$$MR_A = 6 - (2/5)Q_A = 0 = MC$$

$$(2/5)Q_A = 6$$

$$(Q_A)_1 = 6/(2/5) = 15$$

FIGURE 9.1 DUOPOLY MINERAL SPRINGS EXAMPLE: COURNOT CASE

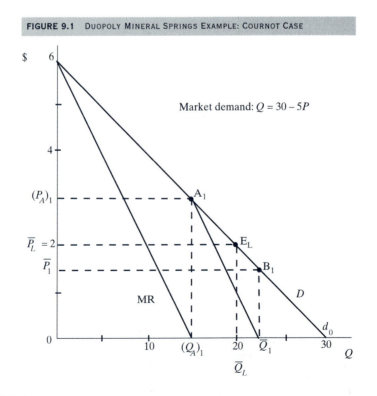

and

$$(P_A)_1 = 6 - (1/5)(Q_A)_1 = 6 - (1/5)15 = \$3.00$$

The total revenues for firm A initially (i.e., before firm B enters the market) are

$$(TR_A)_1 = (P_A)_1 \cdot (Q_A)_1 = (\$3.00)(15) = \$45.00$$

With the entrance of firm B, however, the monopoly of firm A disappears and the market becomes a duopoly. As a consequence, we will see that firm A will not be able to retain its initial output, price, or total revenues. Firm B, assuming that firm A will maintain an output of $(Q_A)_1 = 15$, regards the rest of the market demand (given by the lower portion of the demand curve, see $A_1 d_0$ in Figure 9.1) as available. The equation for this residual market demand is

$$Q_B = Q - (Q_A)_1 = 30 - 5P_B - 15 = 15 - 5P_B$$

or, in terms of the unit price charged by firm B,

$$P_B = 3 - (1/5)Q_B$$

Firm B's total revenue and marginal revenue schedules are:

$$TR_B = P_B \cdot Q_B = [3 - (1/5)Q_B]Q_B = 3Q_B - (1/5)Q_B^2$$

$$MR_B = dTR_B/dQ_B = 3 - (2/5)Q_B$$

Setting $MR_B = MC = 0$, firm B's profit-maximizing output, $(Q_B)_1$, and price, $(P_B)_1$, are

$$3 - (2/5)Q_B = 0$$

$$(Q_B)_1 = 3/(2/5) = 7.5$$

and

$$(P_B)_1 = 3 - (1/5)(Q_B)_1 = 3 - (1/5)(7.5) = \$1.50$$

The total quantity produced and sold in the market is now $Q_1 = (Q_A)_1 + (Q_B)_1 = 15 + 7.5 = 22.5$. The market equilibrium price is $\overline{P}_1 = 6 - (1/5)Q_1 = 6 - (1/5)(22.5) = \$1.50$. See point B_1 in Figure 9.1. That is, when firm B enters and charges a price of $(P_B)_1 = \$1.50$, given the identical mineral water sold, firm A can no longer charge a price of $(P_A)_1 = \$3.00$, but would have to lower its price to match firm B's price. Indeed, we would expect that the market sales of $Q_1 = 22.5$ would be split equally between firms A and B, since there is no reason for buyers to prefer the mineral water of one firm over the other and there are no cost differences between the two firms.[3]

---

[3]Note that the traditional representation of the Cournot model would have firm A maintain its initial output, here in period 1 equal to $(Q_A)_1 = 15$, after firm B enters the market. If so, the equilibrium for period 1 would be

$$(\overline{Q}_A)_1 = 15; (\overline{Q}_B)_1 = 7.5; \overline{Q}_1 = 22.5$$
$$(\overline{P}_A)_1 = \$1.50 = (\overline{P}_B)_1 = \overline{P}_1$$

and $(\overline{TR}_A)_1 = (\$1.50)(15) = \$22.50; (\overline{TR}_B)_1 = (\$1.50)(7.5) = \$11.25; \overline{TR}_1 = \$33.75$
Whether the market is split equally (the more intuitive case for a homogeneous good) or asymmetrically, the Cournot model converges to the same final long-run equilibrium. Another reason for the equal distribution of the homogeneous product would be to minimize any consumer opportunity cost of waiting in line for the water.

Consequently, firm A's output would drop, from $(Q_A)_1 = 15$ to $(\overline{Q}_A)_1 = (.5)(22.5) = 11.25$, while firm B's output would increase, from $(Q_B)_1 = 7.5$ to $(\overline{Q}_B)_1 = 11.25$. To summarize, the equilibrium for period 1 is

$$(\overline{Q}_A)_1 = 11.25 = (\overline{Q}_B)_1;\, \overline{Q}_1 = 22.5$$

$$(\overline{P}_A)_1 = \$1.50 = (\overline{P}_B)_1 = \overline{P}_1$$

$$(\overline{TR}_A)_1 = (\$1.50)(11.25) = \$16.875 = (\overline{TR}_B)_1;\, TR_1 = \$33.75$$

In period 2, we assume that firm A again makes the first move. Believing that firm B will maintain its output at $(\overline{Q}_B)_1 = 11.25$, firm A now regards its market as

$$Q_A = Q - (\overline{Q}_B)_1 = 30 - 5P_A - 11.25 = 18.75 - 5P_A$$

or, in terms of its unit price: $P_A = 3.75 - (1/5)Q_A$.
The associated marginal revenue schedule is: $MR_A = 3.75 - (2/5)Q_A$, and the profit-maximizing output and price for firm A are

$$MR_A = 3.75 - (2/5)Q_A = 0$$

$$(Q_A)_2 = 3.75/(2/5) = 9.375$$

$$(P_A)_2 = 3.75 - (1/5)(Q_A)_2 = 3.75 - (1/5)(9.375) = \$1.875.$$

As before, firm B reacts. Assuming that firm A would now maintain $(Q_A)_2 = 9.375$, firm B views its part of the market demand as: $Q_B = Q - (Q_A)_2 = 30 - 5P_B - 9.375 = 20.625 - 5P_B$, or, in terms of the price firm B charges, $P_B = 4.125 - (1/5)Q_B$.
With a marginal revenue schedule of: $MR_B = 4.125 - (2/5)Q_B$, firm B's profit-maximizing output and price are: $(Q_B)_2 = 10.313$ and $(P_B)_2 = \$2.062$.

$$MR_B = 4.125 - (2/5)Q_B = 0$$

$$(Q_B)_2 = 4.125/(2/5) = 10.313$$

and

$$(P_B)_2 = 4.125 - (1/5)(10.313) = \$2.062$$

That is, with the total market output in period 2 of $Q_2 = (Q_A)_2 + (Q_B)_2 = 9.375 + 10.313 = 19.688$, the market equilibrium price is $\overline{P}_2 = 6 - (1/5)Q_2 = 6 - (1/5)(19.688) = \$2.062$. With the homogeneous mineral water, the price charged by firm A actually rises from $(P_A)_2 = \$1.875$ to $(\overline{P}_A)_2 = \$2.062$, since firm B's output is below the level expected by firm A. Again, we would expect the market sales of $\overline{Q}_2 = 19.688$ to be evenly divided between the two firms. For period 2 the equilibrium values are

$$(\overline{Q}_A)_2 = 9.844 = (\overline{Q}_B)_2;\, \overline{Q}_2 = 19.688$$

$$(\overline{P}_A)_2 = \$2.062 = (\overline{P}_B)_2 = \overline{P}_2$$

$$(\overline{TR}_A)_2 = (\$2.062)(9.844) = \$20.298 = (\overline{TR}_B)_2;\, TR_2 = \$40.596$$

One more period should be sufficient to reveal the convergence of the model to a long-run equilibrium. In period 3, firm A, regarding firm B's output from period 2 as given, $(\overline{Q}_B)_2 = 9.844$, assumes it faces a demand of: $Q_A = Q - (\overline{Q}_B)_2 = 30 - 5P_A - 9.844 = 20.156 - 5P_A$, or in terms of its price, $P_A = 4.031 - (1/5)Q_A$.

Setting the associated marginal revenue equal to zero, the profit-maximizing output and price for firm A are

$$MR_A = 4.031 - (2/5)Q_A = 0$$

$$(Q_A)_3 = 4.031/(2/5) = 10.078$$

and

$$(P_A)_3 = 4.031 - (1/5)(Q_A)_3 = 4.031 - (1/5)(10.078) = \$2.015$$

Firm B, reacting, now assumes its demand is: $Q_B = Q - (Q_A)_3 = 30 - 5P_B - 10.078 = 19.922 - 5P_B$, or in terms of its price, $P_B = 3.984 - (1/5)Q_B$. With a marginal revenue schedule of $MR_B = 3.984 - (2/5)Q_B$; firm B's profit-maximizing output and price are $(Q_B)_3 = 9.960$ and $(P_B)_3 = \$1.992$. With a total market quantity of $Q_3 = (Q_A)_3 + (Q_B)_3 = 10.078 + 9.960 = 20.038$, the market equilibrium price is $\overline{P}_3 = \$1.992$. Assuming the market sales are evenly shared by the two identical firms, the equilibrium for period 3 is

$$(\overline{Q}_A)_3 = 10.019 = (\overline{Q}_B)_3; \overline{Q}_3 = 20.038$$

$$(\overline{P}_A)_3 = \$1.992 = (\overline{P}_B)_3 = \overline{P}_3$$

$$(\overline{TR}_A)_3 = (\$1.992)(10.019) = \$19.958 = (\overline{TR}_B)_3; \overline{TR}_3 = \$39.916$$

The convergence to a long-run equilibrium should be evident. We summarize with Table 9.1 below for a market demand of: $Q = d_0 - d_1 P = 30 - 5P$, or, alternatively, $P = (d_0/d_1) - (1/d_1)Q = (30/5) - (1/5)Q = 6 - (1/5)Q$, where each firm assumes that the other will not alter its output, once set.

In sum, we can see that under the Cournot assumption of each firm expecting its rival to maintain its output, once set, this duopoly model is stable. The market price

TABLE 9.1   Cournot Duopoly Model: Market Demand of $Q = 30 - 5P$ and Zero Marginal Costs

	Period 1	Period 2	Period 3	...	Period n (limit as n → ∞)
Quantity					
Market	22.5	19.688	20.038	...	$20 = (2/3)d_0$
Firm A	11.25	9.844	10.019	...	$10 = (1/3)d_0$
Firm B	11.25	9.844	10.019	...	$10 = (1/3)d_0$
Price					
Market	$1.50	$2.062	$1.992	...	$\$2.00 = (d_0/d_1) - (1/d_1)(2/3)d_0$ $= (1/3)(d_0/d_1)$

and quantity transacted do converge to long-run equilibrium values of $2.00 and 20 units of output. In Figure 9.1, the long-run equilibrium is indicated by point E_L. Note that the equilibrium prices and quantities converge in an oscillatory manner. One obvious limitation of the Cournot duopoly model, however, is that the firms do not learn from experience—retaining the assumption of a constant rival output despite contrary evidence in every period.

EDGEWORTH CASE

We begin with the same scenario as the Cournot case: two identical mineral springs with a market demand of $Q = 30 - 5P$; zero marginal costs; and firm A, the first to open for business, temporarily acts as a monopolist until firm B enters, at which point the market becomes a duopoly. Instead of assuming that each firm regards its rival's output as fixed, we will illustrate what is known as the Edgeworth case.[4] Here, each firm assumes that its rival's price is fixed. That is, firm B assumes that firm A will not change its price, once set; and firm A assumes that firm B's price, once set, will not change. We will see that with a homogeneous good, the Edgeworth behavioral assumption appears to result in an unstable or indeterminable model.

To illustrate with a specific price change, we will assume that whenever a firm changes its price, believing its rival will not respond, the price change is $.50.[5] We begin with firm A opening and facing a market demand of $Q = 30 - 5P$ [or $P = 6 - (1/5)Q$]. As before, given a marginal cost of zero, firm A's profit-maximizing output and price are: $(Q_A)_1 = 15$ and $(P_A)_1 = \$3.00$, yielding total revenues of $(TR_A)_1 = \$45.00$. See point A_1 in Figure 9.2. Now firm B enters, and assuming firm A will not change its price of $3.00, believes it could capture all the sales by charging a lower price, for example, $(P_B)_1 = \$2.50$. In fact, if firm A does not respond in kind, firm B would sell $Q_B = 30 - 5(2.50) = 17.5$, and firm A's sales would fall to zero. Firm A, however, is likely to match the lower price set by firm B in this period, so the total market sales of 17.5 would be split evenly between the two. Summarizing the market equilibrium for period 1, we have

$$(\overline{Q}_A)_1 = 8.75 = (\overline{Q}_B)_1; \overline{Q}_1 = 17.5$$

$$(\overline{P}_A)_1 = \$2.50 = (\overline{P}_B)_1 = \overline{P}_1$$

$$(\overline{TR}_A)_1 = (\$2.50)(8.75) = \$21.875 = (\overline{TR}_B)_1; \overline{TR}_1 = \$43.75$$

See point B_1 in Figure 9.2.

In period 2, firm A, believing that firm B will hold its price of $(P_B)_1 = \$2.50$, drops its price to $(P_A)_2 = \$2.00$, hoping to gain the entire market, now $(Q_A)_2 = 30 - 5(2) =$

---

[4]Francis Edgeworth (1845 to 1926), an Irish economist, is known for his work in utility theory, as well as in the theory of market behavior. This behavioral assumption of the rival firm holding price constant is also associated with Joseph Bertrand, a French mathematician (1822 to 1900).

[5]This specific price change is, of course, arbitrary. Given a homogeneous good (and no supply limitations), any perceptively lower price would capture all the market sales. The price change of $.50, however, serves to expedite the illustration.

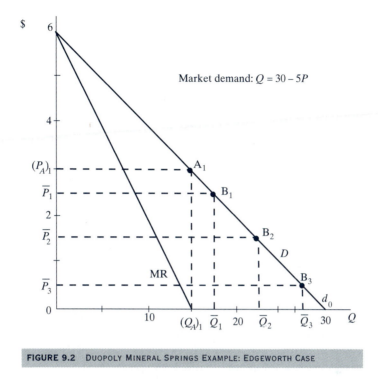

FIGURE 9.2 DUOPOLY MINERAL SPRINGS EXAMPLE: EDGEWORTH CASE

20. Firm B, however, seeing firm A's new price of $2.00, and regarding this as fixed, lowers its price to $(P_B)_2 = \$1.50$, which firm A is forced to match to retain any sales. As a result, the market equilibrium price in period 2 is $\overline{P}_2 = \$1.50$. The market quantity sold is: $\overline{Q}_2 = 30 - 5P_2 = 30 - 5(1.50) = 22.50$, which is assumed to be divided equally between the two firms. Under these rules of the game, where firm A lowers its price, intending to capture all of the market sales; firm B, with the same intention, counters with an even lower price; and then firm A matches firm B's price to complete the transition to a short-run equilibrium; we have for period 2:

$$(\overline{Q}_A)_2 = 11.25 = (\overline{Q}_B)_2; \overline{Q}_2 = 22.50$$

$$(\overline{P}_A)_2 = \$1.50 = (\overline{P}_B)_2 = \overline{P}_2$$

$$(\overline{TR}_A)_2 = (\$1.50)(11.25) = \$16.875 = (\overline{TR}_B)_2; \overline{TR}_2 = \$33.75$$

See point B_2 for the market equilibrium in period 2.

One more period should confirm the unsustainable nature of this Edgeworth model. In period 3, firm A, regarding firm B's price, $(\overline{P}_B)_2 = \overline{P}_2 = \$1.50$, as fixed, lowers its price to $(P_A)_3 = \$1.00$, expecting to sell $(Q_A)_3 = 30 - 5(1.00) = 25$. Firm B, now expecting firm A to maintain $(P_A)_3 = \$1.00$, drops its price to $(P_B)_3 = \$.50$, which, *ceteris paribus*, would yield sales of $(Q_B)_3 = 30 - 5(.50) = 27.50$. Yet, firm A would be compelled to match firm B's lower price, so the market sales of $\overline{Q}_3 = 27.50$ would be shared. The point B_3 in Figure 9.2 illustrates the market equilibrium for period 3.

$$(\overline{Q}_A)_3 = 13.75 = (\overline{Q}_B)_3; \overline{Q}_3 = 27.50$$

$$(\overline{P}_A)_3 = \$.50 = (\overline{P}_B)_3 = \overline{P}_3$$

$$(\overline{TR}_A)_3 = (\$.50)(13.75) = \$6.875 = (\overline{TR}_B)_3; \overline{TR}_3 = \$13.75$$

Clearly both firms are hurt by this rigid price war. As the market price is driven down along the inelastic region (lower-half) of the market demand curve, total revenues (and profits) fall. Using the arbitrary price changes of $.50 and assuming the same behavior, the next period would have firm A dropping its price to $0, at which point the two firms may as well shut down, since none of their fixed costs would be covered. In sum, the Edgeworth assumption that each firm regards its rival's price as fixed, and thus perceives an opportunity to capture the entire market by undercutting its rival's price, results in an unstable model. That is, the model does not converge to a sustainable long-run equilibrium. In practice, price wars do break out on occasion in oligopolistic markets. As illustrated here, such aggressive price competition can be very costly to the involved firms.

Both the Edgeworth case (fixed price assumption) and Cournot case (fixed output assumption) are limited by the inflexible rules of the game that are imposed. That is, in spite of experience to the contrary, neither firm deviates from the initial behavioral assumptions about its rival. Below we present a scenario where firms recognize their interdependence and adopt a mutually beneficial strategy.

CHAMBERLIN CASE

Suppose that, under the Edgeworth case, the two firms did get to the point where the unit price of mineral water reached zero. That is, in period 4, firm A dropped its price to zero. Firm B, now unable to lower its price below firm A's, might instead decide to hold its price at $.50, hoping that firm A would prefer some revenues to none and reverse its price cut. If so, then period 4 would represent a transition to a new regime of cooperation. Both firms would charge the market equilibrium price of $.50 from period 3, with each selling an output of 13.75 and earning total revenues of $6.875.

In period 5 then, firm A might raise its price to $(P_A)_5 = \$1.00$. If matched by firm B, the market output of 20 would be shared and each firm would find its total revenues rising to $10. Such tacit collusion, indicating a change in the rules of the game, might continue with firm A's price hikes matched by firm B, so that neither firm loses market share. Indeed, total revenues (and profits) would continue to rise with the increases in price as long as the demand for mineral water were price inelastic. Once the market price reached $3.00, corresponding to a market output of 15 (see point A_1 in Figure 9.2), further price increases would reduce total revenues (and profits) and would not be sustained. With tacit collusion then, the long-run equilibrium under this price leadership scenario would be a market price of $3.00, with each firm earning total revenues of $22.50, based on outputs of 7.5. Note that this long-run equilibrium corresponds to the profit-maximizing price and output for a monopolist. In effect, by cooperating the two firms are acting as a monopolist and maximizing their joint profits.

Chamberlin reached the same outcome, but much more expediently.[6] Return to the initial Cournot scenario, where firm A is the first to enter the market and acting as a monopolist sets a price of $(P_A)_1 = \$3.00$ and output of $(Q_A)_1 = 15$. Firm B, regarding the remainder of the market as available, $Q_B = Q - (Q_A)_1 = 30 - 5P_B - 15 = 15 - 5P_B$, sets a price of $(P_B)_1 = \$1.50$, intending to sell $(Q_B)_1 = 7.5$ units; although, as we have noted, with the homogeneous mineral water, the market sales of 22.5 would likely be evenly shared. Chamberlin suggested that firm A, at this point, would recognize its interdependence with firm B and reduce its output to $(Q_A)_1 = 7.5$. Firm B, seeing the cutback in output by Firm A, would also recognize the mutually beneficial consequences of holding its output at $(Q_B)_1 = 7.5$. As a result, the two firms share equally the monopoly profits, attaining a long-run equilibrium in period 1 with

$$(\overline{Q}_A)_1 = 7.5 = (\overline{Q}_B); \overline{Q}_1 = 15$$

$$(\overline{P}_A)_1 = \$3.00 = (\overline{P}_B)_1 = \overline{P}_1$$

$$(\overline{TR}_A)_1 = (\$3.00)(7.5) = \$22.50 = (\overline{TR}_B)_1; \overline{TR}_1 = \$45.00$$

Thus, in Chamberlin's case, the duopolists are not bound by any set rules of the game and can adapt to the situation to maximize their joint and individual profits. Open or explicit collusion to share a market or fix prices is illegal in market economies. Tacit or implicit collusion is more difficult to regulate—and also more difficult to sustain, especially as the number of firms in the market increase and as the product becomes more differentiated.

PRACTICE PROBLEM 9.1

Consider two mineral springs, located side by side, and assume that the only costs of production are the fixed costs of sinking the wells. That is, the marginal costs of supplying the mineral water are zero.

Assume the market demand for the mineral water is given by: $Q = 40 - 4P$, where

Q = quantity of mineral water demanded (in hundreds of gallons per day)

P = unit price of mineral water (dollars per gallon)

Suppose that firm A is the first to sink a well and temporarily operates as a monopolist. When firm B enters, the equilibrium market output sold in each period is divided equally between the two firms, since the mineral water is identical.

a) Using the Cournot assumption that each firm regard's the other's output as fixed, find the equilibrium output, price, and total revenue for each firm for the first two periods.

b) Using the Edgeworth assumption that each firm regards the other's price as fixed, find the equilibrium output, price, and total revenue for each firm for the first two periods.

---

[6]Edward Chamberlin (1899 to 1967), an American economist, is best known for developing the theory of monopolistic competition, along with the British economist, Joan Robinson (1903 to 1983).

Assume that when either firm drops its price to capture the market demand, the decrease in price is $1.00.

c) Using the Chamberlin assumption where the firms recognize their interdependence and cooperate, find the equilibrium output, price, and total revenue for each firm.

(The answers are at the end of the chapter.)

THE DUOPOLY MINERAL SPRINGS EXAMPLE REVISITED: GENERAL CASES

We present the three models of the duopoly mineral springs example in general form. We retain the linear specification for the market demand: $Q = d_0 - d_1 P$, or $P = d_0/d_1 - (1/d_1)Q$, which is shared by the two firms, A and B, supplying identical mineral water. We now allow for positive, but constant, marginal cost equal to c, which is assumed to be the same for each firm, that is, $c = c_A = c_B$, as is the fixed cost, C_0. The total cost functions for firms A and B are, respectively: $C_A = C_0 + cQ_A$ and $C_B = C_0 + cQ_B$. The opening scenario is the same as before: firm A initially begins as a monopolist, then firm B enters. The final market output produced, Q, is assumed to be equally shared by the two firms, given the homogeneous good and each firm charging the same price, P.

Cournot Case   Recall that the Cournot assumption is that each firm regards its rival's output as fixed. Accordingly, we assume that: $dQ_A/dQ_B = 0 = dQ_B/dQ_A$. The profit functions for the duopolists are

$$\Pi_A (Q_A, Q_B) = P \cdot Q_A - C_A = [(d_0/d_1) - (1/d_1)Q]Q_A - C_0 - cQ_A$$

$$\Pi_A = (d_0/d_1)Q_A - (1/d_1)Q_A^2 - (1/d_1)Q_A Q_B - C_0 - cQ_A$$

and

$$\Pi_B(Q_A, Q_B) = P \cdot Q_B - C_B = [(d_0/d_1) - (1/d_1)Q]Q_B - C_0 - cQ_B$$

$$\Pi_B = (d_0/d_1)Q_B - (1/d_1)Q_B^2 - (1/d_1)Q_A Q_B - C_0 - cQ_B$$

To find the profit-maximizing output for each firm, assuming the rival's output remains unchanged, we differentiate the profit functions with respect to the firms' outputs, set the results equal to zero, and solve the simultaneous system of equations.

$$d\Pi_A/dQ_A = d_0/d_1 - (2/d_1)Q_A - (1/d_1)Q_B - c = 0$$

$$d\Pi_B/dQ_B = d_0/d_1 - (2/d_1)Q_B - (1/d_1)Q_A - c = 0$$

From these first-order conditions, we have

$$Q_A = \frac{d_0 - Q_B - cd_1}{2} \quad \text{and} \quad Q_B = \frac{d_0 - Q_A - cd_1}{2}$$

Solving simultaneously, we find the equilibrium quantities:

$$\overline{Q}_A = \frac{d_0 - cd_1}{3} \quad \text{and} \quad \overline{Q}_B = \frac{d_0 - cd_1}{3}; \qquad \overline{Q} = \frac{2(d_0 - cd_1)}{3}$$

Substituting $\overline{Q}$ into the market demand schedule, we have the market equilibrium price, $\overline{P}$.

$$\overline{P} = d_0/d_1 - (1/d_1)\overline{Q} = d_0/d_1 - (1/d_1)[(2/3)(d_0 - cd_1)]$$

$$\overline{P} = \frac{d_0 + 2cd_1}{3d_1} = \overline{P}_A = \overline{P}_B$$

Recall that in our numerical example where $d_0 = 30$, $d_1 = 5$, and $c = 0$, we found that the market quantities and price converged in long-run equilibrium to

$$\overline{Q}_A = \frac{d_0 - cd_1}{3} = \frac{30 - (0)(5)}{3} = 10 = \overline{Q}_B; \text{ and } \overline{Q} = \frac{2(d_0 - cd_1)}{3} = \frac{2[30 - (0)(5)]}{3} = 20$$

$$\overline{P} = \frac{d_0 + 2cd_1}{3d_1} = \frac{30 + 2(0)(5)}{(3)(5)} = \$2 = d_0/d_1 - (1/d_1)\overline{Q} = 30/5 - (1/5)(20) = \overline{P}_A = \overline{P}_B$$

If instead we had a positive and constant marginal cost equal to 1, that is, $c = c_A = c_B = 1$, then the long-run equilibrium values would be

$$\overline{Q}'_A = \frac{30 - (1)(5)}{3} = 8.3\overline{3} = \overline{Q}'_B; \qquad \overline{Q}' = \frac{2[30 - (1)(5)]}{3} = 16.6\overline{6}$$

$$\overline{P}' = \frac{30 + 2(1)(5)}{(3)(5)} = \$2.6\overline{6} = 30/5 - (1/5)(16.6\overline{6}) = \overline{P}'_A = \overline{P}'_B$$

Note the first-order conditions:

$$Q_A = \frac{d_0 - Q_B - cd_1}{2} = \frac{d_0 - cd_1}{2} - \frac{Q_B}{2}$$

$$Q_B = \frac{d_0 - Q_A - cd_1}{2} = \frac{d_0 - cd_1}{2} - \frac{Q_A}{2}$$

represent the firms' **reaction functions**, indicating that each firm's output depends on the other's output. We can plot these reaction functions and solve graphically for the equilibrium to this Cournot duopoly model. See Figure 9.3 and point E, the intersection of the reaction functions.

Indeed, we need not go through the sequential rounds of output adjustments to reach this equilibrium. Based on the behavioral assumption that each firm, while considering its rival's output, will not alter its own output once set, that is, $dQ_A/dQ_B = dQ_B/dQ_A = 0$, then the individual firms' pursuit of profit maximization, as shown above, will yield this outcome.

As a final observation on the Cournot model, if we drop the assumption of constant and equal marginal costs ($c = c_A = c_B$), for one of constant, but unequal, marginal costs, $c_A \neq c_B$, then we can show that the profit-maximizing outputs of the two firms are:

$$\overline{Q}_A = \frac{d_0 + (c_B - 2c_A)d_1}{3} \quad \text{and} \quad \overline{Q}_B = \frac{d_0 + (c_A - 2c_B)d_1}{3}$$

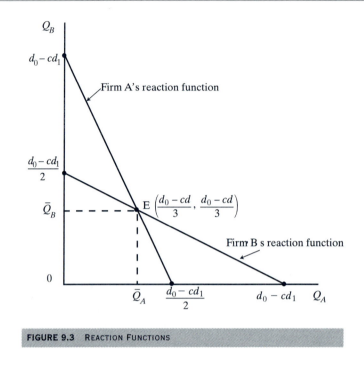

FIGURE 9.3 REACTION FUNCTIONS

Thus, if firm A had a lower constant marginal cost, $c_A < c_B$, it would have a higher profit-maximizing output, $\overline{Q}_A > \overline{Q}_B$; and greater revenues, $TR_A > TR_B$; and greater profits, $\Pi_A > \Pi_B$ (assuming identical fixed costs). Here, despite the homogeneous product which dictates a single market price for the outputs of the two firms, we do not find the total market sales evenly split, since firm A has an absolute cost advantage.[7]

PRACTICE PROBLEM 9.2

Using the example from Practice Problem 9.1 and the Cournot behavioral assumption, suppose that the constant marginal costs of production for the two firms are identical and equal to $2: $c_A = 2.00 = c_B$.

a) Derive the reaction functions of the two firms and then determine the equilibrium outputs for the two firms and the market price.

b) Suppose instead that the constant marginal costs differ: $c_A = \$2.50$ and $c_B = \$1.50$. Derive the new reaction functions of the two firms and then determine the equilibrium outputs for the two firms and the market price.

(The answers are at the end of the chapter.)

Edgeworth Case The Edgeworth assumption is that each firm regards its rival's price as fixed. Accordingly, we assume that $dP_A/dP_B = dP_B/dP_A = 0$. This behavioral assumption leads each firm to drop its price below its rival's price, with the intent of

---

[7]For a duopoly to exist, $Q_B > 0$, which implies that $d_0 > (c_A - 2c_B)d_1$. Otherwise, firm B would have no sales. That is, unless the market price, $\overline{P}$, exceeds firm B's average variable cost (here equal to its constant marginal cost, c_B), then firm A, with the lower constant marginal cost, would become a monopolist.

gaining all the market sales. In effect, each firm regards the entire market demand as its own. The demand functions expected by the two firms are

$$Q_A = d_0 - d_1 P_A \quad \text{or} \quad P_A = d_0/d_1 - (1/d_1)Q_A$$

and

$$Q_B = d_0 - d_1 P_B \quad \text{or} \quad P_B = d_0/d_1 - (1/d_1)Q_B$$

As we have illustrated above, the result is a price war, with the market price driven down to the marginal cost of production (equal to zero in the initial numerical example). Here, in this general model, we assume a constant and identical marginal cost, that is, $c = c_A = c_B$.

We write the profit functions for the firms in terms of the prices charged.

$$\Pi_A (P_A) = P_A \cdot Q_A - C_A = (d_0 - d_1 P_A) P_A - C_0 - c(d_0 - d_1 P_A)$$

$$= d_0 P_A - d_1 P_A^2 - C_0 - cd_0 + cd_1 P_A$$

$$\Pi_B (P_B) = P_B \cdot Q_B - C_B = (d_0 - d_1 P_B)P_B - C_0 - c(d_0 - d_1 P_B)$$

$$= d_0 P_B - d_1 P_B^2 - C_0 - cd_0 + cd_1 P_B$$

To find the firms' profit-maximizing prices, where each assumes that the other's price will not change, we differentiate the profit functions with respect to the firms' prices, set the results equal to zero, and solve.

$$d\Pi_A/dP_A = d_0 - 2d_1 P_A + cd_1 = 0$$

$$d\Pi_B/dP_B = d_0 - 2d_1 P_B + cd_1 = 0$$

We can see the assumed independence of the firms. Each believes that it can change its price without any response from the other. From these first-order conditions, we find:

$$\overline{P}_A = \frac{d_0 + cd_1}{2d_1} \quad \text{and} \quad \overline{P}_B = \frac{d_0 + cd_1}{2d_1}$$

The associated quantities are found by substituting $\overline{P}_A$ and $\overline{P}_B$ into the demand equations.

$$\overline{Q}_A = d_0 - d_1\overline{P}_A = d_0 - d_1\left(\frac{d_0 + cd_1}{2d_1}\right) = \frac{d_0 - cd_1}{2}$$

$$\overline{Q}_B = d_0 - d_1\overline{P}_B = d_0 - d_1\left(\frac{d_0 + cd_1}{2d_1}\right) = \frac{d_0 - cd_1}{2}$$

The identical profit-maximizing prices and outputs for the two firms should not be surprising, given that each firm assumes it can unilaterally lower its price and "monopolize" the market. In fact, as we will see, each firm's supposed profit-maximizing price and output correspond to those of a monopolist. If the firms A and B, however, attempt to sell $\overline{Q}_A$ and $\overline{Q}_B$, the market quantity would be $\overline{Q} = \overline{Q}_A + \overline{Q}_B = d_0 - cd_1$, yielding a market equilibrium price of $\overline{P} = (d_0/d_1) - (1/d_1)Q = c$. That is, the market equilibrium price would be driven down to equal the marginal cost, c.

Recall that price equaling marginal cost characterizes the long-run equilibrium in a perfectly competitive market—as do zero economic profits. Here, with the assumption of constant and equal marginal costs, which are also the constant and equal average variable costs, neither firm would cover any of its fixed costs when the market equilibrium price is driven down to the marginal cost. We might expect though, as discussed in the earlier numerical example of the Edgeworth case, that the two firms would eventually realize the naivety of assuming that each other would not respond to a price cut, and begin to cooperate by jointly raising prices until the monopolist's profit-maximizing price was reached. At this point, the market might stabilize with the two firms sharing monopoly profits.

We illustrate the Edgeworth case where, before any cooperation, each firm attempts to produce a monopolist's profit-maximizing output.

$$\overline{Q}_A = \frac{d_0 - cd_1}{2} = \overline{Q}_B$$

In the initial numerical example, the parameters are: $d_0 = 30$, $d_1 = 5$, and $c = 0$. Therefore

$$\overline{Q}_A = \frac{30 - (0)(5)}{2} = 15 = \overline{Q}_B$$

But, $\overline{Q} = \overline{Q}_A + \overline{Q}_B = 15 + 15 = 30$, and the market equilibrium price is

$$\overline{P} = d_0/d_1 - (1/d_1)\overline{Q}) = 30/5 - (1/5)(30) = \$0 = c$$

If instead, the marginal cost equalled 1, that is, $c = 1$, then

$$\overline{Q}'_A = \frac{30 - (1)(5)}{2} = 12.5 = \overline{Q}'_B$$

So, $\overline{Q}' = \overline{Q}'_A + \overline{Q}'_B = 25$, and $\overline{P}' = 30/5 - (1/5)(25) = \$1 = c$.

Note that if firm A had a lower (constant) marginal cost than firm B, $c_A < c_B$, then its profit-maximizing price would be less than firm B's:

$$\overline{P}_A = \frac{d_0 + c_A d_1}{2d_1} < \frac{d_0 + c_B d_1}{2d_1} = \overline{P}_B.$$

The corresponding outputs would be

$$\overline{Q}_A = \frac{d_0 - c_A d_1}{2} > \frac{d_0 - c_B d_1}{2} = \overline{Q}_B.$$

If firm A did charge a lower price than firm B, then firm A could capture the entire market demand.

To illustrate, we use the market demand, $Q = 30 - 5P$, with parameters $d_0 = 30$ and $d_1 = 5$, and assume the following marginal costs for firms A and B: $c_A = .75$ and

$c_B = 1.5$. Firms A and B, assuming the other will not alter its price, set the profit-maximizing prices:

$$\overline{P}_A = \frac{d_0 + c_A d_1}{2d_1} = \frac{30 + .75(5)}{2(5)} = \$3.375$$

$$\overline{P}_B = \frac{d_0 + c_B d_1}{2d_1} = \frac{30 + 1.5(5)}{2(5)} = \$3.75$$

The associated outputs are

$$\overline{Q}_A = \frac{d_0 - c_A d_1}{2} = \frac{30 - .75(5)}{2} = 13.125$$

$$\overline{Q}_B = \frac{d_0 - c_B d_1}{2} = \frac{30 - 1.5(5)}{2} = 11.25$$

The total market output of $\overline{Q} = \overline{Q}_A + \overline{Q}_B = 13.125 + 11.25 = 24.375$, however, would reduce the market-clearing price to $\overline{P} = 6 - (1/5)\overline{Q} = 6 - (1/5)(24.375) = \$1.125$. This price is lower than the marginal cost (and average variable cost) of firm B. So, firm B may exit, leaving firm A as a monopolist, with $\overline{Q}_A = 13.125$ and $\overline{P}_A = \$3.375$. Firm A could force the exit of firm B by lowering its price to $P_A = \$.75$, which would cover its marginal and average variable costs, but could not be matched by firm B, since firm B has to charge a price at least equal to $P_B = \$1.5 = c_B$.

PRACTICE PROBLEM 9.3

Using the example from Practice Problem 9.1, where the market demand is $Q = 40 - 4P$, suppose that the constant marginal costs of production for the two firms are identical: $c = \$2.00 = c_A = c_B$.

a) Determine the profit-maximizing prices set by firms A and B and the associated outputs under the Edgeworth behavioral assumption. What would be the market equilibrium price given the total output in the market?

b) If instead the constant marginal costs differed between the two firms with $c_A = \$2.50$ and $c_B = \$1.50$, determine the profit-maximizing prices set by firms A and B and the associated outputs under the Edgeworth behavioral assumption. What would be the market equilibrium price given the total output in the market? Would one firm emerge as a monopolist? Why?

(The answers are at the end of the chapter.)

Chamberlin Case The Chamberlin case begins like the Cournot case. Firm A opens, initially as a monopolist. Firm B enters, assumes firm A will not alter its output, and regards the remainder of the market demand as available. Firm B's additional output, however, would drive down the market price. Firm A, recognizing its mutual dependence with firm B, then reduces its output by enough to restore the monopolist's profit-maximizing level of output. Firm B, also recognizing the benefit of cooperating, maintains its output. Both firms share the market, acting like a monopolist and maximizing their combined and individual profits.

As a monopolist, the profit function to be maximized is

$$\Pi(Q) = PQ - C$$

where:

$$Q = Q_A + Q_B \quad (\text{with } Q_A = Q_B)$$

and

$$C = C_A + C_B = 2C_0 + cQ_A + cQ_B = 2C_0 + cQ$$

Expanding the joint-profit function, we have:

$$\Pi(Q) = [d_0/d_1 - (1/d_1)Q]Q - 2C_0 - cQ$$

Differentiating to find the profit-maximizing level of output gives

$$d\Pi/dQ = d_0/d_1 - (2/d_1)Q - c = 0$$

Solving for $\overline{Q}$,

$$\overline{Q} = \frac{d_0 - cd_1}{2}$$

Therefore,

$$\overline{Q}_A = (1/2)\overline{Q} = \frac{d_0 - cd_1}{4} = \overline{Q}_B$$

The profit-maximizing price, $\overline{P}$, is

$$\overline{P} = d_0/d_1 - (1/d_1)\overline{Q} = d_0/d_1 - (1/d_1)\left(\frac{d_0 - cd_1}{2}\right) = \frac{d_0 + cd_1}{2d_1}$$

Illustrating with the parameter values from the initial numerical example: $d_0 = 30$, $d_1 = 5$, and $c = c_A = c_B = 0$, we have

$$\overline{Q} = \frac{d_0 - cd_1}{2} = \frac{30 - (0)(5)}{2} = 15, \quad \text{so} \quad \overline{Q}_A = (1/2)\overline{Q} = 7.5 = \overline{Q}_B$$

$$\overline{P} = \frac{d_0 + cd_1}{2d_1} = \frac{30 + (0)(5)}{(2)(5)} = \$3 = d_0/d_1 - (1/d_1)\overline{Q} = 30/5 - (1/5)(15) = \overline{P}_A = \overline{P}_B$$

If the marginal cost, however, were equal to 1, that is, $c = c_A = c_B = 1$, then

$$\overline{Q}' = \frac{d_0 - cd_1}{2} = \frac{30 - (1)(5)}{2} = 12.5, \quad \text{so} \quad \overline{Q}_A = (1/2)\overline{Q} = 6.25 = \overline{Q}_B$$

$$\overline{P}' = \frac{d_0 + cd_1}{2d_1} = \frac{30 + (1)(5)}{(2)(5)} = \$3.5$$

$$= d_0/d_1 - (1/d_1)\overline{Q} = 30/5 - (1/5)(12.5) = \overline{P}'_A = \overline{P}'_B$$

In the Chamberlin case, if firm A had a lower (constant) marginal cost than firm B ($c_A < c_B$), then firm A would not need to cooperate with firm B. Indeed, firm A would realize that its absolute cost advantage allows it to operate as a monopolist. As in the Edgeworth case, firm A could drive firm B out of the market. (Note, however, if the firms had rising marginal costs, however, for example, $C_A = C_0 + c_A Q_A^2$ and $C_B = C_0 + c_B Q_B^2$, where $c_A < c_B$, then the firms might still maximize joint profits by cooperating. With the lower marginal cost curve, firm A would enjoy a greater share of the joint monopoly profits than firm B, since firm A would have the greater output.)

PRACTICE PROBLEM 9.4

Using the example from Practice Problem 9.1, where the market demand is $Q = 40 - 4P$, suppose that the constant marginal costs of production for the two firms are identical: $c = c_A = c_B = \$2.00$.

a) Determine the profit-maximizing outputs and price for firms A and B under the Chamberlin behavioral assumption.

b) If instead the constant marginal costs differed between the two firms with $c_A = \$2.50$ and $c_B = \$1.50$, determine the market outcome under the Chamberlin behavioral assumption.

(The answers are at the end of the chapter.)

In conclusion, given the same duopoly model, here the classical mineral springs example, the market outcomes depend critically on the specific behavioral assumptions made about the firms. We summarize in Table 9.2, where the two firms have identical, constant marginal costs.

If the marginal costs of the two firms are constant, but different, then under the Edgeworth and Chamberlin behavioral assumptions, the firm with the lower marginal cost would become a monopolist. See Table 9.3 for a summary of the general cases, where firm A has the cost advantage.

Duopoly is the most basic form of oligopoly. Even so, modeling duopolistic markets is difficult, since consistent rules of behavior have to be assumed. Even in these simple examples with a homogeneous good, linear market demand, and constant mar-

TABLE 9.2 Duopoly Models: Firms with Identical, Constant Marginal Costs

	Equilibrium Output			
Case	*Firm A*	*Firm B*	*Market*	*Equilibrium Price*
Cournot (rival's output constant)	$\dfrac{d_0 - cd_1}{3}$	$\dfrac{d_0 - cd_1}{3}$	$\dfrac{2(d_0 - cd_1)}{3}$	$\dfrac{d_0 + 2cd_1}{3d_1}$
Edgeworth (rival's price constant)	$\dfrac{d_0 - cd_1}{2}$	$\dfrac{d_0 - cd_1}{2}$	$d_0 - cd_1$	c
Chamberlin (cooperation)	$\dfrac{d_0 - cd_1}{4}$	$\dfrac{d_0 - cd_1}{4}$	$\dfrac{d_0 - cd_1}{2}$	$\dfrac{d_0 + cd_1}{2d_1}$

Market demand: $Q = d_0 - d_1 P$ or $P = d_0/d_1 - (1/d_1)Q$
Cost functions: Firm A: $C_A = C_0 + cQ_A$; Firm B: $C_B = C_0 + cQ_B$

TABLE 9.3 Duopoly Models: Firms with Constant, but Different, Marginal Costs

	Equilibrium Output			
Case	Firm A	Firm B	Market	Equilibrium Price
Cournot (rival's output constant)	$\dfrac{d_0 + (c_B - 2c_A)d_1}{3}$	$\dfrac{d_0 + (c_A - 2c_B)d_1}{3}$	$\dfrac{2d_0 - (c_A + c_B)d_1}{3}$	$\dfrac{d_0 + (c_A + c_B)d_1}{3d_1}$
Edgeworth (rival's price constant)	$\dfrac{d_0 - c_A d_1}{2}$	0	$\dfrac{d_0 - c_A d_1}{2}$	$\dfrac{d_0 + c_A d_1}{2d_1}$
Chamberlin (cooperation)	$\dfrac{d_0 - c_A d_1}{2}$	0	$\dfrac{d_0 - c_A d_1}{2}$	$\dfrac{d_0 + c_A d_1}{2d_1}$

Market demand: $Q = d_0 - d_1 P$ or $P = d_0/d_1 - (1/d_1)Q$
Cost functions: Firm A: $C_A = C_0 + c_A Q_A$; Firm B: $C_B = C_0 + c_B Q_B$; where $c_A < c_B$

ginal costs for the two firms, the variability of possible outcomes is evident. When we consider that firms may learn from experience and change their behavior accordingly, the task of modeling duopolies, much less oligopolies, becomes even more challenging.

OLIGOPOLY

Oligopoly is a market characterized by the dominance of a few rival firms. The firms in the market are well aware of each other, realizing that their actions will be noticed— and may be countered—by the others. The product may be homogeneous, but typically is differentiated, so that nonprice competition is important. Through advertising, customer service, product innovation, and aggressive salesmanship, firms compete against each other. Like monopolists, oligopolists are price setters; and like monopolies, oligopolies are characterized by barriers to entry.

As noted earlier, duopoly is the most basic form of oligopoly. The models of duopoly presented in this chapter could be extended to more than two firms. In our discussion of oligopoly, we will simplify the analysis by focusing on the behavior of one firm and its rivals, considered collectively.

To begin, we observe that there is no typical oligopoly, so crafting a standard, textbook theory of oligopolistic behavior has not been possible. Economists, nevertheless, have identified general tendencies that often, if not always, characterize oligopolies. We will address three of these stylized facts below.

First, barriers to entry may allow, but do not guarantee, positive economic profits in the long run. The barriers to entry, including high start-up costs and significant scale economies, limit the number of firms that can exist in the market. The automobile industry readily comes to mind. The costs of designing cars, setting up the assembly lines, arranging for input supplies, and establishing a network of distributorships are usually prohibitive for all but the very large corporations. Oligopolies can exist, however, on a smaller scale; for example, several gasoline stations may service a small town.

Changes in tastes and preferences and technological advances resulting in new products can lead to shifts in demand, so that what was once a profitable oligopoly is no longer even viable. For instance, more health-conscious consumers or an aging population may reduce the demand for hamburgers and result in the closing of some of the once profitable drive-in restaurants in a small town. Or, the increased technological sophistication of automobiles with built-in computers has resulted in greater reliability and fewer repairs, reducing the demand for full-service gasoline stations.

Second, prices in oligopolistic markets tend not to fluctuate much. If a firm knows the demand curve it faces (and thus can derive its marginal revenue curve), then profit maximization requires that it produce where marginal revenue equals marginal cost and charge the corresponding price set from its demand schedule. Any exogenous change in demand or variable cost would alter the profit-maximizing output and price. In many oligopolistic markets, however, prices seem not to change with every shift in demand or variable cost. In part, the firms may not (and likely do not) know the demand curves facing them with any degree of certainty and may not recognize shifts in demand until after significant swings in their sales have occurred. Moreover, frequent price changes can be expensive (e.g., restaurants printing up new menus) and disturbing to regular customers. Finally, as will be developed later, firms may be hesitant to change prices due to the uncertain reactions of their rivals. We will discuss an alternative output-pricing model below.

Third, nonprice competition in oligopolistic markets can be intense. Indeed, if price competition is perceived by the firms in the market as mutually harmful (recall the Edgeworth duopoly case), then there may be greater reliance on nonprice competition. Firms attempt to win customers through product recognition and retain their market shares through brand loyalty. We will focus on one particular type of nonprice competition, advertising, illustrating that the consequences for a firm's profits depend not only on its own advertising, but that of its rivals.

A MODEL OF OUTPUT AND PRICE SELECTION FOR AN OLIGOPOLIST

Suppose that an oligopolist does not know the demand curve it faces, so that it is unable to use the marginal revenue equals marginal cost profit-maximizing rule for output. The firm, however, does form an expectation of its sales for the period in question. The firm's expected sales for period t, S_t^e, may be simply last period's sales, that is, $S_t^e = S_{t-1}$, or, if the firm has a sense of shifting market demand, a projection of last period's sales, that is, $S_t^e = (1 + r_t^e)S_{t-1}$, where r_t^e is the firm's assumed projected rate of growth (or decline) in sales.

The firm also has a desired level of inventories for its product, which may be set as a certain fraction of its expected sales. A firm holds inventories in order to meet unexpected increases in the demand for its product. Any discrepancy between its existing inventories (at the beginning of the period) and its desired inventories (at the end of the period) would be addressed by the firm's **planned inventory investment** over the period t, ΔINV_t^p. Planned inventory investment is then the difference between the firm's output, Q_t, and its expected sales, S_t^e, that is, $\Delta INV_t^p = Q_t - S_t^e$. If the firm produces less than it expects to sell, that is, $Q_t < S_t^e$, then planned inventory disinvestment occurs, $\Delta INV_t^p < 0$.

Any change in inventories that is not planned is referred to as **unplanned inventory investment**, ΔINV_t^u, or unplanned inventory disinvestment (if negative). Unplanned inventory investment in period t is the difference between the firm's expected sales, S_t^e, and its actual sales in the period, S_t, that is, $\Delta INV_t^u = S_t^e - S_t$. While necessary, inventories are costly to hold; consequently, firms may respond to unplanned inventory investment (disinvestment) by decreasing (increasing) production, dropping (raising) prices, or a combination of both in the next period.

Total inventory investment, ΔINV_t, is the sum of planned and unplanned inventory investment. Total inventory investment in period t reduces to the difference between the firm's production, Q_t, and its sales, S_t.

$$\Delta INV_t = \Delta INV_t^p + \Delta INV_t^u$$

$$\Delta INV_t = (Q_t - S_t^e) + (S_t^e - S_t)$$

$$\Delta INV_t = Q_t - S_t$$

The firm's output in period t, Q_t, is equal to the sum of its expected sales and planned inventory investment.

$$Q_t = S_t^e + \Delta INV_t^p$$

The firm sets its price, P_t, as a percentage markup, m_t, over the average total cost of producing this level of output, $ATC_t = ATC(Q_t)$.

$$P_t = (1 + m_t) \cdot ATC(Q_t)$$

The percentage markup reflects the firm's desired rate of per unit economic profits.

Figure 9.4 illustrates three scenarios for the demand for the firm's product in an initial period, $t = 0$. In each case, the firm's output is Q_0, based on its expected sales and planned inventory investment. The total costs of the firm, $(Q_0) \cdot (ATC_0)$, are represented by the area, $ATC_0 F_0 Q_0 0$. Adding the firm's desired percentage markup, m_0, to the average total cost of producing the output, Q_0, gives the price charged by the firm, $P_0 = (1 + m_0) \cdot ATC_0$.

If the demand for the firm's product is D_0, then the output sold by the firm is exactly equal to the sum of expected sales and planned inventory investment. (See point E_0 in Figure 9.4, where the demand curve intersects the price line, P_0, at the output, Q_0.) Total revenues equal $(P_0) \cdot (Q_0)$, and total profits are $(P_0 - ATC_0) \cdot Q_0$. In this case, total inventory investment is zero, since sales equal the output produced. Unplanned inventory investment would also equal zero only if planned inventory investment had been zero, meaning that the quantity demanded of the product at P_0 equaled the expected sales.

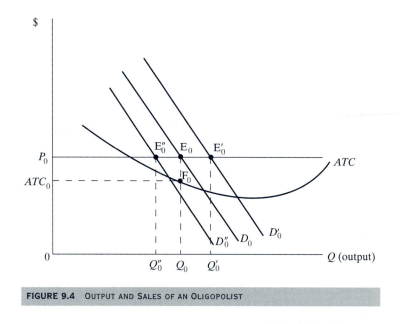

FIGURE 9.4   OUTPUT AND SALES OF AN OLIGOPOLIST

Perhaps a numerical illustration would help. Suppose the firm expects to sell 50 units in this initial period (e.g., the first month of the year), so $S_0^e = 50$; and the firm plans to add 2 units to inventories, so $\Delta INV_0^p = +2$. Therefore the firm produces 52 units, $Q_0 = 52$. If the quantity demanded at the price set by the firm were 52 units, then the actual sales of 52 units, ($S_0 = 52$), equal the production. Since actual sales exceed expected sales by 2 units, however, the unplanned change in inventories equals -2: $\Delta INV_0^u = -2$. So, while the overall inventory investment is zero, the firm's planned inventory investment of 2 units is negated by unplanned inventory disinvestment of 2 units.

Whether the firm retains the level of output, Q_0, depends on its expected sales and planned inventory investment in the next period, which, in turn, would be affected by any unplanned inventory changes in this initial period. In the above example, with the unplanned inventory disinvestment, the firm may well step up the rate of production. The firm also has the option of adjusting its markup, which affects the price it charges for a given output produced. Moreover, to boost sales, the firm might increase its advertising or engage in other forms of nonprice competition.

In sum, the course of action of the firm would depend not only on its satisfaction with the current situation (for instance, whether it experienced unplanned inventory investment or disinvestment), but on its expectation of rivals' actions and reactions to any changes it makes.

If instead the demand curve facing the firm were greater, say $D_0' > D_0$, then sales would equal Q_0', yielding total revenues of $(P_0) \cdot (Q_0')$, given by the area $P_0 E_0' Q_0' 0$. Here the excess of sales over output currently produced is met by inventory disinvestment equal to $Q_0' - Q_0$. The firm experiences increased profits, since revenues are greater, at least in part due to its sales of inventories. If the firm's planned inventory disinvestment had been $Q_0' - Q_0$, then its unplanned inventory investment would be zero.

More likely, the greater demand of D_0' has resulted in some unplanned inventory disinvestment, which may lead the firm in the next period to increase production and perhaps to increase its profit margin—especially if its expected sales are rising.

Finally, suppose that the demand facing the firm in this initial period were only $D_0'' < D_0$. Sales of Q_0'' are less than the current production of Q_0, so the firm's inventory investment is equal to $Q_0 - Q_0''$. Total profits, which may be positive or negative here with the lower demand, are equal to the difference between the total revenues of $(P_0) \cdot (Q_0'')$ and total costs of $(ATC_0) \cdot (Q_0)$, with some of the costs incurred due to the production of the output that is added to the firm's inventories. If the firm had planned inventory investment of $Q_0 - Q_0''$, then there are no unplanned changes in inventories. We might expect though that the firm would respond to the buildup in inventories—especially if some were unplanned—by decreasing production and, perhaps by dropping its price, in the next period. Note, as drawn in Figure 9.4, the firm is currently operating on the declining portion of its ATC curve; therefore, if it decreases output, its average total cost would rise, which for a given markup, would increase its price. Thus, to reduce output and the price it charges, the firm would have to decrease substantially its markup.

Again, the course of action adopted by the firm would depend on its projection of the market in the next period, as well as its unplanned inventory investment (if any) in the current period. To reiterate, an oligopolist's strategy depends on the expected behavior of its rivals, which in turn, is influenced by their perceptions of the firm's behavior. Without more information, for example, on the firm's expected sales and planned inventory investment, we are not able to be more specific about the firm's likely actions in the next period.

To illustrate with a numerical example, suppose an oligopolistic firm expects its sales in this week (S_t^e) to increase by 2% $(r_t^e = .02)$ over last week's total of 10 thousand units $(S_{t-1} = 10)$. The firm also intends to add 800 units of its output to its inventories $(\Delta INV_t^p = .8)$. The firm's short-run total cost function is given by $STC(Q_t) = .04Q_t^3 - .5Q_t^2 + 1.2Q_t + 20$, where Q_t is the output produced by the firm (in thousands of units per week). Assume that the firm sets the unit price it charges, P_t, as a 20% markup $(m_t = .20)$ over the average total cost of production, $ATC(Q_t)$.

To find the level of output produced by the firm, Q_t, we add the expected level of sales, $S_t^e = (1 + r_t^e)S_{t-1}$, to the planned inventory investment, ΔINV_t^p.

$$Q_t = S_t^e + \Delta INV_t^p = (1 + .02)(10) + .8 = 10.2 + .8 = 11.0$$

To derive the average total cost function, $ATC(Q_t)$, we divide the short-run total cost function, $STC(Q_t)$, by output, Q_t.

$$ATC(Q_t) = .04Q_t^2 - .5Q_t + 1.2 + 20/Q_t$$

The average total cost of producing $Q_t = 11.0$ (thousand units per week t) is $2.36.

$$ATC(11.0) = .04(11.0)^2 - .5(11.0) + 1.2 + 20/11.0 = 2.36$$

The oligopolist sets its price, P_t, as a 20% markup over its average total cost of production.

$$P_t = ATC(Q_t) \cdot (1 + m_t) = 2.36\,(1 + .2) = \$2.83$$

Suppose that the demand for the oligopolist's product in week t is given by the schedule: $Q_t^d = 39 - 10P_t$. With the firm's price of $P_t = \$2.83$, the quantity demanded and sold is 10.7 (thousand units per week).

$$Q_t^d = 39 - 10(2.83) = 10.7$$

With an output produced of $Q_t = 11.0$ (thousand units per week), the actual or total change in inventories is equal to .3 (thousand units per week).

$$\Delta INV_t = Q_t - Q_t^d = 11.0 - 10.7 = 0.3.$$

The unplanned inventory investment, ΔINV_t^u, is the difference between the actual and the planned inventory investment.

$$\Delta INV_t^u = \Delta INV_t - \Delta INV_t^p = .3 - .8 = -.5$$

Here, there is unplanned inventory disinvestment equal to .5 (thousand units per week).

The firm's total revenues in week t, TR_t, equal the product of the unit price set and the quantity demanded.

$$TR_t = P_t \cdot Q_t^d = (\$2.83)(10.7) = \$30.28 \text{ (thousand per week).}$$

The firm's total costs, STC_t, are the product of the average total cost of production and the quantity of output produced.

$$STC_t = ATC(Q_t) \cdot Q_t = (\$2.36)(11.0) = \$25.96 \text{ (thousand per week).}$$

Thus, the firm's profits are \$4.32 thousand per week.

$$\Pi(Q_t) = TR(Q_t) - STC(Q_t) = \$30.78 - \$25.96 = \$4.32 \text{ (thousand per week).}$$

Clearly, this level of profits is conditional on the firm's expected sales and planned inventory investment (which summed give the firm's output produced); the firm's short-run total cost function and its desired markup (which determine the price set by the firm); and the market demand for the firm's output (which may not be known by the firm with certainty). In the practice problem below, the sensitivity of the firm's profits to these factors is illustrated.

PRACTICE PROBLEM 9.5

In the above numerical example, find the change in the level of profits of the firm for each of the following changes, *ceteris paribus*. Determine the unplanned inventory investment in each case.

a) The firm expects its sales to increase by 3% (instead of 2%).
b) The firm's markup is 25% (instead of 20%).
c) The market demand for the firm's output is: $Q_t^d = 40 - 10P_t$ (instead of $Q_t^d = 39 - 10P_t$).

(The answers are at the end of the chapter.)

We have set forth, however, a model for an oligopolistic firm's selection of output and price when the firm does not know the demand curve for its product.[8] Such a model may be especially relevant for oligopolists who face demand curves that are conditional on their rival firms' actions. We turn now to the potential consequences for an oligopolist engaging in price and nonprice competition.

THE KINKED DEMAND CURVE AND PRICE RIGIDITY

Another model that may help to explain the relative inflexibility of prices in oligopolistic markets is known as the **kinked demand curve**. Suppose an oligopolistic firm is producing an output, Q_0, equal to its expected sales and planned inventory investment, and charging a price equal, P_0, equal to a percentage markup over its average total cost of production. The firm is considering a price change. Not knowing the reactions of its rival firms to a change in its price, the firm starts with two basic scenarios.

One, any change in its price will be matched by similar price changes by its rivals. If so, the impact on the firm's market share would be minimal—if any—since it should neither gain nor lose customers to other firms with no change in its relative price. The demand curve facing the firm when its price changes are matched is assumed to be

$$Q^d = d_0 - d_1 P \quad \text{or} \quad P = d_0/d_1 - (1/d_1)Q \quad \text{where} \quad d_0, d_1 > 0$$

The second scenario is that any change in its price will be ignored or not matched by its rivals. In this case, the firm would expect that unilaterally changing its price would significantly affect its sales and market share. For example, customers would shift to this firm from other firms if it were the only one to lower its price. The demand curve assumed when its price changes are not matched is

$$Q^d = d_0' - d_1'P \quad \text{or} \quad P = d_0'/d_1' - (1/d_1')Q \quad \text{where} \, d_0', d_1' > 0$$

The demand curve facing the firm when its rivals match its price changes would be less price elastic than the one when its price changes are not matched. To reflect this condition, and to ensure the common initial price-output combination, the restrictions on the demand parameters are:

i) $d_1' > d_1$: the quantity demanded of the firm's output is more sensitive to a price change when its rivals do not match its price change;

ii) $d_0' > d_0$: the quantity intercept is greater when rivals do not match its price change; and

iii) $d_0'/d_1' < d_0/d_1$: the price intercept is smaller when rivals do not match its price change.

Figure 9.5 illustrates. The intersection of the two possible demand curves, indicating the initial output (Q_0) and price (P_0) of the firm, is represented by point A, where

---

[8]Note that we are dealing with the short-run behavior of the oligopolist. The long-run decisions of a firm involving the selection of the cost-minimizing combination of capital and labor for producing the selected level of output are addressed in Chapters 10 and 11.

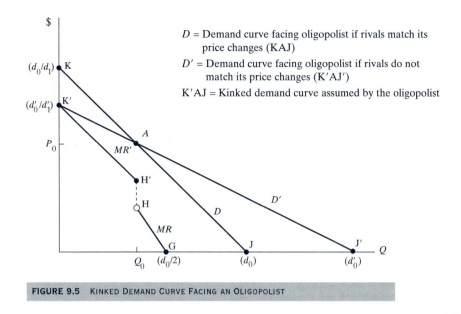

FIGURE 9.5 KINKED DEMAND CURVE FACING AN OLIGOPOLIST

$$Q_0 = \frac{d_0 d_1' - d_0' d_1}{d_1' - d_1} \quad \text{and} \quad P_0 = \frac{d_0' - d_0}{d_1' - d_1}$$

As stated, the firm does not know what its rivals will do if it changes its price. Facing uncertainty, the firm may actually adopt a third, worst-case scenario. That is, if it increases its price, then it does so alone—rivals do not match a price increase. Consequently the firm would expect not only sales to decline with its higher price, but its market share would fall also as it loses customers to other firms. The demand curve AK' is considered relevant for a price increase. Conversely, the firm would expect that if it decreases its price, hoping to boost sales and win customers from its rivals, then its rivals would also lower their prices to protect their market shares. If the firm's price cuts were matched, then its relevant demand curve is AJ. Under this scenario, the firm believes that its demand curve is the kinked demand curve, K'AJ.

Discontinuous Marginal Revenue Curve The marginal revenue curve associated with this kinked demand curve is discontinuous, given by the line segments K'H' and HG, with a vertical segment, H'H, that corresponds to the initial output produced, Q_0. The discontinuous marginal revenue curve reflects a total revenue function that is continuous, but not smooth. Recall from Chapter 2 that, for a function to be differentiable, it has to be smooth and continuous. Here the kinked demand curve and associated total revenue function are not smooth, and so are not differentiable, at the kink or sharp point in the demand curve. Thus, the derived marginal revenue curve is discontinuous at the level of output corresponding to the kink in the demand curve.

To demonstrate, the total and marginal revenue functions associated with the two demand schedules are

Demand schedule D (rivals match the firm's price changes): $Q^d = d_0 - d_1P$

$$\text{Total revenue: } TR = (d_0/d_1)Q - (1/d_1)Q^2$$

$$\text{Marginal revenue: } MR = (d_0/d_1) - (2/d_1)Q$$

Demand schedule D' (rivals do not match the firm's price changes): $Q^d = d_0' - d_1'P$

$$\text{Total revenue: } TR' = (d_0'/d_1')Q - (1/d_1')Q^2$$

$$\text{Marginal revenue: } MR' = (d_0'/d_1') - (2/d_1')Q$$

At point A, the initial price-output combination of the firm, the total revenues associated with the two demand curves are equal: $TR(Q_0) = TR'(Q_0) = P_0 \cdot Q_0$. The slopes of the two total revenue curves at point A, however, are not equal. Evaluated at the output, Q_0, the marginal revenue when rivals do not match the firm's price changes, $MR'(Q_0)$, exceeds the marginal revenue when rivals match the firm's price changes, $MR(Q_0)$. That is,

$$MR'(Q_0) = (d_0'/d_1') - (2/d_1')\left[\frac{d_0d_1' - d_0'd_1}{d_1' - d_1}\right] > (d_0/d_1) - (2/d_1)\left[\frac{d_0d_1' - d_0'd_1}{d_1' - d_1}\right] = MR(Q_0)$$

Simplifying, the inequality becomes

$$d_0'd_1d_1 - d_0'd_1d_1' > -d_0d_1'd_1' + d_0d_1d_1'$$

or
$$d_0'd_1(d_1 - d_1') > d_0d_1'(d_1 - d_1')$$

Dividing through by $(d_1 - d_1') < 0$ reverses the inequality and yields

$$d_0'd_1 < d_0d_1'$$

or
$$d_0'/d_1' < d_0/d_1$$

which is true. (Recall the initial restrictions on the demand parameters.) The gap in the marginal revenue curve, HH', associated with the kinked demand curve is equal to: $d_0/d_1 - d_0'/d_1' > 0$.

The significance of the vertical gap (H'H) in the marginal revenue curve is that shifts in the marginal cost curve falling within this range, for example, due to changes in factor prices or technology, would not affect the firm's profit-maximizing output or price. Thus, a vertical gap in the marginal revenue curve associated with a kinked demand curve contributes to the price stability often observed in oligopolistic markets, since the sensitivity of output price to changes in marginal cost is reduced. In other words, if the firm were equating the assumed marginal revenue to marginal cost, then the firm's output, Q_0, and price, P_0, are consistent with a range of marginal cost curves. This is in contrast to a continuous marginal revenue curve, where any shift in the marginal cost curve would alter the profit-maximizing output and price set by the firm.

In sum, referring to the kinked demand curve, K'AJ, in Figure 9.5, increases (decreases) in the marginal cost curve that are confined within the vertical gap, HH', of the marginal revenue curve, while increasing (decreasing) the average variable cost and average total cost curves and decreasing (increasing) the profit-margin and total profits of the firm, leave the profit-maximizing output, Q_0, and price, P_0, unchanged.

Price Stability   Another explanation derived from the kinked demand curve for the relative stability of prices in oligopolistic markets reflects the impact of changes in the firm's price on its revenues and profits. As we can see from Figure 9.5, the kink in the demand curve, point A, which indicates the firm's initial output and price, occurs in the price elastic regions of the two demand curves: K′AJ′ (rivals do not match price changes) and KAJ (rivals match price changes). We know this since the corresponding marginal revenue curves, K′H and HG, are positive up to the output level $d_0/2$, which exceeds Q_0.[9]

If the firm raises its price above P_0, and its rivals do not follow with their own price hikes, the firm would be moving up the demand curve AK′, and its total revenues would be declining—likely more than its total costs.[10] That is, with an unmatched price increase and a price-elastic demand, the firm finds its sales declining not only because of its absolutely higher price, but with the shift in some of its customers to its rivals due to their now relatively lower prices. In short, a unilateral price increase would likely be perceived by the firm as unprofitable, especially if sales to rivals were difficult to recover, once lost.

On the other hand, if the firm were to lower its price below P_0, which induces its rivals to cut their own prices, the firm would be moving down the demand curve, AJ. The firm's total revenues would rise until its sales reached $d_0/2$; beyond this point, the firm's marginal revenue becomes negative, so its total revenues begin to decline. Its total costs, however, rise continually with its production, and would likely outweigh any increase in revenues realized. Moreover, the difficulty with cutting prices—as the Edgeworth duopoly model illustrated—is putting an end to the ensuing price war. As firms attempt to undercut their rivals, eventually they move down into the price-inelastic region of their demand curves; so that as total costs continue to increase, total revenues begin to fall.

In short, an oligopolist, not knowing its rivals' reactions, may perceive that it is better off not to change its price. Yet, even in oligopolistic markets, prices, while fairly stable, are not absolutely rigid. The question becomes then, when would an oligopolist change its price. With respect to price increases, a firm may pass along significant increases in average costs (e.g., higher wages), especially when its rivals are expected to incur the same increased costs. A firm may also raise its price when it expects significant increases in sales, especially when its inventories are low and its average total cost is rising with its production. Furthermore, firms, particularly if few in number, may adopt a form of price leadership, whereby they tacitly collude to match a price increase.

---

[9]Note, if the initial output, Q_0, corresponding to the kink in the demand curve, were not less than the output level, $d_0/2$, which indicates the unitary elastic point on the demand curve, *KAJ*, then the relevant lower portion of the marginal revenue curve, HG, would lie below the quantity axis.

[10]Indeed, if Q_0 were the profit-maximizing output, then any departure from it would reduce profits. Given that the firm initially produces the output, Q_0 (equal to its expected sales and planned inventory investment), and not knowing its rivals reactions to changes in its price, has to speculate on the likely demand curve facing it, (here the kinked demand curve, K′AJ), the output produced, Q_0, will then be the profit-maximizing output if the firm's marginal cost curve falls within the vertical gap of the marginal revenue curve.

Such coordinated price hikes are more likely when the firms experience higher costs or when the market demand is growing. In industries characterized by frequent technological advances (e.g., software for personal computers) or annual style changes (e.g., automobiles), price increases often accompany the introduction of new models.

With respect to price decreases, firms in an oligopoly may pass along significantly lower costs of production. Examples include the technological progress in the production of personal computers that has reduced their prices, and the lowering of air fares when jet fuel prices plunge. Indeed, price cuts induced by lower costs of production can be profitable. In contrast, price cuts prompted by accumulating inventories and sluggish sales can be costly to the firms involved. Nevertheless, if the market has chronic excess capacity, price competition may force the exit of weaker firms, which restores the profitability of the remaining firms, who can then more easily raise their prices. Indeed, a barrier to entry in some markets may be the threat of sharp price cuts by the established firms with the ability to weather negative economic profits for a while. Typically though, oligopolists prefer nonprice competition, the costs of which are passed on to consumers in the form of higher prices.

Before introducing the analytical technique of game theory, we will use a simple numerical example to illustrate a kinked demand curve.

An Example of a Kinked Demand Curve   Suppose that an oligopolist is currently producing an output of $Q_0 = 4$ (hundred thousand units per week) and charging a price of $P_0 = \$3$. The firm believes that if it lowers its price below $P_0 = \$3$, then the demand curve, $Q^d = 10 - 2P$, is relevant. That is, for every \$.1 decrease in its price, the quantity demanded of its output is expected to increase by .2 (hundred thousand units per week). If the firm maintains or increases its price above $P_0 = \$3$, however, it believes that the demand curve, $Q^d = 16 - 4P$, is relevant. That is, for every \$.1 increase in its price, the firm expects the quantity demanded of its output to decrease by .4 (hundred thousand units per week). Consistent with the theory of the kinked demand curve, the demand facing the firm for price increases is more price elastic—since the firm believes its rivals would not match a price increase, but would match a price decrease.

We write the firm's kinked demand schedule and associated total and marginal revenue schedules below.

Demand schedule D (rivals match the firm's price decreases)

for $P < 3$, $Q^d = 10 - 2P$ [or, for $Q > 4$, $P = 5 - (1/2)Q$]

Total revenue: $TR = 5Q - (1/2)Q^2$

Marginal revenue: $MR = 5 - Q$

Demand schedule D' (rivals do not match the firm's price increases)

for $P \geq 3$, $Q^d = 16 - 4P$ [or, for $Q \leq 4$, $P = 4 - (1/4)Q$]

Total revenue: $TR' = 4Q - (1/4)Q^2$

Marginal revenue: $MR' = 4 - (1/2)Q$

Figure 9.6 illustrates the kinked demand curve, K'AJ, and the discontinuous marginal revenue curve. Note that at $Q_0 = 4$, the marginal revenue corresponding to the upper part of the demand curve, MR' (for $P \geq 3$), is equal to $2; that is, $MR'(4) = 4 - (1/2)(4) = 2$. (See point H'.) The marginal revenue corresponding to the lower part of the demand curve at $Q_0 = 4$, MR (for $P < 3$), is equal to $1; that is, $MR(4) = 5 - 1(4) = 1$. (See point H, indicated by an open dot, since this point is not actually part of the discontinuous marginal revenue curve.) Thus, the vertical gap in the firm's marginal revenue curve at the selected output of $Q_0 = 4$ is equal to $1; that is, $MR'(4) - MR(4) = \$2 - \$1 = \$1$.

Suppose further that the firm's short-run total cost function is given by: $STC(Q) = .067Q^3 - .4Q^2 + 1.3Q + 8$. The associated average total cost and marginal cost functions are

$$ATC(Q) = STC(Q)/Q = .067Q^2 - .4Q + 1.3 + 8/Q$$

$$MC(Q) = dSTC(Q)/dQ = .2Q^2 - .8Q + 1.3$$

The minimum marginal cost occurs at an output of $Q = 2$ and is equal to $.5.

$$dMC(Q)/dQ = .4Q - .8 = 0$$

$$Q = 2$$

$$MC(2) = .2(2)^2 - .8(2) + 1.3 = .5$$

Note that in this example, the marginal cost curve cuts the discontinuous marginal revenue curve in the vertical gap, $H'H$. The marginal cost at the firm's selected output of $Q_0 = 4$ is equal to $1.3; that is, $MC(4) = .2(4)^2 - .8(4) + 1.3 = 1.3$.

The firm's profits at $Q_0 = 4$ and $P_0 = \$3$ are equal to $.91 (hundred thousand per week).

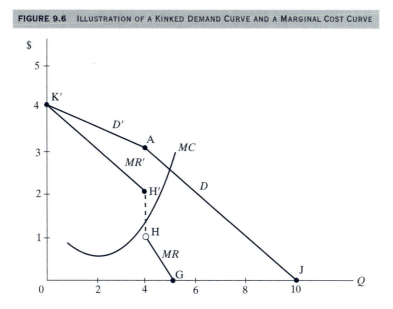

FIGURE 9.6 ILLUSTRATION OF A KINKED DEMAND CURVE AND A MARGINAL COST CURVE

$$\Pi(4) = TR'(4) - STC(4)$$

$$= (3)(4) - [.067(4)^3 - .4(4)^2 + 1.3(4) + 8]$$

$$= 12 - 11.09$$

$$= \$.91 \text{ (hundred thousand per week)}$$

The markup or profit margin of the firm, m_0, equals 8.3%. To derive this, recall that the firm's price is set by: $P_0 = (1 + m_0) \cdot ATC_0$. Here $ATC_0 = ATC(Q_0) = ATC(4) = .067(4)^2 - .4(4) + 1.3 + 8/(4) = 2.77$. So, for $P_0 = 3$, we can solve for the implied percentage markup.

$$P_0 = 3 = (1 + m_0) \cdot ATC_0$$

$$3 = (1 + m_0) \, 2.77$$

$$m_0 = (3/2.77) - 1 = .083$$

Now, consider the impact on the firm's profits of a $.30 increase in its price to $P_1 = \$3.30$, which is not matched by its rivals. The quantity demanded and sold of the firm's output declines to $Q_1 = 16 - 4P_1 = 16 - 4(3.3) = 2.8$ (hundred thousand units per week). The total revenues decline to $TR_1' = (3.3)(2.8) = \$9.24$ (hundred thousand per week). Total costs fall to $STC_1 = .067(2.8)^3 - .4(2.8)^2 + 1.3(2.8) + 8 = \$9.97$ (hundred thousand per week). Total profits are reduced to: $\Pi(Q_1) = TR_1' - STC_1 = \$9.24 - \$9.97 = -\$.73$ (hundred thousand per week). In this example, a unilateral increase in the firm's price not only reduces its profits, but results in negative economic profits. [Note that if the firm's rivals matched its price hike to $P_1 = \$3.30$, that is, if the demand $Q^d = 10 - 2P$ were relevant for price increases, then we can show that the firm's sales would only decrease to 3.4 (hundred thousand units per week) and its profits would only fall to $.79 (hundred thousand per week).]

If instead, the firm considered dropping its price by $.30 to $P_2 = \$2.70$, which it assumes will be matched by its rivals, then the quantity demanded and sold of the firm's output increases to $Q_2 = 10 - 2(2.7) = 4.6$ (hundred thousand units per week). Since the firm would still be operating with a price-elastic demand, its total revenues rise to $TR_2 = (2.7)(4.6) = \$12.42$ (hundred thousand per week). Total costs, however, increase even more to $STC_2 = .067(4.6)^3 - .4(4.6)^2 + 1.3(4.6) + 8 = \$12.04$ (hundred thousand per week). Total profits, while lower, are still positive: $\Pi(Q_2) = TR_2 - STC_2 = \$12.42 - \$12.04 = \$.38$ (hundred thousand per week).[11] As discussed earlier, a problem facing firms is ending price cutting once it begins. [Note that if the firm's rivals did not match its price decrease to $P_2 = \$2.70$, then the firm's quantity sold

---

[11]Note, in this example, any change in price would reduce profits, since, $Q_0 = 4$, once set, becomes the profit-maximizing output. That is, here the marginal cost curve cuts the discontinuous marginal revenue curve associated with the kinked demand curve at $Q_0 = 4$. The marginal cost curve, however, need not intersect the vertical gap of the marginal revenue curve, corresponding to the firm's selected output (assumed to be based on the firm's expected sales and planned inventory investment). If marginal cost does not equal marginal revenue at the output indicating the kink in the demand curve, then that level of output would not maximize the firm's profits.

would increase to 5.2 (hundred thousand units per week) and its profits would decline only to $.68 (hundred thousand per week.]

This example illustrates how an oligopolist, uncertain of its rivals' reactions, would tend not to change its price. The situation facing an oligopolist, however, is even more complicated. In particular, we need to incorporate more fully the possible behavior of the rivals into the analysis. Game theory allows for the modeling of this interdependence.

PRACTICE PROBLEM 9.6

Suppose that an oligopolist is currently producing an output of $Q_0 = 4$ (hundred thousand units per week) and charging a price of $P_0 = \$6.00$. The firm assumes that if it lowers its price, then the demand schedule, $Q^d = 10 - P$, is relevant. On the other hand, if the firm maintains or increases its price from $P_0 = \$6.00$, then the demand schedule, $Q^d, = 16 - 2P$, is assumed to be relevant.

a) Derive the firm's kinked demand schedule and associated, discontinuous marginal revenue schedule. Determine the vertical gap in the marginal revenue curve.

b) If the firm's short-run total cost function is: $STC(Q) = .05Q^3 - .15Q^2 + 1.8Q + 12$, then determine the firm's percentage mark-up and its initial level of profits.

c) Find the effect on the firm's profits if it increases its price by $.50. Find the effect on the firm's profits if instead it decreases its price by $.50.

(The answers are at the end of the chapter.)

USING SIMPLE GAME THEORY

Game theory is a technique often used to analyze the strategic interaction of oligopolists. The underlying premise in game theory is that to understand the behavior of parties whose welfares are interdependent, the possible strategies of the parties and the expected outcomes need to be defined. We will restrict our attention to the most basic form of game theory with two parties or players (the firm and its rivals, who we assume are sufficiently alike that we can consider them collectively) and two strategies or choices (e.g., hold price constant or cut price; maintain advertising expenditures or increase advertising expenditures).

The general form of a two player-two strategy game is given in Figure 9.7. The 2×2 matrix indicates the players' expected payoffs for the combinations of strategies. The first element of the ordered pair, A_{ij}, $(i = 1, 2; j = 1, 2)$, indicates the expected payoff for player A if it selects strategy i and player B selects strategy j. Similarly, the second element of the ordered pair, B_{ij}, indicates player B's expected payoff if player A selects strategy i and it selects strategy j. For instance, if player A choose strategy 1 and player B choose strategy 2, then the outcome would be the upper right-hand cell, with A's expected payoff equal to A_{12} and B's expected payoff equal to B_{12}.

Sometimes one or both players will have a *dominant strategy,* which is a superior strategy regardless of the strategy selected by the other player. For example, strategy 1 would be a dominant strategy for player A if $A_{11} > A_{21}$ and $A_{12} > A_{22}$. If both play-

Player *B*

Strategy 1   Strategy 2

	Strategy 1	Strategy 2
Strategy 1	(A_{11}, B_{11})	(A_{12}, B_{12})
Strategy 2	(A_{21}, B_{21})	(A_{22}, B_{22})

Player A

A_{ij} = Expected payoff for player *A* when it chooses strategy *i* and
player *B* chooses strategy *j*
B_{ij} = Expected payoff for player *B* when player *A* chooses strategy *i* and it chooses strategy *j*
where $i = 1, 2; j = 1, 2;$ and *A* is the row player and *B* is the
column player.

FIGURE 9.7   BASIC TWO PLAYER-TWO STRATEGY GAME

ers have dominant strategies, then the solution or outcome of the game is straightforward—and given by the intersection of the dominant strategies. If only one player (e.g.,
A) has a dominant strategy, then the rival player (B) is assumed to recognize this and
select the strategy yielding the best available outcome.

A *Nash equilibrium* is an outcome where neither player would alter their selected
strategy given the other's chosen strategy.[12] The intersection of dominant strategies, as
well as a player's selection of the best option when the rival player has a dominant
strategy, indicate Nash equilibria. In games where there is no dominant strategy for
either player, we will inspect each outcome to see if either player would want to switch
strategy. If not, then that outcome represents a Nash equilibrium. In a game, there may
be zero, one, or multiple Nash equilibria.

The games illustrated here assume that the two players are not able to collaborate or
openly collude—as is true in the U.S. economy where it is illegal for firms to conspire to
fix prices or divide up markets. Moreover, given that the oligopolistic firms face demand
curves that are negatively sloped and likely shifting, the games are "variable sum," meaning that the players have some common interests, such as avoiding costly price competition and maintaining entry barriers. We should be mindful, however, that the games
presented here do not fully capture the complexities of oligopolistic behavior. The rigor-
ous analysis possible with game theory extends well beyond the relatively simple treatment offered below. Nevertheless, the examples do provide insight into oligopolies.

PRICE COMPETITION

In general, the profitability for an oligopolist in cutting its price is directly related to:
the level of its inventories; how far below capacity (the output corresponding to the
minimum average total cost) is its production (which affects how the firm's average

[12]The namesake of this equilibrium, John Nash (1928–   ), is a mathematical economist who shared the
1994 Nobel Prize in Economics for his contributions to game theory.

total cost changes with its output); and the price elasticity of demand for its product (which is higher the more similar is its product to its rivals' products and the smaller are the price cuts of its rivals in response to its decrease in price). Thus, very favorable conditions for a firm to decrease its price would be surplus inventories, significant excess capacity, and a high price elasticity of demand for its product.

Conversely, an oligopolist would find a price hike to be more profitable, the leaner are its inventories; the more its production exceeds its capacity output; and the less price elastic is the demand for its product. While an oligopolist would usually prefer that its rivals do not match any decrease in its price; it would usually prefer that any price increase be matched by its rivals. (Recall that in the theory of the kinked demand curve, the firm actually expects the opposite reactions: its price cuts are matched, but its price hikes are not.) We say "usually" because, as the games below illustrate, the consequences of a given price change for a firm's profits depend not only on response of its rivals, but also on the changes in the firm's marginal and average total costs as it alters its output.

Return to the numerical example of the oligopolist who, based on its expected sales and planned inventory investment, selects an output of $Q_0 = 4$ (hundred thousand units per week) and sets a price of $P_0 = \$3$, a desired markup over its average total cost of production. With the given total cost schedule: $STC(Q) = .067Q^3 - .4Q^2 + 1.3Q + 8$, the firm's profits are $\$.91$ (hundred thousand per week). The firm, however, might not know whether this is indeed a profit-maximizing level of output and does not know for sure what its rivals would do if it were to change its price. The firm considers two basic reactions for its rivals. If the rivals match its price changes, the relevant demand schedule is assumed to be $Q^d = 16 - 4P$. If the rivals do not match its price changes, the firm assumes the demand schedule, $Q^d = 10 - 2P$, is operational.

In the following examples, the two players are the oligopolistic firm and its rivals, considered as an aggregate. We assume that the rivals collectively have a larger share of the market than the firm, yet individually have cost schedules that are similar to the firm's. The payoffs in the game matrices indicate the expected profits of the firm and its rivals. When possible, we use the firm's expected profits calculated from the given demand and total cost schedules. The rival firms' profit payoffs, however, are hypothetical, although consistent with their larger share of the market. What mostly matters for these games is the ranking or relative ordering of the payoffs, not the exact magnitudes.

Price Increases The first game deals with a possible price increase. Refer to Game 1 below for the expected profit payoffs (in hundred thousand dollars per week). The two strategies are "no change in price" and "price increase." To be specific, assume the firm is considering a price increase of $\$.30$ from $P_0 = \$3.00$ to $P_1 = \$3.30$. If neither the firm nor its rivals change prices, the firm's profits remain at $\$.91$, and we assume that the rivals' profits would be unchanged at $\$1.5$. (As stated earlier, the expected profits for the rivals are hypothetical.) If the firm unilaterally raises its price to $\$3.30$, then we showed that its profits would decline to $-\$.73$; and we assume that its rivals profits rise to $\$2.4$, reflecting their gains in market share. If the firm maintained its price, but its

Game 1: Possible Price Increase

RIVALS

		No change in price	Price increase	
FIRM	No change in price	(.91, 1.5) *	(1.4, .3)	*Firm's dominant strategy*
	Price increase	(−.73, 2.4)	(.79, 1.2)	

Rival's dominant strategy

rivals increased their prices, we assume the firm's expected profits increase to $1.4, while the profits of the rival firms decline to $.3. Finally, if the firm and its rivals jointly raise prices (which would not likely affect market shares), the firm's profits would be $.79, and its rivals' profits would be $1.2.

In this game, the firm has a dominant strategy of not changing its price: since .91 > −.73 (if its rivals do not change their prices) and 1.4 > .79 (if rivals do raise their prices). Similarly, the rivals have a dominant strategy of not changing price (1.5 > .3 and 2.4 > 1.2). The solution appears to be clear. Prices would not be increased and the status quo would prevail. We use an asterisk, *, to indicate the solution, here the cell in the upper left-hand corner of the game matrix. In this game, the firm and its rivals achieve their second best outcomes. The highest expected profits would be when the other player(s) unilaterally increased price(s), *ceteris paribus*.

This outcome of price stability will not always be the case. If firms in the market are operating beyond capacity, so that average total costs would fall as production declines, and if firms tacitly collude, then a price increase may be profitable. Firms that form a cartel, where legal, can jointly raise prices by restricting output. As noted earlier, significant increases in costs may compel firms to raise prices. And, with growth in market demand, firms may be encouraged to raise their prices without a loss in sales. Consider such an increase in demand that boosts the expected sales of the firms in the market. Refer to Game 1A with the hypothetical profit expectations.

We see that across the board, regardless of the combination of strategies, expected profits are higher. Even so, the firm and its rivals still have dominant strategies of not changing price; so it appears that the firm would earn profits of 1.2, while its rivals' profits would be 2.0. (See the upper left-hand cell, where the dominant strategies intersect.) This outcome, however, is only the third-best for the players. A coordinated price increase would be mutually beneficial for the firms—if not for the consumers. (See the lower-right-hand cell, identified by **, which gives the second-best outcome for the players.) The question is how to achieve this tacit collusion.

One scenario, a form of price leadership, would be for the firm to increase its price unilaterally, hoping that its rivals would not undercut it by holding their prices constant

Game 1A: Possible Price Increase with an Increase in Market Demand

RIVALS

		No change in price	Price increase	
FIRM	No change in price	(1.2, 2.0) *	(1.6, 1.8)	*Firm's dominant strategy*
	Price increase	(1.0, 2.4)	(1.4, 2.2) **	

*Rival's dominant
strategy*

(in which case the firm's profits would decline to 1.0, while its rivals' profits increase to 2.4). If the firm does announce or signal a price increase and its rivals acquiesce and raise their prices, then the preferred outcome of greater profits for all is attained: 1.4 for the firm and 2.2 for the rivals. If instead, the rivals did not follow the firm's lead, then the firm could roll back its price (e.g., offering rebates) and the game would return to the initial outcome of no change in prices (the cell with the *). Whether price stability or a coordinated price hike prevail would depend on the leader's credible initiative and the followers' recognition of the mutual benefits. Similar price leadership has been practiced by the domestic automobile industry in the United States when one of the major manufacturers announces its price increases for the new models, and the other firms soon follow with similar price markups.

Price Decreases Return now to the initial situation with the firm producing an output of $Q_0 = 4$ (hundred thousand units per week), charging a price of $3.00, and earning profits of $.91 (hundred thousand per week). Suppose the firm is contemplating a price cut of $.30 to $P_1 = \$2.70$. We showed earlier that a price decrease of $.30, if matched by the rival firms, would reduce the firm's profits to $.38. If not matched, the price cut would drop the firm's profits only to $.68. It seems that the firm would be reluctant to lower its price. We need to consider, however, its rivals' strategies and expected outcomes. Refer to Game 2, where the hypothetical expected profits for the rivals are given, along with those for the firm if its rivals cut their prices and it does not (assumed to be equal to $-.1$). In this game we see that unmatched price decreases, whether by the firm or its rivals, while increasing the market shares of the price cutters, would not be profitable—since costs would rise faster than revenues as production increases. Price stability would seem to be the likely outcome.

To explore further, neither the firm nor its rivals have dominant strategies in this game. Consequently, we will check each outcome to see whether either firm would want to switch its strategy.

Begin with the outcome in the upper left-hand corner of the payoff matrix that corresponds to constant prices. Given the prices set by its rivals, the firm would not want to cut its price unilaterally, since its profits would fall from .91 to .68. Similarly,

Game 2: Possible Price Decrease

	RIVALS	
	No change in price	Price decrease
FIRM — No change in price	(.91, 1.5) *	(−.1, 1.2)
FIRM — Price decrease	(.68, .4)	(.38, .8) *

the rival firms would not want to cut their prices, given the firm's price, since doing so would decrease their profits from 1.5 to 1.2. Thus, the status quo in prices represents a Nash equilibrium.

Unmatched price cuts would not be acceptable to either the firm or its rivals. For example, if the firm considered unilaterally cutting its price, giving it profits of .68 and its rivals collective profits of .4, then the firm and its rivals would want to switch: the firm back to its initial price and the rivals to price decreases.

Mutual price decreases also represent a Nash equilibrium, albeit with lower profits all around. That is, if the firm and its rivals were to cut prices, then neither would want to return to the prices initially set. The game then has two Nash equilibria. Perhaps since the "preferred" Nash equilibria (with no change in prices) involves the status quo, it may be the one that would prevail.

If unmatched price decreases were profitable, that is, the revenue gains exceeded the higher cost as production rises, however, the outcome would be clearer. Refer to Game 2A. Here firm and its rivals have dominant strategies of cutting prices. Any ensuing price competition, however, could be increasingly expensive for the firm and its rivals, as firms moved beyond their capacity outputs and the increases in the costs of production accelerated, while the gains in total revenues declined.

Game 2A: Possible Price Decrease: More Favorable Conditions

	RIVALS		
	No change in price	Price decrease	
FIRM — No change in price	(.91, 1.5)	(−.4, 1.9)	
FIRM — Price decrease	(1.2, .2)	(.38, .8) *	*Firm's dominant strategy*

Rival's dominant strategy

Game 2B: Firm Develops New Cost-Reducing Technology

	RIVALS	
	No change in price	Price decrease
FIRM — No change in price	(1.3, 1.5)	(.4, 1.2)
FIRM — Price decrease	(1.7, .2)	(1.4, .6) *

Firm's dominant strategy

As suggested, price cutting may be profitable when in response to a decrease in costs. Suppose the firm develops a new technology that reduces its costs of production. As a result, the firm realizes greater profits at any level of output. Indeed, with the assumed kinked demand curve, if the cost curves shift down far enough, that is, the new marginal cost curve intersects the marginal revenue curve to the right of the vertical gap, then the firm's profit-maximizing output would increase. The firm's decision is whether or not to pass along its lower costs to consumers through a price cut. Refer to Game 2B, and the expected profits, where we assume that the rival firms do not have the new technology. With the superior cost conditions, the firm can consider deeper cuts in its price than previously.

The firm now has a dominant strategy of a price decrease. Its rivals do not have a dominant strategy, and so do the best they can. With the firm cutting its price, the highest profits for the rivals would be .6, realized when they cut also their prices.

Price Cutting as a Barrier to Entry   The threat of price cuts by established firms in a market can serve as a barrier to entry. To illustrate, suppose that the established firms are earning profits of 4 (hundred thousand dollars per week) before the entrance of a new firm. When the new firm enters, the demand curves facing the established firms shift left and their profits fall. Refer to Game 3 where the expected profits are given after the entrance of a new firm.

Game 3: Entrance of New Firm

	ESTABLISHED FIRMS	
	No change in price	Price decrease
NEW FIRM — No change in price	(.5, 3.5)	(−1, 3)
NEW FIRM — Price decrease	(1.0, 2.5) *	(−.5, 2)

New firm's dominant strategy

Established firms' dominant strategy

The new firm expects to earn positive economic profits if the established firms hold their prices constant. The new firm's profits would be greater, however, if it could undercut the prices of the established firms. In contrast, if the established firms cut their prices, the new firm would expect to earn negative economic profits, and may exit the market after this initial period (e.g., after the first year).

In the matrix for Game 3, the new firm has a dominant strategy of cutting prices. The established firms, perhaps fearing a price war, have a dominant strategy of not changing their prices. The intersection of the dominant strategies (the lower left-hand cell) gives the solution to the game. The new firm undercuts the prices of the established firms and earns profits of 1 (hundred thousand dollars per week); and the established firms, holding their prices, earn profits of 2.5 (hundred thousand dollars per week).

There may be a more interesting outcome to this game, however. Despite having a dominant strategy of not changing their prices, the established firms may try to drive the new firm out of the market. Suppose the established firms believe that the new firm, with a high probability, would exit if it earned negative economic profits in its first year. If the new firm did exit, then the profits of the established firms might rebound to their initial level of 4, provided that their prices also returned to the levels existing before the new firm broke into the market. Taking a 2-year horizon and using a discount factor of 10 percent for profits in the second year, the established firms compare the present value of 2 years of annual profits of 2.5 (using their dominant strategy of not changing prices) with the present value of a profit of 2.0 in the first year (when they cut prices to meet the new firm's lower price) and $4p^e$ in the second year (after the new firm has exited and their price cuts have been reversed). The expected probability that the new firm would exit after receiving negative economic profits in the first year is given by p^e. Solving for the value of this expected probability that would make the riskier strategy of matching price cuts with the new firm in the first year more profitable, we have

$$2 + 4p^e/(1.1) > 2.5 + 2.5/(1.1)$$

$$2 + 3.64p^e > 2.5 + 2.27$$

$$3.64p^e > 2.77$$

$$p^e > .76$$

That is, if the established firms believed that the probability of the new firm exiting if it earns negative economic profits in the first year is greater than 76%, then they may want to abandon their dominant strategy and match the price cuts of the new firm. Moreover, setting a precedent of decreasing prices when new firms break into the market may discourage other attempts to enter in the future. As noted, if successful in driving out the new firm, the established firms then have to find a way to raise prices jointly in order to recover their initial level of profits.

PRACTICE PROBLEM 9.7

Consider the following game, where the costs of the inputs used by the firm and its rivals have increased. The options are to hold prices constant or to increase prices. The payoffs are the expected profits.

RIVALS

	No change in price	Price increase
No change in price	(.5, 1.2)	(.6, .9)
Price increase	(.2, 1.4)	(.7, 1.5)

FIRM

Find the solution to this game.

(The answers are at the end of the chapter.)

ADVERTISING

Through advertising a firm hopes to increase the demand for its product. That is, advertising is intended not only to inform consumers about the characteristics of a product and the conditions for its sale, such as price, financing terms, and vendor locations, but to extol the merits of the product relative to its competitors. To the extent advertising provides useful and truthful information, consumers benefit, as their search times and transactions costs are reduced. Moreover, by increasing the information readily available, advertising may promote a convergence of prices across the product brands in a market. Advertising also subsidizes the mass media. The advertising revenues earned serve to lower the prices of newspapers, periodicals, and television programming.

Advertising, of course, adds to the costs of a firm. Indeed, advertising expenditures can be considered like a fixed cost, in that they do not necessarily vary with the output of a firm. As such, the average cost of a given advertising message declines as the sales of a firm rise. The costs of advertising are passed on to consumers in the form of higher prices for the promoted products. Furthermore, since a firm's rivals also advertise, the effectiveness of the firm's own advertising on increasing its sales will be somewhat neutralized.

We incorporate the effects of advertising on a firm's revenues and costs in developing a decision rule for the firm's profit-maximizing level of advertising. Then we use game theory to illustrate how firms can easily "overadvertise."

Optimal Advertising for a Firm Consider an oligopolist (or a monopolistic competitor) seeking to determine the profit-maximizing level of advertising. The firm's output, Q, is directly related to its advertising expenditures, A; that is, $Q = Q(A)$, where $dQ/dA > 0$. Advertising increases the demand for the firm's product, given by: $P = P(Q)$, where P is the unit price of the output and $dP/dQ < 0$.

The firm's total costs are equal to the total costs of production, $C = C(Q)$, where $dC/dQ > 0$, plus the costs of advertising, A. Consistent with the focus of this model, we write the profits of the firm as a function of its advertising expenditures: $\Pi = \Pi(A)$, where

$$\Pi(A) = P[Q(A)] \cdot Q(A) - C[Q(A)] - A$$

To find the condition for the profit-maximizing level of advertising, we differentiate the profit function and set the result equal to zero.[13]

$$d\Pi/dA = (dP/dQ)(dQ/dA) \cdot Q + P \cdot (dQ/dA) - (dC/dQ)(dQ/dA) - 1 = 0$$

Combining like terms, we have

$$[(dP/dQ) \cdot Q + P](dQ/dA) - (dC/dQ)(dQ/dA) - 1 = 0$$

Letting:

$$MR_Q = MR(Q) = [(dP/dQ) \cdot Q + P] = \text{the firm's marginal revenue of output}$$

$$MC_Q = MC(Q) = dC/dQ = \text{the firm's marginal cost of output}$$

and

$$MP_A = dQ/dA = \text{the firm's marginal product of advertising}$$

we can write

$$MR_Q \cdot MP_A - MC_Q \cdot MP_A - 1 = 0$$

or

$$(MR_Q - MC_Q) \cdot MP_A = 1$$

To maximize profits, a firm should advertise up to the point where the last dollar spent on advertising just increases net revenues by a dollar. To elaborate, the left-hand side of this equation gives the marginal profitability of a dollar spent on advertising, which equals the product of the additional output sold due to the advertising (MP_A) and the difference between the marginal revenue and marginal cost of the additional output ($MR_Q - MC_Q$).

Alternatively, we can write the decision rule for the profit-maximizing level of advertising as:

$$MR_Q \cdot MP_A = 1 + MC_Q \cdot MP_A$$

Here the left-hand side of the equation gives the marginal revenue product of advertising, that is, the additional revenues generated by another dollar of advertising. The right-hand side indicates the additional cost of another dollar of advertising, which equals the dollar of advertising itself (1) plus the marginal cost of producing the additional output sold, $MC_Q \cdot MP_A$.

---

[13]Recall, given a demand function, $P = P(Q)$, the associated total and marginal revenue functions are

$$TR(Q) = P(Q) \cdot Q$$

$$\text{and } MR(Q) = (dP/dQ) \cdot Q + P$$

The decision rule for the optimal level of advertising is more complicated when an oligopolist considers its rivals' advertising expenditures. Let

$$A' = \text{advertising expenditures of the firm's rivals}$$

Rivals' advertising would be expected to reduce the demand for the firm's output. Moreover, the firm might assume that the rivals' advertising expenditures are directly related to its own advertising, that is, $A' = A'(A)$, where $dA'/dA > 0$. Thus, we can write the output of the firm as:

$$Q = Q[A, A'(A)], \quad \text{where} \quad \delta Q/\delta A > 0, \delta Q/\delta A' < 0, \text{and } dA'/dA > 0$$

The firm's profit function to be maximized is

$$\Pi(A) = P(Q[A, A'(A)]) \cdot Q[A, A'(A)] - C[Q(A, A'(A)] - A$$

Differentiating with respect to the firm's advertising and setting the result equal to zero, we have:

$$dΠ/dA = (dP/dQ) \cdot [(\delta Q/\delta A) + (\delta Q/\delta A')(dA'/dA)] \cdot Q + P \cdot [(\delta Q/\delta A)$$

$$+ (\delta Q/\delta A')(dA'/dA)] - (dC/dQ) \cdot [(\delta Q/\delta A) + (\delta Q/\delta A')(dA'/dA)] - 1 = 0$$

Letting:

$$MR_Q = MR(Q) = (dP/dQ) \cdot Q + P = \text{the firm's marginal revenue of output}$$

$$MC_Q = MC(Q) = \text{the firm's marginal cost of output}$$

and

$$MP_A^* = [(\delta Q/\delta A) + (\delta Q/\delta A')(dA'/dA)]$$

where MP_A^* is the firm's marginal product of advertising incorporating its rivals' advertising. Simplifying, the decision rule for the oligopolistic firm's profit-maximizing level of advertising is now: $[MR_Q - MC_Q] \cdot MP_A^* = 1$

As before, a firm should advertise up to the point where the last dollar it spends on advertising just increases its net revenues by a dollar. Assessing the firm's marginal product of advertising, however, is more difficult. An increase of one dollar in the firm's advertising may be expected to increase its rivals' advertising, which would likely reduce the demand for the firm's output, $(\delta Q/\delta A')(dA'/dA) < 0$, which, at least in part, offsets the direct effect of the firm's own advertising on its demand, $(\delta Q/\delta A) > 0$. In particular, the oligopolist can only speculate on the effect of its advertising expenditures on its rivals' advertising. We can use game theory to illustrate this uncertainty.

Uncertainty in Advertising In markets characterized by product differentiation, firms need to advertise. Consumers have to be informed about the available products and firms use advertising to shore up brand loyalties.

Suppose an oligopolist is considering whether to maintain or increase its current level of advertising. Its rivals are contemplating the same decision. See Game 4, where the hypothetical expected profits (in hundred thousand dollars per week) are given.

Game 4: Advertising

RIVALS

	Maintain advertising	Increase advertising
Maintain advertising	(.5, 1)	(.3, 1.2)
Increase advertising	(.6, .6)	(.4, .8) *

FIRM

Firm's dominant strategy

Rivals' dominant strategy

The highest profits for the firm (.6) are realized with an unmatched increase in its advertising expenditures. The same is true for its rivals (profits of 1.2). The next highest profits for both parties, however, would be achieved when the existing levels of advertising expenditures are maintained. Yet, both the firm and its rivals have dominant strategies of increasing advertising. The resulting advertising "war" yields only the third highest level of profits: .4 for the firm and .8 for the rival firms'.

In short, fearful of losing market share, the firms increase advertising—although the additional costs exceed the additional revenues generated—in part due to the canceling-out effect of the competitive advertising. Consumers end up paying higher prices for the more heavily advertised products. Nevertheless, advertising expenditures, while perhaps inflated, would not continue to rise unabated. Recognition of the likely diminishing returns to advertising limits this form of non-price competition.

In our discussion of duopoly and oligopoly, we highlighted the role of uncertainty. Firms may not know the demand curves they face—in part because their rivals' actions and reactions are not known. Consequently, to model these forms of imperfect competition, we must impose rules of behavior on the firms. Game theory provides a useful framework for modeling such interdependent decision making.[14] In the simple games for oligopolists presented, we abstracted by aggregating the firm's rivals—assuming that the rivals behaved similarly enough to be considered collectively as one. In practice, of course, this need not be the case, which adds to the challenge of modeling and understanding this prevalent form of industrial organization. In the next two chapters, using the technique of constrained optimization, we continue our study of the firm. Then, in Chapter 12, we analyze consumer behavior.

---

[14]Needless to say, the applications of game theory extend well beyond the theory of oligopolistic behavior to include any situation of strategic interaction in the social sciences.

❖ KEY TERMS

Economics

- duopoly (p. 279)
- game theory (p. 309)
- kinked demand curve (p. 302)
- planned inventory investment (p. 298)
- oligopoly (p. 296)
- reaction functions (p. 289)
- unplanned inventory investment (p. 298)

Mathematics

- dominant strategy (p. 309)
- Nash equilibrium (p. 310)

❖ PROBLEMS

1. Consider two strawberry fields situated side-by-side, where customers pick their own strawberries. The market demand schedule is: $Q^d = 60 - 4P$, where

   Q = quantity demanded of strawberries (in hundred boxes per week)

   P = price of a box of strawberries (in dollars)

   Assume that the marginal costs of supplying strawberries to the farmers, A and B, who own the fields, are zero. Further, assume that farmer A is the first to open for business, and temporarily operates as a monopolist. When farmer B enters, however, the equilibrium market output sold in each period is divided evenly between the two farmers, since the strawberries in the two fields are homogeneous.

   a) Using the Cournot assumption that each farmer regards the other's output as fixed, find the equilibrium output, price, and total revenue for each farmer for the first two periods. Derive the reaction functions of farmers A and B and then determine the long-run equilibrium values for output, price, and total revenue for each farmer.

   b) Using the Edgeworth assumption that each farmer regards the other's price as fixed, find the equilibrium output, price, and total revenue for each farmer for the first two periods. Assume when each farmer sets a lower price in order to capture all of the market sales, the price decrease is $.75. Determine the long-run equilibrium values for output, price, and total revenue for each farmer.

   c) Using the Chamberlin assumption, where the farmers recognize their interdependence and cooperate, find the equilibrium output, price, and total revenue for each farmer.

   d) Which of the three models, (Cournot, Edgeworth, or Chamberlin) do you consider to be the most realistic? Discuss why.

2. Repeat the analysis in Problem 1, parts a)–c) when the marginal cost of supplying strawberries equals $1.50 for each farmer.

3. Repeat the analysis in Problem 1, parts a)–c) when the marginal costs of supplying strawberries differ between the firms, with $MC_A = c_A = \$1.00$ and $MC_B = c_B = \$2.00$.

4. Repeat the analysis in Problem 1, part c) only, when the marginal costs of supplying strawberries for farmers A and B are, respectively: $MC_A = c_A = .8Q_A$ and $MC_B = c_B = 1.2Q_B$.

5. Given an oligopolist who does not know the demand curve for its output. The firm, however, expects sales equal to 9 (thousand units per week) and has planned inventory investment equal to 1 (thousand units per week). The short-run total cost function of the firm is:

$$STC(Q) = .083Q^3 - 2Q^2 + 18Q + 5$$

where Q = output of the firm (thousand units per week).

The oligopolist sets the price for its output, P, equal to a percentage markup, m, over the average total cost of producing the selected level of output. The markup of the firm is 20%, that is, $m = .20$.

Find the price set by the firm, the total revenue, total cost, and total profit, and the unplanned inventory investment for the firm if the market demand for its output is
a) $Q^d = 26 - 2P$
b) $Q^d = 24 - 2P$

6. Given an oligopolist producing an output of $Q_0 = 10$ (thousand units per week) and charging a price of $P_0 = \$8.2$. The total cost function of the oligopolist is

$$STC(Q) = .083Q^3 - 2Q^2 + 19.5Q + 5$$

Not knowing its rivals' reactions to a change in its price, the firm assumes that the demand schedule it faces is

$$Q^d = 30.5 - 2.5P \quad \text{(if its rivals match any changes in its price)}$$

$$Q^{d'} = 92 - 10P \quad \text{(if its rivals do not match any change in its price)}$$

a) Determine the initial profits of the firm.
b) If the firm assumes that its rivals would not match an increase in its price, but would match a decrease in its price, plot the firm's kinked demand curve and associated marginal revenue curve.
c) Find the firm's profits if it were to increase its price from $P_0 = \$8.2$ to $P_1 = \$8.5$ when
   i) its rivals do not match its price increase
   ii) its rivals match its price increase.
d) Find the firm's profits if it were to decrease its price from $P_0 = \$8.2$ to $P_2 = \$8.0$ when
   i) its rivals match its price decrease
   ii) its rivals do not match its price decrease.
e) Does it appear that this oligopolist would want to change its price? Discuss.

7. Repeat the analysis in Problem 5 when the oligopolist's total cost function is

$$STC(Q) = .083Q^3 - 2Q^2 + 18Q + 5$$

8. For each of the following games, with the expected profit payoffs (in hundred thousand dollars per month), find the solution and explain your reasoning.

a) Game 1

Possible Price Decrease with a Decrease in the Costs of Production for All Firms

		RIVALS	
		No change in price	Price decrease
FIRM	No change in price	(12, 33)	(7, 36)
	Price decrease	(15, 29)	(10, 31)

b) Game 2

Possible Price Increase with a Shift in Consumers' Tastes in Favor of Firm's Product

		RIVALS	
		No change in price	Price increase
FIRM	No change in price	(10, 14)	(12, 10)
	Price increase	(8, 16)	(11, 12)

c) Game 3

Possible Price Increase after Firm Negotiates a Costly Labor Contract

		RIVALS	
		No change in price	Price increase
FIRM	No change in price	(2, 10)	(3, 8)
	Price increase	(1, 12)	(4, 9)

d) Game 4

Possible Price Decrease with a Decrease in the Market Demand

		RIVALS	
		No change in price	Price decrease
FIRM	No change in price	$(-1, -3)$	$(-2, 1)$
	Price decrease	$(2, -6)$	$(0, 0)$

e) Game 5

Possible Price Decrease with an Increase in Firm's Inventories

		RIVALS	
		No change in price	Price decrease
FIRM	No change in price	$(-1, 5)$	$(-3, 6)$
	Price decrease	$(2, 2)$	$(0, 1)$

f) Game 6

Possible Decrease in Advertising Expenditures

		RIVALS	
		No change in advertising	Decrease in advertising
FIRM	No change in advertising	$(5, 12)$	$(6, 10)$
	Decrease in advertising	$(4, 13)$	$(7, 15)$

g) Game 7

Possible Increase in Advertising Expenditures with Rivals' Increase in Inventories

RIVALS

	No change in advertising	Increase in advertising
No change in advertising	$(4, 2)$	$(3, 4)$
Increase in advertising	$(2, 0)$	$(1, 3)$

FIRM

❖ ANSWERS TO PRACTICE PROBLEMS

9.1 a) Under the Cournot assumption, the equilibrium output, price, and total revenue for firms A and B for the first two periods are

Period 1: $(\overline{Q}_A)_1 = 15 = (\overline{Q}_B)_1; (\overline{P}_A)_1 = \$2.5 = (\overline{P}_B)_1; (\overline{TR}_A)_1 = \$37.5 = (\overline{TR}_B)_1$

Period 2: $(\overline{Q}_A)_2 = 13.125 = (\overline{Q}_B)_2; (\overline{P}_A)_2 = \$3.438 = (\overline{P}_B)_2; (\overline{TR}_A)_2 = \$45.124 = (\overline{TR}_B)_2$

b) Under the Edgeworth assumption, the equilibrium output, price, and total revenue for firms A and B for the first two periods are

Period 1: $(\overline{Q}_A)_1 = 12 = (\overline{Q}_B)_1; (\overline{P}_A)_1 = \$4 = (\overline{P}_B)_1; (\overline{TR}_A)_1 = \$48 = (\overline{TR}_B)_1$

Period 2: $(\overline{Q}_A)_2 = 16 = (\overline{Q}_B)_2; (\overline{P}_A)_2 = \$2 = (\overline{P}_B)_2; (\overline{TR}_A)_2 = \$32 = (\overline{TR}_B)_2$

c) Under the Chamberlin assumption, the equilibrium output, price, and total revenue for firms A and B are: $\overline{Q}_A = 10 = \overline{Q}_B; \overline{P}_A = \$5 = \overline{P}_B; \overline{TR}_A = \$50 = \overline{TR}_B$.

9.2 a) The reaction functions are: firm A, $Q_A = 16 - (1/2)Q_B$ and firm B, $Q_B = 16 - (1/2)Q_A$. The equilibrium outputs for the two firms are: $\overline{Q}_A = 10.\overline{6} = \overline{Q}_B$. The market price is $\overline{P} = \$4.6$.

b) The new reaction functions are: firm A, $Q_A = 15 - (1/2)Q_B$ and firm B, $Q_B = 17 - (1/2)Q_A$. The new equilibrium outputs and market price are: $\overline{Q}_A = 8.\overline{6}$, $\overline{Q}_B = 12.\overline{6}$, and $\overline{P} = \$4.\overline{6}$.

9.3 a) The prices set by firms A and B and associated outputs are: $\overline{P}_A = \$6 = \overline{P}_B$ and $\overline{Q}_A = 16 = \overline{Q}_B$. The market equilibrium price is $\overline{P} = \$2 = c_A = c_B$.

b) The new prices set by firms A and B and associated outputs are: $\overline{P}_A = \$6.25$ and $\overline{P}_B = \$5.75; \overline{Q}_A = 15$ and $\overline{Q}_B = 17$. The market equilibrium price is $\overline{P} = \$2$. Firm B would likely emerge as a monopolist since the market price of $P = \$2$ is less than firm A's marginal cost (and average variable cost) of $c_A = \$2.50$.

9.4 a) The profit-maximizing outputs and price for firms A and B are: $Q_A = 8 = Q_B$ and $\overline{P}_A = \overline{P}_B = \overline{P} = \$6$.

b) With the lower constant marginal cost of production, firm B becomes a monopolist with a profit-maximizing output of $\overline{Q}_B = \overline{Q} = 17$ and price of $P_B = \overline{P} = \$5.75$.

9.5 a) Profits equal \$3.32 (thousand per week), a decrease of \$1.00 thousand per week. Unplanned inventory investment equals $-.1$ (thousand units per week).

b) Profits equal \$2.07 (thousand per week), a decrease of \$2.25 (thousand per week). Unplanned inventory investment equals $+.7$ (thousand units per week).

c) Profits equal \$7.15 (thousand per week), an increase of \$2.83 (thousand per week). Unplanned inventory investment equals -1.5 (thousand units per week).

9.6 a) The firm's kinked demand schedule is: $Q^d = 10 - P$ (for $P < 6$) and $Q^d = 16 - 2P$ (for $P \geq 6$). The firm's marginal revenue schedule is: $MR = 10 - 2Q$ (for $Q > 4$) and $MR' = 8 - Q$ (for $Q \leq 4$). The vertical gap in the marginal revenue curve occurs at $Q = 4$ and equals $MR'(4) - MR(4) = \$4.00 - \$2.00 = \$2.00$.

b) The firm's percentage markup is 20% ($m = .2$). The initial level of profits equals \$4.00 (hundred thousand per week).

c) The increase in the firm's price reduces its profits to \$2.10 (hundred thousand per week). The decrease in the firm's price reduces its profits to \$3.13 (hundred thousand per week).

9.7 There are no dominant strategies in this game. The two solutions are the Nash equilibria represented in the upper left-hand cell (where neither the firm nor its rivals change prices) and the lower right-hand cell (where the firm and its rivals increase prices).

THEORY OF THE FIRM: CONSTRAINED OPTIMIZATION

So far we have dealt with unconstrained or free optima. That is, we have found extreme values for objective functions without any restrictions placed on the choice or independent variables—except for requiring economic relevance in terms of non-negative prices and quantities. Under constrained optimization we seek to find extrema subject to a set of conditions placed on the choice variables. Common examples in economics are households seeking the utility-maximizing combination of expenditures on goods and services under a budget constraint and firms seeking the cost-minimizing combination of inputs for producing selected levels of output.

We begin this chapter by illustrating the difference between unconstrained and constrained optimization with a specific example. Next we present a general technique for constrained optimization known as the Lagrange multiplier method. In the second part of the chapter we apply constrained optimization to firm behavior in the long run.

OPTIMIZATION UNDER CONSTRAINTS: AN EXAMPLE

Consider an unregulated monopolist providing services to two types of customers, say a power company furnishing electricity to residential and commercial users. Suppose the profit function of the monopolist is given to be

$$\Pi(x, y) = 64x - 2x^2 + 4xy - 4y^2 + 32y - 14$$

where x and y are the quantities of service provided to the two types of customers. The monopolist seeks to determine the profit-maximizing levels of service for each of the customers.

The first-order conditions are

$$\Pi_x = \delta\Pi/\delta x = 64 - 4x + 4y = 0$$

$$\Pi_y = \delta\Pi/\delta y = 4x - 8y + 32 = 0$$

We can solve for the critical values of x and y using Cramer's rule. Rewriting the first-order conditions to isolate the choice variables on the left-hand side:

$$-4x + 4y = -64$$

$$4x - 8y = -32$$

and then writing the system in matrix notation:

$$\begin{bmatrix} -4 & 4 \\ 4 & -8 \end{bmatrix} \begin{bmatrix} x \\ y \end{bmatrix} = \begin{bmatrix} -64 \\ -32 \end{bmatrix}$$

we can see that the coefficient matrix is nonsingular, $\begin{vmatrix} -4 & 4 \\ 4 & -8 \end{vmatrix} = 16 \neq 0$, so a unique solution exists. We use the subscript "0" to identify the initial equilibrium values. Applying Cramer's rule, we find

$$\bar{x}_0 = \frac{\begin{vmatrix} -64 & 4 \\ -32 & -8 \end{vmatrix}}{\begin{vmatrix} -4 & 4 \\ 4 & -8 \end{vmatrix}} = \frac{640}{16} = 40$$

$$\bar{y}_0 = \frac{\begin{vmatrix} -4 & -64 \\ 4 & -32 \end{vmatrix}}{\begin{vmatrix} -4 & 4 \\ 4 & -8 \end{vmatrix}} = \frac{384}{16} = 24$$

The associated level of profits is then:

$$\bar{\Pi}(\bar{x}, \bar{y}) = 64\bar{x} - 2\bar{x}^2 + 4\bar{x}\bar{y} - 4\bar{y}^2 + 32\bar{y} - 14$$

$$= 64(40) - 2(40)^2 + 4(40)(24) - 4(24)^2 + 32(24) - 14$$

$$= 1,650$$

We check the second-order conditions by partially differentiating the first-order conditions with respect to the choice variables and evaluating the Hessian.

$$\Pi_{xx} = \frac{\delta(\delta\Pi/\delta x)}{\delta x} = -4$$

$$\Pi_{xy} = \frac{\delta(\delta\Pi/\delta y)}{\delta x} = 4$$

$$\Pi_{yx} = \frac{\delta(\delta\Pi/\delta x)}{\delta y} = 4$$

$$\Pi_{yy} = \frac{\delta(\delta\Pi/\delta y)}{\delta y} = -8$$

$$|H| = \begin{vmatrix} \Pi_{11} & \Pi_{12} \\ \Pi_{21} & \Pi_{22} \end{vmatrix} = \begin{vmatrix} \Pi_{xx} & \Pi_{xy} \\ \Pi_{yx} & \Pi_{yy} \end{vmatrix} = \begin{vmatrix} -4 & 4 \\ 4 & -8 \end{vmatrix}$$

Consistent with a maximum we find: $|H_1| = -4 < 0$ and $|H_2| = |H| = 16 > 0$. Therefore, the unconstrained profit-maximizing levels of outputs are $\bar{x}_0 = 40$ and $\bar{y}_0 = 24$, yielding a level of profits of $\bar{\Pi}_0 = 1,650$.

Now suppose that the government regulates the monopolist by requiring a total output or level of services provided equal to 79 units, that is, $x + y = 79$. For example, in the case of natural monopolies, like public utilities, the economies of scale in production are large relative to the market demand. That is, the market demand curve intersects the long-run average-cost curve of the natural monopolist on the region of decreasing average costs. Consequently, competition is not economically feasible; however, an unregulated monopolist would produce a profit-maximizing output significantly below the level that captures all of the scale economies. Regulatory commissions have required the natural monopolist to produce a higher level of output, (where the long-run average cost curve intersects the market demand), and charge a lower unit price (equal to the long run average cost, which incorporates a "normal" rate of profits or "fair" return on the invested capital).

Here, we assume that the monopolist is still free to determine the profit-maximizing mix of the outputs so long as the total output constraint is satisfied. We can see that the services provided to the two types of customers are no longer independent. Here, we can write $x = 79 - y$. The problem becomes one of constrained optimization. The regulated monopolist seeks to maximize profits, $\Pi(x, y) = 64x - 2x^2 + 4xy - 4y^2 + 32y - 14$, subject to the constraint, $x + y = 79$.

Fortunately, we can easily turn this problem into one with one choice variable by incorporating the constraint into the objective function. Substituting $(79 - y)$ in for x in the objective function gives

$$\Pi(y) = 64(79 - y) - 2(79 - y)^2 + 4(79 - y)y - 4y^2 + 32y - 14$$

which reduces to: $\Pi(y) = -7,440 + 600y - 10y^2$. Finding the critical point, and identifying the new equilibrium values with the subscript "1," we have

$$d\Pi/dy = 600 - 20y = 0$$

$$\bar{y}_1 = 30$$

Thus,

$$\bar{x}_1 = 79 - \bar{y}_1 = 49$$

Checking the second-order condition is easy. For a maximum we need

$$\frac{d(d\Pi/dy)}{dy} = \frac{d^2\Pi}{dy^2} < 0$$

Here

$$\frac{d^2\Pi}{dy^2} = -20 < 0.$$

The profit-maximizing level of profits under the output constraint is

$$\overline{\Pi}(\overline{y}_1) = -7{,}440 + 600\overline{y} - 10\overline{y}^2 = -7{,}440 + 600(30) - 10(30)^2 = 1{,}560.$$

Not surprisingly, compared to the unconstrained maximum, the level of profits has decreased.

While substituting the constraint directly into the objective function seems straightforward enough in this example—and even made the optimization simpler—this technique quickly becomes unwieldy as the number of choice variables increases. Furthermore, using this technique of substitution is possible only if the constraint is expressed in explicit functional form. An alternative approach, however, is available for solving constrained optimization problems. The Lagrange multiplier method incorporates the constraint into an expanded objective function called the *Lagrangian*.

USING THE LAGRANGE MULTIPLIER METHOD

Return to the problem of the regulated monopolist seeking to maximize profits, $\Pi(x,y) = 64x - 2x^2 + 4xy - 4y^2 + 32y - 14$, subject to the total output constraint, $x + y = 79$. We set up the Lagrangian function with three variables: the original choice variables, x and y, representing the outputs to the two types of customers, and an additional variable, λ, known as the *Lagrange multiplier*. The Lagrangian function, written in general form as $L(\lambda, x, y)$, consists of the original objective function, $\Pi(x, y)$, plus the product of the Lagrange multiplier, λ, and the constraint, expressed as $79 - x - y = 0$.

$$L(\lambda, x, y) = 64x - 2x^2 + 4xy - 4y^2 + 32y - 14 + \lambda \cdot (79 - x - y)$$

We proceed as before with the first-order conditions, except now there are three "choice" variables to consider. Partially differentiating the Lagrangian function with respect to $\lambda, x,$ and y and setting the results equal to zero gives the following:
First-order conditions:

$$\delta L / \delta \lambda = 79 - x - y = 0$$

$$\delta L / \delta x = 64 - 4x + 4y - \lambda = 0$$

$$\delta L / \delta y = 4x - 8y + 32 - \lambda = 0$$

Note that the first of these conditions, $\delta L / \delta \lambda = 79 - x - y = 0$, ensures that the output constraint, $x + y = 79$, is satisfied.

We can solve this system of three equations in three variables using Cramer's rule. Rewriting the first-order conditions as

$$-x - y = -79$$

$$-4x + 4y - \lambda = -64$$

$$4x - 8y - \lambda = -32$$

the system in matrix notation is

$$\begin{bmatrix} 0 & -1 & -1 \\ -1 & -4 & 4 \\ -1 & 4 & -8 \end{bmatrix} \begin{bmatrix} \lambda \\ x \\ y \end{bmatrix} = \begin{bmatrix} -79 \\ -64 \\ -32 \end{bmatrix}$$

The determinant of the coefficient matrix does not vanish, so a unique solution exists (which we knew from our earlier working of this problem). The optimal values for x, y, and λ are

$$\bar{\lambda}_1 = \frac{\begin{vmatrix} -79 & -1 & -1 \\ -64 & -4 & 4 \\ -32 & 4 & -8 \end{vmatrix}}{\begin{vmatrix} 0 & -1 & -1 \\ -1 & -4 & 4 \\ -1 & 4 & -8 \end{vmatrix}} = \frac{-240}{+20} = -12$$

$$\bar{x}_1 = \frac{\begin{vmatrix} 0 & -79 & -1 \\ -1 & -64 & 4 \\ -1 & -32 & -8 \end{vmatrix}}{\begin{vmatrix} 0 & -1 & -1 \\ -1 & -4 & 4 \\ -1 & 4 & -8 \end{vmatrix}} = \frac{+980}{+20} = 49$$

and $\bar{y}_1 = 79 - \bar{x}_1 = 30$, as before when we substituted the constraint directly into the objective function. The constrained maximum level of profits is $\bar{\Pi}_1 = 1,560$. With the Lagrange multiplier method, however, we obtain additional information—the value of the Lagrange multiplier, $\bar{\lambda}$.

We will interpret the Lagrange multiplier more formally later. For now, consider the effect of tightening the output constraint on the regulated monopolist by 1 unit. That is, suppose the monopolist were required to produce 80 units of output, up from 79 units, for example, to accommodate growth in market demand. The new constraint is $x + y = 80$. The constraint has become more binding because the monopolist is pushed further from the unconstrained optimum output of 64 units (where $\bar{x}_0 = 40$ and $\bar{y}_0 = 24$).

The new Lagrangian function is

$$L(\lambda, x, y) = 64x - 2x^2 + 4xy - 4y^2 + 32y - 14 + \lambda \cdot (80 - x - y)$$

Taking the first-order conditions and solving we find: $\bar{x}_2 = 49.6$, $\bar{y}_2 = 30.4$, and $\bar{\lambda}_2 = -12.8$. The new constrained level of profits is $\bar{\Pi}_2 = 1,547.6$. (You may want to confirm these results by solving yourself.) Note that tightening the constraint by one unit reduces profits by approximately 12 units. We will develop this notion below.

PRACTICE PROBLEMS 10.1 AND 10.2

10.1 Given the objective function, $z = 50x - 3x^2 + 6xy - 4y^2 + 30y - 200$:

    a) Find the critical values for the variables x and y.

     b) Find the optimum value for z.

     c) Check the second-order conditions to establish the type of extremum.

     d) Find the new critical values for the variables x and y given the constraint:
        $x + y = 80$.

     e) Find the constrained optimum value of z.

     f) Find the value of the Lagrange multiplier.

10.2 Given the objective function, $z = -20x + 5x^2 + 4xy + 2y^2 - 10y + 25$:

     a) Find the critical values for the variables x and y.

     b) Find the optimum value for z.

     c) Check the second-order conditions to establish the type of extremum.

     d) Find the new critical values for the variables x and y given the constraint:
        $2x + y = 3$.

     e) Find the constrained optimum value of z.

     f) Find the value of the Lagrange multiplier.

(The answers are at the end of the chapter.)

LAGRANGE MULTIPLIER METHOD

We begin with the simplest case: the objective function has two choice variables and there is one constraint. We can then extend the analysis, adding choice variables and constraints—with the proviso that the number of choice variables must be equal to or greater than the number of constraints.

The general optimization problem with two choice variables, x and y, and one constraint, is to optimize $z = z(x, y)$, subject to a constraint, represented by $g(x, y) = c$, where c is a constant. The Lagrangian function is:

$$L(\lambda, x, y) = z(x, y) + \lambda \cdot [c - g(x, y)]$$

where, as before, λ, is the Lagrange multiplier. In effect, we incorporate the constraint into an expanded objective function, the Lagrangian, and add a variable, the Lagrange multiplier.

To find the extremum for the Lagrangian function, we solve the first-order conditions. Partially differentiating the Lagrangian with respect to the Lagrange multiplier and the choice variables and setting the results equal to zero gives the first-order conditions:

$$\delta L/\delta \lambda = c - g(x, y) = 0 \qquad \text{(The constraint is satisfied.)}$$

$$\delta L/\delta x = z_x - \lambda g_x = 0$$

$$\delta L/\delta y = z_y - \lambda g_y = 0$$

where $z_x = \delta z/\delta x$, $z_y = \delta z/\delta y$, $g_x = \delta g/\delta x$, and $g_y = \delta g/\delta y$ are first-order partial derivatives. The first-order conditions imply that

$$z_x = \lambda g_x \quad \text{and} \quad z_y = \lambda g_y$$

or

$$z_x/g_x = \lambda = z_y/g_y$$

Recall that for an unconstrained optimization for the objective function, $z = z(x, y)$, the first-order conditions required for $dz = z_x\, dx + z_y dy = 0$ are, for any dx and dy, arbitrary changes in the choice variables (not both equal to zero), that $z_x = z_y = 0$. Now, with a constraint, $g(x, y) = c$, changes in the choice variables, dx and dy, are no longer independent. To see that the variations in x and y are related, totally differentiate the constraint, $g(x, y) = c$.

$$dg = g_x\, dx + g_y\, dy = dc$$

Since c is a given constant, $dc = 0$. Thus,

$$g_x\, dx + g_y\, dy = 0$$

Isolating dy, we find

$$dy = -(g_x/g_y)\, dx$$

Arbitrary changes in x, (dx), determine the change in y, (dy), along with the values of the first-order partials, $(g_x$ and $g_y)$, from the constraint function. Note, here we require $g_y \neq 0$, and for that matter, $g_x \neq 0$, since we could have as easily solved for dx.

Before deriving the second-order conditions, we need to return to the Implicit Function Theorem and extend the analysis to a simultaneous system of n equations with n endogenous variables.

IMPLICIT FUNCTIONS IN SIMULTANEOUS EQUATIONS SYSTEMS

Recall from Chapter 6 that the Implicit Function Theorem established the conditions whereby a general function of the form, $F(y; x_1, x_2, \ldots x_m) = 0$, defined an implicit function, $y = f(x_1, x_2, \ldots x_m)$. Now we extend the Implicit Function Theorem to a system of equations.

IMPLICIT FUNCTION THEOREM FOR A SYSTEM OF EQUATIONS

Given a set of n simultaneous equations with n endogenous variables, $y_1, y_2, \ldots y_n$, and m exogenous variables, $x_1, x_2, \ldots x_m$, written in general form as

$$F^1\, (y_1, y_2, \ldots y_n; x_1, x_2, \ldots x_m) = 0$$

$$F^2\, (y_1, y_2, \ldots y_n; x_1, x_2, \ldots x_m) = 0$$

$$\vdots$$

$$F^n\, (y_1, y_2, \ldots y_n; x_1, x_2, \ldots x_m) = 0$$

If this system of simultaneous equations, $F^1, F^2, \ldots F^n$, has continuous partial derivatives with respect to all of the y and x variables, and if at a point, $(y_{10}, y_{20}, \ldots y_{n0}; x_{10}, x_{20}, \ldots x_{m0})$, satisfying the equations, the following Jacobian determinant

$$|J| = \left| \frac{\delta(F^1, F^2, \ldots F^n)}{\delta(y_1, y_2, \ldots y_n)} \right| = \begin{vmatrix} \delta F^1/\delta y_1 & \delta F^1/\delta y_2 & \cdots & \delta F^1/\delta y_n \\ \delta F^2/\delta y_1 & \delta F^2/\delta y_2 & \cdots & \delta F^2/\delta y_n \\ \cdot & \cdot & & \cdot \\ \cdot & \cdot & & \cdot \\ \cdot & \cdot & & \cdot \\ \delta F^n/\delta y_1 & \delta F^n/\delta y_2 & \cdots & \delta F^n/\delta y_n \end{vmatrix}$$

is nonsingular, that is, $|J| \neq 0$, in an m-dimensional neighborhood around the point $(x_{10}, x_{20}, \ldots x_{m0})$, then the n implicit functions in the m exogenous variables

$$y_1 = f^1 (x_1, x_2, \ldots x_m)$$

$$y_2 = f^2 (x_1, x_2, \ldots x_m)$$

$$\cdot$$
$$\cdot$$
$$\cdot$$

$$y_n = f^n (x_1, x_2, \ldots x_m)$$

are defined. Moreover, the n implicit functions are continuous and have continuous partial derivatives.

Recall from Chapter 8, if $|J| \neq 0$, then the functions, $F^1, F^2, \ldots F^n$, are functionally independent. We will make use of the Implicit Function Theorem for a system of equations frequently—in particular, for the second-order conditions for constrained optimization problems, for comparative statics, and for clarifying the meaning of the Lagrange multiplier.

INTERPRETATION OF THE LAGRANGE MULTIPLIER

Return to the objective function with two choice variables, $z = z(x, y)$, to be optimized subject to the constraint, $g(x, y) = c$. To find the constrained optimum, we set up the Lagrangian $L(\lambda, x, y) = z(x, y) + \lambda \cdot [c - g(x, y)]$. The first-order conditions are

$$\delta L/\delta \lambda = c - g(x, y) = 0$$

$$\delta L/\delta x = z_x - \lambda g_x = 0$$

$$\delta L/\delta y = z_y - \lambda g_y = 0$$

Solving the first-order conditions would give the critical point and the optimum values for the choice variables, $(\bar{x}, \bar{y})$, as well as the value for the Lagrange multiplier, $(\bar{\lambda})$.

Consider these first-order conditions as a system of simultaneous equations

$$F^j (\lambda, x, y; c) = 0 \qquad j = 1, 2, 3$$

with c as the only exogenous variable in the system, satisfying the Implicit Function Theorem. That is, assume that this system of equations has continuous partial derivatives and, at the constrained critical point, $(\lambda_0, \overline{x}_0, \overline{y}_0)$, the following Jacobian is non-singular.

$$|J| = \left|\frac{\delta(F^1, F^2, F^3)}{\delta(\lambda, x, y)}\right| = \begin{vmatrix} \delta F^1/\delta\lambda & \delta F^1/\delta x & \delta F^1/\delta y \\ \delta F^2/\delta\lambda & \delta F^2/\delta x & \delta F^2/\delta y \\ \delta F^3/\delta\lambda & \delta F^3/\delta x & \delta F^3/\delta y \end{vmatrix}$$

$$= \begin{vmatrix} 0 & -g_x & -g_y \\ -g_x & z_{xx} - \lambda g_{xx} & z_{yx} - \lambda g_{yx} \\ -g_y & z_{xy} - \lambda g_{xy} & z_{yy} - \lambda g_{yy} \end{vmatrix} \neq 0$$

Then we can say that the first-order conditions, $F^j(\lambda, x, y; c) = 0$ define a set of implicit functions

$$\overline{\lambda} = \lambda(c)$$

$$\overline{x} = x(c)$$

and

$$\overline{y} = y(c)$$

where each endogenous variable in the system can be written as a function of all the exogenous variables in the system (here only c) and the optimum values ($\overline{x}$, $\overline{y}$, and $\overline{\lambda}$) are evaluated at the critical point found from the solution of the first-order conditions. (Recall that if $|J| \neq 0$, then the first-order conditions represent functionally independent equations.) Intuitively, with a change in the constraint, dc, we would expect to find new optimum values for the choice variables and the objective function.

That is, since the optimum value for z, call it $\overline{z}$, depends on the optimum values of λ, x, and y,

$$\overline{z} = z(\overline{x}, \overline{y}) + \overline{\lambda} \cdot [c - g(\overline{x}, \overline{y})]$$

taking the total derivative of $\overline{z}$ with respect to c (a comparative static experiment) gives

$$d\overline{z}/dc = z_x(d\overline{x}/dc) + z_y(d\overline{y}/dc) + [c - g(\overline{x}, \overline{y})](d\overline{\lambda}/dc) + \overline{\lambda} \cdot [1 - g_x(d\overline{x}/dc) - g_y(d\overline{y}/dc)]$$

Collecting like terms, we can write

$$d\overline{z}/dc = (z_x - \overline{\lambda}g_x)(d\overline{x}/dc) + (z_y - \overline{\lambda}g_y)(d\overline{y}/dc) + [c - g(\overline{x}, \overline{y})](d\overline{\lambda}/dc) + \overline{\lambda}$$

From the first-order conditions, at the critical point we have

$$c - g(\overline{x}, \overline{y}) = 0$$

$$z_x - \overline{\lambda}g_x = 0$$

$$z_y - \overline{\lambda}g_y = 0$$

Thus, the first three terms on the right-hand side of the derivative, $d\bar{z}/dc$, drop out and we have

$$d\bar{z}/dc = \bar{\lambda}$$

The optimal value of the Lagrange multiplier indicates the instantaneous effect of an infinitesimal change in the constraint (dc) on the optimal value of the objective function ($d\bar{z}$). Recall the earlier example of the regulated monopolist where the value of $\bar{\lambda}$ was equal to -12 when the constraint was $x + y = 79$. Then, tightening the constraint by 1 unit ($\Delta c = +1$, more than an infinitesimal change) reduced the maximum profits of the monopolist by 12.4 units ($\Delta\Pi = -12.4$, or approximately the value of the Lagrange multiplier).

SECOND-ORDER CONDITIONS

As with an unconstrained optimization, unless we have knowledge about the objective function, for example, strictly concave or strictly convex, we have to check the second-order conditions to determine the type of extremum. Here with our objective function $z = z(x, y)$ subject to $g(x, y) = c$, we know that the variations in the choice variables are no longer independent. In fact, we showed that differentiating the constraint and "solving" for dy gave: $dy = -(g_x/g_y)\, dx$.

Our task is to sign the second-order total differential d^2z. For a critical point from the first-order conditions, showing that $d^2z > 0$ will be sufficient to establish a *relative minimum*. On the other hand, if $d^2z < 0$, we have sufficient conditions for a *relative maximum*. Taking the differential of dz, and remembering that with the constraint, dy "depends" on the values of x and y (which determine g_x and g_y), as well as on the arbitrary dx, we have

$$d(dz) = d^2z = \frac{\delta(dz)}{\delta x}dx + \frac{\delta(dy)}{\delta y}dy$$

$$= \frac{\delta(z_x\, dx + z_y\, dy)}{\delta x}dx + \frac{\delta(z_x\, dx + z_y dy)}{\delta y}dy$$

$$= \left[z_{xx}\, dx + z_{xy}\, dy + z_y\left(\frac{\delta(dy)}{\delta x}\right)\right]dx + \left[z_{yx}\, dx + z_{yy}\, dy + z_y\left(\frac{\delta(dy)}{\delta y}\right)\right]dy$$

$$= z_{xx}\, dx^2 + 2z_{xy}\, dx\, dy + z_{yy}\, dy^2 + z_y\left[\frac{\delta(dy)}{\delta x}dx + \frac{\delta(dy)}{\delta y}dy\right]$$

The first three terms of this expression for d^2z are the same as for the unconstrained optimization. We now have an additional term,

$$z_y\left[\frac{\delta(dy)}{\delta x}dx + \frac{\delta(dy)}{\delta y}dy\right] = z_y\, d(dy) = z_y\, d^2y, \text{ where } d^2y = d(dy).$$

Therefore, with the constrained optimization we can write

$$(1)\ d^2z = z_{xx}\, dx^2 + 2z_{xy}\, dx\,dy + z_{yy}\, dy^2 + z_y\, d^2y$$

We need to deal with the constraint directly. Totally differentiating $g = g(x, y) = c$, we obtain $dg = g_x\, dx + g_y\, dy = dc = 0$ (since c is a constant). Taking the second-order total differential of dg gives

$$d(dg) = d^2g = \frac{\delta(g_x\, dx + g_y\, dy)}{\delta x}\, dx + \frac{\delta(g_x\, dx + g_y\, dy)}{\delta y}\, dy$$

$$= \left[g_{xx}\, dx + g_{xy}\, dy + g_y\, \frac{\delta(dy)}{\delta x} \right] dx + \left[g_{yx}\, dx + g_{yy}\, dy + g_y\, \frac{\delta(dy)}{\delta y} \right] dy$$

$$= g_{xx}\, dx^2 + 2g_{xy}\, dx\, dy + g_{yy}\, dy^2 + g_y\left[\frac{\delta(dy)}{\delta x}\, dx + \frac{\delta(dy)}{\delta y}\, dy \right]$$

$$= g_{xx}\, dx^2 + 2g_{xy}\, dx\, dy + g_{yy}\, dy^2 + g_y\, d(dy)$$

Since $d(dy) = d^2y$, we can write $d(dg) = d^2g$ as

$$(2)\ d^2g = g_{xx}\, dx^2 + 2g_{xy}\, dx\, dy + g_{yy}\, dy^2 + g_y\, d^2y = 0$$

Isolating d^2y in equation (2) on the left-hand side gives

$$d^2y = -\left[\frac{g_{xx}\, dx^2 + 2g_{xy}\, dx\, dy + g_{yy}\, dy^2}{g_y} \right]$$

Note that again we restrict $g_y \neq 0$. Substituting this expression for d^2y into equation (1) for d^2z we find

$$d^2z = z_{xx}\, dx^2 + 2z_{xy}\, dx\, dy + z_{yy}\, dy^2 + z_y\left[\frac{g_{xx}\, dx^2 + 2g_{xy}\, dx\, dy + g_{yy}\, dy^2}{-g_y} \right]$$

Combining like terms, we have

$$(3)\ d^2z = [z_{xx} - (z_y/g_y)\, g_{xx}]\, dx^2 + 2\, [z_{xy} - (z_y/g_y)\, g_{xy}]\, dx\, dy + [z_{yy} - (z_y/g_y)\, g_{yy}]\, dy^2$$

Recall from the first-order conditions that $(z_x/g_x) = (z_y/g_y) = \lambda$; we substitute λ into d^2z and we can write

$$(4)\ d^2z = (z_{xx} - \lambda g_{xx})\, dx^2 + 2(z_{xy} - \lambda g_{xy})\, dx\, dy + (z_{yy} - \lambda g_{yy})\, dy^2$$

Now, if we can sign d^2z for values of dx and dy that satisfy $dg = g_x\, dx + g_y\, dy = 0$, then we can establish the type of extremum.

Let $L_{xx} = z_{xx} - \lambda g_{xx}$, $L_{xy} = z_{xy} - \lambda g_{xy}$, and $L_{yy} = z_{yy} - \lambda g_{yy}$. We can then rewrite equation (4) as

$$(5)\ d^2z = L_{xx}\, dx^2 + 2L_{xy}\, dx\, dy + L_{yy}\, dy^2$$

From the first-order differential of the constraint we showed that: $dy = -(g_x/g_y)\, dx$. Substituting $-(g_x/g_y)\, dx$ for dy in equation (5) gives

$$d^2z = L_{xx}dx^2 - 2(g_x/g_y)L_{xy}\, dx^2 + (-g_x/g_y)^2\, L_{yy}\, dx^2$$

Factoring out $dx^2/(g_y)^2$, we have

$$(6) \ d^2z = [(g_y)^2 \ L_{xx} - 2g_xg_y \ L_{xy} + (-g_x)^2 \ L_{yy}] \ dx^2/(g_y)^2$$

Since $dx^2/(g_y)^2 > 0$ for any dx and g_y, the sign of d^2z depends on the sign of the term in the bracket, $[(g_y)^2 \ L_{xx} - 2g_xg_yL_{xy} + (-g_x)^2 \ L_{yy} \ ]$. This bracketed term is the *negative* of the determinant, $|\overline{H}|$, called a *bordered Hessian*. That is,

$$(g_y)^2 \ L_{xx} - 2g_xg_y \ L_{xy} + (-g_x)^2 \ L_{yy} = - \begin{vmatrix} 0 & -g_x & -g_y \\ -g_x & L_{xx} & L_{xy} \\ -g_y & L_{yx} & L_{yy} \end{vmatrix} = -|\overline{H}|$$

Therefore, if $-|\overline{H}| > 0$, or equivalently $|\overline{H}| < 0$, then $d^2z > 0$ and the extremum is a minimum. If, on the other hand, $-|\overline{H}| < 0$, or $|\overline{H}| > 0$, then $d^2z < 0$ and the extremum is a maximum.

Writing out the bordered Hessian

$$-|\overline{H}| = \begin{vmatrix} 0 & -g_x & -g_y \\ -g_x & z_{xx} - \lambda g_{xx} & z_{xy} - \lambda g_{xy} \\ -g_y & z_{yx} - \lambda g_{yx} & z_{yy} - \lambda g_{yy} \end{vmatrix}$$

we find that the bordered Hessian is identical to the Jacobian obtained by partially differentiating the first-order conditions with respect to the variables, λ, x, and y.[1] That is,

$$|\overline{H}| = |J| = \left| \frac{\delta(F^1, F^2, F^3)}{\delta(\lambda, x, y)} \right| = \left| \frac{\delta(\delta L/\delta \lambda, \delta L/\delta x, \delta L/\delta y)}{\delta(\lambda, x, y)} \right|$$

In sum, given $z = z(x, y)$, subject to $g(x, y) = c$, a critical point or extremum established with the first-order conditions is

a relative minimum: if $|\overline{H}| < 0$, and d^2z is positive definite $(d^2z > 0)$.

a relative maximum: if $|\overline{H}| > 0$, and d^2z is negative definite $(d^2z < 0)$.

Note that if $|\overline{H}| = 0$, then $|J| = 0$, and the first-order conditions are functionally dependent equations.

To illustrate, return to the example of the regulated monopolist, seeking to maximize its profits, $\Pi(x, y) = 64x - 2x^2 + 4xy - 4y^2 + 32y - 14$, subject to the total output constraint, $x + y = 79$. The Lagrangian is

$$L(\lambda, x, y) = 64x - 2x^2 + 4xy - 4y^2 + 32y - 14 + \lambda \cdot (79 - x - y)$$

The first-order conditions are

$$\delta L/\delta \lambda = 79 - x - y = 0 \quad \text{(The output constraint is satisfied.)}$$

$$\delta L/\delta x = 64 - 4x + 4y - \lambda = 0$$

$$\delta L/\delta y = 4x - 8y + 32 - \lambda = 0$$

---

[1]Technically, the bordered Hessian, $|\overline{H}|$, is equivalent to the transpose of the associated Jacobian, $|J'|$. Since the determinant of a matrix, $|J|$, equals the determinant of its transpose, $|J'|$, we can write: $|\overline{H}| = |J| = |J'|$.

Solving the first-order conditions we found the optimum values: $\bar{x} = 49, \bar{y} = 30$, and $\bar{\lambda} = -12$, where the interpretation of $\bar{\lambda}$ is the instantaneous impact on profits of an infinitesimal change in the constraint, $\delta\bar{\Pi}/\delta c = \bar{\lambda}$, and c indicates the total output constraint, here $c = 79$.

Setting up the bordered Hessian, $|\bar{H}|$, by partially differentiating the first-order conditions with respect to λ, x, and y, we obtain

$$|\bar{H}| = \left| \frac{\delta(\delta L/\delta\lambda, \ \delta L/\delta x, \ \delta L/\delta y)}{\delta(\lambda, \ x, \ y)} \right| = |J|$$

$$\left| \frac{\delta(\delta L/\delta\lambda, \ \delta L/\delta x, \ \delta L/\delta y)}{\delta(\lambda, \ x, \ y)} \right| = \begin{vmatrix} \dfrac{\delta(\delta L/\delta\lambda)}{\delta\lambda} & \dfrac{\delta(\delta L/\delta x)}{\delta\lambda} & \dfrac{\delta(\delta L/\delta y)}{\delta\lambda} \\ \dfrac{\delta(\delta L/\delta\lambda)}{\delta x} & \dfrac{\delta(\delta L/\delta x)}{\delta x} & \dfrac{\delta(\delta L/\delta y)}{\delta x} \\ \dfrac{\delta(\delta L/\delta\lambda)}{\delta y} & \dfrac{\delta(\delta L/\delta x)}{\delta y} & \dfrac{\delta(\delta L/\delta y)}{\delta y} \end{vmatrix} = \begin{vmatrix} 0 & -1 & -1 \\ -1 & -4 & 4 \\ -1 & 4 & -8 \end{vmatrix}$$

So

$$|\bar{H}| = 0 \begin{vmatrix} -4 & 4 \\ 4 & -8 \end{vmatrix} + 1 \begin{vmatrix} -1 & 4 \\ -1 & -8 \end{vmatrix} - 1 \begin{vmatrix} -1 & -4 \\ -1 & 4 \end{vmatrix} = 0 + 12 - (-8) = 20 > 0$$

Thus, we do have a constrained maximum at $\bar{x} = 49$ and $\bar{y} = 30$.

PRACTICE PROBLEMS 10.3 AND 10.4

10.3 Return to Practice Problem 10.1 and check the second-order condition for the constrained optimization: maximize $z = 50x - 3x^2 + 6xy - 4y^2 + 30y - 200$, subject to the constraint, $x + y = 80$.

10.4 Return to Practice Problem 10.2 and check the second-order condition for the constrained optimization: minimize $z = -20x + 5x^2 + 4xy + 2y^2 - 10y + 25$, subject to the constraint, $2x + y = 3$.

(The answers are at the end of the chapter.)

EXTENSION OF LAGRANGE MULTIPLIER METHOD TO *N* CHOICE VARIABLES

Given an objective function in n choice variables, $z = z(x_1, x_2, \ldots x_n)$, to be optimized subject to the constraint, $g = g(x_1, x_2, \ldots x_n) = c$, we form the Lagrangian $L(\lambda, x_1, x_2, \ldots x_n) = z(x_1, x_2, \ldots x_n) + \lambda \cdot [c - g(x_1, x_2, \ldots x_n)]$
The first-order conditions are

$$\delta L/\delta\lambda = c - g(x_1, x_2, \ldots x_n) = 0 \qquad \text{(The constraint is satisfied.)}$$

$$\delta L/\delta x_1 = z_1 - \lambda g_1 = 0$$

$$\delta L/\delta x_2 = z_2 - \lambda g_2 = 0$$

.
.

$$\delta L/\delta x_n = z_n - \lambda g_n = 0$$

where

$$z_i = \delta z/\delta x_i \quad \text{and} \quad g_i = \delta g/\delta x_i \quad (i = 1 \dots n)$$

Solving the first-order conditions, which represent $(n + 1)$ simultaneous equations in $(n + 1)$ variables, λ and the n choice variables, gives the relative extremum. To confirm the type of extremum, we check the second-order conditions. The bordered Hessian, $|\overline{H}|$, is formed by partially differentiating the first-order conditions with respect to the Lagrange multiplier and the n choice variables.

$$|\overline{H}| = \left| \frac{\delta(\delta L/\delta \lambda, \ \delta L/\delta x_1, \ \delta L/\delta x_2, \ \dots \ \delta L/\delta x_n)}{\delta(\lambda, \ x_1, \ x_2, \ \dots \ x_n)} \right|$$

$$= \begin{vmatrix} 0 & g_1 & g_2 & \cdots & g_n \\ g_1 & L_{11} & L_{12} & \cdots & L_{1n} \\ g_2 & L_{21} & L_{22} & \cdots & L_{2n} \\ \vdots & & & & \\ g_n & L_{n1} & L_{n2} & \cdots & L_{nn} \end{vmatrix}$$

where

$$L_{ij} = \frac{\delta(\delta L/\delta x_j)}{\delta x_i} \quad (i, j = 1 \dots n)$$

The principal minors of the bordered Hessian are

$$|\overline{H}_2| = \begin{vmatrix} 0 & g_1 & g_2 \\ g_1 & L_{11} & L_{12} \\ g_2 & L_{21} & L_{22} \end{vmatrix}, |\overline{H}_3| = \begin{vmatrix} 0 & g_1 & g_2 & g_3 \\ g_1 & L_{11} & L_{12} & L_{13} \\ g_2 & L_{21} & L_{22} & L_{23} \\ g_3 & L_{31} & L_{32} & L_{33} \end{vmatrix}, |\overline{H}_4|, |\overline{H}_5|, \text{ etc.}$$

We state below, without proof, the sufficient conditions for identifying a constrained extremum.

For a relative minimum, the principal minors of the bordered Hessian are all negative:

$$|\overline{H}_2|, |\overline{H}_3|, |\overline{H}_4| \dots |\overline{H}_n| = |\overline{H}| < 0$$

For a relative maximum, the principal minors of the bordered Hessian alternate in sign as:

$$|\overline{H}_2| > 0, |\overline{H}_3| < 0, |\overline{H}_4| > 0, \text{ etc.}$$

EXTENSION OF LAGRANGE MULTIPLIER METHOD TO *M* CONSTRAINTS

We begin again with an objective function in n choice variables, $z = z(x_1, x_2, \ldots x_n)$, but allow for m constraints, $g^k (x_1, x_2, \ldots x_n) = c_k$, where $k = 1 \ldots m$. Note that we restrict the number of constraints to be less than the number of choice variables, here $m < n$. If we had the same number of constraints as choice variables, the search for the optimum would be reduced to the one point that satisfied all the constraints. If we had more constraints than choice variables, the system would be *overdetermined* and there would be no solution.[2]

The Lagrangian function is

$$L(\lambda_1, \lambda_2, \ldots \lambda_m, x_1, x_2, \ldots x_n) = z(x_1, x_2, \ldots x_n) + \lambda_1 \cdot [c_1 - g^1 (x_1, x_2, \ldots x_n)]$$

$$+ \lambda_2 \cdot [c_2 - g^2 (x_1, x_2, \ldots x_n)] + \cdots + \lambda_m \cdot [c_m - g^m(x_1, x_2, \ldots x_n)]$$

The $(n + m)$ first-order conditions are:

$$\left. \begin{array}{l} \delta L/\delta\lambda_1 = c_1 - g^1 (x_1, x_2, \ldots x_n) = 0 \\[4pt] \delta L/\delta\lambda_2 = c_2 - g^2 (x_1, x_2, \ldots x_n) = 0 \\[2pt] \cdot \\ \cdot \\ \cdot \\ \delta L/\delta\lambda_m = c_m - g^m (x_1, x_2, \ldots x_n) = 0 \end{array} \right] \quad \text{(The } m \text{ constraints are satisfied.)}$$

$$\delta L/\delta x_1 = z_1 - \lambda_1 g_1^1 - \lambda_2 g_1^2 - \ldots - \lambda_m g_1^m = 0$$

$$\delta L/\delta x_2 = z_2 - \lambda_1 g_2^1 - \lambda_2 g_2^2 - \ldots - \lambda_m g_2^m = 0$$

$$\cdot$$
$$\cdot$$
$$\cdot$$

$$\delta L/\delta x_n = z_n - \lambda_1 g_n^1 - \lambda_2 g_n^2 - \ldots - \lambda_m g_n^m = 0$$

where $\lambda_1, \lambda_2, \ldots \lambda_m$ are the m Lagrange multipliers and $g_i^k = \delta g^k/\delta x_i$ ($i = 1 \ldots n, k = 1 \ldots m$) are the partial derivatives of the kth constraint with respect to the ith choice variable. The solution to these $(n + m)$ simultaneous equations gives the constrained optimum.

---

[2]A simple example illustrates the point. Suppose the goal is to maximize the objective function, $z = xy$, subject to the constraint, $x + y = 3$. The Lagrangian is: $L(\lambda, x, y) = xy + \lambda \cdot (3 - x - y)$. We can show that the optimal values of $x, y,$ and z are $\bar{x} = 1.5, \bar{y} = 1.5,$ and $\bar{z} = 2.25$. If the objective function were subject to two constraints, say $x + y = 3$ and $x - y = 1$, then the Lagrangian is: $L(\lambda_1, \lambda_2, x, y) = xy + \lambda_1 \cdot (3 - x - y) + \lambda_2 \cdot (1 - x + y)$. Here with two constraints and two choice variables, the only ordered pair that satisfies both constraints is $\bar{x} = 2, \bar{y} = 1$. The optimal value of z is $\bar{z} = 1$. Finally, if we add a third constraint, say, $-x - y = 5$, then the system is overdetermined. The Lagrangian is $L(\lambda_1, \lambda_2, \lambda_3, x, y) = xy + \lambda_1 \cdot (3 - x - y) + \lambda_2 \cdot (1 - x + y) + \lambda_3 \cdot (5 + x + y)$. There is no ordered pair (x, y), however, that can satisfy the three constraints.

To form the bordered Hessian, we partially differentiate the first-order conditions with respect to the m Lagrange multipliers and n choice variables.

$$|\overline{H}| = \left| \frac{\delta(\delta L/\delta\lambda_1, \; \delta L/\delta\lambda_2, \; \dots \; \delta L/\delta\lambda_m, \; \delta L/\delta x_1, \; \delta L\delta x_2, \; \dots \; \delta L/\delta x_n)}{\delta(\lambda_1, \lambda_2, \; \dots \; \lambda_m, x_1, x_2, \dots x_n)} \right|$$

$$|\overline{H}| = \begin{vmatrix} 0 & 0 & \dots & 0 & g_1^1 & g_2^1 & \dots & g_n^1 \\ 0 & 0 & \dots & 0 & g_1^2 & g_2^2 & \dots & g_n^2 \\ \cdot & \cdot & & \cdot & \cdot & \cdot & & \cdot \\ \cdot & \cdot & & \cdot & \cdot & \cdot & & \cdot \\ 0 & 0 & \dots & 0 & g_1^m & g_2^m & \dots & g_n^m \\ g_1^1 & g_1^2 & \dots & g_1^m & L_{11} & L_{12} & \dots & L_{1n} \\ g_2^1 & g_2^2 & \dots & g_2^m & L_{21} & L_{22} & \dots & L_{2n} \\ \cdot & \cdot & & \cdot & \cdot & \cdot & & \cdot \\ \cdot & \cdot & & \cdot & \cdot & \cdot & & \cdot \\ g_n^1 & g_n^2 & \dots & g_n^m & L_{n1} & L_{n2} & \dots & L_{nn} \end{vmatrix}$$

The dimension of this bordered Hessian is $(n + m)$ by $(n + m)$. The principal minors of the bordered Hessian are derived as before. For example, $|\overline{H}_i|$, is the determinant of order $(i + m)$ by $(i + m)$, formed by going along the principal diagonal up to, and including, the L_{ii} element $(i = 2 \dots n)$.

For an extremum from the first-order conditions to be a relative minimum, the principal minors of this bordered Hessian must all take on the same sign, namely, $(-1)^m$. So for an even number of constraints, we need the principal minors of the bordered Hessian all to be positive. For an odd number of constraints, the sufficient condition for an extremum to be a relative minimum is that the principal minors of the bordered Hessian all be negative.

For an extremum from the first-order conditions to be a relative maximum, the principal minors of the bordered Hessian have to alternate in sign, with the sign of $|\overline{H}_{m+1}|$ given by $(-1)^{m+1}$. As before, if we have prior knowledge about the objective function (strictly concave for a maximum and strictly convex for a minimum), we do not have to check the second-order conditions.

We can now apply the Lagrangian technique of constrained optimization to the theory of the firm. Before addressing the long run behavior of a firm, specifically, finding the least cost combination of inputs for producing a selected level of output, we will review production functions. Some of the basic properties of production functions will be illustrated with two well-known examples: the Cobb-Douglas and CES production functions.

PRODUCTION FUNCTIONS

A **production function** describes the relationship between the output of a commodity and the required sets of inputs for a given state of technology. More formally, a production function represents the technically-efficient input combinations for producing given amounts of outputs. **Technically efficient** input combinations refer to the minimum levels of the inputs required to produce the designated outputs. In particular, the marginal products of the inputs are always positive, since additional units of an input would not be used if output were not increased.

In Chapter 6, we examined short-run production and cost functions, where physical capital was the fixed factor and output varied with labor. In this chapter, we study long-run production and cost functions, where all factors are variable.

The general form of a production function is

$$Q = Q(x_1, x_2, \ldots x_n)$$

where Q = output of a commodity (expressed in units per period of time)

x_i = input i (expressed in units per period of time), $i = 1 \ldots n$,

and we assume that $\delta Q / \delta x_i > 0$, that is, the marginal products of the n inputs are positive.

A widely used example is the **Cobb-Douglas production function**, which can be written in general as:

$$Q = A x_1^{b_1} x_2^{b_2} \ldots x_n^{b_n}$$

where A = index of technology $(A > 0)$

and b_i = transformation parameter $(b_i > 0, i = 1 \ldots n)$

The transformation parameters indicate the relationships between the inputs and output, and, along with A, are regarded as exogenous.

Again, to be able to illustrate graphically, we will restrict our attention to the standard two-factor case, with physical capital (K) and labor (L) as the primary factors of production.[3] The Cobb-Douglas production function then reduces to $Q = AK^a L^b$, where a and b represent the transformation parameters, and we assume $0 < a < 1$, $0 < b < 1$.

The **CES production function**, where CES stands for constant elasticity of substitution, with the two factors of capital and labor, takes the general form

$$Q = A \cdot [uK^{-p} + (1 - u)L^{-p}]^{-r/p}$$

where, in addition to the index of technology (A), we have

u = distribution parameter $(0 < u < 1)$

p = substitution parameter $(p > -1$ and $p \neq 0)$

r = returns to scale parameter $(r > 0)$

---

[3]Implicitly all other inputs used by firms (e.g., natural resources and intermediate goods) are available as needed, and so firms seek the optimal mix of capital and labor.

Returns to Scale Production functions may be distinguished by the property of returns to scale. A general function, $y = f(x_1, x_2, \ldots x_n)$, is said to be *homogeneous of degree r* if multiplication of each of the independent variables $(x_1, x_2, \ldots x_n)$ by a scalar c changes the value of the function by the proportion c^r. That is, $c^r y = f(cx_1, cx_2, \ldots cx_n)$.

For the production function, $Q = Q(x_1, x_2, \ldots x_n)$, if we multiply each of the inputs by a constant c and the output is multiplied by c^r, then the production function is homogeneous of degree r. That is, $Q = Q(x_1, x_2, \ldots x_n)$ and $Q(cx_1, cx_2, \ldots cx_n) = c^r \cdot Q(x_1, x_2, \ldots x_n) = c^r \cdot Q$. If $r = 1$, then the production function is *linearly homogeneous* or homogeneous of degree 1. A linearly homogeneous production function exhibits **constant returns to scale**. For example, a 10% increase (decrease) in all inputs results in a 10% increase (decrease) in output. If $r > 1$, then **increasing returns to scale** are indicated. A 10% increase (decrease) in all inputs results in a more than 10% increase (decrease) in output. If $r < 1$, then **decreasing returns to scale** are present. A 10% increase (decrease) in all inputs results in a less than 10% increase (decrease) in output.

Returning to the two-factor Cobb-Douglas production function, we can see that the sum of the transformation parameters, the exponents a and b, indicates the returns to scale. That is, $r = a + b$. To demonstrate, starting with a general Cobb-Douglas production function, $Q = AK^a L^b$, multiplying the inputs of capital and labor by a constant c gives:

$$A(cK)^a (cL)^b = Ac^{a+b} K^a L^b = c^{a+b} Q$$

If $a + b = 1$, then we have constant returns to scale.

If $a + b > 1$, then we have increasing returns to scale.

If $a + b < 1$, then we have decreasing returns to scale.

For the CES production function, $Q = A[uK^{-p} + (1-u)L^{-p}]^{-r/p}$, multiplying the inputs by a constant c yields

$$A[u(cK)^{-p} + (1-u)(cL)^{-p}]^{-r/p} = A[c^{-p}(uK^{-p} + (1-u)L^{-p})]^{-r/p} =$$

$$= c^r \cdot A[uK^{-p} + (1-u)L^{-p}]^{-r/p} = c^r \cdot Q$$

and we can see directly that r, the returns to scale parameter, gives the degree of homogeneity.

To illustrate, consider the Cobb-Douglas production function: $Q = K^3 L^6$. We can recognize that this production function is characterized by decreasing returns to scale—since the sum of the exponents is less than one: $.3 + .6 = .9 < 1$. Consequently, if we scale up the inputs by say 20%, that is, multiply the factors K and L by 1.2, then the increase in output would be less than 20%.

$$(1.2K)^3 (1.2L)^6 = (1.2)^3 K^3 (1.2)^6 L^6 = (1.2)^9 K^3 L^6 = (1.2)^9 Q = 1.178Q < 1.2Q$$

Next, consider the CES production function: $Q = [.4K^{-3} + .6L^{-3}]^{-1/4}$. It is not as obvious that this production function is also characterized by decreasing returns to scale. Here $p = 3$ and $r/p = 1/4$, so $r = 3/4$. If we scale up inputs by 20% here, we have

$$[.4(1.2K)^{-3} + .6(1.2L)^{-3}]^{-1/4} = [(1.2)^{-3}(.4K^{-3} + .6L^{-3})]^{-1/4} = (1.2)^{3/4}[.4K^{-3} + .6L^{-3}]^{-1/4}$$

$$= (1.2)^{3/4} Q = 1.147Q < 1.2Q$$

We can see that output increases by less than 20% (here by 14.7%) when the factors are increased by 20%, so this CES production function is characterized by decreasing returns to scale.

PRACTICE PROBLEM 10.5

Determine the returns to scale of the following production functions:

a) $Q = .5K^{.7}L^{.3}$

b) $Q = [.5K^{-2} + .5L^{-2}]^{-.6}$

(The answers are at the end of the chapter.)

ISOQUANTS

An **isoquant** is a graph of all the technically efficient input combinations for producing a selected level of output. Isoquants are derived from a production function, and thus reflect a given level of technology. We sketch an isoquant, Q_0, for the general two-factor production function, $Q = A \cdot Q(K, L)$, in Figure 10.1. The curve, indicating all the technically efficient combinations of capital and labor that can produce the level of output, Q_0, is just one of a family of isoquants associated with the production func-

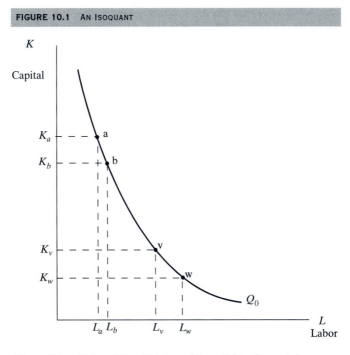

FIGURE 10.1   AN ISOQUANT

Given $(K_v - K_w) = (K_a - K_b)$, then $(L_w - L_v) > (L_b - L_a)$

tion. On this isoquant, the combinations of capital and labor represented by points a, b, v, and w, are all capable of producing the level of output of Q_0. Isoquants further from the origin represent higher levels of output. Note that an increase in technology, represented by a rise in A, would shift the isoquant Q_0 in toward the origin—allowing the same output to be produced with fewer inputs.

The slope of an isoquant, known as the **marginal rate of technical substitution** (*MRTS*), indicates the rate at which one input can be substituted for the other, while maintaining the same level of output. We can derive the expression for the *MRTS* and show that the isoquants are negatively sloped and strictly convex.

Begin with the general production function, $Q = A \cdot Q(K, L)$. Totally differentiating, we obtain

$$dQ = dA \cdot Q(K, L) + A \cdot (Q_K \, dK + Q_L \, dL)$$

where $Q_K = \delta Q / \delta K$ = marginal product of capital

and $Q_L = \delta Q / \delta L$ = marginal product of labor

Along an isoquant, technology is given, $(dA = 0)$, and output is constant, $(dQ = 0)$. Therefore

$$dQ = 0 = A \cdot (Q_K \, dK + Q_L \, dL)$$

Solving for dK/dL, the generic expression for the slope of any curve in the K-L space (with K on the vertical axis), we find the marginal rate of technical substitution:

$$dK/dL = -Q_L/Q_K = MRTS$$

So, given that the marginal products of capital and labor are positive, an isoquant will have a negative slope. Intuitively, if a firm uses less capital, $(dK < 0)$, then it must use more labor, $(dL > 0)$, to maintain the same level of output.

To determine the curvature of the isoquant, we examine the behavior of the slope, $(dK/dL = -Q_L/Q_K)$, as we vary the input combination. Note that moving along an isoquant, the levels of the two inputs are related, so we can write $K = K(L)$, with $dK/dL < 0$. Any change in labor will dictate the required change in capital to keep output constant. The curvature of the isoquant is given by

$$\frac{d(dK/dL)}{dL} = \frac{d^2K}{dL^2} = \frac{d[-Q_L(K(L), L]/Q_K(K(L), L))}{dL} = \frac{dMRTS}{dL}$$

Note that the values of the marginal products of capital and labor depend on the amounts of capital and labor used. Applying the quotient rule for differentiation, we have

$$\frac{d^2K}{dL^2} = \frac{[-Q_{KL}(dK/dL) - Q_{LL}]Q_K - [Q_{KK}(dK/dL) + Q_{LK}](-Q_L)}{(Q_K)^2}$$

Substituting in $(-Q_L/Q_K)$ for dK/dL, and then expressing the terms in the numerator over a common denominator, we get

$$\frac{d^2K}{dL^2} = \frac{-Q_{LL}(Q_K)^2 + 2Q_L Q_K Q_{KL} - Q_{KK}(Q_L)^2}{(Q_K)^3} > 0$$

since $Q_{LL} = \delta(Q_L)/\delta L < 0$ and $Q_{KK} = \delta(Q_K)/\delta K < 0$, consistent with the law of diminishing returns. Recall, according to the **law of diminishing returns**, the marginal product of a factor of production declines as the use of the factor increases, *ceteris paribus*. Here, moving along an isoquant, using more labor (capital) reduces the marginal product of labor (capital). Also, $Q_{KL} = \delta(Q_L)/\delta K = Q_{LK} = \delta(Q_K)/\delta L > 0$. The cross-partials are positive, since the marginal product of labor (capital) increases as the use of capital (labor) increases. In sum, the slope of an isoquant is negative and strictly convex.

In Figure 10.1 we can see that the negative slope of the isoquant is increasing (i.e., becoming less negative) as we move down the isoquant, substituting labor for capital. The *MRTS* is approaching zero ($dK/dL = -Q_L/Q_K \rightarrow 0$, since as $L \uparrow$ and $K \downarrow$, $Q_L \downarrow$ and $Q_K \uparrow$). In words, as labor is substituted for capital, increasingly more units of labor are required to replace each unit of capital in order to maintain the same rate of output. In moving from input combinations *a* to *b*, compared to combinations *v* to *w*, the reductions in capital are equal, $(K_a - K_b) = (K_v - K_w)$, while the increases in labor required are greater, $(L_w - L_v) > (L_b - L_a)$.

We can demonstrate that the isoquants derived from a Cobb-Douglas production function, $Q = AK^aL^b$, where $0 < a < 1$ and $0 < b < 1$, are strictly convex, since the marginal products of capital and labor are positive ($Q_K > 0$, $Q_L > 0$); both capital and labor are subject to diminishing returns ($Q_{KK} < 0$, $Q_{LL} < 0$); and the cross-partials are positive ($Q_{KL} = Q_{LK} > 0$).

$$Q_L = \delta Q/\delta L = bAK^aL^{b-1} > 0$$

$$Q_K = \delta Q/\delta K = aAK^{a-1}L > 0$$

$$Q_{LL} = \delta(Q_L)/\delta L = (b-1)bAK^aL^{b-2} < 0 \quad (b < 1)$$

$$Q_{KK} = \delta(Q_K)/\delta K = (a-1)aAK^{a-2}L^b < 0 \quad (a < 1)$$

$$Q_{KL} = \delta(Q_L)/\delta K = Q_{LK} = \delta(Q_K)/\delta L = abAK^{a-1}L^{b-1} > 0$$

Recall that the marginal rate of technical substitution, indicated by the slope of an isoquant, is equal to the negative ratio of the marginal products of the two factors. For the general Cobb-Douglas production function, $Q = AK^aL^b$, with capital on the vertical axis, the *MRTS* equals

$$MRTS = -Q_L/Q_K = \frac{-bAK^aL^{b-1}}{aAK^{a-1}L^b} = \frac{-bK}{aL} = dK/dL$$

To confirm that the isoquants are strictly convex, with negative but increasing slopes, we show that the derivative of the *MRTS* with respect to labor is positive.

$$\frac{dMRTS}{dL} = \frac{d(dK/dL)}{dL} = \frac{d(-bK/aL)}{dL} = \frac{-b \cdot (dK/dL) \cdot (aL) + bK \cdot a}{(aL)^2}$$

Substituting in $(-bK/aL)$ for dK/dL, we have

$$\frac{dMRTS}{dL} = \frac{d^2K}{dL^2} = \frac{-b \cdot (-bK/aL) \cdot (aL) + abK}{a^2L^2} = \frac{bK(b + a)}{a^2L^2} > 0$$

For example, given the Cobb-Douglas production function, $Q = 2K^{.6}L^{.5}$, we can show that both capital and labor are subject to diminishing returns. The marginal products are

$$Q_L = K^{.6}L^{-.5} > 0$$

$$Q_K = 1.2K^{-.4}L^{.5} > 0$$

Taking the second-order partial differentials, we have

$$Q_{LL} = \delta Q_L/\delta L = -.5K^{.6}L^{-1.5} < 0$$

$$Q_{KK} = \delta Q_K/\delta K = -.48K^{-1.4}L^{.5} < 0$$

Note that this production function exhibits increasing returns to scale, since the sum of the exponents exceeds one: $.6 + .5 > 1$.

The marginal rate of technical substitution is

$$MRTS = -Q_L/Q_K = \frac{-K^{.6}L^{-.5}}{1.2K^{-.4}L^{.5}} = \frac{-K}{1.2L} < 0$$

The associated isoquants have negative slopes. Moreover, the isoquants are strictly convex, since the negative slopes are increasing, that is, the *MRTS* becomes less negative as the use of labor increases. Intuitively, as the firm uses more labor (and less capital) to produce a given output, the rate at which labor has to be substituted for capital is increasing.

$$dMRTS/dL = \frac{d(-Q_L/Q_K)}{dL} = \frac{d(-K/1.2L)}{dL} = \frac{-dK/dL \cdot (1.2L) + K \cdot (1.2)}{(1.2L)^2}$$

$$= \frac{(-K/1.2L) \cdot (1.2L) + 1.2K}{(1.2L)^2} = \frac{-K + 1.2K}{(1.2L)^2} = \frac{.2K}{(1.2L)^2} > 0$$

PRACTICE PROBLEM 10.6

For the Cobb-Douglas production function, $Q = 3K^{.5}L^{.4}$

a) Find the marginal products of labor and capital.
b) Show that both labor and capital are subject to diminishing returns.
c) Demonstrate that the cross-partials Q_{KL} and Q_{LK} are positive and equal.
d) Find the *MRTS* and show that the isoquants are strictly convex.

(The answers are at the end of the chapter.)

COST MINIMIZATION

An example of constrained optimization for the firm would be the selection of the cost-minimizing combination of factors for producing a given level of output. In the long run, all the factors of production are variable, and a firm seeks to minimize the total costs of producing the selected level of output. That is, the profit-maximizing firm needs to determine the **economically efficient** or least-cost factor combination.

We will illustrate using the general two-factor production function, $Q = Q(K, L)$, where Q is the output of the firm and K and L are the physical capital and labor, respectively, used by the firm. We will assume that the firm has determined the profit-maximizing level of output, Q_0. Exogenous to the firm are the user costs of labor and capital. The **user cost of labor**, w, is the comprehensive wage rate per unit of labor, which includes not only the wage directly paid but the taxes and benefits paid by the firm on each unit of labor. The **user cost of capital**, r, sometimes referred to as the rental rate, is the cost to the firm of using a unit of physical capital. This refers to either the cost to the firm of renting a unit of physical capital or to the user cost to the firm if it owns the physical capital. In this latter case, the user cost of capital, expressed per dollar of physical capital, includes the interest cost (measured by the interest that has to be paid on the funds borrowed to purchase the unit of physical capital or the opportunity cost to the firm of using its own funds) and the depreciation cost of the unit of physical capital (i.e., the loss in the value of the unit of capital due to wear and tear and technological obsolescence). The total cost of production, C, is equal to the sum of the costs of capital and labor: $C = r_0K + w_0L$, where r_0 and w_0 are the given user costs of capital and labor.

The objective of the firm, then, is to minimize the total cost of production, $C = r_0K + w_0L$, subject to the output constraint, $Q = Q(K, L) = Q_0$. Setting up the Lagrangian function, $\mathscr{L}$, we have

$$\mathscr{L}(\lambda, K, L) = r_0K + w_0L + \lambda \cdot [Q_0 - Q(K, L)]$$

The first-order conditions are

$$\delta\mathscr{L}/\delta\lambda = Q_0 - Q(K, L) = 0 \quad \text{(The output constraint is satisfied.)}$$

$$\delta\mathscr{L}/\delta K = r_0 - \lambda Q_K = 0$$

$$\delta\mathscr{L}/\delta L = w_0 - \lambda Q_L = 0$$

where Q_K and Q_L are the marginal products of capital and labor, respectively. Solving these simultaneous equations yields the optimal values of capital and labor, $\overline{K}$ and $\overline{L}$, as well as the value of the Lagrange multiplier, λ. From the second and third equations, we find that at the critical point, $r_0/Q_K = w_0/Q_L = \lambda$, or rearranging, $(Q_K/r_0) = (Q_L/w_0) = (1/\lambda)$. Thus, to minimize the total cost of producing a given level of output, Q_0, a firm should allocate its expenditures over its factors of production such that the marginal products per dollar spent are equal. Here, with the two factors, the economically efficient combination is where the ratio of the marginal product of capital to the user cost of capital is equal to the ratio of the marginal product of labor to the user cost of labor. The Lagrange multiplier at the point of constrained cost minimization represents the marginal cost of production, $\lambda = \delta\overline{C}/\delta Q_0$, that is, the instantaneous change in the minimum long-run cost associated with an infinitesimal change in output.

Isocost Lines   Before we illustrate this problem of constrained cost minimization graphically, we need to review isocost lines. For given user costs of the factors, an **isocost line** represents all the combinations of factors that have the same total cost to a firm. In Figure 10.2, we depict two of the isocost lines of the firm. All the combinations of capital and labor lying on the isocost line C_0 cost the same to the firm. For example, the maximum amount of capital the firm could purchase for a total cost of C_0 would be C_0/r_0 units, the vertical intercept of the isocost line. At this point, the firm would not be able to afford any labor. Similarly, the maximum amount of labor the firm could purchase, with no capital expenditures, would be equal to C_0/w_0, the horizontal intercept of the isocost line. The slope of the isocost line is equal to the negative of the ratio of the user costs of the factors. Here with capital on the vertical axis, the slope of the isocost line, C_0, is given by $-w_0/r_0$, the negative of the wage-rental ratio.

An increase in the total costs of a firm, necessary for producing more output, is represented by a parallel shift outward of the isocost line. For example, in Figure 10.2, the isocost line C_1 represents a higher total cost than the isocost line C_0. A change in the ratio of the user costs of the factors would alter the slope of an isocost line.

Graphically in Figure 10.3, we illustrate the goal of the firm: to find the least-cost combination of capital and labor for producing a selected level of output, represented by the isoquant Q_0. For the given user costs of capital and labor, the lowest isocost line the firm could reach and still produce the output Q_0 would be at the point of tangency, E_0, between the isoquant, Q_0, and the isocost line, $\overline{C} = r_0K + w_0L$. At this point of tangency, the slope of the isoquant, given by the value of the marginal rate of technical substitution, $-Q_L/Q_K$, is equal to the slope of the isocost line, given by the negative of

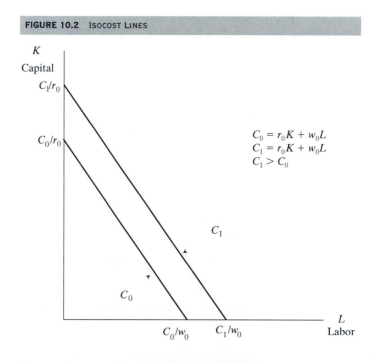

FIGURE 10.2   ISOCOST LINES

$C_0 = r_0K + w_0L$
$C_1 = r_0K + w_0L$
$C_1 > C_0$

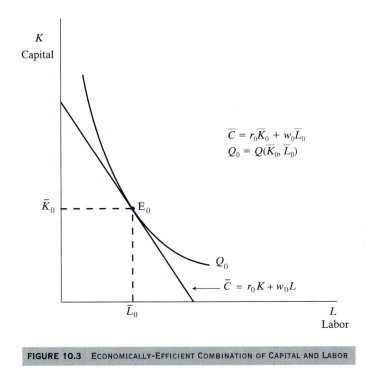

$$\overline{C} = r_0 \overline{K}_0 + w_0 \overline{L}_0$$
$$Q_0 = Q(\overline{K}_0, \overline{L}_0)$$

Q_0

$\overline{C} = r_0 K + w_0 L$

FIGURE 10.3 ECONOMICALLY-EFFICIENT COMBINATION OF CAPITAL AND LABOR

the wage-rental ratio, $-w_0/r_0$. We can see that this is the same condition we derived from the first-order conditions, since $-(Q_L/Q_K) = -w_0/r_0$, after multiplying through by $-(Q_K/w_0)$, is equivalent to: $Q_L/w_0 = Q_K/r_0$.

Second-Order Conditions We need to confirm that the critical point found from solving the first-order conditions is indeed a minimum. We derive the bordered Hessian $|\overline{H}|$ in the same way as we obtain the associated Jacobian, by differentiating the first-order conditions.

$$|\overline{H}| = |J| = \left| \frac{\delta(\delta\mathscr{L}/\delta\lambda, \, \delta\mathscr{L}/\delta K, \, \delta\mathscr{L}/\delta L)}{\delta(\lambda, \, K, \, L)} \right|$$

$$|\overline{H}| = \begin{vmatrix} 0 & -Q_K & -Q_L \\ -Q_K & -\lambda Q_{KK} & -\lambda Q_{KL} \\ -Q_L & -\lambda Q_{LK} & -\lambda Q_{LL} \end{vmatrix}$$

and expanding along the first row, we have

$$|\overline{H}| = Q_K \begin{vmatrix} -Q_K & -\lambda Q_{KL} \\ -Q_L & -\lambda Q_{LL} \end{vmatrix} - Q_L \begin{vmatrix} -Q_K & -\lambda Q_{KK} \\ -Q_L & -\lambda Q_{LK} \end{vmatrix}$$

$$= \lambda(Q_K)^2 Q_{LL} - \lambda Q_K Q_L Q_{KL} - \lambda Q_L Q_K Q_{LK} + \lambda(Q_L)^2 Q_{KK}$$

$$= \lambda \cdot [(Q_K)^2 Q_{LL} - 2Q_K Q_L Q_{KL} + (Q_L)^2 Q_{KK}]$$

For a constrained minimum we need $|\overline{H}| < 0$. Since $\overline{\lambda} > 0$, recall that $\overline{\lambda}$ refers to the marginal cost of production; $Q_{LL} < 0$ and $Q_{KK} < 0$, due to diminishing returns to labor and capital; and $Q_{LK} = Q_{KL} > 0$, positive cross-partials, that is, the marginal product of capital (labor) is increased with an increase in labor (capital); we can sign the term in the brackets as negative, making $|\overline{H}| < 0$ and establishing a minimum. Note that the negativity of the bordered Hessian here also reflects the strict convexity of the isoquants, where

$$d^2K/dL^2 = \frac{-Q_{LL}(Q_K)^2 + 2Q_L Q_K Q_{KL} - Q_{KK}(Q_L)^2}{(Q_K)^3} > 0$$

Consider the following example. A firm seeks to minimize the cost of producing 434 units of output. The production function is $Q = 10K^{.7}L^{.1}$, and the user costs of capital and labor are $r_0 = \$28$ and $w_0 = \$10$. The constrained minimization problem is to minimize the total cost, $C = r_0 K + w_0 L = 28K + 10L$, subject to the output constraint, $Q_0 = 434 = 10K^{.7}L^{.1}$. The Lagrangian function is: $\mathscr{L}(\lambda, K, L) = 28K + 10L + \lambda \cdot (434 - 10K^{.7}L^{.1})$ The first-order conditions are

$$\delta\mathscr{L}/\delta\lambda = 434 - 10K^{.7}L^{.1} = 0 \qquad \text{(The output constraint is satisfied.)}$$

$$\delta\mathscr{L}/\delta K = 28 - \lambda(7K^{-.3}L^{.1}) = 0$$

$$\delta\mathscr{L}/\delta L = 10 - \lambda(1K^{.7}L^{-.9}) = 0$$

From the second and third equations we can solve for λ, and show that

$$\frac{28}{7K^{-.3} L^{.1}} = \overline{\lambda} = \frac{10}{1K^{.7} L^{-.9}}$$

or $4K^{.3}L^{-.1} = 10K^{-.7}L^{.9}$. Multiplying both sides by $K^{.7}L^{.1}$, and "solving" for K in terms of L, we have $\overline{K} = 2.5\overline{L}$. Substituting this expression back into the output constraint, we have reduced the system of three equations in three unknowns, to one equation in one unknown: $434 = 10K^{.7}L^{.1} = 10(2.5L)^{.7}L^{.1} = 10(1.9)L^{.8}$. Solving for $\overline{L}$, we find the cost-minimizing quantity of labor to be $\overline{L}_0 = 49.9$. Therefore, $\overline{K}_0 = 2.5\overline{L} = 124.8$. The long-run marginal cost of output, $\overline{\lambda}_0$, equals $\$11.5$.

$$\overline{\lambda}_0 = 4\overline{K}_0^3\overline{L}_0^{-.1} = 4(124.8)^3 (49.9)^{-.1} = 11.5 = 10\overline{K}_0^{-.7}\overline{L}_0^{.9} = 10(124.8)^{-.7}(49.9)^{.9}$$

To check the second-order conditions, we evaluate the bordered Hessian, $|\overline{H}|$, where

$$|\overline{H}| = \left| \frac{\delta(\delta\mathscr{L}/\delta\lambda, \delta\mathscr{L}/\delta K, \delta\mathscr{L}/\delta L)}{\delta(\lambda, K, L)} \right|$$

We can evaluate each of the second-order partials at the critical point, $(\overline{\lambda}_0, \overline{K}_0, \overline{L}_0)$. For the first row of $|\overline{H}|$, we have

$$\frac{\delta(\delta\mathscr{L}/\delta\lambda)}{\delta\lambda} = 0$$

$$\frac{\delta(\delta\mathcal{L}/\delta K)}{\delta\lambda} = -7K^{-.3}L^{.1} = -7(124.8)^{-.3}(49.9)^{.1} = -2.43$$

$$\frac{\delta(\delta\mathcal{L}/\delta L)}{\delta\lambda} = -1K^{.7}L^{-.9} = -1(124.8)^{.7}(49.9)^{-.9} = -.87$$

For the second row of $|\overline{H}|$,

$$\frac{\delta(\delta\mathcal{L}/\delta\lambda)}{\delta K} = -.7(10)K^{-.3}L^{.1} = -7(124.8)^{-.3}(49.9)^{.1} = -2.43$$

$$\frac{\delta(\delta\mathcal{L}/\delta K)}{\delta K} = -.3(-7\lambda)K^{-1.3}L^{.1} = 2.1(11.5)(124.8)^{-1.3}(49.9)^{.1} = .07$$

$$\frac{\delta(\delta\mathcal{L}/\delta L)}{\delta K} = -.7\lambda K^{-.3}L^{-.9} = -.7(11.5)(124.8)^{-.3}(49.9)^{-.9} = -.06$$

and, for the third row of $|\overline{H}|$,

$$\frac{\delta(\delta\mathcal{L}/\delta\lambda)}{\delta L} = -.1(10)K^{.7}L^{-.9} = -1(124.8)^{.7}(49.9)^{-.9} = -.87$$

$$\frac{\delta(\delta\mathcal{L}/\delta K)}{\delta L} = -.1(7\lambda)K^{-.3}L^{-.9} = -.7(11.5)(124.8)^{-.3}(49.9)^{-.9} = -.06$$

$$\frac{\delta(\delta\mathcal{L}/\delta L)}{\delta L} = -.9(-\lambda)K^{.7}L^{-1.9} = -.9(-11.5)(124.8)^{.7}(49.9)^{-1.9} = .18$$

The bordered Hessian is equal to

$$|\overline{H}| = \begin{vmatrix} 0 & -2.43 & -.87 \\ -2.43 & .07 & -.06 \\ -.87 & -.06 & .18 \end{vmatrix} = 2.43\begin{vmatrix} -2.43 & -.87 \\ -.06 & .18 \end{vmatrix} - .87\begin{vmatrix} -2.43 & -.87 \\ .07 & -.06 \end{vmatrix}$$

$$|\overline{H}| = -1.19 - .18 = -1.37 < 0$$

The positive definite bordered Hessian confirms our constrained minimization. In sum, the cost-minimizing combination of producing 434 units of output is 124.8 units of capital and 49.9 units of labor. $Q_0 = 434 = 10\overline{K}_0^{.7}\overline{L}_0^{.1} = 10(124.8)^{.7}(49.9)^{.1}$. The minimum cost is $\overline{C}_0 = 28\overline{K}_0 + 10\overline{L}_0 = \$28(124.8) + \$10(49.9) = \$3,993.4$.

PRACTICE PROBLEM 10.7

a) Find the cost-minimizing combination of capital (K) and labor (L) for producing an output of $Q_0 = 100$, given the production function, $Q = 2K^{.4}L^{.6}$, and the user costs of capital and labor, $r_0 = \$15$ and $w_0 = \$6$, respectively.

b) Determine the marginal cost of output.

c) Determine the minimum cost.

d) Check the second-order condition.

(The answers are at the end of the chapter.)

COMPARATIVE STATICS ON THE LEAST-COST EQUILIBRIUM OF THE FIRM

To investigate the effects on the cost-minimizing combination of capital and labor of changes in output or the user costs of the factors, we return to the first-order conditions from the general model. We invoke the Implicit Function Theorem and then totally differentiate the system of equations evaluated at the critical point.

Rewriting the first-order conditions at the critical point, $(\bar{\lambda}, \bar{K}, \bar{L})$, we have

$$Q_0 - Q(\bar{K}, \bar{L}) = 0$$

$$r_0 - \bar{\lambda} Q_K(\bar{K}, \bar{L}) = 0$$

$$w_0 - \bar{\lambda} Q_L(\bar{K}, \bar{L}) = 0$$

which represents a system of continuous equations with continuous partial derivatives. Moreover, the associated Jacobian, $|J|$, which is equivalent to the bordered Hessian $|\bar{H}|$, does not equal zero. (Recall, we established that $|\bar{H}| < 0$.). Therefore, we can assert that the implicit functions

$$\bar{\lambda} = \lambda(Q_0, r_0, w_0)$$

$$\bar{K} = K(Q_0, r_0, w_0)$$

$$\bar{L} = L(Q_0, r_0, w_0)$$

are defined and are continuous, with continuous partial derivatives. Consequently, we can do comparative statics on these first-order conditions, even though we cannot solve explicitly for the endogenous variables in terms of the exogenous variables of the model. Totally differentiating, we obtain

$$dQ_0 - Q_K \, d\bar{K} - Q_L \, d\bar{L} = 0$$

$$dr_0 - d\bar{\lambda} Q_K - \bar{\lambda}(Q_{KK} \, d\bar{K} + Q_{LK} \, d\bar{L}) = 0$$

$$dw_0 - d\bar{\lambda} Q_L - \bar{\lambda}(Q_{KL} \, d\bar{K} + Q_{LL} \, d\bar{L}) = 0$$

Writing this system of equations in matrix form, with the vector of exogenous changes on the right-hand side gives

$$\begin{bmatrix} 0 & -Q_K & -Q_L \\ -Q_K & -\bar{\lambda} Q_{KK} & -\bar{\lambda} Q_{LK} \\ -Q_L & -\bar{\lambda} Q_{KL} & -\bar{\lambda} Q_{LL} \end{bmatrix} \begin{bmatrix} d\bar{\lambda} \\ d\bar{K} \\ d\bar{L} \end{bmatrix} = \begin{bmatrix} -dQ_0 \\ -dr_0 \\ -dw_0 \end{bmatrix}$$

Suppose that we want to find the effect of a change in output on the optimal amount of capital, that is, $\delta\bar{K}/\delta Q_0$. Using Cramer's rule we can solve for $d\bar{K}$, after setting $dr_0 = dw_0 = 0$.

$$dK = \frac{\begin{vmatrix} 0 & -dQ_0 & -Q_L \\ -Q_K & 0 & -\bar{\lambda}Q_{LK} \\ -Q_L & 0 & -\bar{\lambda}Q_{LL} \end{vmatrix}}{|\bar{H}|} = \frac{dQ_0 \begin{vmatrix} -Q_K & -\bar{\lambda}Q_{LK} \\ -Q_L & -\bar{\lambda}Q_{LL} \end{vmatrix}}{|\bar{H}|}$$

$$d\bar{K} = \frac{dQ_0 (\bar{\lambda}Q_{LL}Q_K - \bar{\lambda}Q_L Q_{LK})}{|\bar{H}|}$$

where

$$|\bar{H}| = \lambda \cdot [(Q_K)^2 \, Q_{LL} - 2Q_K Q_L Q_{KL} + (Q_L)^2 \, Q_{KK}] < 0$$

Dividing through by dQ_0, and then converting to the partial derivative, we have

$$\delta\bar{K}/\delta Q_0 = \frac{\bar{\lambda} \cdot (Q_{LL} \, Q_K - Q_L Q_{LK})}{|\bar{H}|} > 0$$

since $\bar{\lambda} > 0$, $Q_{LL} < 0$, $Q_K > 0$, $Q_L > 0$, and $Q_{LK} > 0$. Similarly, we can show that $\delta\bar{L}/\delta Q_0 > 0$. Both of these comparative static results are intuitive. An increase in the output of the firm would require increases in the levels of the cost-minimizing factors of production. The firm's demands for capital and labor are derived from the demand for the firm's output.

We can do four additional comparative static experiments in this model: $\delta\bar{K}/\delta r_0$, $\delta\bar{K}/\delta w_0$, $\delta\bar{L}/\delta r_0$, and $\delta\bar{L}/\delta w_0$. For example, we would expect that an increase in the user cost of capital would increase the use of labor, *ceteris paribus*, as the firm substitutes labor for capital in producing the given level of output. To show this, we solve for $d\bar{L}$, with $dQ_0 = 0$ and $dw_0 = 0$.

$$dL = \frac{\begin{vmatrix} 0 & -Q_K & 0 \\ -Q_K & -\bar{\lambda}Q_{KK} & -dr_0 \\ -Q_L & -\bar{\lambda}Q_{KL} & 0 \end{vmatrix}}{|\bar{H}|} = \frac{dr_0 \begin{vmatrix} 0 & -Q_K \\ -Q_L & -\bar{\lambda}Q_{KL} \end{vmatrix}}{|\bar{H}|} = \frac{dr_0 (-Q_L Q_K)}{|\bar{H}|}$$

Now, dividing through by dr_0 and converting to partial derivatives, we get

$$\delta\bar{L}/\delta r_0 = \frac{-Q_L Q_K}{|\bar{H}|} > 0 \quad \text{(since } |\bar{H}| < 0, \text{ and } Q_K > 0, Q_L > 0)$$

We could also show that $\delta\bar{K}/\delta r_0 < 0$, consistent with the law of demand. That is, for a given level of output and given user cost of labor, a rise in the user cost of capital would reduce the quantity demanded of capital, as a firm would shift to a less capital-intensive method of production.

To illustrate, return to the earlier example of a firm seeking the least cost combination of capital and labor for producing $Q_0 = 434$ units of output. The firm's production function is $Q = 10K^{.7}L^{.1}$, and the user costs of labor and capital are $w_0 = \$10$ and $r_0 = \$28$. We showed that the cost-minimizing combination is $\bar{K}_0 = 124.8$ and $\bar{L}_0 = 49.9$. The marginal cost of output equals $\bar{\lambda}_0 = \$11.5$ and the minimum total cost is $\bar{C}_0 = \$3,993.4$.

We can do comparative statics directly since we have the explicit cost and production functions. First, consider an increase in the firm's selected output to $Q_1 = 450$. The optimization problem for the firm becomes: minimizing $C = 28K + 10L$ subject to $Q = 10K^{.7} L^{.1} = 450$. The Lagrangian function is: $\mathscr{L}(\lambda, K, L) = 28K + 10L + \lambda \cdot (450 - 10K^{.7}L^{.1})$. Solving, we would find the new cost-minimizing combination to be: $\overline{K}_1 = 130.8$ and $\overline{L}_1 = 52.3$. The increase in output results in an increase demand for capital and labor. The marginal cost of production rises to $\lambda_1 = \$11.6$ and the minimum total cost of now $\overline{C}_1 = \$4,185.4$. (For practice, you may want to confirm these results.)

Instead, consider an increase in the user cost of capital from $r_0 = \$28$ to $r_2 = \$30$. The optimization for the firm is minimizing the total cost, $C = 30K + 10L$, of producing the level of output, $Q_0 = 434$, given the production function, $Q = 10K^{.7}L^{.1}$. The Lagrangian function is: $\mathscr{L}(\lambda, K, L) = 30K + 10L + \lambda \cdot (434 - 10K^{.7}L^{.1})$. Solving we would find the new cost-minimizing factor combination to be: $\overline{K}_2 = 123.9$ and $\overline{L}_2 = 53.1$. As expected, an increase in the user cost of capital, *ceteris paribus*, induces the firm to substitute away from capital (the quantity demanded of capital is inversely related to its price) and use a more labor-intensive method of production. Moreover, at the selected level of output, the marginal cost of production is higher, $\lambda_2 = \$12.2$, as is the minimum total cost of production, $C_2 = \$4,248.0$.

Graphically, a change in the user cost of capital affects the slope of the isocost lines. The firm moves along the given isoquant — here substituting labor for capital. In contrast, with an increase in the output of the firm, there is a move to a higher isoquant. The isocost line shifts out in a parallel fashion until a new point of tangency is reached with the isoquant representing the higher level of output. We will further develop these comparative statics below.

Expansion Paths   Graphically we can illustrate the comparative statics of varying output levels on the cost-minimizing combinations of capital and labor. Holding constant the user costs of capital and labor, hence the slope of the isocost lines, changes in the firm's output will result in movements to new isoquants. In each case, the new least-cost combination of capital and labor will be defined by the condition that the given slope of the isocost line $(-w/r)$ equals the slope of the isoquant $(MRTS = -Q_L/Q_K)$ at the point of tangency between the isocost line and isoquant.

See Figure 10.4, and the isoquants representing three levels of output, $Q_3 > Q_2 > Q_1$. The points of tangency, E_1, E_2, and E_3, indicate the economically-efficient combinations of capital and labor for producing the three levels of output. If we draw a curve through these (and other) equilibrium points, we obtain the firm's output-expansion path. More formally, the **output-expansion path** of a firm is the locus of the least-cost combinations of capital and labor for producing varying levels of output, holding constant technology and the ratio of the user costs of labor and capital.

For any production function homogeneous of degree r, the output-expansion path is a ray from the origin. In the two-factor case here, given the wage-rental ratio, as the firm's output increases, the economically efficient capital-labor ratio $(\overline{K}/\overline{L})$ is constant. Recall that for a production function homogeneous of degree r, a c^r-fold increase in output is attained with a c-fold increase in capital and labor. If the user cost ratio is

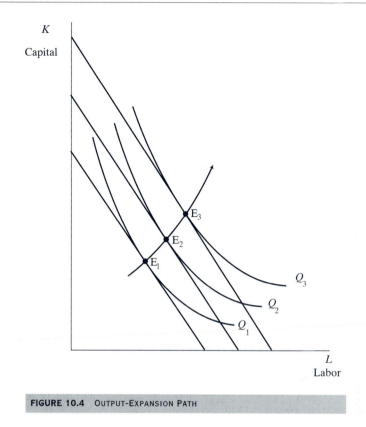

FIGURE 10.4   OUTPUT-EXPANSION PATH

unchanged, then the firm would not alter the ratio of capital to labor as the level of output changes.

We can derive the output-expansion path for the general two-factor Cobb-Douglas and CES production functions. For each level of output, the cost-minimizing combination of capital and labor, $\overline{K}$ and $\overline{L}$, occurs at the point of tangency between an isoquant and isocost line, where the (negative) ratio of the marginal products equals the (negative) ratio of the user costs: $-Q_L/Q_K = -w_0/r_0$, or simply, $Q_L/Q_K = w_0/r_0$.

Applied to the Cobb-Douglas production function, $Q = AK^aL^b$, $(0 < a < 1, 0 < b < 1)$, which is homogeneous of degree $a + b$, the cost-minimizing condition is

$$Q_L/Q_K = \frac{bA\overline{K}^a\overline{L}^{b-1}}{aA\overline{K}^{a-1}\overline{L}^b} = w_0/r_0$$

Reducing, we have $b\overline{K}/a\overline{L} = w_0/r_0$. Solving for $\overline{K}$ gives the equation for the output-expansion path, $\overline{K} = (a/b)(w_0/r_0)\overline{L}$, which is a ray from the origin, with a slope equal to $d\overline{K}/d\overline{L} = (a/b)(w_0/r_0)$.

Recall from the previous example, given the user costs of capital and labor of $r_0 = \$28$ and $w_0 = \$10$, an increase in the firm's selected output from $Q_0 = 434$ to $Q_1 = 450$ increased the cost-minimizing factor combination from $K_0 = 124.8$ and $L_0 = 49.9$ to $K_1 = 130.8$ and $L_1 = 52.3$. The capital-labor ratio is unchanged, however: $\overline{K}_0/\overline{L}_0 =$

124.8/ 49.9 = 2.5 = 130.8/52.3 = $\overline{K}_1/\overline{L}_1$. This Cobb-Douglas function is homogeneous of degree .8, equal to the sum of the exponents of capital and labor ($a = .7$ and $b = .1$, respectively). The associated expansion path is a ray from the origin with a slope equal to 2.5: $\overline{K} = (a/b)(w_0/r_0)\overline{L} = (.7/.1)(10/28)\overline{L} = 2.5\overline{L}$.

Applied to the CES production function, $Q = A[uK^{-p} + (1-u)L^{-p}]^{-r/p}$, which is homogeneous of degree r, the ratio of the marginal products at the cost-minimizing combinations of K and L is

$$\frac{Q_L}{Q_K} = \frac{-(r/p)A[u\overline{K}^{-p} + (1-u)\overline{L}^{-p}]^{-r/p-1}(-p(1-u)\overline{L}^{-p-1})}{-(r/p)A[u\overline{K}^{-p} + (1-u)\overline{L}^{-p}]^{-r/p-1}(-p(u)\overline{K}^{-p-1})}$$

$$= \frac{(1-u)\overline{L}^{-p-1}}{u\overline{K}^{-p-1}} = \frac{(1-u)\overline{K}^{p+1}}{u\overline{L}^{p+1}}$$

Setting the ratio of the marginal products equal to the ratio of user costs gives

$$\frac{(1-u)\overline{K}^{p+1}}{u\overline{L}^{p+1}} = w_0/r_0$$

Then, solving for $\overline{K}$, we obtain the equation for the output-expansion path.

$$\overline{K} = [u/(1-u)]^{1/p+1}(w_0/r_0)^{1/p+1}\overline{L}$$

Thus, the output-expansion path for the CES production function is also a ray from the origin with a slope equal to $d\overline{K}/d\overline{L} = [u/(1-u)]^{1/p+1}(w_0/r_0)^{1/p+1}$.

To illustrate, consider the CES production function, $Q = 2[.4K^{-2} + .6L^{-2}]^{-1/3}$. The marginal productivities of labor and capital are

$$Q_L = -(2/3)[.4K^{-2} + .6L^{-2}]^{-4/3}(-1.2L^{-3})$$

$$Q_K = -(2/3)[.4K^{-2} + .6L^{-2}]^{-4/3}(-.8K^{-3})$$

If the user costs of capital and labor are: $r_0 = \$28$ and $w_0 = \$10$, then at the cost-minimizing combinations of capital and labor (i.e., at the points of tangency of the isoquants and isocost lines) the condition, $MRTS = -Q_L/Q_K = -w_0/r_0$, holds. Here, after simplifying, we have

$$Q_L/Q_K = 1.2L^{-3}/.8K^{-3} = 10/28$$

Solving for $\overline{K}$, the optimal amount of capital, we find the equation for the expansion path.

$$1.2K^3 = (10/28)(.8L^3)$$

$$K^3 = .24L^3$$

$$\overline{K} = (.24)^{1/3}\overline{L}$$

$$\overline{K} = .62\overline{L}$$

Here the CES production function is homogeneous of degree $r = 2/3$. That is, $p = 2$ and $r/p = 1/3$, so $r = (1/3)p = (1/3)(2) = 2/3$.

PRACTICE PROBLEM 10.8

Assuming the user costs of capital and labor are $r_0 = \$15$ and $w_0 = \$40$, find the equation for the expansion path for each of the following production functions.

a) $Q = 3K^{.8}L^{.2}$

b) $Q = 3(.8K^{-3} + .2L^{-3})^{-1/2}$

(The answers are at the end of the chapter.)

Elasticity of Substitution   Another important concept related to the comparative statics of a firm is **elasticity of substitution**, or the degree to which the firm can change its cost-minimizing ratio of factors in response to a change in the user cost ratio. The elasticity of substitution between capital and labor is defined to be σ (sigma), where

$$\sigma = \frac{d(\overline{K}/\overline{L})/(\overline{K}/\overline{L})}{d(w/r)/(w/r)} \cong \frac{\text{percentage change in the optimal capital-labor ratio}}{\text{percentage change in the wage-rental ratio}}$$

We expect $\sigma > 0$, since an increase in the relative price of labor $(w/r) \uparrow$ would induce a profit-maximizing (cost-minimizing) firm to use a more capital-intensive production process $(\overline{K}/\overline{L}) \uparrow$. See Figure 10.5, where a rise in the relative price of labor, reflected in a steeper isocost line, C_2 (compared to C_1) moves the firm along the isoquant Q_0 from E_1 to E_2, where $\overline{K}_2/\overline{L}_2 > \overline{K}_1/\overline{L}_1$.

The degree to which a firm can substitute the factors of production is reflected in the shape of its isoquants. Two extreme cases can be illustrated. In Figure 10.6a, the

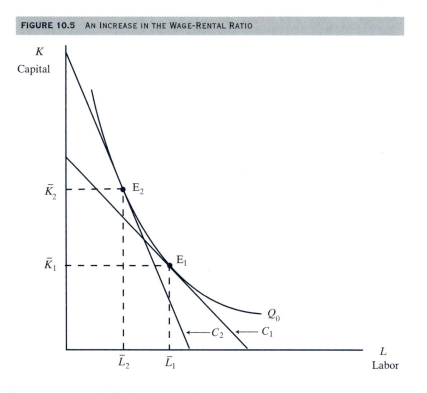

FIGURE 10.5 AN INCREASE IN THE WAGE-RENTAL RATIO

right-angle isoquant represents a **fixed-coefficients production function,** Q = minimum $(K/a, L/b)$, where a and b are constants indicating the fixed capital-output and labor-output ratios, respectively. For each level of output there is only one optimal combination of capital and labor—regardless of the user cost ratio. For example, for the output, Q_0, the optimal combination is $\overline{K}_0$ and $\overline{L}_0$, for any wage-rental ratio, w_0/r_0, where $\overline{K}_0 = aQ_0$ and $\overline{L}_0 = bQ_0$. For fixed-coefficients production functions, the elasticity of substitution is zero, $\sigma = 0$. A firm's capital-labor ratio is independent of the wage-rental ratio.

In Figure 10.6b, the isoquant is linear, indicating that capital and labor are perfect substitutes. The underlying production function is $Q = aK + bL$, where a and b are the fixed marginal products of capital and labor: $dQ/dK = a$ and $dQ/dL = b$. The slope of the isoquant is constant and equal to $-b/a$. For any isocost line with a flatter slope than the isoquant, here if $|-w_0/r_0| < |-b/a|$, the firm would use only labor. See point Q_0/b with isocost line C_1 in Figure 10.6b.

On the other hand, if the slope of the isocost line were steeper than the slope of the isoquant, $|-w_0/r_0| > |-b/a|$, then the firm would use only capital. See point Q_0/a and the isocost line C_2.

Finally, if the slopes of the isocost line and isoquant were equal, $|-w_0/r_0| = |-b/a|$, the firm could use any combination of capital and labor on the isoquant; however, the slightest change in the ratio of user costs would drive the cost-minimizing firm to one of the extreme combinations, Q_0/a or Q_0/b. In sum, for linear production functions and linear isoquants, the factors are perfect substitutes and the elasticity of substitution equals infinity, $\sigma = \infty$.

For the Cobb-Douglas production function, $Q = AK^aL^b$, the elasticity of substitution is equal to one. To demonstrate, return to the equation for the output-expansion path, $\overline{K} = (a/b)(w/r)\overline{L}$. Dividing through by $\overline{L}$ gives the optimal capital-labor ratio:

FIGURE 10.6 RIGHT-ANGLE ISOQUANTS AND LINEAR ISOQUANTS

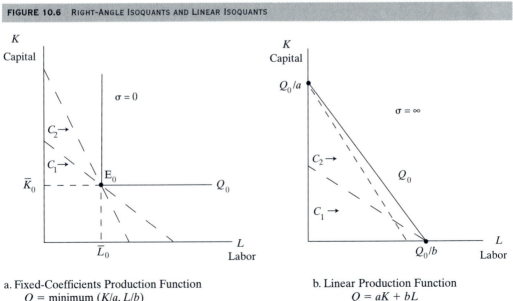

a. Fixed-Coefficients Production Function
   Q = minimum $(K/a, L/b)$

b. Linear Production Function
   $Q = aK + bL$

$K/L = (a/b)(w/r)$. Taking the natural logarithm of both sides, we have: $\ln(\overline{K/L}) = \ln(a/b) + \ln(w/r)$. Now, taking the derivative of both sides with respect to $\ln(w/r)$ yields the elasticity of substitution.

$$\frac{d \ln(\overline{K/L})}{d \ln(w/r)} = 1 = \sigma = \frac{d(\overline{K/L})/(\overline{K/L})}{d(w/r)/(w/r)}$$

In words, for the Cobb-Douglas production function, a 1% increase in the ratio of the user cost of labor to the user cost of capital would induce a 1% increase in the optimal capital-labor ratio.

Recall the earlier example of the firm's minimization of the total cost ($C = 28K + 10L$) of producing a selected level of output ($Q_0 = 434 = 10K^{.7}L^{.1}$). An increase in the user cost of capital from $r_0 = \$28$ to $r_2 = \$30$ led to a shift in the optimal combination of capital and labor from $\overline{K}_0 = 124.8$ and $\overline{L}_0 = 49.9$ to $\overline{K}_2 = 123.9$ and $\overline{L}_2 = 53.1$. Here, the wage-rental ratio fell from $w_0/r_0 = 10/28 = .357$ to $w_1/r_1 = 10/30 = .333$, or by 6.7%, which led to a fall in the cost-minimizing capital-labor ratio of 6.7%, from $\overline{K}_0/\overline{L}_0 = 124.8/49.9 = 2.5$ to $\overline{K}_2/\overline{L}_2 = 123.9/53.1 = 2.33$. This is consistent with the unitary elasticity of substitution of the Cobb-Douglas production function.

For the CES production function, rewriting the output-expansion path in terms of the optimal capital-labor ratio gives: $\overline{K/L} = [u/(1 - u)]^{1/p+1} (w/r)^{1/p+1}$. Taking the natural logarithm of both sides, we have

$$\ln(\overline{K/L}) = [1/(p + 1)] \ln[u/(1 - u)] + [1/(p + 1)] \ln(w/r)$$

Differentiating both sides of this equation with respect to $\ln(w/r)$, as before, yields the elasticity of substitution.

$$\frac{d \ln(\overline{K/L})}{d \ln(w/r)} = 1/(p + 1) = \sigma = \frac{d(\overline{K/L})/(\overline{K/L})}{d(w/r)/(w/r)}$$

Thus, for the CES production function, as the name indicates, the elasticity of substitution is constant and is equal to $1/(p + 1)$, where $p > -1$ and $p \neq 0$.

To illustrate, take the CES production function, $Q = 2 (.4K^{-2} + .6L^{-2})^{-1/3}$. For a wage-rental ratio of $w_0/r_0 = 10/28 = .357$, the expansion path is given by: $\overline{K} = (.4/.6)^{1/3} (10/28)^{1/3} \overline{L} = .62\overline{L}$, so the capital-labor ratio along the expansion path equals $(\overline{K/L})_0 = .62$. If the user cost of capital increases to $r_2 = \$30$, then the expansion path becomes: $\overline{K} = (.4/.6)^{1/3} (10/30)^{1/3} \overline{L} = .606\overline{L}$. The capital-labor ratio along the new expansion path is: $(\overline{K/L})_2 = .606$. The 6.7% decrease in the wage-rental ratio, from $w_0/r_0 = .357$ to $w_0/r_2 = .333$ led to a 2.2% decrease in the optimal capital-labor ratio, from $(\overline{K/L})_0 = .62$ to $(\overline{K/L})_2 = .606$. The elasticity of substitution is $\sigma = 2.2/6.7 \cong 1/3 = 1/(p + 1)$.

PRACTICE PROBLEM 10.9

Determine the elasticity of substitution for the following production functions.

a) $Q = 3K^{.8} L^{.2}$

b) $Q = 3(.8K^{-3} + .2L^{-3})^{-1/2}$

(The answers are at the end of the chapter.)

In the next chapter we continue our analysis of constrained optimization for the firm with the technique of mathematical programming and multiple constraints. Here the optimization occurs under conditions where not all of the constraints need be binding.

❖ KEY TERMS

Economics

- CES production function (p. 343)
- Cobb-Douglas production function (p. 343)
- constant returns to scale (p. 344)
- decreasing returns to scale (p. 344)
- economically efficient (p. 349)
- elasticity of substitution (p. 359)

- fixed coefficients production function (p. 359)
- increasing returns to scale (p. 344)
- isocost line (p. 350)
- isoquant (p. 345)
- law of diminishing returns (p. 347)
- marginal rate of technical substitution (p. 346)

- output-expansion path (p. 356)
- production function (p. 342)
- technically efficient (p. 343)
- user cost of capital (p. 349)
- user cost of labor (p. 349)

Mathematics

- bordered Hessian (p. 338)
- homogeneous of degree r (p. 344)

- Lagrange multiplier (p. 330)
- Lagrangian (p. 330)

- linearly homogeneous (p. 344)
- overdetermined (p. 341)

❖ PROBLEMS

1. Given the objective function, $z(x,y) = 40x - 2x^2 + xy - 3y^2 + 20y - 40$:
   a) Find the critical values for the variables x and y.
   b) Find the optimum value for z.
   c) Check the second-order conditions to establish the type of relative extremum.
   d) Now add the constraint, $x + y = 10$, and find the new critical values for x and y.
   e) Find the constrained optimum value for z.
   f) Find the value of the Lagrange multiplier.
   g) Check the second-order condition for the constrained optimization.

2. Repeat parts a)–c) of Problem 1 for the objective function, $z(x,y) = -25x + 5x^2 - 2xy + 2y^2 - 15y + 12$. Then add the constraint, $3x + y = 15$, and repeat parts d)–g).

3. Repeat parts d)–g) in Problem 2 if, instead, the constraint is $3x + y = 18$.

4. Given the production functions:
   i) $Q = 2K^{.4}L^{.6}$ ii) $Q = 2(.4K^{-2} + .6L^{-2})^{-1/2}$ iii) $Q = .4K + .6L$
   for each find:
   a) the marginal products of labor and capital. Are labor and capital each subject to diminishing returns?

    b) the returns to scale

    c) the elasticity of substitution

    d) the equation for the output-expansion path, given that the user costs of labor and capital are respectively: $w_0 = \$10$ and $r_0 = \$20$.

5. Given a firm with a production function, $Q = 1.5K^4L^6$, seeking the cost-minimizing combination of capital and labor for producing $Q_0 = 200$ units of output, assume that the user costs of capital and labor to the firm are, respectively, $r_0 = \$20$ and $w_0 = \$12$.

    a) Find the cost-minimizing combination of K and L.

    b) Determine the marginal cost of production.

    c) Determine the minimum total cost.

    d) Check the second-order condition.

    e) If the firm decreases its output to $Q_1 = 190$, find the new cost-minimizing combination of K and L.

    f) If the user cost of capital declines to $r_2 = \$15$, find the new cost-minimizing combination of K and L for producing $Q_0 = 200$.

6. Repeat the analysis in Problem 5, parts a)–c), only where the firm's production function is given by $Q = 1.5(.4K^{-2} + .6L^{-2})^{-1/2}$.

7. A firm with a Cobb-Douglas production function, $Q = AK^aL^b$, $(0 < a < 1, 0 < b < 1)$, where A is an index of technology, facing user costs of labor and capital equal to w_0 and r_0, respectively, seeks to find the cost-minimizing combination of capital and labor for producing a selected level of output equal to Q_0.

    a) Set up the Lagrangian function.

    b) Derive the first-order conditions and solve for the optimal values of K and L.

    c) Solve for and interpret the optimal value of the Lagrange multiplier.

    d) Check the second-order conditions.

    e) Find and sign (if possible) the following comparative static results.

        i) $\delta\bar{L}/\delta A$ ii) $\delta\bar{L}/\delta w_0$ iii) $\delta\bar{L}/\delta Q_0$

Do these results make economic sense? Discuss.

Note: For this problem you do not have to use the Implicit Function Theorem to do comparative statics since you can solve explicitly for the equilibrium values of the endogenous variables.

8. A firm with a general production function, $Q = A \cdot Q(K, L)$, where A is an index of technology, facing user costs of labor and capital equal to w_0 and r_0, respectively, seeks to find the cost-minimizing combination of capital and labor for producing a selected level of output of Q_0.

    a) Set up the Lagrangian function.

    b) Derive and interpret the first-order conditions.

    c) Interpret the optimal value of the Lagrange multiplier.

    d) Check the second-order conditions.

e) Using the Implicit Function Theorem and Cramer's rule, find and sign (if possible) the following comparative static results.
  i) $\delta\bar{L}/\delta A$ ii) $\delta\bar{L}/\delta w_0$ iii) $\delta\bar{L}/\delta Q_0$

Do these results make economic sense? Discuss.

❖ ANSWERS TO PRACTICE PROBLEMS

10.1 a) The critical values are: $\bar{x}_0 = 48.3$ and $\bar{y}_0 = 40.0$.
  b) The optimal value of z is: $\bar{z}_0 = 1,608.\bar{3}$.
  c) $|H_1| = -6 < 0$ and $|H_2| = 12 > 0$, consistent with a maximum.
  d) The critical values are: $\bar{x}_1 = 43.8$ and $\bar{y}_1 = 36.2$.
  e) The constrained optimum value of z is: $\bar{z}_1 = 1,592.3$.
  f) The value of the Lagrange multiplier is: $\bar{\lambda}_1 = 3.85$.

10.2 a) The critical values are: $\bar{x}_0 = 1.\bar{6}$ and $\bar{y}_0 = .8\bar{3}$.
  b) The optimal value of z is: $\bar{z}_0 = 9.72$.
  c) $|H_1| = 10 > 0$ and $|H_2| = 24 > 0$, consistent with a minimum.
  d) The critical values are: $\bar{x}_1 = 1.2$ and $\bar{y}_1 = .6$.
  e) The constrained optimum value of z is: $\bar{z}_1 = 5.8$.
  f) The value of the Lagrange multiplier is: $\bar{\lambda}_1 = -2.8$.

10.3 The bordered Hessian is $|\overline{H}| = 26 > 0$, which is consistent with a constrained maximum.

10.4 The bordered Hessian is $|\overline{H}| = -10 < 0$, which is consistent with a constrained minimum.

10.5 a) $Q = .5K^{.7}L^{.3}$ is characterized by constant returns to scale, $r = 1.0$.
  b) $Q = [.5K^{-2} + .5L^{-2}]^{-.6}$ is characterized by increasing returns to scale, $r = 1.2$.

10.6 a) The marginal products are: $Q_L = 1.2K^{.5}L^{-.6} > 0$ and $Q_K = 1.5K^{-.5}L^{.4} > 0$.
  b) $Q_{LL} = -.72K^{.5}L^{-1.6} < 0$ and $Q_{KK} = -.75K^{-1.5}L^{.4} < 0$.
  c) $Q_{KL} = .6K^{-.5}L^{-.6} = Q_{LK} > 0$
  d) $dMRTS/dL = 1.44K/L^2 > 0$

10.7 a) The cost-minimizing combination of capital and labor is: $\bar{K}_0 = 22.6$ and $\bar{L}_0 = 84.8$.
  b) The marginal cost of output is: $\bar{\lambda}_0 = \$8.5$.
  c) The minimum total cost is: $\bar{C} = \$847.8$.
  d) The bordered Hessian equals $|\overline{H}| = -.55 < 0$, which is consistent with a constrained minimum.

10.8 a) $\overline{K} = 10.\bar{6}\,\overline{L}$.
  b) $\overline{K} = 1.8\overline{L}$.

10.9 a) The elasticity of substitution is: $\sigma = 1$.
  b) The elasticity of substitution is: $\sigma = 1/4$.

THEORY OF THE FIRM: INEQUALITY CONSTRAINTS

A central concern in economics is the optimal allocation of resources. In Chapter 10 we modeled a firm's pursuit of the cost-minimizing combination of capital and labor for producing a selected level of output. In the next chapter we will examine a household's objective of achieving the greatest satisfaction from its expenditures on goods and services out of a given income.

In these classical constrained optimization problems, the choice variables are strictly related. That is, the relationship between the choice variables is specified by an equality constraint. For example, the firm's selected level of output was to be exactly produced. There were no restrictions, save being nonnegative, on the factors of capital and labor available to the firm in the long run. Moreover, the number of equality constraints could not exceed the number of choice variables—so with two choice variables (capital and labor) we dealt with one constraint (producing the selected level of output).

We may want to allow greater flexibility to the firm. The output constraint need not be binding or hold exactly, and the strict relationships between the choice variables embodied in equality constraints may be loosened to bounded relationships represented by inequality constraints. On the other hand, we may want to impose additional conditions on a firm's optimization. For example, a labor contract may commit a firm to using at least a minimum amount of labor. Or, environmental standards may limit the maximum amount of an input a firm can use.

Mathematical programming provides techniques for analyzing allocation problems where the constraints on the economic activity need not be binding. We begin with linear programming, which, while limited in applications due to the linear specification for the involved functions, is conceptually straightforward, useful for illustrating the important principle of duality, and important for the transition to the more advanced technique of nonlinear programming.

LINEAR PROGRAMMING

When restricted to linear functions—both for the objective function and the constraints—the analysis is called *linear programming*. We begin with the general formulation of a linear programming problem in maximization. Given a linear objective function, z, in n choice variables, $x_1, x_2, \ldots x_n$, and m linear constraints, the problem can be written as:

$$\text{maximize: } z = c_1 x_1 + c_2 x_2 + \cdots + c_n x_n$$

$$\text{subject to: } a_{11} x_1 + a_{12} x_2 + \cdots + a_{1n} x_n \leq r_1$$

$$a_{21} x_1 + a_{22} x_2 + \cdots + a_{2n} x_n \leq r_2$$

$$.$$
$$.$$
$$.$$

$$a_{m1} x_1 + a_{m2} x_2 + \cdots + a_{mn} x_n \leq r_m$$

$$\text{and } x_j \geq 0 \qquad j = 1 \ldots n$$

The c_j, $(j = 1 \ldots n)$, are the exogenous coefficients of the n choice variables in the objective function, and the a_{ij}, $(i = 1 \ldots m, j = 1 \ldots n)$, are the exogenous coefficients of the n choice variables in the m constraints. Note that the n choice variables, x_j, are subject to n nonnegativity restrictions $(x_j \geq 0)$. Most variables in economics (e.g., prices, quantities, and incomes) assume only nonnegative values.

There are m linear constraints, and, in contrast to the classical constrained optimization problems of the previous chapter, we allow for nonbinding constraints. That is, the constraints are expressed as weak inequalities ($\leq$ for a maximization problem). Accordingly, the number of constraints may exceed the number of choice variables, that is, $m > n$. The $r_i, i = 1 \ldots m$, are constants that represent the upper limits or bounds for the constraints.

We can write the system in matrix notation as:

$$\text{maximize: } z = \mathbf{cx}$$

$$\text{subject to: } \mathbf{Ax} \leq \mathbf{r}$$

$$\text{and } \mathbf{x} \geq \mathbf{0}$$

$$\text{where } \mathbf{c} = [c_1 \, c_2 \ldots c_n] \text{ and}$$

$$\mathbf{x} = \begin{bmatrix} x_1 \\ x_2 \\ . \\ . \\ x_n \end{bmatrix} \quad \mathbf{A} = \begin{bmatrix} a_{11} & a_{12} & \cdots & a_{1n} \\ a_{21} & a_{22} & \cdots & a_{2n} \\ . \\ . \\ a_{m1} & a_{m2} & \cdots & a_{mn} \end{bmatrix} \quad \mathbf{r} = \begin{bmatrix} r_1 \\ r_2 \\ . \\ . \\ r_m \end{bmatrix}$$

An Example in Linear Programming To illustrate, consider an entrepreneur, who seeks to maximize the total revenues generated across n production activities given fixed quantities available of m inputs. Specifically, consider a farmer seeking the optimal planting of two crops ($n = 2$) given fixed quantities of land, labor hours, and fertilizer available ($m = 3$).

The farmer's total revenues are a linear combination of the unit prices and quantities of the two crops. The goal of the farmer is to maximize $R = P_1 x_1 + P_2 x_2$, where

$$R = \text{total revenues from the sale of the two crops}$$

$$P_1 = \text{unit price of crop 1}$$

$$P_2 = \text{unit price of crop 2}$$

$$x_1 = \text{quantity produced of crop 1}$$

and $$x_2 = \text{quantity produced of crop 2.}$$

The unit prices are assumed to be set in the market and exogenous to the farmer. The farmer is searching for the revenue-maximizing output combination of the two crops.

The farmer faces resource constraints, however, reflected in the quantities of land (input 1), labor hours (input 2), and fertilizer (input 3) available in the production period. We assume fixed coefficients production functions for each crop, where there are no substitutions possible over the required inputs. The resource constraints are:

$$a_{11} x_1 + a_{12} x_2 \le r_1 \quad \text{(land constraint)}$$

$$a_{21} x_1 + a_{22} x_2 \le r_2 \quad \text{(labor constraint)}$$

$$a_{31} x_1 + a_{32} x_2 \le r_3 \quad \text{(fertilizer constraint)}$$

where r_1, r_2, and r_3 are the total amounts of land, labor hours, and fertilizer, respectively, available to the farmer during the period; and a_{ij} ($i = 1, 2, 3$, and $j = 1, 2$) is the fixed quantity of input i required to produce one unit of output j. Finally, we have the nonnegativity restrictions: $x_j \ge 0$. That is, the output of each crop is zero or positive.

To make this example more concrete, suppose that we have the following values:

$$P_1 = \$5, P_2 = \$3, r_1 = 36 \text{ acres}, r_2 = 40 \text{ hours}, r_3 = 28 \text{ bags of fertilizer, and}$$

$$a_{11} = 6, a_{12} = 2, a_{21} = 5, a_{22} = 5, a_{31} = 2, a_{32} = 4$$

The linear programming problem is then:

maximize: $R = 5x_1 + 3x_2$

subject to: $6x_1 + 2x_2 \le 36$

$\qquad\qquad 5x_1 + 5x_2 \le 40$

$\qquad\qquad 2x_1 + 4x_2 \le 28$

and $\qquad x_1, x_2 \ge 0$

Here, to plant each unit of crop 1 (e.g., each unit equals a hundred bushels) requires 6 acres of land, 5 hours of labor, and 2 bags of fertilizer. Each unit of crop 2 (in hundreds of bushels) requires 2 acres of land, 5 hours of labor, and 4 bags of fertilizer. We can say that crop 1 is relatively land-intensive, while crop 2 is fertilizer-intensive. There are a total of 36 acres of land, 40 hours of labor, and 28 bags of fertilizer available to the farmer.

The resource constraints illustrate the production limitations on the farmer. For example, the land constraint $(6x_1 + 2x_2 \leq 36)$ indicates the output combinations of the two crops that are possible with the land available. That is, the sum of the land allocated to crop 1 (the 6 acres of land for each unit of output, $6x_1$) and the land allocated to crop 2 (2 acres of land for each unit of output, $2x_2$) cannot exceed the 36 acres of land available.

With two choice variables, x_1 and x_2, the quantities of the two crops planted, we can graphically illustrate the possible output combinations. In Figure 11.1 the three resource constraints are plotted. The intersection of the areas underneath the linear constraints defines the *feasible region* for solutions. See the shaded area OABCD. Any output combination in the feasible region, including the boundary ABCD, satisfies all of the constraints. To find the coordinates of the *extreme points*, A, B, C, and D, we can

FIGURE 11.1   RESOURCE CONSTRAINTS AND THE FEASIBLE REGION

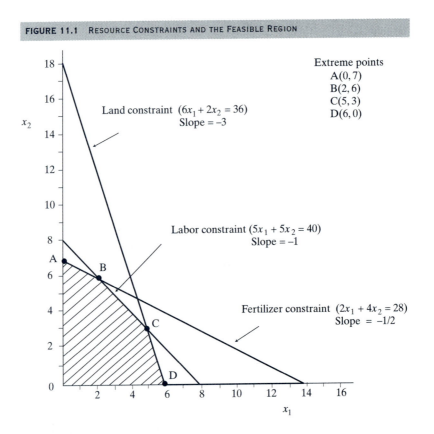

solve simultaneously using the two relevant intersecting constraints. For example, for the coordinates of the extreme point B, we use the labor and fertilizer constraints, written as equalities.

$$5x_1 + 5x_2 = 40 \text{ (labor constraint)}$$

$$2x_1 + 4x_2 = 28 \text{ (fertilizer constraint)}$$

From the labor constraint, we can "solve" for x_1 as: $x_1 = 8 - x_2$. Substituting for x_1 into the fertilizer constraint and solving for x_2 gives:

$$2(8 - x_2) + 4x_2 = 28$$

$$16 - 2x_2 + 4x_2 = 28$$

$$2x_2 = 12$$

So $x_2 = 6$ and $x_1 = 8 - 6 = 2$. The coordinates of the extreme point B are $(2, 6)$. Similarly, we can find the coordinates of the extreme point C $(5, 3)$ involving the land and fertilizer constraints. The extreme points A $(0, 7)$ and D $(6, 0)$ each involve only one constraint.

Intuitively, given the farmer's objective of maximizing total revenues, which, for exogenous market prices for the two crops would imply output combinations as far from the origin as possible, we would restrict our search to the combinations lying on the boundary of (not within) the feasible region. We could begin by evaluating the objective function at each of the extreme points. Doing so for $R = 5x_1 + 3x_2$ gives:

$$A(0, 7): R = 5(0) + 3(7) = 21$$

$$B(2, 6): R = 5(2) + 3(6) = 28$$

$$C(5, 3): R = 5(5) + 3(3) = 34$$

$$D(6, 0): R = 5(6) + 3(0) = 30.$$

The output combination represented by point $C, \bar{x}_1 = 5$ and $\bar{x}_2 = 3$, maximizes the total revenues of the farmer: $\bar{R} = 34$.

Graphically, we could sketch parallel **isorevenue lines**, $R = 5x_1 + 3x_2$, or, equivalently, $x_2 = R/3 - (5/3)x_1$, with slopes equal to $-5/3$. The isorevenue line furthest from the origin, but still intersecting the boundary of feasible region, represents the maximum total revenue. The highest isorevenue line is $x_2 = 34/3 - (5/3)x_1$, where $R = 34$, and intersects the boundary of the feasible region at point C. We note that the slope of the line segment BC of the feasible region equals -1, and the slope of the line segment CD is equal to -3. The slope of the isorevenue lines, (not plotted in Figure 11.1), equals the negative of the ratio of unit prices of the two crops, $-P_1/P_2 = -5/3$, which falls between the slopes of the adjacent line segments BC and CD. Thus, for the given relative prices of the two crops, point C is as far from the origin as the feasible region of solutions allows.

For different relative price ratios, we might (but need not) obtain different revenue-maximizing combinations of the two crops. The table below summarizes the revenue-maximizing output combinations for all the relative price ratios (P_1/P_2). You should confirm these results.

Relative Price Ratio (P_1/P_2)	Revenue-Maximizing Output-Combination
$P_1/P_2 < 1/2$	A: $x_1 = 0, x_2 = 7$.
$P_1/P_2 = 1/2$	Any combination on the line segment AB
$1/2 < P_1/P_2 < 1$	B: $x_1 = 2, x_2 = 6$
$P_1/P_2 = 1$	Any combination on the line segment BC
$1 < P_1/P_2 < 3$	C: $x_1 = 5, x_2 = 3$
$P_1/P_2 = 3$	Any combination on the line segment CD
$P_1/P_2 > 3$	D: $x_1 = 6, x_2 = 0$

THE SIMPLEX METHOD

As we know, a limitation to graphical analysis is the severe dimensional constraint imposed; that is, we can represent only two, or at most three, choice variables. To solve linear programming problems with any number of choice variables ($n \geq 2$), the *simplex method* can be used.

Consider the general maximization problem with a linear objective function of n choice variables subject to m inequality constraints.

$$\text{maximize:} \quad z = c_1 x_1 + c_2 x_2 + \cdots + c_n x_n$$

$$\text{subject to:} \quad a_{11} x_1 + a_{12} x_2 + \cdots + a_{1n} x_n \leq r_1$$

$$a_{21} x_1 + a_{22} x_2 + \cdots + a_{2n} x_n \leq r_2$$

$$\cdot$$
$$\cdot$$
$$\cdot$$

$$a_{m1} x_1 + a_{m2} x_2 + \cdots + a_{mn} x_n \leq r_m$$

and the nonnegativity restrictions $x_j \geq 0$ $(j = 1 \ldots n)$

We first convert the inequality constraints into equalities by adding *dummy variables*, $s_1, s_2, \ldots s_m$, known as *slack variables* in maximization problems. These slack variables are also "added" to the objective function; but in order not to affect the optimal value of the variable to be maximized, the coefficients assigned to the slack variables in the objective function are all equal to zero. Thus, we can write:

$$\text{maximize:} \quad z = c_1 x_1 + c_2 x_2 + \cdots + c_n x_n + 0s_1 + 0s_2 + \cdots + 0s_m$$

$$\text{subject to:} \quad a_{11} x_1 + a_{12} x_2 + \cdots + a_{1n} x_n + s_1 = r_1$$

$$a_{21} x_1 + a_{22} x_2 + \cdots + a_{2n} x_n + s_2 = r_2$$

$$.$$
$$.$$
$$.$$

$$a_{m1} x_1 + a_{m2} x_2 + \cdots + a_{mn} x_n + s_m = r_m$$

$$x_j \geq 0$$

We now have $(n + m)$ endogenous variables, (the n choice variables and the m slack variables). Recall, for a unique solution to a linear system with n endogenous variables, there must be n simultaneous equations. With m constraints, a solution to this general system of m linear equations will consist of only m of the $(n + m)$ endogenous variables.

With the simplex method, on each trial solution, we set n of the $(n + m)$ endogenous variables equal to zero, and then solve the m equations for the m remaining variables. We continue to evaluate the feasible solutions as long as the optimal value of the dependent variable, z, increases on each trial. When no further improvement is realized, we have found the optimal values for the included m variables.

Below we illustrate for our example of the farmer with two crops and three resource constraints. Recall the problem:

$$\text{maximize:} \quad R = 5x_1 + 3x_2 \quad \text{(total revenue function)}$$

$$\text{subject to:} \quad 6x_1 + 2x_2 \leq 36 \ \text{(land constraint)}$$

$$5x_1 + 5x_2 \leq 40 \ \text{(labor constraint)}$$

$$2x_1 + 4x_2 \leq 28 \ \text{(fertilizer constraint)}$$

$$\text{and } x_1, x_2 \geq 0$$

Adding the three slack variables to the three constraints and the objective function, we get

$$\text{maximize:} \quad R = 5x_1 + 3x_2 + 0s_1 + 0s_2 + 0s_3$$

$$\text{subject to:} \quad 6x_1 + 2x_2 + s_1 = 36$$

$$5x_1 + 5x_2 + s_2 = 40$$

$$2x_1 + 4x_2 + s_3 = 28$$

$$\text{and } x_1, x_2 \geq 0$$

We then set up the *simplex tableau*, a table that we can manipulate to obtain the solution to the linear programming problem. All of the variables of the problem are aligned at the top of the tableau, beginning with the dependent variable, the choice variables, the slack variables, and finally the constant, representing the resource constraints. The objective function is rewritten as: $R - 5x_1 - 3x_2 - 0s_1 - 0s_2 - 0s_3 = 0$. The coefficients of the rewritten objective function are represented in row 0 of the tableau. The coefficients of the constraints are represented in rows 1–m (here $m = 3$) of the tableau. The initial tableau, **I**, is given below.

I	R	x_1	x_2	s_1	s_2	s_3	Constant
row 0	1	−5	−3	0	0	0	0
row 1	0	6	2	1	0	0	36
row 2	0	5	5	0	1	0	40
row 3	0	2	4	0	0	1	28

Remember that this system of three equations (the three constraints) in five endogenous variables (the 2 choice variables and 3 slack variables) requires that only three of the endogenous variables enter into the solution (the other two being set equal to zero). With the simplex method, we systematically rotate sets of three endogenous variables through the objective function until we no longer increase the value of the dependent variable to be maximized.

Recall also that m linearly independent vectors form the basis for m-space. Regarding the 3×5 matrix formed by rows 1, 2, and 3 and the columns under x_1, x_2, s_1, s_2, and s_3 as the one that is relevant for the feasible set of solutions, we can see that the initial tableau provides one possible solution. The three column vectors under the slack variables are linearly independent and thus form a basis for 3-space. We can quickly reject this set ($s_1 = 36$, $s_2 = 40$, and $s_3 = 28$) as the solution, however, since if all of the slack variables were the nonzero variables in the solution set, then the two choice variables would be equal to zero ($x_1 = 0$, $x_2 = 0$), and the value of the total revenues (to be maximized), would be zero. This trial solution corresponds to the origin of the feasible region, illustrated in Figure 11.1. No resources are used, no output is produced, and total revenues are zero.

So we move on, forming a new basis for the 3-space by replacing one of the slack variables with one of the choice variables. In the simplex method, for a maximization problem, we select the variable to include by finding the largest negative value in row 0. Here, it is −5, corresponding to the choice variable, x_1. Intuitively, this makes sense. If we are seeking to maximize total revenues, then we would begin with the output with the largest unit price. The column under the selected variable becomes the *pivot column*, which will be manipulated to become linearly independent with two other columns that will then form a basis for 3-space.

We then need to select a *pivot element* in this column. The decision rule is to divide each positive element in the pivot column into its corresponding element in the last column of constants. The resulting ratios are called *displacement quotients*. The three displacement quotients in the x_1 pivot column are $36/6 = 6$, $40/5 = 8$, and $28/2 = 14$. The element with the smallest displacement quotient, here the 6 (underlined in Tableau **I**) becomes the pivot element. Note that selecting the smallest displacement quotient also makes sense, since we are concerned with resource constraints. Dividing the unit input requirements into the total supply of the input and taking the smallest ratio may indicate the tightest resource constraint.

Next, we set the pivot element equal to 1 by dividing the row containing the pivot element by 6. The transformed row 1, indicated by row 1′, is given below.

$$\text{row 1}' \quad [0 \quad 1 \quad 1/3 \quad 1/6 \quad 0 \quad 0 \quad 6]$$

Through the addition of multiples of row 1' to the other rows, we can eliminate the nonzero elements in the pivot column. Recall from Chapter 5 that among the properties of determinants of matrices useful in solving a system of linear equations is: Multiplying any row of a determinant by a constant k and adding the result to any other row of the determinant, does not change the value of the determinant. Here, in our row manipulation we are also multiplying the terms in the rows under the constants.

To eliminate the -5 in row 0 of the pivot column, we multiply row 1' by 5 and add to row 0, obtaining the new row 0' (with the desired zero in the transformed row underlined for emphasis).

$$\text{row } 0' \quad [1 \quad \underline{0} \quad -4/3 \quad 5/6 \quad 0 \quad 0 \quad 30]$$

To eliminate the 5 in row 2 of the pivot column, we multiply row 1' by -5 and add to row 2, obtaining the new row 2'.

$$\text{row } 2' \quad [0 \quad \underline{0} \quad 10/3 \quad -5/6 \quad 1 \quad 0 \quad 10]$$

Finally, to eliminate the 2 in row 3 of the pivot column, we multiply row 1' by -2 and add to row 3, obtaining the new row 3'.

$$\text{row } 3' \quad [0 \quad \underline{0} \quad 10/3 \quad -1/3 \quad 0 \quad 1 \quad 16]$$

The new simplex tableau, labeled **II**, is illustrated below.

II	R	x_1	x_2	s_1	s_2	s_3	Constant
row 0'	1	0	$-4/3$	5/6	0	0	30
row 1'	0	1	1/3	1/6	0	0	6
row 2'	0	0	$\underline{10/3}$	$-5/6$	1	0	10
row 3'	0	0	10/3	$-1/3$	0	1	16

With this simplex tableau, the basis for the 3-space is the three linearly independent columns under x_1, s_2, and s_3. The variables x_2 and s_1 are set equal to zero. In this trial solution, $x_1 = 6$, $s_2 = 10$, and $s_3 = 16$, with $x_2 = 0$ and $s_1 = 0$. With only the first constraint binding, since the associated slack variable, s_1, equals zero, the total revenues would be equal to 30: $R = 5x_1 + 3x_2 = 5(6) + 3(0) = 30$. Note, the value of the objective function for this solution can be found in row 0' under the constant column.

As long as there is a negative value in the top row of the simplex tableau, row 0' here, we continue on and try a new basis. The new pivot column is x_2, containing the largest negative element in row 0'; in fact, in this example, the only negative element in row 0'. The pivot element is the 10/3 found in row 2', since its displacement quotient, $10/(10/3) = 3$, is the smallest for the positive elements in the pivot column.

Before securing a 1 for the pivot element by dividing row 2' through by 10/3, we could add -1 times row 2' to row 3' to eliminate the nonzero element present there. Row 3' then becomes row 3''.

$$\text{row } 3'' \quad [0 \quad 0 \quad \underline{0} \quad 1/2 \quad -1 \quad 1 \quad 6]$$

Now, dividing through row 2′ by 10/3 gives row 2″.

$$\text{row 2″} \quad [0 \quad 0 \quad 1 \quad -1/4 \quad 3/10 \quad 0 \quad 3]$$

To eliminate the $-4/3$ in the pivot column of row 0″, we multiply row 2″ by 4/3 and add to row 0′. The new row 0″ is:

$$\text{row 0″} \quad [1 \quad 0 \quad \underline{0} \quad 1/2 \quad 2/5 \quad 0 \quad 34]$$

Finally, to eliminate the 1/3 in the pivot column of row 1′, we multiply row 2″ by $-1/3$ and add the result to row 1′, obtaining row 1″:

$$\text{row 1″} \quad [0 \quad 1 \quad \underline{0} \quad 1/4 \quad -1/10 \quad 0 \quad 5]$$

(As an aside, as much fun as row manipulation is, we can appreciate the value of computer programs that, given an initial simplex tableau, can generate all the row manipulations involved in solving a linear programming problem.)

The new simplex tableau, labeled **III**, is

III	R	x_1	x_2	s_1	s_2	s_3	Constant
row 0″	1	0	0	1/2	2/5	0	34
row 1″	0	1	0	1/4	−1/10	0	5
row 2″	0	0	1	−1/4	3/10	0	3
row 3″	0	0	0	1/2	−1	1	6

Since there are no longer any negative elements in the top row, row 0″ here, we have reached the final simplex tableau and our solution to the maximization linear programming problem. The three linearly independent columns that form a basis for 3-space are x_1, x_2, and s_3. Combining with the first column of the final tableau for the dependent variable, R, we can write out the solution in matrix form.

$$\begin{bmatrix} 1 & 0 & 0 & 0 \\ 0 & 1 & 0 & 0 \\ 0 & 0 & 1 & 0 \\ 0 & 0 & 0 & 1 \end{bmatrix} \begin{bmatrix} R \\ \bar{x}_1 \\ \bar{x}_2 \\ \bar{s}_3 \end{bmatrix} = \begin{bmatrix} 34 \\ 5 \\ 3 \\ 6 \end{bmatrix}$$

or

$$\bar{R} = 34, \bar{x}_1 = 5, \bar{x}_2 = 3, \text{ and } \bar{s}_3 = 6 \quad \text{(with } \bar{s}_1 = 0 \text{ and } \bar{s}_2 = 0\text{)}$$

Not surprisingly, this is the same solution we found graphically earlier by evaluating the extreme points of the feasible region. Note that $\bar{s}_3 = 6$ means that the third constraint (in this example, the fertilizer constraint) is not binding. The other two constraints, (land and labor), corresponding to the slack variables s_1 and s_2, however, are binding. We write out the solution below. The optimum value of the objective function: $\bar{R} = P_1 \bar{x}_1 + P_2 \bar{x}_2 = 5(5) + 3(3) = 34$ (or \$3,400 since the outputs of the two crops are in hundreds of bushels).

constraints: $6\bar{x}_1 + 2\bar{x}_2 + \bar{s}_1 = 6(5) + 2(3) + 0 = 36$ (acres of land)

$$5\bar{x}_1 + 5\bar{x}_2 + \bar{s}_2 = 5(5) + 5(3) + 0 = 40 \text{ (hours of labor)}$$

$$2\bar{x}_1 + 4\bar{x}_2 + \bar{s}_3 = 2(5) + 4(3) + 6 = 28 \text{ (bags of fertilizer)}$$

In fact, the final tableau provides information in addition to the solution values of the choice variables, the optimum value of the objective function, and which of the constraints are binding. The value of the element in the row directly under each slack variable gives the marginal value or **shadow price** of the associated input or resource. Similar to Lagrange multipliers, the shadow price indicates how much the optimum value of the objective function would change with a one unit increase in the amount of the resource available.

In this example, the 1/2 in row 0″ under the s_1 of the final tableau indicates that a 1-unit increase in the quantity of resource 1 (one acre of land) available to the farmer would increase total revenues by 1/2 of a unit (here, $.5 times a hundred bushels or $50). Similarly, the 2/5 under the s_2 slack variable shows that a 1-unit increase in the quantity of resource 2 (1 hour of labor) would increase total revenues by 2/5 of a unit (here, $.4 times a hundred bushels or $40). With the fertilizer constraint nonbinding ($s_3 = 6$, or 6 bags of fertilizer remaining), the element in Row 0″ under the s_3 slack variable equals zero. Relaxing a nonbinding constraint would not affect the optimum value of the objective function. In this example, another bag of fertilizer would not increase the farmer's total revenues.

Finally, the optimum value of the objective function will be equal to the sum of the products of the shadow prices and quantities of the available resources. Here we have

$$\bar{R} = (1/2)(36) + (2/5)(40) + (0)(28) = 34$$

The intuition is that the market value of the total output of the two crops (the total revenues earned by the farmer) is equal to the weighted sum of the marginal values of the resources used.

To illustrate the concept of a shadow price, we will increase the amount of resource 1 by 1 unit (here, relax the land constraint by one acre, giving the farmer now 37 acres of land) and show how the farmer's maximum total revenues increase by 1/2 of a unit (here by $50). The new revenue maximization problem is written below, with the change in the resource constraint underlined.

$$\text{maximize: } R = 5x_1 + 3x_2 + 0s_1 + 0s_2 + 0s_3$$

$$\text{subject to: } 6x_1 + 2x_2 + s_1 = \underline{37}$$

$$5x_1 + 5x_2 + s_2 = 40$$

$$2x_1 + 4x_2 + s_3 = 28$$

The associated simplex tableaus are

I	R	x_1	x_2	s_1	s_2	s_3	Constant
row 0	1	−5	−3	0	0	0	0
row 1	0	6	2	1	0	0	37
row 2	0	5	5	0	1	0	40
row 3	0	2	4	0	0	1	28

II	R	x_1	x_2	s_1	s_2	s_3	Constant
row 0′	1	0	−4/3	5/6	0	0	185/6
row 1′	0	1	1/3	1/6	0	0	37/6
row 2′	0	0	10/3	−5/6	1	0	55/6
row 3′	0	0	10/3	−1/3	0	1	94/6

III	R	x_1	x_2	s_1	s_2	s_3	Constant
row 0″	1	0	0	1/2	2/5	0	207/6 = 34.5
row 1″	0	1	0	1/4	−1/10	0	63/12 = 5.25
row 2″	0	0	1	−1/4	3/10	0	11/4 = 2.75
row 3″	0	0	0	1/2	−1	1	39/6 = 6.5

Note: In this example the only changes in the simplex tableaus are in the final column of constants. This need not be the case. A change in a resource constraint could be large enough to affect the displacement quotients. We can read off the solution values from the final simplex tableau **III**.

$$\bar{x}_1 = 63/12 = 5.25 \quad \text{and} \quad \bar{x}_2 = 11/4 = 2.75$$

$$\bar{s}_3 = 39/6 = 6.5 \quad \text{and} \quad \bar{s}_1 = \bar{s}_2 = 0$$

$$\bar{R} = 5\bar{x}_1 + 3\bar{x}_2 = 5(5.25) + 3(2.75) = 34.5$$

We see that the optimum values of the two crops have changed. Not surprisingly, relaxing the land constraint increased the optimal planting of the land-intensive crop, x_1, from 5 to 5.25 units (or from 500 bushels to 525 bushels). The optimal planting of the fertilizer-intensive crop, x_2, declined from 3 to 2.75 (or from 300 bushels to 275 bushels). Both the land and labor constraints are still binding: $\bar{s}_1 = \bar{s}_2 = 0$. The associated shadow prices for land and labor, found in row 0″ of the final tableau, remain as 1/2 and 2/5, respectively—consistent with the fixed-coefficients production functions assumed. There is even more slack in the fertilizer constraint: here $\bar{s}_3 = 6.5$, indicating that 6.5 bags of fertilizer are now left over. Finally, as predicted, the maximum value of the total revenues increased by 1/2 a unit, from 34 to 34.5 (or from $3,400 to $3,450). See the value in row 0″ under the constant in the final column: $\bar{R} = 207/6 = 34.5$.

Summary of the Simplex Procedure for a Maximization   The steps involved in a maximization linear programming problem with n choice variables and m constraints using the simplex method are:

1. Convert the m inequality constraints into m equality constraints by adding a slack variable to each constraint. Also add the m slack variables with zero coefficients to the objective function.

2. Set up the initial simplex tableau with the variables aligned at the top: the dependent variable, n choice variables, m slack variables, and the constant. The top row of coefficients represents the objective function. The m rows of coefficients beneath represent the m constraints.

3. To find the pivot column, select the most negative coefficient in the top row. To find the pivot element, take the smallest displacement quotient, found by dividing the positive coefficients in the pivot column into the constant terms in the corresponding rows of the last column of the tableau.

4. Initialize the pivot element to a 1 by dividing the coefficients in the row of the pivot element by the coefficient of the pivot element. Use row manipulation to obtain zeros in the other rows of the pivot column.

5. The new simplex tableau should contain m linearly independent columns which form a basis for a trial solution space. The value of the objective function (the dependent variable to be maximized) and the values of the included m choice and slack variables of the trial solution space can be found in the constant column.

6. As long as there are negative coefficients in the top row of the tableau, we repeat steps 3–5, trying a new basis for the solution space.

7. The final simplex tableau for a maximization will contain no negative coefficients in the top row. The m linearly independent columns identify the m choice and slack variables included in the solution. The n other variables are equal to zero. The optimum values of the objective function and the included m variables are given in the last column of the tableau. The coefficients in the top row under the slack variables that are equal to zero (indicating binding resource constraints) give the shadow prices of those resources. The shadow price of a resource that is not binding (indicated by a positive value for the associated slack variable) is zero.

PRACTICE PROBLEM 11.1

Consider a farmer seeking to maximize the total revenues (R) from the sale of two crops (x_1 and x_2). The unit prices of the two crops are: $P_1 = \$4$ and $P_2 = \$6$. Each crop requires the inputs of land, labor, and fertilizer and is characterized by a fixed coefficients production function. In particular, each unit of crop 1 produced requires 1 unit of land, 3 units of labor, and 4 units of fertilizer. Each unit of crop 2 produced requires 2 units of land, 2 units of labor, and 1 unit of fertilizer. Available to the farmer are 20 units of land, 30 units of labor, and 32.5 units of fertilizer.

a) Set up the linear programming problem.

b) Identify the extreme points of the feasible region.

c) Using the simplex method, solve for the revenue-maximizing outputs of the two crops. Determine the maximum revenues for the farmer.

d) Determine which constraints are binding and the shadow prices for land, labor, and fertilizer.

(The answers are at the end of the chapter.)

DUALITY

Every constrained maximization problem can be transformed into a counterpart constrained minimization, and vice versa. For example, given the technology and factor prices, a firm's minimizing the total cost, $\overline{C}$, of producing a given output, Q_0, is equivalent to producing the maximum output, $\overline{Q}$, for a given total cost, C_0, where $\overline{C} = C_0$ and $Q_0 = \overline{Q}$.

So too, in linear programming, where the objective function and constraints are linear, we can convert constrained maximization (minimization) problems into constrained minimization (maximization) problems. We had a hint of this duality in the maximization example of the farmer using the simplex method. We showed that the optimum value of the objective function (maximum total revenues) was equal to not only the sum of the products of the unit prices and quantities of the crops sold, but to the sum of the products of the shadow prices and quantities available of the resources.

We refer to the initial problem, whether formulated as a constrained maximization or constrained minimization, as the *primal*, and its counterpart, as the *dual*. We begin with the general case. Then we will return to our example of the farmer and constrained revenue maximization, illustrating duality and solving using the simplex method for a constrained minimization.

If the primal is a maximization, here with n choice variables and m constraints, then the dual is a minimization with m choice variables and n constraints. We denote the dependent variable of the primal as z, and the dependent variable of the dual as z^*.

Primal	*Dual*
maximize: $z = c_1 x_1 + c_2 x_2 + \cdots + c_n x_n$	minimize: $z^* = r_1 y_1 + r_2 y_2 + \cdots + r_m y_m$
subject to: $a_{11} x_1 + a_{12} x_2 + \cdots + a_{1n} x_n \leq r_1$	subject to: $a_{11} y_1 + a_{21} y_2 + \cdots + a_{m1} y_m \geq c_1$
$a_{21} x_1 + a_{22} x_2 + \cdots + a_{2n} x_n \leq r_2$	$a_{12} y_1 + a_{22} y_2 + \cdots + a_{m2} y_m \geq c_2$
.	.
.	.
$a_{m1} x_1 + a_{m2} x_2 + \cdots + a_{mn} x_n \leq r_m$	$a_{1n} y_1 + a_{2n} y_2 + \cdots + a_{mn} y_m \geq c_n$
$x_j \geq 0 \ (j = 1 \ldots n)$	$y_i \geq 0 \ (i = 1 \ldots m)$

Expressed in matrix notation we have:

Primal	*Dual*
maximize: $z = \mathbf{cx}$	minimize: $z^* = \mathbf{r'y}$
subject to: $\mathbf{Ax} \leq \mathbf{r}$	subject to: $\mathbf{A'y} \geq \mathbf{c'}$
$\mathbf{x} \geq 0$	$\mathbf{y} \geq 0$

where $\mathbf{c} = [c_1 \ c_2 \dots c_n]$ and $\mathbf{r'} = [r_1 \ r_2 \dots r_m]$

$$\mathbf{A} = \begin{bmatrix} a_{11} & a_{12} & \cdots & a_{1n} \\ a_{21} & a_{22} & \cdots & a_{2n} \\ . & & & \\ . & & & \\ a_{m1} & a_{m2} & \cdots & a_{mn} \end{bmatrix} \quad \mathbf{x} = \begin{bmatrix} x_1 \\ x_2 \\ . \\ . \\ x_n \end{bmatrix} \quad \text{and} \quad \mathbf{y} = \begin{bmatrix} y_1 \\ y_2 \\ . \\ . \\ y_m \end{bmatrix}$$

and $\mathbf{A'}$ is the transpose of $\mathbf{A}$, $\mathbf{r'}$ is the transpose of $\mathbf{r}$, and $\mathbf{c'}$ is the transpose of $\mathbf{c}$.

Note the following:

1. If the primal is a maximization, then the inequality constraints are expressed as upper limits ($\leq$). For the dual, a minimization, the inequality constraints are expressed as lower limits ($\geq$).
2. The coefficients, $(c_1, c_2, \dots c_n)$, of the choice variables for the objective function of the primal are the constants in the constraints of the dual. Similarly, the constants $(r_1, r_2, \dots r_m)$ in the constraints of the primal are the coefficients of the choice variables for the objective function of the dual.
3. The transpose of the coefficient matrix for the constraints in the primal is the coefficient matrix for the constraints in the dual.

$$\mathbf{A} = \begin{bmatrix} a_{11} & \cdots & a_{1n} \\ . & & \\ . & & \\ . & & \\ a_{m1} & \cdots & a_{mn} \end{bmatrix} \quad \text{and} \quad \mathbf{A'} = \begin{bmatrix} a_{11} & \cdots & a_{m1} \\ . & & \\ . & & \\ a_{1n} & & a_{mn} \end{bmatrix}$$

Although we have illustrated the general case of a maximization as the primal, the same rules apply if the primal is a minimization, as shown below.

Primal	*Dual*
minimize: $z = c_1 x_1 + c_2 x_2 + \cdots + c_n x_n$	maximize: $z^* = r_1 y_1 + r_2 y_2 + \cdots + r_m y_m$
subject to: $a_{11} x_1 + a_{12} x_2 + \cdots + a_{1n} x_n \geq r_1$	subject to: $a_{11} y_1 + a_{21} y_2 + \cdots + a_{m1} y_m \leq c_1$
.	.
.	.
.	.
$a_{m1} x_1 + a_{m2} x_2 + \cdots + a_{mn} x_n \geq r_m$	$a_{1n} y_1 + a_{2n} y_2 + \cdots + a_{mn} y_m \leq c_n$
$x_j \geq 0 \ (j = 1 \dots n)$	$y_i \geq 0 \ (i = 1 \dots m)$

Recall the maximization problem for the farmer, where the maximum revenues from the sale of two crops, x_1 and x_2, were sought, subject to the resource constraints of the available land, labor, and fertilizer.

$$\text{maximize:} \quad R = 5x_1 + 3x_2$$

$$\text{subject to:} \quad 6x_1 + 2x_2 \leq 36 \quad \text{(land)}$$

$$5x_1 + 5x_2 \leq 40 \quad \text{(labor)}$$

$$2x_1 + 4x_2 \leq 28 \quad \text{(fertilizer)}$$

$$x_1, x_2 \geq 0$$

where we found that $\bar{x}_1 = 5, \bar{x}_2 = 3$, and $\bar{R} = 34$, and that the land and labor constraints were binding (with positive shadow prices of .5 and .4, respectively). The third constraint, fertilizer, however, was not binding; thus the shadow price or marginal value of fertilizer was zero.

The corresponding dual problem can be written as:

$$\text{minimize:} \quad R^* = 36y_1 + 40y_2 + 28y_3$$

$$\text{subject to:} \quad 6y_1 + 5y_2 + 2y_3 \geq 5$$

$$2y_1 + 5y_2 + 4y_3 \geq 3$$

$$y_1, y_2 \geq 0$$

The interpretation of the dual is that the farmer is seeking to minimize the weighted sum of the shadow prices or marginal values of the resources available, R^*, subject to the constraints that the value of the resources used to produce each unit of output is greater than or equal to the unit prices of the outputs. Note that we cannot easily graph the minimization problem, since with three choice variables, y_1, y_2, and y_3, a three-dimensional graph would be required. For a problem with four or more choice variables, graphing would not be possible.

The simplex procedure for a minimization, while similar to that for a maximization, is initially a bit more complex. First, we convert the inequality constraints to equalities by subtracting dummy variables called *surplus variables*. Here, with two constraints, we need two surplus variables. The surplus variables, t_1 and t_2, will also be added to the objective function, with zero coefficients, however, so that the value of the objective function is unaffected.

Second, in a minimization problem, the feasible set of solutions will not include the origin, which provided a useful starting point for the trial solutions for a maximization. Consequently, we need to add *artificial variables* to every constraint and to the objective function in such a way that the artificial variables do not enter the solution, but do provide a starting point for the search. We do this by giving the artificial variables, v_1 and v_2, very large coefficients (100 here) in the objective function—so that these "dummy resources" are so abundant as to have zero shadow prices and, consequently, would not be relevant when the objective is to minimize the resource cost.

Adding the surplus variables (t_1 and t_2), and the artificial variables (v_1 and v_2) to this constrained minimization problem, we obtain:

minimize: $R^* = 36y_1 + 40y_2 + 28y_3 + 0t_1 + 0t_2 + 100v_1 + 100v_2$

subject to: $6y_1 + 5y_2 + 2y_3 - t_1 + v_1 = 5$

$2y_1 + 5y_2 + 4y_3 - t_2 + v_2 = 3$

$y_1, y_2, y_3 \geq 0$

We rewrite the objective function as: $R^* - 36y_1 - 40y_2 - 28y_3 - 0t_1 - 0t_2 - 100v_1 - 100v_2 = 0$, and then form the initial simplex tableau.

I	R^*	y_1	y_2	y_3	t_1	t_2	v_1	v_2	Constant
row 0	1	-36	-40	-28	0	0	-100	-100	0
row 1	0	6	5	2	-1	0	1	0	5
row 2	0	2	$\underline{5}$	4	0	-1	0	1	3

As with the maximization problem, the objective function is represented in the top row (row 0) and the constraints in the rows below (rows 1 and 2 here). We see that this problem includes three choice variables, (y_1, y_2, y_3), two surplus variables, (t_1, t_2), and two artificial variables (v_1, v_2). The solution space will include only two of these variables; consequently we seek a basis for 2-space with two linearly independent column vectors in the simplex tableau.

To begin, we need to get the artificial variable columns in form of unit vectors; so we multiply row 1 by 100 and row 2 by 100 and add the resulting rows to row 0. Row 0 is now:

row 0   [1   764   960   572 -100 -100 0   0   800]

To determine the pivot column, we look for the largest positive coefficient in the new row 0. Intuitively, if the goal is to minimize the resource cost, the most abundant resource would be the logical place to start. In this example, the pivot column is the one under the y_2 choice variable.

The pivot element is found by dividing each positive coefficient in the pivot column into the constant term for the rows representing the constraints. The smallest of the resulting displacement quotients identifies the pivot element. Here, the smallest displacement quotient indicates the lowest ratio of the unit price of an output to the shadow price of the most abundant resource—revealing the most binding constraint. The displacement quotients are $5/5 = 1$ for row 1 and $3/5 = .6$ for row 2. Therefore, the pivot element is the 5 in row 2, and is underlined in the simplex tableau.

We then convert the pivot element to one by dividing the row through by its coefficient, 5. The resulting row is:

row 2′   [0   2/5 $\underline{1}$ 4/5   0 $-1/5$ 0   1/5   3/5]

We use row manipulation of row 2′ to obtain zeros elsewhere in the pivot column. Multiplying row 2′ by -960 and adding to row 0 gives:

row 0′   [1   380 $\underline{0}$ -196 -100 92   0 -192 224]

Multiplying row 2' by −5 and adding to row 1 gives:

$$\text{row 1}' \quad [0 \ \ 4 \ \ \underline{0} \ \ -2 \ \ -1 \ \ 1 \ \ 1 \ \ -1 \ \ 2]$$

The new simplex tableau **II** is:

II	R*	y_1	y_2	y_3	t_1	t_2	v_1	v_2	Constant
row 0'	1	380	0	−196	−100	92	0	−192	224
row 1'	0	4	0	−2	−1	1	1	−1	2
row 2'	0	2/5	1	4/5	0	−1/5	0	1/5	3/5

For a minimization, we continue on as long as there is a positive coefficient remaining in the top row, not including the 1 under the dependent variable $R*$ and the coefficient under the constant term. If we were to stop with tableau **II**, the two variables entering the solution space would be y_2 and v_1, as indicated by the two linearly independent columns of the 2×7 matrix formed by the two constraint rows and seven columns for the choice, surplus, and artificial variables. Recall that v_1 and v_2 are the artificial variables used to get the simplex process started and are not intended to be part of the solution. Indeed, we assigned inflated values for these dummy resources to ensure zero shadow prices.

Repeating the process, the largest positive coefficient in the top row is the 380 under the y_1 column. The pivot element in this column is the 4 in row 1' (with a displacement quotient of 2/4 = .5, compared to (3/5)/(2/5) = 1.5 for the coefficient in row 2'). Dividing row 1' through by 4 to get a 1 as the pivot element, we get:

$$\text{row 1}'' \quad [0 \ \ \underline{1} \ \ 0 \ \ -1/2 \ \ -1/4 \ \ 1/4 \ \ 1/4 \ \ -1/4 \ \ 1/2]$$

Multiplying row 1'' by −380 and adding to row 0' gives us the desired zero in the pivot column of row 0'.

$$\text{row 0}'' \quad [1 \ \ \underline{0} \ \ 0 \ \ -6 \ \ -5 \ \ -3 \ \ -95 \ \ -97 \ \ 34]$$

Multiplying row 1'' by −2/5 and adding to row 2' gives the desired 0 in the pivot column of row 2'.

$$\text{row 2}'' \quad [0 \ \ \underline{0} \ \ 1 \ \ 1 \ \ 1/10 \ \ -3/10 \ \ -1/10 \ \ 3/10 \ \ 2/5]$$

The new tableau is **III**.

III	R*	y_1	y_2	y_3	t_1	t_2	v_1	v_2	Constant
row 0''	1	0	0	−6	−5	−3	−95	−97	34
row 1''	0	1	0	−1/2	−1/4	1/4	1/4	−1/4	1/2
row 2''	0	0	1	1	1/10	−3/10	−1/10	3/10	2/5

This is the final tableau since there are no other positive elements in the top row for the columns representing the choice, surplus, and artificial variables. We can read off the solution directly and we can express the solution values in matrix notation. For the latter, taking the two linearly independent columns that form the basis for the solution space and adding the column corresponding to the dependent variable, R^*, we can write the solution as:

$$\begin{bmatrix} 1 & 0 & 0 \\ 0 & 1 & 0 \\ 0 & 0 & 1 \end{bmatrix} \begin{bmatrix} R^* \\ \bar{y}_1 \\ \bar{y}_2 \end{bmatrix} = \begin{bmatrix} 34 \\ 1/2 \\ 2/5 \end{bmatrix}$$

The 3×1 matrix on the right-hand side of the solution represents the column of constants in the final simplex tableau. Alternatively, reading from the tableau directly, the two linearly independent columns corresponding to the choice variables, y_1 and y_2, indicate the optimal shadow prices for resources 1 and 2 (here land and labor, respectively): $\bar{y}_1 = 1/2 = .5$ and $\bar{y}_2 = 2/5 = .4$. Accordingly, we know that the land and labor constraints are binding, since the optimal shadow prices are positive. The marginal value of resource 3 (fertilizer) is zero: $\bar{y}_3 = 0$, indicating that this resource is in surplus.

The other variables are also equal to zero: $\bar{t}_1 = 0, \bar{t}_2 = 0, \bar{v}_1 = 0$, and $\bar{v}_2 = 0$. The zero values for the surplus variables, t_1 and t_2, indicate that both constraints are binding; that is, the value of the resources used to produce a unit of output is equal to the unit price of the output for both crops. Recall that the zero values for the artificial variables, v_1 and v_2, are intended.

Finally, the optimum value for the objective function, here, the minimum value for R^*, the total resource cost of producing the two crops, is 34, and is found in the constant column of the top row: $R^* = 34 = 36\bar{y}_1 + 40\bar{y}_2 + 28\bar{y}_3 = 36(.5) + 40(.4) + 28(0)$.

Summary of the Simplex Procedure for a Minimization The steps involved in a minimization linear programming problem with m choice variables and n constraints using the simplex method are:

1. Convert the n inequality constraints into n equality constraints by subtracting a surplus variable from each constraint. Also add the surplus variables with zero coefficients to the objective function.

2. Add an artificial variable to each constraint. Also, add the artificial variables with arbitrarily large coefficients to the objective function. The coefficients attached to the artificial variables in the objective function need to be sufficiently large to ensure that the artificial variables are optimally equal to zero.

3. Set up the initial simplex tableau with the variables aligned at the top: the dependent variable, m choice variables, n surplus variables, and n artificial variables and the constant. The top row of coefficients represents the objective function. The n rows of coefficients beneath represent the n constraints.

4. Convert the n artificial variable columns into n unit vectors by multiplying the n constraint rows by the coefficients of the artificial variables and adding to the top row.

5. To find the pivot column, select the largest positive coefficient in the top row. For the pivot element, take the smallest displacement quotient by dividing the positive

coefficients in the pivot column into the constant terms in the corresponding rows of the last column of the tableau.

6. Initialize the pivot element to a 1 by dividing the coefficients in the row of the pivot element by the coefficient of the pivot element. Use row manipulation to obtain zeros in the other rows of the pivot column.

7. The new simplex tableau should contain n linearly independent columns which form a basis for a trial solution space. The value of the objective function (the dependent variable to be minimized) and the values of the included n choice, surplus, and artificial variables of the trial solution space can be found in the constant column.

8. As long as there are positive coefficients in the top row of the tableau (except for the 1 representing the dependent variable and the constant term), we repeat steps 5 through 7, trying a new basis for the solution space.

9. The final simplex tableau will contain no positive elements in the top row (except for the 1 representing the dependent variable and the constant term). The n linearly independent columns identify the n choice and surplus variables included in the solution. The m other variables are set equal to zero. The optimum values of the objective function and the included n variables are given in the last column of the tableau.

PRACTICE PROBLEM 11.2

Consider the dual minimization problem to Practice Problem 11.1.
a) Set up this linear programming problem.
b) Using the simplex method, solve for the shadow prices or marginal values for the resources (y_1, y_2, and y_3) that minimize the total resource cost, R^*. What is the minimum total resource cost?

(The answers are at the end of the chapter.)

TWO DUALITY THEOREMS

Comparing the final simplex tableaus for the primal maximization and dual minimization (reproduced below), reinforces the concept of duality. Each tableau contains all the relevant information for the basic problem at hand.

Primal (maximization)

III	R	x_1	x_2	s_1	s_2	s_3	Constant
row 0″	1	0	0	1/2	2/5	0	34
row 1″	0	1	0	1/4	−1/10	0	5
row 2″	0	0	1	−1/4	3/10	0	3
row 3″	0	0	0	1/2	−1	1	6

Dual (minimization)

III	R^*	y_1	y_2	y_3	t_1	t_2	v_1	v_2	Constant
row 0″	1	0	0	−6	−5	−3	−95	−97	34
row 1″	0	1	0	−1/2	−1/4	1/4	1/4	−1/4	1/2
row 2″	0	0	1	1	1/10	−3/10	−1/10	3/10	2/5

We observe a correspondence between the top row of the primal (dual) and the constant column of the dual (primal) in the tableaus. We cite, without proof, two duality theorems in linear programming.

Duality Theorem I: *Given that the solutions exist, the optimum values of the primal and dual objective functions are equal.*

In this example, the optimum value of the primal, $\overline{R}$, indicates the maximum revenues for the farmer from the two crops planted, $\overline{x}_1$ and $\overline{x}_2$, given the unit prices of the two crops, $P_1 = \$5$ and $P_2 = \$3$. $\overline{R} = P_1 \overline{x}_1 + P_2 \overline{x}_2 = \$5(5) + \$3(3) = \$34$

The optimum value of the dual, $\overline{R}^*$, indicates the minimum resource cost for producing the outputs of the two crops from the optimum values of the shadow prices ($\overline{y}_1, \overline{y}_2$, and $\overline{y}_3$) of the resources available to the farmer: $r_1 = 36$ units of land, $r_2 = 40$ units of labor, and $r_3 = 28$ units of fertilizer: $\overline{R}^* = r_1 \overline{y}_1 + r_2 \overline{y}_2 + r_3 \overline{y}_3 = 36(\$.5) + 40(\$.4) + 28(\$0) = \$34$.

In short, $\overline{R} = \overline{R}^*$ shows that the value of the outputs (maximum total revenues) equals the value of the inputs used (minimum of the weighted shadow prices). The second duality theorem follows.

Duality Theorem II: *If the optimum value of a choice variable in the primal (dual) is non-zero (i.e., enters the solution space), then the optimum value of the counterpart dummy variable in the dual (primal) is zero.*

Here, the choice variables in the primal maximization are the quantities of the two crops planted, x_1 and x_2, which are optimally, $\overline{x}_1 = 5$ and $\overline{x}_2 = 3$. The corresponding dummy variables in the dual are the surplus variables, t_1 and t_2, both of which are optimally equal to zero, indicating that both of the constraints in the dual are binding. That is, $\overline{t}_1 = 0$ and $\overline{t}_2 = 0$ show that the marginal value of the resources used equals the unit price of the output produced for crops 1 and 2, respectively. Note that we find $\overline{x}_1 = 5$ and $\overline{x}_2 = 3$ in the constant column of the tableau for the maximization and -5 and -3 in the top row under the surplus variables, t_1 and t_2 of the minimization. (Recall that we subtracted the surplus variables in the constraints of the minimization problem.)

The choice variables in the dual minimization are the marginal values or shadow prices of the resources, y_1, y_2, and y_3, which are optimally: $\overline{y}_1 = 1/2 = .5, \overline{y}_2 = 2/5 = .4$, and $\overline{y}_3 = 0$. The corresponding dummy variables in the primal are the slack variables, s_1, s_2, and s_3, which are optimally: $\overline{s}_1 = 0, \overline{s}_2 = 0$, and $\overline{s}_3 = 6$, indicating that resource constraints 1 and 2 are binding (thus, the positive shadow prices $\bar{y}_1 = .5$ and $\bar{y}_2 = .4$), while resource 3 is nonbinding (with 6 units of the resource unutilized, the shadow price of resource 3 is zero: $\bar{y}_3 = 0$.)

Turning to the final simplex tableau, the nonzero shadow prices for the resources are found in the top row of the primal and the constant column of the dual. The 6 in the constant column of the primal tableau, representing the third constraint row (row 3″), corresponds to the -6 in the top row of the dual under the y_3 variable. As noted above, there are 6 units of resource 3 unused.

The relationship described in Duality Theorem II between the choice variables and counterpart dummy variables is known as *complementary slackness*. In fact, since either of the final tableaus contain all the information for the solution of the linear programming problem, we can select either of the primal or dual problems to solve.

In this example, the maximization problem, which served as the primal, had the advantage that it could be graphed. On the other hand, the dual minimization had fewer constraints and thus involved less row manipulation during the simplex procedure. The maximization of total revenues subject to resource constraints, however, may be more intuitive than the minimization of the resource cost (the weighted sum of the shadow prices of the resources used) of producing outputs of given values. Before leaving linear programming, we should note the possibility of nonunique solutions.

PRACTICE PROBLEM 11.3

For Practice Problems 11.1 and 11.2:
a) Write out the final simplex tableaus.
b) Show that Duality Theorem I holds.
c) Show that Duality Theorem II holds

(The answers are at the end of the chapter.)

Multiple Solutions   Note that the duality theorems presume that the solutions of the primal and dual exist. Indeed, in this problem there was a unique output combination for the two crops that maximized the farmer's total revenues ($\bar{x}_1 = 5$ and $\bar{x}_2 = 3$), and there was a unique combination of shadow prices that minimized the resource cost ($\bar{y}_1 = .5, \bar{y}_2 = .4$, and $\bar{y}_3 = 0$). It is possible that the solutions, even while existing, may not be unique. Refer back to Figure 11.1 and the primal maximization problem. Instead of occurring at an extreme point, here point C, the solution could have occurred along one of the constraints forming the feasible region. For example, if the ratio of the output prices had been equal to 3, that is, $P_1/P_2 = 3$, then the solution would include any combination of the outputs along the border of the feasible region given by the line segment CD. Here the slope of the land constraint equals the slope of the isorevenue lines (and the slope of the objective function). There would not be a unique combination of the outputs of the two crops that maximized the total revenues.

For example, suppose that the revenue maximization problem (the primal here) were changed and the unit price of output 1 were $P_1' = \$9$ (instead of $P_1 = \$5$). The total revenue function to be maximized would be: $R' = P_1' x_1 + P_2 x_2 = 9x_1 + 3x_2$. Solving the primal using the simplex method, we would find: $\bar{x}_1' = 6$ and $\bar{x}_2' = 0$ (the output combination represented by point D, an extreme point on the feasible region in Figure 11.1). The maximum total revenues would be: $\bar{R}' = \$9\bar{x}_1 + \$3\bar{x}_2 = \$9(6) + \$3(0) = \$54$. We would find that constraints 2 (labor) and 3 (fertilizer) are not binding: $\bar{s}_2' = 10$ and $\bar{s}_3' = 16$, with $\bar{s}_1' = 0$, consistent with the binding constraint for resource 1 (land). (For practice, you may want to confirm these results yourself.)

Setting up the dual, the change in the unit price of output 1 does not affect the objective function, but does affect the first constraint. In the course of solving with the simplex method, we would find in the second round tableau a tie for the smallest displacement quotients in the pivot column. Arbitrarily selecting one of the coefficients with the smallest displacement quotient as the pivot element would, after one more round, yield the solution: $\bar{y}_1' = 1.5$ and $\bar{y}_2' = 0$. The other variables would take on zero values: $\bar{y}_3' = 0, \bar{t}_1' = 0, \bar{t}_2' = 0, \bar{v}_1' = 0$, and $\bar{v}_2' = 0$. Here, with only constraint 1 (land) binding, only the shadow price for resource 1 is optimally nonzero. Selecting the other coefficient with the smallest displacement quotient as the pivot element, however, ultimately would yield the solution: $\bar{y}_1' = 1.5$ and $\bar{t}_2' = 0$. The other variables taking on zero values are: $\bar{y}_2' = 0, \bar{y}_3' = 0, \bar{t}_1' = 0, \bar{v}_1' = 0$, and $\bar{v}_2' = 0$. Again, the only positive shadow price is associated with the binding land constraint. The minimum resource cost is: $\bar{R}^{*\prime} = 36\bar{y}_1' + 40\bar{y}_2' + 28\bar{y}_3' = 36(1.5) + 40(0) + 28(0) = 54$, which is consistent with Duality Theorem I: $\bar{R}' = \bar{R}^{*\prime}$.

We note that, depending on the arbitrary choice for the pivot element between the two coefficients with the smallest displacement quotients, different variables enter the solution space for the dual ($\bar{y}_2' = 0$ or $\bar{t}_2' = 0$). Moreover, both the primal and the dual have zero values for variables that enter the solution space: $\bar{x}_2' = 0$ for the primal, and either $\bar{y}_2' = 0$ or $\bar{t}_2' = 0$ for the dual. Tied displacement quotients and the existence of optimum values of zero for the variables that enter the solution space are indicative of nonunique or multiple solutions to a linear programming problem. Indeed, as we can see in Figure 11.1, since the slope of the objective function (for total revenues) in the primal is equal to the slope of one of the constraints (land), any output combination on the line segment CD of the feasible region would maximize total revenues. For instance, the output combinations of ($\bar{x}_1' = 5$ and $\bar{x}_2' = 3$) and ($\bar{x}_1' = 5.5$ and $\bar{x}_2' = 1.5$) also yield total revenues of 54. Only for the output combination represented by point C (5, 3), however, would we find the labor constraint also to be binding.

Linear programming, while an improvement over classical optimization problems where the constraints must be binding, and thus the number of constraints cannot exceed the number of choice variables, is nevertheless limited by the requirement that the objective function and constraints must be linear. In the remainder of this chapter we introduce the technique of nonlinear programming. Then we apply nonlinear programming to the theory of the firm.

AN INTRODUCTION TO NONLINEAR PROGRAMMING

As the name suggests, nonlinear programming allows for nonlinear objective and constraint functions. Consistent with linear programming, however, are the nonnegativity restrictions on the choice variables, the allowance for more constraints than choice variables, and the property of duality. We begin by setting out the general nonlinear programming problem, using a maximization for the primal and a minimization for the dual. The general conditions for the solution of nonlinear programming problems are discussed and other examples are presented.

As noted above, economic variables commonly assume nonnegative values, for example, quantities, prices, incomes, and expenditures. Negative economic magnitudes, however, do occur. For example, economic profits can be negative (economic losses); real rates of interest are negative when the inflation rate exceeds the nominal rate of interest; and recessions are characterized by declines in real national output and negative growth rates.

In classical optimization, we seek the optimal value(s) of an objective function subject to equality constraints—where the number of constraints is less than the number of choice variables in the model. While the choice variables are not explicitly restricted to be nonnegative, economists using the classical optimization technique would evaluate the solution values for their economic relevance. With nonlinear programming, the constraints need not be strictly binding, that is, all, some, or none of the inequality constraints could hold as equalities. Moreover, the nonnegativity restrictions on the choice variables are imposed at the outset as part of the model. The method of the Lagrange multiplier, employed in classical constrained optimization, however, is also used for solving nonlinear programming problems.

THE NONLINEAR PROGRAMMING PROBLEM

For a maximization, the general nonlinear programming problem can be written as:

$$\text{maximize:} \quad z = z\,(x_1, x_2, \ldots x_n)$$

$$\text{subject to:} \quad g^1\,(x_1, x_2, \ldots x_n) \le r_1$$

$$g^2\,(x_1, x_2, \ldots x_n) \le r_2$$

$$.$$
$$.$$

$$g^m\,(x_1, x_2, \ldots x_n) \le r_m$$

$$\text{and } x_j \ge 0 \quad (j = 1 \ldots n)$$

The dependent variable, z, in the objective function to be maximized, is a function of the n choice variables, $x_1, \ldots x_n$. The m inequality constraints, $g^1, \ldots g^m$, are also functions of the n choice variables; where, as in linear programming, there is no necessary relationship between the number of choice variables, n, and the number of inequality constraints, m. The choice variables, however, are restricted to be nonnegative. The m exogenous variables, $r_1, \ldots r_m$, represent the constants in the inequality constraints.

For the general minimization problem, we can write:

$$\text{minimize:} \quad z^* = z^*(y_1, y_2, \ldots y_m)$$

$$\text{subject to:} \quad h^1(y_1, y_2, \ldots y_m) \geq c_1$$

$$h^2(y_1, y_2, \ldots y_m) \geq c_2$$

$$.$$

$$.$$

$$h^n(y_1, y_2, \ldots y_m) \geq c_n$$

$$\text{and } y_i \geq 0 \quad (i = 1 \ldots m)$$

Here, the dependent variable, z^*, in the objective function to be minimized, is a function of m choice variables, $y_1, \ldots y_m$. The n inequality constraints, $h^1, \ldots h^n$, are also functions of these m choice variables, which are restricted to be nonnegative. The n exogenous variables, $c_1, \ldots c_n$, represent the constants in the inequality constraints.

The Lagrange Multiplier Method in Nonlinear Programming: Maximization We begin with the general maximization problem:

$$\text{maximize:} \quad z = z(x_1, x_2, \ldots x_n)$$

$$\text{subject to:} \quad g^1(x_1, x_2, \ldots x_n) \leq r_1$$

$$g^2(x_1, x_2, \ldots x_n) \leq r_2$$

$$.$$

$$.$$

$$g^m(x_1, x_2, \ldots x_n) \leq r_m$$

$$\text{and } x_j \geq 0 \quad (j = 1 \ldots n)$$

As with linear programming, we can convert the inequality constraints into equalities by adding nonnegative slack variables. That is, to each constraint, we add a slack variable, s_i, defined to be

$$s_i = r_i - g^i(x_1, x_2, \ldots x_n) \geq 0 \quad (i = 1 \ldots m)$$

The problem can then be rewritten as

$$\text{maximize:} \quad z = z(x_1, x_2, \ldots x_n)$$

$$\text{subject to:} \quad g^1(x_1, x_2, \ldots x_n) + s_1 = r_1$$

$$g^2 (x_1, x_2, \ldots x_n) + s_2 = r_2$$

.

.

$$g^m (x_1, x_2, \ldots x_n) + s_m = r_m$$

$$\text{and } x_j \geq 0, s_i \geq 0 \quad (j = 1 \ldots n; i = 1 \ldots m)$$

We set up the Lagrangian function, L, and derive the first-order conditions—mindful of the nonnegativity restrictions on the choice and slack variables. The Lagrangian is a function of the $(n + 2m)$ endogenous variables: the n choice variables, $x_1, \ldots x_n$; the m slack variables, $s_1, \ldots s_m$; and the m Lagrange multipliers, $\lambda_1, \ldots \lambda_m$.

$$L(x_1, \ldots x_n, \lambda_1, \ldots \lambda_m, s_1, \ldots s_m) = z (x_1, \ldots x_n) + \lambda_1 \cdot [r_1 - g^1 (x_1, \ldots x_n) - s_1]$$

$$+ \cdots + \lambda_m \cdot [r_m - g^m (x_1, \ldots x_n) - s_m]$$

The first-order conditions, incorporating the nonnegativity restrictions are

$$\delta L/\delta x_1 = z_1 - \lambda_1 g_1^1 - \ldots - \lambda_m g_1^m \leq 0; \quad x_1 \geq 0; \quad \text{and} \quad (x_1)(\delta L/\delta x_1) = 0$$

.

.

$$\delta L/\delta x_n = z_n - \lambda_n g_n^1 - \ldots - \lambda_m g_n^m \leq 0; \quad x_n \geq 0; \quad \text{and} \quad (x_n)(\delta L/\delta x_n) = 0$$

$$\delta L/\delta \lambda_1 = r_1 - g^1 (x_1, \ldots x_n) - s_1 = 0$$

.

.

$$\delta L/\delta \lambda_m = r_m - g^m (x_1, \ldots x_n) - s_m = 0$$

$$\delta L/\delta s_1 = - \lambda_1 \leq 0; \quad s_1 \geq 0; \quad \text{and} \quad (s_1)(\delta L/\delta s_1) = 0$$

.

.

$$\delta L/\delta s_m = - \lambda_m \leq 0; \quad s_m \geq 0; \quad \text{and} \quad (s_m)(\delta L/\delta s_m) = 0$$

where $z_j = \delta z/\delta x_j, (j = 1 \ldots n)$, and $g_j^i = \delta g^i/\delta x_j, (i = 1 \ldots m; j = 1 \ldots n)$, represent the first-order partial derivatives.

The first-order conditions can be written more concisely as:

$$\delta L/\delta x_j = z_j - \sum_{i=1}^{m} \lambda_i g_j^i \leq 0; \quad x_j \geq 0; \quad \text{and } (x_j)(\delta L/\delta x_j) = 0 \quad (j = 1 \ldots n)$$

$$\delta L/\delta \lambda_i = r_i - g^i (x_1, \ldots x_n) - s_i = 0 \quad (i = 1 \ldots m)$$

$$\delta L/\delta s_i = -\lambda_i \leq 0; \quad s_i \geq 0; \quad \text{and} \quad (s_i)(\delta L/\delta s_i) = 0 \; (i = 1 \ldots m)$$

We can see that the nonlinear programming problem is potentially more complicated than the classical constrained optimization. In addition to the explicit nonnegativity restrictions on the choice variables and the included slack variables, there are *complementary slackness conditions:*

$$(x_j)(\delta L/\delta x_j) = 0, \quad (j = 1 \ldots n), \quad \text{and } (s_i)(\delta L/\delta s_i) = 0, \quad (i = 1 \ldots m).$$

If, in solving the first-order conditions, all of the choice variables, $x_1, \ldots x_n$, are positive at the optimum point, then the complementary slackness conditions, $(x_j)(\delta L/\delta x_j) = 0$, imply that the first-order partials of the Lagrangian function equal zero: $(\delta L/\delta x_j) = 0$, just as in classical constrained optimization. That is, the marginal conditions for optimization (maximization here) hold for each choice variable.

The value of a choice variable (or variables), however, could equal zero. (Recall in linear programming when we solved using the simplex method, in searching for a basis, we set the variables not included in the solution space equal to zero.) For example, say the value of the kth choice variable equals zero in the solution to the nonlinear programming problem, $x_k = 0$. One possibility is that the optimum value of this kth choice variable actually is equal to zero, $\bar{x}_k = 0$ (and the nonnegativity restriction is not needed), so $\delta L/\delta x_k = 0$ also. The other possibility, is that the optimum value of the kth choice variable is negative, $\bar{x}_k < 0$, which violates the nonnegativity restrictions on the choice variables. In this case, we have $\delta L/\delta x_k \leq 0$, since if we could reduce the value of x_k below zero, then the value of the Lagrangian function (and the objective function to be maximized) would increase. In sum, the complementary slackness conditions, when the optimum values of choice variables would be negative if they were unconstrained, imply that $\delta L/\delta x_j < 0, j = 1 \ldots n$; that is, the associated first-order conditions for the choice variable are inequalities to incorporate these possibilities.

The first-order conditions for the Lagrange multipliers, $\delta L/\delta \lambda_i = r_i - g^i (x_1, \ldots x_n) - s_i = 0$, simply state the m inequality constraints. The first-order conditions for the slack variables, $\delta L/\delta s_i = \lambda_i; s_i \geq 0$; and $(s_i)(\delta L/\delta s_i) = 0$, also reflect the m inequality constraints. If the ith constraint is binding, then the associated slack variable equals zero: $s_i = 0$ when $g^i (x_1, \ldots x_n) = r_i$. For a binding constraint, the value of the Lagrange multiplier is positive, $\lambda_i > 0$, indicating that a relaxation of the constraint would increase the optimum value of the objective function. Conversely, if the ith constraint is not binding, then the ith slack variable is positive: $s_i > 0$ when $g^i (x_1, \ldots x_n) < r_i$. The optimum value of the ith Lagrange multiplier in this case is zero, $\lambda_i = 0$, since relaxing a nonbinding constraint has no effect on the optimum value of the objective function.

Summarizing,

$$\text{If } r_i - g^i (x_1, \ldots x_n) = 0, \text{ then } s_i = 0 \text{ and } \lambda_i > 0$$

$$\text{If } r_i - g^i (x_1, \ldots x_n) > 0, \text{ then } s_i > 0 \text{ and } \lambda_i = 0$$

The complementary slackness conditions for the first-order conditions associated with the slack variables capture these relationships: $(s_i)(\delta L/\delta s_i) = (s_i)(\lambda_i) = 0, (i = 1 \ldots m)$. In fact, we can drop the slack variables from the problem, since $s_i = r_i - g^i (x_1, \ldots x_n)$ and $(\delta L/\delta s_i) = \lambda_i$.

We return to the original maximization problem.

$$\text{maximize: } z = z\,(x_1, \ldots x_n)$$

$$\text{subject to: } g^1\,(x_1, \ldots x_n) \leq r_1$$

$$\cdot$$
$$\cdot$$
$$\cdot$$

$$g^m\,(x_1, \ldots x_n) \leq r_m$$

$$\text{and } x_j \geq 0, \quad j = 1 \ldots n$$

Setting up the Lagrangian function, without the slack variables, $s_i = r_i - g^i\,(x_1, \ldots x_n)$, we have

$$L(x_1, \ldots x_n, \lambda_1, \ldots \lambda_m) = z\,(x_1, \ldots x_n) + \sum_{i=1}^{m} \lambda_i \cdot [r_i - g^i\,(x_1, \ldots x_n)]$$

The first-order conditions for a maximization are

$$\delta L/\delta x_j = z_j - \sum_{i=1}^{m} \lambda_i\, g^i_j \leq 0; \quad x_j \geq 0; \quad \text{and } (x_j)(\delta L/\delta x_j) = 0, (j = 1 \ldots n)$$

$$\delta L/\delta \lambda_i = r_i - g^i\,(x_1, \ldots x_n) \geq 0; \quad \lambda_i \geq 0; \quad \text{and } (\lambda_i)(\delta L/\delta \lambda_i) = 0, (i = 1 \ldots m)$$

Solving these first-order conditions, known as the *Kuhn-Tucker conditions*, will give the optimal values for the choice variables and the Lagrange multipliers in the nonlinear programming maximization problem.

The Lagrange Multiplier Method in Nonlinear Programming: Minimization   We now turn to the general nonlinear programming minimization problem,

$$\text{minimize: } z^* = z^*(y_1, \ldots y_m)$$

$$\text{subject to: } h^1\,(y_1, \ldots y_m) \geq c_1$$

$$\cdot$$
$$\cdot$$
$$\cdot$$

$$h^n\,(y_1, \ldots y_m) \geq c_n$$

$$y_1, \ldots y_m \geq 0$$

The Lagrangian is

$$L^*(y_1, \ldots y_m, \lambda_1^*, \ldots \lambda_n^*) = z^*(y_1, \ldots y_m) + \lambda_1^* \cdot [c_1 - h^1\,(y_1, \ldots y_m)]$$

$$+ \cdots + \lambda_n^* \cdot [c_n - h^n\,(y_1, \ldots y_m)]$$

The first-order conditions (Kuhn-Tucker conditions) are

$$\delta L^*/\delta y_1 = z_1^* - \lambda_1^* h_1^1 \ldots - \lambda_n^* h_1^n \geq 0; \quad y_1 \geq 0; \quad (y_1)(\delta L^*/\delta y_1) = 0$$

$$\cdot$$
$$\cdot$$

$$\delta L^*/\delta y_m = z_m^* - \lambda_1^* h_m^1 \ldots - \lambda_n^* h_m^n \geq 0; \quad y_m \geq 0; \quad (y_m)(\delta L^*/\delta y_m) = 0$$

$$\delta L^*/\delta \lambda_1^* = c_1 - h^1(y_1, \ldots y_m) \leq 0; \quad \lambda_1^* \geq 0; \quad (\lambda_1^*)(\delta L^*/\delta \lambda_1^*) = 0$$

.

.

$$\delta L^*/\delta \lambda_n^* = c_n - h^n(y_1, \ldots y_m) \leq 0; \quad \lambda_n^* \geq 0; \quad (\lambda_n^*)(\delta L^*/\delta \lambda_n^*) = 0$$

$$\text{where } z_i^* = \delta z^*/\delta y_i \quad (i = 1 \ldots m)$$

$$\text{and } h_i^j = \delta h^j/\delta y_i \quad (i = 1 \ldots m; j = 1 \ldots n)$$

are the first-order partial derivatives.

Note again that the first-order conditions (the Kuhn-Tucker conditions) incorporate the nonnegativity restrictions on the choice variables and Lagrange multipliers and the complementary slackness conditions, as well as the marginal conditions, that is, the partials of the Lagrangian with respect to the choice variables and Lagrange multipliers. The inequalities on the marginal conditions, however, are reversed from those for the maximization problem. Here, in the minimization, we have: $\delta L^*/\delta y_i \geq 0$ and $\delta L^*/\delta \lambda_j^* \leq 0$.

Solving the Kuhn-Tucker conditions will give the optimal values for the choice variables and Lagrange multipliers. Later in this chapter, we will discuss some second-order conditions for establishing the type of extrema. First, we illustrate with a nonlinear programming maximization problem. Then we will apply nonlinear programming to a firm's long-run objective of cost minimization.

A Numerical Example   Given the following problem:

$$\text{maximize: } z = xy^2$$

$$\text{subject to: } x + 2y \leq 80$$

$$x + y \leq 50$$

$$x, y \geq 0$$

The graph of the feasible region is shown in Figure 11.2. The extreme points on the feasible region are: A(0, 40), B(20, 30) and C(50, 0). Given the objective function, we can rule out the corner points A and C, since if either of the choice variables equals zero, the value of z is zero, and clearly not a maximum. Thus, the optimal combination, $(\bar{x}, \bar{y})$, would be found either on the open line segment between points A and B (where only the first constraint, $x + 2y \leq 80$, is binding), or at point B (where both constraints are binding), or on the open line segment between points B and C (where only the second constraint, $x + y \leq 50$, is binding).

The Lagrangian function is:

$$\mathcal{L}(x, y, \lambda_1, \lambda_2) = xy^2 + \lambda_1 \cdot (80 - x - 2y) + \lambda_2 \cdot (50 - x - y)$$

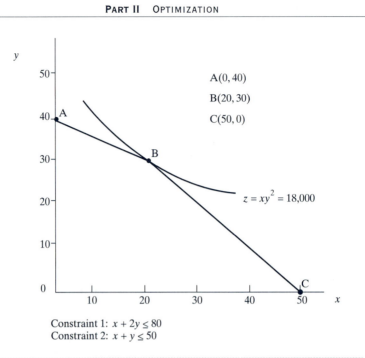

Constraint 1: $x + 2y \leq 80$
Constraint 2: $x + y \leq 50$

FIGURE 11.2   NONLINEAR PROGRAMMING PROBLEM: BOTH CONSTRAINTS ARE BINDING

The Kuhn-Tucker conditions are:

$$\delta\mathcal{L}/\delta x = y^2 - \lambda_1 - \lambda_2 \leq 0; \qquad x \geq 0; \qquad (x)(\delta\mathcal{L}/\delta x) = 0$$

$$\delta\mathcal{L}/\delta y = 2xy - 2\lambda_1 - \lambda_2 \leq 0; \qquad y \geq 0; \qquad (y)(\delta\mathcal{L}/\delta y) = 0$$

$$\delta\mathcal{L}/\delta\lambda_1 = 80 - x - 2y \geq 0; \qquad \lambda_1 \geq 0; \qquad (\lambda_1)(\delta\mathcal{L}/\delta\lambda_1) = 0$$

$$\delta\mathcal{L}/\delta\lambda_2 = 50 - x - y \geq 0; \qquad \lambda_2 \geq 0; \qquad (\lambda_2)(\delta\mathcal{L}/\delta\lambda_2) = 0$$

The optimal values for the choice variables, x and y, and the Lagrange multipliers, λ_1 and λ_2, must satisfy the Kuhn-Tucker conditions.

To solve, we find the slope of the curves associated with the objective function, $z = xy^2$. Totally differentiating the objective function, we have: $dz = y^2 dx + 2xy\, dy$. For a given value of z, which sets the curve in the x-y plane and makes $dz = 0$, we can solve for $dy/dx = -y^2/2xy = -y/2x$ (where $x \neq 0$).

We begin by evaluating the slope of a curve at the point B (20, 30) on the boundary of the feasible region, where both constraints are binding.

$$dy/dx \, (20, 30) = -30/2(20) = -3/4$$

(Note, at this point, the value of the objective function is: $z(20, 30) = 18{,}000$.) We see that the slope of the curve associated with the objective function at point B lies between the slopes of the two constraints.

$$-1/2 \quad < -3/4 < \quad -1$$

(slope of $x + 2y = 80$) $\qquad$ (slope of $x + y = 50$)

This implies that moving away from this point along either constraint would reduce the value of the objective function, that is, force a movement to a lower curve, $z = xy^2$ < 18,000. Refer to Figure 11.2, where we can see that in moving from point B toward point A (with x decreasing and y increasing), the distance between the curve, $z = xy^2 = 18{,}000$, and the line segment AB is increasing. Similarly, moving from point B along the line segment BC the distance between the curve and the binding constraint is increasing.

Indeed, we can confirm that the point $(\bar{x}, \bar{y}) = (20, 30)$ satisfies the Kuhn-Tucker conditions. Note that with both constraints binding, the optimal values of the Lagrange multipliers are positive ($\lambda_1 > 0$ and $\lambda_2 > 0$). To solve for these values, we use the marginal conditions for the partials of the Lagrangian with respect to the choice variables, evaluated at the critical point, $\bar{x} = 20$ and $\bar{y} = 30$.

$$\delta \mathcal{L}/\delta x = \bar{y}^2 - \bar{\lambda}_1 - \bar{\lambda}_2 = 900 - \bar{\lambda}_1 - \bar{\lambda}_2 = 0$$

$$\delta \mathcal{L}/\delta y = 2\overline{xy} - 2\bar{\lambda}_1 - \bar{\lambda}_2 = 1200 - 2\bar{\lambda}_1 - \bar{\lambda}_2 = 0$$

Solving the two simultaneous equations for $\bar{\lambda}_1$ and $\bar{\lambda}_2$, we find: $\bar{\lambda}_1 = 300$ and $\bar{\lambda}_2 = 600$. Recall, the optimal value of a Lagrange multiplier indicates the (instantaneous) impact on the optimal value of the dependent variable, here $\bar{z}$, of an (infinitesimal) change in the constraint.

In sum, the first-order conditions for the nonlinear maximization are satisfied as shown below. The optimal values are: $\bar{x} = 20$ and $\bar{y} = 30$, which yield $\bar{z} = 18{,}000$; and $\bar{\lambda}_1 = 300, \bar{\lambda}_2 = 600$.

$$\delta \mathcal{L}/\delta x = \bar{y}^2 - \bar{\lambda}_1 - \bar{\lambda}_2 = 0 \le 0; \quad \bar{x} = 20 \ge 0; \quad (\bar{x})(\delta \mathcal{L}/\delta x) = 0$$

$$\delta \mathcal{L}/\delta y = 2\overline{xy} - 2\bar{\lambda}_1 - \bar{\lambda}_2 = 0 \le 0; \quad \bar{y} = 30 \ge 0; \quad (\bar{y})(\delta \mathcal{L}/\delta y) = 0$$

$$\delta \mathcal{L}/\delta \lambda_1 = 80 - \bar{x} - 2\bar{y} = 0 \ge 0; \quad \bar{\lambda}_1 = 300 \ge 0; \quad (\bar{\lambda}_1)(\delta \mathcal{L}/\delta \lambda_1) = 0$$

$$\delta \mathcal{L}/\delta \lambda_2 = 50 - \bar{x} - \bar{y} = 0 \ge 0; \quad \bar{\lambda}_2 = 600 \ge 0; \quad (\bar{\lambda}_2)(\delta \mathcal{L}/\delta \lambda_2) = 0$$

To illustrate a nonlinear programming problem where there is a nonbinding constraint, we take the same objective function and introduce two new constraints. The optimization becomes

$$\text{maximize:} \quad z = xy^2$$

$$\text{subject to:} \quad 3x + 4y \le 180$$

$$2x + y \le 80$$

$$x, y \ge 0$$

In Figure 11.3 the feasible region is illustrated by the area 0ABC. Again, given this objective function, the corner points A and C can be ruled out, since a zero value for

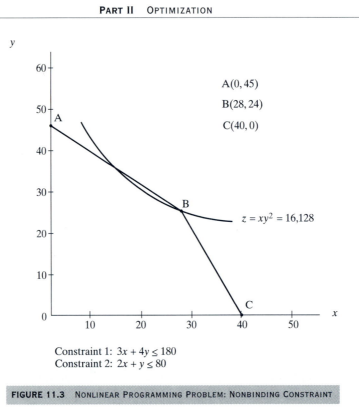

Constraint 1: $3x + 4y \leq 180$
Constraint 2: $2x + y \leq 80$

FIGURE 11.3   NONLINEAR PROGRAMMING PROBLEM: NONBINDING CONSTRAINT

a choice variable results in a zero value for the objective function. At point B, where $x = 28$ and $y = 24$, the value of the objective function is: $z = xy^2 = (28)(24)^2 = 16{,}128$. The slope of the curve associated with this objective function passing through point B is: $dy/dx = -y/2x = -24/(2)28 = -3/7 = -.429$. This is less (in absolute value) than the slope of either constraint: $dy/dx = -3/4$ for $3x + 4y = 180$ and $dy/dx = -2$ for $2x + y = 80$. In fact, moving from point B up along the constraint $3x + 4y = 180$ toward point A would initially increase the value of the objective function. Refer to Figure 11.3 where a portion of this binding constraint lies above the curve, $z = xy^2 = 16{,}128$. Therefore, there exists a higher curve, $z = xy^2 > 16{,}128$, that is tangent to the binding constraint represented by the line segment AB. The other constraint, $2x + y \leq 80$, represented by the line segment BC, however, is not binding.

With respect to the Lagrangian function for this nonlinear maximization, we have:

$$\mathcal{L}(x, y, \lambda_1, \lambda_2) = xy^2 + \lambda_1 \cdot (180 - 3x - 4y) + \lambda_2 \cdot (80 - 2x - y)$$

The associated Kuhn-Tucker conditions are

$$\delta\mathcal{L}/\delta x = y^2 - 3\lambda_1 - 2\lambda_2 \leq 0; \qquad x \geq 0; \qquad (x)(\delta\mathcal{L}/\delta x) = 0$$

$$\delta\mathcal{L}/\delta y = 2xy - 4\lambda_1 - \lambda_2 \leq 0; \qquad y \geq 0; \qquad (y)(\delta\mathcal{L}/\delta y) = 0$$

$$\delta\mathcal{L}/\delta\lambda_1 = 180 - 3x - 4y \geq 0; \qquad \lambda_1 \geq 0; \qquad (\lambda_1)(\delta\mathcal{L}/\delta\lambda_1) = 0$$

$$\delta\mathcal{L}/\delta\lambda_2 = 80 - 2x - y \geq 0; \qquad \lambda_2 \geq 0; \qquad (\lambda_2)(\delta\mathcal{L}/\delta\lambda_2) = 0$$

With the critical values for the choice variables, $\bar{x}$ and $\bar{y}$, positive (since the constrained maximization occurs between the points A and B along the line segment AB), the marginal conditions both hold exactly: $\delta\mathcal{L}/\delta x = 0$ and $\delta\mathcal{L}/\delta y = 0$. Moreover, with the second constraint not binding, the associated Lagrange multiplier equals zero: $\bar{\lambda}_2 = 0$. From the marginal conditions and binding constraint we can solve for the optimal values of x, y, and λ_1:

$$\delta\mathcal{L}/\delta x = y^2 - 3\lambda_1 - 0 = 0; \quad \text{so} \quad y^2 = 3\lambda_1 \quad \text{or} \quad y^2/3 = \lambda_1$$

$$\delta\mathcal{L}/\delta y = 2xy - 4\lambda_1 - 0 = 0; \quad \text{so} \quad 2xy = 4\lambda_1 \quad \text{or} \quad xy/2 = \lambda_1$$

Therefore, $y^2/3 = xy/2$, or $(2/3)y = x$.
Substituting $(2/3)y$ for x into the binding constraint $(3x + 4y = 80)$, we find

$$3(2/3)y + 4y = 80, \text{ or } \bar{y} = 30. \text{ Solving for } \bar{x} \text{ gives } \bar{x} = (2/3)\bar{y} = (2/3)(30) = 20$$

To solve for the Lagrange multiplier, λ_1, we use

$$\bar{y}^2/3 = \bar{\lambda}_1 = \bar{x}\bar{y}/2$$

$$(30)^2/3 = 300 = \bar{\lambda}_1 = (30)(20)/2$$

Thus, the critical values are: $\bar{x} = 20$ and $\bar{y} = 30$, which yield $\bar{z} = 18{,}000$, and $\bar{\lambda}_1 = 300$, $\bar{\lambda}_2 = 0$. The Kuhn-Tucker conditions for a maximum are met:

$$\delta\mathcal{L}/\delta x = \bar{y}^2 - 3\bar{\lambda}_1 - 2\bar{\lambda}_2 = 0 \leq 0; \quad \bar{x} = 20 \geq 0; \quad (\bar{x})(\delta\mathcal{L}/\delta x) = 0$$

$$\delta\mathcal{L}/\delta y = 2\bar{x}\bar{y} - 4\bar{\lambda}_1 - \bar{\lambda}_2 = 0 \leq 0; \quad \bar{y} = 30 \geq 0; \quad (\bar{y})(\delta\mathcal{L}/\delta y) = 0$$

$$\delta\mathcal{L}/\delta\lambda_1 = 180 - 3\bar{x} - 4\bar{y} = 0 \geq 0; \quad \bar{\lambda}_1 = 300 \geq 0; \quad (\bar{\lambda}_1)(\delta\mathcal{L}/\delta\lambda_1) = 0$$

$$\delta\mathcal{L}/\delta\lambda_2 = 80 - 2\bar{x} - \bar{y} = 10 \geq 0; \quad \bar{\lambda}_2 = 0 \geq 0; \quad (\bar{\lambda}_2)(\delta\mathcal{L}/\delta\lambda_2) = 0$$

We return now to the theory of the firm, in particular, to the long-run decision on the cost-minimizing combination of capital and labor for producing a selected level of output. As we will see, with nonlinear programming, additional constraints on the behavior of the firm can be modeled.

PRACTICE PROBLEM 11.4

Given the following nonlinear programming problem:

$$\text{maximize:} \quad z = xy$$

$$\text{subject to:} \quad 4x + y \leq 50$$

$$2x + 2y \leq 70$$

$$x, y \geq 0$$

a) Graph the feasible region.
b) Set up the Lagrangian.
c) Solve for the critical values for the choice variables, x and y, and for the Lagrange multipliers, λ_1 and λ_2.

d) Find the constrained maximum value for z.

e) Show that the Kuhn-Tucker conditions are satisfied.

(The answers are at the end of the chapter.)

COST MINIMIZATION

To highlight the potential economic realism gained with nonlinear programming, we begin with a classical constrained optimization version of the firm's long-run allocation of capital and labor for producing a given level of output.

Given the user costs of capital and labor, $r_0 = 5$ and $w_0 = 2$, respectively, and the firm's production function, $Q = K^8 L^4$, where Q = units of output, K = units of capital, and L = units of labor; find the cost-minimizing combination of capital and labor for producing a level of output of $Q_0 = 20$. (We might note that this Cobb-Douglas production function is characterized by increasing returns to scale. You might want to review the section on production functions in Chapter 10 if unclear why.)

The classical constrained minimization problem can be written as

$$\text{minimize: } C = r_0 K + w_0 L = 5K + 2L$$

$$\text{subject to: } K^a L^b = K^8 L^4 = Q_0 = 20$$

where C is the total cost of producing the output. The Lagrangian function is

$$\mathcal{L}(K, L, \lambda) = 5K + 2L + \lambda \cdot (20 - K^8 L^4)$$

Here, we list the two choice variables, K and L, before the Lagrange multiplier, λ—in contrast to the practice in Chapter 10—although the order of the choice variables and Lagrange multiplier(s) as arguments in the objective function is somewhat arbitrary. The first-order conditions for a constrained optimization are

$$\delta \mathcal{L}/\delta K = 5 - .8\lambda K^{-.2} L^4 = 0$$

$$\delta \mathcal{L}/\delta L = 2 - .4\lambda K^8 L^{-.6} = 0$$

$$\delta \mathcal{L}/\delta \lambda = 20 - K^8 L^4 = 0 \qquad \text{(The output constraint is met.)}$$

From the first two marginal conditions, we can solve for λ.

$$5/(.8K^{-.2} L^4) = \lambda = 2/(.4K^8 L^{-.6})$$

$$6.25 K^2/L^4 = \lambda = 5L^6/K^8$$

$$\text{Moreover,} \qquad 6.25K = 5L$$

$$\text{and} \qquad K = .8L$$

Substituting into the output constraint, we find

$$20 - K^8 L^4 = 0$$

$$(.8L)^{.8} L^{.4} = 20$$

$$.837L^{1.2} = 20$$

$$\overline{L} = 14.06$$

$$\text{So, } \overline{K} = .8\overline{L} = .8(14.06) = 11.25$$

$$\text{and } \overline{\lambda} = 6.25(\overline{K}^2/\overline{L}^4) = 6.25(11.25)^2/(14.06)^4 = 3.52$$

Recall that the Lagrange multiplier here indicates the marginal cost of output, $\overline{\lambda} = \delta\overline{C}/\delta\overline{Q}_0$. Finally, the minimum cost of producing $Q_0 = 20$ is $\overline{C} = 84.37$.

$$\overline{C} = 5\overline{K} + 2\overline{L} = 5(11.25) + 2(14.06) = 84.37$$

Recall from Chapter 10 that, at the cost-minimizing combination of capital and labor, the marginal rate of technical substitution, $MRTS$, indicating the slope of the isoquant, is equal to the negative of the ratio of the user costs, $-w_0/r_0$, indicating the slope of the tangential isocost line. The $MRTS$ is the negative of the ratio of the marginal product of labor, MP_L, to the marginal product of capital, MP_K. Here, with $Q = K^{.8}L^{.4}$,

$$MRTS = \frac{-MP_L}{MP_K} = \frac{-\delta Q/\delta L}{\delta Q/\delta K} = \frac{-.4K^{.8}L^{-.6}}{.8K^{-.2}L^{.4}} = -K/2L$$

At the optimum point, $\overline{K}_0 = 11.25$ and $\overline{L}_0 = 14.06$, so the $MRTS = -11.25/2(14.06) = -.4$. This equals the negative ratio of the user cost of labor, $w_0 = 2$, to the user cost of capital, $r_0 = 5$, $-w_0/r_0 = -2/5 = -.4$.

As an exercise, you should check the second-order conditions (i.e., evaluate the associated bordered Hessian) to confirm that the optimum combination of capital and labor found above is indeed a minimum.

Now suppose that the firm has a labor contract with a union that commits it to employing a minimum of 18 units of labor: $L_1 \geq 18$. Given the same production function, $Q = K^{.8}L^{.4}$, and the same user costs of capital and labor, $r_0 = 5$ and $w_0 = 2$, the firm seeks the cost-minimizing combination of capital and labor for producing at least 20 units of output, $Q_0 \geq 20$, and using at least 18 units of labor, $L_1 \geq 18$. We write this nonlinear programming problem as

$$\text{minimize:} \quad C = 5K + 2L$$

$$\text{subject to:} \quad K^{.8}L^{.4} \geq 20$$

$$L \geq 18$$

$$\text{and} \quad K \geq 0, L \geq 0$$

Note that, given the minimum employment requirement, the nonnegativity restriction for labor, $L \geq 0$, is redundant here. Figure 11.4 illustrates. The tangency of the isocost line AB with the isoquant, $Q_0 = 20$, at point E_0 gives the classical constrained optimum, where $\overline{K}_0 = 11.25$ and $\overline{L}_0 = 14.06$. If the firm is also constrained to using at least

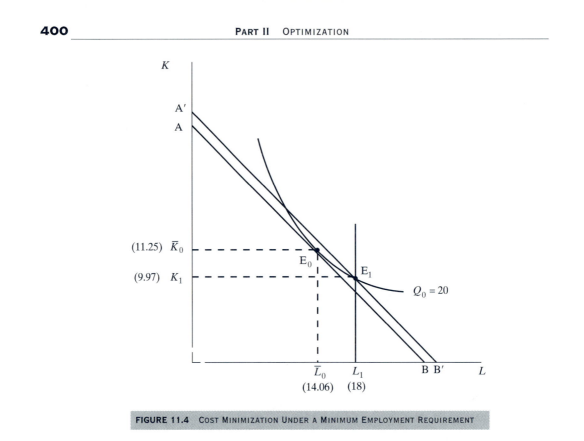

FIGURE 11.4　Cost Minimization Under a Minimum Employment Requirement

18 units of labor (see the vertical line L_1E_1) where, as in this case, the minimum employment exceeds the cost minimizing labor, $L_1 > \overline{L}_0$, then the firm is pushed to a higher isocost line, A′B′.

We will work through the nonlinear programming problem, aided by Figure 11.4. The Lagrangian function is

$$\mathcal{L}(K, L, \lambda_1, \lambda_2) = 5K + 2L + \lambda_1 \cdot (20 - K^{.8}L^{.4}) + \lambda_2 \cdot (18 - L)$$

The Kuhn-Tucker conditions for a minimum are

$$\delta\mathcal{L}/\delta K = 5 - .8\lambda_1 K^{-.2}L^{.4} \geq 0; \qquad K \geq 0; \qquad \text{and } (K)(\delta\mathcal{L}/\delta K) = 0$$

$$\delta\mathcal{L}/\delta L = 2 - .4\lambda_1 K^{.8}L^{-.6} \geq 0; \qquad L \geq 0; \qquad \text{and } (L)(\delta\mathcal{L}/\delta L) = 0$$

$$\delta\mathcal{L}/\delta\lambda_1 = 20 - K^{.8}L^{.4} \leq 0; \qquad \lambda_1 \geq 0; \qquad \text{and } (\lambda_1)(\delta\mathcal{L}/\delta\lambda_1) = 0$$

$$\delta\mathcal{L}/\delta\lambda_2 = 18 - L \leq 0; \qquad \lambda_2 \geq 0; \qquad \text{and } (\lambda_2)(\delta\mathcal{L}/\delta\lambda_2) = 0$$

Recall that compared to a maximization, for a minimization problem in nonlinear programming the inequalities for the first-order partials of the Lagrangian function are reversed in the Kuhn-Tucker conditions. That is, for a minimization, the first-order partials of the Lagrangian with respect to the choice variables are "greater than or equal to zero," while the first-order partials with respect to the Lagrange multipliers are "less than or equal to zero." With a constrained minimization, we have the possibility that the optimum value(s) of the choice variable(s) could be negative, if unrestricted; thus, the value of the Lagrangian function (and the objective function to be minimized) would decrease if the value(s) of the choice variable(s) could be reduced below zero.

Since we found in the classical constrained optimization, without the employment constraint, the cost-minimizing combination of capital and labor to be: $\overline{K}_0 = 11.25$ and $\overline{L}_0 = 14.06$; we see that the union requirement of employing at least 18 units of labor forces the firm to use more labor than otherwise would be optimal. To determine the amount of capital required to produce at least 20 units of output with the given 18 units of labor, we plug into the production function.

$$Q_0 = 20 = K^{.8}L^{.4} = K^{.8} (18)^{.4}$$

Solving for K, we get:

$$K^{.8} = 20/(18)^{.4} = 20/ (3.178) = 6.293$$

$$(K^{.8})^{1.25} = (6.293)^{1.25}$$

$$\overline{K} = 9.97$$

Therefore, the employment-constrained factor combination for producing $Q_0 = 20$ is: $\overline{K}_1 = 9.97$ and $\overline{L}_1 = 18$. See point E_1, the intersection of the isoquant, $Q_0 = 20$, and the labor constraint, $L_1 = 18$, in Figure 11.4. The new isocost line, $A'B'$, parallel to the isocost line, AB, cuts the isoquant, Q_0, at point E_1. Further, we can show that the marginal rate of technical substitution at point E_1 is less, in absolute value, than the slope of the isocost line, $A'B'$.

$$MRTS = \frac{-\delta Q/\delta L}{\delta Q/\delta K} = \frac{-.4K^{.8}L^{-.6}}{.8K^{-.2}L^{.4}} = -K/2L$$

At point E_1, where $\overline{K}_1 = 9.97$ and $\overline{L}_1 = 18$, the $MRTS = -9.97/ 2(18) = -.277$, compared to the slope of the isocost line(s), $-w_0/r_0 = -2/5 = -.4$. If not constrained by the union, the firm would like to use less labor and more capital to produce $Q_0 = 20$.

As illustrated, the slope of the isoquant is flatter than the slope of the isocost line at point E_1, the employment-constrained, cost-minimizing combination of capital and labor required to produce $Q_0 = 20$. If the firm used more than 18 units of labor to produce $Q_0 = 20$, the total cost would rise even more. That is, the intersection with the isoquant $Q_0 = 20$ would require an even higher isocost line than $A'B'$.

To confirm that the point E_1 represents the new constrained cost-minimizing combination of capital and labor, we can show that the Kuhn-Tucker conditions are satisfied. First, we will use these conditions to solve for the Lagrange multipliers. At point E_1, both constraints are binding, $\delta \mathscr{L}/\delta \lambda_1 = 0$ and $\delta \mathscr{L}/\delta \lambda_2 = 0$, so $\lambda_1 > 0$ and $\lambda_2 > 0$. Since $\overline{K}_1 = 9.97 > 0$ and $\overline{L}_1 = 18 > 0$, the marginal conditions also hold: $\delta \mathscr{L}/\delta K = 0$ and $\delta \mathscr{L}/\delta L = 0$. We can use these to solve for λ_1 and λ_2.

$$\delta \mathcal{L}/\delta K = 5 - .8\lambda_1\, K^{-.2}L^{.4} = 5 - .8\lambda_1\, (9.97)^{-.2}\,(18)^{.4} = 0$$

$$5 - 1.605\lambda_1 = 0$$

$$\overline{\lambda}_1 = 3.12$$

and

$$\delta \mathcal{L}/\delta L = 2 - .4\lambda_1\, K^{.8}L^{-.6} - \lambda_2 = 2 - .4(3.12)(9.97)^{.8}(18)^{-.6} - \lambda_2 = 0$$

$$2 - 1.385 - \lambda_2 = 0$$

$$\overline{\lambda}_2 = .61$$

Thus, the cost-minimization solution is: $\overline{K}_1 = 9.97, \overline{L}_1 = 18, \overline{\lambda}_1 = 3.12$, and $\overline{\lambda}_2 = .61$. The minimum cost of producing $Q_0 = 20$ is $\overline{C}_1 = 5\overline{K}_1 + 2\overline{L}_1 = 5(9.97) + 2(18) = 85.85$.

While $\overline{\lambda}_1 = \delta \overline{C}/\delta Q_0$ indicates the marginal cost of production, the Lagrange multiplier, $\overline{\lambda}_2 = \delta \overline{C}/\delta L_1$ indicates the marginal cost of the employment constraint, for a given level of output. For example, a tightening of the employment constraint by .1 units of labor, to $L_1' \geq 18.1$, would increase the total cost of producing 20 units of output by approximately .061 units. (We say approximately because, strictly speaking, the Lagrange multipliers refer to infinitesimal changes in the constraints.)

The Kuhn-Tucker conditions for a minimum are met at point E_1, with $\overline{K} = 9.97$, $\overline{L} = 18, \overline{\lambda}_1 = 3.12$, and $\overline{\lambda}_2 = .61$.

$$\delta \mathcal{L}/\delta K = 5 - .8\overline{\lambda}_1 \overline{K}^{-.2}\overline{L}^{.4} = 0 \geq 0; \quad \overline{K} = 9.97 \geq 0; \quad \text{and } (\overline{K})(\delta \mathcal{L}/\delta K) = 0$$

$$\delta \mathcal{L}/\delta L = 2 - .4\overline{\lambda}_1 \overline{K}^{.8}\overline{L}^{-.6} - \overline{\lambda}_2 = 0 \geq 0; \quad \overline{L} = 18 \geq 0; \quad \text{and } (\overline{L})(\delta \mathcal{L}/\delta L) = 0$$

$$\delta \mathcal{L}/\delta \lambda_1 = 20 - \overline{K}^{.8}\overline{L}^{.4} = 0 \leq 0; \quad \overline{\lambda}_1 = 3.12 \geq 0; \quad \text{and } (\overline{\lambda}_1)(\delta \mathcal{L}/\delta \lambda_1) = 0$$

$$\delta \mathcal{L}/\delta \lambda_2 = 18 - \overline{L} = 0 \leq 0; \quad \overline{\lambda}_2 = .61 \geq 0; \quad \text{and } (\overline{\lambda}_2)(\delta \mathcal{L}/\delta \lambda_2) = 0$$

Duality   To illustrate the property of duality, we convert this constrained cost minimization problem into a constrained output maximization. That is, given the primal:

$$\text{minimize:} \quad C = 5K + 2L$$

$$\text{subject to:} \quad Q = K^{.8}L^{.4} \geq 20$$

$$L \geq 18$$

$$\text{and } K \geq 0, L \geq 0$$

with a solution: $\overline{K}_1 = 9.97, \overline{L}_1 = 18, \overline{\lambda}_1 = 3.12$, and $\overline{\lambda}_2 = .61$ and a minimum cost of $\overline{C} = 85.85$ for producing $Q_0 = 20$ units of output; the counterpart dual is

$$\text{maximize:} \quad Q = K^{.8}L^{.4}$$

$$\text{subject to:} \quad C = 5K + 2L \leq 85.85$$

$$-L \leq -18$$

$$\text{and } K \geq 0, L \geq 0$$

Note that we write the employment constraint, $L \geq 18$, as $-L \leq -18$, to be consistent with the general "less than or equal to" constraints in the maximization problem.

We can again refer to Figure 11.4. The isocost line, $A'B'$, represents a total cost of 85.85. With the employment constraint, $L \geq 18$, the relevant feasible region is the lower part of this isocost line, E_1B'. Consequently, the highest isoquant that can be reached is $Q_0 = 20$. If the firm were not required to use at least 18 units of labor, then for the total cost indicated by the isocost line, $A'B'$, a greater output could be produced. That is, there would be an isoquant, Q_1, where $Q_1 > 20$, that is tangent to the isocost line between points A' and E_1.

The solution to this maximization is straightforward, since we know that the employment constraint is binding. We use the isocost line, $5K + 2L = 85.85$ to solve for $\overline{K}$, where $\overline{L} = 18$.

$$5K + 2L = 5K + 2(18) = 85.85$$

$$5K = 49.85$$

$$\overline{K} = 9.97$$

Thus, the maximum output is: $\overline{Q} = \overline{K}_1^8 \overline{L}_1^4 = (9.97)^{.8}(18)^{.4} = (6.294)(3.178) = 20.0$

We can use the Kuhn-Tucker conditions to solve for the Lagrange multipliers, λ_1^* and λ_2^*. The Lagrangian function for the dual maximization problem is

$$\mathscr{L}^*(K, L, \lambda_1^*, \lambda_2^*) = K^8L^4 + \lambda_1^* \cdot (85.85 - 5K - 2L) + \lambda_2^* \cdot (L - 18)$$

The Kuhn-Tucker conditions are

$$\delta\mathscr{L}^*/\delta K = .8K^{-2}L^4 - 5\lambda_1^* \leq 0; \quad K \geq 0; \quad \text{and } (K)(\delta\mathscr{L}^*/\delta K) = 0$$

$$\delta\mathscr{L}^*/\delta L = .4K^8L^{-6} - 2\lambda_1^* - \lambda_2^* \leq 0; \quad L \geq 0; \quad \text{and } (L)(\delta\mathscr{L}^*/\delta L) = 0$$

$$\delta\mathscr{L}^*/\delta\lambda_1^* = 85.85 - 5K - 2L \geq 0; \quad \lambda_1^* \geq 0; \quad \text{and } (\lambda_1^*)(\delta\mathscr{L}^*/\delta\lambda_1^*) = 0$$

$$\delta\mathscr{L}^*/\delta\lambda_2^* = L - 18 \geq 0; \quad -\lambda_2^* \geq 0; \quad \text{and } (\lambda_2^*)(\delta\mathscr{L}^*/\delta\lambda_2^*) = 0$$

Note that here we write the nonnegativity restriction for the Lagrange multiplier, λ_2^*, as $-\lambda_2^* \geq 0$, since in this formulation, $\lambda_2^* = \delta\overline{Q}/\delta L_1 < 0$. That is, an increase in the minimum employment requirement, L_1, would reduce the output that could be produced for a given total cost, since the firm is forced to substitute relatively less productive labor for capital.

From the marginal condition, $\delta\mathscr{L}^*/\delta K = 0$, with $\overline{K}_1 = 9.97$ and $\overline{L}_1 = 18$, we have

$$.8\overline{K}^{-2}\overline{L}^4 - 5\lambda_1^* = 0$$

$$.8(9.97)^{-2}(18)^{.4} = 5\lambda_1^*$$

$$1.60 = 5\lambda_1^*$$

$$\overline{\lambda_1^*} = .32$$

From the second marginal condition, $\delta\mathcal{L}*/\delta L = 0$, with $\overline{K}_1 = 9.97$, $\overline{L}_1 = 18$, and $\overline{\lambda}_1^* = .32$, we have

$$.4\overline{K}^8\overline{L}^{-.6} - 2\overline{\lambda}_1^* - \lambda_2^* = 0$$

$$.4(9.97)^{.8}(18)^{-.6} - 2(.32) = \lambda_2^*$$

$$.44 - .64 = \lambda_2^*$$

$$\overline{\lambda}_2^* = -.20$$

The interpretations of the Lagrange multipliers are as follows. In the dual maximization problem, $\overline{\lambda}_1^* = \delta\overline{Q}/\delta C_0$, or the reciprocal of the marginal cost of output. Here, $\overline{\lambda}_1^* = .32 = 1/(3.12) = 1/\overline{\lambda}_1$, where $\overline{\lambda}_1$ is the Lagrange multiplier from the primal minimization problem. The second Lagrange multiplier in the dual indicates the effect on the maximum output from a change in the employment constraint: $\lambda_2^* = \delta\overline{Q}/\delta L_1 < 0$. Here $\overline{\lambda}_2^* = -.20$, so, for example, a tightening of the employment constraint by .1 units of labor to $L_1' = 18.1$, would reduce output by approximately .02 units.

Finally, we observe that the solution $\overline{K}_1 = 9.97$, $\overline{L}_1 = 18$, $\overline{\lambda}_1^* = .32$, and $\overline{\lambda}_2^* = -.20$, with $\overline{Q} = 20$, satisfies the Kuhn-Tucker conditions.

$$\delta\mathcal{L}*/\delta K = .8\overline{K}^{-.2}\overline{L}^{.4} - 5\overline{\lambda}_1^* = 0 \le 0; \quad \overline{K} = 9.97 \ge 0; \quad \text{and } (\overline{K})(\delta\mathcal{L}*/\delta K) = 0$$

$$\delta\mathcal{L}*/\delta L = .4\overline{K}^8\overline{L}^{-.6} - 2\overline{\lambda}_1^* - \overline{\lambda}_2^* = 0 \le 0; \quad \overline{L} = 18 \ge 0; \quad \text{and } (\overline{L})(\delta\mathcal{L}*/\delta L) = 0$$

$$\delta\mathcal{L}*/\delta\lambda_1^* = 85.85 - 5\overline{K} - 2\overline{L} = 0 \le 0; \quad \overline{\lambda}_1^* = .32 \ge 0; \quad \text{and } (\overline{\lambda}_1^*)(\delta\mathcal{L}*/\delta\lambda_1^*) = 0$$

$$\delta\mathcal{L}*/\delta\lambda_2^* = \overline{L} - 18 = 0 \le 0; \quad -\overline{\lambda}_2^* = -(-.20) \ge 0; \quad \text{and } (\overline{\lambda}_2^*)(\delta\mathcal{L}*/\delta\lambda_2^*) = 0$$

PRACTICE PROBLEM 11.5

Given the nonlinear programming problem:

$$\text{minimize:} \quad z = x + 2y$$

$$\text{subject to:} \quad xy \ge 100$$

$$x \ge 10$$

$$x, y \ge 0$$

a) Graph the feasible region.
b) Set up the Lagrangian.
c) Solve for the critical values for the choice variables, x and y, and for the Lagrange multipliers, λ_1 and λ_2.
d) Find the constrained minimim value for z.
e) Show that the Kuhn-Tucker conditions are satisfied.

(The answers are at the end of the chapter.)

Second-Order Conditions   Recall in the classical constrained optimization problems in Chapter 10, to determine the type of extremum identified by the first-order conditions, the signs of the associated bordered Hessians would be evaluated. We also stated that knowledge about the objective function to be optimized could make it unnecessary to check the second-order conditions. In particular, if the objective function to be maximized were concave, then the critical point would be an absolute maximum. If the objective function to be minimized were convex, then the critical point would be an absolute minimum.

In this introduction to nonlinear programming, we have focused on the first order conditions, known as the Kuhn-Tucker conditions. We will briefly discuss some additional requirements to establish the constrained optima as absolute extrema.[1]

Sufficient conditions for a solution satisfying the Kuhn-Tucker conditions for a maximum to establish an absolute maximum are that the objective function be differentiable and concave and that each constraint function be differentiable and convex. Sufficient conditions for a solution satisfying the Kuhn-Tucker conditions for a minimum to establish an absolute minimum are that the objective function be differentiable and convex and that each constraint function be differentiable and concave.

Recall from the discussion of functions of one variable, $y = f(x)$, in Chapter 6, that linear functions are both concave and convex. We will illustrate using examples from the present chapter. First, we should elaborate on the mathematical properties of concavity and convexity of functions.

Given a function, $y = f(x_1, x_2, \ldots x_n)$, defined over n-space, and u and v as any two members of the domain of this function, $u = (x_1', x_2', \ldots x_n')$ and $v = (x_1'', x_2'', \ldots x_n'')$, and given the two points, $M = [u, f(u)]$ and $N = [v, f(v)]$; then the function $y = f(x_1, x_2, \ldots x_n)$ is:

concave if and only if $\quad sf(u) + (1 - s)f(v) \leq f[su + (1 - s)v]$

convex if and only if $\quad sf(u) + (1 - s)f(v) \geq f[su + (1 - s)v]$

where s is a scalar, $0 < s < 1$. If we replace the "less than or equal" sign ("greater than or equal" sign) with a "less than" sign ("greater than" sign), that is, if we just allow for the strict inequality, then the function y is *strictly concave (strictly convex)*.

The expression, $sf(u) + (1 - s)f(v)$, with $0 < s < 1$, represents the value of the function for a point lying on the line segment between the points M and N and evaluated at $[su + (1 - s)v]$. The expression, $f[su + (1 - s)v]$, with $0 < s < 1$, represents the associated point on the hypersurface connecting the points M and N, that is, the value of the function $y = f(x_1, x_2, \ldots x_n)$ at $[su + (1 - s)v]$.

Consider a very simple example in two dimensions, $y = f(x) = x^2$, which is a parabola with the minimum at the origin. We know that this function is strictly convex, since $d^2y/dx^2 = 2 > 0$. Let us restrict our attention to nonnegative values of x, that is, $x \geq 0$, or the right half of the parabola. Taking any two values of x in the domain, say $u = 1$ and $v = 3$, and the corresponding points on the function, $M = [u, f(u)] = (1,1)$

---

[1]For a more extensive treatment of the conditions for establishing the type of extremum in nonlinear programming problems, see Alpha C. Chiang, *Fundamental Methods of Mathematical Economics,* Third Edition, New York: McGraw-Hill, 1984, Chapter 21, "Nonlinear Programming," especially pages 731–746.

and $N = [v, f(v)] = (3, 9)$, and an arbitrary value for s, say $s = .4$, we can show that the function $y = x^2$ is strictly convex according to the requirement:

$$sf(u) + (1 - s)f(v) > f[su + (1 - s)v]$$

$$.4(1) + .6(9) > f[.4(1) + .6(3)] = f(2.2) = (2.2)^2$$

$$5.8 > 4.84$$

Figure 11.5 illustrates. We see that the line segment connecting the points M and N lies entirely above the curve between points M and N. Therefore, the value of the function for a point on the line segment, $sf(u) + (1 - s)f(v)$, (see point B), will exceed the value of the function for the corresponding point on the curve, $f[su + (1 - s)v]$. (See point A.)

We illustrate with an example from the firm, seeking to minimize the total cost of producing a given level of output, subject to a minimum level of employment imposed by a labor union. Recall the problem:

$$\text{minimize:}\quad C = 5K + 2L$$

$$\text{subject to:}\quad Q = K^{.8}L^{.4} \geq 20$$

$$L \geq 18$$

FIGURE 11.5   THE STRICTLY CONVEX FUNCTION, $y = x^2$

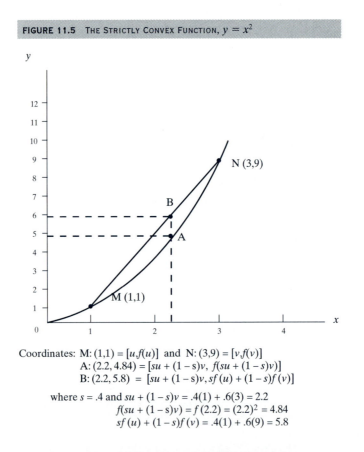

Coordinates: M: $(1,1) = [u, f(u)]$ and N: $(3,9) = [v, f(v)]$
A: $(2.2, 4.84) = [su + (1 - s)v, f(su + (1 - s)v)]$
B: $(2.2, 5.8) = [su + (1 - s)v, sf(u) + (1 - s)f(v)]$

where $s = .4$ and $su + (1 - s)v = .4(1) + .6(3) = 2.2$
$f(su + (1 - s)v) = f(2.2) = (2.2)^2 = 4.84$
$sf(u) + (1 - s)f(v) = .4(1) + .6(9) = 5.8$

$$\text{and} \qquad K \geq 0, L \geq 0$$

Here the objective function is linear, and so qualifies as a convex function consistent with the sufficient conditions for an absolute minimum. Moreover, the employment constraint is linear, and so qualifies as a concave function. We need to determine if the output constraint function, $Q = K^{.8}L^{.4}$, is also concave. That is, for concavity, we need: $sf(u) + (1 - s)f(v) \leq f[su + (1 - s)v]$, where u and v are any two combinations of capital and labor and s is a scalar, $0 < s < 1$. For example, let: $u = (10, 5), v = (20, 10)$, and $s = .6$. We have

$$f(u) = K^{.8}L^{.4} = (10)^{.8}(5)^{.4} = (6.310)(1.904) = 12.014$$

$$f(v) = K^{.8}L^{.4} = (20)^{.8}(10)^{.4} = (10.986)(2.512) = 27.597$$

$$su + (1 - s)v = .6(10, 5) + .4(20, 10) = (14, 7)$$

$$f[su + (1 - s)v] = f(14, 7) = (14)^{.8}(7)^{.4} = (8.259)(2.178) = 17.988$$

$$sf(u) + (1 - s)f(v) = .6(12.014) + .4(27.597) = 7.208 + 11.039 = 18.247$$

Therefore, $sf(u) + (1 - s)f(v) = 18.247 \geq 17.988 = f[su + (1 - s)v]$.

So, the production function, $Q = K^{.8}L^{.4}$, is not concave. This production function, characterized by increasing returns to scale, is strictly convex. We see that a doubling of inputs, from $K_1 = 10$ and $L_1 = 5$, to $K_2 = 20$ and $L_2 = 10$, more than doubles output, from $Q_1 = 12.014$ to $Q_2 = 27.597$. Because the production function constraint is not concave, we have not established the sufficient conditions for the solution, $\overline{K} = 9.97$ and $\overline{L} = 18$, to be an absolute cost-minimizing combination of factors. We should note there are less stringent conditions for establishing absolute extremum in nonlinear programming problems, although these conditions are better addressed in more advanced presentations of nonlinear programming. For our purposes here, since we can graph the problem (refer back to Figure 11.4 for a sketch), and can check points in the neighborhood of the solution identified by the Kuhn-Tucker conditions, we will assume that the optimal combination of capital and labor found is cost-minimizing.

PRACTICE PROBLEM 11.6

Determine if the production function, $Q = K^{.5}L^{.3}$ is strictly concave. Use the factor combinations (K, L) of $(10, 10)$ and $(20, 20)$, and let $s = .6$.

(The answers are at the end of the chapter.)

In Chapter 12 we analyze consumer behavior, where households seek the most satisfaction from their expenditures. We will apply the same techniques of constrained optimization developed in the last two chapters.

❖ KEY TERMS

Economics

- isorevenue lines (p. 369)
- shadow price (p. 375)

Mathematics

❖ PROBLEMS

1. Consider a farmer seeking to maximize the total revenues (R) from the sale of two crops (x_1 and x_2). The unit prices of the two crops are: $P_1 = \$10$ and $P_2 = \$4$. Each crop requires the inputs of land, labor, and fertilizer and is characterized by a fixed-coefficients production function. In particular, each unit produced of crop 1 requires 5 units of land, 2 units of labor, and 7.5 units of fertilizer. Each unit produced of crop 2 requires 5 units of land, 1 unit of labor, and 2 units of fertilizer. Available to the farmer are 80 units of land, 20 units of labor, and 61 units of fertilizer.
   a) Set up the linear programming problem.
   b) Sketch the feasible region.
   c) Using the simplex method, solve for the revenue-maximizing outputs of the two crops. Determine the maximum revenues of the farmer.
   d) Determine which constraint(s) are binding and the shadow prices of land, labor, and fertilizer.

2. Consider the dual minimization problem to the above Problem 1.
   a) Set up the linear programming problem.
   b) Using the simplex method, solve for the shadow prices for the resources, y_1, y_2, and y_3, that minimize the total resource cost, R^*. What is the minimum total resource cost?
   c) Confirm that Duality Theorem I holds.
   d) Confirm that Duality Theorem II holds.

3. A firm manufactures two products, x_1 and x_2, using two different machines, M_1 and M_2. It takes 30 minutes of machine time on M_1 and 20 minutes of machine time on M_2 to produce each unit of x_1. It takes 15 minutes of machine time on M_1 and 30 minutes of machine time on M_2 to produce each unit of x_2. The market price of x_1 is \$200 per unit and the market price of x_2 is \$240 per unit. The firm operates 40 hours (2,400 minutes) per week. The firm seeks to maximize the total revenues from the sales of its two products.
   a) Set up the linear programming problem.
   b) Graph the feasible region.

c) Solve for the revenue-maximizing rates of output for x_1 and x_2 using the simplex method.

d) Find the shadow prices of a minute of time on each machine.

e) Suppose that the unit price of x_2 increases to $300. Repeat parts a)–d).

f) Suppose, instead, that it only takes 24 minutes of machine time on $M1$ and 16 minutes of machine time on $M2$ to produce each unit of x_1. Repeat parts a)–d).

4. Consider the dual, that is, the counterpart minimization problem, to the initial revenue maximization in the above Problem 3.

a) Set up the linear programming problem.

b) Graph the feasible region.

c) Solve using the simplex method.

d) Confirm that Duality Theorems I and II hold.

5. Given a firm seeking to minimize the total cost of producing $Q_0 = 200$ units of output. The firm's production function is $Q = 2K^{.4}L^{.6}$ and the user costs of capital and labor are $r_0 = 40$ and $w_0 = 20$, respectively.

a) Using classical constrained optimization (as in Chapter 10), set up the Lagrangian function, derive the first-order conditions, and solve for the cost-minimizing combination of capital and labor for producing $Q_0 = 200$ units of output.

b) Calculate the marginal cost of output and the minimum total cost of production.

c) Check the second-order conditions.

6. Convert the case of the firm in question 4 into a nonlinear programming problem by assuming that the firm has a maximum of 45 units of capital available, $K \leq 45$. Set up the nonlinear programming problem of minimizing the total cost of producing at least $Q_0 = 200$ units of output subject to the capital constraint, $K \leq 45$.

a) Write out the Lagrangian function and the Kuhn-Tucker conditions.

b) Determine the cost-minimizing combination of capital and labor. Confirm, if possible, that this solution is an absolute minimum.

c) Calculate the marginal cost of output and the minimum cost of producing $Q_0 = 200$ units of output.

d) Suppose that the user cost of capital increases to $r'_0 = 60$. Repeat parts a)–c) of this problem.

❖ ANSWERS TO PRACTICE PROBLEMS

11.1 a) maximize: $R = 4x_1 + 6x_2$

subject to: $1x_1 + 2x_2 \leq 20$ (land constraint)

$\quad\quad\quad\quad\ 3x_1 + 2x_2 \leq 30$ (labor constraint)

$\quad\quad\quad\quad\ 4x_1 + 1x_2 \leq 32.5$ (fertilizer constraint)

$\quad\quad\quad\quad\ x_1, x_2 \geq 0$

b) The extreme points (x_1, x_2) are: A(0, 10), B(5, 7.5), C(7, 4.5), and D(8.125, 0).

c) The revenue-maximizing outputs of the two crops are: $\bar{x}_1 = 5$ and $\bar{x}_2 = 7.5$. The maximum revenues are: $\bar{R} = 65$.

d) The land and labor constraints are binding. The shadow prices of land and labor are, respectively, 2.5 and .5. The shadow price of fertilizer equals zero.

11.2 a) minimize: $R^* = 20y_1 + 30y_2 + 32.5y_3$

        subject to: $1y_1 + 3y_2 + 4y_3 \geq 4$

                 $2y_1 + 2y_2 + 1y_3 \geq 6$

                 $y_1, y_2, y_3 \geq 0$

b) The resource cost-minimizing shadow prices are: $\bar{y}_1 = 2.5, \bar{y}_2 = .5$, and $\bar{y}_3 = 0$. The minimum total resource cost is: $\bar{R}^* = 65$.

11.3 a) The final simplex tableaus are:

Primal (maximization of total revenues, R)

III	R	x_1	x_2	s_1	s_2	s_3	Constant
row 0″	1	0	0	5/2	1	0	65
row 1″	0	0	1	3/4	−1/2	0	7.5
row 2″	0	1	0	−1/2	1/2	0	5
row 3″	0	0	0	3	−7/4	1	5

Dual (minimization of total resource cost, R^*)

III	R^*	y_1	y_2	y_3	t_1	t_2	v_1	v_2	Constant
row 0″	1	0	0	−5	−5	−7.5	−95	−75	65
row 1″	0	0	1	21/12	−1/2	1/4	1/2	−1/4	.5
row 2″	0	1	0	−5/4	1/2	−3/4	−1/2	3/4	2.5

b) primal: $\bar{R} = 4\bar{x}_1 + 6\bar{x}_2 = 4(5) + 6(7.5) = 65$

    dual: $\bar{R}^* = 20\bar{y}_1 + 30\bar{y}_2 + 32.5\bar{y}_3 = 20(2.5) + 30(.5) + 32.5(0) = 65$

    $\bar{R} = \bar{R}^* = 65$

c) $\bar{x}_1 = 5$ (primal) and $\bar{t}_1 = 0$ (dual); $\bar{x}_2 = 7.5$ (primal) and $\bar{t}_2 = 0$ (dual)

    $\bar{y}_1 = 2.5$ (dual) and $\bar{s}_1 = 0$ (primal); $\bar{y}_2 = .5$ (dual) and $\bar{s}_2 = 0$ (primal);

    $\bar{y}_3 = 0$ (dual) and $\bar{s}_3 = 5$ (primal).

11.4 a) The extreme points of the feasible region are: A(0, 35), B(5, 30), and C(12.5, 0).

b) The Lagrangian is: $\mathcal{L}(x, y, \lambda_1, \lambda_2) = xy + \lambda_1 \cdot (50 - 4x - y) + \lambda_2 \cdot (70 - 2x - 2y)$

c) The critical values are: $\bar{x} = 6.25, \bar{y} = 25, \bar{\lambda}_1 = 6.25$, and $\bar{\lambda}_2 = 0$.

d) The constrained maximum value of z is: $\bar{z} = 156.25$.

e) The Kuhn-Tucker conditions are satisfied:

$$\delta\mathcal{L}/\delta x = \bar{y} - 4\bar{\lambda}_1 - 0 = 0 \leq 0; \bar{x} = 6.25 \geq 0; (\bar{x})(\delta\mathcal{L}/\delta x) = 0$$

$$\delta\mathcal{L}/\delta y = \bar{x} - \bar{\lambda}_1 - 0 = 0 \leq 0; \bar{y} = 25 \geq 0; (\bar{y})(\delta\mathcal{L}/\delta y) = 0$$

$$\delta\mathcal{L}/\delta\lambda_1 = 50 - 4\bar{x} - \bar{y} = 0 \geq 0; \bar{\lambda}_1 = 6.25 \geq 0; (\bar{\lambda}_1)(\delta\mathcal{L}/\delta\lambda_1) = 0$$

$$\delta\mathcal{L}/\delta\lambda_2 = 70 - 2\bar{x} - 2\bar{y} = 7.5 \geq 0; \bar{\lambda}_2 = 0 \geq 0; (\bar{\lambda}_2)(\delta\mathcal{L}/\delta\lambda_2) = 0$$

11.5 a) The feasible region is formed by the intersection of the areas $x \geq 10$ and $y \geq 100/x$.

   b) The Lagrangian is: $\mathcal{L}(x, y, \lambda_1, \lambda_2) = x + 2y + \lambda_1 \cdot (100 - xy) + \lambda_2 \cdot (10 - x)$

   c) The critical values are: $\bar{x} = 14.14$, $\bar{y} = 7.07$, $\bar{\lambda}_1 = .14$, and $\bar{\lambda}_2 = 0$.

   d) The constrained minimum value of z is: $\bar{z} = 28.28$.

   e) The Kuhn-Tucker conditions are satisfied:

$$\delta\mathcal{L}/\delta x = 1 - \bar{\lambda}_1\bar{y} - \bar{\lambda}_2 = 0 \geq 0; \bar{x} = 14.14 \geq 0; (\bar{x})(\delta\mathcal{L}/\delta x) = 0$$

$$\delta\mathcal{L}/\delta y = 2 - \bar{\lambda}_1\bar{x} = 0 \geq 0; \bar{y} = 7.07 \geq 0; (\bar{y})(\delta\mathcal{L}/\delta y) = 0$$

$$\delta\mathcal{L}/\delta\lambda_1 = 100 - \bar{x}\bar{y} = 0 \leq 0; \bar{\lambda}_1 = .14 \geq 0; (\bar{\lambda}_1)(\delta\mathcal{L}/\delta\lambda_1) = 0$$

$$\delta\mathcal{L}/\delta\lambda_2 = 10 - \bar{x} < 0 \leq 0; \bar{\lambda}_2 = 0 \geq 0; (\bar{\lambda}_2)(\delta\mathcal{L}/\delta\lambda_2) = 0$$

11.6 Given $Q = K^{.5}L^{.3}$, let $f(u) = Q(10, 10) = (10)^{.5}(10)^{.3} = 6.30$; $f(v) = Q(20, 20) = (20)^{.5}(20)^{.3} = 10.986$; and $s = .6$, so $su + (1 - s)v = (14, 14)$ and $Q(14, 14) = (14)^{.5}(14)^{.3} = 8.259$. Since $sf(u) + (1 - s)f(v) = .6(6.30) + .4(10.986) = 8.18 < 8.259 = f[su + (1 - s)v]$, the function, $Q = K^{.5}L^{.3}$, is strictly concave.

THEORY OF CONSUMER BEHAVIOR

In this chapter, the household, the basic unit of consumption, is addressed. The same techniques of optimization developed in the last two chapters are applied to consumer behavior.

We begin with the classical constrained optimization of a household seeking to maximize the total utility or satisfaction it derives from its expenditures on goods and services out of a given budgeted income. The Implicit Function Theorem is used in the comparative static analysis to identify the substitution and income effects of a change in the unit price of a good consumed by the household. Then the labor-leisure trade-offs of an individual are modeled within the framework of utility maximization.

Next, applying the technique of nonlinear programming, we illustrate the importance of the nonnegativity restrictions on the choice variables, here the goods consumed by the household. In the last part of the chapter, a time constraint is added to the model of utility maximization, since households should consider not just the relative monetary prices, but the relative time costs in their optimal allocation of expenditures.

UTILITY MAXIMIZATION

Consider a hypothetical household, whose total utility, U, is a function of its consumption of two goods, x and y. That is, $U = U(x, y)$, where

U = total utility of the household over the period

x = quantity (number of units) of good x consumed by the household over the period

y = quantity (number of units) of good y consumed by the household over the period

Note, although we could extend the model to n goods, we will restrict our analysis here to just two goods, in order to illustrate graphically.

Furthermore, consistent with the **law of diminishing marginal utility**, we assume positive, but diminishing, marginal utilities associated with the consumption of each

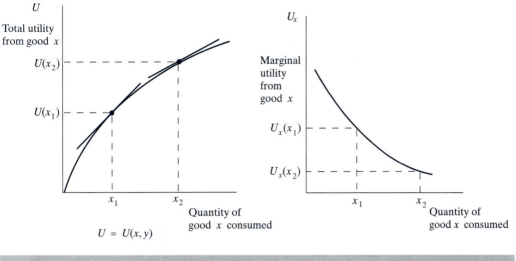

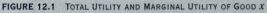

$$U = U(x, y)$$

FIGURE 12.1 TOTAL UTILITY AND MARGINAL UTILITY OF GOOD x

good. That is, while successive units consumed of any good add to the total utility of the household, the subsequent gains to utility are smaller. Clearly, a rational household would not consume additional units of a good if the marginal utilities were zero or negative, that is, if total utility did not increase or even began to decrease.[1]

Mathematically, we can write these assumptions as

$$U_x = \delta U / \delta x > 0 \quad \text{and} \quad U_{xx} = \delta U_x / \delta x < 0$$

$$U_y = \delta U / \delta y > 0 \quad \text{and} \quad U_{yy} = \delta U_y / \delta y < 0$$

For good x, we illustrate the total utility and marginal utility in Figure 12.1, where we hold constant the consumption of all other goods (here, good y) during the period. In panel a, the total utility curve for good x is strictly concave; and in panel b, the marginal utility curve for x is strictly convex. Indeed, the slope of the curve for the total utility associated with good x is given by the value of the marginal utility of good x. We can see that, as the consumption of good x rises, $x_2 > x_1$, the total utility received from good x increases, $U(x_2) > U(x_1)$, but the marginal utility of good x decreases, $U_x(x_2) < U_x(x_1)$. The same conditions are assumed for good y.

INDIFFERENCE CURVES

Graphically, if we plot all the combinations of the two goods, x and y, that yield the same level of total utility, say U_0, to the household, we obtain an **indifference curve**. Refer to Figure 12.2. Each of the combinations of the goods represented by the points a, b, v, and

---

[1]You might have witnessed, or even experienced yourself, however, occasions when the consumption of a good was carried to the point of negative marginal utility (disutility). Examples would include drinking alcoholic beverages to the point of becoming sick or passing out; eating so much at a buffet as to become stuffed and uncomfortable; or sunbathing to the point of getting sunburned. This behavior, while characteristic of human nature, would be considered irrational by economists; since it would be inconsistent with the objective of utility maximization. Even economists though, while understanding the law of diminishing marginal utility, have been guilty of these foibles.

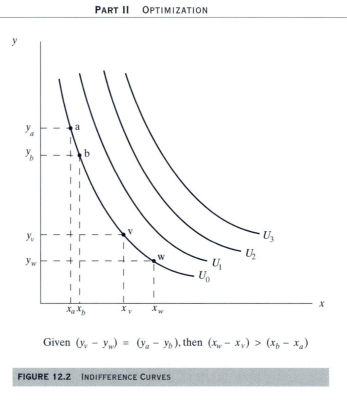

Given $(y_v - y_w) = (y_a - y_b)$, then $(x_w - x_v) > (x_b - x_a)$

FIGURE 12.2   INDIFFERENCE CURVES

w provides the same satisfaction or total utility to the household—so the household would be indifferent among these and any other combination of the two goods lying on the curve, U_0. If we vary the level of total utility, we can obtain other indifference curves for the household, the set of which comprise the household's **indifference mapping**. Indifference curves farther from the origin represent higher levels of total utility. The indifference mapping reflects the tastes and preferences of the household.

Moreover, with the assumption of positive and diminishing marginal utilities, we can show that the indifference curves are negatively sloped and strictly convex to the origin. Totally differentiating the utility function, $U = U(x, y)$, we get

$$dU = (\delta U/\delta x)dx + (\delta U/\delta y)dy = U_x \, dx + U_y \, dy$$

Since total utility is constant along an indifference curve, $dU = 0$, we can write

$$dU = 0 = U_x \, dx + U_y \, dy$$

Solving for dy/dx, which represents the slope of any curve in this x-y plane, we find the slope of an indifference curve, $dy/dx = -U_x/U_y$. (Note that $U_y \neq 0$.)

That is, the slope of an indifference curve is equal to the negative ratio of the marginal utilities of the two goods.[2] Given that the marginal utilities of goods x and y are always positive, the slope of an indifference curve is always negative.

---

[2]*Note:* If we had represented good y on the horizontal axis and good x on the vertical axis, the slope of the indifference curve would be given by $dx/dy = -U_y/U_x$, with $U_x \neq 0$.

The slope of an indifference curve, known as the **marginal rate of substitution** (MRS), indicates the rate at which the household is willing to trade off a unit of one of the goods for units of the other good in order to remain equally satisfied. Thus, $dy/dx = MRS = -(U_x/U_y) < 0$. Intuitively, if the household consumes less of good y ($dy < 0$), then more of good x ($dx > 0$) would be required for the household to remain equally satisfied.

When indifference curves are strictly convex, the negative slope increases (i.e., becomes less negative and approaches zero) as we move down an indifference curve, substituting good x for good y. Reflecting the law of diminishing marginal utility, as the consumption of good x increases, the marginal utility of good x declines ($x \uparrow \rightarrow U_x \downarrow$); and, as the consumption of good y decreases, the marginal utility of good y rises ($y \downarrow \rightarrow U_y \uparrow$). Thus, as good x is substituted for good y, the marginal rate of substitution decreases in absolute value ($|MRS| = |-U_x/U_y| \downarrow$ as $x \uparrow$ and $y \downarrow$), since the household becomes less willing to give up good y for good x. In other words, the household will require more units of good x to compensate for the loss of each unit of good y.

Formally, the curvature of an indifference curve can be found by differentiating the slope, $dy/dx = MRS$, with respect to x, the variable of the horizontal axis. Using the quotient rule for differentiation, we have

$$d^2y/dx^2 = \frac{d(dy/dx)}{dx} = \frac{d[-U_x(x, y)/U_y(x, y)]}{dx}$$

$$= \frac{(-U_{xx} - U_{yx} \, dy/dx)U_y - (-U_x)(U_{xy} + U_{yy} \, dy/dx)}{(U_y)^2}$$

and substituting $(-U_x/U_y)$ for dy/dx, we have

$$d^2y/dx^2 = \frac{-U_{xx}U_y - U_{yx} \, U_y(-U_x/U_y) + U_x \, U_{xy} + U_x \, U_{yy}(-U_x/U_y)}{(U_y)^2}$$

Since $U_{xy} = U_{yx}$, we can write

$$d^2y/dx^2 = \frac{-U_{xx}(U_y)^2 + 2U_{yx} \, U_x U_y - (U_x)^2 \, U_{yy}}{(U_y)^3} > 0$$

The negative slope of an indifference curve is increasing, that is, becoming less negative, $d^2y/dx^2 > 0$, since: $U_x > 0$ and $U_y > 0$; $U_{xx} < 0$ and $U_{yy} < 0$, due to the law of diminishing marginal utility; and $U_{xy} = U_{yx} > 0$, that is, as the consumption of good x (good y) increases along an indifference curve, the consumption of the good y (good x) must fall, which increases the marginal utility of good y (good x).

The strict convexity of the indifference curves is illustrated in Figure 12.2. In particular, for the indifference curve, U_0, the increasing reluctance of the household to sacrifice units of good y for good x, as the consumption of y falls and the consumption of x rises, is shown in comparing the movement from combinations a to b to the movement from combinations v to w. In the latter case, the same loss in good y, here ($y_v -$

$y_w) = (y_a - y_b)$, requires a greater gain in good x, $(x_w - x_v) > (x_b - x_a)$, to maintain the same level of utility.

To illustrate, consider the utility function, $U = x^{.6} y^{.7}$. We can show that the marginal utilities are positive but diminishing for the two goods x and y.

$$U_x = .6x^{-.4}y^{.7} > 0 \quad \text{and} \quad U_{xx} = -.24x^{-1.4}y^{.7} < 0$$

$$U_y = .7x^{.6}y^{-.3} > 0 \quad \text{and} \quad U_{yy} = -.21x^{.6}y^{-1.3} < 0$$

The cross-partials, however, are positive, indicating that an increase in the consumption of one of the goods would increase the marginal utility of the other good.

$$U_{xy} = .42x^{-.4}y^{-.3} = U_{yx} > 0$$

The marginal rate of substitution, *MRS*, is equal to the negative of the ratio of the marginal utilities.

$$MRS = -U_x/U_y = \frac{-.6x^{-.4}y^{.7}}{.7x^{.6}y^{-.3}} = -.86y/x < 0$$

The slope of any indifference curve associated with this utility function is negative. To determine the curvature of the indifference curves, we differentiate the marginal rate of substitution with respect to good x (arbitrarily placing good x on the horizontal axis, with good y on the vertical axis of the graph for the indifference curves.)

$$dMRS/dx = \frac{d(dy/dx)}{dx} = \frac{d(-U_x/U_y)}{dx} = \frac{d(-.86y/x)}{dx}$$

$$= \frac{-.86 \, (dy/dx) \cdot x - (-.86y)}{x^2}$$

Substituting in $-.86y/x$ for (dy/dx), we have

$$dMRS/dx = \frac{-.86(-.86y/x) \cdot x + .86y}{x^2} = \frac{.74y + .86y}{x^2} = \frac{1.6y}{x^2} > 0$$

With negative, but increasing, slopes, the indifference curves are strictly convex.

Change in Tastes   As noted earlier, the indifference mapping reflects the tastes and preferences of the household. Changes in tastes and preferences would affect the indifference curves. For example, a shift in the preferences of the household in favor of good y could rotate the indifference curves in a counterclockwise manner, that is, the indifference mapping would appear flatter. See Figure 12.3, where the new indifference curves are represented by U'_0, U'_1, and U'_2. For a given quantity of good y, the marginal rate of substitution, $MRS = -U_x/U_y$, would be greater, that is, less negative. The household would require more units of good x to compensate for a given reduction in good y when the taste for good y has increased. For example, consider point h on indifference curves U_0 and U'_0, and a quantity of good y equal to y_h. For a given decrease in the consumption of good y, to say y_g, the increase in good x required would now be greater, $(x'_g - x_h) > (x_g - x_h)$.

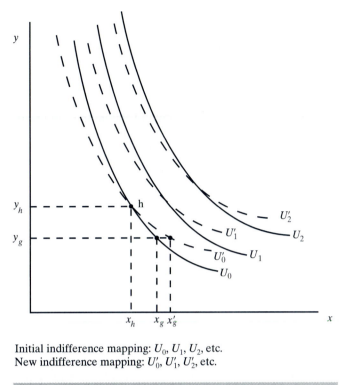

Initial indifference mapping: U_0, U_1, U_2, etc.
New indifference mapping: U'_0, U'_1, U'_2, etc.

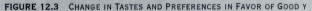

FIGURE 12.3   CHANGE IN TASTES AND PREFERENCES IN FAVOR OF GOOD Y

To illustrate, return to the utility function, $U = x^{.6}y^{.7}$, with the associated marginal rate of substitution, $MRS = -.86y/x$. Suppose a change in tastes in favor of good y results in a new utility function, $U' = x^{.4}y^{.8}$. The new marginal rate of substitution, MRS', is:

$$MRS' = -U'_x/U'_y = \frac{-.4x^{-.6}y^{.8}}{.8x^{.4}y^{-.2}} = -.5y/x$$

For any combination of goods x and y, that is, for any y/x ratio, the new marginal rate of substitution is reduced in absolute value: $|MRS'| = |-.5y/x| < |-.86y/x| = |MRS|$. Therefore, with a shift in preferences toward good y, the household is less willing to trade off good y for good x. At any combination of the two goods, the new indifference mapping would be flatter.

PRACTICE PROBLEM 12.1

Given the utility function for goods x and y, $U = x^{.7}y^{.2}$:
a) Show that the marginal utilities for x and y are positive but diminishing.
b) Derive the marginal rate of substitution.
c) Show that the indifference curves are strictly convex.

(The answers are at the end of the chapter.)

THE BUDGET CONSTRAINT

Given nonsatiation, or positive marginal utilities associated with the consumption of the goods, there is no unconstrained maximum utility. Higher utility curves indicate greater utility. The household's income, however, is limited. We will assume that for a given disposable income (that is, income after taxes paid and any transfers received by the household) over the planning period, the household determines the income to be budgeted for consumption expenditures on goods x and y. The difference between the total disposable income of the household and that budgeted for consumption represents the planned saving of the household. We will further assume that all of the income budgeted for consumption is spent.[3] Thus, the budgeted income of the household, I, can be considered as predetermined by the household and exogenous to our analysis.

For a given budgeted income, the quantities of goods x and y that the household could purchase depends on the unit prices of the goods, P_x and P_y, which are assumed to be set in the market and exogenous to the household. The household's budget constraint can be written as

$$P_x x + P_y y = I$$

where P_x = the unit price of good x

$\quad P_y$ = the unit price of good y

$\quad\quad I$ = the income budgeted by the household over the period for spending on goods x and y

In short, the sum of total expenditures on x (i.e., $P_x x$) and the total expenditures on y (i.e., $P_y y$) equals the budgeted income. (Note, the notation, P_x and P_y, for the unit prices of the two goods, should not be confused with the notation used elsewhere in the text for partial derivatives.)

The income constraint, illustrated in Figure 12.4, represents all of the combinations of the two goods that expend all of the household's budgeted income, given the unit prices of the two goods. The slope of the budget line can be found by solving the equation for good y (represented on the vertical axis), $y = I/P_y - (P_x/P_y)x$. The slope is given by $dy/dx = -(P_x/P_y)$, or the negative of the ratio of the unit price of good x to the unit price of good y.

A change in the ratio of the unit prices of the two goods would affect the slope of the budget line. *Ceteris paribus*, an increase in the price of good x would rotate the budget line in a clockwise direction from the vertical intercept (since the same amount of good y could be purchased with all of the household's income). The budget line becomes steeper. See Figure 12.5a. An increase in the unit price of good y would rotate the budget line in a counterclockwise direction from the horizontal intercept (since the

---

[3]There is also the possibility that a household dissaves, using part of its wealth for spending on goods x and y, or assumes debt by taking out loans to finance its spending, meaning that the budgeted income exceeds its disposable income. In any case, we assume that the budgeted income of the household is exhausted in the period for expenditures on goods x and y.

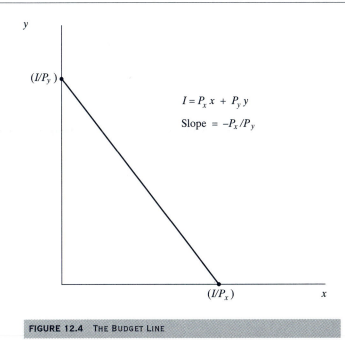

$$I = P_x x + P_y y$$

$$\text{Slope} = -P_x/P_y$$

FIGURE 12.4   THE BUDGET LINE

same amount of good x could be purchased with all of the household's income). The budget line becomes flatter.

A change in the income budgeted by the household, *ceteris paribus,* would shift the budget line in a parallel fashion. For example, an increase in the budgeted income would result in a parallel shift of the budget line to the right. The slope of the budget line is unchanged. See Figure 12.5b.

FIGURE 12.5   CHANGES IN THE BUDGET LINE

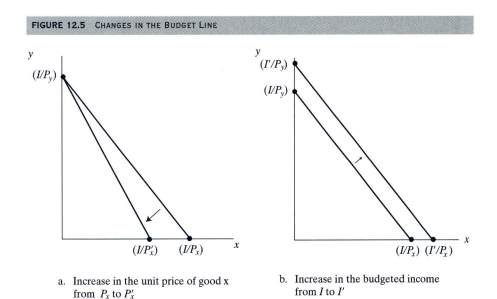

a. Increase in the unit price of good x
    from P_x to P_x'

b. Increase in the budgeted income
    from I to I'

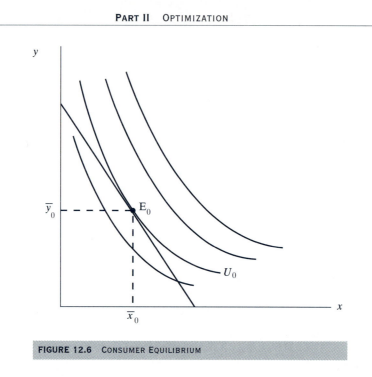

FIGURE 12.6   CONSUMER EQUILIBRIUM

CONSUMER EQUILIBRIUM

Superimposing the indifference mapping on the given budget constraint allows us to determine graphically the constrained maximum utility for the household. Refer to Figure 12.6. The highest indifference curve the household could reach occurs with the tangency of the budget line and the indifference curve U_0, yielding the utility-maximizing consumption combination of $\bar{x}_0$ and $\bar{y}_0$.

At the point of tangency, E_0, the slope of the indifference curve, $MRS = -(U_x/U_y)$, indicating the rate at which the household is willing, based on its tastes and preferences, to trade off good y for good x, is equal to the slope of the budget line, $-(P_x/P_y)$, indicating the rate at which the household is able, based on the relative unit prices, to trade off good y for good x. Rearranging, we obtain the condition for constrained utility-maximization: $(U_x/P_x) = (U_y/P_y)$. That is, to maximize its total utility, a household should arrange its expenditures such that the marginal utility per dollar spent is equal across the commodities.

UTILITY MAXIMIZATION USING THE LAGRANGIAN METHOD

We can model this problem of utility maximization mathematically. The objective function is $U = U(x, y)$ and the constraint is $P_x x + P_y y = I$. We seek to maximize $U = U(x, y)$ subject to $P_x x + P_y y = I$. Setting up the Lagrangian, $\mathcal{L}$, we have

$$\mathcal{L}(\lambda, x, y) = U(x, y) + \lambda \cdot [I - P_x x - P_y y]$$

Deriving the first-order conditions gives

$$\delta\mathcal{L}/\delta\lambda = I - P_x x - P_y y = 0 \qquad \text{(The budget constraint is satisfied.)}$$

$$\delta\mathcal{L}/\delta x = U_x - \lambda P_x = 0$$

$$\delta\mathcal{L}/\delta y = U_y - \lambda P_y = 0$$

Working with the last two first-order conditions, we can show that at the critical point, that is, the utility-maximizing combination,

$$U_x/P_x = U_y/P_y = \lambda$$

As expected from our earlier graphical analysis, the utility-maximizing combination of goods x and y will be characterized by equal marginal utilities per dollar spent. Furthermore, recall that we can interpret the Lagrange multiplier as the (instantaneous) effect on the optimal value of the objective function, here utility, of an (infinitesimal) change in the constraint, here income. Thus, $\lambda = \delta U/\delta I$, or in economic terms, the marginal utility of income.

Second-Order Conditions   Unless we know that the objective function is strictly concave, and therefore the constrained optimization will yield a maximum from solving the first-order conditions, we need to check the second-order conditions. That is, we need to evaluate the bordered Hessian.

To derive the bordered Hessian, we totally differentiate the first-order conditions and form the determinant, $|\overline{H}|$, which is equivalent to the associated Jacobian, $|J|$.

$$|\overline{H}| = \left| \frac{\delta(\delta\mathcal{L}/\delta\lambda, \ \delta\mathcal{L}/\delta x, \ \delta\mathcal{L}/\delta y)}{\delta(\lambda, x, y)} \right| = |J|$$

$$|\overline{H}| = \begin{vmatrix} 0 & -P_x & -P_y \\ -P_x & U_{xx} & U_{xy} \\ -P_y & U_{yx} & U_{yy} \end{vmatrix}$$

and expanding along the first column we have

$$|\overline{H}| = P_x(-P_x U_{yy} + P_y U_{yx}) - P_y(-P_x U_{xy} + P_y U_{xx})$$

$$= -(P_x)^2 \, U_{yy} + P_x P_y U_{yx} + P_x P_y U_{xy} - (P_y)^2 \, U_{xx}$$

$$= -(P_x)^2 \, U_{yy} + 2P_x P_y U_{xy} - (P_y)^2 \, U_{xx}$$

For a relative maximum, we need for the bordered Hessian to be negative definite, that is, $|\overline{H}| > 0$. The first term, $-(P_x)^2 \, U_{yy}$, and the third term, $-(P_y)^2 \, U_{xx}$, are positive, due to our assumptions of diminishing marginal utilities. The middle term, $2P_x P_y U_{xy}$, is also positive, given the second-order cross-partial derivative, $U_{xy} = U_{yx}$, is positive, as we expect to be the case along an indifference curve.[4]

---

[4]Actually, for $|\overline{H}| > 0$, all we need is that the following inequality hold: $-(P_x)^2 U_{yy} - (P_y)^2 U_{xx} > 2P_x P_y U_{xy}$.

Consider the following example: a household's utility function is $U = (x - 1)^{.5} \cdot (y - 4)^{.5}$; the unit prices of x and y are $P_x = \$2$ and $P_y = \$3$, respectively; and the budgeted income of the household is $I = \$24$. The constrained optimization problem then is to maximize $U = U(x, y) = (x - 1)^{.5} (y - 4)^{.5}$ subject to $P_x x + P_y y = 2x + 3y = 24 = I$.

Here, the household must have at least one unit of good x and four units of good y before any satisfaction is derived. Beyond these minimum levels or thresholds required before realizing any utility, for example, games of tennis or hours in the gym each week, the consumption of each of the goods provides positive, but diminishing, marginal utility to the household.

$$\delta U / \delta x = U_x = .5(x - 1)^{-.5} (y - 4)^{.5} > 0$$

$$\delta U / \delta y = U_y = .5(x - 1)^{.5} (y - 4)^{-.5} > 0$$

and

$$\delta U_x / \delta x = U_{xx} = -.25(x - 1)^{-1.5} (y - 4)^{.5} < 0$$

$$\delta U_y / \delta y = U_{yy} = -.25(x - 1)^{.5} (y - 4)^{-1.5} < 0$$

Moreover, the cross-partials are positive.

$$\delta U_y / \delta x = U_{xy} = U_{yx} = \delta U_x / \delta y = .25(x - 1)^{-.5} (y - 4)^{-.5} > 0$$

Setting up the Lagrangian function we have

$$\mathcal{L}(\lambda, x, y) = (x - 1)^{.5} (y - 4)^{.5} + \lambda \cdot [24 - 2x - 3y]$$

The first-order conditions are

$$\delta \mathcal{L} / \delta \lambda = 24 - 2x - 3y = 0 \quad \text{(The budget constraint is satisfied.)}$$

$$\delta \mathcal{L} / \delta x = .5(x - 1)^{-.5} (y - 4)^{.5} - 2\lambda = 0$$

$$\delta \mathcal{L} / \delta y = .5(x - 1)^{.5} (y - 4)^{-.5} - 3\lambda = 0$$

Solving the second and third equations for λ, and then equating, we obtain

$$\frac{.5(x - 1)^{-.5}(y - 4)^{.5}}{2} = \lambda = \frac{.5(x - 1)^{.5} (y - 4)^{-.5}}{3}$$

or

$$\frac{(y - 4)}{2} = \frac{(x - 1)}{3}$$

and

$$3y - 12 = 2x - 2$$

We "solve" for x in terms of y to get

$$x = 1.5y - 5$$

Substituting this expression for x into the budget constraint, we have reduced the system of three equations (the first-order conditions) in three unknowns (λ, x, and y) to one equation (the budget constraint) in one unknown (here y).

$$2x + 3y = 24$$

$$2(1.5y - 5) + 3y = 24$$

$$6y = 34$$

$$\bar{y} = 5.66\bar{6} = 5.67$$

Therefore, $\bar{x} = 1.5\bar{y} - 5 = 1.5(5.67) - 5 = 3.5$

The constrained utility-maximizing combination is then $\bar{x} = 3.5$ and $\bar{y} = 5.67$, yielding a total utility of $\bar{U} = (\bar{x} - 1)^{.5} (\bar{y} - 4)^{.5} = (3.5 - 1)^{.5} (5.67 - 4)^{.5} = 2.04$.

We can also find the value for λ, which represents the marginal utility of income.

$$\bar{\lambda} = \frac{.5(\bar{x} - 1)^{-.5} (\bar{y} - 4)^{.5}}{2} = \frac{.5(3.5 - 1)^{-.5} (5.67 - 4)^{.5}}{2} = .204 = \delta\bar{U}/\delta I$$

To check the second-order conditions, we need to evaluate the bordered Hessian, $|\bar{H}|$.

$$|\bar{H}| = \left| \frac{\delta(\delta\mathcal{L}/\delta\lambda, \delta\mathcal{L}/\delta x, \delta\mathcal{L}/\delta y)}{\delta(\lambda, x, y)} \right|$$

Furthermore, with the explicit utility function given, we can evaluate each of the partials at the critical point, $(\bar{\lambda}, \bar{x}, \bar{y})$, where $\bar{\lambda} = .204, \bar{x} = 3.5$, and $\bar{y} = 5.67$.

For the first row of $|\bar{H}|$, we have

$$\frac{\delta(\delta\mathcal{L}/\delta\lambda)}{\delta\lambda} = 0; \qquad \frac{\delta(\delta\mathcal{L}/\delta x)}{\delta\lambda} = -2; \qquad \text{and} \qquad \frac{\delta(\delta\mathcal{L}/\delta y)}{\delta\lambda} = -3$$

For the second row of $|\bar{H}|$, we have

$$\frac{\delta(\delta\mathcal{L}/\delta\lambda)}{\delta x} = -2$$

$$\frac{\delta(\delta\mathcal{L}/\delta x)}{\delta x} = -.25(x - 1)^{-1.5} (y - 4)^{.5} = -.25(3.5 - 1)^{1.5}(5.67 - 4)^{.5}$$

$$= -.25(.253)(1.292) = -.082$$

$$\frac{\delta(\delta\mathcal{L}/\delta y)}{\delta x} = -.25(x - 1)^{-.5} (y - 4)^{-.5} = .25(3.5 - 1)^{-.5}(5.67 - 4)^{-.5}$$

$$= .25(.632)(.774) = .122$$

In addition, for the third row of $|\bar{H}|$, we have

$$\frac{\delta(\delta\mathcal{L}/\delta\lambda)}{\delta y} = -3$$

$$\frac{\delta(\delta\mathcal{L}/\delta x)}{\delta y} = \frac{\delta(\delta\mathcal{L}/\delta y)}{\delta x} = .122 \qquad \text{(from above)}$$

$$\frac{\delta(\delta\mathcal{L}/\delta y)}{\delta y} = -.25(x-1)^{.5}(y-4)^{-1.5} = -.25(3.5-1)^{.5}(5.67-4)^{-1.5}$$

$$= -.25(.632)(.463) = -.073$$

The bordered Hessian is equal to

$$|\overline{H}| = \begin{vmatrix} 0 & -2 & -3 \\ -2 & -.082 & .122 \\ -3 & .122 & -.073 \end{vmatrix} = 2 \begin{vmatrix} -2 & -3 \\ .122 & -.073 \end{vmatrix} - 3 \begin{vmatrix} -2 & -3 \\ -.082 & .122 \end{vmatrix}$$

$$|\overline{H}| = 2(.512) - 3(-.49) = 2.494 > 0$$

The second-order condition checks out. The bordered Hessian is negative definite, $|\overline{H}| > 0$, and we have a constrained-utility maximization.

PRACTICE PROBLEM 12.2

Given the utility function, $U = 2x^{.6}y^{.3}$, and the unit prices of the two goods, $P_x = \$4$ and $P_y = \$1$, and the budgeted income, $I = \$90$:

a) Set up the Lagrangian and find the utility-maximizing combination of the two goods subject to the budget constraint.

b) Determine the marginal utility of income, $\bar{\lambda}$, and the maximum utility, $\overline{U}$.

c) Check the second-order conditions.

(The answers are at the end of the chapter.)

COMPARATIVE STATICS ON CONSUMER EQUILIBRIUM

Return to the general two-good model, where a household seeks to maximize its total utility, $U = U(x, y)$, subject to a budget constraint, $P_x x + P_y y = I$. Consider the first-order conditions, listed below, as a set of equations that satisfy the Implicit Function Theorem.

$$\delta\mathcal{L}/\delta\lambda = I - P_x x - P_y y = 0$$

$$\delta\mathcal{L}/\delta x = U_x - \lambda P_x = 0$$

$$\delta\mathcal{L}/\delta y = U_y - \lambda P_y = 0$$

That is, these first-order conditions have continuous partial derivatives and, at the critical point, the associated Jacobian, which is the bordered Hessian, does not equal zero: $|J| = |\overline{H}| \neq 0$. (Note that in establishing the second-order conditions for a utility maximum, we showed that $|\overline{H}| > 0$.) Then, the first-order conditions define implicit functions, where the equilibrium values of each of the endogenous variables can be written as a function of the exogenous variables in the system. Moreover, these implicit functions define the household's demand functions for the two goods. For given tastes and preferences, the household's quantities demanded of the two goods are functions of the unit prices of the two goods and the budgeted income.

$$\bar{\lambda} = \lambda(P_x, P_y, I)$$

$$\bar{x} = x(P_x, P_y, I)$$

$$\bar{y} = y(P_x, P_y, I)$$

Furthermore, if we evaluate the first-order conditions at the critical point, $(\bar{\lambda}, \bar{x}, \bar{y})$,

$$I - P_x \bar{x} - P_y \bar{y} = 0$$

$$U_x(\bar{x}, \bar{y}) - \bar{\lambda}P_x = 0$$

$$U_y(\bar{x}, \bar{y}) - \bar{\lambda}P_y = 0$$

which yield the conditions for constrained utility maximization; that is, the budget constraint is satisfied and the marginal utility per dollar spent is equal for both goods and equal to the marginal utility of income ($U_x/P_x = U_y/P_y = \bar{\lambda}$), then we can do comparative static analysis on the equilibrium. This is the beauty of the Implicit Function Theorem. Even though we cannot solve explicitly for the equilibrium values of the endogenous variables in terms of the exogenous variables of the system, we can still do comparative statics to assess the effects on the equilibrium of changes in the exogenous variables. Here we cannot solve explicitly for the endogenous variables because we have not imposed a specific functional form on the objective function, $U = U(x, y)$, the utility of the household.

We begin by totally differentiating the first-order conditions evaluated at the critical point and arrange the resulting system in matrix notation. Totally differentiating we get

$$dI - dP_x \bar{x} - P_x d\bar{x} - dP_y \bar{y} - P_y d\bar{y} = 0$$

$$U_{xx} d\bar{x} + U_{yx} d\bar{y} - d\bar{\lambda} P_x - \bar{\lambda} dP_x = 0$$

$$U_{xy} d\bar{x} + U_{yy} d\bar{y} - d\bar{\lambda} P_y - \bar{\lambda} dP_y = 0$$

In matrix notation, the system becomes

$$\begin{bmatrix} 0 & -P_x & -P_y \\ -P_x & U_{xx} & U_{yx} \\ -P_y & U_{xy} & U_{yy} \end{bmatrix} \begin{bmatrix} d\bar{\lambda} \\ d\bar{x} \\ d\bar{y} \end{bmatrix} = \begin{bmatrix} -dI + dP_x \bar{x} + dP_y \bar{y} \\ \bar{\lambda} dP_x \\ \bar{\lambda} dP_y \end{bmatrix}$$

A Change in Budgeted Income We can now use Cramer's rule to do comparative statics. For example, consider the effect on the utility-maximizing consumption of good x of a change in the household's budgeted income. The comparative static result we seek is $\delta \bar{x}/\delta I$.

Holding constant all other exogenous variables, that is, $dP_x = 0$ and $dP_y = 0$, the vector of exogenous changes becomes:

$$\begin{bmatrix} -dI \\ 0 \\ 0 \end{bmatrix}$$

Solving for $d\bar{x}$, according to Cramer's rule, we replace the second column of the matrix of second-order partials with the new vector of exogenous changes. Then taking the ratio of the determinants, we have

$$d\bar{x} = \frac{\begin{vmatrix} 0 & -dI & -P_y \\ -P_x & 0 & U_{yx} \\ -P_y & 0 & U_{yy} \end{vmatrix}}{|\bar{H}|} = \frac{dI \begin{vmatrix} -P_x & U_{yx} \\ -P_y & U_{yy} \end{vmatrix}}{|\bar{H}|} = \frac{dI(-P_x U_{yy} + P_y U_{yx})}{|\bar{H}|}$$

where

$$|\bar{H}| = \begin{vmatrix} 0 & -P_x & -P_y \\ -P_x & U_{xx} & U_{xy} \\ -P_y & U_{yx} & U_{yy} \end{vmatrix} = \begin{vmatrix} 0 & -P_x & -P_y \\ -P_x & U_{xx} & U_{yx} \\ -P_y & U_{xy} & U_{yy} \end{vmatrix} = |J|$$

$$= P_x (-P_x U_{yy} + U_{xy}P_y) - P_y (-P_x U_{yx} + P_y U_{xx})$$

$$|\bar{H}| = -(P_x)^2 U_{yy} + 2 P_x P_y U_{xy} - (P_y)^2 U_{xx}$$

Recall that earlier when we were establishing the second-order conditions for a constrained utility-maximization, we asserted that $|\bar{H}| > 0$, since $U_{xx} < 0$ and $U_{yy} < 0$ (according to the law of diminishing marginal utility) and $U_{xy} = U_{yx} > 0$ (given an indifference curve for two goods, an increase in the consumption of one of the goods would mean a decrease in the consumption of the other good, hence a rise in the marginal utility of this other good). Now, we are considering a change in income and movement between indifference curves. Consequently, an increase in the consumption of one good need not imply a decrease in the consumption of the other good. In short, we can no longer assume that the cross-partials, U_{xy} and U_{yx}, are positive.

We divide both sides of the equation by dI to get

$$d\bar{x}/dI = \frac{-P_x U_{yy} + P_y U_{yx}}{|\bar{H}|}$$

and since we held the unit prices of the two goods constant ($dP_x = dP_y = 0$), we can write this derivative, $d\bar{x}/dI$, as a partial derivative

$$\delta\bar{x}/\delta I = \frac{-P_x U_{yy} + P_y U_{yx}}{|\bar{H}|}$$

We cannot sign this partial derivative, although we can say that

$$\delta\bar{x}/\delta I > 0 \quad \text{if } x \text{ is a normal good}$$

and

$$\delta\bar{x}/\delta I < 0 \quad \text{if } x \text{ is an inferior good.}$$

Figure 12.7 illustrates the effect on the consumption of good x with an increase in the budgeted income. In Figure 12.7a, x is a normal good in this income range, so the quantity demanded and consumed by the household rises with its income. In Figure 12.7b, x is an inferior good in this income range, and the quantity demanded and consumed of good x declines with the rise in the household's income. Note that y is a normal good in both examples. In fact, in the two-good model, both goods could not be inferior, since an increase (a decrease) in income would have to be accompanied by an increase (a decrease) in the consumption of at least one of the goods.

A Change in the Unit Price of a Good Consider now the effect of a change in the price of one of the goods, specifically, the impact on the consumption of good x from a decrease in the price of good x. We return to our system of equations acquired by totally differentiating the first-order conditions, rewritten below in matrix notation.

$$
\begin{bmatrix}
0 & -P_x & -P_y \\
-P_x & U_{xx} & U_{yx} \\
-P_y & U_{xy} & U_{yy}
\end{bmatrix}
\begin{bmatrix}
d\overline{\lambda} \\
d\overline{x} \\
d\overline{y}
\end{bmatrix}
=
\begin{bmatrix}
-dI + dP_x\overline{x} + dP_y\overline{y} \\
\overline{\lambda}\, dP_x \\
\lambda dP_y
\end{bmatrix}
$$

The comparative static result we seek is $\delta\overline{x}/\delta P_x$; so we hold constant all of the other exogenous variables in the system. The resulting vector of exogenous changes that we substitute in using Cramer's rule to solve for $d\overline{x}$ is

$$
\begin{bmatrix}
dP_x\overline{x} \\
\overline{\lambda}\, dP_x \\
0
\end{bmatrix}
$$

since $dI = 0$ and $dP_y = 0$. Thus, applying Cramer's rule, we have

FIGURE 12.7 EFFECTS OF AN INCREASE IN INCOME ON CONSUMER EQUILIBRIUM

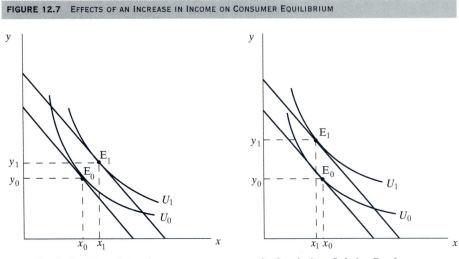

a. Good x is a Normal Good

b. Good x is an Inferior Good

$$dx = \frac{\begin{vmatrix} 0 & dP_x\bar{x} & -P_y \\ -P_x & \bar{\lambda}\,dP_x & U_{yx} \\ -P_y & 0 & U_{yy} \end{vmatrix}}{|H|} = \frac{-dP_x\bar{x}\begin{vmatrix} -P_x & U_{yx} \\ -P_y & U_{yy} \end{vmatrix} + \bar{\lambda}\,dP_x\begin{vmatrix} 0 & -P_y \\ -P_y & U_{yy} \end{vmatrix}}{|H|}$$

$$d\bar{x} = \frac{-dP_x\bar{x}(-P_xU_{yy} + P_yU_{yx})}{|H|} + \frac{-\bar{\lambda}\,dP_x(P_y)^2}{|H|}$$

Dividing through by dP_x and converting to partial derivatives (since all other exogenous variables have been held constant), we obtain

$$\delta\bar{x}/\delta P_x = -\bar{x}\cdot\frac{(-P_xU_{yy} + P_yU_{yx})}{|H|} + \frac{-\bar{\lambda}(P_y)^2}{|H|}$$

We can write the partial derivative, $\delta\bar{x}/\delta P_x$, which gives us the (instantaneous) effect on the quantity demanded and consumed of good x of an (infinitesimal) change in the price of good x as

$$\delta\bar{x}/\delta P_x = -\bar{x}\cdot(\delta\bar{x}/\delta I) + \frac{-\bar{\lambda}(P_y)^2}{|H|}$$

You might recall from microeconomic theory that a change in the unit price of a good on the quantity demanded of the good can be broken down into a substitution effect and an income effect. Consider a fall in the price of good x. A utility-maximizing household would increase its consumption of good x, substituting away from other, now relatively more expensive, goods that satisfy a similar need. The **substitution effect** is negative: a fall (rise) in the price of a good results in an increase (a decrease) in the quantity demanded of the good. The substitution effect is represented by the term $-\bar{\lambda}(P_y)^2/|H|$. (Note that since $\bar{\lambda} = \delta\bar{U}/\delta I > 0$, a negative substitution effect implies that $|H| > 0$.)

The **income effect**, represented by $-\bar{x}\cdot(\delta\bar{x}/\delta I)$, however, may be negative or positive. For normal goods, $\delta\bar{x}/\delta I > 0$, and the income effect reinforces the substitution effect. That is, a fall in the price of good x would not only increase the incentive to consume more of good x (substitution effect), but would increase the ability out of a given money or nominal income to purchase more of good x (the income effect). For inferior goods, $\delta\bar{x}/\delta I < 0$, so the income effect modifies or works against the substitution effect. In fact, the income effect may dominate the negative substitution effect. To elaborate, a fall in the price of good x, for any given quantity of good x consumed, represents a rise in the real income of the household, that is, less of its nominal income is required to purchase the quantity of good x. If good x is inferior, then an increase in the real income of the household would reduce the consumption of good x. It is theoretically possible, although rarely documented in practice, that a fall (rise) in the unit price of a good would decrease (increase) the consumption of the good. Such a good, known as a **Giffen good**, would have a positively sloped demand curve (at least over some price range) for the household. In sum, a Giffen good is an inferior good that constitutes a relatively large share of a household's budget (i.e., $\bar{x}$ would be significant.)

For a Giffen good,

$$\delta\bar{x}/\delta P_x = -\bar{x} \cdot (\delta\bar{x}/\delta I) + \frac{-\bar{\lambda}(P_y)^2}{|H|} > 0$$

since:

$$-\bar{x} \cdot (\delta\bar{x}/\delta I) > \frac{\bar{\lambda}(P_y)^2}{|H|} > 0 \qquad \text{(where } \delta\bar{x}/\delta I < 0\text{).}$$

In Figure 12.8 we illustrate a Giffen good, where, *ceteris paribus*, a fall in the price of good x decreases the quantity demanded and consumed of good x. An example of a Giffen good might be a staple food for a poor household. Consider a household subsisting largely on cassava, a starchy root grown in the tropics. A fall in the price of cassava might free up enough purchasing power for the given modest income to allow the household to reduce its consumption of cassava and afford a more varied diet.

THE LABOR-LEISURE TRADEOFF

We turn to another application of utility theory: an individual's allocation of time between work and play. Consider an individual with a given amount of discretionary time during each week to divide between her job and her leisure. The individual seeks

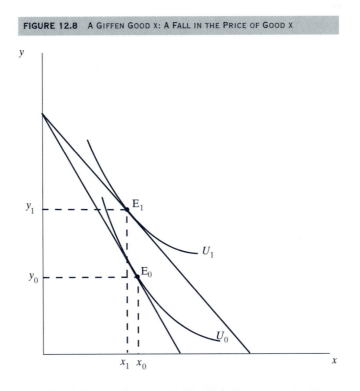

FIGURE 12.8 A GIFFEN GOOD X: A FALL IN THE PRICE OF GOOD X

to maximize her total utility, U, which is a function of the income she earns, I, and the hours of leisure she enjoys, F, (where F stands for free time). Exogenous to the individual is the wage rate per hour she can earn, w. Let T be the hours per week that the individual decides to allocate between work and play. Note that T can vary across individuals. For instance, not everyone needs the same amount of sleep or has the same amount of responsibilities outside of paid employment, for example, childcare or household chores.

The constrained utility-maximization problem is then: maximize $U = U(I, F)$, subject to $I = w \cdot (T - F)$, where

U = total utility of the individual

I = income earned by the individual in a week

F = leisure hours consumed by the individual in a week

w = wage rate per hour the individual earns

T = number of discretionary hours in a week to be allocated between work and leisure. So $T - F$ = number of hours worked in a week.

We assume that T is predetermined by the individual. Note that the income earned by the individual is endogenous. Income gives the individual the ability to consume goods and services that, in turn, provide satisfaction. Leisure hours too contribute to the individual's utility. The more leisure the individual chooses, however, the lower will be the income earned.

We assume positive, but diminishing, marginal utilities for income and leisure.

$$\delta U / \delta I = U_I > 0 \quad \text{and} \quad \delta U_I / \delta I = U_{II} < 0$$

$$\delta U / \delta F = U_F > 0 \quad \text{and} \quad \delta U_F / \delta F = U_{FF} < 0$$

The Lagrangian function is $\mathcal{L}(\lambda, I, F) = U(I, F) + \lambda \cdot [w \cdot (T - F) - I]$
The first-order conditions are

$$\delta \mathcal{L} / \delta \lambda = w(T - F) - I = 0$$

$$\delta \mathcal{L} / \delta I = U_I - \lambda = 0$$

$$\delta \mathcal{L} / \delta F = U_F - \lambda w = 0$$

The first equation states that in the constrained utility-maximization, the income earned per week is equal to the product of the wage rate per hour and the number of hours worked per week. From the second and third equations, we can solve for λ, obtaining the condition:

$$U_I = U_F / w = \overline{\lambda} = \delta \overline{U} / \delta T$$

Recall that the optimal value of the Lagrange multiplier, $\overline{\lambda}$, represents the effect (instantaneous) on the optimal value of the objective function (here total utility, $\overline{U}$) of a change (infinitesimal) in the constraint (here discretionary time, T). Thus, to maximize her total utility, the individual should allocate her time such that the marginal utility per dollar of income, U_I, is equal to the marginal utility of leisure per dollar wage that she could earn, U_F/w. Each of these marginal utilities per dollar, in turn, would be equal to the marginal utility of discretionary time, $\lambda = \delta U/\delta T$.

To check the second-order conditions, we totally differentiate the first-order conditions and evaluate the resulting bordered Hessian.

$$|\overline{H}| = \begin{vmatrix} \delta(\delta\mathcal{L}/\delta\lambda,\ \delta\mathcal{L}/\delta I,\ \delta\mathcal{L}/\delta F) \\ \delta(\lambda, I, F) \end{vmatrix} = \begin{vmatrix} 0 & -1 & -w \\ -1 & U_{II} & U_{IF} \\ -w & U_{FI} & U_{FF} \end{vmatrix} = -U_{FF} + 2w\,U_{FI} - w^2 U_{II}$$

$|\overline{H}| > 0$, and we have a constrained maximization if $U_{FI} = U_{IF} > 0$, or even if $|-U_{FF} - w^2\,U_{II}| > |2w\,U_{FI}|$. Along an indifference curve representing trade-offs in income and leisure, we expect that $U_{FI} > 0$, that is, if leisure is substituted for income earned, the marginal utility of income would rise.

Drawing on the Implicit Function Theorem, we can do comparative statics by totally differentiating the first-order conditions evaluated at the critical point, $(\overline{\lambda}, \overline{I}, \overline{F})$. That is, from

$$w(T - \overline{F}) - \overline{I} = 0$$

$$U_I(\overline{I}, \overline{F}) - \overline{\lambda} = 0$$

$$U_F(\overline{I}, \overline{F}) - \overline{\lambda}w = 0$$

we totally differentiate to get

$$dw(T - \overline{F}) + w \cdot (dT - d\overline{F}) - d\overline{I} = 0$$

$$U_{II}\,d\overline{I} + U_{FI}\,d\overline{F} - d\overline{\lambda} = 0$$

$$U_{IF}\,d\overline{I} + U_{FF}\,d\overline{F} - d\overline{\lambda}\,w - \overline{\lambda}\,dw = 0$$

Arranging in matrix notation, we have

$$\begin{bmatrix} 0 & -1 & -w \\ -1 & U_{II} & U_{FI} \\ -w & U_{IF} & U_{FF} \end{bmatrix} \begin{bmatrix} d\overline{\lambda} \\ d\overline{I} \\ d\overline{F} \end{bmatrix} = \begin{bmatrix} -dw\,(T - \overline{F}) - w\,dT \\ 0 \\ \overline{\lambda}\,dw \end{bmatrix}$$

We again note that the determinant of the coefficient matrix for this set of equations is identical to the bordered Hessian, $|\overline{H}|$. Applying Cramer's rule we can find four comparative static results in this model: $\delta\overline{I}/\delta T$, $\delta\overline{I}/\delta w$, $\delta\overline{F}/\delta T$, and $\delta\overline{F}/\delta w$. We will assess two of these.

First, to find the impact of a change in discretionary time, T, on the utility-maximizing income earned, we solve for $d\overline{I}$, where the vector of exogenous changes is

$$\begin{bmatrix} -w\,dT \\ 0 \\ 0 \end{bmatrix}.$$

With Cramer's rule, we have

$$dI = \frac{\begin{vmatrix} 0 & -w\,dT & -w \\ -1 & 0 & U_{FI} \\ -w & 0 & U_{FF} \end{vmatrix}}{\begin{vmatrix} 0 & -1 & -w \\ -1 & U_{II} & U_{FI} \\ -w & U_{IF} & U_{FF} \end{vmatrix}} = \frac{w\,dT(-U_{FF} + wU_{FI})}{|H|}$$

or dividing through by dT and expressed in terms of the partial derivative, (since $dw = 0$), we get

$$\delta \bar{I}/\delta T = \frac{-wU_{FF} + w^2 U_{FI}}{|H|}$$

While we might expect $\delta \bar{I}/\delta \bar{T} > 0$, and a rise (fall) in discretionary time to increase (decrease) the income earned, we cannot unambiguously sign this partial derivative. That is, although we assume $U_{FF} < 0$ (diminishing marginal utility of leisure) and note that along an indifference curve, $U_{FI} > 0$; when we change the amount of time to be allocated, there will be a movement to a new indifference curve. For example, an increase in discretionary time could be associated with an increase in both hours worked (income earned) and leisure hours; or with an increase in either one (income earned or leisure hours), with the other held constant or even decreasing. Without a specific form for the utility function, we cannot be more definite.

Similarly, when we examine the impact of a change in the wage rate on the utility-maximizing amount of leisure hours, $\delta \bar{F}/\delta w$, we will see that the comparative static result is indeterminate. Here we hold constant the number of discretionary hours ($dT = 0$), and we allow for a change in the wage rate. The vector of exogenous changes becomes

$$\begin{bmatrix} -dw\,(T - \bar{F}) \\ 0 \\ \bar{\lambda}\,dw \end{bmatrix}$$

Solving for $d\bar{F}$, we have

$$d\bar{F} = \frac{\begin{vmatrix} 0 & -1 & -dw\,(T - F) \\ -1 & U_{II} & 0 \\ -w & U_{IF} & \bar{\lambda}\,dw \end{vmatrix}}{|H|} = \frac{1[-\bar{\lambda}\,dw + U_{IF}\,dw\,(T - \bar{F})] - w[U_{II}\,dw\,(T - \bar{F})]}{|H|}$$

$$d\bar{F} = \frac{dw[-\bar{\lambda} + U_{IF}\,(T - \bar{F}) - w\,U_{II}\,(T - \bar{F})]}{|H|}$$

Dividing through by dw and converting to a partial derivative, we have

$$\delta \bar{F}/\delta w = \frac{-\bar{\lambda} + (T - \bar{F})(U_{IF} - wU_{II})}{|H|}$$

Here, although we can sign $-\bar{\lambda} < 0$ ($\bar{\lambda} = \delta \bar{U}/\delta T$); $T - \bar{F} > 0$ ($T > \bar{F}$); and $U_{II} < 0$ (diminishing marginal utility of income), we cannot sign U_{IF}. For example, with an increase in the wage that could be earned, we might expect an individual to substitute away from leisure—as the opportunity cost of an hour of leisure, represented by w, increases—and work more hours. This substitution effect of a wage increase is consistent with a positively-sloped supply curve of labor for the individual, where the number of hours of labor supplied rises with the wage rate. There is also an income effect from a wage increase. For a given amount of hours worked, when the wage rate rises, the income earned is greater. If leisure is a normal good, as would be expected, the individual may "purchase" more leisure and actually work fewer hours. Consequently, we could find an individual's supply curve of labor bending backward, that is, assuming a negative slope for higher wages, when the income effect dominates the substitution effect. We illustrate this possibility in Figure 12.9, where for wage rates higher than w^*, we have $\delta F/\delta w > 0$, and an increase in leisure hours consumed (decrease in hours worked) as the wage rate rises. Typically, however, we draw upward-sloping labor supply curves, implicitly assuming that the substitution effect dominates over the wage range considered.

As you can see, using the Implicit Function Theorem for comparative statics may not establish definite signs for the partial derivatives of interest. Nevertheless, even though the comparative static results from general models of constrained utility-maximization could not be unambiguously signed, we still were able to draw insight

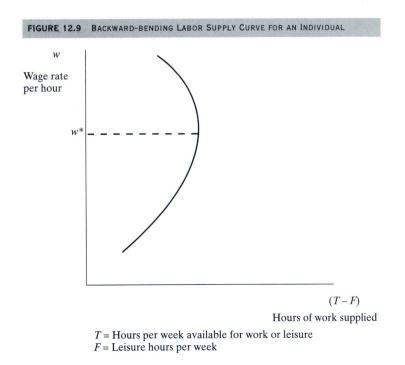

FIGURE 12.9   BACKWARD-BENDING LABOR SUPPLY CURVE FOR AN INDIVIDUAL

w

Wage rate per hour

w^*

$(T - F)$

Hours of work supplied

T = Hours per week available for work or leisure
F = Leisure hours per week

into the underlying economic behavior, for example, identifying the substitution and income effects associated with a price change.

PRACTICE PROBLEM 12.3

For the labor-leisure model just discussed,

maximize: $U = U(I, F)$

subject to: $I = w \cdot (T - F)$

Find and sign, if possible, the comparative static: $\delta \bar{I} / \delta w$.

(The answers are at the end of the chapter.)

NONLINEAR PROGRAMMING AND UTILITY MAXIMIZATION

Recall from the last chapter that with nonlinear programming we allow for inequality constraints and impose nonnegativity restrictions on the choice variables. Moreover, the number of inequality constraints may exceed the number of choice variables— unlike the classical constrained optimization with binding equality constraints.

We will continue with utility functions with two choice variables and add a second constraint for allotted time. We begin our application of nonlinear programming to the theory of consumer behavior, however, with an illustration of the significance of the nonnegativity restrictions on the choice variables.

Nonnegativity Restrictions: An Example   Consider a household seeking to maximize its utility, U, a function of the consumption of two goods, x and y, subject to a budget constraint, $P_x x + P_y y = I$. The utility function is given to be: $U = U(x, y) = (1 + x) \cdot (1 + y)$. The exogenous unit prices of the two goods and the budgeted income are: $P_x = \$4$, $P_y = \$1$, and $I = \$1$.

Using the technique of classical constrained optimization, with equality constraints (here, only one), and no restrictions on the choice variables, x and y, we have:

$$\text{maximize } U = (1 + x)(1 + y)$$

$$\text{subject to: } 4x + y = 1$$

The Lagrangian function is: $\mathcal{L}(x, y, \lambda) = (1 + x)(1 + y) + \lambda \cdot (1 - 4x - y)$. The first-order conditions are:

$$\delta \mathcal{L} / \delta x = (1 + y) - 4\lambda = 0$$

$$\delta \mathcal{L} / \delta y = (1 + x) - \lambda = 0$$

$$\delta \mathcal{L} / \delta \lambda = 1 - 4x - y = 0$$

Solving by substitution, we have from the first two equations

$$\frac{1+y}{4} = \bar{\lambda} = \frac{1+x}{1}$$

which is the familiar condition for utility maximization: the marginal utility per dollar spent must be equal across the commodities and equal to the marginal utility of income, given by the optimum value of the Lagrange multiplier, $\bar{\lambda}$. Writing y in terms of x, we have: $y = 3 + 4x$, and substituting into the budget constraint, represented by $\delta\mathcal{L}/\delta\lambda = 1 - 4x - y = 0$, assumed to be binding in classical optimization, we get

$$1 - 4x - y = 1 - 4x - (3 + 4x) = 0$$

$$-2 - 8x = 0$$

$$\bar{x} = -1/4$$

and

$$\bar{y} = 3 + 4(-1/4) = 2.$$

The marginal utility of income is $\bar{\lambda} = \dfrac{1+2}{4} = \dfrac{1+(-1/4)}{4} = 3/4$

The maximum utility is: $U = (1 + \bar{x})(1 + \bar{y}) = [1 + (-1/4)](1 + 2) = 9/4 = 2.25$

The answer, however, doesn't make economic sense. The optimum quantity consumed of good x is $-1/4$ units. In this example, classical optimization "fails" as a method of solution since *a priori*, it doesn't restrict the choice variables to economically meaningful values.

Actually, the utility function assumed is a bit unusual. While the marginal utilities are positive for each good: that is, for $U = (1 + x)(1 + y)$,

$$\delta U/\delta x = 1 + y > 0 \qquad \text{(for } y > -1)$$

$$\delta U/\delta x_2 = 1 + x > 0 \qquad \text{(for } x > -1)$$

diminishing marginal utility does not hold for either good: $\delta^2 U/\delta x^2 = 0 = \delta^2 U/\delta y^2$.

The marginal rate of substitution, *MRS*, indicating the slope of the indifference curve, however, is negative:

$$dy/dx = MRS = \frac{-\delta U/\delta x}{\delta U/\delta y} = \frac{-(1 + y)}{(1 + x)} < 0 \qquad \text{(for } x > -1, y > -1)$$

In addition, the indifference curves are strictly convex:

$$dMRS/dx = \frac{-[-1(1 + y)]}{(1 + x)^2} = \frac{(1 + y)}{(1 + x)^2} > 0 \quad \text{(for } x > -1, y > -1)$$

At the utility-maximizing point, $\bar{x} = -1/4$ and $\bar{y} = 2$, the slope of the indifference curve, *MRS*, equals the slope of the budget line, $-P_x/P_y$, consistent with a point of tangency.

$$MRS = \frac{-(1 + \bar{y})}{(1 + \bar{x})} = \frac{-(1 + 2)}{1 + (-1/4)} = -4 = -4/1 = -P_x/P_y$$

Thus, while everything seems in order, with the exception of no diminishing marginal utilities associated with the consumption of each good, the utility-maximizing combination must be rejected, since the optimum quantity consumed of one of the goods is negative.

Using nonlinear programming for this utility maximization, we have

$$\text{maximize: } U = (1 + x)(1 + y)$$

$$\text{subject to: } 4x + y \leq 1$$

$$\text{and } x, y \geq 0$$

where the nonnegativity restrictions on the choice variables are included. Note also that the budget constraint need not be binding.

The Lagrangian function is the same:

$$\mathcal{L}(x, y, \lambda) = (1 + x)(1 + y) + \lambda \cdot (1 - 4x - y)$$

The first-order conditions (Kuhn-Tucker conditions) for a maximum are

$$\delta\mathcal{L}/\delta x = (1 + y) - 4\lambda \leq 0; \quad x \geq 0; \quad \text{and } (x)(\delta\mathcal{L}/\delta x) = 0$$

$$\delta\mathcal{L}/\delta y = (1 + x) - \lambda \leq 0; \quad y \geq 0; \quad \text{and } (y)(\delta\mathcal{L}/\delta y) = 0$$

$$\delta\mathcal{L}/\delta\lambda = 1 - 4x - y \geq 0; \quad \lambda \geq 0; \quad \text{and } (\lambda)(\delta\mathcal{L}/\delta\lambda) = 0$$

In addition to the marginal conditions being inequalities ($\delta\mathcal{L}/\delta x \leq 0$ and $\delta\mathcal{L}/\delta y \leq 0$), and the possibility of a nonbinding budget constraint, there are nonnegativity restrictions on the choice variables and Lagrange multiplier, and complementary slackness conditions: $(x)(\delta\mathcal{L}/\delta x) = 0$, $(y)(\delta\mathcal{L}/\delta y) = 0$, and $(\lambda)(\delta\mathcal{L}/\delta\lambda) = 0$.

In the classical constrained optimization solution the marginal conditions and the budget constraint hold exactly. Therefore, $\delta\mathcal{L}/\delta\lambda = 0$ and we found: $x = -1/4$ and $y = 2$. Here, we reject the solution for x as a violation of the nonnegativity restriction. So, in accordance with the complementary slackness condition, we set $x = 0$. From the budget constraint, if $x = 0$, then $y = 1$. From the marginal condition, $\delta\mathcal{L}/\delta y = 0$, and consistent with the complementary slackness condition for $y > 0$, we can solve for the Lagrange multiplier, $\lambda = 1 + x = 1 + 0 = 1$. We confirm that the solution, $\bar{x} = 0, \bar{y} = 1$, and $\bar{\lambda} = 1$, satisfies the Kuhn-Tucker conditions.

$$\delta\mathcal{L}/\delta x = (1 + y) - 4\lambda = (1 + 1) - 4(1) = -2 \leq 0; x = 0 \geq 0;$$

$$\text{and } (x)(\delta\mathcal{L}/\delta x) = (0)(-2) = 0$$

$$\delta\mathcal{L}/\delta y = (1 + x) - \lambda = (1 + 0) - 1 = 0 \leq 0; y = 1 \geq 0; \text{and } (y)(\delta\mathcal{L}/\delta y) = (1)(0) = 0$$

$$\delta\mathcal{L}/\delta\lambda = 1 - 4x - y = 1 - 4(0) - 1 = 0 \geq 0; \lambda = 1 \geq 0;$$

$$\text{and } (\lambda)(\delta\mathcal{L}/\delta\lambda) = (1)(0) = 0$$

The solution works. Another "solution" to try would have set $y = 0$, so $x = 1/4$ and $\lambda = 1/4$. The combination, $(x, y) = (1/4, 0)$, represents the other intercept of the budget constraint. This "solution," however, does not satisfy the Kuhn-Tucker conditions. In particular, the marginal condition, $\delta\mathscr{L}/\delta y \leq 0$, is not met: $\delta\mathscr{L}/\delta y = (1 + x) - \lambda = (1 + 1/4) - 1/4 = 1 > 0$.

Note that while the budget constraint is still binding, the marginal utility of income is greater in the nonlinear programming problem $(\bar\lambda = 1)$ than in the classical constrained optimization problem $(\bar\lambda = 3/4)$. The maximum total utility, however, is lower in the nonlinear programming version: $\bar{U} = (1 + \bar{x})(1 + \bar{y}) = (1 + 0)(1 + 1) = 2$, versus $\bar{U} = 2.25$. Both of these outcomes make sense here, since in the nonlinear programming problem there is an additional binding constraint, the nonnegativity restriction on the choice variable, x.

UTILITY MAXIMIZATION WITH TWO CONSTRAINTS

We now turn to a nonlinear programming problem of utility maximization with two constraints. Again we will restrict the analysis to two dimensions (two goods) for graphical purposes. We begin with the general formulation, then follow with a specific example.

Assume that a household seeks to maximize its total utility, U, which is a function of the consumption of two goods, x and y. We assume positive, but diminishing, marginal utilities for each good. The household faces an income budget constraint and a discretionary time constraint:

$$P_x x + P_y y \leq I \quad \text{(budget constraint)}$$

$$t_x x + t_y y \leq T \quad \text{(time constraint)}$$

where P_x and P_y are the unit prices of the two goods; t_x and t_y are the unit time costs of the two goods, that is, the time required to consume a unit of each good; I is the budgeted income of the household, and T is the discretionary time available to the household for the consumption of the two goods. The unit prices, unit time costs, budgeted income, and available time are assumed to be exogenously determined.

The nonlinear programming problem is

$$\text{maximize: } U = U(x, y)$$

$$\text{subject to: } P_x x + P_y y \leq I$$

$$t_x x + t_y y \leq T$$

$$\text{and } x, y \geq 0$$

Setting up the Lagrangian function, we have:

$$\mathscr{L}(x, y, \lambda_1, \lambda_2) = U(x, y) + \lambda_1 \cdot (I - P_x x - P_y y) + \lambda_2 \cdot (T - t_x x - t_y y)$$

The Kuhn-Tucker conditions for a maximization are:

$$\delta\mathscr{L}/\delta x = U_x - \lambda_1 P_x - \lambda_2 t_x \leq 0; \quad x \geq 0; \quad \text{and } (x)(\delta\mathscr{L}/\delta x) = 0$$

$$\delta\mathcal{L}/\delta y = U_y - \lambda_1 P_y - \lambda_2 t_y \leq 0; \qquad y \geq 0; \qquad \text{and } (y)(\delta\mathcal{L}/\delta y) = 0$$

$$\delta\mathcal{L}/\delta\lambda_1 = I - P_x x - P_y y \geq 0; \qquad \lambda_1 \geq 0; \qquad \text{and } (\lambda_1)(\delta\mathcal{L}/\delta\lambda_1) = 0$$

$$\delta\mathcal{L}/\delta\lambda_2 = T - t_x x - t_y y \geq 0; \qquad \lambda_2 \geq 0; \qquad \text{and } (\lambda_2)(\delta\mathcal{L}/\delta\lambda_2) = 0$$

where U_x and U_y refer to the marginal utilities for goods x and y, respectively: $U_x = \delta U/\delta x$ and $U_y = \delta U/\delta y$.

To illustrate the feasible region in Figure 12.10, we will assume that the slope of the budget constraint, $-P_x/P_y$, is steeper than the slope of the time constraint, $-t_x/t_y$. That is, we assume: $|P_x/P_y| > |t_x/t_y|$ or $|P_x/t_x| > |P_y/t_y|$. Good x is relatively expensive monetarily, and good y is relatively time-consuming. We also assume that $I/P_y > T/t_y$, that is, the vertical intercept of the budget constraint is greater than the vertical intercept of the time constraint; and that $I/P_x < T/t_x$, that is, the horizontal intercept of the budget constraint is less than that for the time constraint. The feasible region is given by the area $OABC$. In the maximization of total utility, we can confine our search for a solution to the exterior border, ABC.

There are five possibilities for a solution, given a utility function with strictly convex indifference curves. The utility-maximizing solution could occur at point A, between points A and B, at point B, between points B and C, or at point C. We will explore each of these possibilities.

To begin, recall that the slope of an indifference curve at any point is given by the marginal rate of substitution, *MRS*. With the graphical orientation depicted in Figure 12.10, the marginal rate of substitution is: $MRS = dy/dx = -U_x/U_y$, or the negative ratio of the marginal utility of good x to the marginal utility of good y. The optimum

---

FIGURE 12.10   A FEASIBLE REGION FOR UTILITY MAXIMIZATION

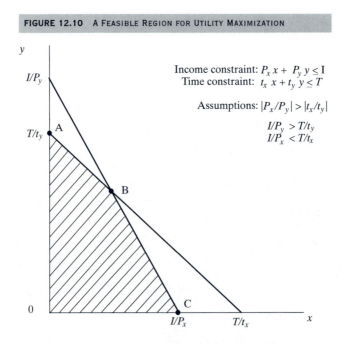

Income constraint: $P_x x + P_y y \leq I$
Time constraint: $t_x x + t_y y \leq T$

Assumptions: $|P_x/P_y| > |t_x/t_y|$

$I/P_y > T/t_y$
$I/P_x < T/t_x$

combination of the two goods will depend on the values of the *MRS*, the ratio of unit prices, and the ratio of unit time costs.

At point A, only the time constraint is binding, and all of the discretionary time is allotted to the consumption of good *y*. Consequently $y = T/t_y$ and $x = 0$. There are two cases to consider. First, the optimum value of *x* is negative, which violates the non-negativity restriction, $x \geq 0$. This would occur when the marginal rate of substitution at the combination of the two goods represented by point A ($x = 0$, $y = T/t_y$) was smaller (in absolute value) than the unit time cost ratio: that is, if $U_x/U_y < t_x/t_y$. Here a "flatter" indifference curve would intersect the feasible region at point A. See Figure 12.11 and the indifference curves U_0' and U_1'. If not for the nonnegativity restriction on *x*, the utility-maximizing point would be A', at the tangency of the indifference curve, U_1', and the time constraint. This case is similar to the earlier utility-maximization example that illustrated the importance of the nonnegativity restrictions. With respect to the Kuhn-Tucker conditions, we have here:

$$\delta \mathcal{L}/\delta x < 0; \quad x = 0; \quad \text{and } (x)(\delta \mathcal{L}/\delta x) = 0$$

$$\delta \mathcal{L}/\delta y = 0; \quad y > 0; \quad \text{and } (y)(\delta \mathcal{L}/\delta y) = 0$$

FIGURE 12.11   CORNER SOLUTIONS FOR UTILITY-MAXIMIZATION

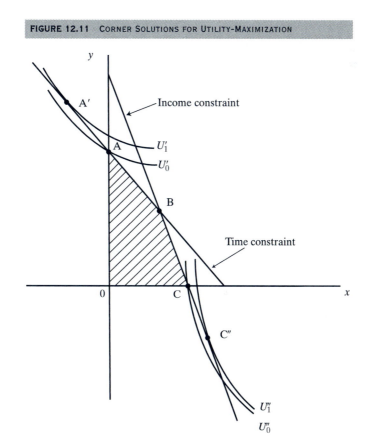

$$\delta\mathcal{L}/\delta\lambda_1 > 0; \quad \lambda_1 = 0; \quad \text{and } (\lambda_1)(\delta\mathcal{L}/\delta\lambda_1) = 0$$

$$\delta\mathcal{L}/\delta\lambda_2 = 0; \quad \lambda_2 > 0; \quad \text{and } (\lambda_2)(\delta\mathcal{L}/\delta\lambda_2) = 0$$

Since the income constraint is not binding at point A, the marginal utility of income is zero: $\lambda_1 = \delta U/\delta I = 0$. Conversely, with the time constraint binding, the marginal utility of time is positive: $\lambda_2 = \delta U/\delta T > 0$. Note also from the second marginal condition, $\delta\mathcal{L}/\delta y = 0$, we have at the utility-maximizing combination: $U_y/t_y = \lambda_2$.

Alternatively, it may be the case at point A that the optimum value of x is zero. If so, an indifference curve would be tangent to the time constraint at point A, that is, $U_x/U_y = t_x/t_y$, and the marginal condition would also hold for good 1: $\delta\mathcal{L}/\delta x = 0$ now. Therefore, from the first two marginal conditions, we can show that: $U_x/t_x = U_y/t_y = \lambda_2$.

We next shift to the other extreme possibility, represented by point C. At point C, the horizontal intercept of the budget constraint, where $x = I/P_x$ and $y = 0$, we also have two cases to consider. First, the optimum value of y is negative: see point C″ in Figure 12.11, the point of tangency between the indifference curve, U_1'' and the extended budget line. Since this violates the nonnegativity restriction, $y \geq 0$, we are constrained to the indifference curve, U_0'', which intersects the budget line at point C. Here the marginal rate of substitution exceeds the ratio of unit prices $|MRS| > |P_x/P_y|$. The relevant Kuhn-Tucker conditions are

$$\delta\mathcal{L}/\delta x = 0; \quad x > 0; \quad \text{and } (x)(\delta\mathcal{L}/\delta x) = 0$$

$$\delta\mathcal{L}/\delta y < 0; \quad y = 0; \quad \text{and } (y)(\delta\mathcal{L}/\delta y) = 0$$

$$\delta\mathcal{L}/\delta\lambda_1 = 0; \quad \lambda_1 > 0; \quad \text{and } (\lambda_1)(\delta\mathcal{L}/\delta\lambda_1) = 0$$

$$\delta\mathcal{L}/\delta\lambda_2 > 0; \quad \lambda_2 = 0; \quad \text{and } (\lambda_2)(\delta\mathcal{L}/\delta\lambda_2) = 0$$

That is, the marginal conditions only hold for x, $\delta\mathcal{L}/\delta x = 0$; and from this, we have $U_x/P_x = \lambda_1$, since $\lambda_2 = 0$. The income constraint is binding, so the marginal utility of income is positive: $\delta U/\delta I = \lambda_1 > 0$. The time constraint is not binding, $\delta\mathcal{L}/\delta\lambda_2 > 0$, so the marginal utility of time is zero: $\delta U/\delta T = \lambda_2 = 0$.

The other case associated with a utility-maximization at point C is that the optimal value of y is zero. If so, then an indifference curve is tangent to the budget line at point C, and $MRS = -U_x/U_y = -P_x/P_y$. Moreover, the marginal condition for y also holds, $\delta\mathcal{L}/\delta y = 0$, so we have $U_y/P_y = U_x/P_x = \lambda_1$, from solving for λ_1, the marginal utility of income, from the marginal conditions with $\lambda_2 = 0$.

The third possibility would be a utility-maximization on the line segment between the points A and B. Here both choice variables are positive, $\bar{x} > 0$ and $\bar{y} > 0$, so both marginal conditions hold, $\delta\mathcal{L}/\delta x = 0$ and $\delta\mathcal{L}/\delta y = 0$. The income constraint is not binding, so $\lambda_1 = 0$. The marginal conditions reduce to: $U_x/t_x = \lambda_2 = U_y/t_y$, where λ_2 is the marginal utility of time. Alternatively, at the point of tangency, we have $-U_x/U_y = -t_x/t_y$, or the slope of the indifference curve equals the slope of the time line; thus the rate at which the household is willing to trade off the two goods (MRS) is equal to the rate at which the two goods can be traded off in time. The Kuhn-Tucker conditions are

$$\delta\mathcal{L}/\delta x = 0; \quad x > 0; \quad \text{and } (x)(\delta\mathcal{L}/\delta x) = 0$$

$$\delta\mathcal{L}/\delta y = 0; \quad y > 0; \quad \text{and } (y)(\delta\mathcal{L}/\delta y) = 0$$

$$\delta\mathcal{L}/\delta\lambda_1 > 0; \quad \lambda_1 = 0; \quad \text{and } (\lambda_1)(\delta\mathcal{L}/\delta\lambda_1) = 0$$

$$\delta\mathcal{L}/\delta\lambda_2 = 0; \quad \lambda_2 > 0; \quad \text{and } (\lambda_2)(\delta\mathcal{L}/\delta\lambda_2) = 0$$

The fourth possibility is a tangency between points B and C, along the binding income constraint. Here too, both choice variables are positive, so the associated marginal conditions hold as equalities. The marginal utility of time, however, is equal to zero, since the time constraint is not binding. Consequently, at the utility-maximizing combination of the two goods, we have: $U_x/P_x = U_y/P_y = \lambda_1$, or the marginal utility per dollar spent is equal for both goods and equal to the marginal utility of income. Alternatively, the slope of the tangential indifference curve, $-U_x/U_y$, is equal to the slope of the budget line, $-P_x/P_y$. The Kuhn-Tucker conditions are

$$\delta\mathcal{L}/\delta x = 0; \quad x > 0; \quad \text{and } (x)(\delta\mathcal{L}/\delta x) = 0$$

$$\delta\mathcal{L}/\delta y = 0; \quad y > 0; \quad \text{and } (y)(\delta\mathcal{L}/\delta y) = 0$$

$$\delta\mathcal{L}/\delta\lambda_1 = 0; \quad \lambda_1 > 0; \quad \text{and } (\lambda_1)(\delta\mathcal{L}/\delta\lambda_1) = 0$$

$$\delta\mathcal{L}/\delta\lambda_2 > 0; \quad \lambda_2 = 0; \quad \text{and } (\lambda_2)(\delta\mathcal{L}/\delta\lambda_2) = 0$$

Finally, the fifth possibility is that the utility-maximizing combination of the two goods occurs at point B, where both constraints are binding and both choice variables are positive. Solving for the intersection of the two constraints gives the coordinates of this point:

$$x = \frac{t_y I - P_y T}{t_y P_x - t_x P_y} \quad \text{and} \quad y = \frac{T P_x - t_x I}{t_y P_x - t_x P_y}$$

where $t_y P_x \neq t_x P_y$ or $t_x/t_y \neq P_x/P_y$, which we assumed to be the case from the beginning; that is, the budget and time constraints do not have the same slope. The marginal conditions, $\delta\mathcal{L}/\delta x = 0$ and $\delta\mathcal{L}/\delta y = 0$, give

$$\frac{U_x - \lambda_2 t_x}{P_x} = \frac{U_y - \lambda_2 t_y}{P_y} = \lambda_1$$

That is, at the utility-maximizing point, the net marginal utility per dollar spent is equal for the two goods and equal to the marginal utility of income. By the net marginal utility, we mean the marginal utility of the good less the product of the marginal utility of time and the unit time cost of the good. Alternatively, we could write

$$\frac{U_x - \lambda_1 P_x}{t_x} = \frac{U_y - \lambda_1 P_y}{t_y} = \lambda_2$$

At the utility-maximizing combination, the net marginal utility per unit of time expended is equal for the two goods and equal to the marginal utility of time. Here, net marginal utility refers to the marginal utility of the good less the product of the marginal utility of income and the unit price of the good.

For the combination represented by point B to be the utility-maximizing combination, the indifference curve intersects the border of the feasible region at point B, and the marginal rate of substitution must be between (or equal to one of) the slopes of the budget and time constraints. In particular, $|t_x/t_y| \leq |MRS| = |- U_x/U_y| \leq |P_x/P_y|$. We allow for the equality of the slope of either constraint with the slope of the indifference curve at point B.

The Kuhn-Tucker conditions are

$$\delta\mathcal{L}/\delta x = 0; \quad x > 0; \quad \text{and } (x)(\delta\mathcal{L}/\delta x) = 0$$

$$\delta\mathcal{L}/\delta y = 0; \quad y > 0; \quad \text{and } (y)(\delta\mathcal{L}/\delta y) = 0$$

$$\delta\mathcal{L}/\delta\lambda_1 = 0; \quad \lambda_1 > 0; \quad \text{and } (\lambda_1)(\delta\mathcal{L}/\delta\lambda_1) = 0$$

$$\delta\mathcal{L}/\delta\lambda_2 = 0; \quad \lambda_2 > 0; \quad \text{and } (\lambda_2)(\delta\mathcal{L}/\delta\lambda_2) = 0$$

A Numerical Example   To illustrate with an example, consider the following utility-maximization problem.

$$\text{maximize: } U = x^{.4} y^{.2}$$

$$\text{subject to: } 6x + 4y \leq 120 \quad \text{(budget constraint)}$$

$$x + 2y \leq 30 \quad \text{(time constraint)}$$

and $x, y \geq 0$.

Assume that x and y are the quantities of two leisure activities consumed per month. The budgeted income for these activities is $I = \$120$ per month, and the unit prices are $P_x = \$6$ and $P_y = \$4$. The allotted time per month is $T = 30$ hours, where each unit of activity x requires one hour of leisure time and each unit of activity y requires two hours of leisure time: $t_x = 1$ and $t_y = 2$. Figure 12.12 illustrates the feasible region, denoted by area $OABC$. The Lagrangian function is:

$$\mathcal{L}(x, y, \lambda_1, \lambda_2) = x^{.4} y^{.2} + \lambda_1 \cdot (120 - 6x - 4y) + \lambda_2 \cdot (30 - x - 2y)$$

The Kuhn-Tucker conditions are:

$$\delta\mathcal{L}/\delta x = .4x^{-.6} y^{.2} - 6\lambda_1 - \lambda_2 \leq 0; \quad x \geq 0; \quad \text{and } (x)(\delta\mathcal{L}/\delta x) = 0$$

$$\delta\mathcal{L}/\delta y = .2x^{.4} y^{-.8} - 4\lambda_1 - 2\lambda_2 \leq 0; \quad y \geq 0; \quad \text{and } (y)(\delta\mathcal{L}/\delta y) = 0$$

$$\delta\mathcal{L}/\delta\lambda_1 = 120 - 6x - 4y \geq 0; \quad \lambda_1 \geq 0; \quad \text{and } (\lambda_1)(\delta\mathcal{L}/\delta\lambda_1) = 0$$

$$\delta\mathcal{L}/\delta\lambda_2 = 30 - x - 2y \geq 0; \quad \lambda_2 \geq 0; \quad \text{and } (\lambda_2)(\delta\mathcal{L}/\delta\lambda_2) = 0$$

We might begin by deriving the marginal rate of substitution or the slope of an indifference curve. Totally differentiating the utility function, $U = x^{.4} y^{.2}$, we get

$$dU = .4x^{-.6} y^{.2} dx + .2x^{.4} y^{-.8} dy$$

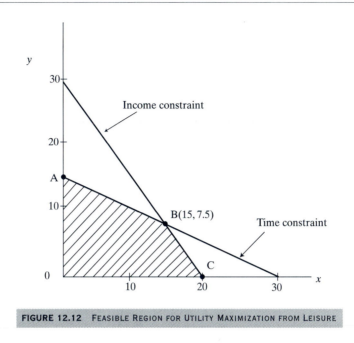

FIGURE 12.12 FEASIBLE REGION FOR UTILITY MAXIMIZATION FROM LEISURE

Along an indifference curve, utility is constant, so $dU = 0$. Solving for dy/dx yields the expression for the slope of an indifference curve and the marginal rate of substitution:

$$.4x^{-.6} y^{.2} dx + .2 x^{.4} y^{-.8} dy = 0$$

$$dy/dx = \frac{-.4x^{-.6} y^{.2}}{.2x^{.4} y^{-.8}} = -2y/x = MRS$$

We note that the slopes of the income and time constraints are, respectively:

$$-P_x/P_y = -3/2 \quad \text{and} \quad -t_x/t_y = -1/2$$

We can rule out point A, where $x = 0$, as a utility-maximizing combination, since the MRS is undefined for $x = 0$. In fact, for this utility function, $U = x^{.4}y^{.2}$, total utility would be equal to zero if the consumption of either good were zero. So, point C, where $y = 0$, can also be eliminated.

Evaluating the MRS at point B, $(x = 15, y = 7.5)$, where both constraints are binding, we find $MRS = -2y/x = -2 (7.5)/15 = -1$. The slope of the indifference curve at point B lies between the slopes of the income and time constraints, implying that this point represents the utility-maximizing combination. To check the Kuhn-Tucker conditions for $x = 15$ and $x = 7.5$, we have $\delta\mathcal{L}/\delta x = 0$ and $\delta\mathcal{L}/\delta y = 0$. Since both constraints are binding, we know that $\delta\mathcal{L}/\delta\lambda_1 = 0$ and $\delta\mathcal{L}/\delta\lambda_2 = 0$.

$$\delta\mathcal{L}/\delta x = .4(15)^{-.6} (7.5)^{.2} - 6\lambda_1 - \lambda_2 = 0$$

$$\delta\mathcal{L}/\delta y = .2(15)^{.4} (7.5)^{-.8} - 4\lambda_1 - 2\lambda_2 = 0$$

or

$$.118 - 6\lambda_1 - \lambda_2 = 0$$

and

$$.118 - 4\lambda_1 - 2\lambda_2 = 0$$

Solving for λ_1 and λ_2 through elimination, we multiply $\delta\mathscr{L}/\delta x = 0$ by -2 and add to $\delta\mathscr{L}/\delta y = 0$.

$$-.236 + 12\lambda_1 + 2\lambda_2 = 0$$
$$\underline{.118 - 4\lambda_1 - 2\lambda_2 = 0}$$
$$-.118 + 8\lambda_1 = 0$$

so

$$\lambda_1 = -.118/-8 = .0148$$

and substituting:

$$.118 - 4(.0148) - 2\lambda_2 = 0$$
$$2\lambda_2 = .0588$$
$$\lambda_2 = .0294$$

Thus, the utility-maximizing combination of the two goods is: $\bar{x} = 15$ and $\bar{y} = 7.5$. The marginal utilities of income and time are: $\bar{\lambda}_1 = .0148$ and $\bar{\lambda}_2 = .0294$. The maximum utility is: $U = \bar{x}^{.4}\bar{y}^{.2} = (15)^{.4} (7.5)^{.2} = (2.954)(1.496) = 4.419$
The Kuhn-Tucker conditions for a maximization are met:

$$\delta\mathscr{L}/\delta x = 0 \leq 0; \quad \bar{x} = 15 \geq 0; \quad \text{and } (\bar{x})(\delta\mathscr{L}/\delta x) = 0$$
$$\delta\mathscr{L}/\delta y = 0 \leq 0; \quad \bar{y} = 7.5 \geq 0; \quad \text{and } (\bar{y})(\delta\mathscr{L}/\delta y) = 0$$
$$\delta\mathscr{L}/\delta\lambda_1 = 0 \geq 0; \quad \bar{\lambda}_1 = .0148 \geq 0; \quad \text{and } (\bar{\lambda}_1)(\delta\mathscr{L}/\delta\lambda_1) = 0$$
$$\delta\mathscr{L}/\delta\lambda_2 = 0 \geq 0; \quad \bar{\lambda}_2 = .0294 \geq 0; \quad \text{and } (\bar{\lambda}_2)(\delta\mathscr{L}/\delta\lambda_2) = 0$$

Recall from Chapter 11 that sufficient conditions to establish an absolute maximum for a solution satisfying the Kuhn-Tucker conditions for a maximum are that the objective function be differentiable and concave and that each constraint function be differentiable and convex. Here the objective function is the utility function, $U = x^{.4}y^{.2}$, which is differentiable. For this utility function to be concave, we need: $sf(u) + (1 - s)f(v) \leq f[su + (1 - s)v]$, where u and v are any two combinations of the goods x and y and s is a scalar, $0 < s < 1$.

Let $u = (5, 10)$ and $v = (10, 20)$. Then using the utility function, $U = x^{.4}y^{.2}$, we have:

$$f(u) = (5)^{.4} (10)^{.2} = (1.904)(1.585) = 3.018$$

$$f(v) = (10)^{.4} (20)^{.2} = (2.512)(1.821) = 4.574$$

Let $s = .6$, so $su + (1 - s)v = .6(5, 10) + .4(10, 20) = (7, 14)$, and

$$f[su + (1 - s)v] = (7)^{.4} (14)^{.2} = (2.178)(1.695) = 3.692.$$

Plugging into the sufficient condition to establish a concave function, we find:

$$sf(u) + (1 - s)f(v) = .6(3.018) + .4(4.574) = 3.641 \leq 3.692 = f[su + (1 - s)v]$$

Therefore, the utility function, $U = x^{.4}y^{.2}$, is concave, and, in fact, strictly concave. The linear constraint functions (the budget and time constraints) are convex—as well as concave. We conclude that the solution, $\bar{x} = 15$ and $\bar{y} = 7.5$, represents an absolute maximum.

Suppose now that the tastes of the household change in favor of activity y, and that the new utility function is $U' = x^{.2}y^{.6}$. Given the same budget and time constraints, will the new utility-maximizing combination of the two activities change?

The new nonlinear programming problem is:

$$\text{maximize: } U = x^{.2}y^{.6}$$

$$\text{subject to: } 6x + 4y \leq 120 \text{ (budget constraint)}$$

$$x + 2y \leq 30 \text{ (time constraint)}$$

and

$$x, y \geq 0$$

The new Lagrangian is:

$$\mathcal{L}'(x, y, \lambda_1, \lambda_2) = x^{.2}y^{.6} + \lambda_1 \cdot (120 - 6x - 4y) + \lambda_2 \cdot (30 - x - 2y)$$

The Kuhn-Tucker conditions are:

$$\delta\mathcal{L}'/\delta x = .2x^{-.8}y^{.6} - 6\lambda_1 - \lambda_2 \leq 0; \quad x \geq 0; \quad \text{and } (x)(\delta\mathcal{L}'/\delta x) = 0$$

$$\delta\mathcal{L}'/\delta y = .6x^{.2}y^{-.4} - 4\lambda_1 - 2\lambda_2 \leq 0; \quad y \geq 0; \quad \text{and } (y)(\delta\mathcal{L}'/\delta y) = 0$$

$$\delta\mathcal{L}'/\delta\lambda_1 = 120 - 6x - 4y \geq 0; \quad \lambda_1 \geq 0; \quad \text{and } (\lambda_1)(\delta\mathcal{L}'/\delta\lambda_1) = 0$$

$$\delta\mathcal{L}'/\delta\lambda_2 = 30 - x - 2y \geq 0; \quad \lambda_2 \geq 0; \quad \text{and } (\lambda_2)(\delta\mathcal{L}'/\delta\lambda_2) = 0$$

The new marginal rate of substitution, MRS', is derived by totally differentiating the new utility function, $U' = x^{.2}y^{.6}$, setting the result equal to zero, and solving for dy/dx, the slope of an indifference curve.

$$dU' = .2x^{-.8}y^{.6} \, dx + .6x^{.2}y^{-.4} \, dy = 0$$

$$dy/dx = \frac{-.2x^{-.8}y^{.6}}{.6x^{.2}y^{-.4}} = -y/3x = MRS'$$

As before, we can rule out the corner points A and C (refer to Figure 12.12), since the total utility of the household equals zero if the consumption of either commodity were zero. At point B, ($x = 15$ and $y = 7.5$), where both constraints are binding, the marginal rate of substitution equals $-.167$, that is, $MRS' = -y/3x = -7.5/(3)(15) = -.167$, which is less, in absolute value, than the slope of the time constraint. Thus, at point B an indifference curve has a flatter slope than the time constraint, implying that the utility-maximizing combination of the two activities lies on a higher indifference curve that is tangent to the binding portion of the time constraint, that is, on the line segment between points A and B. Put another way, at point B, we have

$$|MRS'| = |- U_x/U_y| = .167 < .5 = |-t_x/t_y| = |\text{slope of the time constraint}|$$

or rearranging, $U_x/U_y < t_x/t_y$ and $U_x/t_x < U_y/t_y$. The ratio of the marginal utility of leisure activity y to its unit time cost exceeds that for leisure activity x. Consequently, the household should consume more of leisure activity y and less of leisure activity x in any given time period, moving up and to the left along the binding time constraint.

To find the utility-maximizing combination, we know that the marginal rate of substitution has to be equal to the slope of the time constraint—consistent with a tangency of an indifference curve with the time constraint line.

$$MRS' = -y/3x = -1/2 = -t_x/t_y$$

or

$$y = (3/2)x = 1.5x$$

Also, the point has to lie on the time constraint, satisfying the equation, $x + 2y = 30$. Simultaneously solving the two equations by substituting $y = 1.5x$ into the time constraint, we obtain

$$x + 2(1.5x) = 30$$

$$4x = 30$$

$$\bar{x} = 7.5 \quad \text{and} \quad \bar{y} = (1.5)(7.5) = 11.25$$

To solve for the marginal utility of time, λ_2, we note that since $\bar{x} > 0$ and $\bar{y} > 0$, then $\delta\mathcal{L}'/\delta x = 0$ and $\delta\mathcal{L}'/\delta y = 0$, respectively, consistent with the complementary slackness conditions. Furthermore, the nonbinding income constraint, $\delta\mathcal{L}'/\delta\lambda_1 > 0$, means that the Lagrange multiplier indicating the marginal utility of income is zero: $\lambda_1 = 0$.

$$\delta\mathcal{L}'/\delta x = .2x^{-.8}y^{.6} - 6\lambda_1 - \lambda_2 = .2(7.5)^{-.8}(11.25)^{.6} - 6(0) - \lambda_2 = 0$$

$$\delta\mathcal{L}'/\delta y = .6x^{.2}y^{-.4} - 4\lambda_1 - 2\lambda_2 = .6(7.5)^{.2}(11.25)^{-.4} - 4(0) - 2\lambda_2 = 0$$

or

$$.17 - \lambda_2 = 0$$

and

$$.34 - 2\lambda_2 = 0$$

Thus,

$$\bar{\lambda}_2 = .17$$

To confirm that the income constraint is not binding:

$$\delta\mathcal{L}'/\delta\lambda_1 = 120 - 6\bar{x} - 4\bar{y} = 120 - 6(7.5) - 4(11.25) = 120 - 45 - 45 = 30 > 0$$

The unspent income equals $30.

In sum, the new utility-maximizing combination of the two goods (leisure activities) after the change in tastes in favor of good y is: $\bar{x} = 7.5$ and $\bar{y} = 11.25$. The marginal utility of income and time are, respectively: $\bar{\lambda}_1 = 0$ and $\bar{\lambda}_2 = .17$. The maximum total utility is: $\overline{U}' = \bar{x}^2 \bar{y}^{.6} = (7.5)^2 (11.25)^{.6} = (1.496)(4.273) = 6.392$. Finally, this solution satisfies the Kuhn-Tucker conditions, since

$$\delta\mathscr{L}'/\delta x = 0 \le 0; \quad \bar{x} = 7.5 \ge 0; \quad \text{and } (\bar{x})(\delta\mathscr{L}'/\delta x) = 0$$

$$\delta\mathscr{L}'/\delta y = 0 \le 0; \quad \bar{y} = 11.25 \ge 0; \quad \text{and } (\bar{y})(\delta\mathscr{L}'/\delta y) = 0$$

$$\delta\mathscr{L}'/\delta\lambda_1 = 30 \ge 0; \quad \bar{\lambda}_1 = 0 \ge 0; \quad \text{and } (\bar{\lambda}_1)(\delta\mathscr{L}'/\delta\lambda_1) = 0$$

$$\delta\mathscr{L}'/\delta\lambda_2 = 0 \ge 0; \quad \bar{\lambda}_2 = .17 \ge 0; \quad \text{and } (\bar{\lambda}_2)(\delta\mathscr{L}'/\delta\lambda_2) = 0$$

Thus, the change in tastes in favor of good y results in a new utility-maximizing combination with increased consumption of good y in this nonlinear programming problem. We can show that this utility function is also strictly concave, and combined with the linear constraint functions, we have sufficient conditions to establish the combination, $\bar{x} = 7.5$ and $\bar{y} = 11.25$ as an absolute maximum.

PRACTICE PROBLEM 12.4

Return to the previous problem:

$$\text{maximize:} \quad U = x^2 y^{.6}$$

$$\text{subject to:} \quad 6x + 4y \le 120 \text{ (budget constraint)}$$

$$x + 2y \le 30 \text{ (time constraint)}$$

$$x, y \ge 0$$

and suppose that the unit price of activity x doubles from \$6 to \$12, so that the new budget constraint is: $12x + 4y \le 120$.
a) Find the new utility-maximizing combination of the two activities, x and y, and the maximum utility.
b) Find the marginal utilities of income and time.

(The answers are at the end of the chapter.)

This concludes our discussion of optimization. With Chapter 13 we begin the final part of this text: Macroeconomic Analysis. We will use many of the same mathematical techniques—especially in solving the models and in conducting comparative static experiments. The basic difference is the unit of analysis—no longer the individual household, or firm, or even an individual commodity market, but the macroeconomy. The markets we deal with are aggregate markets: for national output and the aggregate price level, for money and the interest rate, and for national employment and the wage rate.

❖ KEY TERMS

Economics

- Giffen good (p. 428)
- income effect (p. 428)
- indifference curve (p. 413)
- indifference mapping (p. 414)
- law of diminishing marginal utility (p. 412)
- marginal rate of substitution (p. 415)
- substitution effect (p. 428)

❖ PROBLEMS

1. For each of the following utility functions, where $0 < a < 1$:

   i) $U = x^a y^{1-a}$ ii) $U = a \ln x + (1 - a) \ln y$ iii) $U = [a x^{-2} + (1 - a) y^{-2}]^{-1/2}$

   a) Show that the marginal utilities for x and y are positive but diminishing.
   b) Derive the marginal rate of substitution.

2. Given a household's utility is a function of its consumption of two goods, x and y, where $U = U(x,y) = 2 \ln x + \ln y$, its budgeted income is $36, and the unit prices of the two goods are $P_x = \$2$ and $P_y = \$4$.

   a) Show that the consumption of each good provides positive, but diminishing, marginal utility to the household.
   b) Find the utility-maximizing combination of the two goods. What is the total utility of the household at this optimum?
   c) Find the marginal utility of income when the household's utility is maximized.
   d) Check the second-order conditions.
   e) Find the new utility-maximizing combination of goods x and y if the household increases its budgeted income from $36 to $36.30. Find the change in total utility associated with this change in income. Compare this with the optimum value of the Lagrange multiplier.

3. Given the utility function, $U = 10[.4x^{-3} + .6y^{-2}]^{-1/3}$, a budgeted income of $I = \$100$, and unit prices of the two goods, $P_x = \$6$ and $P_y = \$2$.

   a) Find the utility-maximizing combination of the two goods, x and y, subject to the income constraint.
   b) Determine the marginal utility of income and the maximum utility.
   c) Check the second-order conditions.

4. Given an individual, seeking to maximize his utility, which is a function of his consumption of goods and services per week, X, and his leisure hours per week, F, subject to a budget constraint. His utility function is: $U = X^a F^b$ $(0 < a < 1, 0 < b < 1)$. The budget constraint of this individual is given by: $P_X X = M + w \cdot (T - F)$, where

   X = quantity of goods and services consumed per week

   F = leisure hours consumed per week

   P_X = price index for goods and services

M = nonwage income of the individual

w = wage rate per hour the individual earns

T = number of discretionary hours in the week to be allocated between work and leisure.

a) Set up the Lagrangian function, then derive and interpret the first-order conditions.
b) Check the second-order conditions.
c) Find and sign (if possible):
   i) $\delta\overline{F}/\delta M$ and   ii) $\delta\overline{F}/\delta w$.

Discuss whether these comparative static results make economic sense.

5. Given the following linear programming problem for utility maximization:

$$\text{maximize: } U = 5x + y$$

$$\text{subject to: } x + y \le 8 \quad \text{(time constraint)}$$

$$3x + y \le 12 \quad \text{(budget constraint)}$$

$$x \le 3 \quad \text{(ration constraint)}$$

$$x, y \ge 0$$

where x and y are the quantities of the two goods under consideration and the individual is seeking to maximize her total utility (U) subject to three constraints:
- Up to 8 hours of time available for the consumption of the two goods. A unit of x and a unit of y each require 1 hour for consumption.
- Up to $12 of income is budgeted for the consumption of the two goods. The unit prices are P_x = $3 and P_y = $1.
- A maximum of 3 units of x are available under the allotment of ration coupons.
a) Graph the feasible region. Find the solution by testing the extreme points. Plot the highest indifference curve the individual can attain given the constraints.
b) Solve the linear programming problem using the simplex method. Which constraints are binding? Find the shadow prices associated with time, income, and ration coupons.
c) Set up the dual, that is, the counterpart minimization problem. Solve using the simplex method. Relate the solutions for the maximization and minimization problems using Duality Theorems I and II.
d) What simplifying assumption is implicit in the linear objective function for the primal? Is this consistent with the usual assumptions we make about consumer behavior?

6. Given a household seeking to maximize its total utility, $U = x^{.5}y^{.4}$, subject to an income constraint. The budgeted income is: I = $500 per month and the unit prices of the two goods are P_x = $50 and P_y = $20.

a) Set up the Lagrangian and then find the utility-maximizing combination of the two goods, x and y, subject to the income constraint.

b) Determine the marginal utility of income and the maximum utility.

c) Check the second-order conditions.

Now add a second constraint, where the maximum available time for the consumption of these two goods is $T = 40$ hours per month and the unit time costs are $t_x = 5$ hours and $t_y = 1$ hour. Assume now that the budgeted income of $500 is a maximum that the household is willing to spend each month on the consumption of goods x and y.

d) Set up the nonlinear programming problem.

e) Graph the feasible region.

f) Write out the Lagrangian function and the Kuhn-Tucker conditions.

g) Find the utility-maximizing quantities of the two goods and the maximum total utility.

h) Determine the marginal utilities of income and time. Determine whether there is any unspent income or unused time.

i) Determine, if possible, whether the utility-maximizing combination of the two goods constitutes an absolute maximum.

7. Refer to Problem 6 above. Suppose that the time cost of y increases from $t_y = 1$ to $t'_y = 1.25$ (hours). Repeat steps d)–h).

8. Refer to Problem 6 above. Suppose that the maximum budgeted income for the consumption of these two goods increases from $I = 500 to $I' = 600 per month. Repeat steps d)–h).

❖ **ANSWERS TO PRACTICE PROBLEMS**

12.1 a) $U_x = .7x^{-3} y^{.2} > 0$ and $U_{xx} = -.21x^{-1.3} y^{.2} < 0$
$U_y = .2x^{.7} y^{-.8} > 0$ and $U_{yy} = -.16x^{.7} y^{-1.8} < 0$

b) $MRS = -U_x/U_y = -3.5y/x < 0$

c) $dMRS/dx = d(-3.5y/x)/dx = 15.75y/x^2 > 0$

12.2 a) The Lagrangian is: $\mathcal{L}(\lambda, x, y) = 2x^{.6} y^{.3} + \lambda \cdot (90 - 4x - y)$. The utility-maximizing combination of the two goods is: $\bar{x} = 15$ and $\bar{y} = 30$.

b) The marginal utility of income is: $\bar{\lambda} = .28$. The maximum utility is: $\bar{U} = 28.17$.

c) The bordered Hessian equals: $|\bar{H}| = .23 > 0$, consistent with a maximum.

12.3 $\delta\bar{I}/\delta w = \dfrac{(T - \bar{F})(-U_{FF} + wU_{FI}) + w\bar{\lambda}}{|H|}$ can't be signed; the sign of U_{FI} is indeterminate.

12.4 a) The utility-maximizing combination is: $\bar{x} = 6$ and $\bar{y} = 12$. The maximum utility is $\bar{U} = 6.36$.

b) The marginal utilities of income and time are respectively: $\bar{\lambda}_1 = .005$ and $\bar{\lambda}_2 = .152$.

BASIC MACROECONOMIC MODELS: INPUT-OUTPUT ANALYSIS AND A SIMPLE KEYNESIAN MODEL

In microeconomics we attempt to explain the behavior of individual economic agents, primarily households and firms, and the outcomes of individual markets, such as a local market for unskilled labor or the national market for automobiles. Economists develop decision rules for optimal behavior: the maximization of utility for households and the maximization of profits for firms. The outcomes of the markets— the prices and quantities transacted—reflect not only the underlying motivations and characteristics of the agents involved, but also the degree of government regulation.

In these last three chapters we study macroeconomic models. In macroeconomics the unit of analysis is the national economy. The markets modeled are aggregate markets, such as the labor market, the money and bond markets, and the product market for goods and services. In all of these markets, there is an international dimension with the export and import of goods, services, and assets.

We are concerned with the interdependence of these aggregate markets in the determination of national employment, the level of prices, and real national output. There are macroeconomic goals or objectives, such as full employment, price stability, and economic growth. Yet, quantifying these concepts—much less reaching a consensus on the relative importance of these objectives or agreeing on how best to achieve these objectives—can be difficult. Indeed, macroeconomics is characterized by considerable controversy—over how the macroeconomy works (or doesn't) and on the efficacy of fiscal and monetary policies to promote national objectives.

In our discussion of macroeconomic models, we will note areas of policy relevance, as well as the points of controversy. We will begin in this chapter with input-output analysis, where the linkages across sectors or industries of the economy are explicitly modeled. Here the final demands for the outputs of the sectors, and collectively the aggregate demand, are exogenous. We then present a basic version of the Keynesian model, where real national output is the endogenous variable of interest. In contrast, the focus in the Simple Keynesian Model is on aggregate demand. Indeed, aggregate supply is assumed to be perfectly elastic. In the last part of the chapter, the Simple Keynesian Model is extended to two countries to illustrate the foreign repercussions effect.

In Chapter 14, we return to the one-country Simple Keynesian Model and add a money market and interest-sensitive expenditures, deriving what is known as the *IS-LM* model. The *IS-LM* model is then extended to incorporate aggregate supply constraints and changes in the aggregate price level. In Chapter 15 we move to growth models and dynamic macroeconomic analysis.

INPUT-OUTPUT ANALYSIS

The sectors of an economy are linked together. The production of many final goods requires not only the primary factors of labor and capital, but the outputs of other sectors as **intermediate goods**. For instance, the manufacture of automobiles requires the intermediate goods of tires and headlights, which, in turn, require the intermediate goods of rubber and glass, respectively. Therefore, the total demand for any product, (e.g., tires), will be equal to the sum of all the intermediate demands (e.g., by automobile manufactures) and final demands (e.g., by consumers and firms purchasing tires directly). Input-output models account for the linkages across the sectors or industries of an economy.

As we will illustrate, a primary use of input-output analysis is for consistency planning—identifying total input requirements and resource constraints consistent with sectoral output targets. Input-output models were used extensively in command economies, where the central authorities established production goals and allocated resources across the sectors.

THE INPUT-OUTPUT TABLE

The **input-output (I-O) table** records the purchases and sales across the sectors of an economy over a given period of time. Below we set out a basic I-O table under the following key assumptions:

1. Each sector or industry is characterized by a fixed coefficients production function. That is, there is a fixed or inflexible relationship between the level of output of any sector and the levels of required inputs. Irrespective of relative input prices, no factor substitution is possible.
2. The production of output in each sector is characterized by constant returns to scale. That is, an $r\%$ increase (decrease) in the output of a sector requires an $r\%$ increase (decrease) in all of the inputs.
3. Technology is given. The fixed coefficients production functions are set and reflect a given state of technology.

In Figure 13.1 we illustrate an I-O table. In constructing an I-O table, the entries can be in physical units (e.g., tons of steel or hours of service) or in terms of monetary value (e.g., dollars or pesos). We will use monetary value and assume constant unit prices for inputs and outputs in order to have fixed relationships between monetary values and physical quantities. Doing so greatly facilitates the interpretation of the I-O table and the derivation of the I-O relationships.

The I-O table can be divided vertically according to the type of demand (interindustry demands and final demands) and horizontally according to the type of input (domestic intermediate goods, domestic primary factors of production, and imports). In this general model we will consider n sectors or industries, two primary factors of production (capital and labor), and initially four types of final demand (personal consumption expenditures, C; investment expenditures, I; government purchases of goods and services, G; and exports, E).

Referring to Figure 13.1, the Xs indicate the value of output. For example,

$$X_i = \text{value of the output of sector } i \ (i = 1 \dots n)$$

FIGURE 13.1   GENERAL INPUT-OUTPUT TABLE

Purchases by:		Intermediate Users Sectors/Industries					Final Demands				Total Demand
		1	**2**	**3**	**...**	**n**	**C**	**I**	**G**	**E**	**X**
Sales by:	1	X_{11}	X_{12}	X_{13}	...	X_{1n}	C_1	I_1	G_1	E_1	X_1
	2	X_{21}	X_{22}	X_{23}	...	X_{2n}	C_2	I_2	G_2	E_2	X_2
	3	X_{31}	X_{32}	X_{33}	...	X_{3n}	C_3	I_3	G_3	E_3	X_3
Sectors/					...		...				
Industries	.	.	.	.	...	.	.	.	.	.	.
	.	.	.	.	...	.	.	.	.	.	.
	n	X_{n1}	X_{n2}	X_{n3}	...	X_{nn}	C_n	I_n	G_n	E_n	X_n
Payments	**W**	W_1	W_2	W_3	...	W_n	W_C		W_G		W
	R	R_1	R_2	R_3	...	R_n					R
Imports	**M**	M_1	M_2	M_3	...	M_n	M_C	M_I	M_G		M
Total supply	**X**	X_1	X_2	X_3	...	X_n	C	I	G	E	

where

X_i = value of the output of sector i ($i = 1 \dots n$)

X_{ij} = sales by sector i to sector j, or the value of inputs from sector i used to produce the output of sector j ($i = 1 \dots n; j = 1 \dots n$)

W_j = wages in sector j ($j = 1 \dots n$)

R_j = interest and profits in sector j

M_j = imports of sector j

C_i = personal consumption expenditures for the output of sector i

I_i = investment expenditures for the output of sector i

G_i = government purchases of the output of sector i

E_i = exports of the output of sector i

$M_C, M_I,$ and M_G = imports of final goods by consumers, firms, and the government, respectively

When there are two subscripts attached, X_{ij}, interindustry transactions are indicated. The first subscript, i, indicates the sector of origin (the provider of inputs), and the second subscript, j, indicates the sector of destination (the user of the inputs). Therefore,

X_{ij} = sales by sector i to sector j, or the value of the inputs of sector i used to produce the output of sector j ($i = 1 \ldots n; j = 1 \ldots n$).

Other key variables are

W_j = wages in sector j (the payments to labor in sector j)
R_j = interest and profits in sector j (the payments to the owners of capital in sector j)
C_i = personal consumption expenditures on the output of sector i
I_i = investment expenditures for the output of sector i
G_i = government purchases of the output of sector i
E_i = exports of the output of sector i
M = imports

The $n \times n$ matrix in the upper left quadrant of the I-O table represents the interindustry transactions or the sales of intermediate goods, $X_{ij}, i = 1 \ldots n, j = 1 \ldots n$. The $n \times 4$ matrix in the upper right quadrant represents the final demands for the output of sector i: by consumers (C_i), firms (I_i), the government (G_i), and foreigners (E_i). The $3 \times n$ matrix in the lower left quadrant represents the factor payments by each sector to labor (W_j) and the owners of capital (R_j), and payments to foreigners for imports (M_j). Finally, the lower right quadrant, with relatively few entries, accounts for the final consumption of labor (e.g., domestic help hired by households, W_C, and the employees of the government, W_G), and imports of final goods by consumers (M_C), firms (M_I), and the government (M_G).

Next, reading across any of the first n rows shows how the output of a sector is allocated across users—as inputs into the production of the n sectors and for final demands. For example, the total demand for the output of sector i can be written as

$$X_i = \sum_{j=1}^{n} X_{ij} + F_i \qquad i = 1 \ldots n$$

where $\sum_{j=1}^{n} X_{ij}$ = the total interindustry demand for the output of sector i, or sales by sector i to the n sectors

and F_i = the total final demand for the output of sector i. $F_i = C_i + I_i + G_i + E_i$

Dropping down to the next two rows, we have the total payments to labor and the owners

$$W = \sum_{j=1}^{n} W_j + (W_C + W_G)$$

and

$$R = \sum_{j=1}^{n} R_j$$

The next row indicates the total value of imports into the economy: imports of inputs $\left(\sum_{j=1}^{n} M_j \right)$ plus imports of final goods and services by consumers, firms, and the government (M_C, M_I, and M_G, respectively).

$$M = \sum_{j=1}^{n} M_j + (M_C + M_I + M_G)$$

Reading down any of the first n columns gives the input composition of the domestic output of a sector. For example, the value of the output of sector j is made up of the value of the domestic inputs purchased from the n sectors plus the **value added** by domestic labor and capital plus any imported inputs.

$$X_j = \sum_{i=1}^{n} X_{ij} + W_j + R_j + M_j \qquad (j = 1 \ldots n)$$

Reading down the next four columns gives the value of the final demands by consumers, firms for investment, government purchases, and exports to foreigners.

$$C = \sum_{i=1}^{n} C_i + W_C + M_C$$

$$I = \sum_{i=1}^{n} I_i + M_I$$

$$G = \sum_{i=1}^{n} G_i + W_G + M_G$$

$$E = \sum_{i=1}^{n} E_i$$

By definition, the value of the total demand for the output of any sector (representing the total expenditures) must equal the value of the total supply (indicating the total cost of the output). For example, for sector k:

$$X_k = \sum_{j=1}^{n} X_{kj} + F_k = \sum_{i=1}^{n} X_{ik} + W_k + R_k + M_k = X_k \qquad (k = 1 \ldots n)$$

where

$$F_k = C_k + I_k + G_k + E_k$$

Input-Output Coefficients Given the assumption of fixed coefficients production functions, we can derive the input-output coefficients as follows. We noted that the value of the output of sector j (going down the jth column) can be written as

{1} $$X_j = \sum_{i=1}^{n} X_{ij} + W_j + R_j + M_j \qquad (j = 1 \ldots n)$$

Dividing through equation (1) by the value of the output of sector j, X_j, we get

$$\{2\} \qquad 1 = \sum_{i=1}^{n} X_{ij}/X_j + W_j/X_j + R_j/X_j + M_j/X_j$$

Let $a_{ij} = X_{ij}/X_j$, $(i = 1 \ldots n, ; j = 1 \ldots n)$, represent the **input-output coefficients**, also known as the **technical coefficients**, for the n sectors. The input-output coefficient, $a_{ij}, 0 \le a_{ij} < 1$, indicates the share of the output of sector j accounted for by the inputs purchased from sector i. For example, if $a_{13} = .15$, then 15% of the value of the output of sector 3 is due to, or contributed by, inputs purchased from sector 1. The input-output coefficients can equal 0, (if no inputs from sector i are used in the production of sector j), but must be less than 1 (if there is value added by labor and capital in the production of the output of sector j).

The W_j/X_j, R_j/X_j, and M_j/X_j, indicate the shares of wages (payments to labor), interest and profits (payments to the owners of capital), and imports (payments to foreigners) in the output of sector j. Substituting $a_{ij} = X_{ij}/X_j$ in equation (2), we get

$$\{3\} \qquad 1 = \sum_{i=1}^{n} a_{ij} + W_j/X_j + R_j/X_j + M_j/X_j \qquad j = 1 \ldots n$$

We also know that the total demand for the output of sector i is given by

$$\{4\} \qquad X_i = \sum_{j=1}^{n} X_{ij} + F_i \qquad i = 1 \ldots n$$

Substituting $a_{ij} X_j = X_{ij}$ (that is, the product of the share of the inputs from sector i in the output of sector j and the output of sector j must equal the total sales of inputs from sector i to sector j) into equation $\{4\}$, we get

$$\{5\} \qquad X_i = \sum_{j=1}^{n} a_{ij} X_j + F_i \qquad i = 1 \ldots n$$

Expanding, we have

for

$$i = 1: \qquad X_1 = a_{11} X_1 + a_{12} X_2 + \cdots + a_{1n} X_n + F_1$$

$$i = 2: \qquad X_2 = a_{21} X_1 + a_{22} X_2 + \cdots + a_{2n} X_n + F_2$$

$$\vdots$$

$$i = n: \qquad X_n = a_{n1} X_1 + a_{n2} X_2 + \cdots + a_{nn} X_n + F_n$$

Isolating the final demands on the right-hand side gives:

$$(1 - a_{11})X_1 - a_{12} X_2 - \ldots - a_{1n} X_n = F_1$$

$$-a_{21} X_1 + (1 - a_{22})X_2 - \ldots - a_{2n} X_n = F_2$$

$$\vdots$$

$$-a_{n1} X_1 - a_{n2} X_2 - \ldots + (1 - a_{nn})X_n = F_n$$

This system of n linear equations in n unknowns (the sectoral outputs, $X_1, \ldots, X_n$), can be written in matrix notation as $(\mathbf{I} - \mathbf{A})\mathbf{X} = \mathbf{F}$, where $\mathbf{I}$ is the $n \times n$ identity matrix, $\mathbf{A}$ is the $n \times n$ matrix of exogenous input-output coefficients, $\mathbf{X}$ is the $n \times 1$ matrix (vector) of endogenous sectoral outputs, and $\mathbf{F}$ is the $n \times 1$ matrix (vector) of exogenous final demands.

$$
\mathbf{I} = \begin{bmatrix} 1 & 0 & \cdots & 0 \\ 0 & 1 & \cdots & 0 \\ \cdot & \cdot & \cdots & \cdot \\ 0 & 0 & \cdots & 1 \end{bmatrix}, \quad \mathbf{A} = \begin{bmatrix} a_{11} & a_{12} & \cdots & a_{1n} \\ a_{21} & a_{22} & \cdots & a_{2n} \\ \cdot & \cdot & \cdots & \cdot \\ a_{n1} & a_{n2} & \cdots & a_{nn} \end{bmatrix}, \quad \mathbf{X} = \begin{bmatrix} X_1 \\ X_2 \\ \cdot \\ X_n \end{bmatrix}, \quad \text{and } \mathbf{F} = \begin{bmatrix} F_1 \\ F_2 \\ \cdot \\ F_n \end{bmatrix}
$$

The matrix $(\mathbf{I} - \mathbf{A})$ is known as the **Leontief matrix**.[1] The solution to the system, $(\mathbf{I} - \mathbf{A})\mathbf{X} = \mathbf{F}$, if existing, is found by premultiplying both sides of the equation by the inverse of the Leontief matrix,

$$
(\mathbf{I} - \mathbf{A})^{-1} (\mathbf{I} - \mathbf{A})\mathbf{X} = (\mathbf{I} - \mathbf{A})^{-1} \mathbf{F}
$$

Thus,

$$
\overline{\mathbf{X}} = (\mathbf{I} - \mathbf{A})^{-1}\mathbf{F} = \frac{\mathbf{Adj}(\mathbf{I} - \mathbf{A})}{|\mathbf{I} - \mathbf{A}|} \mathbf{F}
$$

where $\overline{\mathbf{X}}$ is the $n \times 1$ matrix (vector) of sectoral output levels required to meet the final demands for the sectoral outputs, given the input requirements set by the sectoral fixed coefficients productions functions. For the solution to exist, the Leontief matrix must be nonsingular, that is,

$$
|\mathbf{I} - \mathbf{A}| \neq 0.
$$

An Example of an Input-Output Table Suppose that we have just three sectors of the economy, for example, agriculture, manufacturing, and services. For simplicity, we will assume a closed economy (no imports or exports), and consider only the level of final demands, F_i, and not the individual components (C_i, I_i, and G_i here). Furthermore, we assume that wage payments by households and the government are zero, so the lower right quadrant in the I-O table is empty, that is, contains only zero entries. Figure 13.2 gives the hypothetical I-O table.

As presented, the I-O table accounts for all the transactions in the economy. Reading across the row for any sector gives the value of the total demand. For example, the total demand for the output of sector 2 of $200 million consists of $65 million in interindustry demands (sectors 1, 2, and 3 use, respectively, $25 million, $20 million, and $20 million worth of output from sector 2 as inputs in their productions) and $135 million in final demands. An example of intraindustry demand for intermediate goods would be steel used in manufacturing automobiles.

---

[1] The economist Wassily Leontief (1906 to 1998) did the pioneering work on input-output tables in the 1940s.

Reading down the column for any sector gives the contributions of the inputs to the value of the total output. For example, the $200 million worth of output of sector 2 is accounted for by $50 million, $20 million, and $30 million worth of inputs purchased from sectors 1, 2, and 3, respectively, $60 million in payments of wages, and $40 million in payments to owners of capital. Note that the sum of the final demands (here $185 million) is equal to the sum of the payments to labor ($115 million) and capital ($70 million).

At this point, we have a set of accounting identities. The contribution of input-output analysis to policy is in assessing the consistency of sectoral output targets, driven by desired growth in final demands, with the expected resource availability.

To demonstrate with this I-O table, assuming the given technology and fixed-coefficients production functions, we can derive the input-output coefficients and form the Leontief matrix. The input-output coefficients are:

$$a_{11} = X_{11}/X_1 = 10/100 = .10, a_{12} = X_{12}/X_2 = 50/200 = .25, a_{13} = X_{13}/X_3 = 0/60 = .0$$

$$a_{21} = X_{21}/X_1 = 25/100 = .25, a_{22} = X_{22}/X_2 = 20/200 = .10, a_{23} = X_{23}/X_3 = 20/60 = .33$$

$$a_{31} = X_{31}/X_1 = 5/100 = .05, a_{32} = X_{32}/X_2 = 30/200 = .15, a_{33} = X_{33}/X_3 = 15/60 = .25$$

The matrix of input-output coefficients is

$$\mathbf{A} = \begin{bmatrix} .10 & .25 & .0 \\ .25 & .10 & .33 \\ .05 & .15 & .25 \end{bmatrix}$$

The Leontief matrix is $(\mathbf{I} - \mathbf{A})$

$$(\mathbf{I} - \mathbf{A}) = \begin{bmatrix} .90 & -.25 & .0 \\ -.25 & .90 & -.33 \\ -.05 & -.15 & .75 \end{bmatrix}$$

The inverse of the Leontief matrix is $(\mathbf{I} - \mathbf{A})^{-1}$

FIGURE 13.2   ILLUSTRATION OF AN INPUT-OUTPUT TABLE (IN MILLIONS OF $)

Purchases by:		Intermediate Users Sectors/Industries			Final Demand	Total Demand
		1	*2*	*3*	*F*	*X*
Sales by:	**1**	10	50	0	40	100
Sectors/Industries	**2**	25	20	20	135	200
	3	5	30	15	10	60
Payments	**W**	40	60	15		115
	R	20	40	10		70
Total Supply	**X**	100	200	60		360

$$(\mathbf{I} - \mathbf{A})^{-1} = \frac{1}{.5115} \begin{bmatrix} .6251 & .1875 & .0833 \\ .2042 & .6750 & .2997 \\ .0825 & .1475 & .7475 \end{bmatrix} = \begin{bmatrix} 1.2221 & .3666 & .1629 \\ .3992 & 1.3196 & .5859 \\ .1613 & .2884 & 1.4614 \end{bmatrix}$$

Note that the main diagonal elements in the inverse of the Leontief matrix are all greater than 1, while the off-diagonal elements are positive and less than 1. (You may need to revisit Chapter 5 to review the calculation of an inverse matrix.)

The system of linear equations, representing the I-O table, can be written as

$$\mathbf{X} = \begin{bmatrix} \overline{X}_1 \\ \overline{X}_2 \\ \overline{X}_3 \end{bmatrix} = \begin{bmatrix} 100 \\ 200 \\ 60 \end{bmatrix} = \begin{bmatrix} 1.2221 & .3666 & .1629 \\ .3992 & 1.3196 & .5859 \\ .1613 & .2884 & 1.4614 \end{bmatrix} \begin{bmatrix} 40 \\ 135 \\ 10 \end{bmatrix} = (\mathbf{I} - \mathbf{A})^{-1} \mathbf{F}$$

To illustrate the use of the input-output model for consistency planning, suppose the goals over the planning horizon were to increase the sectoral outputs enough to produce a new vector of final demands of $\mathbf{F}' = [60\ 140\ 20]$. Suppose further that the available labor was projected to be \$140 million and the available capital to be \$80 million. Recall that we are assuming constant returns to scale and fixed unit prices for inputs and outputs. The question is whether the projected labor and capital will be sufficient for producing sectoral outputs consistent with the desired new levels of final demands.

The new level of sectoral outputs, $\overline{\mathbf{X}}'$, is given by: $\overline{\mathbf{X}}' = (\mathbf{I} - \mathbf{A})^{-1} \mathbf{F}'$

$$\overline{\mathbf{X}}' = \begin{bmatrix} 127.91 \\ 220.41 \\ 79.28 \end{bmatrix} = \begin{bmatrix} 1.2221 & .3666 & .1629 \\ .3992 & 1.3196 & .5859 \\ .1613 & .2884 & 1.4614 \end{bmatrix} \begin{bmatrix} 60 \\ 140 \\ 20 \end{bmatrix}$$

That is, we simply rotate in the new vector of desired final demands, $\mathbf{F}'$, and solve for the new sectoral output levels. Summarizing, to meet the desired increases of \$20 million, \$5 million, and \$10 million in the final demands for the outputs of sectors 1, 2, and 3, respectively, requires increases of \$27.91 million, \$20.41 million, and \$19.28 million in the total sectoral outputs produced. In turn, the required inputs of labor and capital can be found using the fixed shares of wages and payments of interest and profits in the total values of the sectoral outputs with the new levels of sectoral outputs. Returning to Figure 13.2 and the I-O table, the shares of wages (W) and interest and profits (R) in the value of sectoral outputs are

$$W_1/X_1 = 40/100 = .4, \quad W_2/X_2 = 60/200 = .3, \quad W_3/X_3 = 15/60 = .25$$

$$R_1/X_1 = 20/100 = .2, \quad R_2/X_2 = 40/200 = .25, \quad R_3/X_3 = 10/60 = .167$$

The new total wage payments required are

$$[W_1/X_1\ W_2/X_2\ W_3/X_3] \begin{bmatrix} \overline{X}_1 \\ \overline{X}_2 \\ \overline{X}_3 \end{bmatrix} = [.4\ .3\ .25] \begin{bmatrix} 127.91 \\ 220.41 \\ 79.28 \end{bmatrix} = [51.16 + 66.12 + 19.82] = 137.1$$

With the available labor projected to be \$140 million, it appears that there would be more than enough labor to produce the required new sectoral outputs. Indeed, with the fixed coefficients production functions, the surplus labor of \$2.9 million (\$140 − \$137.1) would be unemployed.

The new total payments of interest and profits are

$$[R_1/X_1 \ R_2/X_2 \ R_3/X_3] \begin{bmatrix} \overline{X}_1 \\ \overline{X}_2 \\ \overline{X}_3 \end{bmatrix} = [.2 \ .2 \ .167] \begin{bmatrix} 127.91 \\ 220.41 \\ 79.28 \end{bmatrix} = [25.58 + 44.08 + 13.24] = 82.9$$

In contrast, the required payments to the owners of capital of \$82.9 million would exceed the capital projected to be available (assumed to be \$80 million). Therefore, the new levels of sectoral outputs required to meet the desired new levels of final demands are inconsistent with the projected amount of capital to be available. Either the desired levels of final demands must be pared back or measures taken to increase the amount of physical capital formation, or some combination of these two approaches. With no input substitution allowed with the fixed coefficients production functions, the option of substituting some of the surplus labor for the scarce capital, that is, switching to a more labor-intensive method of production, is not possible.

PRACTICE PROBLEM 13.1

Given the Input-Output Table (in millions of \$) below:

Purchases by		Intermediate Users Sectors/Industries			Final Demand	Total Demand
		1	*2*	*3*	*F*	*X*
Sales by:	**1**	15	60	—	220	—
Sectors/Industries	**2**	75	—	35	300	500
	3	60	70	30	—	200
Payments	**W**	—	230	85		
	R	45	50	45		
Total supply	**X**	—	500	200		

a) Fill in the blanks in the input-output table.
b) Derive the Leontief matrix.
c) Determine the impact (to the nearest tenth or one decimal place) of a decrease of ten in the final demand for the output of sector 1 on the total outputs of sectors 1, 2, and 3.
d) Determine the impact (to the nearest tenth or one decimal place) of a decrease of ten in the final demand for the output of sector 1 on the total wage payments.

Note: In doing your work, carry your calculations out to the nearest ten-thousandth or four decimal places. Then round your answers for the new sectoral outputs and wage payments to the nearest tenth.

(The answers are at the end of the chapter.)

The Usefulness of Input-Output Analysis   This simple example illustrates both the value and limitations of input-output analysis. The value is in explicitly considering the linkages across the sectors of the economy—where an increase in the final demand for the output of one sector requires increases in the outputs of all related sectors. Supply limitations and resource constraints can be identified in the course of planning for the growth of an economy. A realistic modeling of an economy, however, would require a large input-output table with many sectors or industries, disaggregated well beyond three sectors (agriculture, manufacturing, and services). Clearly the data requirements to establish the production functions and linkages across the sectors are substantial and increase with the disaggregation of the economy.

Moreover, the underlying assumptions of fixed coefficients production functions with no input substitution, fixed technologies, and constant unit prices for factors and outputs, are restrictive, and not very realistic, except perhaps in a command economy. The inefficiencies of such a system are readily apparent: the resources required to collect the data and establish the I-O table, to communicate output quotas and allocate resources across all the firms of the economy; and to set the prices of all goods and services in order to allocate the demands over the available supplies. Typically, the choices made by the central planners on what and how much to produce did not reflect the desires of the consumer population—resulting in frequent shortages and surpluses at disequilibrium prices. A system of market-based prices, based on the interactions of firms pursuing profits (and cost-minimization) and utility-maximizing consumers "voting with their dollars," is more efficient.

On the other hand, there are "market failures," including public goods, imperfect competition, externalities, and poverty, that arguably call for government intervention. Nor does this fundamental flaw of command economies diminish the historical record of the Soviet Union's use of central planning to become a military superpower during the first few decades following World War II. Developing economies have used input-output models in industrial planning, for example, to assess the implications of industrial growth strategies fueled by directed investments. Input-output analysis can expose the factors (e.g., skilled labor, capital goods, imported inputs) constraining output growth.

COMPARATIVE STATICS

We conclude our discussion of input-output analysis with an illustration of comparative statics. In the earlier example, we introduced a vector of new final demands and solved for the required new sectoral output levels. From the general solution to the I-O model, however, we can isolate the impact of a change in any final demand on the output of any sector in the economy.

Return to the general solution from the I-O table, $\overline{\mathbf{X}} = (\mathbf{I} - \mathbf{A})^{-1}\mathbf{F}$, which we can write as

$$\begin{bmatrix} \overline{X}_1 \\ \overline{X}_2 \\ . \\ . \\ \overline{X}_n \end{bmatrix} = \begin{bmatrix} b_{11} & b_{12} & \ldots & b_{1n} \\ b_{21} & b_{22} & \ldots & b_{2n} \\ . & . & \ldots & . \\ . & . & \ldots & . \\ b_{n1} & b_{n2} & \ldots & b_{nn} \end{bmatrix} \begin{bmatrix} F_1 \\ F_2 \\ . \\ . \\ F_n \end{bmatrix}$$

where b_{ij}, $(i = 1 \ldots n; j = 1 \ldots n)$, is the (i, j)th element of the inverse of the Leontief matrix, $(\mathbf{I} - \mathbf{A})^{-1}$. Expanding, we have

$$\overline{X}_1 = b_{11}F_1 + b_{12}F_2 + \cdots + b_{1n}F_n$$

$$\overline{X}_2 = b_{21}F_1 + b_{22}F_2 + \cdots + b_{2n}F_n$$

$$\vdots$$

$$\overline{X}_n = b_{n1}F_1 + b_{n2}F_2 + \cdots + b_{nn}F_n$$

or, in general,

$$\overline{X}_i = b_{i1}F_1 + b_{i2}F_2 + \cdots + b_{in}F_n$$

To find the effect of a change in the final demand for the output of sector j on the required equilibrium output of sector i, we take the partial derivative, $\delta \overline{X}_i / \delta F_j = b_{ij}$.

Recall the earlier example of the three-sector economy. In general, the equilibrium solution to the I-O table can be written as

$$\mathbf{X} = \begin{bmatrix} \overline{X}_1 \\ \overline{X}_2 \\ \overline{X}_3 \end{bmatrix} = \begin{bmatrix} 1.2221 & .3666 & .1629 \\ .3992 & 1.3196 & .5859 \\ .1613 & .2884 & 1.4614 \end{bmatrix} \begin{bmatrix} F_1 \\ F_2 \\ F_3 \end{bmatrix}$$

To show this more clearly, we can expand the system into the three linear equations:

$$\overline{X}_1 = 1.2221\, F_1 + .3666\, F_2 + .1629\, F_3$$

$$\overline{X}_2 = .3992\, F_1 + 1.3196\, F_2 + .5859\, F_3$$

$$\overline{X}_3 = .1613\, F_1 + .2884\, F_2 + 1.4614\, F_3$$

To find the effect of a $1 million increase in the final demand for the output of sector 3 on the equilibrium outputs of sectors 1, 2, and 3, respectively, we take the following partial derivatives:

$$\delta \overline{X}_1 / \delta F_3 = b_{13} = .1629$$

Ceteris paribus, a $1 million increase (decrease) in the final demand for the output of sector 3 requires an increase (a decrease) of $.1629 million in the equilibrium output of sector 1.

$$\delta \overline{X}_2 / \delta F_3 = b_{23} = .5859$$

Ceteris paribus, a $1 million increase (decrease) in the final demand for the output of sector 3 requires an increase (a decrease) of $.5859 million in the equilibrium output of sector 2.

$$\delta \overline{X}_3 / \delta F_3 = b_{33} = 1.4614$$

Ceteris paribus, a $1 million increase (decrease) in the final demand for the output of sector 3 requires an increase (a decrease) of $1.4614 million in the equilibrium output of sector 3. That is, an increase in the final demand for the output of sector 3 by $1 million would increase the output of sector 3 not only by this $1 million, but by an additional $.4614 million to meet the intermediate demands from sectors 1, 2, and 3 for inputs from sector 3 as the outputs of these sectors are increased in response to the intermediate demands from sector 3 for inputs.

In an I/O model with n sectors, there are n^2 such comparative static results, given by the n^2 elements in the inverse of the Leontief matrix. We shift the focus now to the modeling of aggregate demand and the determination of national output. We begin with a version of the most basic Keynesian model.

PRACTICE PROBLEM 13.2

Return to the Input-Output table in Practice Problem 13.1. Determine the following impacts (to the nearest tenth), *ceteris paribus*.

a) The impact on the total output of sector 3 of an increase of 10 in the final demand for the output of sector 1.

b) The impact on the total output of sector 3 of an increase of 10 in the final demand for the output of sector 2.

c) The impact on the total output of sector 3 of an increase of 10 in the final demand for the output of sector 3.

d) The impact on the sales by sector 1 to sector 2 of an increase of 10 in the final demand for the output of sector 3.

e) The impact on the wages paid by sector 1 of an increase of 10 in the final demand for the output of sector 3.

(The answers are at the end of the chapter.)

A SIMPLE KEYNESIAN MODEL

In a Simple Keynesian Model there is one sector, for Y, real national output. The economy is assumed to operate with no aggregate supply constraints, that is, with a perfectly elastic aggregate supply, so that any change in the aggregate demand for national output can be met with a corresponding change in production with no change in the aggregate price level. A Simple Keynesian Model, the most basic version of a Keynesian model, is most appropriate for an economy operating well below full employment with substantial excess capacity or underutilized physical capital.[2]

---

[2]John Maynard Keynes (1883 to 1946) revolutionized macroeconomic theory and policy with his most famous work, *The General Theory of Employment, Interest, and Money* (1936), written during the Great Depression. Keynes believed that the fundamental cause of the low-level economic equilibrium and high unemployment was insufficient aggregate demand. Further, he recommended expansionary demand-management policies (particularly an increase in government purchases) to stimulate such a depressed economy. Keynes was reacting to the conventional wisdom, which he labeled the Classical Model, where full employment was the equilibrium condition of the economy. Other macroeconomic schools of thought, Monetarism and New Classical, will be discussed in Chapter 14. We should emphasize that the Simple Keynesian Model presented in this chapter is a very basic version of the complete Keynesian Model, which is also addressed in the next chapter.

To simplify the analysis, we will use a linear model. The equilibrium condition in this single market model is that desired aggregate expenditures on real national output, A, equal the real national output produced, Y. Whenever a dollar of real national output is produced, a dollar of real national income is generated (through wages, interest, and profits). Thus, Y indicates both real national output and real national income. Desired aggregate expenditures on real national output, as we will see, depend on real national income.

Desired aggregate expenditures on real national output are disaggregated by the type or source of expenditures: households, firms, the government, and foreigners.

$$A \equiv C + I + G + X - M$$

where

C = real personal consumption expenditures

I = real investment expenditures

G = real government purchases of goods and services

X = real exports of goods and services

M = real imports of goods and services.

Behavioral assumptions are made for each of these components of spending.

Consumption   Real personal consumption expenditures by households, C, are assumed to be a linear function of real disposable personal income, Y_d.

$$C = C_0 + cY_d$$

The parameter c represents the **marginal propensity to consume**: $c = dC/dY_d, 0 < c < 1$. Every \$1 change in real disposable income induces a less than \$1 change in real personal consumption expenditures. That part of disposable income not used for consumption goes for personal savings.[3] Realizing that not all consumption expenditures depend on disposable income, we include a term, $C_0 > 0$, representing autonomous consumption, which is intended to capture all other influences on real consumption expenditures (e.g., real wealth, cost of consumer credit, and consumer confidence).

Real disposable personal income, Y_d, is defined here to be equal to real national income, Y, less real taxes, T. (We are assuming no transfer payments in this model.) Real taxes, in turn, are a linear function of real national income, $T = tY$, where the parameter $t, 0 < t < 1$, indicates the **marginal rate of taxation**: $t = dT/dY$. Therefore, we have

$$Y_d \equiv Y - T = Y - tY = (1 - t)Y$$

---

[3]Real personal savings, S, in this model is equal to real disposable personal income less real personal consumption expenditures. $S = Y_d - C = Y_d - C_0 - cY_d = -C_0 + (1-c)Y_d$, where $(1-c)$ indicates the **marginal propensity to save**.

and real disposable income is a constant fraction of real national income. Converting the consumption function, we have

$$C = C_0 + cY_d = C_0 + c(1 - t)Y$$

Investment   Real investment expenditures, I, include real business fixed investment (expenditures by firms on new plant, equipment, and machinery); real residential fixed investment (expenditures on new residential construction); and real inventory investment (the change in the stocks of raw materials, semi-finished and finished goods held by firms).

Over the period, inventory investment can be positive, $\Delta INV > 0$, indicating an increase in business inventories, or negative, $\Delta INV < 0$, inventory disinvestment, indicating a decrease in business inventories. Inventory investment can be planned, ΔINV^p, indicating a desired change in business inventories equal to the difference between planned production and expected sales of output; or unplanned, ΔINV^u, indicating a change in inventories resulting from the difference between expected sales and actual sales of output. Unplanned inventory investment, $\Delta INV^u > 0$, would induce firms to cut back on the rate of output produced. Unplanned inventory disinvestment, $\Delta INV^u < 0$, would induce firms to increase the rate of production.

In the Simple Keynesian Model we assume that desired real investment expenditures, I, are exogenous. Firms decide on the level of real business fixed investment based on factors determined outside the scope of the model, for example, business confidence, cost of credit, technological changes. Similarly, residential fixed investment depends on external factors, including consumer confidence, the cost of mortgages, and population growth. Finally, planned inventory investment is assumed to be set at the beginning of the period on the basis of expected sales and the desired level of inventories to hold. Therefore, desired real investment expenditures, equal to the sum of business fixed investment, residential fixed investment, and planned inventory investment are given: $I = I_0$.

Government Purchases, Exports, and Imports   Real government purchases of goods and services (including the wages paid to public employees for the services provided) are assumed to be exogenous. Government purchases reflect expenditure priorities constrained by budgetary considerations. We write $G = G_0$.

Real exports of goods and services, X, are determined by foreign demands, exchange rates, and foreign trade barriers, among other influences exogenous to the model. So, $X = X_0$.

Some of the expenditures by domestic consumers, firms, and government agencies are for imported goods and services. Even exports may contain imported inputs. Therefore, we must subtract real imports of goods and services from personal consumption expenditures, investment expenditures, government purchases, and exports of goods and services to derive desired aggregate expenditures on real national output. We will assume, however, that all induced imports that depend on disposable income are for personal consumption. All other imported goods and services are autonomous, M_0, and depend on exchange rates, import barriers, and other factors exogenous to the model. The import function is

$$M = M_0 + mY_d \qquad 0 < m < c < 1$$

The parameter m is the **marginal propensity to import**: $m = dM/dY_d$. An increase (a decrease) in disposable income will increase (decrease) personal consumption expenditures, some of which will be for imported consumer goods and services. Therefore, the marginal propensity to import, m, while positive, is less than the marginal propensity to consume, c. Writing the import function in terms of real national income, Y, we have

$$M = M_0 + mY_d = M_0 + m(1 - t)Y$$

Desired Aggregate Expenditures   Combining the components of desired aggregate expenditures and simplifying gives

$$A = C + I + G + X - M$$

$$A = C_0 + c(1 - t)Y + I_0 + G_0 + X_0 - M_0 - m(1 - t)Y$$

$$A = A_0 + aY$$

where A_0 = real autonomous expenditures on national output

$$A_0 = C_0 + I_0 + G_0 + X_0 - M_0$$

and

a = marginal propensity to spend on real national output

$$a = (c - m)(1 - t) \qquad 0 < a < 1$$

The **marginal propensity to spend** represents the change in desired aggregate expenditures due to a change in real national income: $a = dA/dY$. Given our assumptions about the marginal propensities to consume and import, $0 < m < c < 1$, and the marginal rate of taxation, $0 < t < 1$, we can say that the marginal propensity to spend is positive and less than one. That is, increasing (decreasing) the production of real national output by \$1 would increase (decrease) real national income by \$1, but increase (decrease) desired real aggregate expenditures on national output by less than \$1 (that is, by $a \cdot \$1$).

EQUILIBRIUM IN THE SIMPLE KEYNESIAN MODEL

As stated earlier, equilibrium in the Simple Keynesian Model is at that level of real national output and income $(\overline{Y}_0)$, where the desired aggregate expenditures on real national output, $A(\overline{Y}_0)$, equal the national output produced, $\overline{Y}_0$. With our derived desired aggregate expenditure schedule, this becomes: $A = A_0 + aY \stackrel{e}{=} Y$. Solving for the equilibrium level of real national output, which we write as $\overline{Y}_0$, we find

$$A_0 + aY = Y$$

$$Y - aY = A_0$$

$$(1-a)Y = A_0$$

$$Y = \frac{A_0}{1 - a} = \overline{Y}_0 \qquad (0 < a < 1)$$

The equilibrium level of real national output and real national income, $\overline{Y}_0$, is a function of the level of desired real autonomous expenditures, A_0, and the marginal propensity to spend, a.

To illustrate, consider the following Simple Keynesian Model.

$C = 40 + .75Y_d$	(real personal consumption expenditures)
$I_0 = 110$	(real investment expenditures)
$G_0 = 180$	(real government purchases of goods and services)
$X_0 = 100$	(real exports of goods and services)
$M = 10 + .25Y_d$	(real imports of goods and services)
$T = .20Y$	(real taxes)
$Y_d \equiv Y - T$	(real disposable income)
$A \equiv C + I + G + X - M$	(desired real aggregate expenditures on national output)
$A(Y) \overset{e}{=} Y$	(equilibrium condition)

This macroeconomic model consists of three behavioral equations (the consumption, import, and tax functions), two identities (real disposable income and desired real aggregate expenditures), and one equilibrium condition. Exogenous are the levels of real autonomous consumption expenditures ($C_0 = 40$), real investment expenditures ($I_0 = 110$), real government purchases ($G_0 = 180$), real exports ($X_0 = 100$), and real autonomous imports ($M_0 = 10$). Also, exogenous are the parameters for the marginal propensity to consume ($c = .75$), the marginal propensity to import ($m = .25$), and the marginal rate of taxation ($t = .20$). There are six endogenous variables: C (real personal consumption expenditures), M (real imports), T (real taxes), Y_d (real disposable income), A (desired real aggregate expenditures on national output), and Y (real national output and, equivalently, real national income).

We can reduce the model of six equations in six endogenous variables to one equation, the equilibrium condition, $A(Y) \overset{e}{=} Y$, in one variable, Y. To solve, we derive the desired real aggregate expenditure schedule. First, we write consumption and imports as functions of real national income, since real disposable income is a function of real national income.

$$Y_d \equiv Y - T = Y - .20Y = .8Y$$

$$C = 40 + .75Y_d = 40 + .75(.8Y) = 40 + .6Y$$

$$M = 10 + .25Y_d = 10 + .25(.8Y) = 10 + .2Y$$

The desired real aggregate expenditure schedule is then

$$A = C + I + G + X - M$$

$$A = 40 + .6Y + 110 + 180 + 100 - 10 - .2Y$$

$$A = 420 + .4Y$$

Real autonomous expenditures on national output, $A_0 = C_0 + I_0 + G_0 + X_0 - M_0$, that is, those expenditures that are independent of the level of real national income, equal 420. The marginal propensity to spend, $a = (c - m)(1 - t) = (.75 - .25)(1 - .2)$, equals .4.

From the equilibrium condition, we set desired real aggregate expenditures, which are a function of real national income, equal to real national output. Solving, we find the equilibrium level of real national output and real national income, $\overline{Y}_0$.

$$A = 420 + .4Y = Y$$

$$420 = .6Y$$

$$\overline{Y}_0 = 700$$

We can easily find the equilibrium values for the other endogenous variables now that we have the equilibrium real national income.

$$\overline{C} = 40 + .6\overline{Y}_0 = 40 + .6(700) = 460$$

$$\overline{M} = 10 + .2\overline{Y}_0 = 10 + .2(700) = 150$$

$$\overline{T} = .2\overline{Y}_0 = .2(700) = 140$$

$$\overline{Y}_d = \overline{Y}_0 - \overline{T} = 700 - 140 = 560$$

$$\overline{A} = \overline{C} + I_0 + G_0 + X_0 - \overline{M} = 460 + 110 + 180 + 100 - 150 = 700$$

Note: $A(\overline{Y}_0) = 420 + .4\overline{Y}_0 = 420 + .4(700) = 700 = \overline{Y}_0$. That is, in equilibrium, desired aggregate real expenditures on national output equal the real national output produced.

PRACTICE PROBLEM 13.3

Given the following Simple Keynesian Model:

$C = 20 + .75Y_d$	(real personal consumption expenditures)
$I_0 = 105$	(real investment expenditures)
$G_0 = 210$	(real government purchases of goods and services)
$X_0 = 50$	(real exports of goods and services)
$M = 10 + .125Y_d$	(real imports of goods and services)
$T = .4Y$	(real taxes)
$Y_d \equiv Y - T$	(real disposable income)

$A \equiv C + I + G + X - M$ (desired real aggregate expenditures on national output)
$A(Y) \overset{e}{=} Y$ (equilibrium condition)

a) Derive the desired real aggregate expenditure schedule. Identify the level of real
    autonomous expenditures and the value of the marginal propensity to spend.
b) Solve for the equilibrium level of real national output (real national income).
c) Find the equilibrium values for real personal consumption expenditures, real imports of
    goods and services, real tax revenues, and real disposable income.

                                              (The answers are at the end of the chapter.)

Keynesian Cross-Diagram   We can depict the equilibrium graphically with the
Keynesian cross-diagram. See Figure 13.3. Desired aggregate expenditures on real
national output, A, are represented on the vertical axis, and real national output (real
national income) is measured on the horizontal axis. The 45° line from the origin represents the locus of possible equilibrium points, since for any point on this line, $A = Y$.
Plotting the desired aggregate expenditure schedule, we see that the vertical intercept
is A_0, real autonomous expenditures (or expenditures on real national output that are
independent of real national income). The slope of the aggregate expenditure schedule is given by the marginal propensity to spend, $0 < a < 1$. The intersection of the
desired aggregate expenditure line, $A = A_0 + aY$, and the 45° equilibrium line gives
the equilibrium value for real national output and real national income. See point E_0
in Figure 13.3, where $A = A_0 + a\overline{Y}_0 = \overline{Y}_0$.

Note, graphically we can see why the marginal propensity to spend must be a
positive fraction less than one. If $a = 1$, then the equilibrium is undefined, since $\overline{Y}_0 =
A_0/(1 - a) = A_0/0$. The desired aggregate expenditure line would be parallel with the

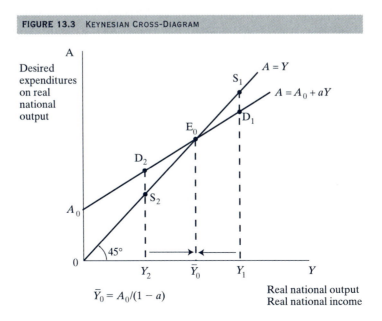

FIGURE 13.3   KEYNESIAN CROSS-DIAGRAM

$\overline{Y}_0 = A_0/(1 - a)$

45° equilibrium line, so no solution would exist. If $a > 1$, then $Y_0 = A_0/(1 - a) < 0$, given that $A_0 > 0$. Here the intersection of the desired aggregate expenditure line and the 45° equilibrium line would occur in the third quadrant (not shown in Figure 13.3), yielding a nonsensical economic equilibrium.

Intuitively, given that real autonomous expenditures on national output are positive, then desired aggregate expenditures dependent on real national income must be less than the real national output produced. If every dollar increase (decrease) in production induced an increase (a decrease) of a dollar or more in desired spending on the output produced, then there would be a perpetual state of excess demand (excess supply) and production would never catch up with desired expenditures.

STABILITY IN THE SIMPLE KEYNESIAN MODEL

The equilibrium in the Simple Keynesian Model is stable. Refer back to Figure 13.3. If the aggregate level of production were Y_1, then an excess supply of goods (*ESG*) would exist, since $A(Y_1) < Y_1$, indicated by the distance, $S_1 - D_1$. The excess supply of goods would result in an unplanned increase in inventories, $\Delta INV^u > 0$, and a cutback in production, $\Delta Y < 0$. As real national output decreased, so would real national income and desired aggregate expenditures. The decrease in output (from S_1 to E_0), greater than the decrease in aggregate expenditures (from D_1 to E_0), would continue until the excess supply of goods (and services) were eliminated and the economy returned to the equilibrium level of production, $\overline{Y}_0$.

Conversely, if the initial level of production were below the equilibrium level, for example, $Y_2 < \overline{Y}_0$, there would be an excess demand for goods (*EDG*), since $A(Y_2) > Y_2$, indicated by the distance, $D_2 - S_2$. The excess demand for goods would be met by running down inventories, that is, unplanned inventory disinvestment, $\Delta INV^u < 0$. To restore inventories to the desired level, firms would step up production, $\Delta Y > 0$. The subsequent rise in real national income and real expenditures on national output (from D_2 to E_0) would be less than the increase in the production (S_2 to E_0). Supply would catch up with the demand at E_0 again, where desired aggregate expenditures on real national output equal the output produced and unplanned inventory investment is zero ($\Delta INV^u = 0$).

In sum, the adjustment mechanism in the Simple Keynesian Model is change in real national output and real national income, triggered by unplanned inventory investment or disinvestment which signals to firms the need to alter the rate of production.

Return to the example with a desired aggregate expenditure schedule, $A = 420 + .4Y$, and equilibrium real national output of $\overline{Y}_0 = 700$. A higher level of output produced, for example, $Y_1 = 750$, would result in an excess supply of goods, here $ESG = 30$, since desired aggregate expenditures would be insufficient to purchase all of the output: $A(750) = 420 + .4(750) = 720 < 750 = Y_1$. The excess supply of goods would increase inventories, which would signal firms to cut back on production until unplanned inventory investment returned to zero, that is, $\overline{Y}_0 = 700$.

Conversely, if the rate of national output produced were less than the equilibrium level, for example, $Y_2 = 600 < 700 = \overline{Y}_0$, an excess demand for goods would result: $A(600) = 420 + .4(600) = 660 > 600 = Y_2$. To meet the excess demand, here $EDG = 60$, firms would run down their inventories where possible. The unplanned inventory disinvestment would prompt firms to step up production.

PRACTICE PROBLEM 13.4

Return to the Simple Keynesian Model in Practice Problem 13.3. Identify the type of disequilibrium and the adjustment that would result if the level of real national output produced were $Y = 640$.

(The answers are at the end of the chapter.)

COMPARATIVE STATICS

The equilibrium level of real national output is conditional upon the given level of real autonomous expenditures, $A_0 = C_0 + I_0 + G_0 + X_0 - M_0$, and the marginal propensity to spend, $a = (c - m)(1 - t)$. Any change in the autonomous expenditures or the marginal propensity to spend would affect the level of desired aggregate expenditures and result in a disequilibrium. Since the model is stable, real output and income would adjust and the economy would move to a new equilibrium.

Change in Autonomous Expenditures   Consider first an increase in government purchases ($\Delta G_0 > 0$).[4] Refer to Figure 13.4. The desired aggregate expenditure line shifts up by the increase in government spending. The resulting excess demand for goods and services (EDG), indicated by the distance, $E' - E_0$, may initially be met by a rundown in inventories, $\Delta INV^u < 0$, or if the type of government spending cannot be met by drawing down inventories (e.g., purchases of new jet fighters or the construction of new highways), then the involved firms would directly hire more labor to meet the increased demand for their output. In any case, national production increases, generating more income and inducing additional spending. The economy moves to a new equilibrium at point E_1, where the new desired aggregate expenditure line, $A' = A'_0 + aY$, intersects the $45°$ equilibrium line. The change in equilibrium real output and income, $\Delta \overline{Y} = \overline{Y}_1 - \overline{Y}_0$, is equal to the final change in desired real aggregate expenditures, ΔA, (indicated by $E_1F = E_0F$), and exceeds the initial change in real autonomous expenditures, here the increase in government purchases (indicated by $E'E_0 = E_1G$), by the amount of induced spending, indicated by GF. This additional spending is due to the multiplier effect.

In fact, we can easily derive the autonomous expenditure multiplier for the Simple Keynesian Model. Returning to the equilibrium value for real national output, $\overline{Y}_0 = A_0/(1 - a)$, we differentiate $d\overline{Y}_0/dA_0 = 1/(1 - a) = K_{A_0}$.

---

[4]The source of the change in autonomous expenditures, ($\Delta G_0, \Delta C_0, \Delta I_0, \Delta X_0$, or ΔM_0) doesn't matter in the Simple Keynesian Model, except that the effect of a change in autonomous imports on national output and income would be in the opposite direction of the other autonomous expenditure changes.

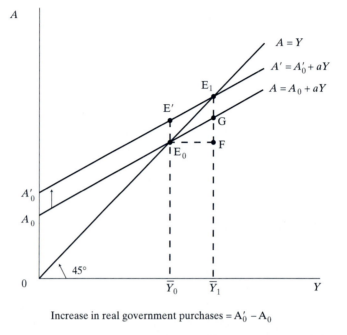

Increase in real government purchases = $A_0' - A_0$

FIGURE 13.4   ILLUSTRATION OF AN INCREASE IN GOVERNMENT PURCHASES

The **autonomous expenditure multiplier**, $K_{A_0} = 1/(1-a)$, exceeds 1, since the marginal propensity to spend, a, is less than 1. In our linear model, the change in equilibrium real national output, $\Delta\overline{Y}$, is a multiple of the initiating change in real autonomous expenditures.

$$\Delta\overline{Y}_0 = K_{A_0} \cdot \Delta A_0 \quad \text{where} \quad K_{A_0} = 1/(1-a) > 1.$$

Graphically, in Figure 13.4, we can see that

$$\Delta\overline{Y} = \overline{Y}_1 - \overline{Y}_0 > A_0' - A_0 = \Delta A_0$$

or

$$E_0\,F = E_1\,F > E_1\,G$$

In the earlier example of the Simple Keynesian Model with a desired aggregate expenditure schedule, $A = 420 + .4Y$, and an equilibrium level of real national output, $Y_0 = 700$, the autonomous expenditure multiplier is $K_{A_0} = 1/(1-.4) = 1.67$. Therefore, any change in autonomous expenditures on real national output of \$1 would generate a change in the equilibrium level of real national output of \$1.67. The additional \$.67 is due to the induced spending from the multiplier effect.

For instance, suppose exports fell by 10 from $X_0 = 100$ to $X_0' = 90$. The new aggregate expenditure schedule is $A' = 410 + .4Y$. Solving for the new equilibrium real national output, we have

$$A' = 410 + .4Y = Y$$

$$410 = .6Y$$

$$\overline{Y}_1 = 683.33$$

We see that the decrease in real national output is equal to 1.67 times the decrease in autonomous spending. $\Delta \overline{Y} = \overline{Y}_1 - \overline{Y}_0 = 683.33 - 700 = -16.67 = 1.67(-10) = K_{A_0} \cdot \Delta A_0$. In this Simple Keynesian Model, an equivalent decrease in autonomous consumption, investment, or government spending, and an equivalent increase in autonomous imports, would have the same multiplier effect.

Change in the Marginal Propensity to Spend   We can also evaluate a change in the marginal propensity to spend, a, which will affect the slope of the desired aggregate expenditure schedule. For example, consider an increase in the marginal rate of taxation, $\Delta t > 0$, so that the real taxes collected at any level of income rise. Refer to Figure 13.5. The increase in the tax rate reduces the marginal propensity to spend, $a = (c - m)(1 - t)$, and rotates the desired aggregate expenditure line clockwise from the vertical intercept, A_0. The new aggregate expenditure line is $A' = A_0 + a'Y$, where $a' = (c - m)(1 - t')$. At the initial equilibrium level of real national output and income, $\overline{Y}_0$, there is now an excess supply of goods and services (ESG), indicated by E_0E'.

To explain, the higher tax rate reduces the level of real disposable income for the initial real national income, and so decreases desired aggregate expenditures on real national output as real consumption expenditures decrease by more than real imports

FIGURE 13.5   ILLUSTRATION OF AN INCREASE IN THE INCOME TAX RATE

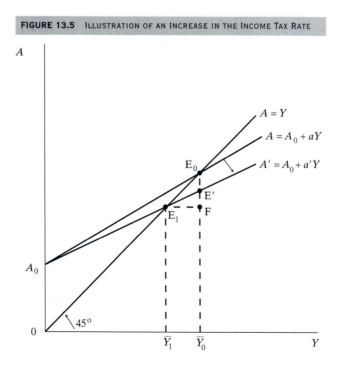

Increase in income tax rate $= t' - t$

of goods and services. The excess supply of goods is reflected in a buildup of inventories, $\Delta INV^u > 0$, which triggers a cutback in production. The decrease in real national output and income (from E_0 to E_1) is greater than the induced decline in spending (from E' to E_1); so the economy moves to a new equilibrium at $\overline{Y}_1$, where $A(\overline{Y}_1) = \overline{Y}_1$, and unplanned inventory investment is again equal to zero.

We can derive the tax rate multiplier for the Simple Keynesian Model by differentiating the equilibrium level of real national output, $\overline{Y}_0$, with respect to the tax rate, t.

$$\overline{Y}_0 = \frac{A_0}{(1 - a)} = \frac{A_0}{[1 - (c - m)(1 - t)]}$$

Therefore

$$d\overline{Y}_0/dt = \frac{-A_0(c - m)}{[1 - (c - m)(1 - t)][1 - (c - m)(1 - t')]} = \frac{-A_0(c - m)}{(1 - a)(1 - a')}$$

$$d\overline{Y}_0/dt = \frac{-(c - m)\overline{Y}_0}{(1 - a')} = -(c - m)\overline{Y}_0 K'_{A_0}$$

Note that according to the quotient rule for differentiation, we would have the initial denominator squared $(1 - a)^2$ in the denominator of the derivative. Instead, we have the product of the initial denominator, $(1 - a)$, and the "new" denominator, $(1 - a')$, that is, with the new tax rate, t', since the multiplier effect that unfolds will incorporate this new marginal propensity to spend, $a' = (c - m)(1 - t')$. Moreover, since $A_0/(1 - a) = \overline{Y}_0$, we can substitute this initial equilibrium level of real national income into the expression for the tax rate multiplier. Therefore, the **tax rate multiplier**, K_t, of the Simple Keynesian Model is equal to

$$K_t = -(c - m)\overline{Y}_0 K'_{A_0} \qquad \text{where } K'_{A_0} = 1/(1 - a')$$

We can see that the value of the tax rate multiplier depends on the initial level of real national income, $\overline{Y}_0$. For a given change in the tax rate, Δt, the impact on disposable income and spending depends on the initial level of national income. For instance, an increase of .1 in the tax rate (say from $t = .3$ to $t' = .4$) would decrease disposable income by \$20 billion if national income were \$200 billion, but by \$25 billion if national income were \$250 billion. The corresponding initial change in desired aggregate expenditures with the change in disposable income, $(\Delta A_0 = -(c - m)\overline{Y}_0 \Delta t)$, will set off the multiplier process, where the new multiplier is based on the new income tax rate, t', that is, $K'_{A_0} = 1/(1 - a')$, where $a' = (c - m)(1 - t')$.

$$\Delta \overline{Y} = K_t \Delta t = \frac{-(c - m)\overline{Y}_0 \Delta t}{(1 - a')}$$

In Figure 13.5, the initial decrease in desired aggregate expenditures on real national output due to the increase in the income tax rate is indicated by the distance E_0E'. The subsequent induced decrease in spending is represented by the distance $E'F$.

To illustrate a decrease in the income tax rate return once more to the Simple Keynesian Model, where $A = A_0 + aY = A_0 + (c - m)(1 - t)Y = 420 + (.75 - .25)\cdot$

$(1 - .2)Y = 420 + .4Y$, and the equilibrium real national output is $\overline{Y}_0 = A_0/(1 - a) = 420/.6 = 700$. Suppose now that the tax rate is reduced from $t = .2$ to $t' = .18$, that is, $\Delta t = -.02$. Both the consumption and import expenditures, functions of disposable income, are affected by the change in the tax rate. Real disposable income is now: $Y'_d = Y - t'Y = Y - .18Y = .82Y$. The new consumption and import schedules are

$$C' = 40 + .75Y'_d = 40 + .75(.82Y) = 40 + .615Y$$

$$M' = 10 + .25Y'_d = 10 + .25(.82Y) = 10 + .205Y$$

The new desired aggregate expenditure schedule is:

$$A' = C' + I_0 + G_0 + X_0 - M' = 420 + .615Y + 110 + 180 + 100 - 10 - .205Y$$

$$A' = 420 + .41Y$$

We see that the decrease in the tax rate from $t = .2$ to $t' = .18$ has increased the marginal propensity to spend from $a = .4$ to $a' = .41$.

$$a = (c - m)(1 - t) = (.75 - .25)(1 - .2) = .40$$

$$a' = (c - m)(1 - t') = (.75 - .25)(1 - .18) = .41$$

Solving for the new equilibrium level of real national output, we find

$$A' = 420 + .41Y = Y$$

$$420 = .59Y$$

$$\overline{Y}_1 = 711.86$$

Thus, a decrease in the tax rate by .02, combined with an initial level of real national income of 700, increases equilibrium real national income by 11.86. The implied tax rate multiplier is $K_t = \Delta\overline{Y}/\Delta t = 11.86/(-.02) = -593$.

To elaborate, with the initial income of $\overline{Y}_0 = 700$, a decrease in the tax rate by .02 would raise disposable income by 14, that is, $\Delta Y_d = \overline{Y}_0 \cdot \Delta t = (700)(.02) = 14$. The initial changes in consumption and import expenditures are

$$\Delta C = c\Delta Y_d = .75(14) = 10.5$$

$$\Delta M = m\Delta Y_d = .25(14) = 3.5$$

Consequently, the initial impact on desired spending on national output is: $\Delta A = \Delta C - \Delta M = 10.5 - 3.5 = 7$. The new expenditure multiplier is $K'_{A_0} = 1/(1 - a') = 1/(1 - .41) = 1.695$, which reflects the new tax rate of $t' = .18$. Using the new expenditure multiplier to generate the additional spending induced from the initial increase in desired expenditures from the tax cut, we find the total change in equilibrium real national output: $\Delta\overline{Y} = K'_{A_0} \cdot 7 = (1.695)(7) = 11.86$.

PRACTICE PROBLEM 13.5

Return to the Simple Keynesian Model in Practice Problem 13.3 and find the impact on the equilibrium real national output of each of the following.

a) an increase in real autonomous investment expenditures of 10, that is, $\Delta I_0 = +10$.

b) an increase in the marginal rate of taxation of .1, that is, $\Delta t = +.1$.

In each case derive the new desired aggregate expenditure schedule and solve the model. Calculate the autonomous expenditure and tax rate multipliers.

(The answers are at the end of the chapter.)

As an exercise, you may want to consider the other sources of change in the marginal propensity to spend, for example, an increase in the marginal propensity to consume or in the marginal propensity to import. In Chapter 14, we extend the Simple Keynesian model to incorporate additional markets. To conclude the present chapter, however, we will illustrate a phenomenon known as the foreign repercussions effect.

A TWO-COUNTRY SIMPLE KEYNESIAN MODEL

The addition of a second country to the Simple Keynesian Model is straightforward. We will make the same behavioral assumptions with respect to the components of aggregate demand for the second country, which will be identified with a subscript 2, with the first country designated by the subscript 1. We do not assume, however, that the values for the parameters (the marginal propensities to consume and import and the marginal rate of taxation) or that the real autonomous expenditures are the same for the two countries. In a two-country Simple Keynesian Model, the two countries are linked through trade. In particular, if country 2 represents the rest of the world, then, by definition, the exports of country 1 are the imports of country 2, and the imports of country 1 are the exports of country 2.

Figure 13.6 sets forth the equations of the model. The model can be reduced to two simultaneous equations, the equilibrium conditions: $A_1(Y_1, Y_2) \stackrel{e}{=} Y_1$ and $A_2(Y_1, Y_2) \stackrel{e}{=} Y_2$, in two unknowns, the levels of real national output and income in the two countries: Y_1 and Y_2. Note that: $X_1 = M_2 = M_{20} + m_2 Y_{d2}$ (that is, exports of country 1 equal the imports of country 2) and that: $X_2 = M_1 = M_{10} + m_1 Y_{d1}$ (that is, exports of country 2 equal the imports of country 1).

FIGURE 13.6   TWO-COUNTRY SIMPLE KEYNESIAN MODEL

Country 1	Country 2
$C_1 = C_{10} + c_1 Y_{d1}$	$C_2 = C_{20} + c_2 Y_{d2}$
$I_1 = I_{10}$	$I_2 = I_{20}$
$G_1 = G_{10}$	$G_2 = G_{20}$
$X_1 = M_{20} + m_2 Y_{d2}$	$X_2 = M_{10} + m_1 Y_{d1}$
$M_1 = M_{10} + m_1 Y_{d1}$	$M_2 = M_{20} + m_2 Y_{d2}$
$T_1 = t_1 Y_1$	$T_2 = t_2 Y_2$
$Y_{d1} \equiv Y_1 - T_1$	$Y_{d2} \equiv Y_2 - T_2$
$A_1 \equiv C_1 + I_1 + G_1 + X_1 - M_1$	$A_2 \equiv C_2 + I_2 + G_2 + X_2 - M_2$
$A_1(Y_1, Y_2) \stackrel{e}{=} Y_1$	$A_2(Y_1, Y_2) \stackrel{e}{=} Y_2$

Forming the desired aggregate expenditure schedules in the two countries we get country 1:

$$A_1 = C_1 + I_1 + G_1 + X_1 - M_1$$

$$A_1 = C_{10} + c_1 (1 - t_1)Y_1 + I_{10} + G_{10} + M_{20} + m_2 (1 - t_2)Y_2 - M_{10} - m_1(1 - t_1)Y_1$$

$$A_1 = A_{10} + a_1Y_1 + m_2(1 - t_2)Y_2$$

where

$$A_{10} = C_{10} + I_{10} + G_{10} + M_{20} - M_{10}$$

and

$$a_1 = (c_1 - m_1)(1 - t_1)$$

country 2:

$$A_2 = C_2 + I_2 + G_2 + X_2 - M_2$$

$$A_2 = C_{20} + c_2(1 - t_2)Y_2 + I_{20} + G_{20} + M_{10} + m_1(1 - t_1)Y_1 - M_{20} - m_2(1 - t_2)Y_2$$

$$A_2 = A_{20} + a_2Y_2 + m_1(1 - t_1)Y_1$$

where

$$A_{20} = C_{20} + I_{20} + G_{20} + M_{10} - M_{20}$$

and

$$a_2 = (c_2 - m_2)(1 - t_2)$$

Setting desired aggregate expenditures equal to real national output in each country in accordance with the respective equilibrium conditions gives

$$A_{10} + a_1Y_1 + m_2(1 - t_2)Y_2 = Y_1$$

or

$$(1 - a_1)Y_1 - m_2(1 - t_2)Y_2 = A_{10} \qquad \{1\}$$

and

$$A_{20} + a_2Y_2 + m_1(1 - t_1)Y_1 = Y_2$$

or

$$-m_1(1 - t_1)Y_1 + (1 - a_2)Y_2 = A_{20} \qquad \{2\}$$

Clearly, the equilibrium levels of real national output (and real national income) in the two countries are simultaneously determined. Writing the system in matrix notation, we have

$$\begin{bmatrix} (1 - a_1) & -m_2(1 - t_2) \\ -m_1(1 - t_1) & (1 - a_2) \end{bmatrix} \begin{bmatrix} Y_1 \\ Y_2 \end{bmatrix} = \begin{bmatrix} A_{10} \\ A_{20} \end{bmatrix}$$

We will focus on the equilibrium value for real national output and comparative statics for country 1, in order to compare with the single-country Simple Keynesian Model presented earlier. Using Cramer's rule, we solve for $\overline{Y}_1$.

$$\overline{Y}_1 = \frac{\begin{vmatrix} A_{10} & -m_2(1-t_2) \\ A_{20} & (1-a_2) \end{vmatrix}}{\begin{vmatrix} (1-a_1) & -m_2(1-t_2) \\ -m_1(1-t_1) & (1-a_2) \end{vmatrix}} = \frac{A_{10}(1-a_2) + m_2(1-t_2)A_{20}}{(1-a_1)(1-a_2) - m_1(1-t_1)m_2(1-t_2)} = \overline{Y}_{10}$$

The reduced form solution for real national output (real national income) in country 1, $\overline{Y}_{10}$, is entirely in terms of the exogenous variables of the model: the parameters representing the marginal propensities to consume and import and the marginal rate of taxation and real autonomous expenditures on national outputs in both countries.

To illustrate, consider the following two-country model:

Country 1	*Country 2*
$C_1 = 40 + .75Y_{d1}$	$C_2 = 30 + .9Y_{d2}$
$I_1 = 110$	$I_2 = 85$
$G_1 = 180$	$G_2 = 95$
$X_1 = 4 + .16Y_{d2}$	$X_2 = 10 + .25Y_{d1}$
$M_1 = 10 + .25Y_{d1}$	$M_2 = 4 + .16Y_{d2}$
$T_1 = .20Y_1$	$T_2 = .25Y_2$
$Y_{d1} \equiv Y_1 - T_1$	$Y_{d2} \equiv Y_2 - T_2$
$A_1 \equiv C_1 + I_1 + G_1 + X_1 - M_1$	$A_2 \equiv C_2 + I_2 + G_2 + X_2 - M_2$
$A_1(Y_1, Y_2) \overset{e}{=} Y_1$	$A_2(Y_1, Y_2) \overset{e}{=} Y_2$

Note that the equations for country 1 are the same as in the earlier Simple Keynesian Model, except for the exports of country 1, which now equal the imports of country 2, which depend on the real income of country 2. We do this to make the distinction between the two models clearer when we do comparative statics. Similarly, the imports of country 1 are the exports of country 2. The economies are interdependent and we have a simultaneous model.

We reduce this system of 14 equations in 14 endogenous variables ($C_1, X_1, M_1, T_1,$ $Y_{d1}, A_1,$ and Y_1 for country 1 and $C_2, X_2, M_2, T_2, Y_{d2}, A_2,$ and Y_2 for country 2) into a system of two equations (the equilibrium conditions) in the two key endogenous variables (the real national outputs in countries 1 and 2, Y_1 and Y_2). First, converting the consumption and import expenditures into functions of national income, we have

$$Y_{d1} = Y_1 - T_1 = Y_1 - .20Y_1 = .80Y_1$$

$$C_1 = 40 + .75Y_{d1} = 40 + .75(.80Y_1) = 40 + .6Y_1$$

$$M_1 = 10 + .25Y_{d1} = 10 + .25(.80Y_1) = 10 + .2Y_1$$

for country 1 and

$$Y_{d2} = Y_2 - T_2 = Y_2 - .25Y_2 = .75Y_2$$

$$C_2 = 30 + .9Y_{d2} = 30 + .9(.75Y_2) = 30 + .675Y_2$$

$$M_2 = 4 + .16Y_{d2} = 4 + .16(.75Y_2) = 4 + .12Y_2$$

for country 2.

The desired aggregate expenditure schedules are

$$A_1 = C_1 + I_1 + G_1 + X_1 - M_1$$

$$A_1 = 40 + .6Y_1 + 110 + 180 + 4 + .12Y_2 - 10 - .2Y_1$$

$$A_1 = 324 + .4Y_1 + .12Y_2$$

and

$$A_2 = C_2 + I_2 + G_2 + X_2 - M_2$$

$$A_2 = 30 + .675Y_2 + 85 + 95 + 10 + .2Y_1 - 4 - .12Y_2$$

$$A_2 = 216 + .555Y_2 + .2Y_1$$

We see that the desired aggregate expenditures for each country depend not only on that country's real national income, but also on the other country's real national income.

The two equilibrium conditions are

$$A_1 (Y_1, Y_2) \overset{e}{=} Y_1$$

and

$$A_2 (Y_1, Y_2) \overset{e}{=} Y_2$$

which in this model are

$$A_1 = 324 + .4Y_1 + .12Y_2 = Y_1$$

and

$$A_2 = 216 + .555Y_2 + .2Y_1 = Y_2$$

Simplifying, we have

$$.6Y_1 - .12Y_2 = 324$$

and

$$-.2Y_1 + .445Y_2 = 216$$

Arranging in matrix notation and solving using Cramer's rule gives

$$\begin{bmatrix} .6 & -.12 \\ -.2 & .445 \end{bmatrix} \begin{bmatrix} Y_1 \\ Y_2 \end{bmatrix} = \begin{bmatrix} 324 \\ 216 \end{bmatrix}$$

$$\overline{Y}_1 = \frac{\begin{vmatrix} 324 & -.12 \\ 216 & .445 \end{vmatrix}}{\begin{vmatrix} .6 & -.12 \\ -.2 & .445 \end{vmatrix}} = \frac{170.1}{.243} = 700$$

$$\overline{Y}_2 = \frac{\begin{vmatrix} .6 & 324 \\ -.2 & 216 \end{vmatrix}}{\begin{vmatrix} .6 & -.12 \\ -.2 & .445 \end{vmatrix}} = \frac{194.4}{.243} = 800$$

The exports of country 1 (imports of country 2) are: $\overline{X}_1 = 4 + .12\overline{Y}_2 = 4 + .12(800) = 100 = \overline{M}_2$. The imports of country 1 (exports of country 2) are: $\overline{M}_1 = 10 + .2\overline{Y}_1 = 10 + .2(700) = 150 = \overline{X}_2$.

PRACTICE PROBLEM 13.6

Suppose in the above illustration of the two-country model, the marginal propensity to import for country 1 had been $m_1' = .30$, instead of $m_1 = .25$. Resolve the model to find the equilibrium levels of real national outputs in the two countries.

(The answers are at the end of the chapter.)

The Foreign Repercussions Effect   In deriving the autonomous expenditure multiplier in the two-country model, we need to be careful in distinguishing domestic autonomous expenditures, that is, C_{10}, I_{10}, and G_{10}, from the foreign trade autonomous expenditures, that is, $M_{10} = X_{20}$ and $X_{10} = M_{20}$. For example, the domestic autonomous expenditure multiplier associated with changes in C_{10}, I_{10}, or G_{10}, for country 1 is

$$(K_{A_{10}})^f = d\overline{Y}_{10}/dC_{10} = d\overline{Y}_{10}/dI_{10} = d\overline{Y}_{10}/dG_{10}$$

$$= \frac{(1 - a_2)}{(1 - a_1)(1 - a_2) - m_1(1 - t_1)m_2(1 - t_2)}$$

where the superscript f indicates the incorporation of the foreign repercussions effect—soon to be identified. We can divide the numerator and denominator by $(1 - a_2)$ and get

$$(K_{A_{10}})^f = \frac{1}{(1 - a_1) - \dfrac{m_1(1 - t_1)m_2(1 - t_2)}{(1 - a_2)}}$$

which we can more easily compare with the autonomous expenditure multiplier of the single-country model, $K_{A_{10}} = 1/(1 - a_1)$. The difference in the two multipliers is the subtraction of the term $m_1(1 - t_1)m_2(1 - t_2)/(1 - a_2)$ in the denominator for the two-country model. This term, which is positive, represents the **foreign repercussions effect**, so its subtraction reduces the denominator of the domestic autonomous expenditure multiplier of the two-country model. In general, the foreign repercussions effect refers to the reverberations on an economy from the impacts of changes in the economy on foreign economies. Therefore, we can state

$$((K_{A_{10}})^f > K_{A_{10}}$$

or the incorporation of foreign repercussions enhances the autonomous expenditure multiplier for changes in real autonomous consumption, investment, or government purchases.

To illustrate why, consider an increase in real government purchases, $\Delta G_{10} > 0$. Beginning in equilibrium, an increase in government spending on real national output in country 1 results in an excess demand for goods and services (EDG_1). Inventories may be run down ($\Delta INV^u < 0$) and production will be increased to meet the greater demand. The final change in country 1's real national output would be a multiple of the increase in real autonomous expenditures: $\Delta Y_1 = K_{A_{10}} \cdot \Delta G_{10}$, where $K_{A_{10}} = 1/(1 - a_1)$. When we consider foreign repercussions, however, we find additional induced spending. The rise in real national income in country 1 increases its imports, $\Delta M_1 = m_1(1 - t_1)\Delta Y_1$, which are the exports of country 2. The increase in country 2s exports creates an excess demand for goods and services there (EDG_2) and a rise in the production and income in country 2 ($\Delta Y_2 > 0$). The increase in country 2s real income, in turn, increases its spending on imports, $\Delta M_2 = m_2(1 - t_2)\Delta Y_2$, which are the exports of country 1. The foreign repercussions of a secondary stimulus with an increase in the exports of country 1 augments the multiplier effect, producing a greater expansion in real national output and income in country 1. The final change in real output and income in country 1 is: $\Delta \overline{Y}_1 = (K_{A_{10}})^f \cdot \Delta G_{10}$.

Schematically, we can illustrate the process of adjustment with a flow chart:

$$G_{10}\uparrow \Rightarrow EDG_1 \Rightarrow (\Delta INV^u)_1 < 0 \Rightarrow Y_1\uparrow$$

(where $\Delta \overline{Y}_1 = K_{A_{10}} \cdot \Delta G_{10}$ in the single-country, Simple Keynesian Model)

in addition, with foreign repercussions,

as $Y_1\uparrow \Rightarrow M_1\uparrow \Rightarrow EDG_2 \Rightarrow (INV^u)_2 < 0 \Rightarrow Y_2\uparrow \Rightarrow M_2\uparrow = X_1\uparrow \Rightarrow Y_1\uparrow$ again

(where $\Delta \overline{Y}_1 = (K_{A_{10}})^f \cdot \Delta G_{10}$ in the two-country, Simple Keynesian Model.)

In sum, incorporating the foreign repercussions effect in this two-country Simple Keynesian Model increases the value of the autonomous expenditure multiplier for changes in autonomous consumption, investment, and government purchases. In a very basic way, we can see the international business cycle, where growth (a decline) in output and income in one country spills over with positive (negative) effects on the output and income of other countries.

We can illustrate with the two country Simple Keynesian Model. Recall the desired aggregate expenditure schedules were: $A_1 = 324 + .4Y_1 + .12Y_2$ and $A_2 = 216 + .555Y_2 + .2Y_1$. The equilibrium real national outputs were: $\overline{Y}_1 = 700$ and $\overline{Y}_2 = 800$. Suppose now that government purchases in country 1 increased by 10 to $G'_{10} = 190$. The new desired aggregate expenditure schedule in country 1 is: $A'_1 = 334 + .4Y_1 + .12Y_2$. Solving simultaneously, we would find: $\overline{Y}'_1 = 718.31$ and $\overline{Y}'_2 = 808.23$. The implied autonomous expenditure multiplier for country 1 incorporating the foreign repercussions effect is $(K_{A_{10}})^f = \Delta \overline{Y}/\Delta G_{10} = 18.31/10 = 1.83$.

To confirm, we can calculate the multiplier directly:

$$(K_{A_{10}})^f = \cfrac{1}{(1 - a_1) - \cfrac{m_1(1 - t_1)m_2(1 - t_2)}{(1 - a_2)}} = \cfrac{1}{(1 - .4) - \cfrac{.25(1 - .2).16(1 - .25)}{1 - .555}}$$

$$= \cfrac{1}{.6 - .024/.445} = \cfrac{1}{.6 - .054} = 1.83$$

This autonomous expenditure multiplier exceeds the one for the single-country Simple Keynesian Model, where the country 1 had the same conditions: $K_{A_0} = 1/(1 - .4) = 1/.6 = 1.67$. The difference is due to the foreign repercussions effect, which augments the impact of a change in government spending on the equilibrium real national income in an economy.

What about autonomous changes in imports or exports? Do foreign repercussions enhance the multiplier effect here too? Suppose country 1 attempts to stimulate its economy by erecting import barriers to trade, so that $\Delta M_{10} < 0$. We derive the comparative static result, $d\overline{Y}_{10}/dM_{10}$, from

$$\overline{Y}_0 = \frac{A_{10}(1 - a_2) + m_2(1 - t_2)A_{20}}{(1 - a_1)(1 - a_2) - m_1(1 - t_1)m_2(1 - t_2)}$$

by differentiating

$$d\overline{Y}_{10}/dM_{10} = \frac{-(1 - a_2) + m_2(1 - t_2)}{(1 - a_1)(1 - a_2) - m_1(1 - t_1)m_2(1 - t_2)}$$

which can be simplified to

$$d\overline{Y}_{10}/dM_{10} = \cfrac{-1}{(1 - a_1) + \cfrac{m_2(1 - t_2)[1 - c_1(1 - t_1)]}{1 - c_2(1 - t_2)}} = (K_{M_{10}})^f$$

Compared to the autonomous expenditure multiplier for the single-country model

$$d\overline{Y}_{10}/dM_{10} = \frac{-1}{1 - a_1} = K_{M_{10}}$$

we again see an extra term in the denominator for the multiplier for the two-country model, which represents the foreign repercussions effect. This term, $\dfrac{m_2(1 - t_2)[1 - c_1(1 - t_1)]}{1 - c_2(1 - t_2)}$, is also positive; so adding it makes the denominator larger and the multiplier smaller (in absolute value). That is, $|(K_{M_{10}})^f| < |K_{M_{10}}|$.

To explain, consider the consequences of a decrease in autonomous imports in country 1 due to its imposition of trade barriers. The fall in imports diverts domestic demand in country 1 towards domestic output, resulting in an excess demand for goods (EDG_1) and an expansion of real national output and income in country 1. Ignoring the foreign repercussions, the increase in real income in country 1 would be $\Delta \overline{Y}_1 = $

$K_{M_{10}} \cdot \Delta M_{10} > 0$. The decrease in autonomous imports in country 1, however, would be an equivalent decrease in autonomous exports of country 2, reducing desired real aggregate expenditures for country 2's output and resulting in an excess supply of goods in country 2 (ESG_2). Inventories may build up and production would be cut back in country 2. As real income falls in country 2, so would its imports, which are the exports of country 1. The decrease in the exports of country 1 would offset, in part, its initial autonomous decrease in imports, and therefore modify the expansion in its real national output and income. In sum, the final increase in real income in country 1 would be less due to the foreign repercussions effect: $\Delta \overline{Y}_1 = (K_{M_{10}})^f \cdot \Delta M_{10} < K_{M_{10}} \cdot \Delta M_{10}$. Note, the improvement in country 1's balance of trade, $X_1 - M_1$, with the imposition of import barriers, would also be less considering the foreign repercussions effect—*a fortiori* if country 2 retaliated with its own import barriers.

Schematically,

$$M_{10}\downarrow \; \Rightarrow EDG_1 \Rightarrow (\Delta INV^u)_1 < 0 \Rightarrow Y_1 \uparrow$$

(where $\Delta \overline{Y}_1 = K_{M_{10}} \cdot \Delta M_{10}$ in the single-country, Simple Keynesian Model)

but, with the foreign repercussions,

with $M_{10} \downarrow \; = X_{20} \downarrow \; \Rightarrow ESG_2 \Rightarrow (\Delta INV^u)_2 > 0 \; \Rightarrow Y_2 \downarrow \; \Rightarrow M_2 \downarrow \; = X_1 \downarrow \; \Rightarrow Y_1 \downarrow$ some

(where $\Delta \overline{Y}_1 = (K_{M_{10}})^f \cdot \Delta M_{10}$ in the two-country, Simple Keynesian Model)

In sum, country 1 does not receive the same boost in real output and income (or improvement in its trade balance) from imposing import barriers to trade when the foreign repercussions effect is considered. Moreover, if country 2 retaliates and imposes its own import barriers and a trade war erupts, then the expansion in real output and income in country 1 would be reduced further. Reduced volumes of trade yield a less efficient allocation of resources and lower global output as countries produce less of their comparative advantage goods.

To illustrate with the numerical example of the two-country model, suppose that country 1 erects trade barriers so that its autonomous imports decline by 2, meaning that the autonomous exports of country 2 decline by 2. The new import function for country 1 (export function for country 2) is: $M_1'' = (10 - 2) + .25Y_{d1} = 8 + .25Y_{d1} = 8 + .25(.8Y_1) = 8 + .2Y_1 = X_2''$. The new desired aggregate expenditure schedules are:

$$A_1'' = 326 + .4Y_1 + .12Y_2$$

$$A_2'' = 214 + .555Y_2 + .2Y_1.$$

Using the equilibrium conditions to solve simultaneously: $A_1'' (Y_1, Y_2) \overset{e}{=} Y_1$ and $A_2'' (Y_1, Y_2) \overset{e}{=} Y_2$, we find $\overline{Y}_1'' = 702.67$ and $\overline{Y}_2'' = 796.71$. (Recall that the initial equilibrium levels of real national output were $\overline{Y}_1 = 700$ and $\overline{Y}_2 = 800$.) The implied multiplier for an autonomous change in imports in country 1 is: $\Delta Y_1 / \Delta M_{10} = +2.67/(-2) = -1.34$. Note that the absolute impact on the equilibrium real national output of country 2 from the decline in its autonomous exports (autonomous imports from

country 1) is greater: $\Delta \overline{Y}_2 / \Delta M_{10} = -3.29/(-2) = -1.65$. This reflects the greater marginal propensity to spend in country 2 ($a_2 = .555$) compared to Country 1 ($a_1 = .4$).
Directly calculating the multiplier, we have

$$(K_{M_{10}})^f = \frac{-1}{(1 - a_1) + \dfrac{m_2(1 - t_2)[1 - c_1(1 - t_1)]}{1 - [c_2(1 - t_2)]}}$$

$$= \frac{-1}{(1 - .4) + \dfrac{.16(1 - .25)[1 - .75(1 - .2)]}{1 - [.9(1 - .25)]}}$$

$$= \frac{-1}{.6 + .148} = -1.34$$

Ignoring the foreign repercussions effect, the expenditure multiplier for a change in autonomous imports for country 1 is $(K_{M_{10}}) = -1/(1 - a_1) = -1/(1 - .4) = -1.67$. Incorporating the foreign repercussions effect with the two-country model reduces this multiplier to $(K_{M_{10}})^f = -1.34$.

The essential point of this two-country model is to highlight one dimension of the economic interdependence of nations. Any autonomous change in expenditures, due perhaps to changes in fiscal and monetary policies, especially in large countries, will have consequences for foreign economies, as well as for the domestic economy. The foreign repercussions can enhance or diminish the multiplier effects on domestic output and income.

PRACTICE PROBLEM 13.7

Return to the two-country model in Practice Problem 13.6, where the marginal propensity to import for country 1 is $m_1' = .30$. Find the impact on the equilibrium real national output of country 1 of each of the following:
a) A decrease in autonomous consumption in country 1 of 5, so the new consumption function for country 1 is: $C_1' = 35 + .75Y_{d1}$.
b) An increase in autonomous exports for country 1 of 5, so the new export function for country 1 (import function for country 2) is: $X_1'' = 9 + .16Y_{d2} = M_2''$.
Compare the multiplier effects with and without the foreign repercussions.

(The answers are at the end of the chapter.)

In the next chapter we extend the Simple Keynesian Model for one country first by adding a second market, the money market, and a second key variable, the nominal rate of interest. Then we incorporate the labor market and aggregate supply constraints, adding two more key endogenous variables, the level of employment and the aggregate price level, to the macro model. In Chapter 15, the final chapter in this book, we turn to dynamic macroeconomic analysis and introduce growth models.

❖ KEY TERMS

Economics

- autonomous expenditure multiplier (p. 472)
- foreign repercussions effect (p. 480)
- input-output coefficients (p. 456)
- input-output table (p. 452)
- intermediate goods (p. 452)

- Leontief matrix (p. 457)
- marginal propensity to consume (p. 464)
- marginal propensity to import (p. 466)
- marginal propensity to save (p. 464)

- marginal propensity to spend (p. 466)
- marginal rate of taxation (p. 464)
- tax rate multiplier (p. 474)
- technical coefficients (p. 456)
- value added (p. 455)

❖PROBLEMS

1. Given the Input-Output Table below (in millions of $):

Purchases by:		Intermediate Users Sectors/Industries			Final Demand	Total Demand
		1	*2*	*3*	*F*	*X*
Sales by:	**1**	15	40	0	95	150
Sectors/	**2**	10	5	30	155	200
Industries	**3**	50	35	10	5	100
Payments	**W**	50	40	30		
	R	25	80	30		
Total Supply	**X**	150	200	100		

a) Find the levels of sectoral outputs needed to meet final demands projected to be in the next period: 100 for sector 1; 145 for sector 2; and 10 for sector 3. Will the new levels of final demands be able to be met with the current amounts of capital and labor? Explain. (Note that the sum of the final demands is unchanged, only the composition has changed.)

b) Find the impacts on the total output levels of sectors 1, 2, and 3 of an increase of 10 in the final demand for the output of sector 2, *ceteris paribus*.

c) Find the impact of an increase of 10 in the final demand for the output of sector 2 on
   i) wages paid in sector 2 (W_2).
   ii) total payments to labor (W) and capital (R).
   iii) sales by sector 1 to sector 2 (X_{12}).
   iv) profits and interest in sector 3 (R_3).

In your work, carry your calculations out to the nearest ten-thousandth (four decimal places). Then round your final answers to the nearest tenth (one decimal place) for the sectoral outputs and factor payments.

2. Given the following Simple Keynesian Model for country 1:

$$C = 10 + .9Y_d$$

$$I_0 = 125$$

$$G_0 = 180$$

$$X_0 = 95$$

$$M = 10 + .1Y_d$$

$$T = .25Y$$

$$Y_d \equiv Y - T$$

$$A \equiv C + I + G + X - M$$

$$A(Y) \overset{e}{=} Y$$

a) Find the equilibrium level of real national income $(\overline{Y}_0)$ and the balance of trade $(X - M)$.

b) Find the impact on the equilibrium level of real national income and the balance of trade of

   i) an increase in real government expenditures of 10.

   ii) a decrease in real autonomous imports of 10.

   iii) a decrease in the marginal rate of taxation by .05 to $t' = .20$.

3. Now add a second country. The two countries, distinguished by the subscripts 1 and 2, are linked through trade.

Country 1	*Country 2*
$C_1 = 10 + .9Y_{d1}$	$C_2 = 5 + .95Y_{d2}$
$I_1 = 125$	$I_2 = 93$
$G_1 = 180$	$G_2 = 170$
$X_1 = 5 + .25Y_{d2}$	$X_2 = 10 + .1Y_{d1}$
$M_1 = 10 + .1Y_{d1}$	$M_2 = 5 + .25Y_{d2}$
$T_1 = .25Y_1$	$T_2 = .4Y_2$
$Y_{d1} \equiv Y_1 - T_1$	$Y_{d2} \equiv Y_2 - T_2$
$A_1 \equiv C_1 + I_1 + G_1 + X_1 - M_1$	$A_2 \equiv C_2 + I_2 + G_2 + X_2 - M_2$
$A_1(Y_1, Y_2) \overset{e}{=} Y_1$	$A_2(Y_1, Y_2) \overset{e}{=} Y_2$

a) Find the equilibrium level of real national income $(\overline{Y}_{10})$ and balance of trade $(X_1 - M_1)$ for Country 1.

b) Find the impact on the equilibrium level of real national income and the balance of trade for Country 1 of:

   i) an increase in real government expenditures in Country 1 of 10.

   ii) a decrease in real autonomous imports of Country 1 of 10.

   iii) a decrease in the marginal rate of taxation in Country 1 by .05 to $t'_1 = .20$.

c) Explain why the effect of an increase in real government expenditures of Country 1 on the equilibrium level of real national income and balance of trade in Country 1 differs between the two models. Calculate the multiplier with and without the foreign repercussions effect.

d) Explain why the effect of a decrease in real autonomous imports in Country 1 on the equilibrium level of real national income and balance of trade in Country 1 differs between the two models. Calculate the multiplier with and without the foreign repercussions effect.

e) Explain why the effect of a decrease in the marginal rate of taxation in Country 1 on the equilibrium level of real national income and balance of trade in Country 1 differs between the two models. Calculate the multiplier with and without the foreign repercussions effect.

Note: The only difference between the two models for Country 1 is the export function. In both models, to find the effects of an increase in real government expenditures, or a decrease in real autonomous imports, or decrease in the marginal rate of taxation, you should solve the models again. For the two-country model, you will need to carry the calculations to four decimal places to minimize the rounding error. Express your final answers, however, rounded to the nearest hundredth.

❖ ANSWERS TO PRACTICE PROBLEMS

13.1 a) $X_{13} = 5, X_1 = 300, X_{22} = 90, F_3 = 40$, and $W_1 = 105$.

b) $(\mathbf{I} - \mathbf{A}) = \begin{bmatrix} .95 & -.12 & -.025 \\ -.25 & .82 & -.175 \\ -.20 & -.14 & .85 \end{bmatrix}$

c) The total changes in sectoral outputs are: $\Delta X_1 = -11.1, \Delta X_2 = -4.1$, and $\Delta X_3 = -3.3$.

d) The total change in wage payments is: $\Delta W = -7.2$.

13.2 a) $\delta \overline{X}_3 / \delta F_1 = b_{31} = .3294$, so $\Delta \overline{X}_3 = +3.3$ with $\Delta F_1 = +10$

b) $\delta \overline{X}_3 / \delta F_2 = b_{32} = .2598$, so $\Delta \overline{X}_3 = +2.6$ with $\Delta F_2 = +10$

c) $\delta \overline{X}_3 / \delta F_3 = b_{33} = 1.2397$, so $\Delta \overline{X}_3 = +12.4$ with $\Delta F_3 = +10$

d) $\delta \overline{X}_2 / \delta F_3 = b_{23} = .2855$, so $\Delta \overline{X}_2 = +2.9$ with $\Delta F_3 = +10; a_{12} = .12$, so $\Delta \overline{X}_{12} = .12 \Delta \overline{X}_2 = (.12)(2.9) = .3$

e) $\delta \overline{X}_1 / \delta F_3 = b_{13} = .0687$, so $\Delta X_1 = .7$ with $\Delta F_3 = +10; W_1/X_1 = .35$, so $\Delta W_1 = (.35)(.7) = +.2$

13.3 a) $A = 375 + .375Y$. Real autonomous expenditures are $A_0 = 375$. The marginal propensity to spend is $a = .375$.

b) The equilibrium level of real national output (real national income) is $\overline{Y}_0 = 600$.

c) The equilibrium values for real personal consumption expenditures, real imports of goods and services, real taxes, and real disposable income are $\overline{C} = 290, \overline{M} = 55, \overline{T} = 240$, and $\overline{Y}_d = 360$.

13.4 If the real national output produced were $Y = 640$, there would be an excess supply of goods, $ESG = 25$. Unplanned inventory investment would occur, leading firms to cut back on production.

13.5 a) The new desired aggregate expenditure schedule is: $A' = 385 + .375Y$. The equilibrium real national output increases by 16 to $\overline{Y}_1 = 616$. The autonomous expenditure multiplier is $K_{A_0} = 1.6$.

   b) The new desired aggregate expenditure schedule is $A'' = 375 + .3125Y$. The equilibrium real national output decreases by 54.55 to $\overline{Y}_2 = 545.45$. The tax rate multiplier is $K_t = -545.\overline{45}$.

13.6 The equilibrium real national outputs are: $\overline{Y}_1 = 664.45$ and $\overline{Y}_2 = 843.75$.

13.7 a) Equilibrium real national output in Country 1 decreases by 8.69. The multipliers with and without the foreign repercussions effect are: $(K_{A_{10}})^f = 1.74$ and $(K_{A_{10}}) = 1.56$.

   b) Equilibrium real national output in Country 1 increases by 6.35. The multipliers with and without the foreign repercussions effect are: $(K_{X_{10}})^f = 1.27$ and $(K_{X_{10}}) = 1.56$.

IS-LM and Aggregate Demand–Aggregate Supply Models

We return to a single-country, Simple Keynesian Model and extend the analysis in two basic ways. First, the interest rate is incorporated in the model as an endogenous variable. The most interest-sensitive components of desired aggregate expenditures are consumer durables (e.g., new automobiles, appliances, furniture), residential fixed investment (new residential construction), and business fixed investment (purchases of new capital goods). Often these expenditures are financed through credit; and a given loan becomes more expensive to pay off the higher is the rate of interest. The second extension is to add the money market—the demand for, and supply of, money balances, which include currency in circulation and checkable deposits.

In the second half of the chapter we incorporate aggregate supply to model more completely the macroeconomy. Specifically, an aggregate production function and labor market are included and two key endogenous variables, labor employment and the aggregate price level, are added.

AN IS-LM MODEL

Below we set forth the equations of an *IS-LM* Model, which consists of two markets, the product and money markets, and two key variables, real national output (real national income) and the nominal rate of interest. We still abstract from aggregate supply constraints—so the *IS-LM* Model is, like the Simple Keynesian Model, demand-determined. Consequently, the aggregate price level is exogenous. Finally, instead of assuming a linear specification, we will write the behavioral equations in general functional form. Later, we will use a linear example of the *IS-LM* model, however, to illustrate an explicit solution.

THE PRODUCT MARKET

As in the Simple Keynesian Model, equilibrium in the product market requires that desired aggregate expenditures on real national output equal the real national output produced. Desired aggregate expenditures, A, are disaggregated into expenditures by households, firms, government, and foreigners: $A = C + I + G + X - M$.

Real personal consumption expenditures, C, are positively related to real disposable personal income, Y_d, and negatively related to the nominal rate of interest, r. Real disposable income is equal to the difference between real national income, Y, and real taxes, $T(Y)$, where real taxes are directly related to real national income. Mathematically,

$$C = C(Y_d, r) = C(Y - T(Y), r)$$

where

$\delta C / \delta Y_d = C_{Y_d} =$ marginal propensity to consume, $0 < C_{Y_d} < 1$

$\delta C / \delta r = C_r =$ interest rate-sensitivity of real personal consumption expenditures, $C_r < 0$

and

$dT/dY = T' =$ marginal rate of taxation, $0 < T' < 1$[1]

Real investment expenditures, I, composed of business fixed investment, residential fixed investment, and inventory investment, are inversely related to the nominal rate of interest, r, and directly related to the exogenous level of business confidence, B_0. While there are other influences on investment spending, we explicitly include in this model the level of business confidence—which can affect both the willingness of firms to invest in new plant, equipment, and machinery and the amount of residential construction undertaken. We will still regard planned inventory investment as given; therefore, any discrepancy between expected sales and actual sales of real national output would be reflected in unplanned inventory investment or disinvestment. Mathematically, we write

$$I = I(r, B_0)$$

where

$\delta I / \delta r = I_r =$ interest rate-sensitivity of real investment expenditures, $I_r < 0$

and

$\delta I / \delta B_0 = I_{B_0} =$ sensitivity of real investment expenditures to the level of business confidence, $I_{B_0} > 0$.

---

[1]Note that we use the prime $(')$ to indicate a first derivative for functions of one variable, $T' = dT/dY$, where $T = T(Y)$. For functions of two or more variables, the partial derivatives are indicated by subscripts, for example, C_{Y_d} and C_r for $\delta C / \delta Y_d$ and $\delta C / \delta r$, respectively, where $C = C(Y_d, r)$.

We continue to assume that real government purchases and real exports of goods and services are exogenous: $G = G_0$ and $X = X_0$. Moreover, like before, real imports of goods and services are directly related to the level of real disposable income:

$$M = M(Y - T(Y))$$

where

$$dM/dY_d = M' = \text{marginal propensity to import}, 0 < M' < C_{Y_d} < 1$$

Summing the components, we get the desired aggregate expenditure schedule,

$$A(Y, r) = C[Y - T(Y), r] + I(r, B_0) + G_0 + X_0 - M[Y - T(Y)]$$

And, in equilibrium, $A(Y, r) \overset{e}{=} Y$.

The *IS* Curve   If we take all of the combinations of real national output (real national income) and the nominal interest rate for which the product market is in equilibrium, we get the *IS* **schedule**.[2]

$$C[Y - T(Y), r] + I(r, B_0) + G_0 + X_0 - M[Y - T(Y)] = Y$$

In Figure 14.1 we sketch the *IS* **curve**. Combinations of real national output and the nominal interest rate on the *IS* curve represent product market equilibrium, where $A(Y, r) = Y$. Points off the *IS* curve indicate a disequilibrium in the product market.

For example, if we begin at point E_1, where $A(Y_1, r_1) = Y_1$, a fall in the interest rate to r_2 would increase desired interest-sensitive expenditures ($r \downarrow \Rightarrow C \uparrow$ and $I \uparrow$). Consequently, there would be an excess demand for goods (EDG), met, at least in part, by a run-down in inventories ($\Delta INV^u < 0$), which induces an increase in real national output produced and real national income earned ($Y \uparrow$). A new product market equilibrium would result at point E_2, where $A(Y_2, r_2) = Y_2$.

Thus, in the product market, there is an inverse relationship between equilibrium values of r and Y. The *IS* curve has a negative slope. In general then, points below the *IS* curve indicate an excess demand for goods and services (EDG); while points above the *IS* curve indicate an excess supply of goods and services (ESG).

---

[2]The label *IS* for the equation indicating product market equilibrium reflects the "Investment = Saving" equilibrium condition for an economy with no government purchases ($G = 0$), no taxes ($T = 0$), and no foreign trade, ($X = M = 0$). That is, in equilibrium, desired aggregate expenditures equal national output: $A = C + I + G + X - M = Y$. Furthermore, the income created in producing the output, Y, can be used for personal consumption, C, private saving, S, and taxes, T: so $Y = C + S + T$. Setting the expenditures on real national output equal to the uses of the real income generated in producing the national output, we get

$$C + I + G + X - M = C + S + T.$$

Subtracting C and adding M to both sides gives:

$$I + G + X = S + T + M$$

This expression represents the "injections = withdrawals" equilibrium condition. That is, product market equilibrium is characterized by the condition that injections into the expenditure stream (from firms, I; government, G; and foreigners, X) must equal withdrawals from the income stream (from savings, S; taxes T; and imports, M). If $G = T = 0$ and $X = M = 0$, then this equilibrium condition reduces to $I = S$.

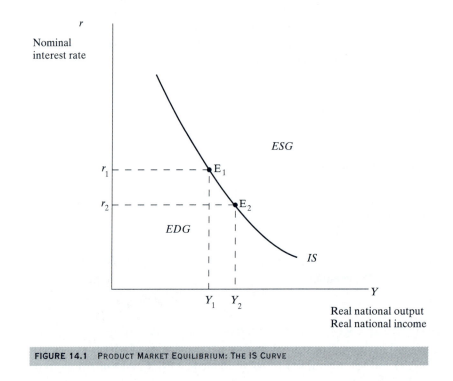

FIGURE 14.1   **PRODUCT MARKET EQUILIBRIUM: THE IS CURVE**

We can demonstrate more rigorously that the *IS* curve has a negative slope, even though we can't "solve" the *IS* schedule for *r* explicitly in terms of *Y*. Return to the equation for the product market equilibrium,

$$C[Y - T(Y), r] + I(r, B_0) + G_0 + X_0 - M[Y - T(Y)] = Y$$

and totally differentiate.

$$C_{Y_d}(dY - T'dY) + C_r\, dr + I_r\, dr + I_{B_0}\, dB + dG_0 + dX_0 - M'(dY - T'dY) = dY$$

Holding constant the exogenous variables, that is, $dB_0 = 0$, $dG_0 = 0$, and $dX_0 = 0$, and isolating the terms involving the differential of the interest rate, dr, on the left-hand side of the equation, we can write

$$(C_r + I_r)\, dr = [1 - (C_{Y_d} - M')(1 - T')]dY$$

The slope of the *IS* curve is given by dr/dY, holding constant real autonomous expenditures:

$$dr/dY\,|_{IS} = \frac{1 - (C_{Y_d} - M')(1 - T')}{C_r + I_r} = \text{slope of the } IS \text{ curve}$$

Since the marginal propensity to import, M', is a positive fraction less than the marginal propensity to consume, C_{Y_d}, which is assumed to be less than one, and the marginal rate of taxation, T', is also a positive fraction less than one, then the numerator,

$1 - (C_{Y_d} - M')(1 - T')$, is positive. Indeed, you might recognize $(C_{Y_d} - M')(1 - T')$ as the marginal propensity to spend from the Simple Keynesian Model, $a = (c - m)(1 - t)$. Here, we are not assuming linear consumption, import, and tax functions, so C_{Y_d}, M', and T' need not be constant. The denominator, $C_r + I_r$, is negative, since real consumption and investment expenditures are inversely related to the nominal interest rate. Therefore, we can confirm that the slope of the IS curve is negative.

We will see that the relative effectiveness of fiscal versus monetary policy depends on the slope (steepness) of the IS curve. The key determinants of the slope are the interest rate sensitivities of real consumption and investment expenditures. Monetarists believe that real consumption and investment expenditures are highly sensitive to the cost of credit, thus $|C_r + I_r|$ is "large," making the slope of the IS curve "small" or the IS curve "flat."[3]

Before exploring further the policy implications, we should first discuss the causes of shifts in the IS curve, and then develop the money market. The IS curve is drawn conditional upon not only the marginal propensities to consume and import, the marginal rate of taxation, and the interest sensitivities of real consumption and investment expenditures—all of which affect the slope of the IS curve—but on the level of real autonomous expenditures on national output, that is, on all those expenditures independent of real national income and the nominal interest rate. Here, in this version of an IS-LM Model, real government purchases, G_0, and real exports of goods and services, X_0, are the exogenous expenditures. We have also included an exogenous component for investment spending, dependent on business confidence. Keynesian economists believe that real investment spending, especially business fixed investment, is volatile, and significantly affected by the state of business confidence.[4] Increases in real government purchases, real exports, or business confidence, which stimulates real investment expenditures, will shift the IS curve to the right—increasing the equilibrium level of real national output at any nominal interest rate. Conversely, decreases in autonomous expenditures would shift the IS curve to the left, reducing the equilibrium level of real national output associated with any nominal interest rate.

With two endogenous variables, Y and r, and only one equation, the IS schedule representing product market equilibrium, there would be an infinite number of solutions to the model. Any combination of the nominal interest rate and real national output on the IS curve represents product market equilibrium. For a unique solution to the IS-LM model, we need to add a second equation—one representing the money market.

---

[3]There is not much controversy over the magnitudes of the marginal propensities to consume or import, or over the marginal rate of taxation. The controversy has centered on the interest rate sensitivities and the magnitude of the denominator of the slope of the IS schedule.

[4]Keynesian economists, or economists who subscribe to Keynesian macroeconomic theory, believe that the economy does not necessarily stabilize at full employment in the short run. Thus, they favor demand-management policies to offset significant shocks to aggregate demand, e.g., shifts in business confidence or consumer spending.

THE MONEY MARKET

In this model, by money, we mean the most narrow definition of the aggregate money supply, $M1$, which consists of currency in circulation (i.e., outside of the vaults of banks) and checkable deposits (i.e., funds held in banks and other depository institutions on which checks can be written to transfer the funds to designated parties). Economic agents, whether households, firms, or government agencies, must choose the composition of their financial assets—generally trading off liquidity for income-earning potential. The **liquidity** of an asset, for example, money, bonds, and stocks, refers to the ease with which the asset can be transferred into a medium of exchange, or a form readily acceptable as a means of payment, without a loss in value. Money is the most liquid of all assets; since money represents immediate purchasing power.

The Demand for Money and the Supply of Money   The demand for real money balances is directly related to the level of real income. As expenditures rise with income, so will the **transactions demand for money** to serve as a medium of exchange.

The opportunity cost of liquidity, however, is the income foregone if wealth were held in a less liquid form, for example, the interest on bonds or saving accounts and dividends on stocks. In general, as the rate of interest rises, individuals will attempt to conserve on money balances and hold more of their financial wealth in less liquid assets until needed for transactions. Keynes added a second reason for the inverse relationship between the quantity demanded of money balances and the rate of interest, which he termed the **speculative demand for money**. Individuals may desire to hold money balances—in excess of those deemed necessary for transactions purposes—in order to take advantage of expected changes in the prices of assets.

We illustrate with bonds. Consider a bond with a 1-year maturity, where

FV = face value of the bond, that is, the denomination of the bond, which is set when the bond is first issued, but not received by the holder of the bond until the bond matures.

INT = interest payment (if any) on the bond, that is, an additional sum, also set when the bond is first issued, but not received until maturity.

d = fraction of the year left before the bond matures, $0 \le d \le 1$. If $d = 1$, the bond is newly issued. If $d = 0$, the bond is at maturity.

P_b = current market price of the bond, that is, the present value of the bond.

r = current market rate of interest, assumed to be indicative of the rate of return that could be earned on comparable assets.

The price of a bond is equal to

$$P_b = \frac{FV + INT}{1 + (d)(r)}$$

For a given face value (FV) and interest payment (INT) on a bond with a 1-year maturity, and at a given point within the year (d), there is an inverse relationship between the price of the bond and the rate of interest. Consider some simple examples. Assume that: $FV = \$10,000$, $INT = \$500$, and $d = 1$ (i.e., a newly issued bond).

$$\text{If } r = .04, \text{ then } P_b = \frac{10,000 + 500}{1 + (1)(.04)} = \$10,096$$

Here the bond sells for a premium when first issued, since its price exceeds its face value.

$$\text{If } r = .05, \text{ then } P_b = \frac{10,000 + 500}{1 + (1)(.05)} = \$10,000$$

$$\text{If } r = .06, \text{ then } P_b = \frac{10,000 + 500}{1 + (1)(.06)} = \$9,906$$

Here the bond sells for a discount when first issued, since its price is less than its face value.

Now, if the bond had been issued 9 months earlier, leaving 3 months until maturity, so $d = .25$, then

$$\text{If } r = .04, \text{ then } P_b = \frac{10,000 + 500}{1 + (.25)(.04)} = \$10,396$$

$$\text{If } r = .05, \text{ then } P_b = \frac{10,000 + 500}{1 + (.25)(.05)} = \$10,370$$

$$\text{If } r = .06, \text{ then } P_b = \frac{10,000 + 500}{1 + (.25)(.06)} = \$10,345$$

Note that as the bond approaches maturity, $d \to 0$, the price of the bond approaches the payoff, that is, the sum of the face value and interest payment.

Speculators attempt to invest in assets that they expect to rise in value or appreciate. If successful in "buying low and selling high," speculators then realize a capital gain. In the case of bonds that can be traded or resold before maturity, speculators seek to time their purchases for when interest rates have peaked, thus bond prices are the lowest. The speculative demand for money refers to the money balances held ready to purchase bonds when interest rates have peaked. Since opinions differ exactly when this will happen, a rise in interest rates and fall in bond prices, in general, will lead to a reduction in money balances as speculators are shifting into bonds in hopes of a future appreciation—if interest rates subsequently reverse direction. The speculative demand for money can be extended to include any money balances held for the purpose of quickly purchasing less liquid assets when there is a potential for appreciation.

We write the demand for real money balances as a general function,

$$L = L(Y, r)$$

where L = quantity demanded of real money balances, that is, currency in circulation plus checkable deposits adjusted for the aggregate price level

and $\delta L/\delta Y = L_Y$ = sensitivity of the quantity demanded of real money balances to real income, $0 < L_Y < 1$

$\delta L/\delta r = L_r$ = sensitivity of the quantity demanded of real money balances to the nominal interest rate, $L_r < 0$

The LM Curve   We will assume that the nominal money supply, M^S, is set by the monetary authorities or the central bank (the Federal Reserve in the case of the U.S. economy), so $M^S = M_0^S$. The aggregate price level, P, is regarded as exogenous in the *IS-LM* Model: $P = P_0$. The condition for money market equilibrium is that the quantity demanded of real money balances equals the real money supply: $L(Y, r) \overset{e}{=} M_0^S/P_0$. The combinations of real national income, Y, and the nominal interest rate, r, that equilibrate the money market represent the **LM schedule**.[5]

An example of the **LM curve** is illustrated in Figure 14.2. Any combination of real national income and nominal interest rate on the *LM* curve yields a demand for real money balances equal to the given real money supply. Combinations off the curve thus indicate disequilibria in the money market. For example, for the combination, E_1, we have $L(Y_1, r_1) = M_0^S/P_0$. If real national income rises to Y_2, the demand for money would increase (for transactions purposes to finance the greater expenditures made possible by the higher income). The increase in the demand for money creates an excess demand for money (*EDM*), which, for a given real money supply, would have to be eliminated by a rise in the nominal rate of interest.

To elaborate, individuals may satisfy their excess demand for money by selling bonds (representing less liquid assets in general). The greater willingness to sell bonds increases the supply of bonds on the market, lowering the market price of bonds and raising the interest rate. The higher interest rate reduces the quantity demanded of money back to the given real money supply. The combination represented by point E_2 gives another possible equilibrium in the money market: $L(Y_2, r_2) = M_0^S/P_0$.

We have demonstrated a positive relationship between real national income and the nominal interest rate in maintaining equilibrium in the money market. The *LM* curve has a positive slope. Before formally deriving the expression for the slope of the *LM* curve, we should note that just as points to the right or below the *LM* curve indicate an excess demand for money (*EDM*), points to the left or above the *LM* curve indicate an excess supply of money (*ESM*).

---

[5]The L in the *LM* schedule stands for liquidity preference, or the desire to hold wealth in the most liquid form, that is, as money balances. The M stands for money supply.

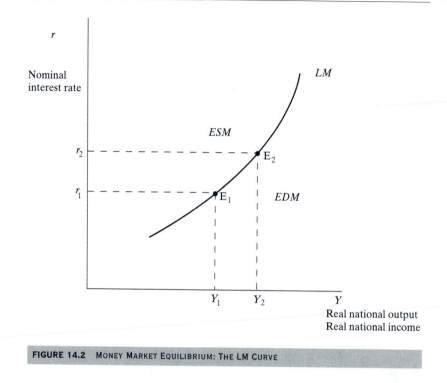

FIGURE 14.2   MONEY MARKET EQUILIBRIUM: THE LM CURVE

Even with our general functional form for the demand for money, $L = L(Y, r)$, we can derive the expression for the slope of the LM curve by differentiating the equilibrium condition for the money market: $L(Y, r) = M_0^S/P_0$. Totally differentiating, we have

$$(\delta L/\delta Y)\, dY + (\delta L/\delta r)\, dr = \frac{dM_0^S \cdot P_0 - M_0^S\, dP_0}{(P_0)^2}$$

or

$$L_Y\, dY + L_r\, dr = dM_0^S/P_0 - (M_0^S/P_0)(dP_0/P_0)$$

Holding constant the nominal money supply and the aggregate price level, $dM_0^S = 0$ and $dP_0 = 0$, we have $L_Y\, dY + L_r\, dr = 0$.

Solving for dr/dY, which expresses the slope of the LM curve, we find

$$dr/dY\,|_{LM} = -L_Y/L_r > 0 \quad \text{since } 0 < L_Y < 1 \quad \text{and } L_r < 0$$

The key partial derivative in explaining the slope of the LM curve is the interest-sensitivity of the demand for real money balances, L_r. Monetarists believe that the demand for real money balances is fairly insensitive to the interest rate, that is, $|L_r|$ is "small," making the LM curve "steep." In the extreme, if $|L_r| = 0$, the LM curve would be vertical.

The *LM* curve is drawn holding constant the real money supply. Any change in the nominal money supply or the aggregate price level would shift the *LM* curve. For example, an increase in the real money supply (with $\Delta M_0^S > 0$ or $\Delta P_0 < 0$) would create an excess supply of money at any level of real national income and reduce the corresponding equilibrium level of the nominal interest rate: the *LM* curve would shift down (or to the right). Conversely, a decrease in the real money supply (with $\Delta M_0^S < 0$ or $\Delta P_0 > 0$) would result in an excess demand for money at any level of real national income and require a higher corresponding equilibrium level of the nominal interest rate: the *LM* curve would shift up (or to the left).

GENERAL EQUILIBRIUM IN THE IS-LM MODEL

The equations for our *IS-LM* Model are listed in Figure 14.3. There are two equilibrium conditions: the product and money market equilibriums (*IS* and *LM* schedules); and two key endogenous variables: real national output (real national income), Y, and the nominal rate of interest, r. General equilibrium requires equilibrium in all of the markets of the model. In the *IS-LM* Model, we need to find the combination of real national output and the nominal interest rate that simultaneously equilibrates the product and money markets. That is, desired aggregate expenditures on real national output, $A(Y, r)$, must equal the real national output produced, Y; and the demand for real money balances, $L(Y, r)$, must equal the real money supply, M_0^S/P_0.

In Figure 14.4, the general equilibrium is indicated by the intersection of the *IS* and *LM* curves. At the common point, E_0, we have both markets clearing: $A(\overline{Y}_0, \overline{r}_0) = \overline{Y}_0$, and $L(\overline{Y}_0, \overline{r}_0) = M_0^S/P_0$. The four regions of disequilibrium are delineated, where

   EDG = excess demand for goods and services (real national output)
   ESG = excess supply of goods and services (real national output)
   EDM = excess demand for real money balances
   ESM = excess supply of real money balances

FIGURE 14.3   EQUATIONS OF THE IS-LM MODEL

$C = C(Y - T(Y), r)$	$0 < C_{Y_d} < 1, C_r < 0$	Real Personal Consumption Expenditures
$I = I(r, B_0)$	$I_r < 0, I_{B_0} > 0$	Real Investment Expenditures
$G = G_0$		Real Government Purchases
$X = X_0$		Real Exports of Goods and Services
$M = M(Y - T(Y))$	$0 < M' < C_{Y_d} < 1$	Real Imports of Goods and Services
$Y_d \equiv Y - T$		Real Disposable Income
$T = T(Y)$	$0 < T' < 1$	Real Taxes
$A \equiv C + I + G + X - M$		Desired Real Aggregate Expenditures on National Output
$L = L(Y, r)$	$0 < L_Y < 1, L_r < 0$	Demand for Real Money Balances
$M^S = M_0^S$		Nominal Money Supply
$P = P_0$		Aggregate Price Level
$A(Y, r) \stackrel{e}{=} Y$		PRODUCT MARKET EQUILIBRIUM: *IS* Schedule
$L(Y, r) \stackrel{e}{=} M_0^S/P_0$		MONEY MARKET EQUILIBRIUM: *LM* Schedule

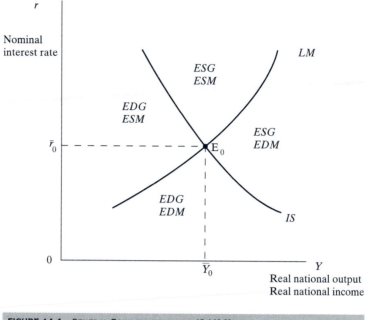

FIGURE 14.4   GENERAL EQUILIBRIUM IN THE IS-LM MODEL

For example, the region to the right of the intersection of the *IS* and *LM* curves represents an excess supply of goods (*ESG*) and an excess demand for money (*EDM*). Disequilibrium in one or both markets will lead to adjustments in both markets until general equilibrium is restored.

In the Keynesian model, general equilibrium need not occur at a level of real national output that is consistent with full employment of the labor force—one of the three primary macroeconomic objectives, along with price stability and healthy growth in real national output.

Consequently, some economists advocate the use of fiscal and monetary policy to demand-manage the economy consistent with the attainment of macroeconomic goals. Since inflation or deflation (changes in the aggregate price level) and economic growth rates are not represented adequately by the *IS-LM* Model, we will focus here on changes in real national output which would be directly related to changes in employment and inversely related to the unemployment rate for a given labor force. Later in this chapter we will extend the *IS-LM* analysis to include endogenous changes in the aggregate price level.

Before doing comparative static analysis with this general *IS-LM* Model, we will illustrate the solution of the equilibrium with a numerical example. For ease of manipulation, we adopt a linear specification. Moreover, we will build on the Simple Keynesian Model illustrated in Chapter 13. Desired real investment expenditures, however, now are a function of the nominal rate of interest, and a money market is added. The equations of this *IS-LM* Model are listed below.

$$C = 55 + .75Y_d - 3r \qquad \text{real personal consumption expenditures}$$
$$I = 140 - 6r \qquad \text{real investment expenditures}$$
$$G_0 = 180 \qquad \text{real government purchases of goods and ser-}$$
vices
$$X_0 = 100 \qquad \text{real exports of goods and services}$$
$$M = 10 + .25Y_d \qquad \text{real imports of goods and services}$$
$$Y_d \equiv Y - T \qquad \text{real disposable income}$$
$$T = .20Y \qquad \text{real taxes}$$
$$A \equiv C + I + G + X - M \qquad \text{desired real aggregate expenditures on}$$
national output
$$L = .2Y - 10r \qquad \text{demand for real money balances}$$
$$M_0^S = 90 \qquad \text{nominal money supply}$$
$$P_0 = 1.0 \qquad \text{aggregate price level}$$
$$A(Y, r) \overset{e}{=} Y \qquad \text{product market equilibrium (\textit{IS} Schedule)}$$
$$L(Y, r) \overset{e}{=} M_0^S/P_0 \qquad \text{money market equilibrium (\textit{LM} Schedule)}$$

To begin, we write the consumption and import functions in terms of real national income, Y, instead of real disposable income, Y_d.

$$Y_d = Y - T = Y - .20Y = .80Y$$

$$C = 55 + .75Y_d - 3r = 55 + .75(.80Y) - 3r = 55 + .6Y - 3r$$

$$M = 10 + .25Y_d = 10 + .25(.80Y) = 10 + .2Y$$

Setting up the desired aggregate expenditure schedule and simplifying, we have

$$A = C + I + G + X - M$$

$$A = 55 + .6Y - 3r + 140 - 6r + 180 + 100 - 10 - .2Y$$

$$A = 465 + .4Y - 9r$$

Now, consistent with the product market equilibrium condition, we equate desired real aggregate expenditures on national output with the national output produced.

$$A = 465 + .4Y - 9r = Y$$

Isolating Y gives us the equation for the IS schedule

$$465 + .4Y - 9r = Y$$

$$.6Y = 465 - 9r$$

$$Y = \frac{465 - 9r}{.6}$$

Note that we could have also isolated r and obtained an equivalent expression for the IS schedule:

$$r = \frac{465 - .6Y}{9}.$$

For the derivation of the *LM* schedule, we begin with the money market equilibrium condition: $L(Y, r) = .2Y - 10r = 90 = 90/1 = M_0^S/P_0$

Isolating *Y* gives us the equation for the *LM* schedule.

$$.2Y - 10r = 90$$

$$Y = 450 + 50r$$

Note, here too, we could have isolated *r*, obtaining an equivalent expression for the *LM* schedule:

$$r = \frac{90 + .2Y}{10}$$

We can solve this system of two equations in two endogenous variables by directly setting the *IS* and *LM* schedules equal.

$$Y = \frac{465 - 9r}{.6} = 450 + 50r$$

Now we have one equation in one variable, *r*, which can be easily solved.

$$465 - 9r = 270 + 30r$$

$$195 = 39r$$

$$\bar{r}_0 = 5.0$$

Substituting the equilibrium value for the nominal interest rate, $\bar{r}_0$, back into either the *IS* or *LM* equations, we obtain the equilibrium value for real national output and real national income, $\bar{Y}_0$.

$$\bar{Y}_0 = \frac{465 - 9(5.0)}{.6} = 450 + 50(5) = 700$$

In sum, the real national output and nominal interest rate that simultaneously equilibrate the product and money markets are: $\bar{Y}_0 = 700$ and $\bar{r}_0 = 5.0$. As a final note, these equilibrium values are conditional on the given values of the exogenous variables (e.g., real exports and the nominal money supply) and parameters (e.g., the marginal propensity to consume and the interest sensitivity of the quantity demanded of real money balances). If any of the exogenous variables or parameters change, then the general equilibrium would be upset and the product and money markets would begin adjustment to a new equilibrium.

PRACTICE PROBLEM 14.1

In the numerical example of an *IS-LM* Model just illustrated, suppose that the investment function were instead $I' = 140 - 5r$ and that the nominal money supply instead equaled $M_0^{s'} = 95$. All the other equations, exogenous variables, and parameters of the model are the same.

a) Derive the *IS* schedule.

b) Derive the *LM* schedule.

c) Find the equilibrium real national output and nominal interest rate.

Note: Carry your calculations out to the thousandth place, then round off your answers to the nearest hundredth place.

(The answers are at the end of the chapter.)

COMPARATIVE STATICS: DEMAND-MANAGEMENT POLICY

There are two basic types of demand-management economic policy. **Fiscal policy**, formulated in the U.S. economy by the President and the Congress, refers to discretionary changes in government expenditures and taxes intended to alter the level (and composition) of aggregate demand. In the *IS-LM* Model, fiscal policy changes affect the *IS* curve. In this general version of the *IS-LM* Model, fiscal policy is limited to changes in real government purchases (ΔG_0); in the earlier linear Simple Keynesian Model, changes in the marginal rate of taxation (Δt) provided another instrument.

Monetary policy, conducted by the Central Bank (the Federal Reserve in the United States), refers to discretionary changes in the money supply intended to alter the level (and composition) of aggregate demand. Changes in the money supply shift the *LM* curve. There are three basic instruments of monetary policy: changes in the **required reserve ratio** (the minimum percentage of checkable deposits that banks must hold as **reserves**, that is, either as cash in their vaults or deposits at the Federal Reserve Bank); changes in the **discount rate** (the rate of interest the Federal Reserve charges banks on the loan of reserves); and **open market operations** (the Federal Reserve's purchase or sale of previously-issued, but yet-to-mature, U.S. government securities or bonds, which injects or withdraws reserves from the banking system). Through changes in the money supply, the Federal Reserve (the Fed) can influence the rate of interest and, indirectly, interest-sensitive expenditures like consumer durables and business and residential fixed investments. We will focus on the third instrument of monetary policy, the Fed's open market purchase or sale of U.S. government bonds.

Fiscal Policy   Consider expansionary fiscal policy, in particular, an increase in real government purchases. We will illustrate the effects on the equilibrium verbally, graphically, and then mathematically. Assume the economy begins in general equilibrium, where both the product and money markets clear. See point E_0 in Figure 14.5, with $\overline{Y}_0$ and $\overline{r}_0$ as the equilibrium levels of real national output and the nominal rate of interest.

The increase in real government purchases creates an excess demand for goods and services, that initially might be met, in part or entirely, by a reduction in inventories. Firms would increase production. Real national output and real national income would rise, inducing additional spending through the multiplier effect. The *IS* curve shifts right to *IS'*, and holding constant the nominal rate of interest, real national output would increase by a multiple of the increase in autonomous government pur-

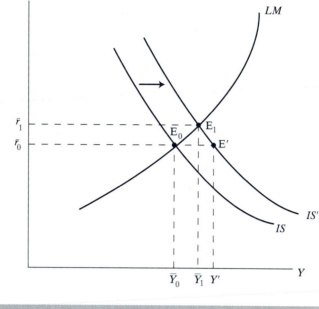

FIGURE 14.5   AN INCREASE IN GOVERNMENT EXPENDITURES: IS-LM MODEL

chases. In the Simple Keynesian Model developed earlier in Chapter 13, $\Delta Y = Y' - \overline{Y}_0 = K_{A_0} \cdot \Delta G_0 = (1/1 - a)\, \Delta G_0$, where a is the marginal propensity to spend.

In the *IS-LM* Model, however, the multiplier effect is modified. The excess demand for goods and services and induced rise in real national income increase the quantity demanded of real money balances (L), which, for a given real money supply, yields an excess demand for money. Seeking to increase their liquidity, individuals sell assets, here, bonds. The increase in the willingness to sell bonds drives the price of bonds down and the interest rate up.[6] The higher interest rate discourages interest-sensitive expenditures (consumer durables and investment), which moderates the excess demand for goods and the increase in real national output and income.

In Figure 14.5, the new equilibrium is at E_1, with $\overline{Y}_1 > \overline{Y}_0$ and $\overline{r}_1 > \overline{r}_0$. The multiplier effect is smaller in the *IS-LM* Model—due to the crowding-out of interest-sensitive expenditures with the expansion of the economy from the initial increase in government purchases. With a flow chart, the sequence of changes are illustrated.

$$G_0 \uparrow \Rightarrow A \uparrow \Rightarrow EDG \Rightarrow \Delta INV^u < 0 \Rightarrow Y \uparrow \Rightarrow L \uparrow \Rightarrow EDM \Rightarrow \text{individuals sell bonds}$$

$$\Rightarrow P_b \downarrow \Rightarrow r \uparrow \Rightarrow C \downarrow \text{ and } I \downarrow \Rightarrow A \downarrow \text{ some and } Y \downarrow \text{ some.}$$

On net, $\Delta G_0 > 0$ results in $\Delta \overline{Y} > 0$ and $\Delta \overline{r} > 0$.

---

[6]Note, if the increase in government purchases increased the government budget deficit, then the government would also have to sell bonds to finance its excess expenditures.

Mathematically, the partial derivatives, $\delta \overline{Y}/\delta G_0$ and $\delta \overline{r}/\delta G_0$, represent the (instantaneous) effects of an (infinitesimal) change in real government purchases on the equilibrium levels of real national output and the nominal interest rate, respectively. But how can we find these partial derivatives when, as in this general model, we cannot solve explicitly for the equilibrium values of $\overline{Y}$ and $\overline{r}$ in terms of the exogenous variables in the system? Recall from Chapter 10 the Implicit Function Theorem for a system of equations, which allows us to do comparative statics even when the endogenous variables cannot be explicitly expressed in terms of the exogenous variables of the model.

In the *IS-LM* Model, the two simultaneous equations are the *IS* and *LM* schedules, representing the product and money market equilibrium conditions. The key endogenous variables are real national output, Y, and the nominal interest rate, r. The exogenous variables are real government purchases, G_0; the level of business confidence, B_0, real exports of goods and services, X_0; the nominal money supply, M_0^S, and the aggregate price level, P_0.

Applying the Implicit Function Theorem, we assume that the following two equations:

$$F^1\ (Y, r; G_0, B_0, X_0, M_0^S, P_0) = 0 \qquad (IS \text{ schedule})$$

$$F^2\ (Y, r; G_0, B_0, X_0, M_0^S, P_0) = 0 \qquad (LM \text{ schedule})$$

which can be written as

$$F^1:\quad C[Y - T(Y), r] + I(r, B_0) + G_0 + X_0 - M[Y - T(Y)] - Y = 0$$

$$F^2:\quad L(Y, r) - M_0^S/P_0 = 0$$

have continuous partial derivatives, and at the general equilibrium point, the associated Jacobian is nonsingular. Thus, implicit functions

$$f^1:\quad \overline{Y} = f^1\ (G_0, B_0, X_0, M_0^S, P_0)$$

$$f^2:\quad \overline{r} = f^2\ (G_0, B_0, X_0, M_0^S, P_0)$$

are defined. We can then proceed to do comparative static experiments.

Totally differentiating the equilibrium conditions evaluated at the initial equilibrium, $(\overline{Y}, \overline{r})$, we have

$$C_{Y_d}(d\overline{Y} - T'd\overline{Y}) + C_r\,d\overline{r} + I_r\,d\overline{r} + I_{B_0}\,dB_0 + dG_0 + dX_0 - M'(d\overline{Y} - T'd\overline{Y}) - d\overline{Y} = 0$$

and

$$L_Y\,dY + L_r\,dr - \frac{(dM_0^S \cdot P_0 - M_0^S dP_0)}{(P_0)^2} = 0$$

Simplifying and moving the exogenous changes to the right-hand side of the equations gives

$$[1 - (C_{Y_d} - M')(1 - T')]d\overline{Y} - (C_r + I_r)\,d\overline{r} = I_{B_0}\,dB_0 + dG_0 + dX_0$$

and

$$L_Y \, d\overline{Y} + L_r \, d\overline{r} = dM_0^S/P_0 - (M_0^S/P_0)(dP_0/P_0)$$

Arranging in matrix notation yields

$$\begin{bmatrix} 1 - (C_{Y_d} - M')(1 - T') & -(C_r + I_r) \\ L_Y & L_r \end{bmatrix} \begin{bmatrix} d\overline{Y} \\ d\overline{r} \end{bmatrix} = \begin{bmatrix} I_{B_0} dB_0 + dG_0 + dX_0 \\ dM_0^S/P_0 - (M_0^S/P_0)(dP_0/P_0) \end{bmatrix}$$

We can find any comparative static result of interest, here, $\delta\overline{Y}/\delta G_0$, by using Cramer's rule and holding constant all other exogenous variables, that is, $dB_0 = dX_0 = dM_0^S = dP_0 = 0$. As part of the solution, and to verify that the two equations (representing the product and money market equilibria) are functionally independent, we find the Jacobian, $|J|$, which is the determinant of the coefficient matrix of partial derivatives.

$$|J| = \begin{vmatrix} 1 - (C_{Y_d} - M')(1 - T') & -(C_r + I_r) \\ L_Y & L_r \end{vmatrix}$$

$$= [1 - (C_{Y_d} - M')(1 - T')]L_r + L_Y (C_r + I_r)$$

$|J| < 0$, since $(C_{Y_d} - M')(1 - T') < 1$, $L_r < 0$; and $L_Y > 0$, $(C_r + I_r) < 0$. So, we have established that $|J| \neq 0$ and the *IS* and *LM* schedules are functionally independent. Applying Cramer's rule, we solve for $\overline{Y}$.

$$d\overline{Y} = \frac{\begin{vmatrix} dG_0 & -(C_r + I_r) \\ 0 & L_r \end{vmatrix}}{|J|} = \frac{dG_0 L_r}{|J|}$$

Dividing through by dG_0 and converting to a partial derivative, since all the other exogenous changes are held constant, we have

$$\delta\overline{Y}/\delta G_0 = \frac{L_r}{|J|} > 0 \quad \text{(since } L_r < 0 \text{ and } |J| < 0\text{)}$$

As demonstrated graphically and explained verbally, the effect of a change in real government purchases on equilibrium real national output, *ceteris paribus,* is positive. In fact, we have derived the expression for the government expenditure multiplier in this *IS-LM* Model.

$$\delta\overline{Y}/\delta G_0 = \frac{L_r}{|J|} = \frac{L_r}{[1 - (C_{Y_d} - M')(1 - T')]L_r + L_Y(C_r + I_r)}$$

Dividing numerator and denominator by L_r, we can more easily compare with the Simple Keynesian government expenditure multiplier, $K_{A_0} = \dfrac{1}{1 - a} = \dfrac{1}{1 - (c - m)(1 - t)}$.

$$\delta\overline{Y}/\delta G_0 = \frac{1}{1 - (C_{Y_d} - M')(1 - T') + \dfrac{L_Y (C_r + I_r)}{L_r}}$$

Other than the general functional form used for the *IS-LM* Model (compared with the linear specification used for the Simple Keynesian Model), the difference is the addition of the positive term $\dfrac{L_Y (C_r + I_r)}{L_r}$ in the denominator, which reduces the multiplier effect in the *IS-LM* Model.

Effectiveness of Fiscal Policy   We can see that the size of the government expenditure multiplier depends directly on the magnitude of the interest-sensitivity of money demand, $|L_r|$, and inversely on the magnitude of the interest-sensitivities of real consumption and real investment expenditures, $|C_r + I_r|$.[7] Expressed in terms of the slopes of the *IS* and *LM* curves, we can say that fiscal policy is more effective, that is, $\delta \overline{Y}/\delta G_0$ is larger, the flatter the *LM* curve (indicated by a larger value for $|L_r|$), and the steeper the *IS* curve (indicated by a smaller value for $|C_r + I_r|$).

Recall that an increase in real government purchases creates not only an excess demand for goods, but an excess demand for money. For a given real money supply, how far the interest rate must rise to reequilibrate the money market depends inversely on the interest-sensitivity of money demand, $|L_r|$. If the demand for real money balances is very interest-sensitive, $|L_r|$ is large, then only a small increase in the nominal interest rate is required. Moreover, how much any increase in the interest rate will reduce desired aggregate expenditures depends directly on the interest-sensitivities of real consumption and real investment $|C_r + I_r|$. If consumption and investment expenditures are not very sensitive to the interest rate, then the increase in real national output and real national income from the higher government purchases will not be offset much.

Monetarists believe that the demand for real money balances is rather interest-insensitive, $|L_r|$ is small, but that real consumption and investment expenditures are quite interest-sensitive, $|C_r + I_r|$ is large. Consequently, an increase in real government purchases "crowds out" or reduces almost an equivalent amount of interest-sensitive expenditures. Accordingly, Monetarists hold that fiscal policy is ineffective, that is, $\delta \overline{Y}/\delta G_0$, representing the government expenditure multiplier, approaches zero. Moreover, in general, a change in autonomous expenditures would not have a significant effect on real national output in the Monetarist model.

Before we discuss monetary policy in the *IS-LM* Model, we should calculate the effect of a change in real government purchases on the equilibrium nominal interest rate, $\delta \overline{r}/\delta G_0$. Returning to the system of comparative statics represented in matrix notation,

$$\begin{bmatrix} 1 - (C_{Y_d} - M')(1 - T') & -(C_r + I_r) \\ L_Y & L_r \end{bmatrix} \begin{bmatrix} d\overline{Y} \\ d\overline{r} \end{bmatrix} = \begin{bmatrix} I_{B_0} dB_0 + dG_0 + dX_0 \\ dM_0^S/P_0 - (M_0^S/P_0)(dP_0/P_0) \end{bmatrix}$$

---

[7]The marginal propensity to spend, $(C_{Y_d} - M')(1 - T')$ and the sensitivity of real money demand to real income, L_Y, are also directly and inversely related, respectively, to the size of the government expenditure multiplier, $\delta \overline{Y}/\delta G_0$. The magnitudes of the interest-sensitivities, however, are the more controversial and uncertain.

We now solve for $d\bar{r}$, holding constant all other exogenous changes except dG_0. Applying Cramer's rule, we have

$$d\bar{r} = \frac{\begin{vmatrix} 1 - (C_{Y_d} - M')(1 - T') & dG_0 \\ L_Y & 0 \end{vmatrix}}{|J|} = \frac{L_Y \, dG_0}{|J|}$$

Dividing through by dG_0 and expressing as a partial derivative, we find

$$\delta\bar{r}/\delta G_0 = \frac{-L_Y}{|J|} > 0 \qquad (\text{since } L_Y > 0 \text{ and } |J| < 0)$$

That is, as expected, an increase (a decrease) in real government purchases would increase (decrease) the equilibrium nominal rate of interest.

PRACTICE PROBLEM 14.2

Return to the initial numerical example of an *IS-LM* Model in this chapter, where the investment schedule is $I = 140 - 6r$ and the nominal money supply is $M_0^S = 90$. Recall that the *IS* and *LM* schedules were $Y = (465 - 9r)/.6$ and $Y = 450 + 50r$, respectively. The equilibrium real national output and nominal interest rate were $\bar{Y}_0 = 700$ and $\bar{r}_0 = 5.0$

a) Find the impact on the equilibrium real national output and the nominal interest rate from a decrease of 10 in real government purchases of goods and services, that is, $\Delta G_0 = -10$.

b) What is the implied government expenditure multiplier for this *IS-LM* Model? How does this compare with the government expenditure multiplier in the underlying Simple Keynesian Model where we ignore the interest rate effect?

Note: Carry out your calculations to the nearest thousandth place and then round off your answers to the nearest hundredth place.

(The answers are at the end of the chapter.)

Monetary Policy Similarly, we can use the above system to examine the effects of a change in the money supply on equilibrium real national output and the nominal interest rate. We will derive the comparative static results, then illustrate graphically and discuss the transition to a new equilibrium.

Consider the effect of a change in the nominal money supply on the equilibrium level of real national output, $\delta\bar{Y}/\delta M_0^S$. Solving for $d\bar{Y}$, holding constant all the other exogenous changes ($dB_0 = dG_0 = dX_0 = dP_0 = 0$), we have, with Cramer's rule,

$$d\bar{Y} = \frac{\begin{vmatrix} 0 & -(C_r + I_r) \\ dM_0^S/P_0 & L_r \end{vmatrix}}{|J|} = \frac{(C_r + I_r)dM_0^S/P_0}{|J|}$$

Dividing through by dM_0^S and expressing as a partial derivative gives

$$\delta\bar{Y}/\delta M_0^S = \frac{(1/P_0)(C_r + I_r)}{|J|} > 0 \qquad (\text{since } C_r < 0, I_r < 0, \text{ and } |J| < 0)$$

Recall that $|J| = [1 - (C_{Y_d} - M')(1 - T')]L_r + (C_r + I_r)L_Y$.

Thus, an increase (a decrease) in the nominal money supply increases (decreases) equilibrium real national output. We can rewrite this money supply multiplier in the *IS-LM* Model as

$$\delta \overline{Y}/\delta M_0^S = \frac{1/P_0}{\dfrac{[1 - (C_{Y_d} - M')(1 - T')]L_r}{C_r + I_r} + L_Y}$$

Effectiveness of Monetary Policy   From money supply multiplier, we can see clearly that monetary policy is more effective, that is, $\delta \overline{Y}/\delta M_0^S$ is larger, and a given change in the nominal money supply has a greater effect on equilibrium real national output: the lower the aggregate price level, P_0; the less sensitive is the real money demand to the interest rate, that is, a smaller $|L_r|$; and the more interest-sensitive are real consumption and investment expenditures, that is, a larger $|C_r + I_r|$.

First, the effect of given change in the nominal money supply on the real money supply is inversely related to the aggregate price level. For instance, an increase of $10 billion in the nominal money supply translates into an increase of $10 billion in the real money supply when the aggregate price level is 1, $P_0 = 1$; but an increase of only $5 billion in the real money supply when the aggregate price level is 2, $P_0' = 2$.

Second, we observe that the conditions under which fiscal policy is less effective (the Monetarist assumptions), make monetary policy more effective: a low interest-sensitivity of real money balances demanded and high interest-sensitivities of real consumption and investment expenditures.[8]

The effect of a change in the nominal money supply on the equilibrium nominal interest rate is given by $\delta \overline{r}/\delta M_0^S$. Solving the system of comparative statics for $d\overline{r}$, holding constant all other exogenous changes except, dM_0^S, we obtain, using Cramer's rule

$$d r = \frac{\begin{vmatrix} 1 - (C_{Y_d} - M')(1 - T') & 0 \\ L_Y & dM_0^S/P_0 \end{vmatrix}}{|J|} = \frac{[1 - (C_{Y_d} - M')(1 - T')]dM_0^S/P_0}{|J|}$$

Converting to the partial derivative, $\delta \overline{r}/\delta M_0^S$, we have

$$\delta \overline{r}/\delta M_0^S = \frac{(1/P_0)[1 - (C_{Y_d} - M')(1 - T')]}{|J|} < 0$$

An increase (decrease) in the nominal money supply, *ceteris paribus*, decreases (increases) the equilibrium nominal rate of interest.

In Figure 14.6 we illustrate the effect of an increase in the nominal money supply on the equilibrium levels of real national output and the nominal interest rate. Beginning in equilibrium at point E_0, suppose the Fed decides to stimulate the economy. Specifically, assume that the Fed engages in open market purchases of U.S. gov-

---

[8]Even so, Monetarists do not advocate demand-management monetary policy due to the lags in policy-making and their belief in the inherent stability of the economy, with its tendency toward full employment.

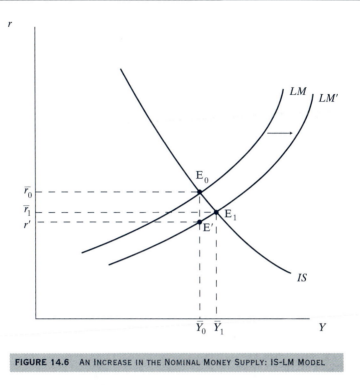

FIGURE 14.6   AN INCREASE IN THE NOMINAL MONEY SUPPLY: IS-LM MODEL

ernment bonds. The increase in the demand for bonds drives up their price and lowers the interest rate. The money supply increases as the Fed pays for its bond purchases with checks, which are deposited in banks, increasing the banks' reserves. Graphically, the *LM* curve shifts to the right with the increase in the money supply. At the initial equilibrium level of real national output, $\overline{Y}_0$, there is now an excess supply of money (*ESM*) and a reduced interest rate (see r'). The lower interest rate stimulates interest-sensitive expenditures (consumer durables and business and residential fixed investment). The increase in desired spending on real national output creates an excess demand for goods, initially met in part or entirely, by a reduction in inventories, leading to greater production. The rise in real national output and income increases the demand for money, which modifies the initial decline in the interest rate. The economy moves to a new equilibrium, indicated by point E_1. The consequences of an increase in the nominal money supply, *ceteris paribus*, are a higher level of real national output and a lower nominal interest rate: $\overline{Y}_1 > \overline{Y}_0$, and $\overline{r}_1 < \overline{r}_0$.

Summarizing the transition to a new equilibrium with a flow chart, we have

$$M_0^S \uparrow \Rightarrow ESM \text{ and } P_b \uparrow \Rightarrow r \downarrow \Rightarrow C \uparrow \text{ and } I \uparrow \Rightarrow A \uparrow \Rightarrow EDG \Rightarrow$$

$$\Delta INV^u < 0 \Rightarrow Y \uparrow \Rightarrow L \uparrow \Rightarrow r \uparrow \text{ a bit.}$$

On net, $\Delta M_0^S > 0$ results in $\Delta \overline{Y} > 0$ and $\Delta \overline{r} < 0$.

For a given change in the nominal money supply, the subsequent changes in equilibrium real national output and the nominal interest rate depend on the interest-sensitivities of money demand, consumption, and investment. A given change in the money supply will have a greater effect on real national output: the less sensitive is the demand for real money balances to the interest rate (the steeper is the *LM* curve) and the more sensitive are real consumption and investment expenditures to the interest rate (the flatter is the IS curve). That is, a larger drop in the interest rate would be required to reequilibrate the money market after the increase in the money supply, and there would be a larger rise in desired spending following the drop in the interest rate.

PRACTICE PROBLEM 14.3

Return to the initial numerical example of the *IS-LM* Model where the *IS* and *LM* schedules are, respectively, $Y = (465 - 9r)/.6$ and $Y = 450 + 50r$. The equilibrium real national output and nominal interest rate are: $\overline{Y}_0 = 700$ and $\overline{r}_0 = 5.0$

a) Find the new equilibrium real national output and nominal interest rate following a decrease of 5 in the nominal money supply, $\Delta M_0^S = -5$, so that the new money supply is $M_0^{S\prime} = 85$.

b) What is the implied money supply multiplier for this *IS-LM* Model? The effectiveness of monetary policy is directly related to which parameters and inversely related to which parameters?

Note: Carry out your calculations to the nearest thousandth place, then round off your answers to the nearest hundredth place.

(The answers are at the end of the chapter.)

In sum, we have illustrated expansionary fiscal policy (here $\Delta G_0 > 0$) and expansionary monetary policy ($\Delta M_0^S > 0$) in the *IS-LM* Model. While both stimulate real national output and income, they differ in their impact on the nominal interest rate and interest-sensitive expenditures. Expansionary fiscal policy drives up the interest rate and crowds out interest-sensitive expenditures. Expansionary monetary policy works by lowering the interest rate and encouraging interest-sensitive expenditures. Note that the effects of contractionary policies would be reversed. Tighter fiscal policy (e.g., $\Delta G_0 < 0$) would result in a lower equilibrium interest rate and real national output. Tighter monetary policy ($\Delta M_0^S < 0$) would result in a higher equilibrium interest rate and lower real national output.

We can do other comparative static experiments in this *IS-LM* Model, illustrating the effect of a change in business confidence which affects investment spending (ΔB_0), or exports (ΔX_0), or the aggregate price level (ΔP_0). The main limitation of the *IS-LM* Model, however, is that the aggregate price level is exogenous. Therefore, we will extend the analysis to incorporate aggregate supply constraints and an endogenous aggregate price level.

PRACTICE PROBLEM 14.4

For the *IS-LM* Model given in Figure 14.3, find and sign the following comparative statics:

a) $\delta \overline{Y}/\delta X_0$ and   b) $\delta \overline{r}/\delta P_0$

(The answers are at the end of the chapter.)

AN AGGREGATE DEMAND-AGGREGATE SUPPLY MODEL

The *IS-LM* Model, like the more basic Simple Keynesian Model, is demand-determined. That is, for a given aggregate price level, general equilibrium is found where desired aggregate expenditures on real national output equal the real national output produced (*IS* schedule) and the demand for real money balances equals the real money supply (*LM* schedule). There are no aggregate supply constraints. Implicitly, any change in desired aggregate expenditures can be met with a corresponding change in real national output produced without any change in the aggregate price level—as if the aggregate supply curve were perfectly elastic.

To extend the analysis and allow for endogenous changes in the aggregate price level, first we will derive an aggregate demand curve, relating the aggregate quantity demanded of real national output to the aggregate price level. Then we will develop an aggregate supply curve, relating the aggregate quantity of real national output supplied or produced to the aggregate price level.

AGGREGATE DEMAND

In the *IS-LM* Model, beginning in equilibrium, a change in the exogenous aggregate price level would affect the real money supply, M_0^S/P_0, and shift the *LM* curve. The resulting disequilibrium in the money market would lead to a change in the nominal interest rate, in turn, affecting interest-sensitive spending and creating a disequilibrium in the product market. The system would move to a new general equilibrium. Thus, we can relate changes in the aggregate price level to changes in the quantity demanded of real national output.

We illustrate mathematically, and then we graphically derive the aggregate demand curve. Return to the system of comparative statics for the *IS-LM* Model, reproduced below.

$$\begin{bmatrix} 1 - (C_{Y_d} - M')(1 - T') & -(C_r + I_r) \\ L_Y & L_r \end{bmatrix} \begin{bmatrix} d\bar{Y} \\ d\bar{r} \end{bmatrix} = \begin{bmatrix} I_{B_0}dB_0 + dG_0 + dX_0 \\ dM_0^S/P_0 - (M_0^S/P_0)(dP_0/P_0) \end{bmatrix}$$

To find the effect of a change in the aggregate price level, dP_0, on the equilibrium level of real national output demanded (and produced) in the *IS-LM* Model, we solve for $d\bar{Y}$, assuming $dB_0 = dG_0 = dX_0 = dM_0^S = 0$. Using Cramer's rule, we have

$$d\bar{Y} = \frac{\begin{bmatrix} 0 & -(C_r + I_r) \\ -(M_0^S/P_0)(dP_0/P_0) & L_r \end{bmatrix}}{|J|} = \frac{-(M_0^S/P_0)(dP_0/P_0)(C_r + I_r)}{|J|}$$

where

$$|J| = [1 - (C_{Y_d} - M')(1 - T')]L_r + (C_r + I_r)L_Y < 0$$

Dividing through by dP_0, and expressing as the comparative static as a partial derivative, we can write

$$\delta \overline{Y}/\delta P_0 = \frac{-(M_0^S/P_0^2)(C_r + I_r)}{|J|} < 0$$

That is, an increase (a decrease) in the aggregate price level, *ceteris paribus*, would decrease (increase) the equilibrium quantity of real national output demanded.

To demonstrate graphically, refer to Figure 14.7. The *IS-LM* equilibrium of Y_0 and r_0, given by point E_0, is conditional upon the price level, P_0, which, along with the nominal money supply, M_0^S, sets the *LM* curve. The corresponding point on the aggregate demand curve, Y^D, is also labeled E_0, with Y_0 and P_0. Now, if the aggregate price level were higher, $P_1 > P_0$, then the real money supply would be lower, $(M_0^S/P_1) < (M_0^S/P_0)$, and the *LM* curve would shift left to $LM(P_1)$. The consequent excess demand for money would lead to a sale of bonds as individuals sought liquidity. The price of bonds would fall and the interest rate would rise. Interest-sensitive consumer durable and investment spending would decline. The economy would move to a new *IS-LM* equilibrium, point E_1, with Y_1 and r_1; and there would be a new point on the aggregate demand curve, Y_1 and P_1. Conversely, a fall in the aggregate price level to P_2 would shift the *LM* curve out, see $LM(P_2)$, and lead to a greater quantity of real national output demanded, Y_2. The corresponding point on the Y^D curve is E_2 with Y_2 and P_2. In short, the aggregate demand curve has a negative slope.

Note that this derivation of the aggregate demand curve, where changes in the aggregate price level are associated with changes in the equilibrium real national output demanded, holds constant all other exogenous factors underlying the *LM* and *IS* curves. For example, at any aggregate price level, a change in the nominal money supply would shift the *LM* and Y^D curves. And, for any aggregate price level, a change in business confidence (B_0), or real government purchases (G_0), or real exports of goods and services (X_0), would shift the *IS* and Y^D curves. In sum, the **aggregate demand curve**, Y^D, relating the aggregate quantity demanded of real national output to the aggregate price level, is drawn holding constant the nominal money supply and the exogenous components of desired aggregate expenditures.[9]

---

[9]Note, changes in the aggregate price level may also affect the quantity demanded of real national output through the *IS* curve. For example, we could write real consumption expenditures as a function of real wealth. Z_0/P_0, where Z_0 is nominal wealth. Real exports and real imports could be written, respectively, as negative and positive functions of the aggregate price level; since, for a given exchange rate, an increase in its aggregate price level would hurt the international competitiveness of a nation. Thus, a rise in the aggregate price level would reduce the quantity demanded of real national output, as personal consumption expenditures declined with real wealth and the nation's trade balance deteriorated.

The higher price level would shift the *IS* curve to the left, further reducing the equilibrium real national output demanded in the *IS-LM* model (but modifying the increase in the equilibrium nominal interest rate) due to the leftward shift in the *LM* curve with the reduction in the real money supply. As a result, the slope of the derived aggregate demand curve would be flatter (i.e., more elastic) when the wealth and international competitive effects of changes in the aggregate price level are incorporated.

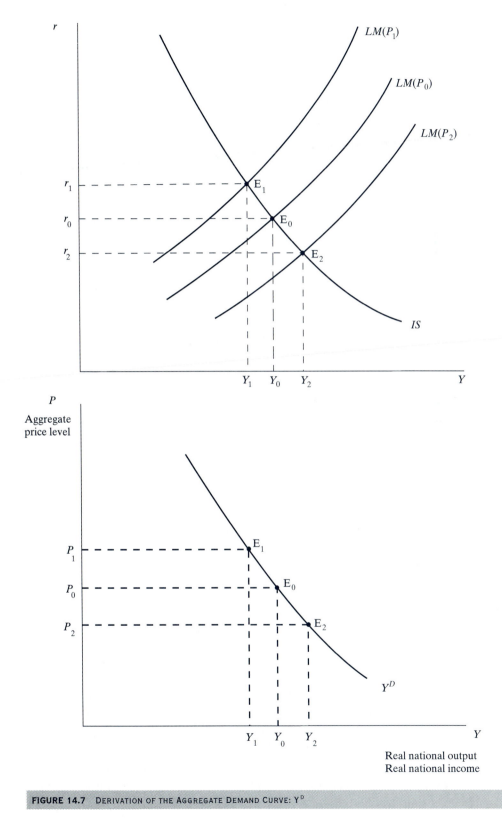

FIGURE 14.7 DERIVATION OF THE AGGREGATE DEMAND CURVE: Y^D

AGGREGATE SUPPLY

Recall from Chapter 6 the short-run production function for a firm, where, for a given technology and fixed capital stock, the firm's output was directly related to the labor it employed. Moreover, in the short run, a firm would experience diminishing returns to labor, that is, eventually the marginal product of labor would decline as employment increased.

Perfectly competitive firms in the output market are price-takers—facing perfectly elastic demand and marginal revenue curves given by the market price for their output. Perfectly competitive firms in the labor market are wage-takers—facing perfectly elastic supply and marginal factor cost of labor curves given by the market wage rate. To maximize profits, a firm would hire labor up to the point where the marginal revenue product of labor (i.e., the change in the firm's total revenues associated with another unit of labor) equals the marginal factor cost of labor (i.e., the change in the firm's total costs associated with another unit of labor). For firms that are perfect competitors in both the product and labor markets, the profit-maximizing decision rule is to equate the value of marginal product of labor (found by multiplying the market price of the firm's output with the firm's marginal product of labor) with the market wage rate.

In a macroeconomic model, we aggregate over the firms in the economy. There is a short-run aggregate production function for real national output,

$$Y = F(K_0, N),$$

where

$$Y = \text{real national output}$$

$$K_0 = \text{fixed capital stock}$$

$$N = \text{employed labor force}$$

Figure 14.8 illustrates a short-run aggregate production function with a positive and strictly concave slope, indicating that diminishing returns to labor set in immediately. That is, the slope of the production function equals the marginal product of labor, $dY/dN = MPN = F_N$. As the level of employment increases, the marginal product of labor declines: $dMPN/dN = d(dY/dN)/dN = d^2Y/dN^2 = F_{NN} < 0$. The curve is drawn for a given physical capital stock, K_0, and technology (reflected in the production function itself). An increase in the physical capital stock, $\Delta K_0 > 0$, would rotate the short-run production function in a counterclockwise direction, increasing the marginal product of labor at every level of employment. Technological progress that raises the productivity of labor would have a similar effect.

With respect to the aggregate labor market, we will assume that the nominal or money wage rate, w, is set in labor contracts, and thus can be considered exogenous in the short run: $w = w_0$. How much of the labor force, N_{LF}, is employed then depends on the demand for labor. The aggregate demand for labor, N^D, is equal to the product of the aggregate price level, P_0, and the marginal product of labor, $MPN = dY/dN$, that

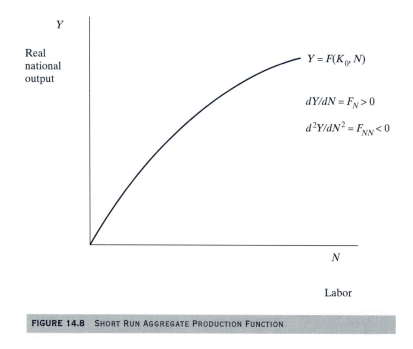

$$Y = F(K_0, N)$$

$$dY/dN = F_N > 0$$

$$d^2Y/dN^2 = F_{NN} < 0$$

Y

Real national output

N

Labor

FIGURE 14.8 SHORT RUN AGGREGATE PRODUCTION FUNCTION

is, $N^D = P_0 \cdot MPN$. Figure 14.9 illustrates this labor market. The equilibrium level of employment is $\overline{N}_0$. We assume there is an excess supply of labor at the exogenous money wage. The difference between the labor force, N_{LF}, and the quantity of labor employed, $\overline{N}_0$, indicates the level of unemployment.[10]

With the aggregate production function and labor market, we can sketch the **aggregate supply curve**, Y^S, which relates the quantity of real national output produced (and supplied) with the aggregate price level. Refer to Figure 14.10. If the price level were P_0, then the labor demand curve is $N^D = P_0 \cdot MPN$, and for the given money wage, w_0, the level of employment is N_0. The real national output produced at this level of labor is Y_0. Thus, one point on the aggregate supply curve is (Y_0, P_0). If the aggregate price level were higher, say $P_1 > P_0$, then for any marginal product of labor, the value of marginal product of labor increases. The relevant labor demand curve is $N^D = P_1 \cdot MPN$. Employment rises to N_1 and real national output produced to Y_1. The associated point on the aggregate supply curve is (Y_1, P_1). Conversely, for a fall in the price level to P_2, the labor demand curve shifts to $N^D = P_2 \cdot MPN$. Employment is N_2 and real national output decreases to Y_2. Therefore, at the aggregate price level of P_2, the quantity supplied of real national output is Y_2.

---

[10]Note, clearly there are other ways to model the aggregate labor market. In particular, we could include an upward-sloping labor supply curve, where the aggregate quantity of labor supplied as a positive function of the real wage (the money wage divided by the aggregate price level). The money wage could be endogenous and adjust to equilibrate the labor market. In this initial aggregate demand-aggregate supply model, however, we assume an exogenous money wage with surplus labor. Indeed, there is always some frictional unemployment in a market economy. Nevertheless, even in this basic model, we might expect that a decrease in the unemployment rate would put upward pressure on the money wages negotiated in the next labor contract.

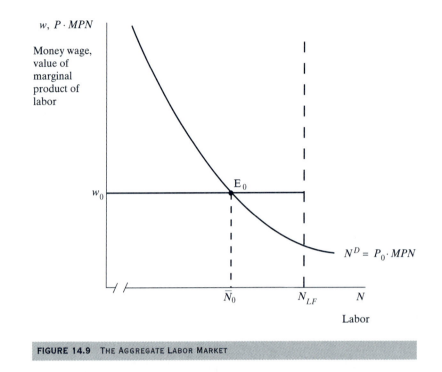

FIGURE 14.9 THE AGGREGATE LABOR MARKET

The aggregate supply curve, Y^S, is drawn holding constant the aggregate production function (which, in turn, reflects a given technology and physical capital stock), and in this model, the money wage, w_0. An increase in the money wage would shift the aggregate supply curve to the left, since at any price level, less labor would be employed and less output would be produced. From another perspective, a higher

FIGURE 14.10 DERIVATION OF THE AGGREGATE SUPPLY CURVE: Y^S

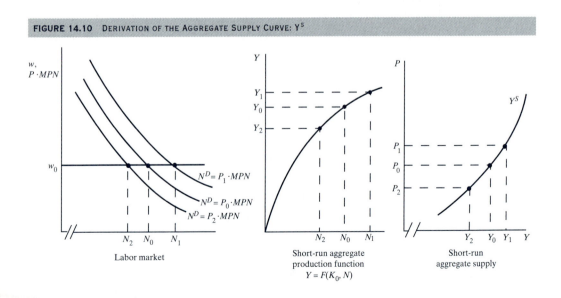

money wage would increase the aggregate price level associated with any quantity of real national output supplied.

GENERAL EQUILIBRIUM IN THE Y^D-Y^S MODEL

Figure 14.11 illustrates the general equilibrium in this aggregate demand-aggregate supply (Y^D-Y^S) model. There are four key endogenous variables: real national output (real national income), Y; the nominal interest rate, r; the aggregate price level, P; and the level of employment, N. The equilibrium values of these variables are simultaneously determined. The general equilibrium, indicated by the points labelled E_0, with $\overline{Y}_0$, $\overline{P}_0$, $\overline{r}_0$, and $\overline{N}_0$, is conditional upon the values of the exogenous variables of the model, here: B_0 (level of business confidence affecting real fixed investment expenditures); G_0 (real government purchases); X_0 (real exports of goods and services); M_0^S (nominal money supply); K_0 (physical capital stock); and w_0 (the money wage).

Graphically, the intersection of the aggregate demand and aggregate supply curves (the former derived from the product and money market equilibria of the *IS-LM* Model with varying price levels, and the latter derived from the aggregate production function and labor market) yields the equilibrium real national output, $\overline{Y}_0$, and aggregate price level, $\overline{P}_0$. The aggregate price level sets the *LM* and N^D curves, establishing the equilibrium nominal interest rate, $\overline{r}_0$, and equilibrium employment, $\overline{N}_0$. Note that the equilibrium real national output ($\overline{Y}_0$) is the output produced by the aggregate production function with the employed labor of $\overline{N}_0$, and the real national

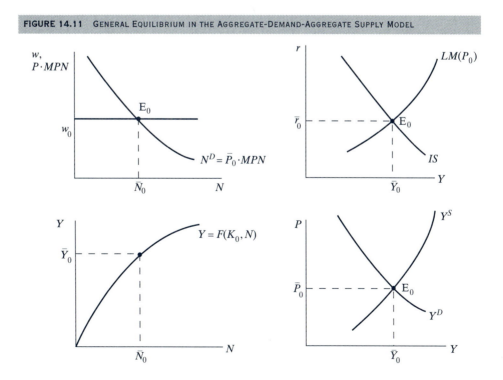

FIGURE 14.11   GENERAL EQUILIBRIUM IN THE AGGREGATE-DEMAND-AGGREGATE SUPPLY MODEL

output (and real national income) consistent with the equilibrium nominal interest rate, $\bar{r}_0$, that yields the product and money market equilibria in the *IS-LM* graph.

Mathematically, we can represent this macroeconomic model with the four equations:

Product Market Equilibrium: $C(Y - T(Y), r) + I(B_0, r) + G_0 + X_0 - M[Y - T(Y)] \overset{e}{=} Y$

Money Market Equilibrium: $L(Y, r) \overset{e}{=} M_0^S/P$

Aggregate Production Function: $Y = F(K_0, N)$

Labor Market Equilibrium: $P \cdot F_N \overset{e}{=} w_0$ (where $F_N = dY/dN = MPN$)

We write these four functions as

F^1: $C[Y - T(Y), r] + I(B_0, r) + G_0 + X_0 - M[Y - T(Y)] - Y = 0$

F^2: $L(Y, r) - M_0^S/P = 0$

F^3: $Y - F(K_0, N) = 0$

F^4: $F_N - w_0/P = 0$

Note that to be consistent with the other equilibrium conditions, we have written the labor market equilibrium condition (equation F^4) in real terms. That is, in equilibrium, the level of employment is where the marginal product of labor (F_N) equals the real wage (w_0/P).

Assuming that the Implicit Function Theorem holds (i.e., the four functions, $F^i(i = 1 \ldots 4)$, have continuous partial derivatives with respect to all the endogenous and exogenous variables in the system and at the general equilibrium point, the associated Jacobian, $|J|$, is nonsingular), then the following implicit functions are defined, where the equilibrium values of the endogenous variables can be written as functions of the exogenous variables of the system.

$$\bar{Y} = Y(B_0, G_0, X_0, M_0^S, K_0, w_0)$$
$$\bar{r} = r(B_0, G_0, X_0, M_0^S, K_0, w_0)$$
$$\bar{P} = P(B_0, G_0, X_0, M_0^S, K_0, w_0)$$
$$\bar{N} = N(B_0, G_0, X_0, M_0^S, K_0, w_0)$$

COMPARATIVE STATICS: AGGREGATE SUPPLY CONSTRAINTS

We can proceed with comparative statics, even though we are unable to solve explicitly for the equilibrium values of the endogenous variables. Totally differentiating the four equations gives

$$C_{Y_d}(dY - T'dY) + C_r dr + I_{B_0} dB_0 + I_r dr + dG_0 + dX_0 - M'(dY - T'dY) - dY = 0$$

$$L_Y \, dY + L_r \, dr - \frac{dM_0^S \cdot P - M_0^S dP}{P^2} = 0$$

$$dY - F_{K_0} \, dK_0 - F_N \, dN = 0$$

$$F_{K_0 N} \, dK_0 + F_{NN} \, dN - \frac{dw_0 \cdot P - w_0 dP}{P^2} = 0$$

where $F_{K_0 N} = \dfrac{\delta(F_N)}{\delta K_0} > 0$, since $F_N = MPN(K_0, N)$, that is, the marginal product of labor is a function of the fixed capital stock and the level of labor employed.

Rearranging, with the endogenous changes on the left-hand sides of the equations and evaluating the variables at their general equilibrium values: $\overline{Y}, \overline{r}, \overline{P}$, and $\overline{N}$, we have

$$[1 - (C_{Y_d} - M')(1 - T')]d\overline{Y} - (C_r + I_r)d\overline{r} = I_{B_0} \, dB_0 + dG_0 + dX_0$$

$$L_Y \, d\overline{Y} + L_r \, d\overline{r} + (M_0^S/P^2) \, d\overline{P} = dM_0^S/P$$

$$d\overline{Y} - F_N \, d\overline{N} = F_{K_0} \, dK_0$$

$$F_{NN} \, d\overline{N} + (w_0/P^2) \, d\overline{P} = -F_{K_0 N} \, dK_0 + dw_0/P$$

Expressing the system of comparative statics in matrix notation gives

$$\begin{bmatrix} 1 - (C_{Y_d} - M')(1 - T') & -(C_r + I_r) & 0 & 0 \\ L_Y & L_r & M_0^S/P^2 & 0 \\ 1 & 0 & 0 & -F_N \\ 0 & 0 & w_0/P^2 & F_{NN} \end{bmatrix} \begin{bmatrix} d\overline{Y} \\ d\overline{r} \\ d\overline{P} \\ d\overline{N} \end{bmatrix}$$

$$= \begin{bmatrix} I_{B_0} \, dB_0 + dG_0 + dX_0 \\ dM_0^S/P \\ F_{K_0} \, dK_0 \\ -F_{K_0 N} \, dK_0 + dw_0/P \end{bmatrix}$$

Note that the *IS-LM* Model is embedded in the first two columns and first two rows of this aggregate demand-aggregate supply model—with the difference that now the aggregate price level is endogenous. We first evaluate the Jacobian of this coefficient matrix of partial derivatives to confirm the functional independence of these four equations and as part of the solution to subsequent comparative static experiments.

Expanding along the first row of the Jacobian, $|J|$, we find

$$[1 - (C_{Y_d} - M')(1 - T')](L_r)(F_N)(w_0/P^2) +$$

$$(C_r + I_r)[(L_Y)(F_N)(w_0/P^2) - (M_0^S/P^2)(F_{NN})] < 0$$

since

$$[1 - (C_{Y_d} - M')(1 - T')] > 0; L_r < 0; F_N > 0; \text{ and } w_0/P^2 > 0$$

and

$$(C_r + I_r) < 0; L_Y > 0; F_{NN} < 0; \text{ and } M_0^S/P^2 > 0$$

Now we are ready for comparative statics. First, we assess the effect of fiscal policy by deriving the government expenditure multiplier, $\delta \overline{Y}/\delta G_0$, for this Y^D-Y^S model. Using Cramer's rule, we solve for $d\overline{Y}$, holding constant all other exogenous variables except real government purchases, that is, assuming that $dB_0 = dX_0 = dM_0^S = dK_0 = dw_0 = 0$.

$$d\overline{Y} = \frac{\begin{bmatrix} dG_0 & -(C_r + L_r) & 0 & 0 \\ 0 & L_r & M_0^S/P^2 & 0 \\ 0 & 0 & 0 & -F_N \\ 0 & 0 & w_0/P^2 & F_{NN} \end{bmatrix}}{|J|} = \frac{dG_0 \, [(L_r)(F_N)(w_0/P^2)]}{|J|}$$

Dividing through by dG_0, expressing the result as a partial derivative, $\delta \overline{Y}/\delta G_0$, and then simplifying by dividing numerator and denominator of the right-hand side by $[(L_r)(F_N)(w_0/P^2)]$, we obtain

$$\delta \overline{Y}/\delta G_0 = \frac{1}{1 - (C_{Y_d} - M')(1 - T') + \dfrac{(C_r + I_r)L_Y}{L_r} - \dfrac{(C_r + I_r)(M_0^S)(F_{NN})}{(L_r)(F_N)(w_0)}} > 0$$

This government expenditure multiplier for the Y^D-Y^S model is smaller than its counterpart for the *IS-LM* Model, due to the subtraction of a negative term, $\dfrac{(C_r + I_r)(M_0^S)(F_{NN})}{(L_r)(F_N)(w_0)}$, in the positive denominator.

We illustrate graphically and then summarize the sequence of changes with a flow chart. Refer to Figure 14.12, where beginning in equilibrium with $\overline{Y}_0, \overline{r}_0, \overline{P}_0$, and $\overline{N}_0$, an increase in real government purchases shifts the *IS* curve to the right to *IS'*. The excess demand for goods and services results in an increase in the production of real national output and a rise in real national income. The transactions demand for money increases with income, leading to an excess demand for money and a selling of bonds, which drives down the market price of bonds and pushes up the interest rate. The higher interest rate discourages interest-sensitive spending, and for a given aggregate price level, the economy would move to a new equilibrium at Y' and r'. (See point E' in the *IS-LM* graph.)

In the aggregate demand-aggregate supply model, however, E' is not the final equilibrium—there are more adjustments. The increase in real government expenditures shifts the Y^D curve to the right by $Y' - \overline{Y}_0$ (the change in the *IS-LM* equilibrium for the aggregate price level, $\overline{P}_0$). As the production of real national output increases to meet the excess demand for goods and services, the aggregate price level rises. That is, in the short run, in order to produce more output, firms hire more labor. Diminishing returns to labor, however, increase the marginal cost of production and the aggregate price level. The higher price level shifts up the labor demand curve, increasing the

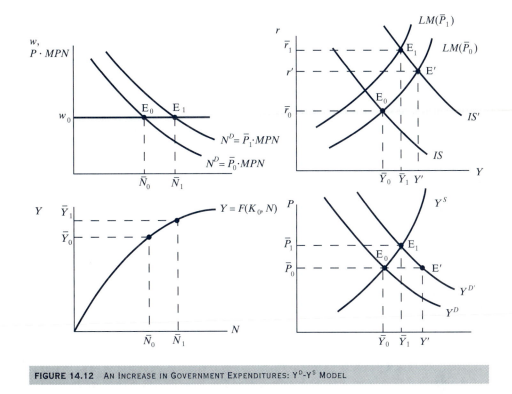

FIGURE 14.12 AN INCREASE IN GOVERNMENT EXPENDITURES: Y^D-Y^S MODEL

value of the marginal product of labor at any level of employment. The new level of employment is $\overline{N}_1$, which is required to produce the greater rate of output, $\overline{Y}_1$. The rise in the aggregate price level to $\overline{P}_1$ reduces the real money supply, shifting the LM curve back to $LM(\overline{P}_1)$. The interest rate rises further to the new equilibrium level of $\overline{r}_1$ and there is a greater decline in interest-sensitive expenditures. The new general equilibrium in the Y^D-Y^S model is indicated by the points labeled E_1, with $\overline{Y}_1, \overline{P}_1, \overline{r}_1$, and $\overline{N}_1$. We can see that incorporating aggregate supply constraints and an endogenous aggregate price level reduces the government expenditure multiplier.

Summarizing the above discussion with a flow chart:

$$G_0 \uparrow \Rightarrow EDG \Rightarrow Y \uparrow \Rightarrow L \uparrow \Rightarrow EDM \Rightarrow \text{individuals sell bonds} \Rightarrow P_b \downarrow \Rightarrow$$

$$r \uparrow \Rightarrow C \downarrow \text{ and } I \downarrow \Rightarrow Y \downarrow \text{ some}$$

(In the *IS-LM* Model, $\Delta Y = Y' - \overline{Y}_0$ and $\Delta r = r' - \overline{r}_0$; but in the Y^D-Y^S model, there are additional adjustments.)

On net, as $Y \uparrow$ from the $EDG \Rightarrow P \uparrow \Rightarrow M_0^S/P \downarrow \Rightarrow EDM \Rightarrow$ individuals sell more bonds $\Rightarrow P_b \downarrow$ more $\Rightarrow r \uparrow$ more $\Rightarrow C \downarrow$ and $I \downarrow$ more $\Rightarrow Y \downarrow$ some more.

Also, with $P \uparrow \Rightarrow N^D \uparrow \Rightarrow N \uparrow$

(In the Y^D-Y^S model, $\Delta Y = \overline{Y}_1 - \overline{Y}_0 < Y' - \overline{Y}_0;$ $\Delta r = \overline{r}_1 - \overline{r}_0 > r' - \overline{r}_0;$
$\Delta P = \overline{P}_1 - \overline{P}_0;$ and $\Delta N = \overline{N}_1 - \overline{N}_0.$)

Effectiveness of Fiscal Policy: Aggregate Supply Constraints   On net then, an increase in real government purchases increases real national output, the aggregate price level, the nominal interest rate, and the level of employment. How much each of the variables increase with the rise in government spending depends on interest rate sensitivities and aggregate supply constraints. To illustrate the importance of aggregate supply constraints and the endogenous price level, return to the expression for the government expenditure multiplier of this Y^D-Y^S model. (Note this multiplier applies in general to changes in autonomous expenditures, specifically in this model, ΔG_0 and ΔX_0.)

$$\delta\overline{Y}/\delta G_0 = \cfrac{1}{1 - (C_{Y_d} - M')(1 - T') + \cfrac{(C_r + I_r)L_Y}{L_r} - \cfrac{(C_r + I_r)(M_0^S)(F_{NN})}{(L_r)(F_N)(w_0)}}$$

This differs from the *IS-LM* government expenditure multiplier due to the subtraction of the negative term, $\dfrac{(C_r + I_r)(M_0^S)(F_{NN})}{(L_r)(F_N)(w_0)}$, in the denominator.

If labor were not subject to diminishing returns, that is, $F_{NN} = 0$, reflecting a constant marginal product of labor, then with the given money wage rate, the Y^D-Y^S government expenditure multiplier would be the same as the *IS-LM* multiplier, since this term would equal zero. This case is most likely in a depressed economy with high unemployment and excess capacity—so that additional labor can be employed without diminishing marginal productivity and without any upward pressure on the money wage.

On the other hand, if the economy were operating in the perfectly inelastic range of the aggregate supply curve (the Classical range), where aggregate supply constraints are absolutely binding and the marginal product of labor is zero, $F_N = 0$, the government expenditure multiplier would equal zero. Any attempt to add labor (if possible) would not increase real national output.

In sum, the effectiveness of fiscal policy in this aggregate demand-aggregate supply model is directly related to the magnitude of the multiplier, $\delta\overline{Y}/\delta G_0$, that is, in turn, directly related to the interest rate sensitivity of the demand for real money balances $|L_r|$; inversely related to the interest rate sensitivities of real consumption and investment expenditures, $|C_r + I_r|$; and inversely related to aggregate supply constraints, reflected here in the marginal product of labor.

Effectiveness of Monetary Policy: Aggregate Supply Constraints   Qualitatively, the impact of monetary policy on real national output, the aggregate price level, and employment, would be similar to fiscal policy. The main difference between monetary and fiscal policy comes through the impact on the nominal interest rate and interest-sensitive expenditures. Expansionary (contractionary) fiscal policy results in a higher (lower) interest rate. In contrast, expansionary (contractionary) monetary policy drives down (up) the interest rate. The relative effectiveness of monetary versus fiscal policy depends on the magnitudes of the interest sensitivities of consumption and investment expenditures and the quantity demanded of real money balances.

Returning to the system of comparative statics in matrix notation for this aggregate demand-aggregate supply model, we can derive the money supply multiplier.

$$
\begin{bmatrix}
1 - (C_{Y_d} - M')(1 - T') & -(C_r + I_r) & 0 & 0 \\
L_Y & L_r & M_0^S/P^2 & 0 \\
1 & 0 & 0 & -F_N \\
0 & 0 & w_0/P^2 & F_{NN}
\end{bmatrix}
\begin{bmatrix}
d\overline{Y} \\
d\overline{r} \\
d\overline{P} \\
d\overline{N}
\end{bmatrix}
$$

$$
=
\begin{bmatrix}
I_{B_0} dB_0 + dG_0 + dX_0 \\
dM_0^S/P \\
F_{K_0} dK_0 \\
-F_{K_0 N} dK_0 + dw_0/P
\end{bmatrix}
$$

The comparative static result we seek is $\delta \overline{Y}/\delta M_0^S$. Consequently, using Cramer's rule we solve for $d\overline{Y}$, and set all the exogenous changes equal to zero except for dM_0^S. That is: $dB_0 = dG_0 = dX_0 = dK_0 = dw_0 = 0$.

$$
d\overline{Y} = \frac{\begin{vmatrix}
0 & -(C_r + I_r) & 0 & 0 \\
dM_0^S/P & L_r & M_0^S/P^2 & 0 \\
0 & 0 & 0 & -F_N \\
0 & 0 & w_0/P^2 & F_{NN}
\end{vmatrix}}{|J|} = \frac{(dM_0^S/P)(C_r + I_r)(F_N)(w_0/P^2)}{|J|}
$$

Dividing through by dM_0^S and converting to partial derivatives (since all the other exogenous changes are set equal to zero), we have

$$
\delta\overline{Y}/\delta M_0^S = \frac{(1/P)(C_r + I_r)(F_N)(w_0/P^2)}{|J|} > 0
$$

since

$$
(C_r + I_r) < 0 \text{ and } F_N > 0 \text{ and } |J| < 0
$$

where

$$
|J| = [1 - (C_{Y_d} - M')(1 - T')](L_r)(F_N)(w_0/P^2)
$$
$$
+ (C_r + I_r)[(L_Y)(F_N)(w_0/P^2) - (M^S/P^2)(F_{NN})]
$$

We can write the money supply multiplier as

$$
\delta\overline{Y}/\delta M_0^S = \frac{1/P}{\dfrac{[1 - (C_{Y_d} - M')(1 - T')]L_r}{(C_r + I_r)} + L_Y - \dfrac{(M_0^S)(F_{NN})}{(C_r + I_r)(F_N)(w_0)}}
$$

which is smaller than the money supply multiplier in the *IS-LM* Model due to the subtraction of the positive term, $(M_0^S)(F_{NN})/[(C_r + I_r)(F_N)(w_0)$, from the negative denominator. This term represents the effect of the aggregate supply constraints. As with fiscal policy, if $F_{NN} = 0$, labor is not subject to diminishing returns and, in effect, there are no aggregate supply constraints which push up the price level as real national output increases, thereby reducing the multiplier effect from expansionary monetary policy. At the other extreme, if $F_N = 0$, then the aggregate supply constraints are absolutely binding in the short run. Consequently, adding labor would not increase the output produced. The denominator of the money supply multiplier becomes "infinitely" negative, so the multiplier is zero.

Finally, as with the *IS-LM* Model money supply multiplier, we see that monetary policy is more effective, that is, a given change in the money supply would yield a greater change in equilibrium real national output, the less sensitive is the quantity demanded of real money balances to the interest rate (i.e., the lower is $|L_r|$); the more interest-sensitive are real consumption and investment expenditures (i.e., the higher are $|C_r|$ and $|I_r|$) ; the less sensitive is the quantity demanded of real money balances to real national income (i.e., the lower is L_Y); and the lower is the aggregate price level, P.

PRACTICE PROBLEM 14.5

Given the macroeconomic model:

Product Market Equilibrium: $C(Y - T(Y), r) + I(B_0, r) + G_0 + X_0 - M(Y - T(Y)) \overset{e}{=} Y$

Money Market Equilibrium: $L(Y, r) \overset{e}{=} M_0^S/P$

Aggregate Production Function: $Y = F(K_0, N)$

Labor Market Equilibrium: $P \cdot F_N = w_0$ or $F_N = w_0/P$

Assuming that the Implicit Function Theorem holds, find and sign the following comparative statics.
a) $\delta\bar{r}/\delta G_0$ and   b) $\delta\bar{r}/\delta M_0^S$

(The answers are at the end of the chapter.)

Note that we could also make labor supply a positive function of the money wage. In other macroeconomic models, labor supply is a positive function of the expected real wage, which is the nominal wage adjusted for an expected price level. If labor supply's expectation of the price level is accurate, then the labor market "clears" with no involuntary unemployment. In particular, New Classicals maintain that with **rational expectations**, labor supply can anticipate and effectively neutralize systematic demand-management fiscal and monetary policies. If so, then short-run policy changes affecting aggregate demand would be offset by changes in aggregate supply—resulting in a zero multiplier effect on real national output. We will not address these models here, although problems 6 and 7 at the end of the chapter illustrate models with an endogenous wage. Instead, we will conclude this chapter with two additional comparative static results from the present Y^D-Y^S model.

Impact of a Change in Business Confidence on Employment   Consider a decrease in business confidence. Intuitively, if businesses become pessimistic about future sales, we would expect a cutback in output and a decrease in the demand for labor. Return to the system of comparative statics, reproduced below.

$$
\begin{bmatrix}
1 - (C_{Y_d} - M')(1 - T') & -(C_r + I_r) & 0 & 0 \\
L_Y & L_r & M_0^S/P^2 & 0 \\
1 & 0 & 0 & -F_N \\
0 & 0 & w_0/P^2 & F_{NN}
\end{bmatrix}
\begin{bmatrix}
dY \\
dr \\
dP \\
dN
\end{bmatrix}
$$

$$
=
\begin{bmatrix}
I_{B_0} dB_0 + dG_0 + dX_0 \\
dM_0^S/P \\
F_{K_0} dK_0 \\
-F_{K_0} dK_0 + dw_0/P
\end{bmatrix}
$$

The comparative static result we seek is $\delta\overline{N}/\delta B_0$. Applying Cramer's rule, we solve for dN, holding constant all other exogenous variables in the model.

$$
d\overline{N} = \frac{
\begin{vmatrix}
1 - (C_{Y_d} - M')(1 - T') & -(C_r + I_r) & 0 & I_{B_0} dB_0 \\
L_Y & L_r & M_0^S/P^2 & 0 \\
1 & 0 & 0 & 0 \\
0 & 0 & w_0/P^2 & 0
\end{vmatrix}
}{|J|}
$$

$$
= \frac{-I_{B_0} dB_0(-L_r)(w_0/P^2)}{|J|}
$$

$$
\delta\overline{N}/\delta B_0 = \frac{(I_{B_0})(L_r)(w_0/P^2)}{|J|} > 0
$$

since

$$
I_{B_0} > 0;\ L_r < 0;\ (w_0/P^2) > 0; \quad \text{and} \quad |J| < 0.
$$

This makes sense. A decrease in business confidence that reduces business investment expenditures would result in an excess supply of goods, a buildup of inventories, and a cutback in production. As production and real national income fall, the aggregate price level would decline, reducing the demand for labor and, at the given money wage, the level of employment. In addition, a decrease in business confidence in this model also reduces the equilibrium interest rate. In terms of a flow chart, with the shifts in curves indicated, the transition to a new equilibrium is

$$
B_0 \downarrow \Rightarrow I \downarrow \Rightarrow ESG \Rightarrow \Delta INV^u > 0 \Rightarrow Y \downarrow \Rightarrow L \downarrow \Rightarrow ESM \Rightarrow
$$
(*IS* curve shifts left.)

$$
\text{individuals buy bonds} \Rightarrow P_b \uparrow \Rightarrow r \downarrow \Rightarrow C \uparrow \text{ and } I \uparrow \Rightarrow Y \uparrow \text{ some}
$$
(Y^D curve shifts left, and, for the initial aggregate price level, $\Delta Y < 0$.)

$$
\text{However, with the } ESG, \text{ as } Y \downarrow \Rightarrow P \downarrow \Rightarrow (M_0^S/P) \uparrow \Rightarrow \text{ adds to } ESM \Rightarrow
$$
(*LM* curve shifts right.)

individuals buy more bonds $\Rightarrow P_b \uparrow$ more $\Rightarrow r \downarrow$ more $\Rightarrow C \uparrow$ and $I \uparrow$ more $\Rightarrow$ $Y \uparrow$ some more

and, with $P \downarrow \Rightarrow N^D \downarrow \Rightarrow N \downarrow$
(N^D curve shifts left.)

In sum, with $\Delta B_0 < 0$, we find: $\Delta \overline{Y} < 0$, $\Delta \overline{P} < 0$, $\Delta \overline{r} < 0$, and $\Delta \overline{N} < 0$

Impact of a Change in the Money Wage on the Aggregate Price Level For the final comparative result to be examined here, consider the effect of an increase in the money wage on the equilibrium aggregate price level, that is, $\delta \overline{P}/\delta w_0$. Using Cramer's rule, we solve for $d\overline{P}$, holding constant all other exogenous variables except the money wage rate.

$$d\overline{P} = \frac{\begin{vmatrix} 1 - (C_{Y_d} - M')(1 - T') & -(C_r + I_r) & 0 & 0 \\ L_Y & L_r & 0 & 0 \\ 1 & 0 & 0 & -F_N \\ 0 & 0 & dw_0/P & F_{NN} \end{vmatrix}}{|J|}$$

$$d\overline{P} = \frac{-(dw_0/P)(-F_N)\{[1 - (C_{Y_d} - M')(1 - T')]L_r + L_Y(C_r + I_r)\}}{|J|}$$

$$\delta \overline{P}/\delta w_0 = \frac{(1/P)(F_N)\{[1 - (C_{Y_d} - M')(1 - T')]L_r + L_Y(C_r + I_r)\}}{|J|} > 0$$

This too makes sense. A rise in the money wage rate would put upward pressure on the aggregate price level. A higher money wage would reduce the level of employment for the existing labor demand. Real national output would fall with less labor employed. The aggregate supply curve would shift left, and for the existing aggregate demand, result in an excess demand for goods and services, putting upward pressure on the aggregate price level as the quantity supplied of real national output rises. On net, the higher money wage would increase the equilibrium aggregate price level, reduce equilibrium real national output and employment, and raise the equilibrium nominal interest rate. With a flow chart, we can detail the transition to the new equilibrium.

$w_0 \uparrow \Rightarrow N \downarrow \Rightarrow Y^S \downarrow$ and $Y \downarrow$ (at initial P_0) $\Rightarrow EDG \Rightarrow \Delta INV^u < 0 \Rightarrow Y \uparrow$ some
(Y^S curve shifts left.)

and $P \uparrow \Rightarrow (M_0^S/P) \downarrow \Rightarrow EDM \Rightarrow$ individuals sell bonds $\Rightarrow P_b \downarrow \Rightarrow r \uparrow$
(LM curve shifts left.)

$\Rightarrow C \downarrow$ and $I \downarrow \Rightarrow Y \downarrow$ some

and as $P \uparrow \Rightarrow N^D \uparrow \Rightarrow N \uparrow$ some
(N^D curve shifts right.)

In sum, with $\Delta w_0 > 0$, we find: $\Delta Y < 0$, $\Delta \overline{P} > 0$, $\Delta \overline{r} > 0$, and $\Delta \overline{N}_0 < 0$.

PRACTICE PROBLEM 14.6

Given the macroeconomic model from Practice Problem 14.5, assume the Implicit Function Theorem holds. Find and sign the comparative static, $\delta \overline{r}/\delta w_0$.

(The answers are at the end of the chapter.)

There are other comparative static experiments we could do with this model. Moreover, this is just one of the macroeconomic models that could have been presented—each differentiated by the assumptions made about the aggregate markets and by the number of included endogenous and exogenous variables. Examples are provided as end-of-chapter problems. We turn now to dynamic analysis in Chapter 15 and an introduction to growth models.

❖ KEY TERMS

Economics

- aggregate demand curve (p. 512)
- aggregate supply curve (p. 515)
- discount rate (p. 502)
- fiscal policy (p. 502)
- *IS* curve (p. 491)
- *IS* schedule (p. 491)

- *LM* curve (p. 496)
- *LM* schedule (p. 496)
- liquidity (p. 494)
- monetary policy (p. 502)
- open market operations (p. 502)
- rational expectations (p. 524)

- required reserve ratio (p. 502)
- reserves (p. 502)
- speculative demand for money (p. 494)
- transactions demand for money (p. 494)

❖ PROBLEMS

1. Find the current market price of a bond with a 1-year maturity, a face value of $5,000, and no interest payment, if the current market rate of interest is 5% and the bond is
   a) newly issued
   b) 3 months old
   c) 6 months old
   d) exactly 1 year old

2. Given the following models:

Simple Keynesian	IS-LM
$C = 20 + .9Y_d$	$C = 20 + .9Y_d$
$I = 95$	$I = 120 - 5r$
$G = 265$	$G = 265$
$X = 80$	$X = 80$
$M = 4 + .15Y_d$	$M = 4 + .15Y_d$
$T = .3Y$	$T = .3Y$
$Y_d \equiv Y - T$	$Y_d \equiv Y - T$
$A \equiv C + I + G + X - M$	$A \equiv C + I + G + X - M$

$$A(Y) \overset{e}{=} Y$$

$$L = .25Y - 8r$$
$$M_0^S/P_0 = 200/1 = 200$$
$$A(Y, r) \overset{e}{=} Y$$
$$L(Y, r) \overset{e}{=} M_0^S/P_0$$

a) Using the Simple Keynesian Model:
   i) Find the aggregate expenditure schedule, A, and then solve for the equilibrium level of real national income, $\overline{Y}_0$.
   ii) Find the impact on the equilibrium level of real national income of a decrease in real government expenditures of 10. Explain the economic transition to the new equilibrium.

b) Using the *IS-LM* Model:
   i) Find the equations for the *IS* and *LM* schedules, and then solve for the equilibrium levels of real national income, $\overline{Y}_0$, and the nominal interest rate, $\overline{r}_0$.
   ii) Find the impact on the equilibrium levels of real national income and the nominal interest rate of a decrease in real government expenditures of 10. Explain the economic transition to the new equilibrium.
   iii) Find the impact on the equilibrium levels of real national income and the nominal interest rate of a decrease in the nominal money supply of 10. Explain the economic transition to the new equilibrium.

3. Given the following *IS-LM* Model:

$$C = C[Y - T(Y), r] \qquad\qquad 0 < C_{Y_d} < 1, C_r < 0$$

$$I = I(r) \qquad\qquad dI/dr = I' < 0$$

$$G = G_0$$

$$X = X_0$$

$$M = M[Y - T(Y), Q_0] \qquad\qquad 0 < M_{Y_d} < C_{Y_d} < 1, M_{Q_0} < 0$$
$$\qquad\qquad\qquad (Q_0 = \text{import barriers})$$

$$T = T(Y) \qquad\qquad 0 < dT/dY = T' < 1$$

$$Y_d \equiv Y - T$$

$$L = L(Y, r) \qquad\qquad 0 < L_Y < 1, L_r < 0$$

$$M^S = M_0^S$$

$$P = P_0$$

$$A \equiv C + I + G + X - M$$

$$A(Y, r) \overset{e}{=} Y \qquad\qquad \text{Product Market Equilibrium}$$

$$L(Y, r) \overset{e}{=} M_0^S/P_0 \qquad\qquad \text{Money Market Equilibrium}$$

Assume that the Implicit Function Theorem holds, that is,

$$F^1 (Y, r; G_0, X_0, Q_0, M_0^S, P_0) = 0 \quad (IS \text{ Schedule})$$

$$F^2 (Y, r; G_0, X_0, Q_0, M_0^S, P_0) = 0 \quad (LM \text{ Schedule})$$

define a set of implicit functions:

$$\overline{Y} = Y(G_0, X_0, Q_0, M_0^S, P_0)$$

and

$$\overline{r} = r (G_0, X_0, Q_0, M_0^S, P_0)$$

a) Find and determine the sign of each of the following:
   i) $\delta\overline{Y}/\delta X_0$ ii) $\delta\overline{Y}/\delta Q_0$ iii) $\delta\overline{Y}/\delta M_0^S$ iv) $\delta\overline{r}/\delta P_0$ v) $\delta\overline{r}/\delta Q_0$ vi) $\delta\overline{r}/\delta M_0^S$
b) Briefly explain (a flow chart is fine) the economic adjustments to the new equilibriums resulting from decreases in each of the following:
   i) aggregate price level (P_0)
   ii) import barriers (Q_0)
   iii) nominal money supply (M_0^S).

4. Given the aggregate demand-aggregate supply model represented by the four equations below:

   Product Market Equilibrium: $C(Y - T(Y), r, Z_0/P) + I(r) + G_0 + X_0 - M[Y - T(Y)] \overset{e}{=} Y$

   Money Market Equilibrium: $L(Y, r) \overset{e}{=} M_0^S/P$

   Aggregate Production Function: $Y = F(K_0, N)$

   Labor Market Equilibrium: $P \cdot F_N \overset{e}{=} w_0 \quad$ (or $F_N \overset{e}{=} w_0/P$)

   and assuming the Implicit Function Theorem holds, so that the equilibrium values of the endogenous variables, $\overline{Y}, \overline{r}, \overline{P},$ and $\overline{N}_0$, can be written as functions of the exogenous variables of the model, $Z_0, G_0, X_0, M_0^S, K_0,$ and w_0, where Z_0 is nominal personal wealth, and $\delta C/\delta Z_0 = C_{Z_0}$, where $0 < C_{Z_0} < 1$:
   a) Find and determine the sign of each of the following:
      i) $\delta\overline{Y}/\delta G_0$ ii) $\delta\overline{r}/\delta Z_0$ iii) $\delta\overline{P}/\delta X_0$ iv) $\delta\overline{N}/\delta M_0^S$
   b) For each of the above, explain the economic transition to the new equilibrium associated with a decrease in that particular exogenous variable.

5. Suppose that the product market equilibrium is given instead by the equation:

   $$C[Y - T(Y), r] + I(r) + G_0 + X(P) - M(Y - T(Y), P) \overset{e}{=} Y$$

   where $X' = dX/dP < 0$ and $M_P = \delta M/\delta P > 0$, that is, real exports of goods and services are inversely related to the aggregate price level, while real imports of goods and services are directly related to the aggregate price level. Assume that the equations for the Money Market Equilibrium, Aggregate Production Function, and Labor Market Equilibrium are the same as in Problem 5.

a) Find and determine the sign of each of the following:

i) $\delta\overline{Y}/\delta G_0$ ii) $\delta\overline{N}/\delta w_0$ iii) $\delta\overline{r}/\delta M_0^S$ iv) $\delta\overline{P}/\delta K_0$

b) For each of the above, explain the economic transition to the new equilibrium associated with an increase in that particular exogenous variable.

6. Given the macroeconomic model represented by the five equations below:

Product Market Equilibrium: $C[Y - T(Y), r] + I(r) + G_0 + X_0 -$
$$M[Y - T(Y)] \overset{e}{=} Y$$

Money Market Equilibrium: $L(Y, r) \overset{e}{=} M_0^S/P$

Aggregate Production Function: $Y = F(K_0, N)$

Labor Supply: $N = N(w)$

Labor Market Equilibrium: $P \cdot F_N \overset{e}{=} w$ (or $F_N \overset{e}{=} w/P$)

In this model, labor supply is a positive function of the money wage, $dN/dw > 0$, and the money wage is an endogenous variable.

Assume that the Implicit Function Theorem holds, so that the equilibrium values of the endogenous variables, $\overline{Y}, \overline{r}, \overline{P}, \overline{N}$, and $\overline{w}$, can be written as functions of the exogenous variables of the model, G_0, X_0, M_0^S, and K_0.

a) Find the government expenditure multiplier, $\delta\overline{Y}/\delta G_0$.

b) Compare this government expenditure multiplier with the one for the above model where the money wage is exogenous, w_0, and the labor market equilibrium condition is given by $P \cdot F_N = w_0$ (or $F_N = w_0/P$).

7. Return to the macroeconomic model in Problem 6, but now assume that labor supply is a function of the real wage, that is, $N = N(w/P)$, where $dN/d(w/P) > 0$. This assumption is consistent with the Classical Model (where labor supply knows the real wage) and with the New Classical Model (when, using rational expectations, labor supply anticipates or accurately predicts the real wage).

a) Find the government expenditure multiplier, $\delta\overline{Y}/\delta G_0$.

b) Explain the difference between this government expenditure multiplier and the one for the Keynesian models in Problem 6.

c) Find and sign $\delta\overline{P}/\delta M_0^S$. Determine the elasticity of the equilibrium aggregate price level to the nominal money supply in this model.

❖ ANSWERS TO PRACTICE PROBLEMS

14.1 a) The *IS* schedule is: $Y = \dfrac{465 - 8r}{.6}$ or $r = \dfrac{465 - .6Y}{8}$.

b) The *LM* schedule is: $Y = 475 + 50r$ or $r = \dfrac{-95 + .2Y}{10}$.

c) The equilibrium real national output and nominal interest rate are: $\overline{Y}_0 = 712$ and $\overline{r}_0 = 4.74$.

14.2 a) The new equilibrium real national output and nominal interest rate are: $\overline{Y}_1 = 687$ and $\overline{r}_1 = 4.74$.

b) The implied government expenditure multiplier for the *IS-LM* Model is: $\Delta\overline{Y}/\Delta G_0 = 1.30$. The government expenditure multiplier for the Simple Keynesian Model is: $K_{A_0} = 1/(1 - a) = 1/(1 - .4) = 1.67$.

14.3 a) The new equilibrium real national output and nominal interest rate are: $\overline{Y}_2 = 694$ and $\overline{r}_2 = 5.38$.

b) The implied money supply multiplier is: $\Delta Y/\Delta M_0^S = -6/-5 = 1.2$. The effectiveness of monetary policy is directly related to the interest sensitivities of consumption and investment expenditures (C_r and I_r) and the marginal propensity to consume (C_{Y_d}). The effectiveness of monetary policy is inversely related to the interest and income sensitivities of the quantity demanded of real money balances (L_r and L_Y, respectively), the marginal propensity to import (dM/dY_d), and the marginal rate of taxation (dT/dY).

14.4 a) $\delta\overline{Y}/\delta X_0 = \dfrac{L_r}{|J|} > 0$

b) $\delta\overline{r}/\delta P_0 = \dfrac{[1 - C_{Y_d} - M'(1 - T')](-M_0^S/P_0^2)}{|J|} > 0$

where $|J| = [1 - (C_{Y_d} - M')(1 - T')]\, L_r + L_Y\,(C_r + I_r) < 0$

14.5 a) $\delta\overline{r}/\delta G_0 = \dfrac{-[(L_Y)(F_N)(w_0/P^2) - (M_0^S/P^2)(F_{NN})]}{|J|} > 0$

b) $\delta\overline{r}/\delta M_0^S = \dfrac{(1/P)[1 - (C_{Y_d} - M')(1 - T')](F_N)(w_0/P^2)}{|J|} < 0$

$|J| = [1 - (C_{Y_d} - M')(1 - T')](L_r)(F_N)(w_0/P^2) + (C_r + I_r)[(L_Y)(F_N)(w_0/P^2) - (M_0^S/P^2)(F_{NN})] < 0$

14.6 $\delta\overline{r}/\delta w_0 = \dfrac{(1/P)[1 - C_{Y_d} - M'(1 - T')](M_0^S/P^2)(-F_N)}{|J|} > 0$

where $|J| < 0$ is the same Jacobian as in Practice Problem 14.5.

GROWTH RATES AND GROWTH MODELS

A s we know, time explicitly enters into the analysis in dynamic models, and solutions are expressed in terms of the time paths of the endogenous variables. In this
final chapter, we study simple dynamic macroeconomic models, where the key variables are growth rates of real national output, labor, and physical capital.

We begin with a general derivation of rates of growth. Then, we focus on economic
growth, measured by the rate of change in per capita real national output.
Differentiating an aggregate production function, we identify the primary sources of
national output growth. In particular, physical capital formation is related to the investment rate, and the factors underlying population change and labor force growth are
described.

The economic growth models are presented, for the most part, as the theories
evolved. We start with the Harrod-Domar Model and the assumption of a fixed-
coefficients production function. The dynamic instability of this model, known as the
"knife-edge" problem, stimulated other efforts to model the economic growth process,
including incorporation of income distribution and a variable saving rate and
allowance for factor substitution. Without technological change or qualitative
improvement in the factors of production, these early growth models were characterized by a long-run or steady-state equilibrium of zero economic growth. We conclude
the chapter with examples of growth models, where steady-state equilibrium is characterized by positive economic growth.

RATES OF GROWTH

In general, a growth rate represents the ratio of the change in a variable, for example,
income, output, the price level, to the variable itself. Given a variable y, which is a function of time, t, $y = f(t)$, the growth rate of y is equal to

$$\frac{dy/dt}{y} = \frac{f'(t)}{f(t)} = \frac{\text{marginal function}}{\text{total function}}$$

Alternatively, we can derive the growth rate by taking the natural logarithm of the function, $\ln y = \ln f(t)$, and then differentiating with respect to time.

$$\frac{d \ln y}{dt} = \frac{d \ln f(t)}{dt} = [1/f(t)]f'(t) = (1/y)(dy/dt) = \frac{dy/dt}{y}$$

Some examples follow. You may want to review the discussion of exponential and logarithmic functions from Chapter 4. For a natural exponential function, $y = Ae^{rt}$, where A and r are constants and e is the base of the natural logarithm, $e = 2.71828. . . ,$ the growth rate of y is equal to

$$dy/dt = rAe^{rt}$$

$$\frac{dy/dt}{y} = \frac{rAe^{rt}}{Ae^{rt}} = r$$

or

$$\ln y = \ln A + rt$$

$$\frac{d \ln y}{dt} = r$$

$$\frac{dy/dt}{y} = r$$

That is, for a natural exponential function of the form, $y = Ae^{rt}$, the parameter r gives the growth rate. For example, let $y = 10e^{.04t}$. Differentiating with respect to t, we have, $dy/dt = .4e^{.04t}$. Dividing through by y we obtain the growth rate:

$$\frac{dy/dt}{y} = \frac{.4e^{.04t}}{10e^{.04t}} = .04$$

For an exponential function with a base b, $(b > 0)$, given by $y = Ab^t$, it is easier to use the natural exponential approach to derive the rate of growth.

$$\ln y = \ln A + t \ln b$$

$$\frac{d \ln y}{dt} = \ln b$$

$$\frac{dy/dt}{y} = \ln b$$

The rate of growth of the exponential function, $y = Ab^t$, $(b > 0)$, is constant and equal to $\ln b$. To illustrate, let $y = 10(2)^t$. Taking the natural logarithm of both sides gives

$$\ln y = \ln 10 + t \ln 2$$

Differentiating with respect to t, we obtain the growth rate of y.

$$\frac{d \ln y}{dt} = (1/y)\, dy/dt = \ln 2$$

$$\frac{dy/dt}{y} = \ln 2$$

For the linear function, $y = A + bt$, the rate of growth is variable with time, t.

$$dy/dt = b$$

$$\frac{dy/dt}{y} = \frac{b}{A + bt} \qquad t > 0 \text{ and } t \neq -A/b$$

For example, let $y = 10 + 2t$. Then $dy/dt = 2$. Dividing through by y gives: $dy/dt/(y) = 2/(10 + 2t)$.

For the power function, $y = At^b$, where t is the variable base, and b is the constant exponent, we have

$$dy/dt = bAt^{b-1}$$

Dividing through by y, we derive the growth rate:

$$\frac{dy/dt}{y} = \frac{bAt^{b-1}}{At^b} = b/t \qquad (t > 0)$$

Here also, for the power function, $y = At^b$, the growth rate is variable with time. As an example, let $y = 10t^2$. Differentiating with respect to t and dividing through by y gives the growth rate

$$dy/dt = 20t$$

$$\frac{dy/dt}{y} = \frac{20t}{10t^2} = 2/t$$

PRACTICE PROBLEM 15.1

For the following functions, find the rate of growth for the dependent variable y.

a) $y(t) = 2e^{.01t}$
b) $y(t) = 5(.01)^t$
c) $y(t) = 4 + .01t$
d) $y(t) = 2t^{.01}$

(The answers are at the end of the chapter.)

ECONOMIC GROWTH

Economic growth is defined to be the percentage change in per capita real national output. Increases in real national output per capita (and real national income per capita) allow for higher average consumption and material standards of living. Along with full employment and price stability, economic growth is one of the primary macroeconomic objectives.

If we let Y = real national output and P = total population in the nation, then $y = Y/P$ is per capita real national output. Differentiating y, we have

$$dy = \frac{dY \cdot P - Y dP}{P^2} = dY/P - (Y/P)dP/P.$$

Dividing through by y (equivalent to multiplying through by the population-output ratio, P/Y), we get the growth rate in real per capita output, dy/y.

$$dy/y = (dY/P)(P/Y) - (Y/P)(dP/P)(P/Y)$$

$$dy/y = dY/Y - dP/P$$

That is, the growth rate in real national output per capita, dy/y, is equal to the difference between the growth rate in real national output, dY/Y, and the population growth rate, dP/P. Strictly speaking, however, this relationship holds only for infinitesimal changes in output and population. For discrete changes, for example, over a year, the relationship is an approximation.

$$\Delta y/y \approx \Delta Y/Y - \Delta P/P$$

Negative economic growth occurs when the population growth rate exceeds the output growth rate.

SOURCES OF OUTPUT GROWTH

We begin with an aggregate production function, where real national output is dependent on the state of technology and the quantities and qualities of the primary factors of production (physical capital, labor, and natural resources).

$$Y(t) = A(t) \cdot F[K^*(t), N^*(t), R^*(t)]$$

with

$Y(t)$ = real national output produced in period t

$A(t)$ = index of technology in period t

$K^*(t)$ = effective physical capital stock in period t

$N^*(t)$ = effective labor employed in period t

$R^*(t)$ = effective natural resources utilized in period t

The state of technology reflects the knowledge applicable to the production of goods and services. *Ceteris paribus*, technological progress through invention and innovation in products and processes permits greater output from a given set of inputs.

Each of the primary factors of production is expressed in effective terms, that is, the physical quantities of the factors are adjusted by an index of the qualities or inherent productivities of the factors.

$$K^*(t) = q_K(t) \cdot K(t) \qquad \text{with } q_K(0) = 1.0$$

$$N^*(t) = q_N(t) \cdot N(t) \qquad \text{with } q_N(0) = 1.0$$

$$R^*(t) = q_R(t) \cdot R(t) \qquad \text{with } q_R(0) = 1.0$$

The quality indices are set equal to unity in the reference period, here the period $t = 0$.

To elaborate, $K(t)$, the physical capital stock in period t, is the quantitative measure of the human-made aids to production: the plant, equipment, and machinery of firms; buildings and residential structures; and the infrastructure (i.e., the transportation system, communications network, and public utilities) that can be used to produce goods and services. The average quality of the capital stock in period t is measured by the index, $q_K(t)$. Technological advances that are embodied in new capital goods, for example, improved memory chips in computers and more energy-efficient machinery, would increase the value of the index, $q_K(t)$.

$N(t)$ is the physical labor employed in period t, a function of the economically active population and the employment rate. With human capital formation through education and training, and improved health and nutrition, the average worker becomes more productive—which would be captured by an increase in the quality index for labor, $q_N(t)$.

$R(t)$ is a measure of the natural resources utilized for production in period t, including the land, forest reserves, minerals, and waterways. With enhanced methods of recovery, for example, harvesting the resources of the ocean and more efficient drilling for petroleum, the natural resources available to a nation can increase over time. Pollution and poor resource management, such as fishing beyond the regeneration potential of present stocks or overgrazing resulting in land erosion, however, can reduce both the quantity and quality of the natural resource base. The quality index for natural resources, $q_R(t)$, indicates the inherent productivity of the natural resources. Examples include the fertility of the farmland, the health of the forests, and the richness of mineral deposits.

Totally differentiating the aggregate production function,

$$Y(t) = A(t) \cdot F[K^*(t), N^*(t), R^*(t)]$$

we obtain

$$dY(t)/dt = (dA(t)/dt) \cdot F[K^*(t), N^*(t), R^*(t)] +$$

$$A(t) \cdot [(\delta F/\delta K^*(t))(dK^*(t)/dt) + (\delta F/\delta N^*(t))(dN^*(t)/dt) + (\delta F/\delta R^*(t))(dR^*(t)/dt)]$$

Multiplying through by the differential, dt, and then dividing through by $Y(t)$, we find

$$dY(t)/Y(t) = dA(t)/A(t) + A(t) \cdot \{[\delta F/\delta K^*(t)][dK^*(t)/Y(t)]$$

$$+ [\delta F/\delta N^*(t)][dN^*(t)/Y(t)] + [\delta F/\delta R^*(t)][dR^*(t)/Y(t)]\}$$

Now, multiplying and dividing the second, third, and fourth terms on the right-hand side of the equation by $K^*(t)$, $N^*(t)$, and $R^*(t)$, respectively, we can write

$$dY(t)/Y(t) = dA(t)/A(t) + \beta_{K*}[dK^*(t)/K^*(t)] + \beta_{N*}[dN^*(t)/N^*(t)]$$
$$+ \beta_{R*}[dR^*(t)/R^*(t)]$$

where

$$\beta_{K*} = A(t) \cdot [\delta F/\delta K^*(t)] \cdot [K^*(t)/Y(t)] = \frac{\delta Y(t)/\delta K^*(t)}{Y(t)/K^*(t)}$$

$$= \frac{\delta Y(t)/Y(t)}{\delta K^*(t)/K^*(t)} = \begin{array}{l}\text{partial output elasticity}\\\text{of effective capital}\end{array}$$

$$\beta_{N*} = A(t) \cdot [\delta F/\delta N^*(t)] \cdot [N^*(t)/Y(t)] = \frac{\delta Y(t)/\delta N^*(t)}{Y(t)/N^*(t)}$$

$$= \frac{\delta Y(t)/Y(t)}{\delta N^*(t)/N^*(t)} = \begin{array}{l}\text{partial output elasticity}\\\text{of effective labor}\end{array}$$

$$\beta_{R*} = A(t) \cdot [\delta F/\delta R^*(t)] \cdot [R^*(t)/Y(t)] = \frac{\delta Y(t)/\delta R^*(t)}{Y(t)/R^*(t)}$$

$$= \frac{\delta Y(t)/Y(t)}{\delta R^*(t)/R^*(t)} = \begin{array}{l}\text{partial output elasticity of}\\\text{effective natural resources}\end{array}$$

The partial output elasticities, β_{K*}, β_{N*}, and β_{R*}, give the ratios of the (instantaneous) percentage changes in real national output to the (infinitesimal) percentage changes in effective physical capital, effective labor, and effective natural resources, respectively, assuming that the other effective primary factors of production and technology are held constant.

The growth rate of real national output, $dY(t)/Y(t)$, then is equal to the growth rate of technology, $dA(t)/A(t)$, plus a weighted sum of the growth rates of the effective primary factors of production, where the weights are the partial output elasticities of the effective factors. The growth rates of the effective primary factors of production, in turn, are equal to the sum of the growth rates of the quantities and quality indices of the factors.

For effective capital, $dK^*(t) = dq_K(t) \cdot K(t) + q_K(t) \cdot dK(t)$

$$dK^*(t)/K^*(t) = dq_K(t)/q_K(t) + dK(t)/K(t)$$

For effective labor, $dN^*(t) = dq_N(t) \cdot N(t) + q_N(t) \cdot dN(t)$

$$dN^*(t)/N^*(t) = dq_N(t)/q_N(t) + dN(t)/N(t)$$

And, for effective natural resources, $dR^*(t) = dq_R(t) \cdot R(t) + q_R(t) \cdot dR(t)$

$$dR^*(t)/R^*(t) = dq_R(t)/q_R(t) + dR(t)/R(t)$$

Again, for discrete changes in the quantities or quality indices, the formulas hold only as approximations.

To illustrate, consider the aggregate production function:

$$Y(t) = A(t) \cdot [K^*(t)]^a \, [N^*(t)]^b \, [R^*(t)]^c \text{ where } 0 < a, b, c < 1$$

(You may recognize this from Chapter 10 as an example of a Cobb-Douglas production function.) Since output, capital, labor, natural resources, and the index of technology are all functions of time, t, we can simplify the notation and write the production function as: $Y = A \cdot (K^*)^a \, (N^*)^b \, (R^*)^c$

Totally differentiating we have

$$dY = dA \cdot [(K^*)^a \, (N^*)^b \, (R^*)^c] \, +$$

$$A \cdot [a(K^*)^{a-1} \, dK^*(N^*)^b \, (R^*)^c + b(K^*)^a \, (N^*)^{b-1} \, dN^*(R^*)^c + c(K^*)^a \, (N^*)^b \, (R^*)^{c-1} \, dR^*]$$

Dividing through by $Y = A \cdot (K^*)^a \, (N^*)^b \, (R^*)^c$ and simplifying, we obtain the growth rate for real national output.

$$dY/Y = dA/A + [a \cdot (dK^*/K^*) + b \cdot (dN^*/N^*) + c \cdot (dR^*/R^*)]$$

We can see that the partial output elasticities for effective capital, effective labor, and effective natural resources are given by the exponents a, b, and c, respectively.

$$(\delta Y/Y)/(\delta K^*/K^*) = a$$

$$(\delta Y/Y)/(\delta N^*/N^*) = b$$

and

$$(\delta Y/Y)/(\delta R^*/R^*) = c$$

Having identified the key sources of output growth, consistent with the early growth models, we will initially work with a simple aggregate production function, $Y(t) = F[K(t), N(t)]$, and focus on physical capital formation and labor force growth. Later we extend the analysis to incoporate technological change and qualitative growth in the factors. We start by relating physical capital formation to the investment rate.

PRACTICE PROBLEM 15.2

Given the aggregate production function, $Y = AK^{.6} \, N^{.3}$:
a) Derive the growth rate for real national output.
b) Determine the partial output elasticities for capital and labor.

(The answers are at the end of the chapter.)

INVESTMENT AND PHYSICAL CAPITAL FORMATION

Gross private domestic investment includes business fixed investment, residential fixed investment, and inventory investment. Business fixed investment refers to expenditures on new plant, equipment, and machinery in the period, and directly adds to the productive capacity of an economy. Residential fixed investment refers to the value of new residential construction during the period, and directly adds to the provision of shelter. Inventory investment refers to changes in the business stocks of goods at various stages of production over the period.

Gross public domestic investment encompasses the capital expenditures by government on buildings, equipment, and the economic infrastructure, including highways, railways, ports, and public utilities—all of which provide essential services like public administration, health care, education, transportation, electricity, and water.

With fixed investment expenditures—whether business, residential, or public— resources are devoted to maintaining or increasing the physical capital stock. Although there is a sacrifice in present consumption, the capital goods produced allow for enhanced future consumption possibilities. Moreover, replacing, modernizing, and expanding the physical capital stock not only can alleviate capacity constraints, but can also increase the productivity of labor. As noted earlier, the latest technologies are often embodied in new capital goods.

Gross fixed investment includes all expenditures on new physical capital, some or all of which are needed to replace the capital that depreciates over the period. **Depreciation** or **capital consumption** is the loss in the value of the physical capital stock due to wear and tear and technological obsolescence. **Net fixed investment** is the difference between gross fixed investment and capital consumption. If gross fixed investment exceeds capital consumption, net fixed investment is positive and the value of the physical capital stock increases over the period. Conversely, if the capital stock is depreciating faster than new expenditures on capital goods, then the physical capital stock is declining in value.

To express the relationship between the rate of net fixed investment and the physical capital stock mathematically, let

$$I(t) = \text{rate of net fixed investment at time } t$$

$$K(t) = \text{physical capital stock at time } t$$

The change in the capital stock reflects the rate of net fixed investment and the length of the period:

$$dK(t) = I(t) \, dt$$

Dividing through by the differential, dt, indicating the length of the period, we have

$$dK(t)/dt = I(t)$$

Integrating both sides with respect to time gives

$$\int dK(t)/dt) \, dt = K(t) + C = \int I(t) \, dt \qquad (C = \text{constant of integration})$$

In order to determine the specific amount of physical capital formation, in addition to the rate of net investment, $I(t)$, we need the length of the time interval, that is, the limits of integration. For example, the definite integral,

$$\int_0^{t_0} I(t) \, dt = K(t_0) \Big]_0^{t_0} = K(t_0) - K(0)$$

gives the change in the physical capital stock between two points in time, $t = 0$ and $t = t_0$.

Figure 15.1 illustrates. The shaded area beneath the curve representing the net investment function, $I(t)$, defined between the two points in time, 0 and t_0, measures the net physical capital accumulation over the interval from 0 to t_0.

Rewriting to solve for the level of the capital stock at time t_0, we have

$$K(t_0) = K(0) + \int_0^{t_0} I(t) \, dt$$

$K(t_0)$, the physical capital stock at a point in time, t_0, is equal to the initial capital stock, $K(0)$, plus the net capital formation over the time interval. Given a rate of net investment, a duration of time, and the initial capital stock, we can determine the capital stock at any future point in time. Moreover, we can derive the equation for the time path of the capital stock, $K(t)$.

For example, let $I(t) = 12t^{1/3}$ be the rate of net investment at time t. Then, given the initial capital stock, $K(0) = 25$, the time path of the capital stock is

$$K(t) = \int I(t) \, dt = \int 12t^{1/3} \, dt = \frac{12t^{4/3}}{4/3} + C = 9t^{4/3} + C$$

Since $K(0) = 25$, we can determine the value of the constant of integration, C, as

$$K(0) = 9(0)^{4/3} + C = 25$$

$$C = 25$$

Therefore, the time path of the physical capital stock is $K(t) = 9t^{4/3} + 25$.

To determine the level of the physical capital stock at any point in time, t_0, we can either use the equation for the time path or add the net physical capital formation over

FIGURE 15.1   THE INVESTMENT RATE AND PHYSICAL CAPITAL FORMATION

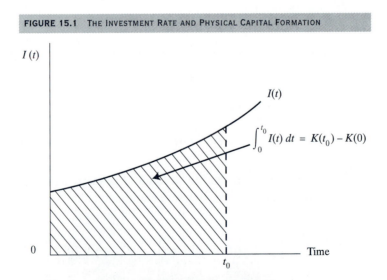

the period to the initial capital stock. To illustrate, to determine the capital stock at the end of 8 years, given an annual rate of net investment of $I(t) = 12t^{1/3}$ and an initial capital stock of $K(0) = 25$, we can set $t = 8$ in the equation for the time path of the capital stock.

$$K(t) = 9t^{4/3} + 25$$

$$K(8) = 9(8)^{4/3} + 25 = 9(16) + 25 = 169$$

Alternatively, we could add the net capital formation over the 8-year period to the initial capital stock.

$$\int_0^8 I(t)\,dt = \int_0^8 12t^{1/3}\,dt = 9t^{4/3}\Big|_0^8 = 9(16) - 9(0) = 144$$

$$K(8) = K(0) + 144 = 25 + 144 = 169$$

Note that, given this particular function for the rate of net fixed investment, the increase in the capital stock is rising in each period or interval of time. For instance, comparing the capital formation in the first and second years of the 8-year period, we have

$$\int_0^1 12t^{1/3}\,dt = 9t^{4/3}\Big|_0^1 = 9(1) - 9(0) = 9$$

$$\int_1^2 12t^{1/3}\,dt = 9t^{4/3}\Big|_1^2 = 9(2)^{4/3} - 9(1)^{4/3} = 9(2.52) - 9(1) = 22.68 - 9 = 13.68$$

PRACTICE PROBLEM 15.3

Given the initial capital stock, $K(0) = 10$ and annual rate of net investment of $I(t) = 2t^5$.
a) Find the time path for the capital stock.
b) Find the value of the capital stock at $t = 2$.
c) Find the net capital formation in the first and second years.

(The answers are at the end of the chapter.)

POPULATION GROWTH

As stated earlier, the economic growth rate is equal to the difference between the growth rates in real national output and population. An increase in population growth, *ceteris paribus*, would reduce economic growth; however, if labor force growth accompanies the population growth, then the net impact on economic growth is less clear, since output growth is also likely to be affected. We begin with the components of population change and then relate labor force growth to population growth.

For a given geographical area, population change is equal to the difference between the births and deaths in the population plus net in-migration to the area over the given period. Net in-migration to the area is the difference between the migration of population to the area (immigration or in-migration) and the migration of population from the area (emigration or out-migration). Formally, consider a period of time of length 1, from $t - 1$ to t. Let

P_t = population of an area at time t

P_{t-1} = population of an area at time $t - 1$

b_t = births to the population during the period from $t - 1$ to t.

d_t = deaths in the population during the period from $t - 1$ to t

nm_t = net in-migration to the area during the period from $t - 1$ to t.

The population in an area at a point in time is a *stock*. If the length of the period is set equal to one, as we assume here, then P_t and P_{t-1}, are the population sizes at the end and beginning of the period, respectively. Births, deaths, and net in-migration are flows, and so defined for a given duration of time.

The population at time t, P_t, is equal to the initial population, P_{t-1}, plus the natural increase (births less deaths) and net in-migration over the period.

$$P_t = P_{t-1} + (b_t - d_t) + nm_t$$

Subtracting the initial population from both sides of the equation, we derive the expression for population change.

$$P_t - P_{t-1} = (b_t - d_t) + nm_t$$

To convert to the population growth rate, the convention is to divide the equation for population change by the midpoint population, or the population size at the midpoint of the period. Assuming an even flow of births, deaths, and net in-migration over the period, the midpoint population, $\overline{P}_t$, is the average of the beginning- and end-of-period populations.

$$\overline{P}_t = .5(P_{t-1} + P_t)$$

The equation for the population growth rate, r_t, is

$$r_t = \frac{P_t - P_{t-1}}{\overline{P}_t} = \left(\frac{b_t}{\overline{P}_t} - \frac{d_t}{\overline{P}_t}\right) + \frac{nm_t}{\overline{P}_t}$$

or

$$r_t = (CBR_t - CDR_t) + NMR_t$$

The ratio of births during the period to the midpoint population is known as the **crude birth rate**, $CBR_t = b_t/\overline{P}_t$. Similarly, the ratio of the deaths during the period to the midpoint population is known as the **crude death rate**, $CDR_t = d_t/\overline{P}_t$. The ratio of the net in-migration during the period (the immigrants less the emigrants) to the midpoint population is the **net in-migration rate**, $NMR_t = nm_t/\overline{P}_t$. The crude birth rate, crude death rate, and net in-migration rate are usually expressed per 1,000 mid-year population. The difference between the crude birth rate and crude death rate is the **crude rate of natural increase**, $CRNI_t = CBR_t - CDR_t$. In a closed population, with no immigration or emigration, the population growth rate is equal to the crude rate of natural increase. In the absence of extraterrestial migration, the earth's population can be regarded as closed.

Consider a simple numerical example. Let

$$P_{t-1} = 40,000 \text{ (population size at the beginning of the year)}$$

$$b_t = 1,000 \text{ (births during the year)}$$

$$d_t = 400 \text{ (deaths during the year)}$$

$$nm_t = -80 \text{ (net in-migration during the year)}$$

Note that here emigration exceeds immigration by 80. The population size of this area at time t, P_t, is equal to

$$P_t = P_{t-1} + (b_t - d_t) + nm_t$$

$$P_t = 40,000 + (1,000 - 400) + (-80)$$

$$P_t = 40,520$$

The mid-year population is: $\overline{P}_t = .5(P_{t-1} + P_t) = .5(40,000 + 40,520) = 40,260$
The population growth rate is $r_t = 1.29\%$.

$$r_t = \frac{40,520 - 40,000}{40,260} = \left(\frac{1,000}{40,260} - \frac{400}{40,260}\right) + \frac{-80}{40,260}$$

$$r_t = .0129 = (.0248 - .0099) + (-.0019)$$

The crude birth rate is .0248 (or 24.8 births per 1,000 mid-year population), and the crude death rate is .0099 (or 9.9 deaths per 1,000 mid-year population), giving a crude rate of natural increase of .0149 (or 14.9 persons per 1,000 mid-year population). The net in-migration rate is $-.0019$ (or -1.9 net in-migrants per 1,000 mid-year population).

Population growth is a continuous process, with births, deaths, and migration occurring throughout the period. We can apply the formula for continuous compounding of interest (refer back to Chapter 4) to measure population growth.

For a given growth rate of population, r, and an initial population, P_0, the population at time t, P_t, is equal to: $P_t = P_0\, e^{rt}$, where e is the base of the natural logarithm: $e = 2.71828. \ldots$ Returning to the previous example, where $P_0 = 40,000$ and $r = .0129$, the population at the end of the year is $P_1 = 40,000\, e^{.0129(1)} = 40,520$. The population at the end of 2 years would be $P_2 = 40,000\, e^{.0129(2)} = 40,000\, e^{.0258} = 41,045$.

On the other hand, if given an initial population and a future population, P_0 and P_t, respectively, we can find the population growth rate, r. Beginning with the equation, $P_t = P_0\, e^{rt}$, and dividing through by P_0, we get

$$P_t/P_0 = e^{rt}$$

Taking the natural logarithm of both sides, we obtain

$$\ln (P_t/P_0) = rt$$

Solving for the population growth rate, r, gives

$$r = (1/t) \ln (P_t/P_0)$$

For example, suppose $P_0 = 2{,}500$, $t = 25$ years, and $P_t = 6{,}000$. Then

$$r = (1/25) \ln (6{,}000/2{,}500) = (1/25) (.8755) = .035$$

The annual population growth rate is 3.5%.

A convenient way to interpret the consequences of a given population growth rate is to calculate the implied doubling time, or the length (in years) for the population to double in size if it were to grow at the constant annual rate of r. Begin again with the equation for the future population, $P_t = P_0 e^{rt}$. Dividing through by P_0, and setting the ratio, P_t/P_0, equal to 2, since we want to find the time required for the population to double in size, gives

$$P_t/P_0 = 2 = e^{rt}$$

Taking the natural logarithm of both sides,

$$\ln 2 = rt$$

and solving for t, we find

$$t = (1/r) \ln 2 = .693/r$$

If the population is growing at an annual rate of 1% ($r = .01$), then the population would double in 69.3 years; at an annual rate of 2% ($r = .02$), the doubling time would be 34.65 years, and so on. A rough approximation for the doubling time is "the rule of 72." Divide the annual population growth rate (in percentage points) into 72 to approximate the time in years required for the population to double. The number 72 is used since it is easily divisible by 2, 3, 4, and 6.

PRACTICE PROBLEM 15.4

Given an initial population, $P_0 = 10{,}000$, and a 1-year interval. Suppose that the births, deaths, and net in-migration over that first year are respectively: $b_1 = 300$, $d_1 = 170$, and $nm_1 = 50$.

a) Determine the population size at the end of the first year, P_1.
b) Determine the crude birth rate, CBR_1, the crude death rate, CDR_1, and the net in-migration rate, NMR_1.
c) Determine the population growth rate and the associated doubling time.
d) Determine the population size at the end of the second year if the population continued to grow at the same rate as in the first year.

(The answers are at the end of the chapter.)

Labor Force Growth   The growth in the labor force is determined by the growth in the population of working age and the labor force participation rates (the percentages of the age groups that are economically active—either employed or unemployed and seeking work). The growth in the population of working age reflects earlier birth rates as well as earlier and current death rates and net in-migration rates. In the advanced economies, generally labor force participation begins at age sixteen. In less developed economies, where child labor is more prevalent, labor force participation begins well before the age of 16.

Formally, the labor force at time t, $(N_{LF})_t$, is equal to the summation of the products of the population at each age, $(P_a)_t$, and the respective labor force participation rates, $(LFPR_a)_t$.

$$(N_{LF})_t = \sum_a (LFPR_a)_t \cdot (P_a)_t$$

where

$(LFPR_a)_t$ = labor force participation rate for population of age a at time t

$(P_a)_t$ = population of age a at time t

For a given labor force, the labor employed depends on the demand for labor, which, in turn, depends on the aggregate demand for goods and services and the aggregate production function.

Returning to the relationship between population growth and economic growth expressed by the equation, $dy/y = dY/Y - dP/P$, we should note that not all population growth has the same consequences for economic growth. That is, the cause or type of population growth can have an impact on output growth, dY/Y.

Consider an increase in the rate of population growth. If the increased population growth rate is due to an increase in the crude birth rate, there would not be a subsequent increase in the labor force growth rate for at least a decade, or until the greater number of children born begin entering the work force. Indeed, if higher birth rates are accompanied by lower female labor force participation rates, then the labor force growth rate—and, depending on the demand for labor, the output growth rate—would decline initially. Therefore, increased population growth due to higher birth rates would most likely reduce economic growth initially.

If the increased population growth rate is instead due to a decrease in the crude death rate, then, likely in addition to the greater number of children surviving, there would be a greater number of working age population surviving, which increases the growth rate of the labor force. Moreover, if the lower death rate reflects improved health, then the average quality of labor may rise. Here, increases in the quantity and quality of labor, associated with increases in the population growth rate from a lower crude death rate, would increase output growth, offsetting in part, entirely, or perhaps even outweighing, the negative direct effects of a larger population on per capita output.

Finally, if the increased population growth rate is due to an increase in the net in-migration rate, then the effects on the output growth rate and the economic growth rate depend on the composition of the migrant flows. For example, an influx of labor, especially skilled labor, would directly contribute to the growth rate of output and increase economic growth. Typically, migration flows are dominated by individuals of labor force age.

In the ensuing discussion of growth models, we will see the importance of the aggregate saving rate. The age composition of a population, reflecting the underlying birth, death, and net in-migration rates, affects the aggregate saving rate of an economy. In particular, in nations with high birth rates and rapid population growth, the populations tend to be young. That is, relatively high percentages of these populations are under the age of 15, resulting in high burdens of dependency and the need to direct significant proportions of national incomes toward the consumption needs of the youth, especially for schooling and health care. Consequently, the saving rates in these nations tend to be low.

HARROD-DOMAR GROWTH MODEL

A well-known early growth model is the Harrod-Domar Model, which, although limited in its application, stimulated other efforts to explain long-run economic growth.[1] Underlying the Harrod-Domar (HD) Model is a fixed-coefficients production function, with real national output, $Y(t)$, a function of the physical capital stock, $K(t)$, and labor, $N(t)$. Natural resources are not included in the aggregate production function—implicitly, natural resources are sufficiently available to accommodate any rate of output growth. Moreover, we abstract from technological progress and qualitative changes in the primary factors of capital and labor.

The structure of the HD Model is given by five equations, listed below.

HD1) $K(t) = vY(t)$ (full-capacity condition)

HD2) $N(t) = uY(t)$ (full-employment condition)

HD3) $I(t) = S(t)$ (product market equilibrium condition)

HD4) $S(t) = sY(t)$ (saving function)

HD5) $N(t) = N(0)e^{nt}$ (labor supply)

Equations HD1) and HD2) represent the fixed-coefficients production function. The parameters v and u are the fixed capital-output ratio, $v = K/Y$, and fixed labor-output ratio, $u = L/Y$, respectively. Recall from Chapter 10 that the fixed-coefficients production function can be written as $Y(t) = \text{minimum } [K(t)/v, N(t)/u]$. With no sub-

---

[1]See Roy Harrod, "An Essay in Dynamic Theory," *Economic Journal* (March 1939), pages 14–33, and Evsey Domar, "Capital Formation, Rate of Growth, and Employment," *Econometrica* (April 1946), pages 137–147, for the seminal articles.

stitution possible between capital and labor, the production of output is limited by the relatively scarce factor—determined by the minimum of $K(t)/v$ and $N(t)/u$.

From another perspective, for a given capital-output ratio, v, the demand for capital is set by the level of output: $K(t) = vY(t)$, as indicated by the full-capacity condition, HD1). Similarly, for a given labor-output ratio, u, the demand for labor is set by the level of output: $N(t) = uY(t)$, as indicated by the full-employment condition, HD2). Intuitively, with a fixed-coefficients production function and constant returns to scale, assuming that the capital stock and labor force are initially fully utilized, maintaining full employment for both factors over time would require that capital, labor, and output all grow at the same rate.

To demonstrate, differentiating equations HD1) and HD2), we have

$$\text{HD1) } K(t) = vY(t)$$

$$dK(t)/dt = v \, dY(t)/dt$$

Dividing the left-hand side of the equation by $K(t)$ and the right-hand side by the equivalent $vY(t)$, we find

$$\frac{dK(t)/dt}{K(t)} = \frac{v \, dY(t)/dt}{vY(t)} = \frac{dY(t)/dt}{Y(t)}$$

then, multiplying through by dt

$$dK(t)/K(t) = dY(t)/Y(t)$$

Similarly for labor

$$\text{HD2) } N(t) = uY(t)$$

$$dN(t)/dt = u \, dY(t)/dt$$

Dividing through by $N(t) = uY(t)$, we obtain

$$\frac{dN(t)/dt}{N(t)} = \frac{u \, dY(t)/dt}{uY(t)} = \frac{dY(t)/dt}{Y(t)}$$

then, multiplying through by dt:

$$dN(t)/N(t) = dY(t)/Y(t)$$

Thus, the full-capacity and full-employment conditions require that the growth rates of output, physical capital, and labor are equal over time.

Equation HD3) gives the equilibrium condition for this one-sector model (for real national output of goods and services). $I(t)$ refers to real net fixed investment expenditures, that is, gross fixed investment less capital consumption (the depreciation of the physical capital stock), and $S(t)$ refers to real net saving, that is, gross saving less the funds set aside for capital consumption. In a simple model for a closed economy, that is, with no foreign trade or foreign investment, the product market equilibrium reduces to domestic investment equals domestic saving. Investment represents the national output used not for consumption, but for the production of capital goods. Saving represents the national income not used for consumption, thus available for the funding of investment expenditures.[2]

Equation HD4) indicates that real net saving is assumed to be a constant fraction, s, of real national income ($0 < s < 1$). The marginal propensity to save, s, assumed to be exogenous, would be dependent on the rate of interest, the distribution of income, and the age-structure of the population.

Equation HD5) gives the labor supply. The labor force is assumed to be growing at a constant rate, n. To illustrate, differentiating HD5) $N(t) = N(0)e^{nt}$, we have

$$dN(t)/dt = nN(0)e^{nt}$$

Dividing through by $N(t)$, the labor supply at time t, we obtain the growth rate for the labor force.

$$[dN(t)/dt]/N(t) = nN(0)e^{nt}/N(0)e^{nt} = n$$

The parameter, n, known as the **natural growth rate of labor**, reflects the growth rate of the population of labor force age and the labor force participation rates.

STEADY-STATE EQUILIBRIUM

To solve the Harrod-Domar Model, we need to find the growth paths of output, capital, and labor that are consistent with product market equilibrium ($I = S$) and full employment of capital and labor. We begin by differentiating equation HD1) $K(t) = vY(t)$,

$$dK(t)/dt = v\,dY(t)/dt \quad \text{or} \quad dK(t) = v\,dY(t)$$

That is, given the fixed coefficients production function, changes in the demand for capital are a fixed multiple, v, of changes in real national output. Recall that changes in the physical capital stock, $dK(t)$, equal real net investment expenditures, $I(t)dt$, and

---

[2]We could incorporate the public sector by disaggregating government purchases into government consumption expenditures, G_C (e.g., civil servant salaries and government payments for services rendered), and government capital expenditures, G_I (e.g., public investment expenditures on capital goods, including the economic infrastructure). Adding government capital expenditures to private domestic investment yields an equilibrium condition for a closed economy:

$$I + G_I = S + (T - G_C)$$

Gross domestic investment, $I + G_I$, is equal to gross domestic saving, $S + (T - G_C)$, where $(T - G_C)$ refers to the current government budget balance. By netting out the capital consumption from gross domestic investment and gross domestic saving, we obtain the condition for product market equilibrium for a closed economy: net domestic investment equals net domestic saving.

By engaging in foreign trade and investment, a nation can relax the condition that gross domestic investment must equal gross domestic saving. For example, gross domestic investment in a nation will exceed gross domestic saving when the nation draws on foreign saving by running a current account deficit in its balance of payments ($M - X + R + F > 0$), where M and X are imports and exports of goods and services, R represents net transfers to the rest of the world, and F represents net factor payments to the rest of the world.

In the growth models discussed in this chapter, we simplify the analysis by using a closed model. We also ignore inventory investment, thus all investment expenditures are for fixed investment.

that in this model, real net saving is a fixed proportion of real national income, $S(t) = sY(t)$.

Setting investment equal to saving, consistent with the product market equilibrium condition, HD3), we have

$$I(t) = dK(t)/dt = v\,dY(t)/dt = sY(t) = S(t)$$

or

$$v\,dY(t)/dt = sY(t).$$

Now, solving for the growth rate of output, $[dY(t)/dt]/Y(t)$, we find

$$[dY(t)/dt]/Y(t) = s/v$$

The growth rate in real national output (and real national income), consistent with the fixed-coefficients production function and product market equilibrium, is known as the **warranted rate of growth** and is equal to the saving rate, s, divided by the capital-output ratio, v. With constant returns to scale and no factor substitution, the required growth rates in physical capital and labor are equal to the growth rate of real national output.

$$\frac{dK(t)/dt}{K(t)} = \frac{dN(t)/dt}{N(t)} = \frac{dY(t)/dt}{Y(t)} = s/v = \text{warranted rate of growth}$$

Steady-State Growth Paths   Given the warranted rate of growth for output, capital, and labor, we can derive the associated growth paths. Beginning with the equation for the output growth rate

$$[dY(t)/dt]/Y(t) = s/v$$

integrating both sides with respect to time, we obtain

$$\int [(dY(t)/dt)/Y(t)]\,dt = \int (s/v)\,dt$$

or

$$\ln Y(t) + C_1 = (s/v)t + C_2$$

and

$$\ln Y(t) = (s/v)t + C$$

where $C = C_2 - C_1$ is the difference between the respective constants of integration from the indefinite integrals for output growth. Converting to exponential form, we can solve for $Y(t)$, deriving the growth path for real national output.

$$Y(t) = e^{(s/v)t+C} = e^{(s/v)t}\,e^C$$

To initialize, we set $t = 0$, so $Y(0) = e^C\,e^{(s/v)0} = e^C$. Therefore, the growth path for real national output is given by: $Y(t) = Y(0)e^{(s/v)t}$.

The growth paths for physical capital and labor can be easily derived. Since $K(t) = vY(t)$ and $N(t) = uY(t)$ from the fixed-coefficients production function, we can write

$$K(t) = vY(0)e^{(s/v)t}$$

and

$$N(t) = uY(0)e^{(s/v)t}.$$

Assuming $K(0) = vY(0)$ and $N(0) = uY(0)$, that is, the initial levels of capital and labor, $K(0)$ and $N(0)$, are equal to the required fixed ratios of the initial output, $Y(0)$, then the growth paths for the physical capital stock and labor are

$$K(t) = K(0)e^{(s/v)t}$$

and

$$N(t) = N(0)e^{(s/v)t}$$

Steady-state equilibrium requires equilibrium in the product market and maintaining full capacity use of the capital stock and full employment of the labor force. The growth rate of labor demand is equal to the warranted rate of growth, s/v. The growth rate of labor supply, however, is independently set by the natural growth rate of the labor force, n. To maintain full employment of labor, the growth paths for labor demand and labor supply must coincide:

growth path for labor demand: $N(t) = N(0)e^{(s/v)t}$

growth path for labor supply: $N(t) = N(0)e^{nt}$ where $N(0) = uY(0)$

In short, the condition for steady-state equilibrium in the Harrod-Domar growth is that

$$\frac{dY(t)/dt}{Y(t)} = \frac{dK(t)/dt}{K(t)} = \frac{dN(t)/dt}{N(t)} = s/v = n$$

This is a very stringent condition. The value of the exogenous parameters representing the saving rate (s), the capital-output ratio (v), and the natural growth rate of the labor force (n), must be such that the warranted rate of growth, s/v, is exactly equal to the natural rate of growth, n. If not—and there is no reason to expect that these parameters would be so aligned—the economy would be out of steady-state equilibrium. Moreover, in the Harrod-Domar Model with a fixed-coefficients production function and exogenous saving rate and natural growth rate of the labor force, there are no adjustment mechanisms to restore steady-state equilibrium. The Harrod-Domar Model is dynamically unstable.

THE KNIFE-EDGE PROBLEM

The dynamic instability of the Harrod-Domar Model is known as the **knife-edge problem**. If initially in equilibrium, then to remain in steady-state equilibrium, the economy must maintain a delicate balance, always equating the warranted rate of growth (s/v) with the natural rate of growth of the labor force (n). Should this not be the case — and recall, the saving rate, capital-output ratio, and natural growth rate are independently determined — the economy would experience either increasing unemployment of labor or increasing excess capacity of the physical capital stock over time.

Surplus Labor and Unemployment   For example, start with an economy in steady-state equilibrium, where $K(0) = vY(0)$, $N(0) = uY(0)$, and $s/v = n$. Real national output, capital, and labor are all growing at the warranted rate of growth, which is equal to the natural rate of growth, so full utilization of both factors is being maintained. Now suppose that, due to a decrease in the death rate (or an increase in the net in-migration rate), the natural growth rate of the labor force increases to $n' > n$. The new natural growth rate of the labor force exceeds the warranted rate of growth: $n' > s/v$. Therefore, the labor supply is growing faster than the labor demand. Usually, in a market economy, an excess supply of labor would exert downward pressure on the wage rate (user cost of labor) and encourage firms to substitute labor for capital. With a fixed-coefficients production function, however, such factor substitution is not possible. Consequently, the excess supply of labor is not absorbed into employment and the output growth rate is not increased. Indeed, as long as the natural rate of growth exceeds the warranted growth rate, the unemployment of labor increases over time.

Moreover, the surplus of labor implies a shortage of capital. Upward pressure on the interest rate and returns to investment in capital might be expected to increase the saving rate, augmenting the supply of funds available for investment and physical capital formation. Yet, the saving rate in the Harrod-Domar Model is also exogenous. In sum, output and capital continue growing at the warranted rate, while the labor force is growing at the higher natural rate:

$$[dY(t)/dt]/Y(t) = [dK(t)/dt]/K(t) = s/v < n' = [dN(t)/dt]/N(t)$$

Surplus Capital and Excess Capacity   Conversely, if an economy in steady-state equilibrium experiences a fall in the natural growth rate of labor to $n'' < n$, then the demand for labor would be growing at a greater rate (s/v) than the supply of labor (n''). The shortage of labor and surplus of capital should drive up the wage rate and drive down the interest rate, inducing firms to substitute capital for labor. Again, with a fixed-coefficients production function, this factor substitution is not possible. Nor would the surplus of capital and likely reduction in the returns to investment decrease the saving rate and rate of capital formation in the Harrod-Domar Model. Consequently, the excess capacity (underutilized capital stock) would continue and even increase over time. In sum, if the warranted rate of growth exceeds the natural growth rate of the labor force, then

$$[dK(t)/dt]/K(t) = s/v > n'' = [dY(t)/dt]/Y(t) = [dN(t)/dt]/N(t)$$

An Illustration of the Harrod-Domar Model   Before turning to the proposed remedies to the knife-edge problem of the Harrod-Domar Model, a numerical example may help to illustrate the dynamic instabilty. Consider the following equations of a HD Model:

HD1) $K(t) = 3Y(t)$ (full-capacity condition)

HD2) $N(t) = 5Y(t)$ (full-employment condition)

HD3) $I(t) = S(t)$ (product market equilibrium condition)

HD4) $S(t) = .075Y(t)$ (saving function)

HD5) $N(t) = 500e^{.025t}$ (labor supply)

where $Y(0) = 100$, $K(0) = 300$, and $N(0) = 500$. The key parameters are: $s = S(t)/Y(t) = .075$; $v = K(t)/Y(t) = 3$; $u = N(t)/Y(t) = 5$; and $n = dN(t)/N(t) = .025$. We note that the warranted rate of growth, $s/v = .075/3 = .025$, is equal to the natural rate of growth, $n = .025$.

We begin by deriving the steady-state growth paths for output, capital, and labor, based on the warranted rate of growth. Differentiating equation HD1) gives

$$dK(t)/dt = 3 \, dY(t)/dt$$

Setting net investment, which is equivalent to the change in the capital stock, equal to net saving, which is given by the product of the saving rate and real national income, we have

$$I(t) = dK(t)/dt = 3dY(t)/dt = .075Y(t) = S(t)$$

or

$$3[dY(t)/dt] = .075Y(t)$$

Solving for the growth rate in real national output, $[dY(t)/dt]/Y(t)$, gives

$$[dY(t)/dt]/Y(t) = .075/3 = .025 = s/v = \text{warranted rate of growth}$$

With the warranted rate of growth, we can obtain the growth path for output. Integrating both sides with respect to time, we have

$$\int ([dY(t)/dt]/Y(t)) \, dt = \int .025 \, dt$$

$$\ln Y(t) + C_1 = .025t + C_2$$

$$\ln Y(t) = .025t + C \quad \text{(where } C = C_2 - C_1)$$

Solving for real national output, $Y(t)$, gives

$$Y(t) = e^{.025t+C} = e^{.025t} e^C$$

Initializing by setting $t = 0$, we have $Y(0) = e^C$.
Thus, the growth path for real national output, given that $Y(0) = 100$, is

$$Y(t) = Y(0)e^{.025t} = 100e^{.025t}$$

The growth paths for capital and labor are, respectively,

$$K(t) = vY(t) = vY(0)e^{.025t} = 3(100)e^{.025t} = 300e^{.025t}$$

$$N(t) = uY(t) = uY(0)e^{.025t} = 5(100)e^{.025t} = 500e^{.025t}$$

Note that the growth path for labor demand is identical to the growth path for labor supply, given by the equation HD5). This economy is in steady-state equilibrium.

To illustrate, we can examine the values for output, capital, labor demand, and labor supply for the points in time, $t = 0, 1$, and 2. We will round off the values to the nearest tenth. Refer to Figure 15.2.

For example, at the end of the first period, $t = 1$, the levels of the physical capital stock, labor (demand and supply), and output are

$$K(1) = 300e^{.025(1)} = 307.6$$

$$N(1) = 500e^{.025(1)} = 512.7$$

$$Y(1) = 100e^{.025(1)} = 102.5$$

Alternatively, we can show that the net saving over this interval from $t = 0$ to $t = 1$ is equal to

$$S_1 = \int_0^1 S(t)dt = \int_0^1 .075Y(t)\, dt = \int_0^1 .075(100)e^{.025t}\, dt = 7.5\int_0^1 e^{.025t}\, dt$$

$$S_1 = \frac{7.5e^{.025t}}{.025}\bigg|_0^1 = 300e^{.025t}\bigg|_0^1 = 300e^{.025(1)} - 300e^{.025(0)} = 307.6 - 300.0 = 7.6$$

FIGURE 15.2   ILLUSTRATION OF HARROD-DOMAR GROWTH MODEL: STEADY-STATE EQUILIBRIUM

Time t	Physical Capital $K(t) = 300e^{.025t}$	Labor Demand $N(t) = 500e^{.025t}$	Labor Supply $N(t) = 500e^{.025t}$	Output $Y(t) = 100e^{.025t}$	Condition
0	300.0	500.0	500.0	100.0	steady-state equilibrium
1	307.6	512.7	512.7	102.5	steady-state equilibrium
2	315.4	525.6	525.6	105.1	steady-state equilibrium
		$N'(t) = 500e^{.03t}$			
3	323.4	538.9	541.6	107.8	unemployed labor = 2.7
4	331.6	552.6	558.1	110.5	unemployed labor = 5.5

Note: After time $t = 2$, the natural growth rate in the labor force increases from $n = .025$ to $n' = .03$.

Equating the net saving with the net investment over this interval, which is equal to the change in the physical capital stock, we can find the level of the capital stock at $t = 1$.

$$K(1) = K(0) + S_1 = 300 + 7.6 = 307.6$$

The rate of output at $t = 1$ is then

$$Y(1) = \text{minimum } [K(1)/3, N(1)/5] = \text{minimum } [307.6/3, 512.7/5]$$

$$= \text{minimum } [102.5, 102.5] = 102.5$$

Similarly, at the warranted rate of growth of 2.5%, the levels of the capital stock, labor, and output for $t = 2$ can be calculated.

Suppose that after $t = 2$, the natural growth rate of the labor force increases to $n' = .03$. Now labor supply is growing faster than labor demand. Refer back to Figure 15.2.

The labor demanded at $t = 3$ is: $N(3) = 500e^{.025(3)} = 525.6e^{.025(1)} = 538.9$.
The labor supplied at $t = 3$ is: $N'(3) = N(2)e^{.03(1)} = 525.6e^{.03(1)} = 541.6$.
The level of output at $t = 3$ is: $Y(3) = \text{minimum } [K(3), N'(3)]$:

$$Y(3) = \text{minimum } [323.4/3, 541.6/5]$$

$$Y(3) = \text{minimum}[107.8, 108.3] = 107.8$$

The surplus labor at $t = 3$, given by the difference between the labor supplied and the labor demanded, is $N'(3) - N(3) = 541.6 - 538.9 = 2.7$.

Projecting the economy one more period to $t = 4$, the capital stock, labor demand, and output continue to grow at the warranted rate of $s/v = .075/3 = .025$; while labor supply grows at the higher natural rate of $n' = .03$. The level of unemployed labor increases to $558.1 - 552.6 = 5.5$.

To reiterate, with no adjustment mechanism in the Harrod-Domar Model, the economy departs further from steady-state equilibrium over time—in this case, with rising unemployment. The surplus labor cannot be absorbed, and the rate of output growth is constrained by the scarce factor, physical capital. This rigidity of the Harrod-Domar Model was not a desirable feature, and so fixes to the knife-edge problem were offered.

PRACTICE PROBLEM 15.5

Given the following Harrod-Domar Model:

HD1)	$K(t) = 4Y(t)$	(full capacity condition)
HD2)	$N(t) = 6Y(t)$	(full employment condition)
HD3)	$I(t) = S(t)$	(product market equilibrium)
HD4)	$S(t) = .12Y(t)$	(saving function)
HD5)	$N(t) = 150e^{.03t}$	(labor supply)

and initial conditions: $K(0) = 100, N(0) = 150,$ and $Y(0) = 25.$

a) Derive the steady-state growth paths for output, capital, and labor and determine whether the model is in steady-state equilibrium.

b) Find the values for $K(1), N(1),$ and $Y(1)$.

c) Suppose at the end of period 1, the natural growth rate of labor supply decreased from $n = .03$ to $n' = .02$. Find the value for $Y(2)$ and determine the type of disequilibrium.

(The answers are at the end of the chapter.)

A VARIABLE SAVING RATE

One remedy to the dynamic instability of the Harrod-Domar Model is to add flexibility through the saving rate. Kaldor allowed for variation in the aggregate saving rate by incorporating the distribution of income into the model.[3]

Kaldor disaggregates national income, Y, into wages, W, and profits, Π. Wages represent the income of labor and profits represent the returns to the owners of the capital. Kaldor assumes that the propensity to save out of profits, s_Π, exceeds the propensity to save out of wages, s_w. Intuitively, capitalists, by their very nature, are inclined to save (and invest) a higher percentage of income earned than are laborers. Moreover, if capitalists generally have higher incomes than laborers, their ability to save would also be greater. Total saving, $S(t)$, can be written as the sum of the saving out of wages, $s_w \cdot W(t)$, and the saving out of profits, $s_\Pi \cdot \Pi(t)$. We replace the saving function, HD4) $S(t) = sY(t)$, in the Harrod-Domar Model, with the Kaldor equation, K4).

$$K4) \quad S(t) = s_w \cdot W(t) + s_\Pi \cdot \Pi(t)$$

where

$$Y(t) = W(t) + \Pi(t), \text{ and } 0 \le s_w < s_\Pi \le 1$$

The aggregate saving rate, s, can be written as a weighted average of the saving rates out of wages and profits, where the weights are the shares of wages and profits in real national income. Dividing through equation K4) by real national income, and then substituting $[1 - \Pi(t)/Y(t)]$ into the equation for $W(t)/Y(t)$, since the shares of wages and profits in national income must sum to one, we can write

$$S(t)/Y(t) = s = s_w \cdot W(t)/Y(t) + s_\Pi \cdot \Pi(t)/Y(t)$$

$$s = s_w \cdot [1 - \Pi(t)/Y(t)] + s_\Pi \cdot \Pi(t)/Y(t)$$

$$s = s_w + (s_\Pi - s_w)\Pi(t)/Y(t)$$

Assuming that $0 \le s_w < s_\Pi \le 1$, we can see that the aggregate saving rate, s, is directly related to the saving rates out of wages and profits and the share of profits in national

---

[3]See Nicholas Kaldor, "Alternative Theories of Distribution," *Review of Economic Studies*, vol. 23, no. 2 (1955–56), pages 83–100.

income. In particular, shifts in the distribution of income would alter the aggregate saving rate for a given level of national income and given saving rates out of wages and profits.

For example, suppose that an economy were thrown out of steady-state equilibrium by an increase in the natural growth rate of the labor force from n to n', so that $n' > n = s/v$. As discussed earlier, unemployment of the surplus labor would result. With a variable saving rate, however, the distribution of income could be shifted in favor of profits, for example, through preferential tax treatment for profits, to increase the aggregate saving rate to s', so that $s'/v = n'$ and the new warranted rate of growth matched the higher natural growth rate, restoring steady-state equilibrium. The new distribution of income consistent with the required higher saving rate can be found by solving for the new share of profits in national income, $[\Pi(t)/Y(t)]'$. From the equation

$$s' = s_w + (s_\Pi - s_w) [\Pi(t)/Y(t)]'$$

we can solve for $[\Pi(t)/Y(t)]'$:

$$[\Pi(t)/Y(t)]' = \frac{s' - s_w}{s_\Pi - s_w}$$

To illustrate, return to the numerical example of the Harrod-Domar Model, where: $s = .075, u = 5, v = 3$, and $n = .025$, with initial conditions, $K(0) = 300, N(0) = 500$, and $Y(0) = 100$. Assume that $W(0) = 80$ and $\Pi(0) = 20$, [or $W(t)/Y(t) = .80$ and $\Pi(t)/Y(t) = .20$], and that $s_w = .04$ and $s_\Pi = .215$. Note that the aggregate saving rate, $s = .075$, is equal to the weighted average of the saving rates out of wages and profits: $s = .04(.80) + .215(.20) = .032 + .043 = .075$. Now, if the natural growth rate of the labor force increases to $n' = .03$, the aggregate saving rate would have to increase to $s' = .09$ to maintain steady-state equilibrium. That is

$$s'/v = n'$$

$$s' = vn'$$

$$s' = 3(.03) = .09$$

For the given saving rates out of wages and profits, the new distribution of income would be

$$[\Pi(t)/Y(t)]' = \frac{s' - s_w}{s_\Pi - s_w} = \frac{.09 - .04}{.215 - .04} = \frac{.05}{.175} = .286$$

and

$$[W(t)/Y(t)]' = 1 - [\Pi(t)/Y(t)]' = 1 - .286 = .714$$

Increasing the share of profits in national income from 20% to 28.6% increases the saving rate to $s' = .09$ and raises the warranted rate of growth to $s'/v = .09/3 = .03$, which is required to match the higher natural growth rate of the labor force. Indeed, the economy might adjust to the initial surplus of labor and shortage of capital resulting from the rise in the natural growth rate of the labor force with downward pressure on the wage rate and upward pressure on the interest rate or returns to capital. If so, the share of wages in national income would tend to fall, while the share of profits would tend to rise, which would work to increase the aggregate saving rate and raise the rate of physical capital accumulation required to maintain steady-state equilibrium.[4]

In fact, following World War II, many less developed countries experienced sharp declines in their death rates due to imported medical technologies that reduced the incidences of diseases like malaria. The higher growth rates in populations and labor forces resulted in surplus labor. The common perception was that physical capital was the scarce factor constraining output growth. Accordingly policy recommendations emphasized increasing the low saving and investment rates in these low-income economies. The policies adopted included setting interest rates below market equilibrium levels to subsidize investment expenditures; setting the official foreign exchange value of the national currency above market-equilibrium levels to subsidize the importation of capital goods; and favorable tax treatment for profits.

We should observe that in steady-state equilibrium, where output is growing at the same rate as the capital stock and the labor force, the capital-labor ratio and output-labor ratio are constant. If the labor force is a constant proportion of the population, then in the steady-state equilibrium in this model, with no technological progess or improvements in the quality of the factors of capital and labor, economic growth is zero. In a sense then, economic growth with rising per capita output and income represents a desirable disequilibrium state.

The primary shortcoming of the Harrod-Domar Model, however, is that if the economy departs from steady-state equilibrium, either rising unemployment (if $s/v < n$) or rising excess capacity (if $s/v > n$) would result. The Kaldor fix of a variable saving rate dependent on the distribution of income does provide a theoretical adjustment mechanism, although the policies required to alter the distribution of income were not always feasible. We turn now to another remedy to the knife-edge problem of the Harrod-Domar Model, one that incorporates flexibility in the aggregate production function.

PRACTICE PROBLEM 15.6

Return to the Harrod-Domar Model in Practice Problem 15.5. Assume that the initial shares of wages and profits in national income are: $(W/Y) = .85$ and $(\Pi/Y) = .15$, and that the saving rates out of wages and profits are: $s_w = .06$ and $s_\Pi = .46$. After period 1, when the natural growth rate of labor supply decreases to $n' = .02$, find the new saving rate and distribution of income that would be consistent with maintaining steady-state equilibrium.

(The answers are at the end of the chapter.)

---

[4]We are ignoring lags in the adjustment of the aggregate saving rate, so that an increase in the natural growth rate of the labor force is immediately matched by the shift in the distribution of income in favor of profits needed to raise the aggregate saving rate and warranted rate of growth. If the adjustment in the saving rate is delayed, then initially a greater increase in the aggregate saving rate may be required to catch up with the already higher natural growth rate of the labor force.

SOLOW GROWTH MODEL

The assumption of a fixed-coefficients production function, while analytically convenient, and even necessary in input-output models, contributes to the knife-edge problem of the Harrod-Domar Model. Solow uses a linearly homogeneous aggregate production function with allowance for factor substitution.[5] The adjustment mechanism in the Solow Model is the flexible capital-labor ratio.

With the two factors of production, capital and labor, and abstracting still from technological progress and qualitative change in the factors, the aggregate production function written in general form is

$$Y(t) = F[K(t), N(t)]$$

Recall from Chapter 10 that a linearly homogeneous production function is characterized by constant returns to scale, meaning that a proportional change in all the inputs results in an equi-proportionate change in output. Thus, multiplying capital and labor in the above production function by the scalar, c, results in a multiplication of real national output by the same scalar:

$$cY(t) = F[cK(t), cN(t)]$$

If we let $c = 1/N(t)$, then

$$Y(t)/N(t) = F[K(t)/N(t), N(t)/N(t)] = F[K(t)/N(t), 1]$$

or

$$y(t) = f[k(t)]$$

where

$y(t) = Y(t)/N(t) =$ output per unit of labor (the average product of labor) at time t

and

$$k(t) = K(t)/N(t) = \text{physical capital-labor ratio at time } t$$

The aggregate production function, $y(t) = f[k(t)]$, is written in intensive form. We assume that output per unit of labor is a positive, but diminishing, function of the capital-labor ratio: $dy(t)/dk(t) > 0$ and $d^2y(t)/dk(t)^2 < 0$.

An example is the following Cobb-Douglas production function, $Y(t) = [K(t)]^a[N(t)]^{1-a}$, with $0 < a < 1$. Dividing through by $N(t)$, we obtain

$$Y(t)/N(t) = [K(t)]^a [N(t)]^{-a}$$

or

$$y(t) = [k(t)]^a$$

---

[5]See Robert Solow, "A Contribution to the Theory of Economic Growth," *Quarterly Journal of Economics*, vol. 70, no. 1 (February 1956), pages 65–94.

Moreover,

$$dy(t)/dk(t) = a[k(t)]^{a-1} > 0$$

and

$$d^2y(t)/dk(t)^2 = (a-1)a[k(t)]^{a-2} < 0$$

Figure 15.3 illustrates a strictly concave, intensive production function, where output per unit of labor rises at a decreasing rate with the capital-labor ratio.

PRACTICE PROBLEM 15.7

Given the production function, $Y(t) = A(t) \cdot [K(t)]^{.3} [N(t)]^{.7}$, where $A(t)$ is an index of technology:

a) Show that this production function is characterized by constant returns to scale.

b) Write the production function in intensive form and show that output per unit of labor is a positive, but diminishing, function of the capital-labor ratio.

(The answers are at the end of the chapter.)

Replacing the Harrod-Domar fixed-coefficients production function, given by equations HD1) and HD2), with the linearly-homogeneous production function with factor substitution, we can write out the basic structural equations of the Solow Model.

S1) $y(t) = f[k(t)]$ (aggregate production function)

FIGURE 15.3 INTENSIVE AGGREGATE PRODUCTION FUNCTION: $Y(T) = F[K(T)]$

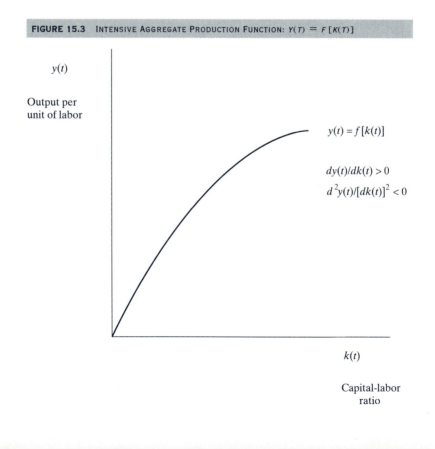

$y(t)$

Output per
unit of labor

$y(t) = f[k(t)]$

$dy(t)/dk(t) > 0$

$d^2y(t)/[dk(t)]^2 < 0$

$k(t)$

Capital-labor
ratio

S2) $I(t) = S(t)$ (product market equilibrium condition)

S3) $S(t) = sY(t)$ (saving function)

S4) $N(t) = N(0)e^{nt}$ (labor supply)

As stated earlier, in the Solow Model the adjustment mechanism is the variable capital-labor ratio, $k(t)$. Intuitively, with factor substitution, full employment of both capital and labor could be maintained. For example, surplus labor resulting from an increase in the natural growth rate of the labor force would depress the user cost of labor relative to the user cost of capital, and encourage firms to use more labor-intensive production processes by substituting labor for capital. Conversely, a shortage of labor and surplus of capital, with upward pressure on wages and downward pressure on interest rates, would induce firms to shift to more capital-intensive methods of production, conserving on the relatively scarce labor. Steady-state equilibrium, however, would still be consistent with a constant capital-labor ratio and constant output per unit of labor.

To illustrate, differentiating the capital-labor ratio, $k(t) = K(t)/N(t)$, we have

$$dk(t)/dt = \frac{[dK(t)/dt] \cdot N(t) - K(t) \cdot [dN(t)/dt]}{[N(t)]^2} = \frac{dK(t)/dt}{N(t)} - \frac{dN(t)/dt}{N(t)} \cdot \frac{K(t)}{N(t)}$$

Dividing through by $k(t)$, we derive the expression for the growth rate in the capital-labor ratio.

$$\frac{dk(t)/dt}{k(t)} = \frac{dK(t)/dt}{K(t)} - \frac{dN(t)/dt}{N(t)}$$

That is, the (instantaneous) growth rate in the capital-labor ratio is equal to the difference between the (instantaneous) growth rates in capital and labor.

Beginning in steady-state equilibrium, a constant capital-labor ratio implies a constant output per unit of labor and equal growth rates in capital, labor, and output. A rising capital-labor ratio, known as **capital deepening**, means a higher growth rate for capital than labor and rising output per unit of labor, which is consistent with positive economic growth.[6] On the other hand, if labor is growing faster than the physical capital stock, resulting in **capital shallowing,** the capital-labor ratio and output per unit of labor are declining, indicative of negative economic growth.[7]

FUNDAMENTAL EQUATION OF THE SOLOW GROWTH MODEL

To derive the steady-state equilibrium condition for the Solow Model, we begin by differentiating the capital-labor ratio.

---

[6]**Capital widening** occurs when the positive growth rate in the capital stock equals the growth rate in labor, resulting in a constant capital-labor ratio, as in steady-state equilibrium.

[7]A rising (falling) capital-labor ratio, *ceteris paribus*, unambiguously results in positive (negative) economic growth with rising (falling) output per capita when the ratio of the employed labor force to the total population is constant.

$$dk(t)/dt = \frac{[dK(t)/dt] \cdot N(t) - K(t) \cdot [dN(t)/dt]}{[N(t)]^2}$$

$$dk(t)/dt = \frac{dK(t)/dt}{N(t)} - \frac{dN(t)/dt}{N(t)} \cdot \frac{K(t)}{N(t)}$$

Now, to maintain product market equilibrium, [given by equation S2)], net saving, $S(t) = sY(t)$, [given by equation S3)], must equal net investment, $I(t)$, which is, by definition, the change in the capital stock, $dK(t)/dt$. Therefore, we substitute $sY(t)$ for $dK(t)/dt$ in the above equation for $dk(t)/dt$. Second, to maintain full employment of the labor force, which is exogenously growing at the rate n [given by equation S4)], we set $[dN(t)/dt]/N(t) = n$. With these substitutions, we have derived the **fundamental equation of the Solow Model**.

$$dk(t)/dt = sY(t)/N(t) - nK(t)/N(t)$$

or

$$dk(t)/dt = sy(t) - nk(t)$$

As noted, in steady-state equilibrium, the capital-labor ratio is constant. Thus, we set $dk(t)/dt = 0$. The steady-state equilibrium condition in the Solow Model is

$$sy(t) - nk(t) = 0$$

or

$$sy(t) = nk(t)$$

The term on the left-hand side, $sy(t)$, indicates the net saving per unit of labor forthcoming, given the aggregate saving rate, s, and the real national income (real national output) per unit of labor, $y(t)$. The right-hand side term, $nk(t)$, indicates the net investment per unit of labor required to maintain the capital-labor ratio, $k(t)$, given the natural growth rate of the labor force, n. If the saving forthcoming just equals the investment required, then the capital-labor ratio will be constant; and the capital stock, labor force, and output will all be growing at the same rate, n, consistent with steady-state equilibrium in this model.

In Figure 15.4 we illustrate this concept. The key endogenous variable, $k(t)$, the capital-labor ratio, is represented on the horizontal axis. Saving per unit of labor, $sy(t)$, measured on the vertical axis, is a strictly concave function of $k(t)$; since $y(t)$, a positive, but decreasing, function of $k(t)$ is multiplied by the constant saving rate, s. The required investment per unit of labor, $nk(t)$, also measured on the vertical axis, is a ray from the origin with a slope equal to the natural growth rate of the labor force, n.

Graphically, the steady-state equilibrium capital-labor ratio, $\bar{k}_0(t)$, is found at the intersection of the $sy(t)$ curve and $nk(t)$ ray. (See point E_0 in Figure 15.4.) At this capital-labor ratio, $s\bar{y}_0(t) = n\bar{k}_0(t)$, where $\bar{y}_0(t) = f[\bar{k}_0(t)]$. The Solow Model is dynamically stable, since any departure of the capital-labor ratio from the steady-state equilibrium value would be corrected.

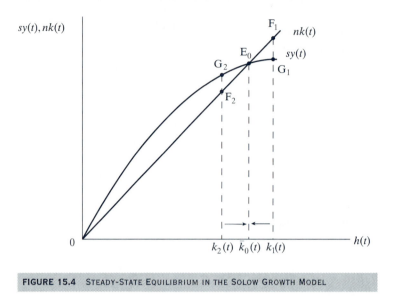

FIGURE 15.4   STEADY-STATE EQUILIBRIUM IN THE SOLOW GROWTH MODEL

For example, suppose the initial capital-labor ratio were $k_1(t) > \bar{k}_0(t)$. At this capital-labor ratio, the saving forthcoming (see point G_1) is insufficient to maintain the capital-labor ratio of $k_1(t)$, given the natural growth rate of the labor force (see point F_1). The shortage of saving (indicated by the gap $F_1 G_1$) would push up the market equilibrium interest rate (and user cost of capital) and encourage firms to shift to less capital-intensive methods of production. Similarly, the surplus of labor at $k_1(t)$ would lower the market wage rate (user cost of labor) and contribute to the substitution of labor for capital. The fall in the capital-labor ratio from $k_1(t)$ to $\bar{k}_0(t)$ reduces the required investment per unit of labor [see the movement from F_1 to E_0 along the ray $nk(t)$] faster than the saving per unit of labor [see the movement from G_1 to E_0 along the curve $sy(t)$], until the equilibrium capital-labor ratio of $\bar{k}_0(t)$ is restored.

Conversely, if the initial capital-labor ratio is too low, for example, $k_2(t) < \bar{k}_0(t)$, then the resulting surplus of saving, that is, beyond what would be required to maintain the current capital-labor ratio of $k_2(t)$, (see the gap $G_2 F_2$ in Figure 15.4), would drive down the interest rate and push up the wage rate, prompting firms to shift to more capital-intensive methods of production. The rise in the capital-labor ratio from $k_2(t)$ to $\bar{k}_0(t)$, increases the investment per unit of labor required (see the movement from F_2 to E_0) faster than the saving per unit of labor forthcoming (see the movement from G_2 to E_0) until the surplus saving is eliminated and the steady-state equilibrium capital-labor ratio of $\bar{k}_0(t)$, is attained.

In sum, the Solow Model is dynamically stable, with adjustments in the capital-labor ratio through factor substitution, induced by changes in the relative user costs of capital and labor, serving to restore steady-state equilibrium. In fact, the steady-state equilibrium condition derived from the fundamental equation of the Solow Model reflects the steady-state equilibrium condition from the Harrod-Domar Model—with one important difference. To demonstrate, return to the steady-state equilibrium condition for the Solow Model:

$$sy(t) = nk(t)$$

Dividing through by the capital-labor ratio, we have

$$sy(t)/k(t) = n$$

and
$$s/v(t) = n,$$

where $v(t) = k(t)/y(t) = K(t)/Y(t)$

That is, the capital-output ratio, $v(t) = K(t)/Y(t)$, in the Solow Model is variable — compared to the steady-state equilibrium condition for the Harrod-Domar Model, $s/v = n$, where the capital-output ratio, v, is fixed. The difference, of course, reflects the assumption of a linearly homogeneous production function with factor substitution in the Solow Model, in contrast to the fixed-coefficients production function of the Harrod-Domar Model.

Changes in the Saving Rate and Natural Growth Rate of the Labor Force   As in the Harrod-Domar Model, without technological progress or qualitative improvement in the factors of production, steady-state equilibrium in the Solow model is characterized by a constant output per unit of labor. Unlike the Harrod-Domar Model, however, where a change in the aggregate saving rate or the natural growth rate of the labor force would throw an economy out of steady-state equilibrium with either rising excess capacity for the capital stock or rising unemployment of labor; in the Solow Model the economy would adjust and restore a steady-state equilibrium.

Consider first an increase in the saving rate from s to s'. Refer to Figure 15.5. At the initial equilibrium capital-labor ratio, $\bar{k}_0(t)$, the higher saving rate creates an excess supply of saving (indicated by the line segment G'_0E_0). Accordingly, the market rate of interest falls, inducing firms to substitute capital for labor. The rise in the capital-labor ratio increases output per unit of labor, which is consistent with economic growth and rising per capita income. Investment per unit of labor rises with the capital-labor ratio (from E_0 to E_1) faster than the saving per unit of labor (from G'_0 to E_1), until the saving-investment equilibrium is restored. The economy moves to a new steady-state equilibrium at $\bar{k}_1(t)$, where again the capital-labor ratio and output per unit of labor are constant, albeit at higher levels. The economic growth that occurred was only temporary — between the steady-state equilibria represented by the points E_0 and E_1.

As noted earlier, the higher saving rate does yield a higher equilibrium level of output per unit labor: $\bar{y}_1(t) = f[\bar{k}_1(t)] > \bar{y}_0(t) = f[\bar{k}_0(t)]$. In contrast, in the dynamically unstable Harrod-Domar Model, an increase in the saving rate from steady-state equilibrium would not increase output per unit of labor, but would result in an increasing amount of excess capacity in the capital stock over time.

Next consider an increase in the natural growth rate of the labor force from n to n'. Refer to Figure 15.6. The higher labor force growth rate results in a shortage of sav-

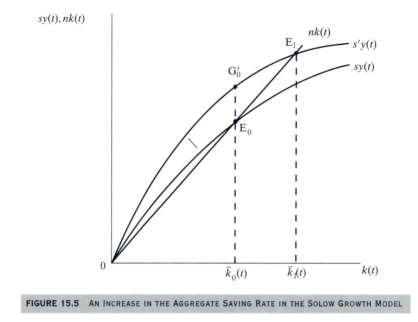

FIGURE 15.5 AN INCREASE IN THE AGGREGATE SAVING RATE IN THE SOLOW GROWTH MODEL

ing needed to maintain the initial steady-state equilibrium capital-labor ratio of $\bar{k}_0(t)$. The shortage of saving (indicated by the line segment $F'_0 E_0$) drives up the market rate of interest, leading firms to adopt less capital-intensive methods of production. The subsequent decline in the capital-labor ratio, from $\bar{k}_0(t)$, to $\bar{k}_1(t)$, reduces the required investment per unit of labor (from F'_0 to E_1) more than the saving per unit of labor

FIGURE 15.6 AN INCREASE IN THE NATURAL GROWTH RATE OF THE LABOR FORCE IN THE SOLOW GROWTH MODEL

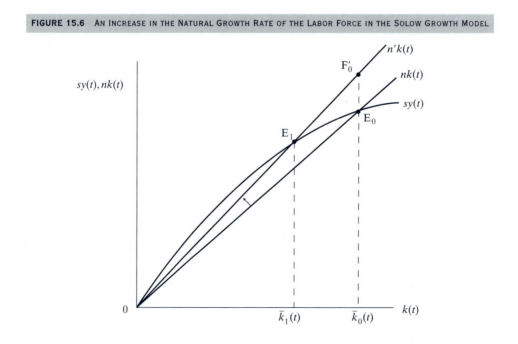

forthcoming (from E_0 to E_1), until the shortfall in saving is eliminated. The economy contracts as the capital-labor ratio and output per unit of labor decline until a new steady-state equilibrium is reached at $\bar{k}_1(t)$.

The net result of the rise in the natural growth rate of the labor force is to reduce the steady-state equilibrium capital-labor ratio and output per unit of labor to $\bar{k}_1(t)$ and $\bar{y}_1(t) = f[\bar{k}_1(t)]$. In contrast, in the Harrod-Domar Model, an increase in the natural growth rate of the labor force from steady-state equilibrium would lead to rising unemployment and falling real national output per unit of labor—as output, capital, and the demand for labor continue to increase at the initial warranted rate, while the labor force grows at the higher natural rate. We would even expect a continual decline in real national income per capita, if like the labor force, the population increases at a greater rate than output.

An Illustration of the Solow Model Before incorporating technological progress and qualitative improvement in the factors into the analysis, we offer a numerical example of the Solow Model. Consider the four structural equations of the Solow model written below:

S1) $Y(t) = [K(t)]^{.4} [N(t)]^{.6}$ (aggregate production function)

S2) $I(t) = S(t)$ (product market equilibrium condition)

S3) $S(t) = .075Y(t)$ (saving function)

S4) $N(t) = 100e^{.025t}$ (labor supply)

The Cobb-Douglas aggregate production function, equation S1), is characterized by constant returns to scale, since the sum of the exponents for the factors equals one. To write the aggregate production function in intensive form, we divide through by $N(t)$:

$$Y(t)/N(t) = [K(t)]^{.4} [N(t)]^{-.4}$$

or

$$\text{S1) } y(t) = [k(t)]^{.4}$$

To derive the fundamental equation of the Solow growth model, we differentiate $k(t) = K(t)/N(t)$:

$$dk(t)/dt = \frac{[dK(t)/dt] \cdot N(t) - K(t) \cdot [dN(t)/dt]}{[N(t)]^2}$$

$$dk(t)/dt = \frac{dK(t)/dt}{N(t)} - \frac{dN(t)/dt}{N(t)} \cdot \frac{K(t)}{N(t)}$$

Substituting in $S(t) = .075Y(t)$ for $dK(t)/dt = I(t)$, consistent with product market equilibrium; and setting $[dN(t)/dt]/N(t) = .025$, consistent with the given natural growth rate of the labor force, we can write

$$dk(t)/dt = .075Y(t)/N(t) - .025 K(t)/N(t)$$

or

$$dk(t)/dt = .075y(t) - .025k(t) \quad \text{(fundamental equation of the Solow Model)}$$

Now, since $y(t) = [k(t)]^{.4}$, and $dk(t)/dt = 0$ in steady-state equilibrium, the equation reduces to

$$0 = .075[k(t)]^{.4} - .025k(t)$$

Solving for the steady-state equilibrium capital-labor ratio, $\bar{k}_0(t)$, we find

$$.075[k(t)]^{.4} = .025k(t)$$

$$3 = [k(t)]^{.6}$$

$$\bar{k}_0(t) = 3^{1.6\overline{6}}$$

$$\bar{k}_0(t) = 6.24$$

The steady-state equilibrium output per unit of labor, $\bar{y}_0(t)$, is

$$\bar{y}_0(t) = [\bar{k}_0(t)]^{.4}$$

$$\bar{y}_0(t) = 6.24^{.4}$$

$$\bar{y}_0(t) = 2.08$$

The steady-state equilibrium capital-output ratio is $\bar{v}_0(t) = \bar{k}_0(t)/\bar{y}_0(t) = 6.24/2.08 = 3$.

In steady-state equilibrium, output, the capital stock, and the labor force are all growing at the natural rate, $n = .025$, which is equal to the warranted rate, $s/\bar{v}_0(t) = .075/3 = .025$. The time path for labor is given by equation S4) $N(t) = 100e^{.025t}$. We can find the time paths for capital and output also. With $N(0) = 100$, and since $\bar{k}_0(t) = 6.24$, then $K(0)/N(0) = 6.24$ and $K(0) = 624$. Similarly, $\bar{y}_0(t) = 2.08$, so $Y(0)/N(0) = 2.08$ and $Y(0) = 208$. The time paths for capital and output are then

$$K(t) = K(0)e^{.025t} = 624e^{.025t}$$

$$Y(t) = Y(0)e^{.025t} = 208e^{.025t}$$

PRACTICE PROBLEM 15.8

Given the Solow Model:

$$\text{S1) } Y(t) = 2[K(t)]^{.5} [N(t)]^{.5}$$

$$\text{S2) } I(t) = S(t)$$

$$\text{S3) } S(t) = .12Y(t)$$

$$\text{S4) } N(t) = 150e^{.03t}$$

a) Derive the fundamental equation of the Solow Model.
b) Solve for the steady-state equilibrium capital-labor ratio, $\bar{k}_0(t)$, output per unit of labor, $\bar{y}_0(t)$ and capital-output ratio, $\bar{v}_0(t)$.

c) Determine the time paths for output, capital, and labor.
d) Determine the warranted rate of growth, s/v.

(The answers are at the end of the chapter.)

Now suppose that the saving rate increases to $s' = .10$. The new saving function is S3)' $S(t) = .10Y(t)$. The new fundamental equation is

$$dk(t)/dt = s'y(t) - nk(t)$$

$$dk(t)/dt = .10y(t) - .025k(t)$$

$$dk(t)/dt = .10[k(t)]^{.4} - .025k(t)$$

Setting $dk(t)/dt = 0$ and solving for the new steady-state equilibrium capital-labor ratio, $\bar{k}_1(t)$, we have

$$0 = .10[k(t)]^{.4} - .025k(t)$$

$$.10[k(t)]^{.4} = .025k(t)$$

$$4 = [k(t)]^{.6}$$

$$4^{1.66} = \bar{k}_1(t)$$

$$\bar{k}_1(t) = 10.08$$

The new steady-state equilibrium output per unit of labor, $\bar{y}_1(t)$, is

$$\bar{y}_1(t) = [\bar{k}_1(t)]^{.4} = 10.08^{.4} = 2.52$$

The new steady-state equilibrium capital-output ratio, $\bar{v}_1(t)$, is

$$\bar{v}_1(t) = \bar{k}_1(t)/\bar{y}_1(t) = 10.08/2.52 = 4$$

As expected, an increase in the saving rate (from $s = .075$ to $s' = .10$) results in increases in the steady-state equilibrium capital-labor ratio (from $\bar{k}_0(t) = 6.24$ to $\bar{k}_1(t) = 10.08$) and output per unit of labor (from $\bar{y}_0(t) = 2.08$ to $\bar{y}_1(t) = 2.52$). The increase in the saving rate would lead initially to a surplus of saving, a decrease in the interest rate, and a shift in favor of more capital-intensive production methods. Consequently, the capital-output ratio rises (from $\bar{v}_0(t) = 3$ to $\bar{v}_1(t) = 4$) to restore steady-state equilibrium, where $s'/v_1(t) = .10/4 = .025 = n$, and capital, labor, and output are again growing at the (annual) rate of 2.5%.

Now suppose that instead of an increase in the saving rate, the natural growth rate of the labor force increases from $n = .025$ to $n' = .03$. The new labor supply function is S4)' $N(t) = 100e^{.03t}$, and the new fundamental equation is

$$dk(t)/dt = sy(t) - n'k(t)$$

$$= .075y(t) - .03k(t)$$

$$= .075[k(t)]^{.4} - .03k(t)$$

Setting $dk(t)/dt = 0$ and solving for $\bar{k}_2(t)$, we have

$$0 = .075[k(t)]^{.4} - .03k(t)$$

$$.075[k(t)]^{.4} = .03k(t)$$

$$2.5 = [k(t)]^{.6}$$

$$\bar{k}_2(t) = [2.5]^{1.66} = 4.61$$

The corresponding steady-state equilibrium output per unit of labor, $\bar{y}_2(t)$, is

$$\bar{y}_2(t) = [\bar{k}_2(t)]^{.4}$$

$$\bar{y}_2(t) = [4.61]^{.4} = 1.84$$

The steady-state equilibrium capital-output ratio becomes $\bar{v}_2(t)$,

$$\bar{v}_2(t) = \bar{k}_2(t)/\bar{y}_2(t) = 4.61/1.84 = 2.5$$

In sum, an increase in the natural growth rate of the labor force (from $n = .025$ to $n' = .03$), results in decreases in the steady-state equilibrium capital-labor ratio (from $\bar{k}_0(t) = 6.24$ to $\bar{k}_2(t) = 4.61$) and output per unit of labor (from $\bar{y}_0(t) = 2.08$ to $\bar{y}_2(t) = 1.84$). The increase in the natural growth rate of the labor force would initially yield a surplus of labor, driving down the market wage rate, and inducing a shift to more labor-intensive production processes. The capital-output ratio falls (from $\bar{v}_0(t) = 3$ to $\bar{v}_2(t) = 2.5$) to restore a steady-state equilibrium, where $s/\bar{v}_2(t) = .075/2.5 = .03 = n'$. Capital, labor, and output are now growing at the (annual) rate of 3.0%.

PRACTICE PROBLEM 15.9

Return to the Solow Model in Practice Problem 15.8, where $\bar{k}_0(t) = 64$, $\bar{y}_0(t) = 16$, and $\bar{v}_0(t) = 4$, and find the new steady-state equilibrium capital-labor ratio, output per unit of labor, and capital-output ratio, for each of the following changes. Determine the warranted rate of growth and the time path for output also.

a) a decrease in the saving rate from $s = .12$ to $s' = .10$.
b) a decrease in the natural growth rate of labor from $n = .03$ to $n' = .025$.

(The answers are at the end of the chapter.)

So far, in the versions of the growth models presented, steady-state equilibrium is characterized by a constant real national output per unit of labor, which is consistent with zero economic growth when the labor force is a constant proportion of the population. In the basic Solow Model presented, positive or negative economic growth with a rising or falling output per unit of labor occurs only during a transition between steady-state equilibria. In particular, increasing the saving rate, while raising the steady-state equilibrium capital-labor ratio and output per unit of labor, only temporarily generates economic growth.

To account for continual economic growth through a rising output per unit of labor, we incorporate technological progress and qualitative improvement in labor and capital into a basic Solow Model.

SUSTAINED ECONOMIC GROWTH

Generally rising per capita real national income is a hallmark of modern economies; although the upward trends in real per capita incomes are periodically interrupted by recessions. To illustrate sustained economic growth, we use the basic Solow Model with a linearly homogeneous Cobb-Douglas production function, incorporating effective labor, effective capital, and neutral technological progress, to derive the growth rate in real national output per unit of labor. We will see that steady-state equilibrium no longer is necessarily characterized by a constant capital-labor ratio.

EFFECTIVE LABOR

Recall the discussion of the sources of economic growth, where the primary factors of production were expressed in effective terms. That is, the physical quantity of a factor, for example, hours of labor, is multiplied by an index of the quality or inherent productivity of the factor. With respect to labor, the effective labor at time t, $N^*(t)$, is the product of $N(t)$, the physical labor at time t, and $q_N(t)$, an index of the average quality of the labor at time t: $N^*(t) = q_N(t) \cdot N(t)$. If we set $q_N(0) = 1.0$, then over time we would expect $q_N(t)$ to rise with increases in the average education and health of the labor force. In other words, with the given technology and physical capital, an average unit of physical labor would be capable of producing more output over time. As demonstrated previously, the (instantaneous) growth rate in effective labor is equal to the sum of the (instantaneous) growth rates in the quality and quantity of labor.

$$\frac{dN^*(t)/dt}{N^*(t)} = \frac{dq_N(t)/dt}{q_N(t)} + \frac{dN(t)/dt}{N(t)}$$

We will continue to assume that the physical labor force is growing at the natural rate, n: $[dN(t)/dt]/N(t) = n$. Further, we will assume that the quality of labor is increasing at a rate of m: $[dq_N(t)/dt]/q_N(t) = m$. Consistent with this assumption, we write the equation for effective labor as: $N^*(t) = e^{mt} N(t)$, where $q_N(t) = e^{mt}$. Differentiating, we have

$$dN^*(t)/dt = me^{mt} N(t) + e^{mt} dN(t)/dt$$

Dividing through by $N^*(t)$, we derive the growth rate for effective labor:

$$\frac{dN^*(t)/dt}{N^*(t)} = m + \frac{dN(t)/dt}{N(t)} = m + n$$

Now incorporating effective labor, $N^*(t) = e^{mt}N(t)$, into the linearly homogeneous Cobb-Douglas production function, we write the Solow Model as:

S1) $Y(t) = [K(t)]^a [N^*(t)]^{1-a}$ (aggregate production function)

S2) $I(t) = S(t)$ (product market equilibrium condition)

S3) $S(t) = sY(t)$ (saving function)

S4) $N(t) = N(0)e^{nt}$ (labor supply)

We can write the aggregate production function given by equation S1) as

$$Y(t) = [K(t)]^a \, [e^{mt} \, N(t)]^{1-a}$$

or

$$Y(t) = e^{m(1-a)t} \, [K(t)]^a \, [N(t)]^{1-a}$$

Transforming the production function into its intensive form by multiplying through by the reciprocal of $N(t)$, we obtain

$$Y(t)/N(t) = e^{m(1-a)t} \, [K(t)]^a \, [N(t)]^{-a}$$

or

$$\text{S1)} \; y(t) = e^{m(1-a)t} \, [k(t)]^a$$

We see that $y(t)$, real national output per unit of labor, for a given capital-labor ratio, $k(t)$, is increasing over time at the rate $m \cdot (1 - a)$, given by the product of the growth rate in the quality of labor, m, and the partial output elasticity of labor, $[\delta Y(t)/Y(t)]/[\delta N(t)/N(t)] = 1 - a$. To demonstrate, we derive the steady-state equilibrium growth rate of real national output per unit of labor incoporating the product market equilibrium condition, $I(t) = S(t)$; the given saving function, $S(t) = sY(t)$; and the natural growth rate of the labor force, n.

Differentiating the intensive production function, $y(t) = e^{m(1-a)t} \, [k(t)]^a$, with respect to time, we have

$$dy(t)/dt = m \cdot (1-a) \, e^{m(1-a)t} \, [k(t)]^a + a \, e^{m(1-a)t} \, [k(t)]^{a-1} \, dk(t)/dt$$

Dividing through by $y(t)$, and simplifying, we obtain the growth rate for real national output per unit of labor.

$$\frac{dy(t)/dt}{y(t)} = m \cdot (1 - a) + a \cdot \left[\frac{dk(t)/dt}{k(t)} \right]$$

Recall that the growth rate in the capital-labor ratio is equal to

$$\frac{dk(t)/dt}{k(t)} = \frac{dK(t)/dt}{K(t)} - \frac{dN(t)/dt}{N(t)}$$

From equations S2) and S3), giving respectively the product market equilibrium condition and the saving function, we can substitute $sY(t)$ in for $dK(t)/dt$. That is,

$$dK(t)/dt = I(t) = S(t) = sY(t)$$

And, from equation S4), we can set the growth rate of labor equal to the natural growth rate of the labor force, $[dN(t)/dt]/N(t) = n$. Thus, the equation for the growth rate of real national output per unit of labor becomes

$$\frac{dy(t)/dt}{y(t)} = m \cdot (1 - a) + a \cdot \left[\frac{dK(t)/dt}{K(t)} - \frac{dN(t)/dt}{N(t)}\right]$$

$$\frac{dy(t)/dt}{y(t)} = m \cdot (1 - a) + a \cdot \left[\frac{sY(t)}{K(t)} - n\right]$$

$$\frac{dy(t)/dt}{y(t)} = m \cdot (1 - a) + a \cdot \left[\frac{sy(t) - nk(t)}{k(t)}\right]$$

Note the expression in the numerator of the term in the brackets, $sy(t) - nk(t)$. This reflects the fundamental equation of the basic Solow Model: $dk(t)/dt = sy(t) - nk(t)$. With no technological progress or qualitative improvement in the factors of production, steady-state equilibrium in the basic Solow Model is characterized by a constant capital-labor ratio, $dk(t)/dt = 0$. Recall that the capital-labor ratio will be constant when the (net) saving per unit of labor forthcoming, $sy(t)$, equals the (net) investment per unit of labor required to maintain the capital-labor ratio for the given natural growth rate in the labor force, $nk(t)$.

Here, with effective labor, if the capital-labor ratio were constant, then the steady-state equilibrium growth rate in real national output per unit of labor would equal the product of the growth rate in the quality of labor, m, and the partial output elasticity of labor, $1 - a$.

$$\frac{dy(t)/dt}{y(t)} = m \cdot (1 - a) \quad \text{when } dk(t)/dt = sy(t) - nk(t) = 0$$

The growth rate in output per unit of labor, however, will be greater than (less than) the product $m \cdot (1 - a)$ when the capital-labor ratio is rising (falling) and saving per unit of labor, $sy(t)$, is greater than (less than) the required investment per unit of labor, $nk(t)$. In fact, with the quality of labor increasing at the rate m, real national output and real national income per unit of labor are increasing at the rate $m \cdot (1 - a)$, independently of the capital-labor ratio. Therefore, for a given saving rate, s, saving per unit of labor forthcoming is rising, which in turn increases the investment per unit of labor and raises the capital-labor ratio in steady-state equilibrium.[8]

Refer to Figure 15.7. Consider a point in time, say $t = 0$, and the corresponding initial equilibrium given by point E_0. Over time, the saving per unit of labor curve, $sy(t)$, is rotating in a counterclockwise fashion with the growth in the quality of labor, which increases the output per unit of labor (e.g., from E_0 to E_0' at the present equilibrium capital-labor ratio (e.g., $\bar{k}(0)$). Consequently the steady-state equilibrium capital-labor ratio is rising, adding to the growth in output per unit of labor. Compare the equilibrium at $t = 1$, indicated by point E_1, with the initial equilibrium at $t = 0$, indicated by point E_0.

---

[8]Note, even if initially, $sy(t) < nk(t)$ and the capital-labor ratio is declining, increases in output per unit of labor, due to the improving quality of labor, would eventually dominate, so that steady-state growth would be characterized by a rising capital-labor ratio.

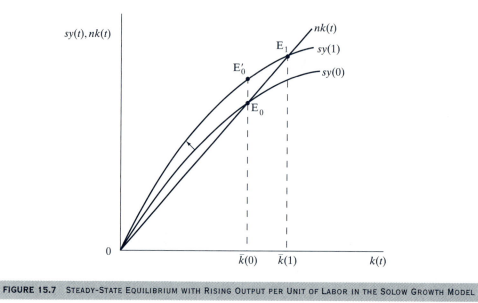

FIGURE 15.7   STEADY-STATE EQUILIBRIUM WITH RISING OUTPUT PER UNIT OF LABOR IN THE SOLOW GROWTH MODEL

In sum, with qualitative growth in labor, steady-state equilibrium is characterized by a rising capital-labor ratio and an even faster rising output per unit of labor.

To illustrate, consider the following Solow Model with effective labor:

S1) $Y(t) = [K(t)]^{.4}[N^*(t)]^{.6}$

S2) $I(t) = S(t)$

S3) $S(t) = .075Y(t)$

S4) $N(t) = 100e^{.025t}$

where $N^*(t) = e^{.01t} N(t)$. Here the quality of labor is growing continuously at the annual rate of .01 or 1%. The production function becomes

$$Y(t) = [K(t)]^{.4}[e^{.01t} N(t)]^{.6} = e^{.006t} [K(t)]^{.4} [N(t)]^{.6}.$$

Dividing through by $N(t)$, we have

$$Y(t)/N(t) = e^{.006t} [K(t)]^{.4}/[N(t)]^{.4}$$

$$y(t) = e^{.006t}[k(t)]^{.4}$$

To derive the growth rate for output per unit of labor, we first differentiate the intensive production function.

$$dy(t)/dt = .006e^{.006t} [k(t)]^{.4} + .4e^{.006t} [k(t)]^{-.6} dk(t)/dt$$

Dividing through by $y(t)$ gives the growth rate for output per unit of labor.

$$\frac{dy(t)/dt}{y(t)} = .006 + .4\left[\frac{dk(t)/dt}{k(t)}\right]$$

We know that the growth rate in the capital-labor ratio equals the difference between the growth rates in capital and labor:

$$\frac{dk(t)/dt}{k(t)} = \frac{dK(t)/dt}{K(t)} - \frac{dN(t)/dt}{N(t)}$$

Incorporating the conditions from the Solow Model, where $dK(t)/dt = I(t) = S(t) = .075Y(t)$ and the natural growth rate for labor is $[dN(t)/dt]/N(t) = n = .025$, we can write for steady-state equilibrium:

$$\frac{dk(t)/dt}{k(t)} = \frac{.075Y(t)}{K(t)} - .025$$

Or, after dividing the numerator and denominator of the first term on the right-hand side by $N(t)$ and then expressing the right-hand side over a common denominator of $k(t)$, we have

$$\frac{dk(t)/dt}{k(t)} = \frac{.075y(t) - .025k(t)}{k(t)}$$

Therefore, we can write the growth rate in output as

$$\frac{dy(t)/dt}{y(t)} = .006 + .4\left[\frac{.075y(t) - .025k(t)}{k(t)}\right]$$

Suppose initially, when $t = 0$, that $k(0) = 6.24$ and $y(0) = 2.08$.[9] Then the term in brackets equals zero:

$$\frac{.075y(0) - .025k(0)}{k(0)} = \frac{.075(2.08) - .025(6.24)}{6.24} = 0.$$

With the quality of labor increasing at at rate of .01 (or 1%) and a partial output elasticity of labor equal to .6, however, the growth rate of output per unit of labor equals .006—for any given capital-labor ratio.

In period 1, for the initial capital-labor ratio of $k(0) = 6.24$, output per unit of labor increases from $y(0) = 2.08$ to $y(1) = e^{.006(1)} y(0) = (1.006)(2.08) = 2.092$. The savings per unit of labor forthcoming would be $sy(1) = (.075)(2.092) = .157$. This exceeds the investment per unit of labor required to maintain the capital-labor ratio of $k(0) = 6.24$ given the natural growth rate of labor of $n = .025$: $sy(1) = .157 > .156 = nk(0) = (.025)(6.24)$. Consequently, the surplus saving drives down the interest rate, encouraging additional investment and a rise in the capital-labor ratio, which, in turn, further increases the growth rate of output in period 1. Here for period 1, we can write

$$\frac{dy(t)/dt}{y(t)} = .006 + .4\left[\frac{.157 - .156}{6.24}\right] = .006 + .00006 = .00606$$

---

[9]These initial values are the steady-state equilibrium values for the capital-labor ratio and output per unit of labor for the Solow Model with a savings rate of $s = .075$, a natural growth rate of labor of $n = .025$, and an aggregate production function of $Y(t) = [K(t)]^{.4}[N(t)]^{.6}$.

So too, in subsequent periods, the steady-state equilibrium growth rate in output will be increasing due to the qualitative growth in labor and the rising capital-labor ratio.

EFFECTIVE CAPITAL

Suppose now, that instead of effective labor, we allow for qualitative improvement in the physical capital stock. The effective physical capital stock at time t, $K^*(t)$, is equal to the physical capital stock at time t, $K(t)$, multiplied by an index of the average quality of capital at time t, $q_K(t)$. That is, $K^*(t) = q_K(t) \cdot K(t)$. Some of the advances in technology are embodied in the latest capital goods produced, for example, more powerful personal computers. If we set $q_K(0) = 1.0$, then with investment in new and superior plant, equipment, and machinery replacing and adding to the older physical capital stock, the index of the average quality of capital would rise over time.

Recall that the (instantaneous) growth rate of the effective capital stock is equal to the sum of the (instantaneous) growth rates in the average quality of the capital stock and the quantity of the physical capital stock.

$$\frac{dK^*(t)/dt}{K^*(t)} = \frac{dq_K(t)/dt}{q_K(t)} + \frac{dK(t)/dt}{K(t)}$$

If we assume that the average quality of the capital stock is growing at a constant (annual) rate of j, then $[dq_K(t)/dt]/q_K(t) = j$. Alternatively, this assumption is reflected in the following equation for the time path of the effective capital stock: $K^*(t) = e^{jt} K(t)$.

The Solow Model with the linearly homogeneous Cobb-Douglas production function and effective capital can be written as

S1) $Y(t) = [K^*(t)]^a [N(t)]^{1-a}$ (aggregate production function)

S2) $I(t) = S(t)$ (product market equilibrium condition)

S3) $S(t) = sY(t)$ (saving function)

S4) $N(t) = N(0)e^{nt}$ (labor supply).

As before, we rewrite the aggregate production function.

$$Y(t) = [e^{jt} K(t)]^a [N(t)]^{1-a}$$

or

$$Y(t) = e^{jat} [K(t)]^a [N(t)]^{1-a}$$

Multiplying through by $1/N(t)$, we obtain the intensive form of the aggregate production function:

$$Y(t)/N(t) = e^{jat} [K(t)]^a [N(t)]^{-a}$$

or

S1) $y(t) = e^{jat} [k(t)]^a$

Proceeding as we did for effective labor, we derive the growth rate for real national output per unit of labor by differentiating the intensive form of the aggregate production function, dividing through by output per unit of labor, and then incorporating the product market equilibrium condition, the saving function, and the natural growth rate for the labor force. The growth rate in real national output per unit of labor is

$$\frac{dy(t)/dt}{y(t)} = ja + a \cdot \left[\frac{dk(t)/dt}{k(t)}\right] = ja + a \cdot \left[\frac{sy(t) - nk(t)}{k(t)}\right]$$

The difference from the growth rate for output per unit of labor using effective capital instead of effective labor is the base growth rate of ja, which is equal to the product of the growth rate in the quality of capital and the partial output elasticity of capital, as opposed to $m \cdot (1 - a)$, which is equal to the product of the growth rate in the quality of labor and the partial output elasticity of labor. Again, in steady-state equilibrium, the growth rate in output per unit of labor will exceed the base rate of ja, since the capital-labor ratio is rising with $sy(t) > nk(t)$.

NEUTRAL TECHNOLOGICAL CHANGE

Another source of sustained economic growth is technological progress. Improved technology through invention and innovation in products and processes yields increased output from a given set of inputs. Consider **neutral technological change** that increases total factor productivity, but does not affect relative factor productivities. The aggregate production function in general form can be written as

$$Y(t) = A(t) \cdot F[K(t), N(t)],$$

where $A(t)$ = index of technology at time t.

Differentiating this production function with respect to time, we have

$$dY(t)/dt = [dA(t)/dt] \cdot F[K(t), N(t)]$$
$$+ A(t) \cdot \{[\delta F/\delta K(t)][dK(t)/dt] + [\delta F/\delta N(t)][dN(t)/dt]\}$$

Dividing through by $Y(t)$, we obtain the growth rate for real national output, which after rearranging, can be written as

$$\frac{dY(t)/dt}{Y(t)} = \frac{dA(t)/dt}{A(t)} + \beta_K \frac{dK(t)/dt}{K(t)} + \beta_N \frac{dN(t)/dt}{N(t)}$$

where

$$\beta_K = \frac{\delta Y(t)/Y(t)}{\delta K(t)/K(t)} = \text{partial output elasticity of capital}$$

and

$$\beta_N = \frac{\delta Y(t)/Y(t)}{\delta N(t)/N(t)} = \text{partial output elasticity of labor}$$

The term, $[dA(t)/dt]/A(t)$, represents the rate of technological change. If we assume that technology increases at a constant rate of g (percent per year), then we can write the general aggregate production function as $Y(t) = e^{gt} F[K(t), N(t)]$.

Incorporating neutral technological change into the model with the linearly homogeneous Cobb-Douglas aggregate production function, we have

S1) $Y(t) = e^{gt} [K(t)]^a [N(t)]^{1-a}$ (aggregate production function)

S2) $I(t) = S(t)$ (product market equilibrium condition)

S3) $S(t) = sY(t)$ (saving function)

S4) $N(t) = N(0)e^{nt}$ (labor supply)

The production function in intensive form is

$$Y(t)/N(t) = e^{gt} [K(t)]^a [N(t)]^{-a}$$

or

S1) $y(t) = e^{gt} [k(t)]^a$

Differentiating with respect to time; dividing through by real national output per unit of labor; and then incorporating the condition for the product market equilibrium, along with the saving function; and setting the growth rate of labor equal to the natural growth rate of the labor force, we derive the expression for the steady-state growth in real national output per unit of labor.

$$dy(t)/dt = ge^{gt} [k(t)]^a + e^{gt} a \cdot [k(t)]^{a-1} dk(t)/dt$$

$$\frac{dy(t)/dt}{y(t)} = g + a \cdot \left[\frac{dk(t)/dt}{k(t)}\right] = g + a \cdot \left[\frac{sy(t) - nk(t)}{k(t)}\right]$$

The growth rate in real national output per unit of labor is equal to the growth rate in technological progress, g, plus a fraction, a (indicating the partial output elasticity of capital) of the ratio of the excess saving per unit of labor to the capital-labor ratio. As with effective labor and effective capital, steady-state equilibrium with neutral technological progress is characterized by a rising capital-labor ratio and an even faster rising output per unit of labor.

It is straightforward to incorporate neutral technological change, effective labor, and effective capital together in the Solow model with a linearly homogeneous, Cobb-Douglas production function. Consider the following:

$$Y(t) = A(t) \cdot [K^*(t)]^a [N^*(t)]^{1-a}$$

where

$$A(t) = e^{gt}$$

$$N^*(t) = q_N(t) \cdot N(t) = e^{mt} N(t)$$

and

$$K^*(t) = q_K(t) \cdot K(t) = e^{jt} K(t)$$

The index of technological change, $A(t)$, is assumed to be increasing at the constant rate of g (percent per year). The quality index for labor, $q_N(t)$, is assumed to be increasing at the constant rate of m (percent per year). The quality index for physical capital, $q_K(t)$, is assumed to be increasing at the constant rate of j (percent per year). The production function can be rewritten as

$$Y(t) = e^{[g+m(1-a)+ja]t} [K(t)]^a [N(t)]^{1-a}$$

or in intensive form as

$$y(t) = e^{[g+m(1-a)+ja]t} [k(t)]^a \quad \text{where } y(t) = Y(t)/N(t) \text{ and } k(t) = K(t)/N(t)$$

The corresponding growth rate in real national output per unit of labor is

$$\frac{dy(t)/dt}{y(t)} = g + m \cdot (1 - a) + ja + a \cdot \left[\frac{dk(t)/dt}{k(t)} \right]$$

$$= g + m \cdot (1 - a) + ja + a \cdot \left[\frac{sv(t) - nk(t)}{k(t)} \right]$$

In general, the steady-state growth rate in real national output per unit of labor is directly related to the growth rates in neutral technological progress (g), the quality of labor (m), and the quality of capital (j). We should note, however, that in practice for any economy, the growth rates in neutral technological progress and the qualities of capital and labor will vary over time, as will the saving rate and the natural growth rate of labor.

Moreover, in practice, distinguishing among the influences of technological change and improvements in the quality of physical capital and labor on economic growth may be difficult. As noted, some of the advances in technology are embodied in the newest capital goods, which may require more educated or better trained labor to be used efficiently. The advances in technology may reflect increased knowledge through human capital formation, which also results in increases in the average quality of labor. Indeed, endogenous growth theory holds that the investment in new physical capital, as well as the production of new intermediate goods, that embody the latest technologies, not only increases the average quality of the capital stock, but may stimulate human capital formation, as labor must learn to use the new technologies.[10] In particular, there may be increasing returns to physical capital formation. If so, then endogenous growth theory may help to explain the rising gap in per capita incomes between the advanced economies, with the resources to undertake the research and development of new technologies and to invest in human capital, and less developed economies with lower incomes and saving rates, and higher population and labor force growth rates.

Growth models and the derivation of steady-state growth rates in output and output per unit of labor, while necessary abstractions from the complex dynamics of mod-

---

[10]For an introduction to endogenous growth theory, see Paul Romer, "The Origins of Endogenous Growth," *The Journal of Economic Perspectives* (Winter 1994), pages 3–22.

ern macroeconomies, do shed insight into longer-run trends and the key factors underlying economic growth. Sustaining increases in output per unit of labor and income per capita remains a primary macroeconomic objective.

❖ KEY TERMS

Economics

- capital deepening (p. 560)
- capital shallowing (p. 560)
- capital widening (p. 560)
- crude birth rate (p. 542)
- crude death rate (p. 542)
- crude rate of natural increase (p. 543)
- depreciation (capital consumption) (p. 539)

- economic growth (p. 534)
- fundamental equation of the Solow Model (p. 561)
- knife-edge problem (p. 550)
- natural growth rate of labor (p. 548)
- net fixed investment (p. 539)
- net in-migration rate (p. 542)

- neutral technological change (p. 575)
- steady-state equilibrium (p. 550)
- warranted rate of growth (p. 549)

❖ PROBLEMS

1. For each of the following rates of net fixed investment, $I(t)$, and initial physical capital stocks, $K(0)$, find the time path of the capital stock, $K(t)$, and the level of the capital stock at time $t = 5$. Find the capital formation in the first and fourth years. (Round off answers to two decimal places.)
   a) $I(t) = 6t^{.5}, K(0) = 10$
   b) $I(t) = 2e^{.25t}, K(0) = 10$

2. Given an initial population at the beginning of year t, P_t; the births during the year, b_t; the deaths during the year, d_t; and the net in-migration during the year, nm_t:
   Find the population at the end of the year, P_{t+1}.
   Find the crude birth rate, crude death rate, and net in-migration rate.
   Find the population growth rate and determine the doubling time (in years) at this annual growth rate.
   Determine the equation for the time path of the population and then find the population size at time $t = 5$. (Assume $P_0 = 10,000$.)
   a) $P_t = 10,000; b_t = 400; d_t = 100; nm_t = -50$
   b) $P_t = 10,000; b_t = 150; d_t = 110; nm_t = 50$

3. Given the Harrod-Domar growth model:

   HD1)　$K(t) = 4Y(t)$　　　(full capacity condition)

   HD2)　$N(t) = 12Y(t)$　　　(full employment condition)

   HD3)　$I(t) = S(t)$　　　(product market equilibrium condition)

HD4) $S(t) = sY(t)$ (saving function)

HD5) $N(t) = 120e^{.02t}$ (labor supply)

a) Derive the steady-state equilibrium growth paths for $Y(t)$, $K(t)$, and $N(t)$. Assume $Y(0) = 10$; $K(0) = 40$, and $N(0) = 120$.

b) Find the equilibrium value for the aggregate saving rate, s, such that the warranted rate of growth equals the natural rate of growth of the labor force.

c) Determine the levels of real national output, the physical capital stock, labor demand, and labor supply at time $t = 4$.

d) Suppose that after $t = 4$, the natural growth rate of the labor force increases to $n' = .025$. Find the levels of real national output, the physical capital stock, labor demand, and labor supply, at time $t = 5$. What is the condition of the economy? Which factor is constraining output growth? Why?

e) Suppose instead that after $t = 4$, the natural growth rate of the labor force decreases to $n'' = .015$. Find the levels of real national output, the physical capital stock, labor demand, and labor supply, at time $t = 5$. What is the condition of the economy? Which factor is constraining output growth? Why?

4. Using the Kaldor saving function, where the aggregate saving rate, s, is a weighted average of the saving rates out of wages, s_w, and profits, s_Π, that is, $s = s_w \cdot (W/Y) + s_\Pi \cdot (\Pi/Y)$, where $s_w = .05$ and $s_\Pi = .25$.

a) Find the distribution of income consistent with the steady-state equilibrium aggregate saving rate for the Harrod-Domar model in problem 3. when the natural growth rate of the labor force is $n = .02$.

b) Find the new distribution of income needed to maintain steady-state equilibrium when the natural growth rate of the labor force increases to $n' = .025$.

c) Instead, find the new saving rate out of profits (s_Π') required to maintain steady-state equilibrium given an unchanged income distribution and saving rate out of wages, $(s_w = .05)$, when the natural growth rate of the labor force increases to $n' = .025$.

d) Find the new distribution of income needed to maintain steady-state equilibrium when the natural growth rate of the labor force decreases to $n'' = .015$.

e) Instead, find the new saving rate out of profits, (s_Π') required to maintain steady-state equilibrium given an unchanged income distribution and saving rate out of wages $(s_w = .05)$, when the natural growth rate of the labor force decreases to $n'' = .015$.

5. Given the Solow growth model:

S1) $Y(t) = 4[K(t)]^{.3} [N(t)]^{.7}$ (aggregate production function)

S2) $I(t) = S(t)$ (product market equilibrium condition)

S3) $S(t) = .08Y(t)$ (saving function)

S4) $N(t) = 80e^{.02t}$ (labor supply)

a) Derive the fundamental equation of the Solow growth model.

b) Solve for the steady-state equilibrium capital-labor ratio, $\bar{k}_0(t)$; output per unit of labor, $\bar{y}_0(t)$; and capital-output ratio, $\bar{v}_0(t)$.

c) Determine the levels of real national output, physical capital stock, and labor at time $t = 4$.

d) Suppose that after $t = 4$, the natural growth rate of the labor force decreases to $n' = .015$. Find the new steady-state equilibrium capital-labor ratio, $\bar{k}_1(t)$; output per unit of labor, $\bar{y}_1(t)$; and capital-output ratio, $\bar{v}_1(t)$. Discuss the transition to the new equilibrium.

e) Suppose instead that after $t = 4$, the saving rate decreases to $s' = .06$. Find the new steady-state equilibrium capital-labor ratio, $\bar{k}_2(t)$; output per unit of labor, $\bar{y}_2(t)$; and capital-output ratio, $\bar{v}_2(t)$. Discuss the transition to the new equilibrium.

f) Suppose that, due to an exogenous increase in technology, the new aggregate production function is: S1)' $Y(t) = 5[K(t)]^{.3} [N(t)]^{.7}$. Find the new steady-state equilibrium capital-labor ratio, $\bar{k}_3(t)$; output per unit of labor, $\bar{y}_3(t)$; and capital-output ratio, $\bar{v}_3(t)$. Discuss the transition to the new equilibrium.

6. Given the Solow growth model with effective labor:

     S1) $Y(t) = 2[K(t)]^{.4} [N^*(t)]^{.6}$ (aggregate production function)

     S2) $I(t) = S(t)$ (product market equilibrium condition)

     S3) $S(t) = .15Y(t)$ (saving function)

     S4) $N(t) = 60e^{.02t}$ (labor supply)

where $N^*(t) = e^{.015t} N(t)$ = effective labor supply at time t

a) Derive the equation for the steady-state equilibrium growth rate for real national output per unit of labor, $[dy(t)/dt]/y(t)$.

b) Given $k(0) = 50$, explain why the initial growth rate in real national output per unit of labor would or would not equal, .009 (.9% per year). Would the growth rate in real national output per unit of labor be constant, increase, or decrease over time? Why?

7. Replace the aggregate production function in the Solow growth model in problem 6. with S1)' $Y(t) = 2[K^*(t)]^{.4} [N(t)]^{.6}$, where $K^*(t) = e^{.015t} K(t)$ = effective physical capital stock at time t.

a) Derive the new equation for the steady-state equilibrium growth rate for real national output per unit of labor, $[dy(t)/dt]/y(t)$.

b) Given $k(0) = 100$, explain why the initial growth rate in real national output per unit of labor would or would not equal .006 (.6% per year). Would the growth rate in real national output per unit of labor be constant, increase, or decrease over time? Why?

8. Replace the aggregate production function in the Solow growth model in problem 6. with S1)' $Y(t) = 2 A(t) [K(t)]^4 [N(t)]^6$, where $A(t) = e^{.015t}$ = index of neutral technological change.

a) Derive the equation for the steady-state equilibrium growth rate for real national output per unit of labor, $[dy(t)/dt]/y(t)$.

b) Given $k(0) = 91.2$, explain why the initial growth rate in real national output per unit of labor would or would not equal .015 (1.5% per year). Would the growth rate in real national output per unit of labor be constant, increase, or decrease over time? Why?

❖ ANSWERS TO PRACTICE PROBLEMS

15.1 a) $\dfrac{dy/dt}{y} = .01$

b) $\dfrac{dy/dt}{y} = \ln(.01) = -4.61$

c) $\dfrac{dy/dt}{y} = \dfrac{.01}{4 + .01t}$

d) $\dfrac{dy/dt}{y} = .01/t$

15.2 a) $dY/Y = dA/A + .6(dK/K) + .3(dN/N)$

b) $(\delta Y/Y)/(\delta K/K) = .6$ and $(\delta Y/Y)/(\delta N/N) = .3$

15.3 a) $K(t) = (4/3)t^{1.5} + 10$

b) $K(2) = (4/3)(2)^{1.5} + 10 = 13.77$

c) $\displaystyle\int_0^1 2t^{.5}\,dt = 1.33$ and $\displaystyle\int_1^2 2t^{.5}\,dt = 2.44$

15.4 a) $P_1 = 10,180$.

b) $CBR_1 = .0297$ or 29.7 births per thousand mid-year population; $CDR_1 = .0168$ or 16.8 deaths per thousand mid-year population; $NMR_1 = .0050$ or .5 net in-migrants per thousand mid-year population.

c) $r_t = .0179$ or 1.79%. The doubling time is 38.7 years.

d) $P_2 = 10,364$

15.5 a) The steady-state growth paths are: $Y(t) = 25e^{.03t}$, $K(t) = 100e^{.03t}$, and $N(t) = 150e^{.03t}$. The model is in steady-state equilibrium since $s/v = .12/4 = .03 = n$.

b) $K(1) = 103.05$, $N(1) = 154.57$, and $Y(1) = 25.76$.

c) $Y(2) = 26.28$. There is surplus capital equal to 1.06.

15.6 The new saving rate and distribution of income for steady-state equilibrium are: $s' = .08$ and $(W/Y)' = .95$, $(\Pi/Y)' = .05$.

15.7 a) $A(t) \cdot [cK(t)]^3 [cN(t)]^7 = c^1 \cdot A(t) \cdot [K(t)]^3[N(t)]^7 = c \cdot Y(t)$

b) $y(t) = A(t) \cdot [k(t)]^3$; $dy(t)/dk(t) = .3A(t) \cdot [k(t)]^{-7} > 0$; $d^2y(t)/dk(t)^2 = -.21A(t) \cdot [k(t)]^{-1.7} < 0$

15.8   a) $dk(t)/dt = .24[k(t)]^{.5} - .03k(t)$

      b) $\bar{k}_0(t) = 64$; $\bar{y}_0(t) = 16$, and $\bar{v}_0(t) = 4$

      c) $Y(t) = 2{,}400e^{.03t}$; $K(t) = 9{,}600e^{.03t}$; $N(t) = 150e^{.03t}$

      d) $s/v = .12/4 = .03$

15.9   a) $\bar{k}_1(t) = 44.\bar{4}$; $\bar{y}_1(t) = 13.\bar{3}$; and $\bar{v}_1(t) = 3.\bar{3}$. The warranted rate of growth is $s/v = .10/3.\bar{3} = .03$. The time path for output is: $Y(t) = 2000e^{.03t}$.

      b) $\bar{k}_2(t) = 92.16$; $\bar{y}_2(t) = 19.2$; $\bar{v}_2(t) = 4.8$. The warranted rate of growth is $s/v = .12/4.8 = .025$. The time path for output is: $Y(t) = 2880e^{.025t}$.

GLOSSARY

ECONOMICS

ADAPTIVE EXPECTATIONS HYPOTHE-SIS The theory that the expected current value of a variable is a function of its past values (Ch. 4)

AGGREGATE DEMAND CURVE The curve representing the relationship between the aggregate quantity demanded of real national output and the aggregate price level (Ch. 14)

AGGREGATE SUPPLY CURVE The curve representing the relationship between the aggregate quantity supplied of real national output and the aggregate price level (Ch. 14)

ALLOCATIVE EFFICIENCY The condition that the market price equals the marginal cost of production of a commodity (Ch. 8)

AUTONOMOUS EXPENDITURE MULTI-PLIER The ratio of the change in equilibrium real national output (real national income) to the initiating change in autonomous real expenditures on national output (Ch. 13)

AVERAGE FACTOR COST OF LABOR The total factor cost of labor per unit of labor; equals the wage rate (Ch. 7)

AVERAGE PRODUCT OF LABOR The output produced per unit of labor (Ch. 6)

AVERAGE REVENUE PRODUCT OF LABOR The revenue generated from the output produced per unit of labor (Ch. 6)

BILATERAL MONOPLY A market characterized by a single buyer (monopsony) and a single seller (monopoly) (Ch. 8)

BLACK MARKET Any illegal transaction to circumvent a legislated price; for example, sale of a commodity for a price above a price ceiling (Ch. 1)

CAPACITY OUTPUT The output of a firm where the average total cost is minimized (Ch. 6)

CAPITAL DEEPENING A rise in the capital-labor ratio (Ch. 15)

CAPITAL SHALLOWING A fall in the capital-labor ratio (Ch. 15)

CAPITAL WIDENING An increase in the capital stock in proportion to the growth in labor to maintain the capital-labor ratio (Ch. 15)

CES PRODUCTION FUNCTION Constant elasticity of substitution production function; with two factors, capital (K) and labor (L), output (Q), can be written as $Q = A \cdot [uK^{-p} + (1 - u)L^{-p}]^{-r/p}$, where $A > 0, 0 < u < 1, p > -1$ and $p \neq 0, r > 0$ (Ch. 10)

COBB-DOUGLAS PRODUCTION FUNC-TION Production function with unitary elasticity of substitution; with two factors of production, capital (K) and labor (L), output (Q) can be written as $Q = A \cdot K^a L^b$, where $A > 0$ and $0 < a, b < 1$ (Ch. 10)

COBWEB MODEL A model of a market where the current quantity supplied (or demanded) is a function of the previous period's price (Ch. 4)

CONSTANT RETURNS TO SCALE Property of a production function where a proportionate change in all of the inputs results in an equiproportionate change in output (Ch. 10)

CONSUMERS' SURPLUS The welfare gained by consumers from being able to purchase a commodity for a price less than the one they would have been willing to pay (Ch. 3)

CONTINUOUS COMPOUNDING Interest compounded continuously over a year as opposed to being compounded at distinct points of time within a year (Ch. 4)

CRUDE BIRTH RATE The ratio of births in a year to the mid-year population (often expressed per thousand mid-year population) (Ch. 15)

CRUDE DEATH RATE The ratio of deaths in a year to the mid-year population (often expressed per thousand mid-year population) (Ch. 15)

CRUDE RATE OF NATURAL INCREASE The difference between the crude birth rate and the crude death rate (Ch. 15)

DEADWEIGHT LOSS A net loss in the sum of consumers' surplus and producers' surplus due to imperfect competition (Ch. 8)

DECREASING COST INDUSTRY An industry with a negatively sloped long run supply curve for its output (Ch. 3)

DECREASING RETURNS TO SCALE Property of a production function where a proportionate change in all of the inputs results in a less than proportionate change in output (Ch. 10)

DEMAND PRICE The unit price buyers would be willing to pay for a given quantity of a commodity (Ch. 3)

DEPRECIATION (CAPITAL CONSUMPTION) The loss in value of the physical capital stock due to wear and tear and technological obsolescence (Ch. 15)

DISCOUNT RATE The interest rate charged by the Federal Reserve on loans to member banks (Ch. 14)

DUOPOLY A market with two suppliers or sellers (Ch. 9)

ECONOMIC GROWTH The percentage change in real national output per capita (Ch. 15)

ECONOMIC MODEL Theoretical framework for the representation and analysis of economic variables (Ch. 1)

ECONOMIC PROFITS The difference between the total revenues earned and the total opportunity costs of production (Ch. 6)

ECONOMIC RENT The additional receipts of a factor above the transfer earnings (Ch. 8)

ECONOMICALLY EFFICIENT The least-cost combination of inputs for producing a given level of output (Ch. 10)

ECONOMIES OF SCALE Declines in the long-run average cost as the volume of production increases (Ch. 8)

EFFECTIVE INTEREST RATE The actual yield realized for a given nominal annual interest rate when interest is compounded more than once during a year (Ch. 4)

ELASTICITY OF SUBSTITUTION The ratio of the percentage change in the cost-minimizing capital-labor ratio to the percentage change in the wage-rental ratio (Ch. 10)

EXCESS DEMAND PRICE The difference between the demand price and supply price for a given quantity of a commodity (Ch. 3)

EXCESS QUANTITY DEMANDED The difference between the quantity demanded and quantity supplied of a commodity at a given unit price of the commodity (Ch. 1)

FISCAL POLICY Discretionary changes in government expenditures and taxes intended to achieve some macroeconomic objective (Ch. 14)

FIXED COEFFICIENTS PRODUCTION FUNCTION A production function where there is only one technically efficient combination of inputs for producing each level of output; with two factors of production, capital (K) and labor (L), output (Q) can be written as $Q = A \cdot \min[K/a, L/b]$ (Ch. 10)

FOREIGN REPERCUSSIONS EFFECT The reverberations on an economy from the consequences of changes in its income and expenditures on foreign economies (Ch. 13)

FUNDAMENTAL EQUATION OF THE SOLOW MODEL The (instantaneous) change in the capital-labor ratio equals the difference between the per capita saving forthcoming and the per capita investment required to maintain the capital-labor ratio given the natural growth rate of the labor force (Ch. 15)

GAME THEORY A method for the analysis of interdependent decision making (Ch. 9)

GIFFEN GOOD An inferior good with a sufficiently strong income effect to yield a positive relationship between the quantity demanded and unit price (Ch. 3)

INCOME EFFECT The impact on the quantity demanded of a commodity due to the change in the real income of the demanders resulting from a change in the unit price of the commodity (Ch. 3)

INCREASING RETURNS TO SCALE Property of a production function where a proportionate change in all inputs results in a greater than proportionate change in output (Ch. 10)

INDIFFERENCE CURVE A curve representing all the combinations of two goods that yield the same utility to a household or consumer (Ch. 12)

INDIFFERENCE MAPPING A family or set of indifference curves reflecting the given tastes and preferences of a household or consumer (Ch. 12)

INFERIOR GOOD A commodity characterized by a negative relationship between the quantity demanded of the commodity and average income of the demanders (Ch. 3)

INPUT-OUTPUT COEFFICIENTS (TECHNICAL COEFFICIENTS) The shares of the output of one sector contributed by inputs purchased from that and other sectors (Ch. 13)

INPUT-OUTPUT TABLE A summary of all the interindustry transactions, final demands, and values added in an economy (Ch. 13)

INTERMEDIATE GOODS The final outputs of sectors used as inputs by other sectors (Ch. 13)

INVENTORY ADJUSTMENT COEFFICIENT A parameter representing the sensitivity of the unit price set by suppliers to the change in inventories from the previous period (Ch. 4)

INVENTORY MODEL A model of a market where the price set by suppliers reflects the change in inventories from the previous period (Ch. 4)

***IS* CURVE** The curve representing the combinations of real national output (real national income) and the nominal interest rate that equilibrate the product market (Ch. 14)

***IS* SCHEDULE** The schedule representing the combinations of real national output (real national income) and the nominal interest rate that equilibrate the product market (Ch. 14)

ISOCOST LINE A line, given the user costs of the factors, that represents all the combinations of factors with the same total cost (Ch. 10)

ISOQUANT A curve representing all the technically efficient combinations of factors for producing a given level of output (Ch. 10)

ISOREVENUE LINES Lines representing combinations of outputs yielding constant revenues for given unit prices of the commodities (Ch. 11)

KINKED DEMAND CURVE A demand curve facing an oligopolist who assumes its rivals will match its price decreases but not its price increases (Ch. 9)

KNIFE-EDGE PROBLEM The dynamic instability that characterizes the Harrod-Domar Model if the warranted rate of growth does not equal the natural rate of growth of labor (Ch. 15)

LAW OF DEMAND The negative relationship hypothesized between the quantity demanded and unit price of a commodity (Ch. 1)

LAW OF DIMINISHING MARGINAL UTILITY The additional utility from a unit of a commodity received by a household or consumer decreases with increases in the number of units of the commodity consumed, holding constant the consumption of all other commodities (Ch. 12)

LAW OF DIMINISHING RETURNS The decline in the marginal product of a variable factor as its use increases in the short run (Ch. 6)

LAW OF SUPPLY The positive relationship hypothesized between the quantity supplied and unit price of a commodity (Ch. 1)

LEONTIEF MATRIX The matrix formed by subtracting the matrix of input-output coefficients from a conformable identity matrix (Ch. 13)

LIQUIDITY The ease with which an asset can be converted into a medium of exchange without a loss in value (Ch. 14)

***LM* CURVE** The curve representing the combinations of real national income (real national output) and the nominal interest rate that equilibrate the money market (Ch. 14)

***LM* SCHEDULE** The schedule representing the combinations of real national income (real national output) and the nominal interest rate that equilibrate the money market (Ch. 14)

MARGINAL COST The ratio of the change in total cost to the change in output produced (Ch. 6)

MARGINAL FACTOR COST OF LABOR The ratio of the change in the total cost of labor to the change in labor employed (Ch. 6)

MARGINAL PRODUCT OF LABOR The ratio of the change in total output produced to the change in labor utilized, holding constant all other factors of production (Ch. 6)

MARGINAL PROPENSITY TO CONSUME The ratio of the change in real personal consumption expenditures to the change in real disposable income (Ch. 13)

MARGINAL PROPENSITY TO IMPORT The ratio of the change in real expenditures on imported goods and services to the change in real disposable income (Ch. 13)

MARGINAL PROPENSITY TO SAVE The ratio of the change in real personal saving to the change in real disposable income (Ch. 13)

MARGINAL PROPENSITY TO SPEND The ratio of the change in real expenditures on national output to the change in real national income (Ch. 13)

MARGINAL RATE OF SUBSTITUTION The rate at which a household or consumer is willing to trade off or substitute one commodity for units of another commodity; equal to the slope of an indifference curve (Ch. 12)

MARGINAL RATE OF TAXATION The ratio of the change in real tax revenues to the change in real national income (Ch. 13)

MARGINAL RATE OF TECHNICAL SUBSTITUTION The rate at which one factor can be substituted for another factor, holding constant the level of output produced; given by the slope of an isoquant (Ch. 10)

MARGINAL REVENUE PRODUCT OF LABOR The additional revenue gener-

ated from employing another unit of labor (Ch. 2)

MARSHALLIAN MARKET SYSTEM A market where quantity is the adjustment mechanism (Ch. 3)

MARSHALLIAN STABILITY An equilibrium property whereby an increase (decrease) in the quantity results in a decrease (increase) in the excess demand price (Ch. 3)

MONETARY POLICY Discretionary changes in the money supply intended to achieve some macroeconomic objective (Ch. 14)

MONOPOLISTIC COMPETITION A market with many firms producing slightly differentiated products (Ch. 7)

MONOPOLY A single supplier or seller in a market (Ch. 8)

MONOPSONY A single demander or buyer in a market (Ch. 8)

NATURAL GROWTH RATE OF LABOR The growth rate of labor supply determined by the growth rate of the population of labor force age and current labor force participation rates (Ch. 15)

NATURAL MONOPOLY A market characterized by sufficiently large economies of scale relative to total demand that competition between two or more firms is not feasible (Ch. 8)

NET FIXED INVESTMENT Gross fixed investment less depreciation (Ch. 15)

NET IN-MIGRATION RATE The ratio of immigrants less emigrants in a year to the mid-year population (often expressed per thousand mid-year population) (Ch. 15)

NEUTRAL TECHNOLOGICAL CHANGE Technological progress that increases total factor productivity but does not affect the relative factor productivities of capital and labor (Ch. 15)

NOMINAL INTEREST RATE The explicit or stated interest rate paid on a sum of money (Ch. 4)

NORMAL GOOD A commodity characterized by a positive relationship between the quantity demanded of the commodity and average income of the demanders (Ch. 3)

OLIGOPOLY A market dominated by a few rival firms (Ch. 9)

OPEN MARKET OPERATIONS The purchase or sale of previously issued, but yet to mature U.S. government securities by the Federal Reserve (Ch. 14)

OUTPUT-EXPANSION PATH The curve or ray from the origin representing the economically efficient combinations of capital and labor for producing different levels of output for a given technology and ratio of the user costs of labor and capital (Ch. 10)

PERFECTLY COMPETITIVE MARKET Market characterized by many suppliers and many demanders of a homogeneous commodity (Ch. 1)

PLANNED INVENTORY INVESTMENT The planned change in inventories over a period; equal to the difference between production and expected sales (Ch. 9)

PRICE CEILING A maximum price above which no transaction can legally occur (Ch. 1)

PRICE DISCRIMINATION A firm's charging different unit prices for a commodity to different consumers for reasons not due to differences in unit costs (Ch. 8)

PRICE ELASTICITY OF DEMAND The ratio of the percentage change in the quantity demanded of a commodity to the percentage change in its unit price (Ch. 3)

PRICE ELASTICITY OF SUPPLY The ratio of the percentage change in the quantity supplied of a commodity to the percentage change in its unit price (Ch. 3)

PRICE FLOOR A minimum price below which no transaction can legally occur (Ch. 1)

PRODUCTION FUNCTION An equation describing the required combinations of inputs for producing output (Ch. 10)

PRODUCERS' SURPLUS The additional revenue earned by suppliers from being able to sell a commodity for a higher price than they would have been willing to accept (Ch. 3)

RATIONAL EXPECTATIONS The hypothesis that expectations are formed using all available information on the economy (Ch. 14)

REACTION FUNCTIONS Functions describing the systematic responses of firms to changes by the other firms (Ch. 9)

REQUIRED RESERVE RATIO The minimum percentage of checkable deposits that must be held by banks as reserves (Ch. 14)

RESERVATION WAGE The minimum wage below which no labor would be supplied (Ch. 8)

RESERVES The cash held by banks in their vaults and the banks' deposits at the Federal Reserve (Ch. 14)

SHADOW PRICE The marginal value or opportunity cost of a unit of a resource (Ch. 11)

SHORT RUN The time period of analysis where at least one factor of production is fixed (Ch. 6)

SHORT-RUN TOTAL COST The sum of total variable cost and total fixed cost (Ch. 6)

SHORTAGE An excess quantity demanded of a commodity at a given unit price (Ch. 1)

SHUT-DOWN RULE A firm should cease production in the short run if its total revenues are less than its total variable costs (or its price is less than its average variable cost) (Ch. 6)

SPECULATIVE DEMAND FOR MONEY The demand for money balances to be able to profit from expected changes in asset prices (Ch. 14)

STATUS GOOD A commodity where the higher the price the greater is the quantity demanded due to the status conveyed to its consumers (Ch. 3)

STEADY-STATE EQUILIBRIUM The growth paths for output, capital, and labor consistent with product market equilibrium and full employment of capital and labor (Ch. 15)

SUBSTITUTION EFFECT The negative impact on the quantity demanded of a commodity from a change in its unit price holding constant the real income of the demanders (Ch. 3)

SUPPLY PRICE The unit price suppliers are willing to accept for a given quantity of a commodity (Ch. 3)

SURPLUS An excess quantity supplied of a commodity at a given unit price (Ch. 1)

TAX RATE MULTIPLIER The ratio of the change in equilibrium real national income to the change in the income tax rate (Ch. 13)

TECHNICALLY EFFICIENT Combinations of the minimum levels of factors capable of producing a given level of output (Ch. 10)

TOTAL EXPENDITURES The total amount spent by consumers for a given quantity of a commodity purchased (Ch. 3)

TOTAL FACTOR COST OF LABOR The total cost associated with employing labor; equals the product of the wage rate and the number of units of labor employed (Ch. 7)

TOTAL FIXED COST The total cost associated with the fixed factor(s) of production (Ch. 6)

TOTAL REVENUES The total amount received by sellers for a given quantity of the commodity sold (Ch. 3)

TOTAL VARIABLE COST The total cost associated with the variable factor(s) of production (Ch. 6)

TRANSACTIONS DEMAND FOR MONEY The demand for money to serve as a medium of exchange (Ch. 14)

TRANSFER EARNINGS The payments to a factor required to employ the factor (Ch. 8)

UNPLANNED INVENTORY INVESTMENT The unplanned change in inventories over a period; equal to the difference between expected sales and actual sales (Ch. 9)

USER COST OF CAPITAL The comprehensive cost (including opportunity cost) of using a unit of capital (Ch. 10)

USER COST OF LABOR The comprehensive cost (including opportunity cost) of using a unit of labor (Ch. 10)

VALUE ADDED The difference between the value of output and the value of inputs purchased (Ch. 13)

VALUE OF MARGINAL PRODUCT OF LABOR The additional revenue generated by another unit of labor employed by a perfectly competitive firm in a product market (Ch. 7)

WALRASIAN STABILITY An equilibrium property whereby an increase (decrease) in the unit price of a commodity results in a decrease (increase) in the excess quantity demanded of the commodity (Ch. 1)

WALRASIAN SYSTEM A system where price is the adjustment mechanism (Ch. 1)

WARRANTED RATE OF GROWTH The growth rate for output and the demands for capital and labor in the Harrod-Domar Model given by the saving rate divided by the capital-output ratio (Ch. 15)

MATHEMATICS

ABSOLUTE EXTREMUM A maximum or minimum value for a dependent variable over the entire domain (s) of the independent variable(s) (Ch. 6)

ADJOINT MATRIX The transpose of a cofactor matrix (Ch. 5)

ANTIDERIVATIVE An integral or function whose derivative is the original function (Ch. 2)

ARTIFICIAL VARIABLES Dummy variables added to linear programming minimization problems and assigned artificially high coefficients in order to establish an initial basis (Ch. 11)

BASIS A set of n linearly independent vectors defined over n-space (Ch. 5)

BEHAVIORAL EQUATION An equation expressing a hypothesized relationship between variables (Ch. 1)

BORDERED HESSIAN A determinant of a matrix consisting of the second-order partial derivatives from a constrained optimization problem (Ch. 10)

CHAIN RULE A procedure for differentiating a function within a function (Ch. 2)

CHOICE VARIABLE A variable that is endogenous and can be varied to achieve some objective (Ch. 6)

COFACTOR A signed minor for the a_{ij} element of a square matrix, where the sign is given by $(-1)^{i+j}$, for $i = 1 \ldots n, j = 1 \ldots n$ (Ch. 5)

COFACTOR MATRIX The matrix formed by replacing each element of an $n \times n$ matrix by its cofactor (Ch. 5)

COMMON LOGARITHM A logarithm with a base of 10 (Ch. 4)

COMPARATIVE STATICS The analysis of comparing different equilibrium states resulting from a change in an exogenous variable in the model (Ch. 3)

COMPLEMENT SET The set of all elements in a universal set not contained in a given subset of the universal set (Ch. 2)

COMPLEMENTARY FUNCTION The solution to a homogeneous first-order difference equation or first-order differential equation (Ch. 4)

COMPLEMENTARY SLACKNESS The relationship between the choice variables in a primal linear programming problem and the counterpart dummy variables in the dual; the relationship between the first-order condition partial derivative of the Lagrangian with respect to a choice variable (Lagrange multiplier) and the value of the choice variable (Lagrange multiplier) in a nonlinear programming problem (Ch. 11)

COMPLEMENTARY SLACKNESS CONDITIONS Part of the first order (Kuhn-Tucker) conditions in a nonlinear programming problem where the product of the partial derivative of the Lagrangian function with respect to a choice variable (Lagrange multiplier) and the choice variable (Lagrange multiplier) equals zero (Ch. 11)

COMPLEX NUMBERS Numbers with a real number component and an imaginary number component (Ch. 4)

CONCAVE A function with a slope (whether positive or negative) that is either constant or decreasing (Ch. 6)

CONFORMABLE Possessing the same dimensions (Ch. 5)

CONSTANT FUNCTION A function where the dependent variable is equal to a constant or takes on a single value only (Ch. 2)

CONSTANT OF INTEGRATION A term representing the initial conditions for an integral (Ch. 2)

CONTINUOUS A function with an unbroken graph (Ch. 2)

CONVEX A function with a slope (whether positive or negative) that is either constant or increasing (Ch. 6)

COORDINATES The location of a point in n-space given by the elements of a vector (Ch. 5)

CRAMER'S RULE A method of solving for an endogenous variable in a system of linear equations (Ch. 5)

CRITICAL POINT A point where the first derivative of a function equals zero (except for a constant function) (Ch. 6)

DECISION VARIABLE Another term for *choice variable*

DEFINITE INTEGRAL An integral with limits of integration (Ch. 2)

DEFINITE SOLUTION The final solution to a first-order difference equation or first-order differential equation that incorporates the initial conditions (Ch. 4)

DERIVATIVE A measure of the rate of change of a function (Ch. 2)

DETERMINANT A scalar associated with a square matrix used in finding the solution to a system of linear equations (Ch. 5)

DIFFERENCE EQUATION An equation where the value of the endogenous variable changes with the different periods of time (Ch. 4)

DIFFERENTIABLE Capable of being differentiated or having a derivative (Ch. 2)

DIFFERENTIAL EQUATION An equation where the value of the endogenous variable changes continuously with time (Ch. 4)

DISPLACEMENT QUOTIENTS The ratio of the constant terms to the positive elements in the pivot column of a simplex tableau (Ch. 11)

DOMAIN The set of values that an independent variable in a function can assume (Ch. 2)

DOMINANT STRATEGY A strategy that results in superior payoffs to a player regardless of the strategy the rival player selects (Ch. 9)

DOT PRODUCT (INNER PRODUCT) The multiplication of two conformable vectors (Ch. 5)

DUAL The counterpart to the primal problem in linear and nonlinear programming (Ch. 11)

DUALITY THEOREM I The optimal value of a primal objective function equals the optimal value of the dual objective function, given that the solutions to the linear programming problems exist (Ch. 11)

DUALITY THEOREM II If the optimal value of a choice variable in the primal (dual) linear programming problem is non-zero then the optimal value of the counterpart dummy variable in the dual (primal) is zero (Ch. 11)

DUMMY VARIABLES The slack variables in linear and nonlinear programming maximization problems and the surplus and artificial variables in linear and nonlinear programming minimization problems (Ch. 11)

DYNAMIC ANALYSIS Analysis where the endogenous variable(s) are dated for different periods or points in time (Ch. 1)

ENDOGENOUS VARIABLE A variable whose value is to be determined, or explained by, other variables in the model (Ch. 1)

EQUILIBRIUM A state or condition in a system characterized by balance that would tend to persist, given the underlying exogenous variables in the system (Ch. 1)

EQUILIBRIUM CONDITION An expression or equation describing the attainment of equilibrium (Ch. 1)

EXISTENCE OF EQUILIBRIUM The property of whether a model has an equilibrium (Ch. 1)

EXOGENOUS VARIABLE A variable whose value is considered to be given or determined by factors outside the model (Ch. 1)

EXPONENT The power to which a given base is raised (Ch. 4)

EXTREME POINTS The corner points of a feasible region where two constraints intersect (Ch. 11)

FEASIBLE REGION The solution space for a linear or nonlinear programming problem formed by the intersection of the inequality constraints (Ch. 11)

FIRST DERIVATIVE The rate of change of a function; given by the slope of the function (Ch. 6)

FIRST DIFFERENCE The difference between the values of an endogenous variable over successive periods (Ch. 4)

FIRST-ORDER An equation where the differential of the endogenous variable is of the first degree only (Ch. 4)

FIRST ORDER CONDITIONS The equations where the first derivatives associated with an objective function are set equal to zero in order to find the critical point(s) (Ch. 6)

FLOW VARIABLE A variable defined or measured for a given duration of time (Ch. 1)

FUNCTION A relationship between a dependent variable and independent variable where there is a unique value for the dependent variable for each value of the independent variable (Ch. 2)

FUNDAMENTAL THEOREM OF CALCULUS The evaluation of a definite integral (Ch. 2)

GENERAL SOLUTION The sum of the particular solution and complementary function for a first-order difference equation or first-order differential equation before incorporating the initial conditions (Ch. 4)

GOAL EQUILIBRIUM The objective to be attained or the variable to be optimized (Ch. 6)

HESSIAN A determinant of a matrix consisting of the second-order partial derivatives from an optimization problem (Ch. 8)

HOMOGENEOUS A system of equations where the constant terms all equal zero (Ch. 5)

HOMOGENEOUS OF DEGREE R The property whereby multiplying all the independent variables in a function by a scalar, c, results in a multiplication of the dependent variable by the scalar c raised to the r power, c^r (Ch. 10)

HYPERSURFACE An n-dimensional surface representing the graph of a multivariate function (Ch. 2)

IDENTITY An equation expressing a relationship that is true by definition (Ch. 1)

IDENTITY MATRIX A square matrix with ones down the main diagonal and zeroes everywhere else (Ch. 5)

IMAGINARY NUMBER A number that is a multiple or fraction of the square root of negative 1 (Ch. 2)

IMPLICIT FUNCTION A function derived from a general equation, where the endogenous variable can be assumed to be a function of the exogenous variables in the equation (Ch. 6)

IMPLICIT FUNCTION THEOREM The conditions that establish when a general equation defines an implicit function (Ch. 6)

INCONSISTENT EQUATIONS A system of equations for which there is no possible solution (Ch. 1)

INDEFINITE INTEGRAL An integral with no limits of integration (Ch. 2)

INFLECTION POINT A point where the curvature of the function changes from strictly convex to strictly concave, or vice versa (Ch. 6)

INTEGER A whole real number (Ch. 2)

INTEGRAL SIGN The elongated s symbol, $\int$, used to identify the process of integration (Ch. 2)

INTEGRAND The function to be integrated (Ch. 2)

IRRATIONAL NUMBER A real number that cannot be expressed as a ratio of two integers or as a repeating decimal (Ch. 2)

JACOBIAN DETERMINANT A determinant composed of the first-order partial derivatives of a system of equations; used to test for the existence and uniqueness of a solution (Ch. 8)

KUHN-TUCKER CONDITIONS The first-order conditions for a nonlinear programming problem (Ch. 11)

LAGRANGE MULTIPLIER A variable that multiplies a constraint function incorporated in a Lagrangian function for a constrained optimization problem (Ch. 10)

LAPLACE EXPANSION A method used for evaluating a determinant of a matrix (Ch. 5)

LEFT-HAND LIMIT The limit of a function as an independent variable approaches a specific value from the negative side or from lesser values of the variable (Ch. 2)

LIMIT The ultimate value that a function approaches as an independent variable approaches a specific value (Ch. 2)

LIMITS OF INTEGRATION The upper and lower values for the variable over which an integral is to be evaluated (Ch. 2)

LINEAR A function whose graph is a straight line; a first-order differential equation where the endogenous variable is raised only to the power of one and is not multiplied by its derivative (Ch. 4)

LINEARLY DEPENDENT Vectors that can be expressed as linear combinations of each other (Ch. 5)

LINEARLY HOMOGENEOUS The property whereby multiplying all the independent variables in a function by a scalar, c, results in a multiplication of the dependent variable of the function by the scalar c (Ch. 10)

LINEARLY INDEPENDENT Vectors that cannot be expressed as linear combinations of each other (Ch. 5)

LINEAR PROGRAMMING A technique for solving optimization problems where the objective function and constraints are linear and there are nonnegativity restrictions on the choice variables (Ch. 11)

LOGARITHM The power to which a given base must be raised to obtain a particular number (Ch. 4)

MAIN DETERMINANT The elements of a matrix where the two subscripts are equal, for example, a_{ij}, where $i = j$, ($i = 1 \ldots n$; $j = 1 \ldots m$) (Ch. 5)

MATRIX A rectangular array of numbers, variables, or functions (Ch. 5)

MINOR The $(n\text{-}1) \times (n\text{-}1)$ subdeterminant associated with an element, a_{ij}, of an $n \times n$ matrix formed by deleting the ith row and jth column of the matrix $i = 1 \ldots n$; $j = 1 \ldots m$) (Ch. 5)

MONOTONIC When the slope of a function is always positive or always negative (Ch. 4)

NASH EQUILIBRIUM An outcome where neither player has an incentive to alter their strategy given the selected strategy of the rival player (Ch. 9)

NATURAL LOGARITHM A logarithm with a base of e, where $e = \lim_{m \to \infty} (1 + 1/m)^m = 2.71828\ldots$ (Ch. 4)

NEGATIVE DEFINITE A negative second-order total differential for a dependent variable of an objective function (Ch. 8)

NONSINGULAR A matrix with a determinant that is not equal to zero, thus a matrix with an inverse (Ch. 5)

NORM The length of a vector (Ch. 5)

NULL SET A set with no elements (Ch. 2)

OBJECTIVE FUNCTION The function that specifies the relationship between the dependent variable to be optimized and the independent variable(s) (Ch. 6)

ORDER The maximum difference between the time periods over which the endogenous variables are defined (Ch. 4)

ORTHOGONAL Perpendicular; two vectors are orthogonal if their dot product equals zero (Ch. 5)

OSCILLATORY When the slope of function systematically changes direction between negative and positive (Ch. 4)

OVERDETERMINED A system of equations where there are more equality constraints than choice variables, so there is no solution

PARAMETER An exogenous variable in an equation, usually in the form of a coefficient (Ch. 1)

PARTIAL DERIVATIVE The ratio of the instantaneous change of a dependent variable to an infinitesimal change in an independent variable holding constant the values of the other independent variables in the model (Ch. 2)

PARTIAL DIFFERENTIAL The instantaneous change in a dependent variable due to an infinitesimal change in an independent variable holding constant the values of the other independent variables in the model (Ch. 2)

PARTIAL EQUILIBRIUM ANALYSIS Comparative statics when there is more than one exogenous variable in the model (Ch. 3)

PARTICULAR INTEGRAL The particular solution to a first-order differential equation (Ch. 4)

PARTICULAR SOLUTION The solution to the static version of a first-order difference equation or first-order differential equation (Ch. 4)

PERIOD ANALYSIS Dynamic analysis where the endogenous variables are assumed to change in finite amounts at distinct points that indicate a change in time periods (Ch. 4)

PIVOT COLUMN The column in a simplex tableau corresponding to the most negative (largest positive) element in the top row for a maximization (minimization) linear programming problem (Ch. 11)

PIVOT ELEMENT The element in the pivot column in a simplex tableau with the smallest displacement quotient (Ch. 11)

POSITIVE DEFINITE A positive second-order total differential for a dependent variable in an objective function (Ch. 8)

PRIMAL The initial linear or nonlinear programming problem under examination (Ch. 11)

PRIME NUMBER A number that can be factored only into itself and one (Ch. 2)

QUADRATIC FORMULA A formula that can be used to find the solution to a quadratic equation of the general form: $ax^2 + bx + c = 0$ (Ch. 3)

RANGE The set of values that the dependent variable can assume or is defined over (Ch. 2)

RATIONAL NUMBER A real number that can be expressed as a ratio of two integers or as a repeating decimal (Ch. 2)

REAL NUMBER Either a rational or irrational number (Ch. 2)

RECTANGULAR HYPERBOLA A strictly convex curve where the areas formed by dropping perpendiculars to the two axes are equal (Ch. 6)

REDUCED FORM EQUATION An equation where an endogenous variable is expressed only in terms of the exogenous variables in the model (Ch. 1)

RELATION A specified association between a dependent variable and an independent variable (Ch. 2)

RELATIVE EXTREMUM A critical point where a dependent variable achieves a maximum or minimum value (Ch. 6)

RELATIVE MAXIMUM A critical point where a dependent variable achieves a maximum value (Ch. 8)

RELATIVE MINIMUM A critical point where a dependent variable achieves a minimum value (Ch. 8)

RIGHT-HAND LIMIT The limit of a function as an independent variable approaches a specific value from the positive side or from greater values of the variable (Ch. 2)

SADDLE POINT A critical point that is a relative maximum from one dimension and a relative minimum from another dimension (Ch. 8)

SCALAR A real number (Ch. 5)

SECOND DERIVATIVE The derivative of a first derivative of a function; gives the rate of change of the rate of change and the curvature of the function (Ch. 6)

SEMI-STABLE An equilibrium that is stable from one perspective or direction, but unstable from another perspective or direction (Ch. 3)

SET A well-defined collection of elements (Ch. 2)

SIMPLEX METHOD A process for solving linear programming problems (Ch. 11)

SIMPLEX TABLEAU A table used to solve linear programming problems with the dependent variable, choice variables, dummy variables, and constant listed in the top row and the objective function and m constraint functions represented in the next $m + 1$ rows, respectively (Ch. 11)

SINGULAR A matrix with a determinant equal to zero, thus the matrix does not have an inverse (Ch. 5)

SLACK VARIABLES The dummy variables used in linear programming maximization problems to turn the inequality constraints into equality constraints (Ch. 11)

SMOOTH No sharp points or sudden changes in the slope of a function (Ch. 2)

SPAN The identification of an n-space by a set of linearly independent vectors (Ch. 5)

SQUARE MATRIX A matrix with an equal number of rows and columns (Ch. 5)

STABILITY OF EQUILIBRIUM A system that tends to return to an equilibrium when not in equilibrium (Ch. 1)

STATIC ANALYSIS Analysis where the endogenous variables are all defined over the same period or point in time (Ch. 1)

STOCK VARIABLE A variable defined for a point in time (Ch. 1)

STRICTLY CONCAVE A function whose slope (whether negative or positive) is continuously decreasing (Ch. 6)

STRICTLY CONVEX A function whose slope (whether negative or positive) is continuously increasing (Ch. 6)

STRUCTURAL EQUATION An equation expressing a behavioral relationship between a dependent and independent variable(s) (Ch. 1)

SUBSET A well-defined collection of elements that is included in another set of elements (Ch. 2)

SURPLUS VARIABLES The dummy variables used in linear programming minimization problems to turn the inequality constraints into equality constraints (Ch. 11)

TOTAL DERIVATIVE The instantaneous change in a dependent variable with respect to an infinitesimal change in an exogenous variable in the model (Ch. 2)

TOTAL DIFFERENTIAL The total change in a dependent variable due to all the possible sources of change in the exogenous variables in the model (Ch. 2)

TRANSPOSE A matrix formed by interchanging the rows with the columns of another matrix (Ch. 5)

UNION The combination of two or more sets that includes the elements in any of the sets (Ch. 2)

UNIQUENESS OF EQUILIBRIUM A model with only one possible equilibrium for any period or point in time given the values of the exogenous variables (Ch. 1)

UNIVERSAL SET The set of all possible elements under consideration (Ch. 2)

VECTOR A point in n-space represented by a directed line segment (Ch. 5)

ZERO MATRIX A matrix where all the elements are zero (Ch. 5)

INDEX